ON RECORD 1979 G. BROWN

CONTENTS

ON RECORD ENTRIES ARE NOT ORDERED ALPHABETICALLY, BUT ORGANIZED INTUITIVELY—A MIXTURE OF SEGUES BY MUSICAL GENRE OR STYLE.

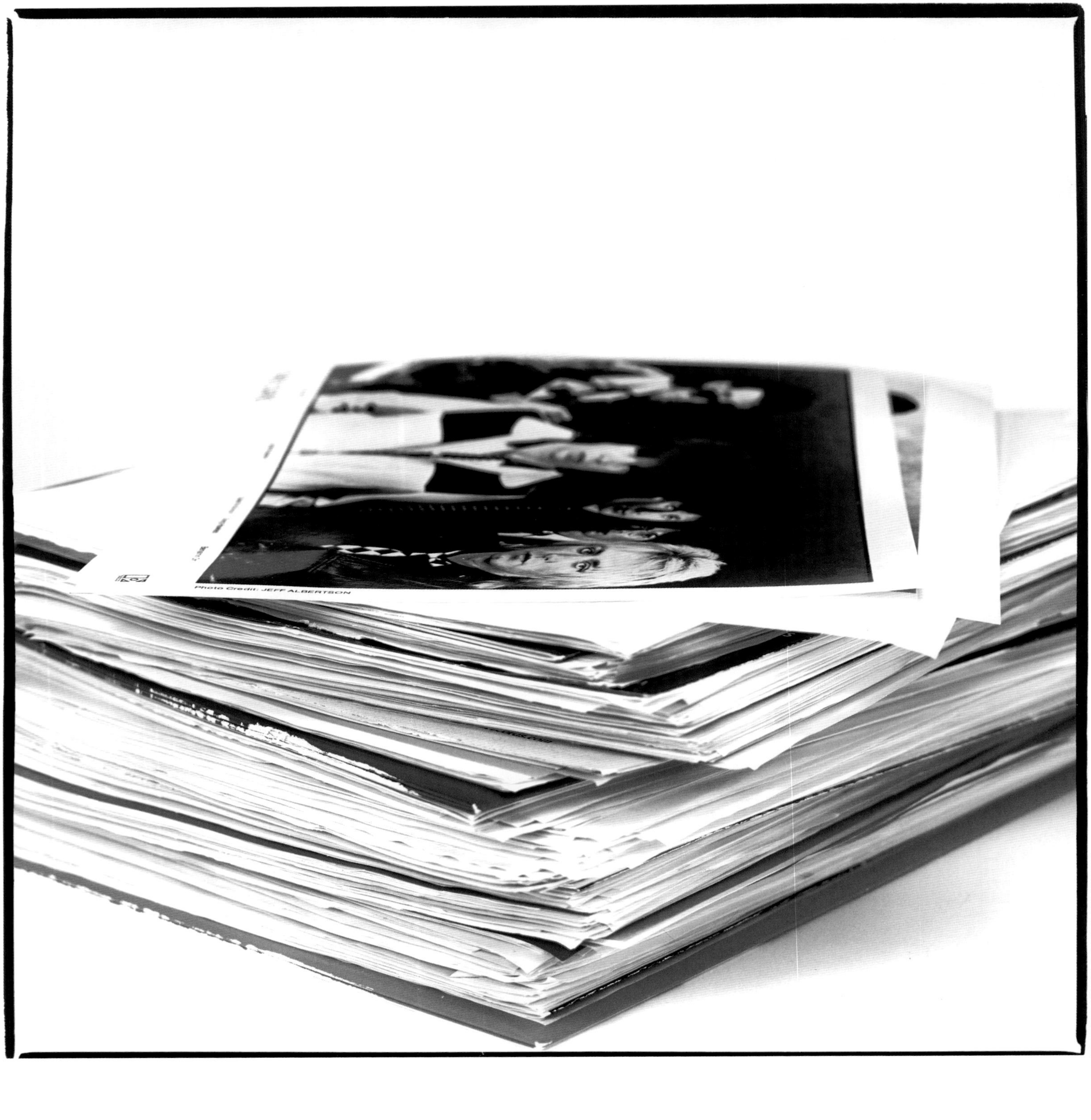

PHOTOGRAPH BY STEPHEN COLLECTOR

ON RECORD VOL. 7 1979

IN 1979, rather than subjecting his client to a litany of phone interviews, Billy Joel's tour publicist decided to fly in a dozen writers from across the country for an informal press conference in Denver, a centrally located city on the tour—and where I was contracted by *The Denver Post*. Before the show, Joel regaled the gathering in his hotel room with his feisty Noo Yawker shtick, then headed over to McNichols Sports Arena to perform. At some point, Joel and his then-wife/manager had a spat. So, instead of gathering backstage after the show, everyone was instructed to meet back at his suite.

Joel was already there, drinking tequila. People stood around uneasily until he put an open hand to his face. "Asshole meter…asshole meter…," he muttered as he shuffled around. He stopped in front of a writer and poured a shot of Cuervo Gold. "I know what you're thinking," Joel sneered. "You think you're gonna watch me get fucked up and then get to write about it. Well, maybe you are—but you're gonna get fucked up, too." The asshole meter detected every scribe before Joel was through.

And then a great party broke out. Joel stood on the outdoor balcony and relieved himself into the parking lot nine stories below—"Ah, rich Corinthian leather," he said in credible Ricardo Montalban-ese as he found his target. Animatedly discussing his music, he shouted, "I have the best goddamn band in the *world*," hitting the wall behind him for emphasis. Unfortunately, a picture frame got in the way—Joel shattered the glass and cut his finger. A record-company honcho was there to overreact: "Billy! Billy! We've got to get you to a hospital!" Without missing a beat, Joel went into his pansy routine. "Ooh, I hurt my widdle hand! Cancel the tour! Ooh, ooh!" The entire room cracked up.

Asked by one of Joel's tour crew what city I was from, I told him. "Oh, Denver—you must be excited about the Broncos." Overhearing this, Joel glared at me. "Raiders," he growled. "Broncos!" I countered. "Raiders," he repeated. Sensing that our dispute would not be resolved verbally, we started throttling each other. The publicist hosting the soiree heard the commotion and saw his diminutive superstar and the local music reporter rolling around on the floor. Priceless. We were laughing so hard, it went down as a draw after ten seconds.

A few years later, Joel wasn't a Raiders fan anymore. "Not since they moved from Oakland to Los Angeles," he told me. "It's not the same—there's something too 'white wine' about the L.A. Raiders." But I'm still behind my Broncos. Don't you love a happy ending?

Bigger things happened in 1979. Disco occupied the top spots on the pop charts—the Bee Gees and Donna Summer reigned supreme. But "My Sharona" by the Knack hit No.1, signaling a potential rock resurgence, and Pink Floyd released *The Wall*. A stampede for seats during a Who concert in Cincinnati killed 11 fans. Musicians United for Safe Energy (MUSE) staged a series of No Nukes concerts at Madison Square Garden. The Sugarhill Gang released "Rapper's Delight," the first rap single to become a Top 40 hit. And I got to interview the artists, hear every album, see dozens of concerts and pore over press kits and photos. I was and am a lucky boy. Please allow me to share. — **G. Brown**

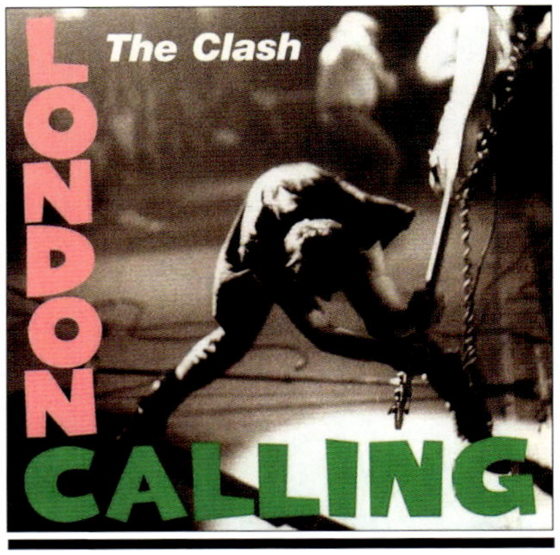

Billboard 200: *London Calling* (#27)
Billboard Hot 100: "Train in Vain (Stand by Me)" (#23)

The Clash managed to leave the faddishness of the punk genre behind through the double album *London Calling*.

THE ENGLISH punk-rock revolution of the mid-Seventies was a misunderstood musical movement in America. British kids, genuinely upset over their on-the-dole lifestyles, had put together bands as their platforms in the rock 'n' roll tradition. Inspired by an early Sex Pistols performance, the Clash formed in 1976. Joe Strummer, Mick Jones and Paul Simonon, who had never picked up an instrument in his life, teamed with drummer Tory Crimes and recorded their first album in a basement.

But the scene was doomed. The Sex Pistols broke up, and American listeners turned away, incapable of sharing the sociological concerns. Left to carry on the battle alone, the Clash's challenge was one of acceptance. The members said publicly that they always could go back to Europe if they didn't make it in the US, but they hungered to find an American audience, even if they were fighting stacked odds because of their image.

So the Clash forged a mighty sound that superseded any political specifics that could dim the power of their music, borrowing from the rough-hewn sound of the Who, the early Rolling Stones and the populist nature of Mott the Hoople, but it was Strummer's blurry howling and Jones' bracing guitar work that gave the Clash its identity. "We want to sell records," Strummer grinned.

London Calling, a stunning statement of purpose, boasted an array of song structures informed by reggae, rockabilly, soul and blues. "Train in Vain" was a near-charming pop song thanks to Jones' sweet vocal in the Keith Richard tradition, and the title track, the first cut on the album, showcased the band's infuriated determination. The Clash became a formidable politically motivated rock ensemble, charged with righteousness and a leftist ideology.

"We're supposed to be people trying to say something to somebody, and I have learned you cannot communicate by repelling anyone," Strummer said. "That's just a microcosm of the real world. You exist here, and there's someone your same age in India looking for a couple of grains of rice. You just can't fall on the floor gnashing your teeth over that thought. That's just the human condition. We make it a point not to brush it under the carpet, but we don't expect the crowd to start wearing sackcloth and ashes."

To fans, the group became the world's mightiest rock band—or at least the only important one.

"We're useless at answers," Strummer stated. "If I knew the answers, I would be removed from the human race—unable to relate to anybody, much less write something that would strike a responsive chord in people. There's only one thing I'm sure of—the only way the Clash is going to carry on is to be for the people, of the people. That's why we're musicians, not politicians." ■

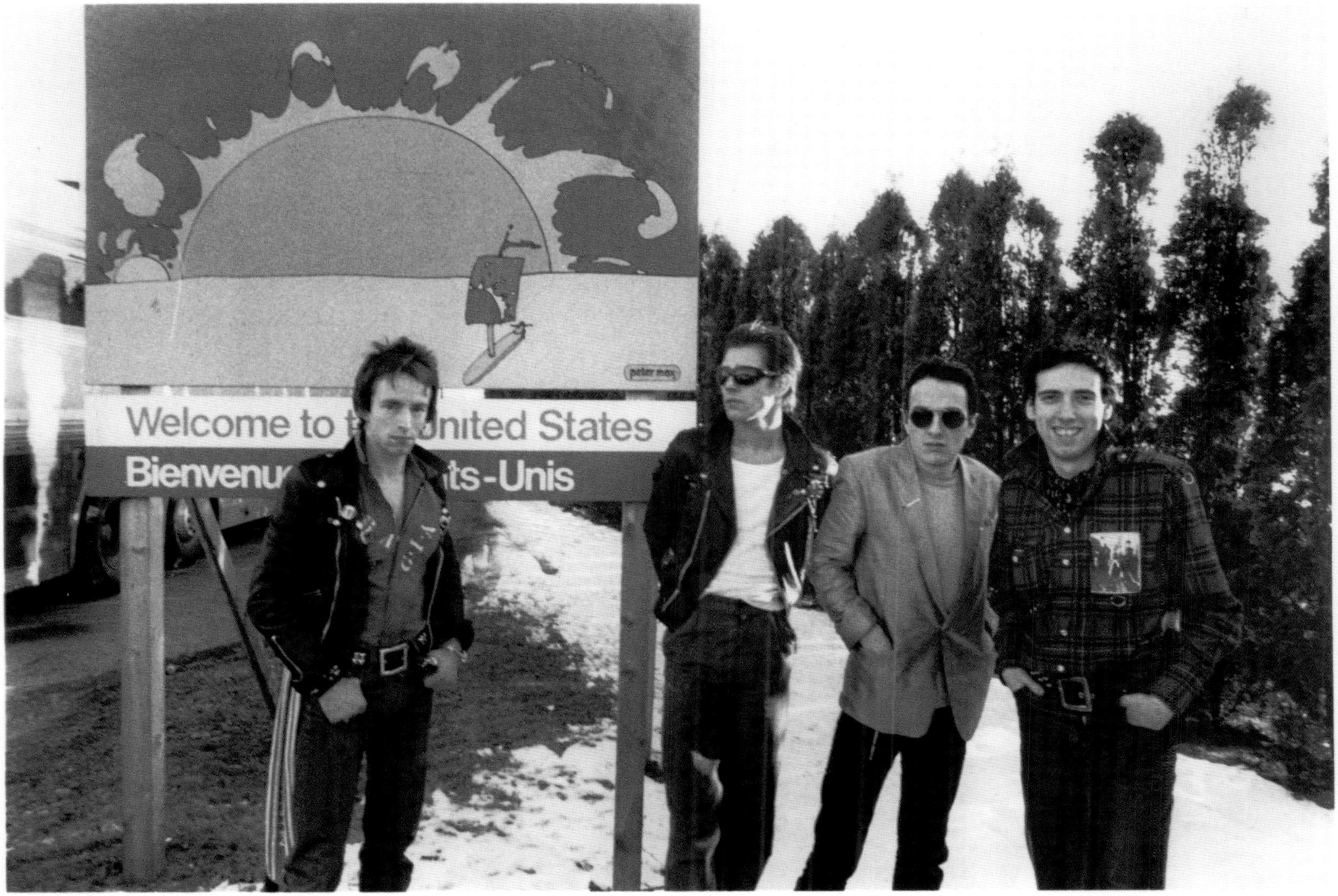

Photo credit: Bob Gruen

THE CLASH

Epic

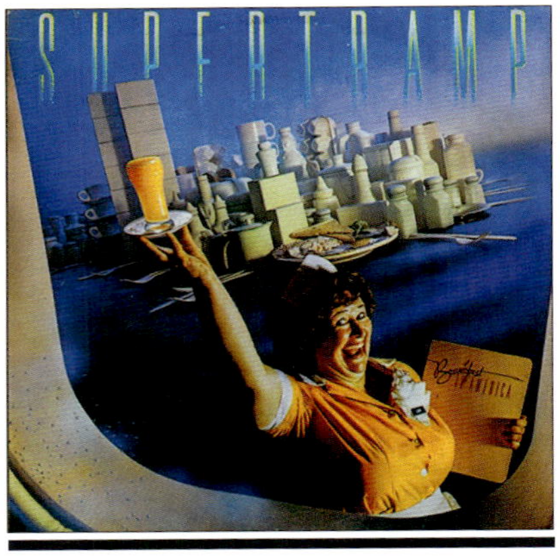

Billboard 200: *Breakfast in America* (No. 1)
Billboard Hot 100: "The Logical Song" (#6); "Goodbye Stranger" (#15); "Take the Long Way Home" (#10); "Breakfast in America" (#62)

Containing four irrepressible singles, *Breakfast in America* propelled Supertramp into the class of supergroups.

THE MEMBERS of Supertramp freely admitted they would never match their progressive masterpiece, 1974's *Crime of the Century*. Yet with 1977's *Even in the Quietest Moments...*, the British act had amassed a huge following, quelling any doubts about its ability to create intriguing, intricately textured rock music. The ensuing tour took Supertramp—Roger Hodgson (guitar), Rick Davies (keyboards), John Helliwell (reeds), Dougie Thomson (bass) and Bob C. Benberg (drums)—to all corners of the earth with a brilliantly precise stage production, a smooth integration of sound and visuals.

Breakfast in America emerged as the best of the band's pop-oriented releases. The masters of "evolved rock" put new emphasis on punchier rhythms and vocal hooks, such as the call-and-response choruses of "Goodbye Stranger." "The Logical Song," "Take the Long Way Home" and the title track were the other neatly constructed singles.

"It's a better album than we've made for a while," Helliwell agreed, "and it's because we're just getting better at playing. Since we came over here to live (the band had moved from England to Los Angeles), Rick and Roger are writing interesting songs about things that they've been experiencing. And we've captured a bit more of a live feel."

Despite the band's seeming effortlessness in producing original material, the making of *Breakfast in America* turned out to be a test for Supertramp. "We started working on it in March of 1978," Helliwell reflected. "We started recording in June—it was supposed to be a two-month album from start to finish—and we didn't actually finish it until December. We got all the basic tracks, but then we kept adding and changing things, and then the mixing took a lot of time, too. We couldn't get it to sound good."

But for the five perfectionists in Supertramp, the attention to craft paid off with a No. 1 album, the band's commercial peak. It was an important concept for a group that lacked a single personality to focus on. "That's exactly what we like," Helliwell admitted. "We're not bothered about individual star complexes. We're just content to play the music." ■

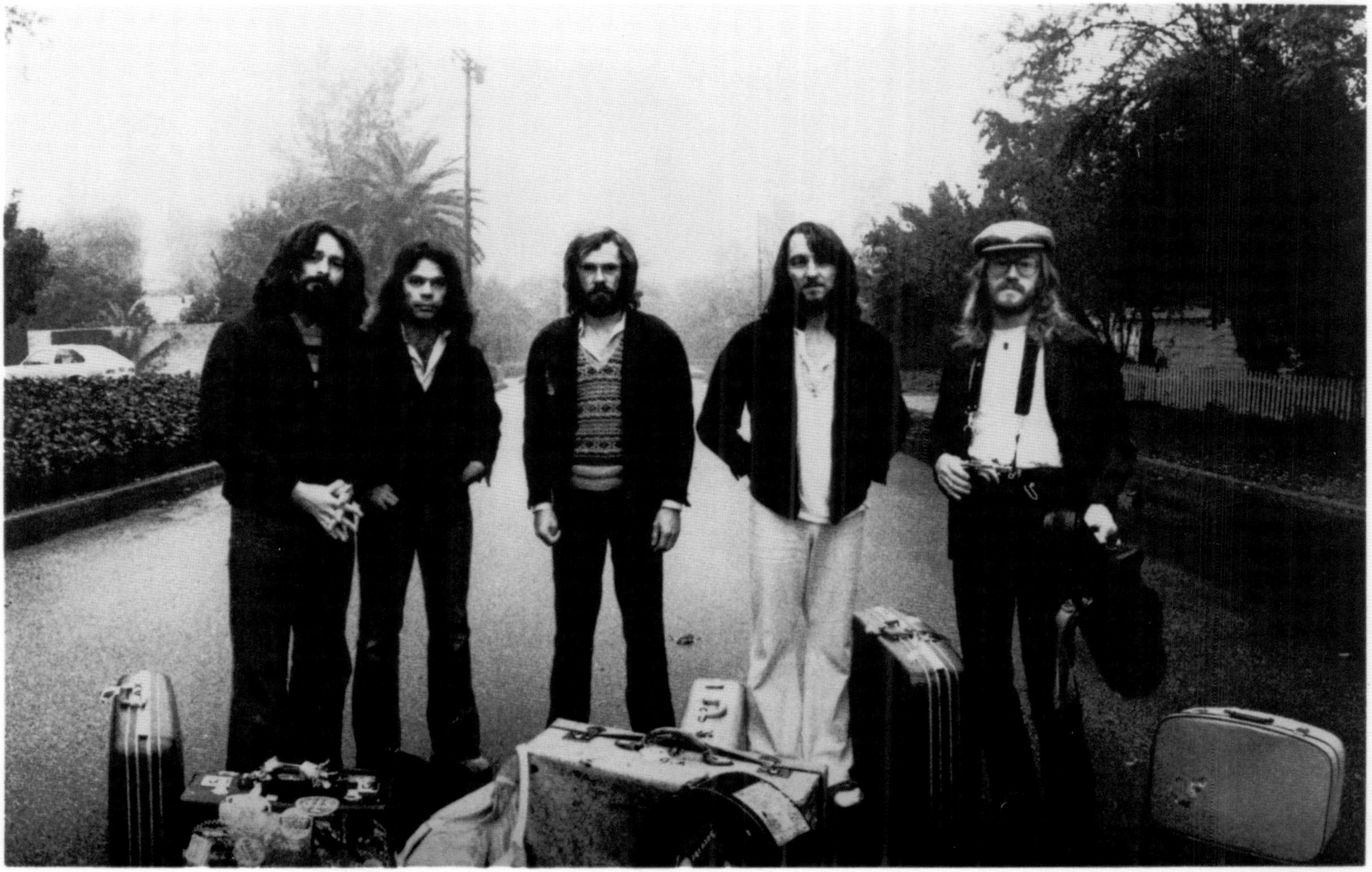

L to R: RICK DAVIES, BOB C. BENBERG, DOUGIE THOMSON, ROGER HODGSON, JOHN A. HELLIWELL,

SUPERTRAMP

A&M RECORDS

Printed in U.S.A.

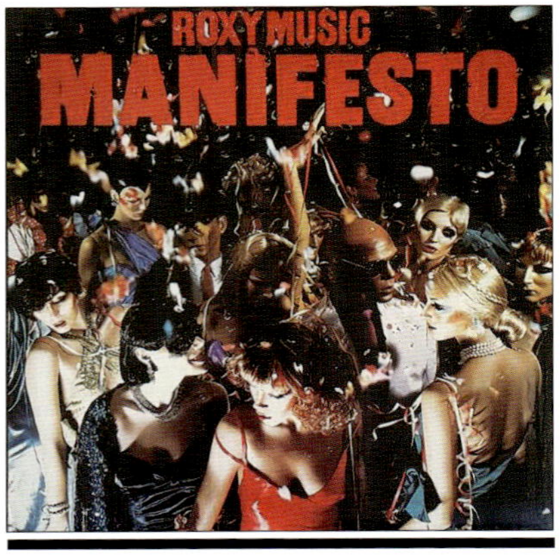

Billboard 200: *Manifesto* (#23)
Billboard Hot 100: "Dance Away" (#44)

After a hiatus, Roxy Music proffered songs for the dance floor and the boudoir on the burnished *Manifesto*.

UPON LEAVING art school and forming Roxy Music in 1972, Bryan Ferry initiated a style of music that resulted in five classic albums in four years, culminating with the brilliant *Siren* and the single "Love Is the Drug" in 1976. The blend of electronics and effects, a shifting, unique musical vocabulary, hypnotizing rhythms and Ferry's mannered vocals and lyrical incisiveness hadn't been approached by any other group.

Yet after building a sizable cult reputation for excellence, the act disbanded after *Siren* to pursue individual projects. For three years the world went Roxyless until the band regrouped to record *Manifesto*.

"I'd always wanted every Roxy album to be an improvement, a step forward," Ferry explained of the suspension of activity. "I felt they had all been a progression, so I needed a break from the studio/tour routine. I wanted to do a solo tour (Ferry's solo albums had outsold Roxy Music releases in Europe), I wanted to live in Los Angeles for a time instead of England, and I wanted to record with other players.

"But I always knew there would be another Roxy album in the future. I wasn't sure who would be in the band, but I'd always intended for there to be one. After I had done what I wanted to do apart from Roxy, it was a natural thing when I returned to England to ring up the others and say, 'Do you want to make another album?' They did."

The Roxy Music lineup had always been formidable—new wave godfather Brian Eno and violinist Eddie Jobson were graduates—and the group's new presence was equally impeccable. Guitarist Phil Manzanera and drummer Paul Thompson brandished their inventive playing, and Andrew Mackay's sharp electronic woodwinds punctuated the musical proceedings.

Manifesto turned out to be Roxy Music's best received album in America. The stylish single "Dance Away" and "Angel Eyes" were two of the band's most accessible tracks, and "Trash" represented its singular blend of instrumental styles.

"When I went off to do solo projects, I thought it would be 18 months until the next Roxy album—it turned out to be three years," Ferry reflected. "I still go to radio stations where they don't even know who I am after heading up 12 albums in seven years. Our career has been hard to follow, and we haven't made any commercial concessions to make it in America. But we're finally making our mark." ■

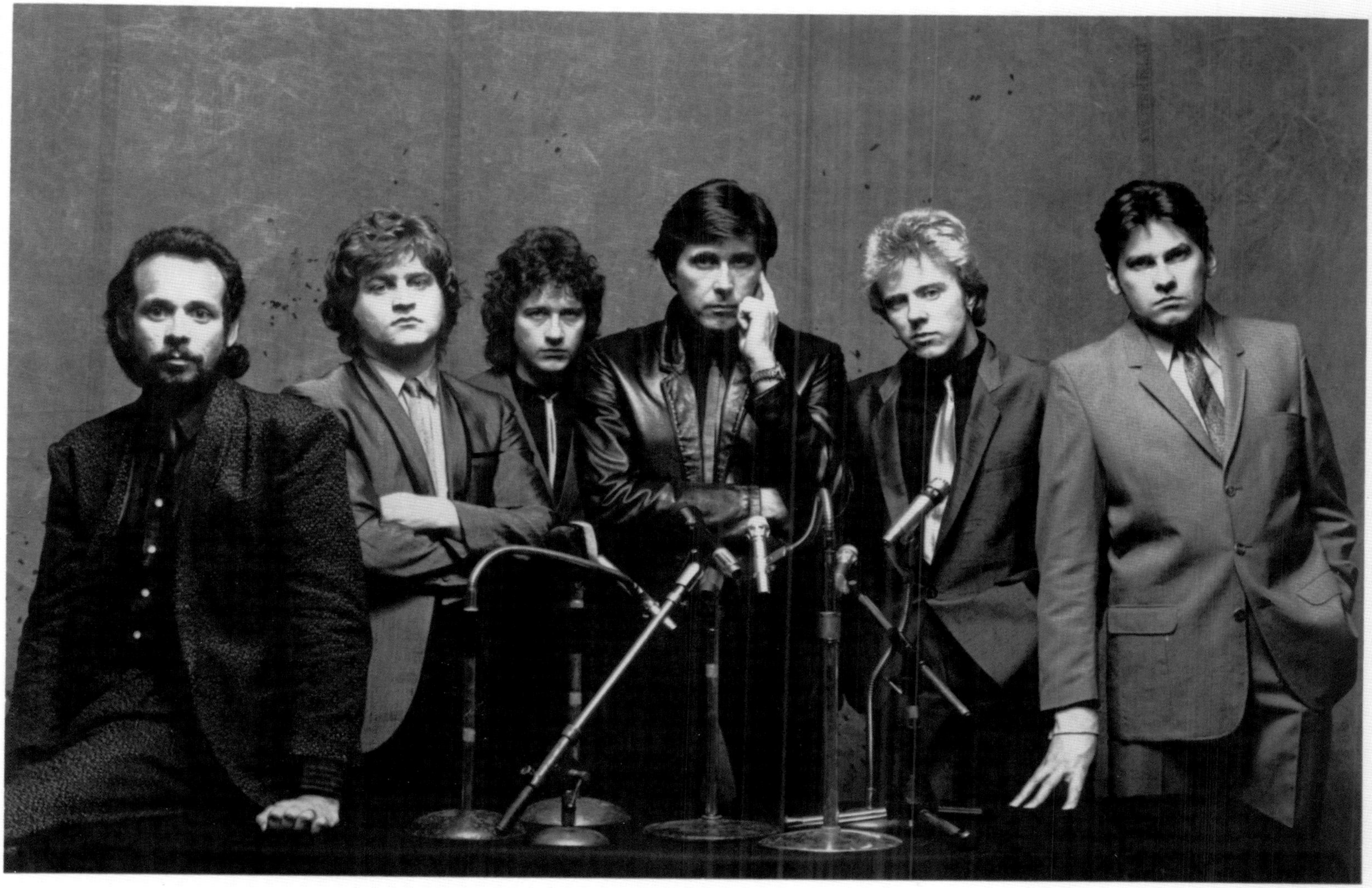

PHIL MANZANERA PAUL THOMPSON DAVE SKINNER BRYAN FERRY GARY TIBBS ANDY MACKAY

ATCO

ROXY MUSIC.

EG RECORDS, INC.
246 East 62nd Street
New York, N.Y 10021
212-355-5200

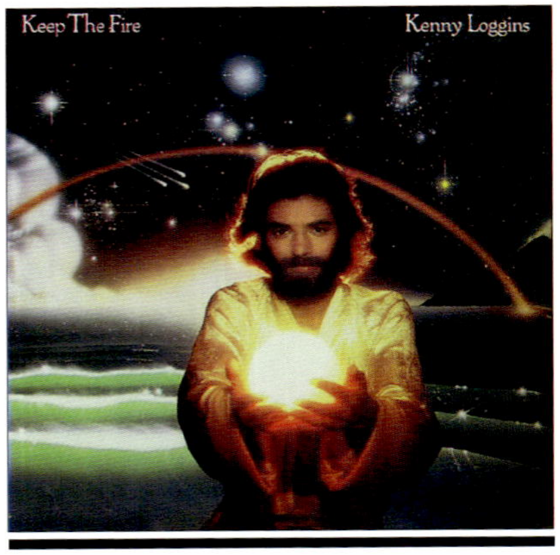

Billboard 200: *Keep the Fire* (#16)
Billboard Hot 100: "This Is It" (#11); "Keep the Fire" (#36)

His third solo album since Loggins & Messina's split, *Keep the Fire* was Kenny Loggins' biggest seller to date.

FROM HIS writing collaborations with Michael McDonald, the soul of the Doobie Brothers, Kenny Loggins' career had received a tremendous boost. The duo had written only two songs together, but both became huge soft-rock successes—"What a Fool Believes" for the Doobies, and "This Is It" for Loggins. The latter appeared on his *Keep the Fire* release.

"Two for two ain't bad," Loggins said, laughing. "I'd like to write more with him, but it's hard for us to get together. I know now how a professional baseball player feels when he's batting a thousand. It feels great, but the potential for a strikeout next time up is even greater. The last thing I said to Michael was, 'Let's get together and write some flops and get them out of the way.'"

Loggins collaborated with his wife Eva on *Keep the Fire*'s title track. He changed producers from jazz maestro Bob James to rock veteran Tom Dowd. "It's actually not that radical a shift," Loggins explained. "They're both into the same concept of communication, but in two different worlds—Bob is the essence of pop jazz and Tommy is more into gutsy rock 'n' roll. But they both believe in simple, efficiently made records. I'm trying to walk the line between those two worlds."

The acceptance of *Keep the Fire* made Loggins' grueling tour schedule a little more bearable, and he planned to sneak a little time off. "A buddy of mine and I are taking a rapids trip down the Colorado River. McDonald told me he'd like to go along, too. We've got to be careful—if we brought Stevie (Nicks of Fleetwood Mac) and Michael Jackson along and the new wave heard about this, they may come gunning for us—they could wipe out the Top 5."

Loggins & Messina, Loggins' formidable partnership with Jim Messina that had produced eight albums, had concluded in 1976. Commenting on Messina's debut solo album, the laid-back *Oasis*, Loggins said, "People change—it's just a guess on my part, but he's probably reacting to what people expected of him. There was no problem with L&M. There was a moment that came, very similar to a love affair, where you realize that you are you and your partner is separate from you. It was a creative decision—time to go on to other things." ■

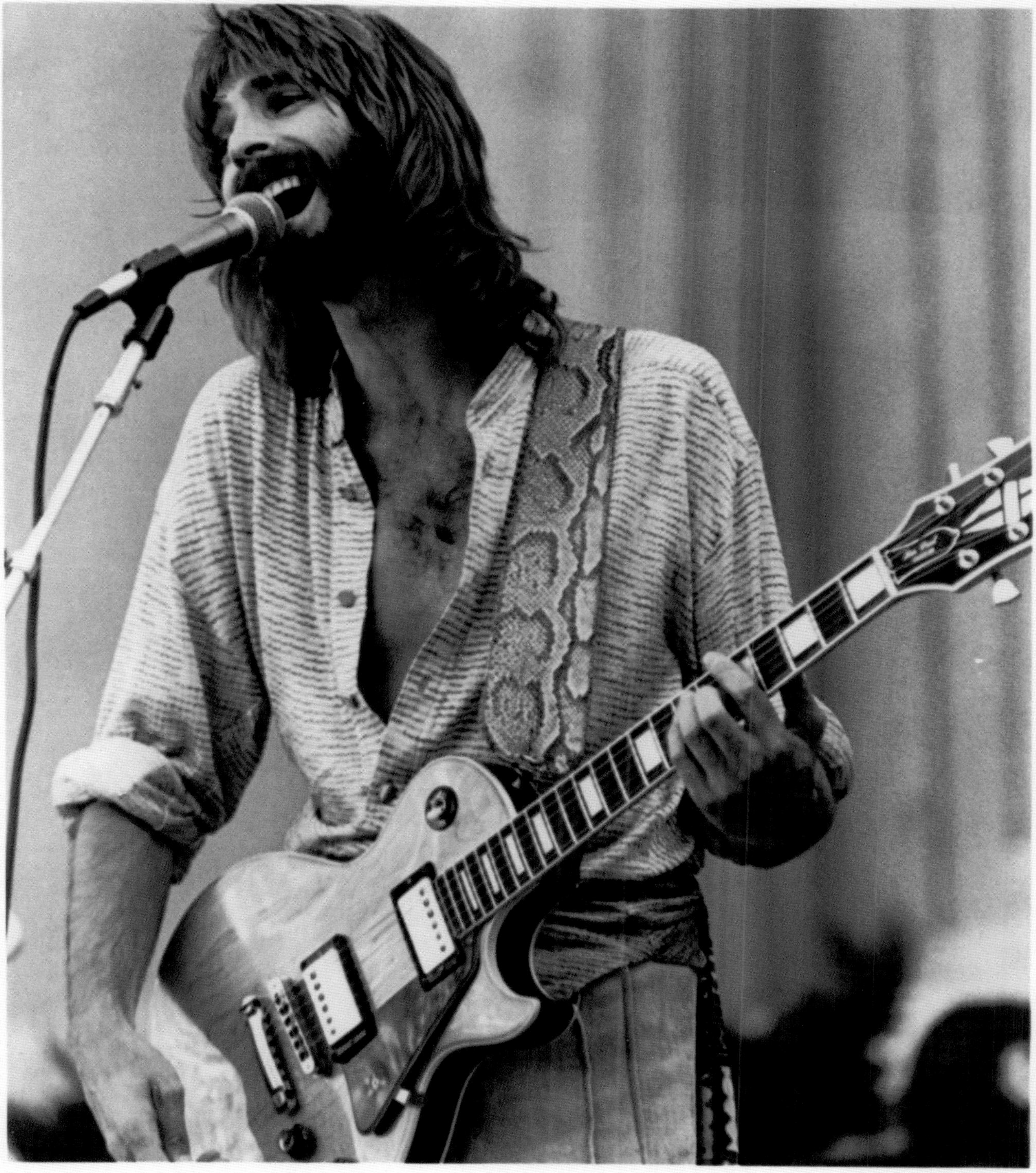

Kenny Loggins

COLUMBIA

7912

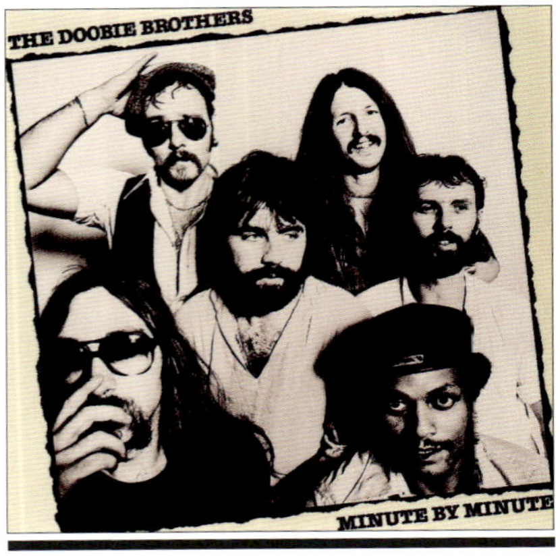

Billboard 200: *Minute by Minute* (No. 1)
Billboard Hot 100: "What a Fool Believes" (No. 1); "Minute by Minute" (#14); "Dependin' on You" (#25)

The Doobie Brothers' career soared with *Minute by Minute*, averring Michael McDonald's dominant presence.

ALTHOUGH HE was earning a good living fronting an R&B cover band in Missouri, the lure of a recording contract was too much to resist. At age 19, Michael McDonald left his native St. Louis for California.

"I came out in 1970 to make a record that never materialized, but it put me into the scene," he explained. "I spent my time working in bands and clubs to support myself, because I never really thought of myself as a songwriter. I wasn't into the publishing thing, beating the streets to peddle my songs."

McDonald passed through Steely Dan's ranks as a recurring contributor. In 1975, he was recruited by the Doobie Brothers when Tom Johnston, who had written and sang a string of hits for the band, became ill with a stomach disorder on the eve of a tour and had to drop out. Johnston rejoined the Doobies after his illness, but he left the band for a solo career in 1977.

The suave familiarity of McDonald's voice and songwriting style came to dominate the Doobies' sound, soaring on *Minute by Minute*, the group's biggest album.

"So much of what we term as disco and dance music is mono-focused," McDonald said. "When I write, I'm trying to emulate Earth, Wind & Fire and Sly & the Family Stone, those kinds of songs. I don't know how that comes off to the public—you get panned for not being more topical or protesting something in the music. But for me, that's not a strong urge. I still enjoy feel-good R&B music."

McDonald's soulful vocals and shuffling rhythms were perfect vehicles to reach the charts—"What a Fool Believes," written with Kenny Loggins, hit No. 1 and earned three Grammys, including Song of the Year and Record of the Year. With McDonald's emergence as the Doobies' artistic focus and a major pop talent, his smoldering good looks catapulted him into the celebrity ranks.

"I've never been inaccessible because I've never had the need to be," the self-effacing performer said. "Rod Stewart and Mick Jagger don't have any choice—they need a bodyguard. But those guys have a mob of 16-year-old girls trying to rip their hair out, while I've got some aunt in Ames, Iowa, wanting autographs for her three daughters." ■

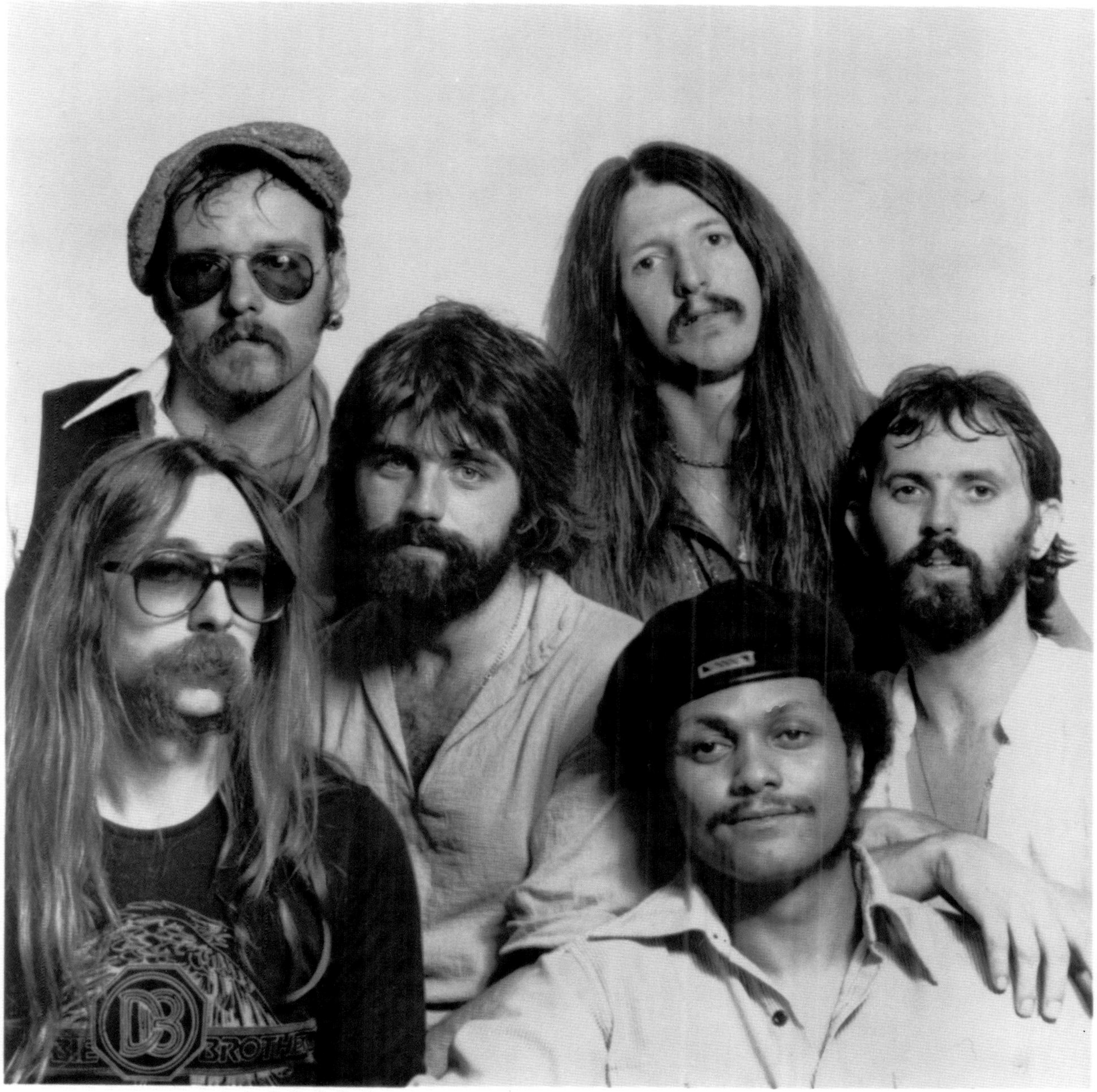

THE DOOBIE BROTHERS

WARNER/REPRISE

JOHN HARTMAN
JEFF BAXTER
MICHAEL McDONALD
PATRICK SIMMONS
TIRAN PORTER
KEITH KNUDSEN

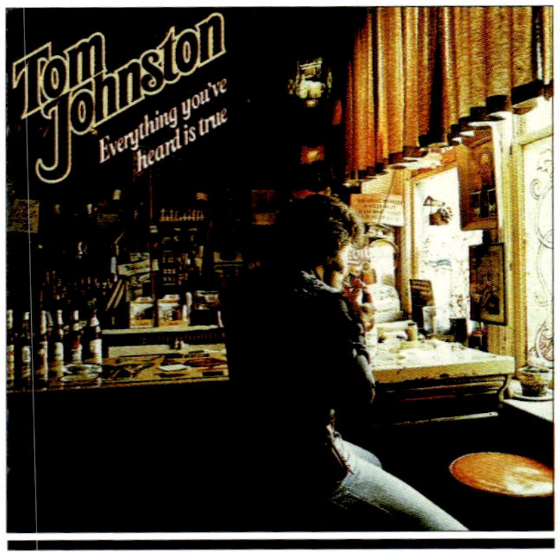

One of the founders of the Doobie Brothers, Tom Johnston landed his first solo hit with "Savannah Nights."

MILLIONS OF people had heard Tom Johnston's music, even though he was far from a household name on his own. Johnston was the sound of the Doobie Brothers back in the early Seventies, penning the hit singles "Listen to the Music," "China Grove" and "Long Train Running." But the Doobies had turned into the Michael McDonald show, and Johnson hoped for some resurrected interest in his style, picking up where he left off upon leaving the Doobies in 1977.

"On my last Doobies album, we started using some session players, and I had never done an album where I didn't know everybody," Johnston explained. "It scared me, to be honest, and I wasn't writing much anyway. I quit when I wanted to quit, and it was the right time—we left amicably, which I'm happy about, and I admire what they're doing."

Johnston took his leave and recovered from the excesses of his trade. "I overdid—I got ridiculously healthy and did zilch for a while." When his weightlifting training was cut short by tendinitis, Johnston regained his zest for music. He reunited with longtime producer Ted Templeman, who sandwiched *Everything You've Heard Is True*, Johnson's first solo record, between his commitments with the Doobies, Van Halen and Nicolette Larson.

Although the album spawned "Savannah Nights," which garnered significant airplay and chart success, parts of the record were taken with tentative experiments such as "Reachin' Out for Lovin' from You," an Al Green-flavored ballad. "It's a pet project, trying some R&B things," Johnston admitted. "I went on a tangent." He then took his act on the road, opening shows for Kenny Loggins.

"I'm finding out that a lot of people don't know who the hell I am," he chuckled. "All of these people are wearing corsages and suits, and they're there to see Kenny. But I'll win them over. I have a crack nine-piece band with horns, and we always get an encore or two. I think that getting out and pounding away is the way to go. But financially, it's a disastrous thing to do." ■

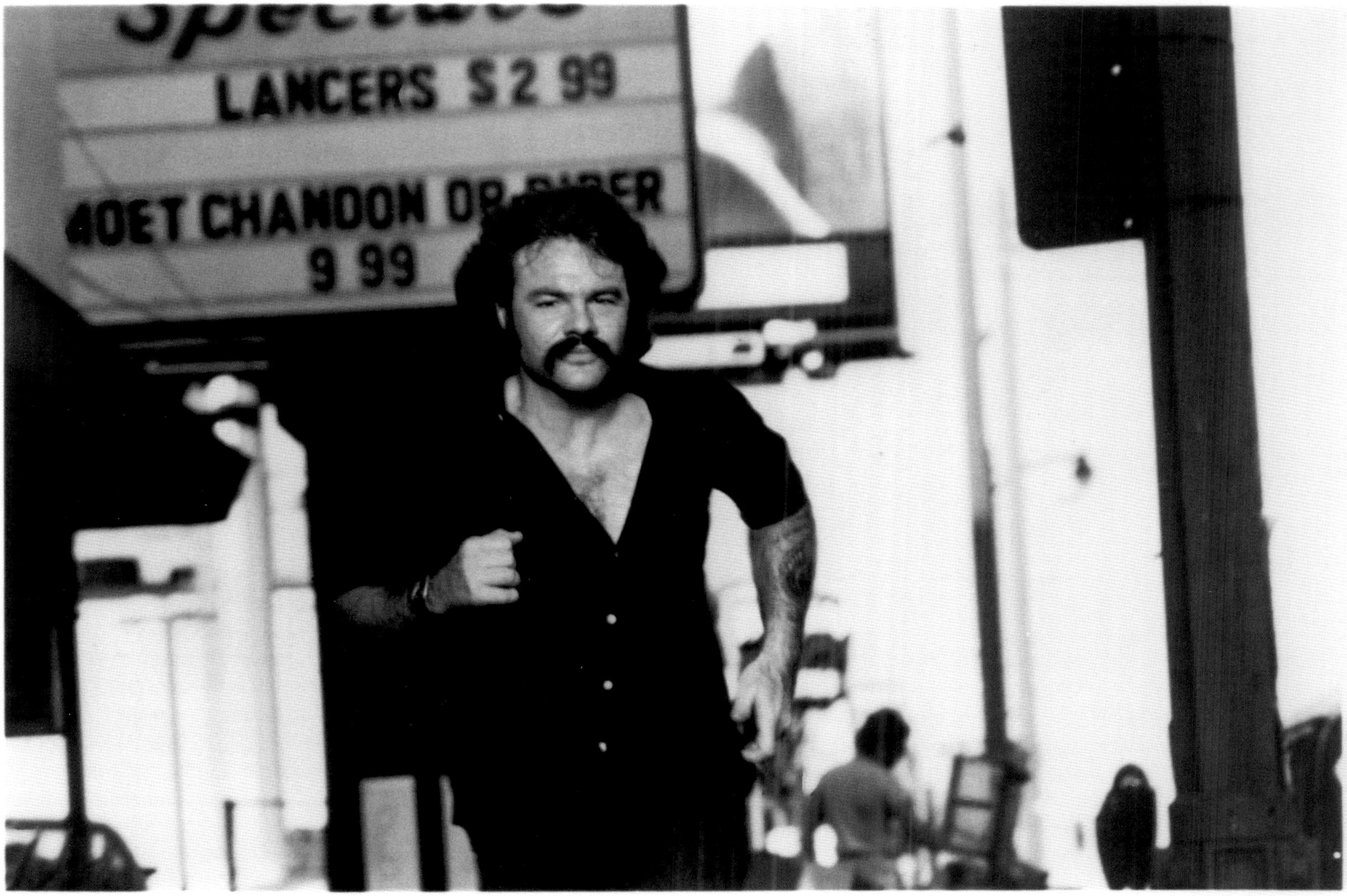

TOM JOHNSTON

BRUCE COHN MANAGEMENT, INC.

David Gest and Associates
Public Relations

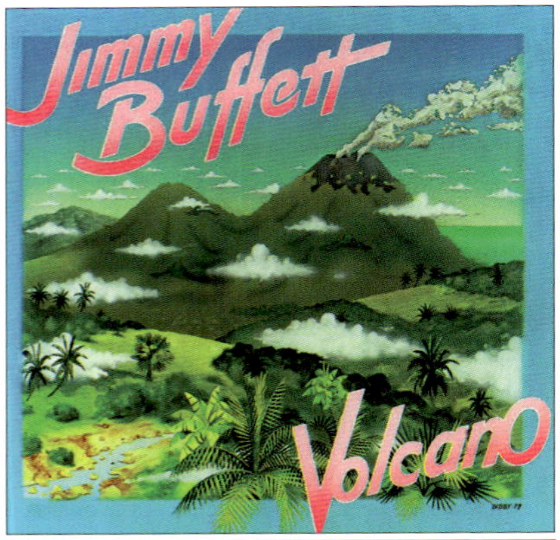

Billboard 200: *Volcano* (#14)
Billboard Hot 100: "Fins" (#35); "Volcano" (#66); "Survive" (#77)

The poet laureate of tropical hedonism, Jimmy Buffett gathered his margarita-fueled wit for the hit "Fins."

STILL A performing animal first and foremost, laid-back Jimmy Buffett maintained his status as a top-drawing concert attraction with Mardi Gras-like performances.

"People all worship the songs, which is fine—even the people who don't like me, like me," Buffett said. "Radio people have an image of me, this guy living in a hammock in Margaritaville out of a job. I don't consider myself a musician—in the lineage from theologians, we're descendants of court jesters. Our job is to make people happy. It's not to save the world. The core of what I do is entertain onstage."

Buffett consistently played to sellout crowds, and there didn't appear to be a designated driver in the bunch of colorful-clad "Parrotheads"—his insane fans, otherwise normal human beings ranging from engineers to fry cooks who all became part of a carnival when he came to town.

"I truly believe that music goes back to tribalism," Buffett commented. "We don't want to get shot at or preached to—you can go downtown or to church to get that. But when you go to a concert, you want to have a good time. I don't apologize for it at all. Some reviewer called me a shameless entertainer, and I thought it was the ultimate compliment!"

Striving to operate within most-fun-allowed-by-law parameters, Parrotheads became part of the party, arrayed in Hawaiian shirts, hula skirts and coconut bras, letting loose as a choir on such Buffett standards as "Come Monday," "Cheeseburger in Paradise" and "Margaritaville" and, until their aim got fuzzy, throwing beach balls and malt beverages onto the stage. His *Volcano* album generated the playful "Fins," a song about horny guys hitting on a girl,

"'Fins' was an 'in' thing with the band, just a term for checking out chicks—a 1979 version of 'Girlwatchers.' But I think it has a little more class. It's really about land sharks who live in bars and feed right after dark."

The Parrotheads picked up on fin and shark themes and started responding to the chorus line of "fins to the left, fins to the right" with steepled hands overhead, swaying from leeward to windward. "Fins" became part of Buffett's concert repertoire, those songs that had made him famous—and he never ignored them.

"Do I get tired of playing them? It doesn't matter. You see the smiles they bring to the audience's faces. If you look at them, they'll tell you when they get tired of the songs. And guess what? They aren't tired of them yet." ■

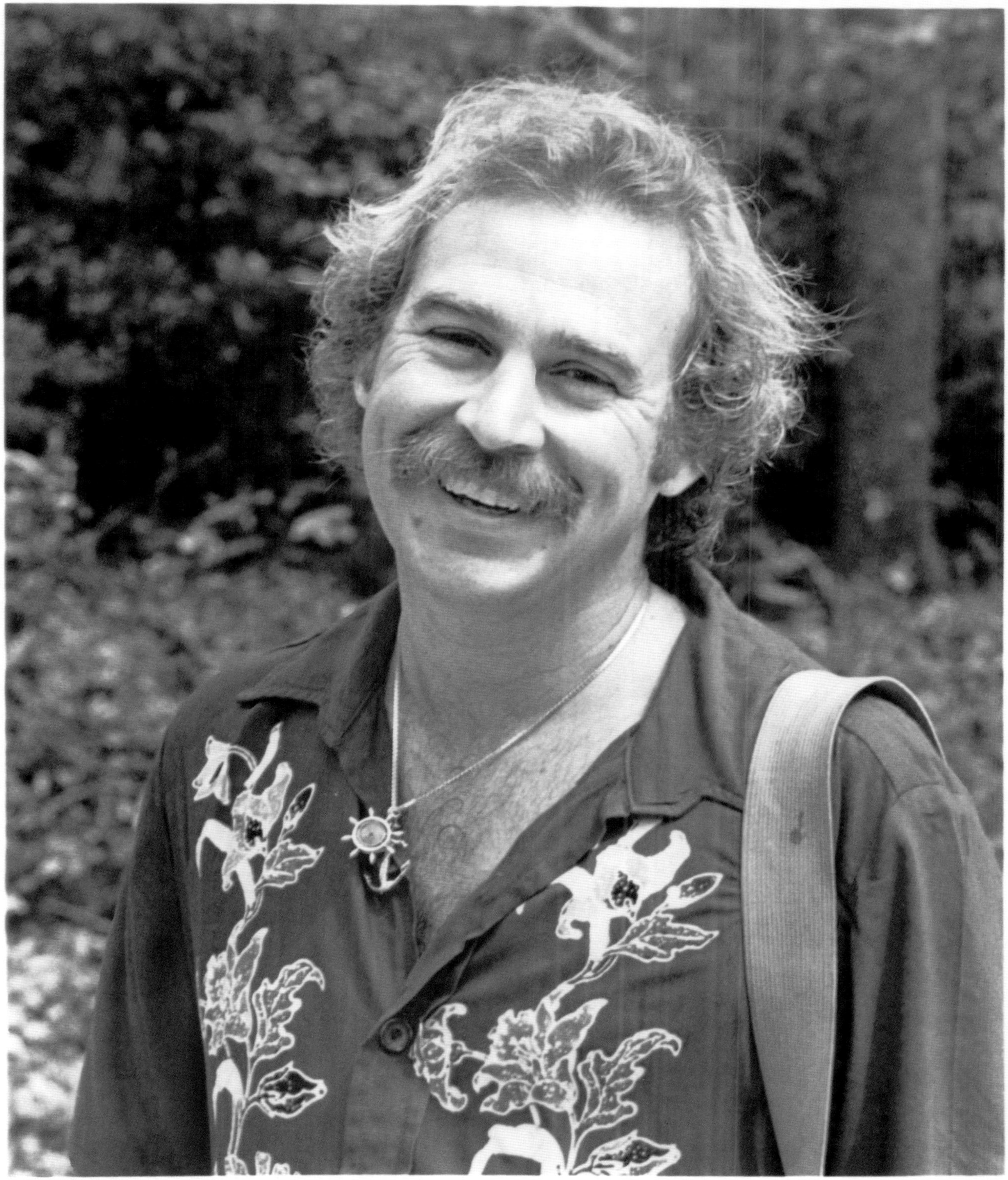

PHOTO CREDIT: TOM CORCORAN

1/80

JIMMY BUFFETT

FRONT LINE
MANAGEMENT COMPANY, INC.
8380 Melrose Ave. Suite 307
Los Angeles, California 90069
(213) 658-6600

EXCLUSIVELY ON
MCA RECORDS

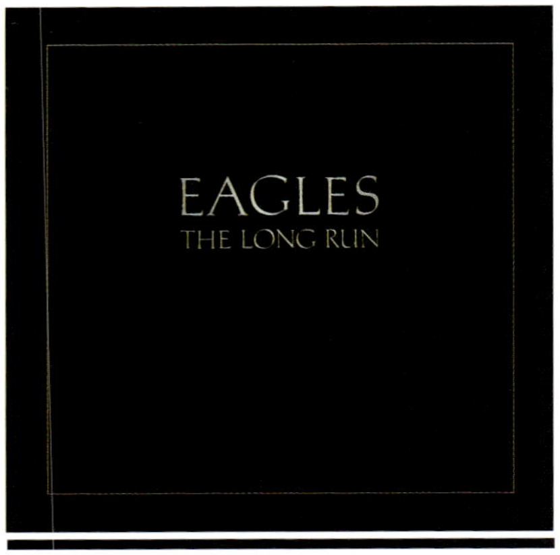

Billboard 200: *The Long Run* (No. 1)
Billboard Hot 100: "Heartache Tonight" (No. 1); "The Long Run" (#8); "I Can't Tell You Why" (#8)

The follow-up to the hugely successful Eagles album *Hotel California* eventually showed up in *The Long Run*.

THE MUCH-ANTICIPATED *The Long Run* reflected the Eagles' belief in their capacity for generating more tunes than they needed, so that every cut finally chosen for inclusion on an album was a monster.

"It's been almost three years since *Hotel California*," guitarist Joe Walsh noted. "We recorded 22 songs, enough for a double album, but we didn't want to hit the public with that. We wanted to release a killer single album, so it took a while for the band to select the best songs, to haggle. It got crazy."

Despite the painful birth, three singles were released from *The Long Run*—"Heartache Tonight," "I Can't Tell You Why" (which new member Timothy B. Schmit brought to the band) and the title track. Walsh had first recorded "In the City" for the soundtrack to the 1979 film *The Warriors*.

"A lot of albums sound like they could be outtakes from the last successful record, but we're not into that. The new album is a very noticeable progression from *Hotel California*. Everyone wrote some great rock 'n' roll tunes—the kind of stuff that started when I joined, like 'Life in the Fast Lane'—but they're even more guitar-oriented. I really think that this is as great an evolution on record as the Beatles made from *Rubber Soul* to *Revolver* and then to *Sgt. Pepper*."

The Long Run topped the charts and sold 7 million copies, but some critics considered it a disappointment. The always affable Walsh had been propelled to solo stardom with his own *...But Seriously, Folks* album in 1978, but he put a follow-up on hold. "I've got a commitment to the Eagles right now. After we tour and establish the new record, I'll probably go in the studio again."

The Eagles embarked on an extensive tour for *The Long Run*—and disbanded the following year. ■

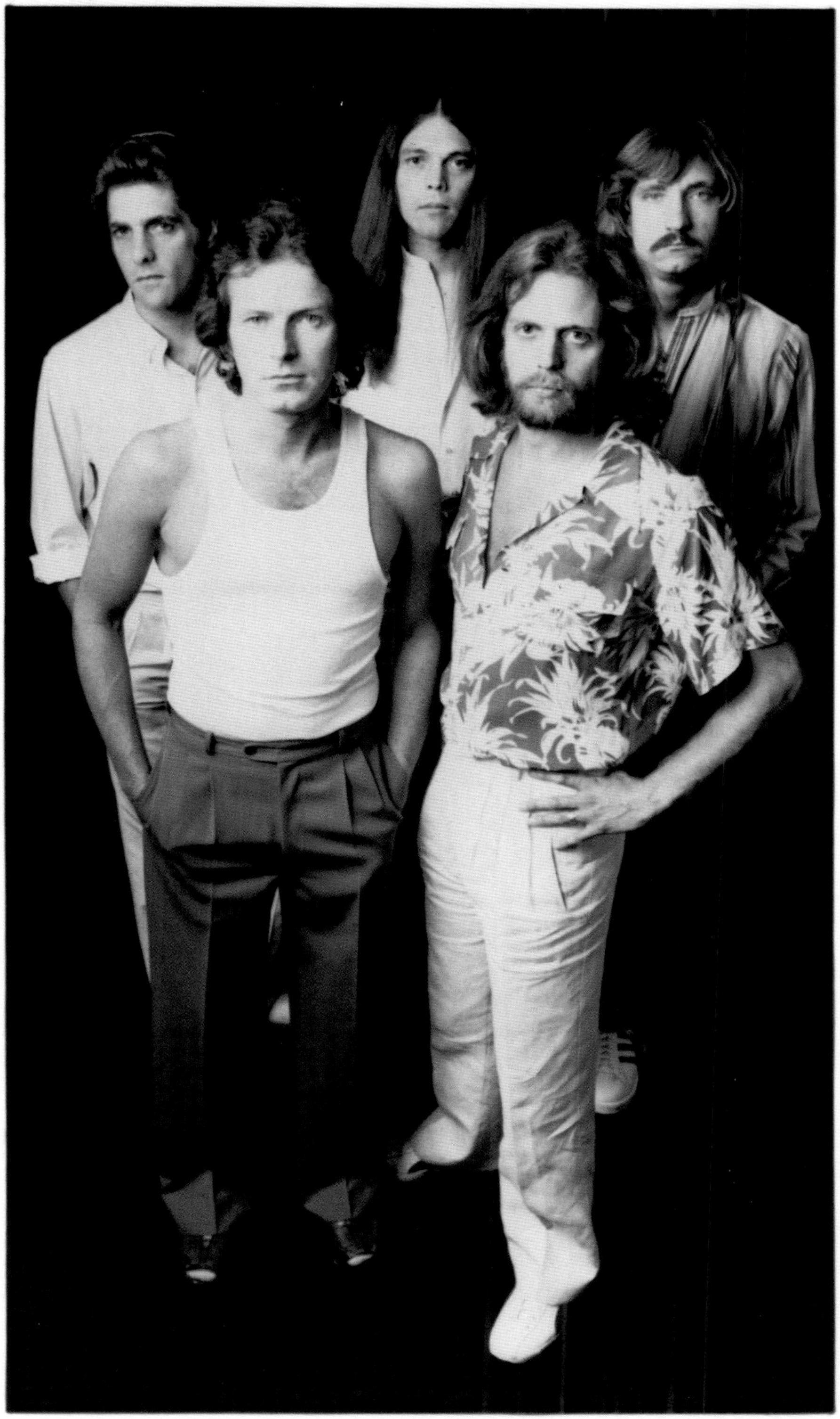

Photo Credit: BRIAN KING /1979

GLENN FREY DON HENLEY TIMOTHY B. SCHMIT DON FELDER JOE WALSH

EAGLES

asylum

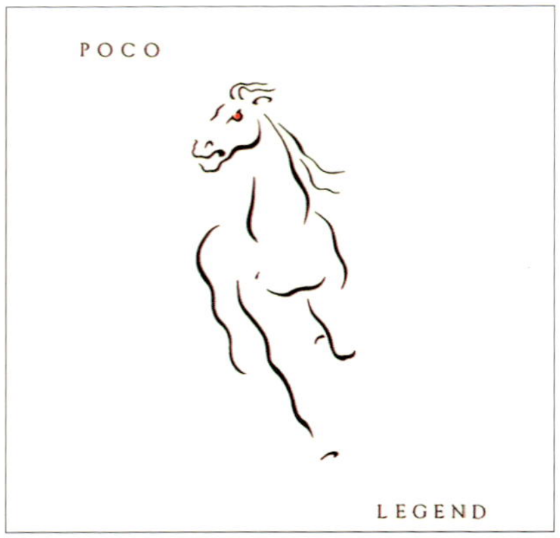

Billboard 200: *Legend* (#14)
Billboard Hot 100: "Crazy Love" (#17); "Heart of the Night" (#20)

Written off by some as a country-rock anachronism, Poco enjoyed a fruitful career rejuvenation with *Legend*.

IN 1968, with Buffalo Springfield in disarray, members Richie Furay and Jim Messina quickly set about assembling a band of their own. They recruited Rusty Young, who had played pedal steel guitar on "Kind Woman" for the final Springfield album. Young called in two buddies from Colorado, George Grantham and Randy Meisner, to play drums and bass, respectively. The new band originally called itself Pogo, but Walt Kelly, the creator of the *Pogo* comic strip, sued.

Poco started out with great commercial promise. Then Meisner left to cofound the Eagles, and guitarist Messina slipped into the Poco bass slot until Timothy B. Schmit signed on in February 1969. In November of that year, Messina split to form a prosperous duo with Kenny Loggins, and guitarist Paul Cotton stepped in to sing and play guitar. In 1973, Furay departed to form the Souther-Hillman-Furay Band—a near-mortal jolt to the group.

Poco plugged on for the next three years, recording such classics as Schmit's "Keep On Tryin'," Young's "Rose of Cimarron" and Cotton's "Indian Summer." But they were left to watch the Eagles adopt the group's sound and emerge as the triumphant synthesis of L.A. country-rock. "We had such a tremendous influence," Young allowed. "But the Eagles were really smart. If they hadn't written a hit song, they went out and found one. They knew how to market."

When Meisner left the Eagles and retired to his native Nebraska, Schmit quit Poco to take his place. Young and Cotton were the last remnants of the traditional Poco lineup when they met keyboardist Kim Bullard. "They were going to start something new called the Cotton-Young Band—they'd had it with the whole Poco thing," Bullard said. "They were writing songs for female vocalists and were auditioning female singers, almost like a Fleetwood Mac situation."

The band ended up recruiting Bullard and an English rhythm section—Steve Chapman on drums and Charlie Harrison on bass—to take on the road for a final tour, releasing one more record under the Poco name in 1979. With *Legend,* its 14th album, Poco finally cracked the top of the charts—the breakthrough, at last.

Young, fittingly, wrote and sang on the gold album's surprise hit single, "Crazy Love," ranked as the No. 1 adult contemporary hit for 1979 by *Billboard.* "That's the irony—when we started this band, I didn't sing or write," Young said. "But I was around great singers and writers, and some of it's bound to rub off. It took a while, but I hit that one song—written in a half-hour. It was a gift."

Cotton's "Heart of the Night" was a second Top 20 hit, and *Legend* (with cover art by graphic artist—and comic—Phil Hartman) lifted Poco's spirits. "A lot of people did us favors and went out on a limb for us over the years," Young said. "We couldn't let them down. We owed them something. We believed in the value of the future, not the past." ■

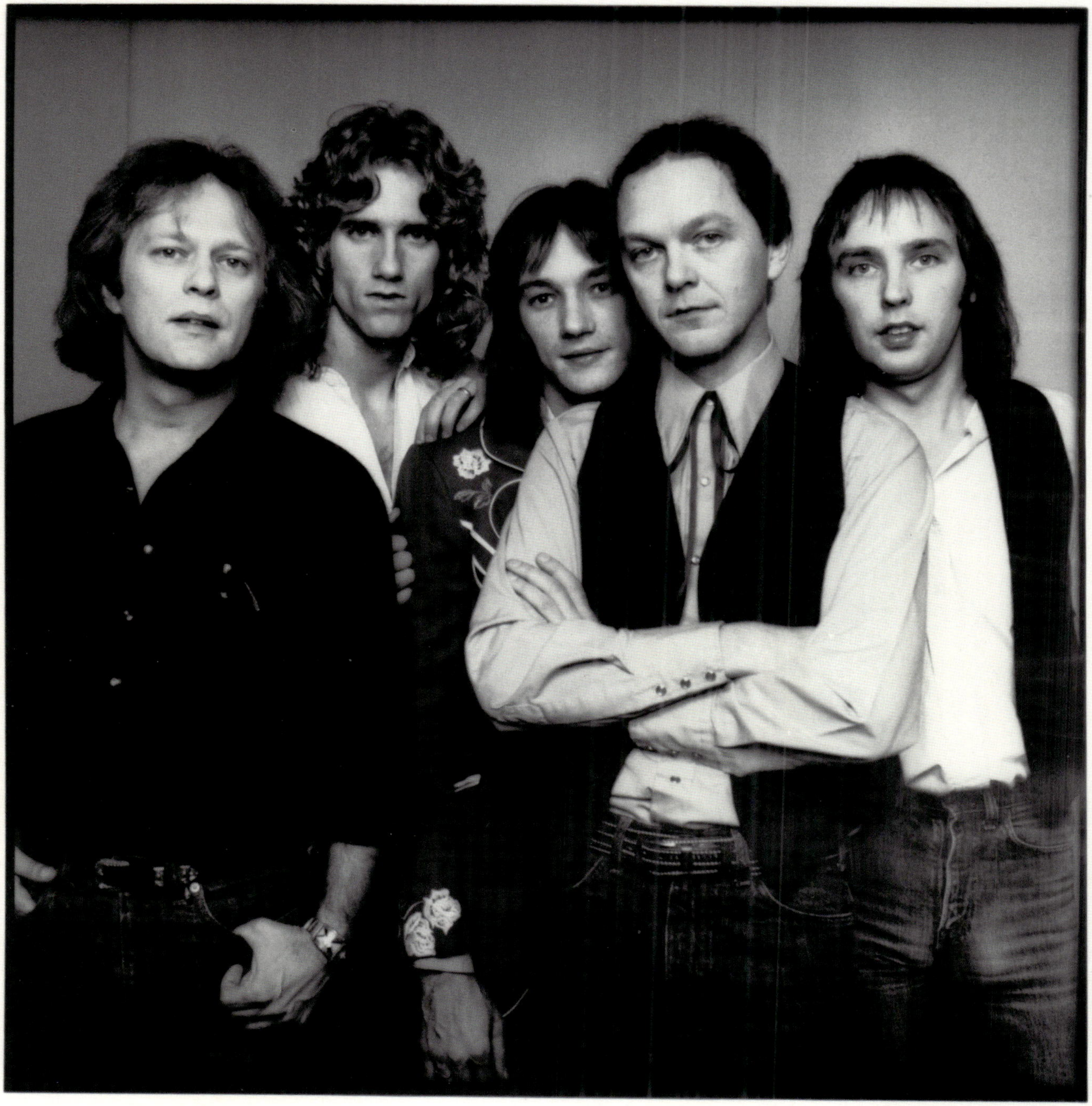

abc Records®

POCO

HARTMANN & GOODMAN
1500
CROSS ROADS OF THE WORLD
HOLLYWOOD
U.S.A
90028

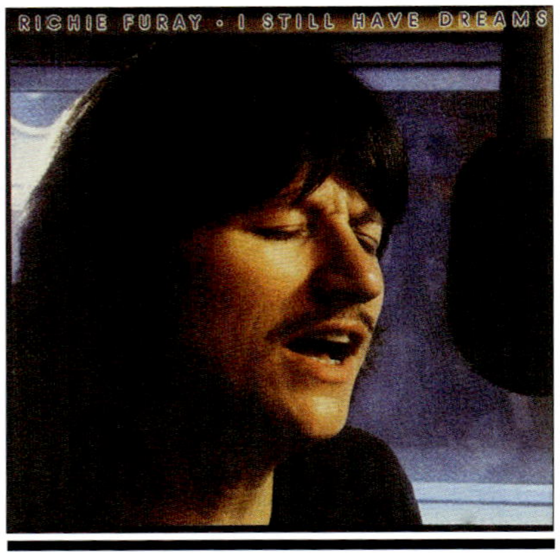

Billboard Hot 100: "I Still Have Dreams" (#39)

Keeping the faith, Richie Furay was rewarded with the title track of *I Still Have Dreams*, his last secular hit.

IN THE spring of 1966, Richie Furay formed Buffalo Springfield with Stephen Stills and Neil Young. The West Coast group had only one major hit (Stills' ominous protest song, "For What It's Worth"), but Furay's songs made the rock band perhaps the first to experiment with a country sound. His best-known track with Springfield was "Kind Woman," which he wrote for his wife, Nancy.

The volatile outfit broke up in 1969, and Furay formed Poco. In the fall of 1970, he and the remaining band members moved to Colorado. Furay provided Poco's most distinctive composition, 1973's "A Good Feeling to Know," but the track failed to make the singles chart. Frustrated by the record's lack of commercial success, Furay left Poco to form the Souther-Hillman-Furay Band, a ready-made supergroup put together by record mogul David Geffen.

By all indications, success was a lock. J.D. Souther was a masterful songwriter in the Eagles mold, Chris Hillman's utilitarian prowess had helped pioneer country rock, and Furay's Buffalo Springfield and Poco roots supposedly clinched it. Furay wrote "Fallin' in Love," SHF's sole hit. But the band never jelled, evaporating after two years.

"David seemed to be the guy who could put his hand on anything—Jackson Browne, Linda Ronstadt, Joni Mitchell, the Eagles," Furay mused. "So why not us? But what looks good on paper doesn't always translate in real life."

Yet while recording the second Souther-Hillman-Furay album at Caribou Ranch in Nederland, Colorado, steel guitarist Al Perkins—a former Flying Burrito Brother and a member of Manassas—suggested Furay consider Christianity as an alternative lifestyle.

"When Chris Hillman wanted Al in the band, I said, 'No way—I know this guy's reputation. He's one of those born-again Christians with a Jesus sticker on his guitar,'" Furay remembered. "I didn't want anything to get in the way of my personal success. But I couldn't deny his musicianship. And I couldn't put my finger on what was different and attractive. This guy was in the middle of rock 'n' roll, and he wasn't getting drunk or doing drugs or chasing women every night. But he was having fun, being creative and enjoying music. When my wife and I separated for seven months, I hit the bottom. That's when I finally prayed with Al, and that's when I found God's plan for me. I was consumed with wanting to be a big rock 'n' roll star, but stars burn out."

Furay gave his life to the Lord and pursued a solo career, becoming one of the first rock stars to make Christian music for the general market. The standout title track of his third solo album, *I Still Have Dreams*, became a Top 40 radio hit.

"It's one of the most fun records I've ever made—I was comfortable with those L.A. musicians," Furay said. "But I'm on another mission—trying to pioneer that there is something to be said in the music. I have it in my mind and in my heart that I'm putting together the rock 'n' roll band for Christ. People know what my life is about." ■

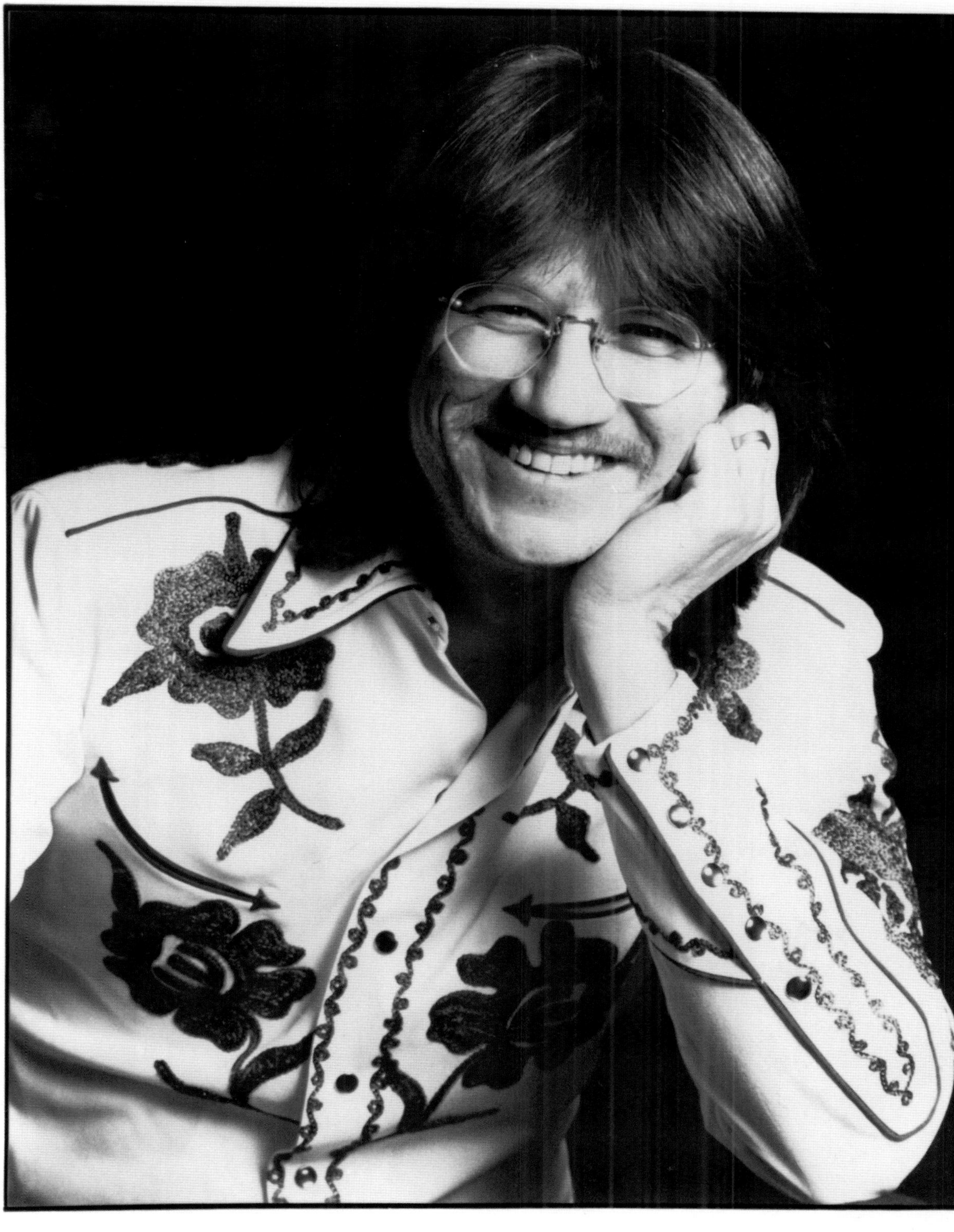

Photo Credit: ANDY KATZ

RICHIE FURAY

asylum

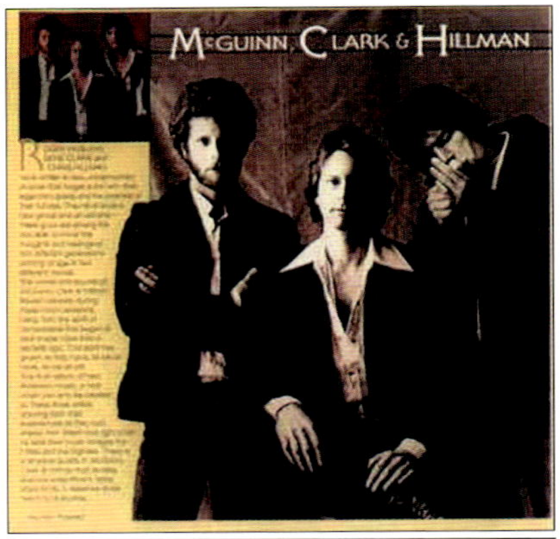

Billboard 200: *McGuinn, Clark & Hillman* (#39)
Billboard Hot 100: "Don't You Write Her Off" (#33)

McGuinn, Clark & Hillman came off as adult folk-rock stylists with a sound that well-nigh evoked the Byrds.

AT THEIR mid-Sixties peak, with Roger McGuinn at the helm, the Byrds were arguably the most important group in American rock music. But McGuinn struggled to keep the band intact before its final 1973 breakup. He renewed his relationship with Gene Clark and Chris Hillman, two of his former partners in the Byrds who had met with success elsewhere. The trio was heard together on *McGuinn, Clark & Hillman.*

McGuinn applied his distinctly sweet voice to only two compositions on the album. One of them, the single "Don't You Write Her Off," rose into the Top 30.

"It's basically the same form as when I first played it for (Gene and Chris). We added some nice counterpoint harmonies in the choruses that sparked it along a little bit. It's bouncy, happy tune with a Caribbean groove," he allowed with his famous faith-in-the-future countenance.

The reunion effort proved short-lived, but he did address a nagging question. Why did the former Jim McGuinn change his name to Roger for 1968's *The Notorious Byrd Brothers* album?

"I was in correspondence with an Indonesian seer at the time," the soft-spoken artist explained. "He told me to send him 10 names that began with the letter R. Being a sci-fi fan, I sent him names like Retro, Rocket and Roger, as in 'Roger Wilco.' He wrote back saying my new name should be Roger—it's supposed to vibrate with my soul. But I don't know that it's done me much good." ■

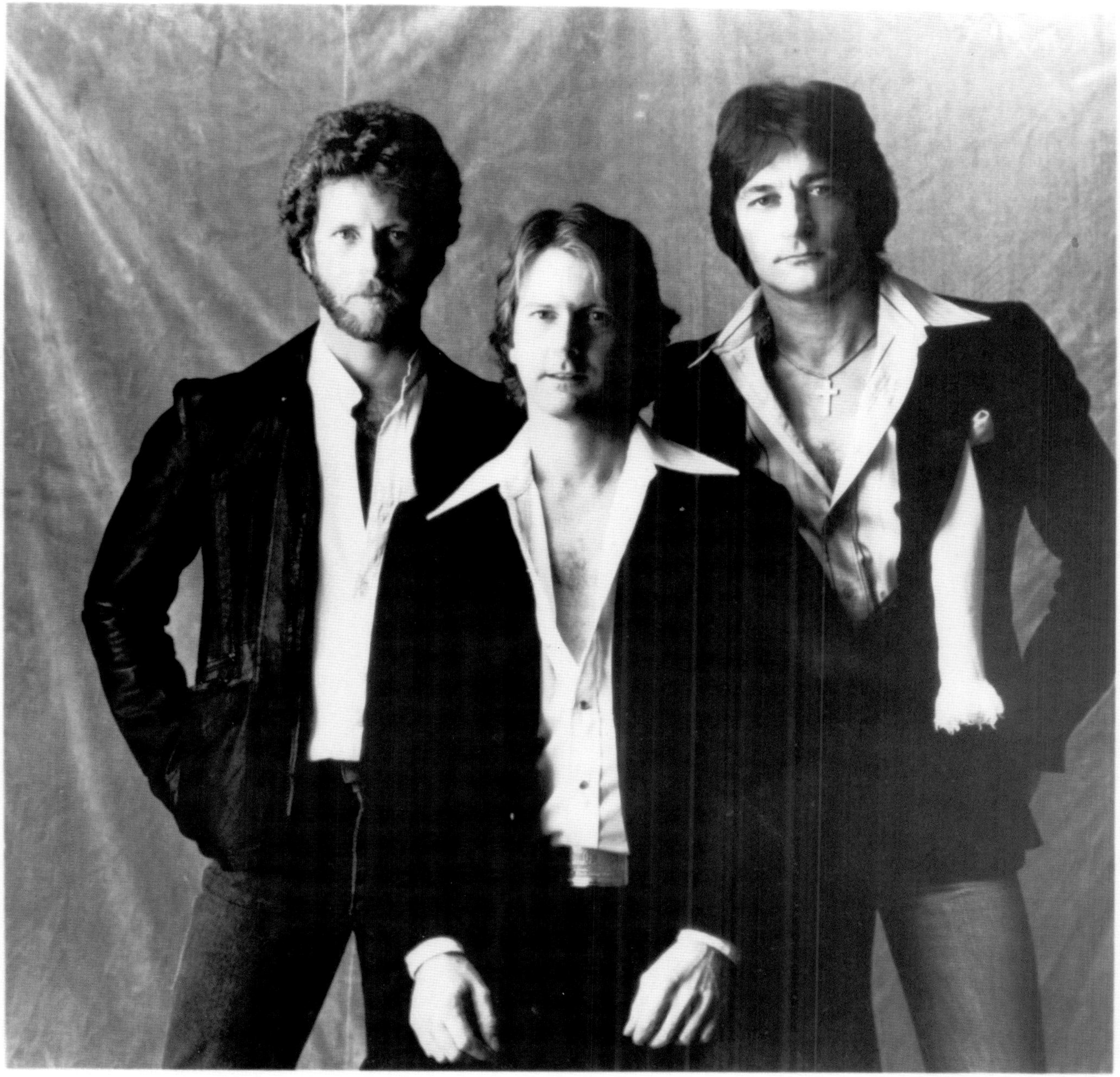

Chris Hillman Roger McGuinn Gene Clark

McGUINN, CLARK & HILLMAN

Capitol RECORDS

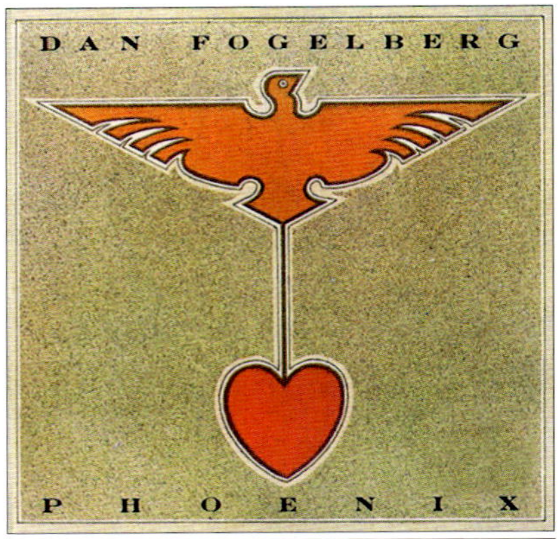

Riding a creative and commercial onrush, Dan Fogelberg composed and recorded the graceful *Phoenix* album.

Billboard 200: *Phoenix* (#3)
Billboard Hot 100: "Longer" (#2); "Heart Hotels" (#21)

DAN FOGELBERG grew up playing in garage bands and, while studying painting at the University of Illinois, realized music was the focus of his creative talent. He left school to follow that muse and headed for the West Coast, finding inspiration during a week in Colorado before moving on. Under the aegis of his manager, Irving Azoff, Fogelberg secured a recording contract.

His first album, *Home Free*, was recorded and produced in Nashville by Norbert Putnam. For his second release, *Souvenirs*, Fogelberg enlisted producer Joe Walsh, who helped him expand on his sparse, countrified folk sound. His growth as a songwriter was most evident on "Part of the Plan," a buoyant, radio-friendly hit single that catapulted him into the commercial firmament at the height of the California rock explosion alongside such hit makers as the Eagles, Jackson Browne and Joni Mitchell.

While touring through Colorado in the mid-Seventies and promoting *Captured Angel*, his third album, Fogelberg learned that a mountain house west of Boulder was on the market. He fell in love with the Nederland spread and bought it from one of his favorite musicians, Chris Hillman, who had played with the Byrds, the Flying Burrito Brothers and Manassas. Fogelberg flew to his Nashville farm, packed up his belongings and hurried back to his Rocky Mountain hideaway.

He plunged into a season of solitude and composing, resulting in the songs for his next album, *Nether Lands*. Written in a more ornate and elaborately conceived idiom, it brought together his signature sound—from-the-heart lyrics with lightly harmonized rock, pop, country and folk ideas with vestiges of classical influences. *Nether Lands* attained to platinum status and endeared him to a loyal legion of fans.

"I grew up with that album," Fogelberg said. "When I made *Nether Lands*, I didn't feel like I was imitating anyone, paying tribute to my influences like the Beatles and Buffalo Springfield. Suddenly it felt like, 'This is my music, this is what I'm about.' When you discover your own voice, it's so incredibly exciting that you never want to let go. Sometimes you go down paths that aren't as good as others, but it's important to be receptive. Once that fire is set in you, I don't know that you can ever extinguish it."

Fogelberg anticipated that his next venture, *Phoenix*, would "tie off the Seventies for me, clean up loose ends and sever the cord." *Phoenix* went to the top of the charts, helped by the hits "Heart Hotels" and "Longer," which he jokingly described as "the song that put me on the elevators." It traversed from sumptuous acoustic flavors to the electric rock of the title track.

The notoriously reserved Fogelberg continued to experiment—paint and photograph and play from the nurturing cocoon of his Colorado hideaway. "It's a pretty calm existence and I cherish that—I'm not a very social person," he said. "I don't want to give anything away—my private life is separate from my musical life. The mountains have been a very healing place for me. You go through a lot of changes in life, but these mountains will always be here." ■

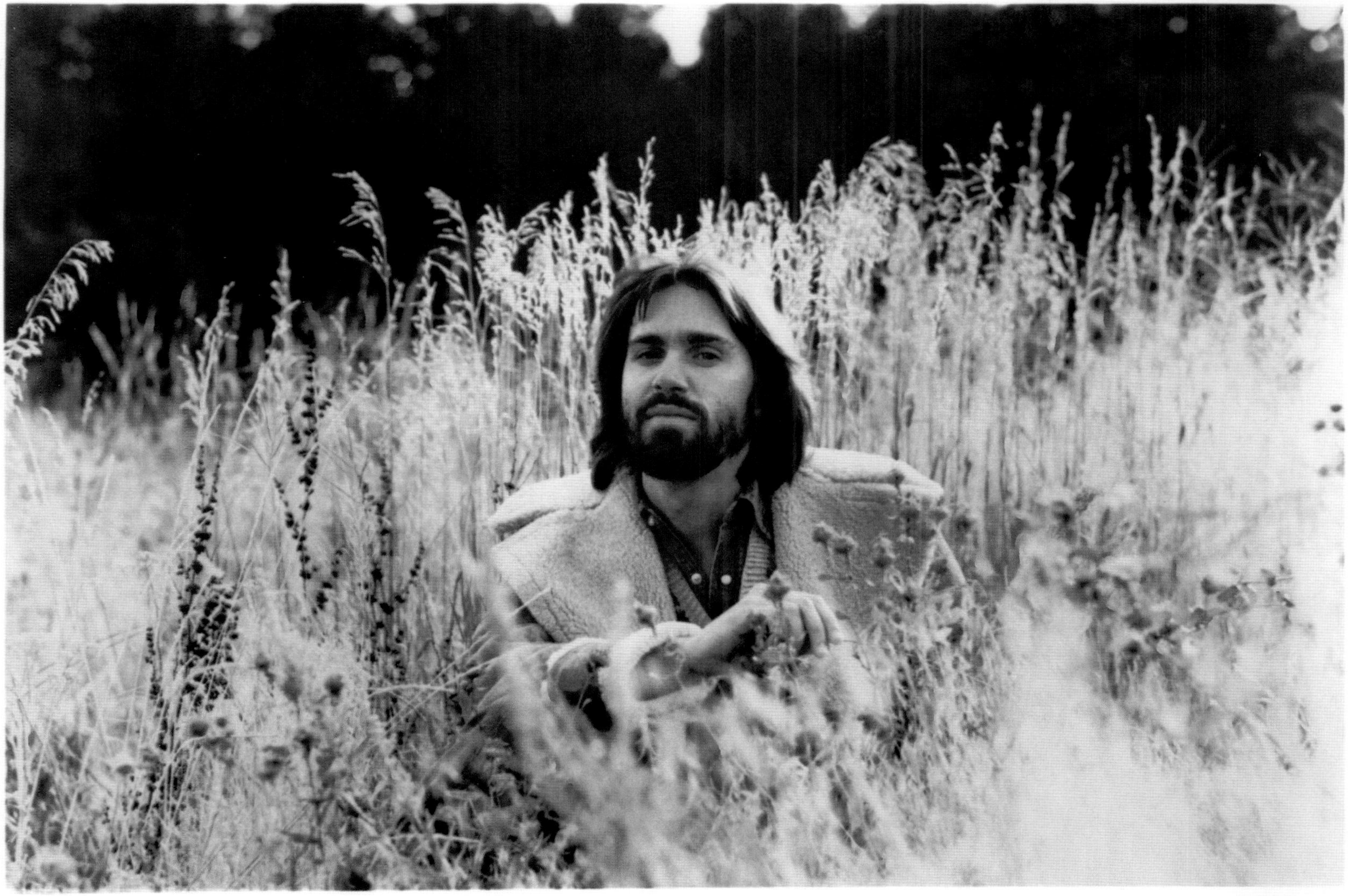

DAN FOGELBERG

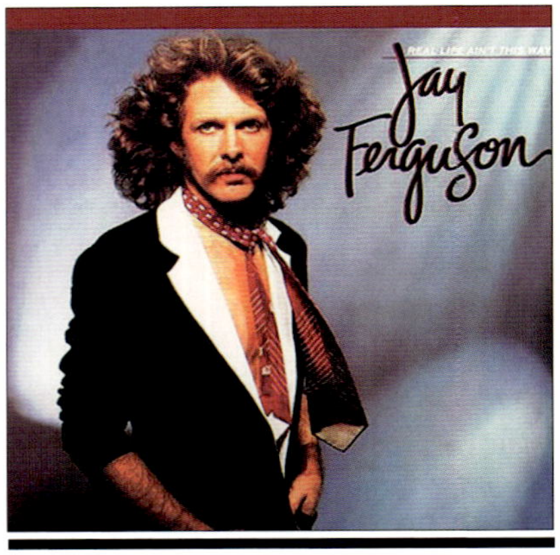

Billboard 200: *Real Life Ain't This Way* (#86)
Billboard Hot 100: "Shakedown Cruise" (#31)

Jay Ferguson followed the Top 40 boom of "Thunder Island" with an equally zestful hit, "Shakedown Cruise."

JAY FERGUSON had been partly responsible for two influential rock bands. In the Sixties, he and high school friend Mark Andes met wunderkind guitarist Randy California and journeyman jazz drummer Ed Cassidy. They formed Spirit and produced four strong albums, including such songs as "I Got a Line on You," "Nature's Way" and "Mr. Skin."

"We had a good combination," Ferguson said, "a good, strong jazz background, that Jimi Hendrix East Coast rock thing and that San Fernando Valley sort of Anglo surfer sound. If it had an English accent or went surfing, we bought it."

Ferguson and Andes decided to leave Spirit to form Jo Jo Gunne (the title of an obscure Chuck Berry tune about a mischievous jungle monkey), a band with a heavier, harder approach. After four albums and a standout single, "Run, Run, Run," the band succumbed to the rigors of constant touring. "It really took the heart out of us," Ferguson recalled. "We were just machines toward the end."

The keyboardist then pursued a solo career. In 1976, he released *All Alone in the End Zone*, produced by long-time friend Bill Szymczyk, who was also producer for the Eagles. The next album, the fruitful *Thunder Island*, started slow but gradually climbed into the charts on the strength of its smash title track.

"*Thunder Island* was 'commercial,' and thus kind of light," Ferguson said. "I didn't want to make another commercial album in exactly that sense."

Real Life Ain't This Way spawned the single "Shakedown Cruise," sparing Ferguson from one-hit-wonder status. "It's sort of a combination of *Two Years Before the Mast* and *A Clockwork Orange*—droogs at sea! It's my personal childhood pirate fantasies brought up to date."

Ferguson also got happy living with his wife and growing produce on their farmland near Santa Barbara. ■

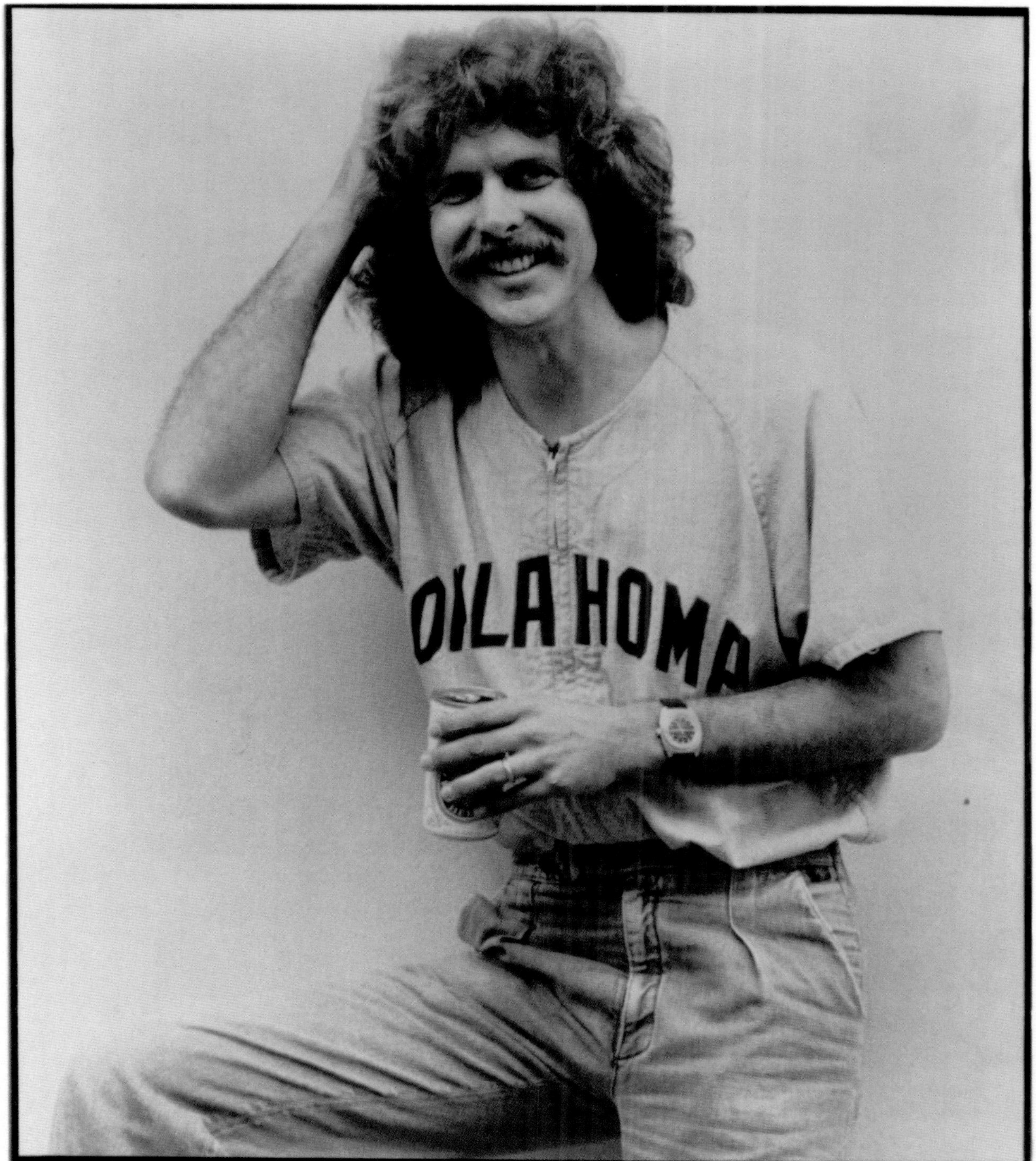

Photo Credit: DAVID GAHR

Jay Ferguson

asylum

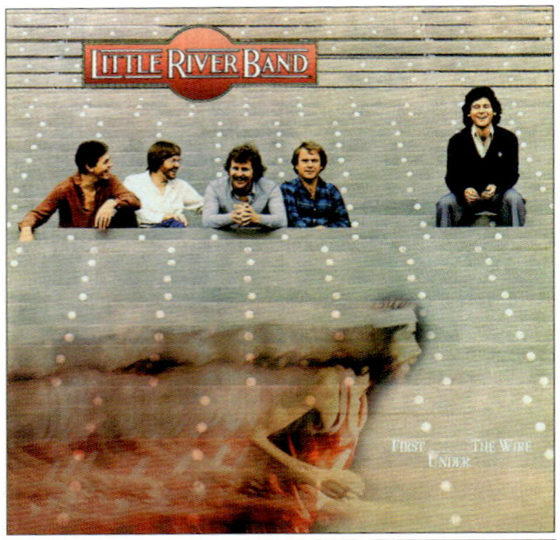

Billboard 200: *First Under the Wire* (#10)
Billboard Hot 100: "Lonesome Loser" (#6); "Cool Change" (#10)

Most outfits would have hocked their amps to gain the repute that Little River Band won with "Cool Change."

THE SONGS "Reminiscing" and "Lady" had established Australia's Little River Band as reliable hitmakers, and two more Top 10 singles, "Lonesome Loser" and the standout "Cool Change" from *First Under the Wire*, further endeared the group to American listeners. LRB's mellow pop sense was carried by the scintillating harmonies of lead singer Glenn Shorrock and rhythm guitarists Beeb Birtles and Graeham Goble.

But audiences still didn't know much about the individual members, for whom performing so far from home had proved an emotionally taxing experience in the past. "With the distance involved, we have to go out for such a long period of time to justify going out at all," guitarist David Briggs explained.

Drummer Derek Pellicci, whose economic but inventive use of syndrums was an interesting sidelight to the group's sound, had returned after suffering serious burns in an accident. Original bassist George McArdle left the band immediately after the recording of *First Under the Wire*.

"George had a 'religious experience,' so he decided he couldn't mix rock 'n' roll with religion," Briggs said. "Now he studies the *Bible* up in the Blue Mountains of Australia. Very dramatic, isn't it? It was a surprise, but you can't fault someone for doing what he wants to."

The group members got to call their own shots Down Under. Shorrock, the affable frontman, had a Top 10 single in Australia, and Birtles and Goble had teamed up for an album. Briggs indulged in a heavy production schedule. "It's not like anybody is going to leave the band as soon as a solo career is established," he assured. "We all play on each other's records anyway." ■

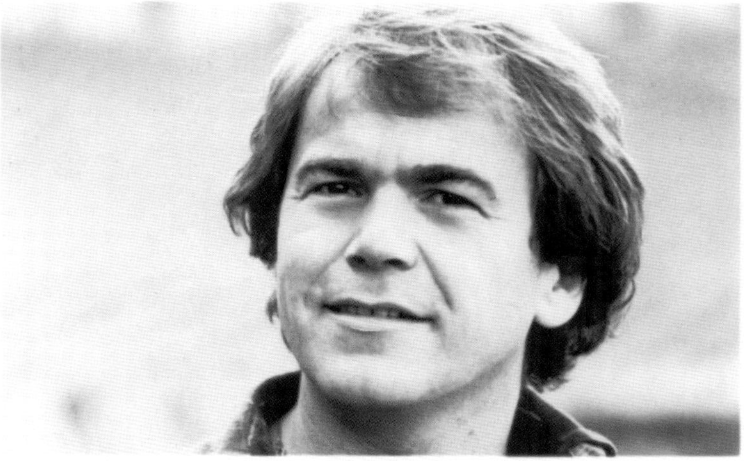

Glenn Shorrock

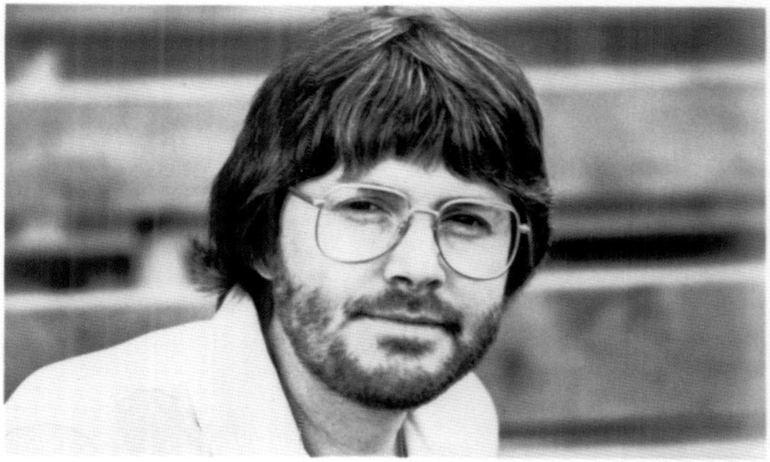

Graham Goble

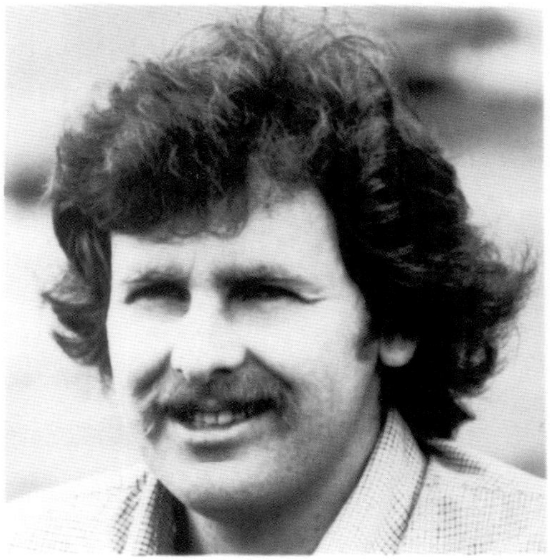

David Briggs

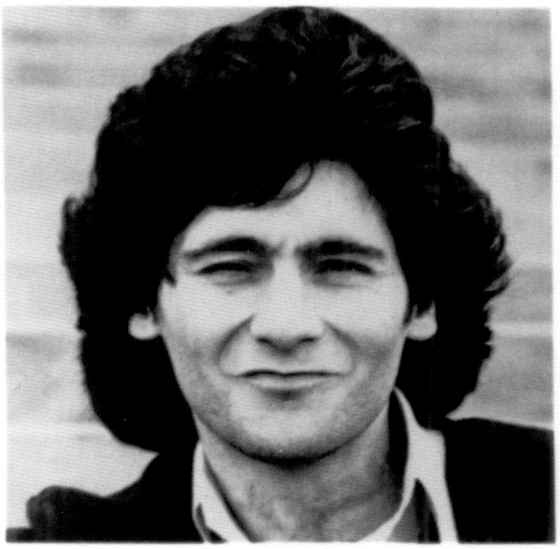

Derek Pellicci

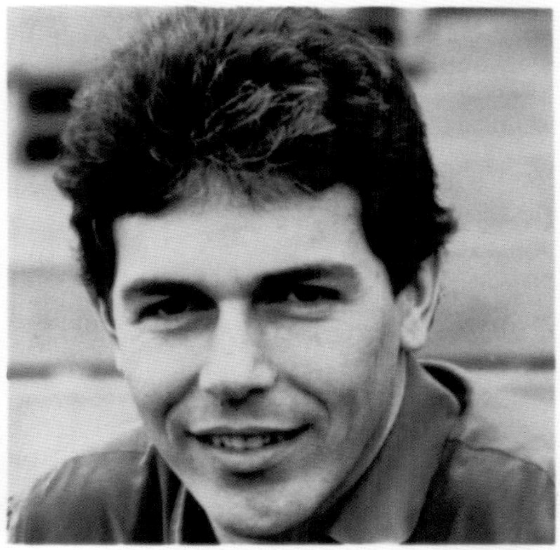

Beeb Birtles

LITTLE RIVER BAND®

Capitol RECORDS

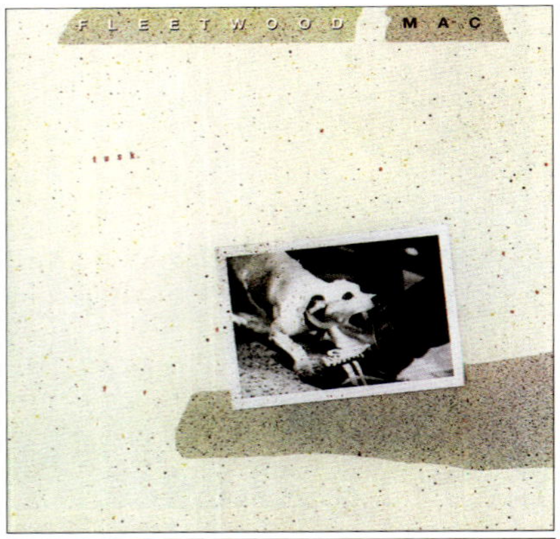

Billboard 200: *Tusk* (#4)
Billboard Hot 100: "Tusk" (#8); "Sara" (#7); "Think About Me" (#20); "Sisters of the Moon" (#86)

Helming *Tusk*, a taxing Fleetwood Mac album, Lindsey Buckingham proved himself a consummate musician.

WITH PARTNER Stevie Nicks in tow, Lindsey Buckingham joined Fleetwood Mac in 1975. Almost instantly, the lanky musician helped propel the ever-morphing British ensemble from the ranks of respected also-rans into the realm of superstar acts. First came the group's self-titled hit album, followed by the wonder of *Rumours*, a work of irresistible soft rock and passionate hard pop that sold more than 13 million copies worldwide.

It was no secret that the landmark record's lyrics detailed the rocky romantic history of the band's members—Buckingham's romantic turmoil with Nicks as well as the disintegration of John and Christine McVie's marriage. How such tensions could produce such genius was an endearing mystery surrounding Fleetwood Mac when the membership reunited for the follow-up to *Rumours*.

"There has definitely been pressure on us," drummer Mick Fleetwood admitted. "People have been telling us we can never manage another *Rumours*, but we set out with the intention of proving them wrong."

An ambitious double album conceived largely by Buckingham, *Tusk* contained 20 tunes written by the band's three resident composers—Buckingham, Nicks and Christine McVie. Its strange charm could be attributed directly to Buckingham's eccentric signature, with his daring arrangements and intricately layered production offsetting his already familiar talents as a singer and guitarist.

"The album was a reaction to the huge success of *Rumours* and what was expected of us, which was to make '*Rumours 2*' and sell another 20 million albums," Buckingham said. "I was very much in a frame of mind to pull a left turn so we didn't fall into the trap of that axiom, 'If it works, run it into the ground.' The reason that all of us got into this in the first place wasn't really about money. It was about being true to what you think is interesting and pursuing that, sometimes at the cost of commerce."

An antic verve marked the album's title track, which was augmented with 112 members of the University of Southern California Trojan Marching Band. Nicks' six-minutes-plus opus "Sara" was edited into a hit single version, and Christine McVie's solid piano and smoky voice shined on the song "Think About Me."

"There was a lot of support from the band during the making of *Tusk*—everyone was really excited about it," Buckingham reported. "But then it became apparent that it wasn't going to sell 10 to 15 million copies like the albums before. Then the attitudes about the music started to change, which was sad for me—it makes me wonder where their priorities are. That's really not the point of doing it. It's to reshape people's preconceptions about pop music."

Despite generally favorable critical reaction, *Tusk* was largely misunderstood in the rock marketplace and put Buckingham on the spot. "It hurt my feelings a little bit. All of a sudden, the band was turning to me saying, 'It's your fault we didn't sell *x* number of albums.' But that was the risk we took in doing something experimental in the first place." ■

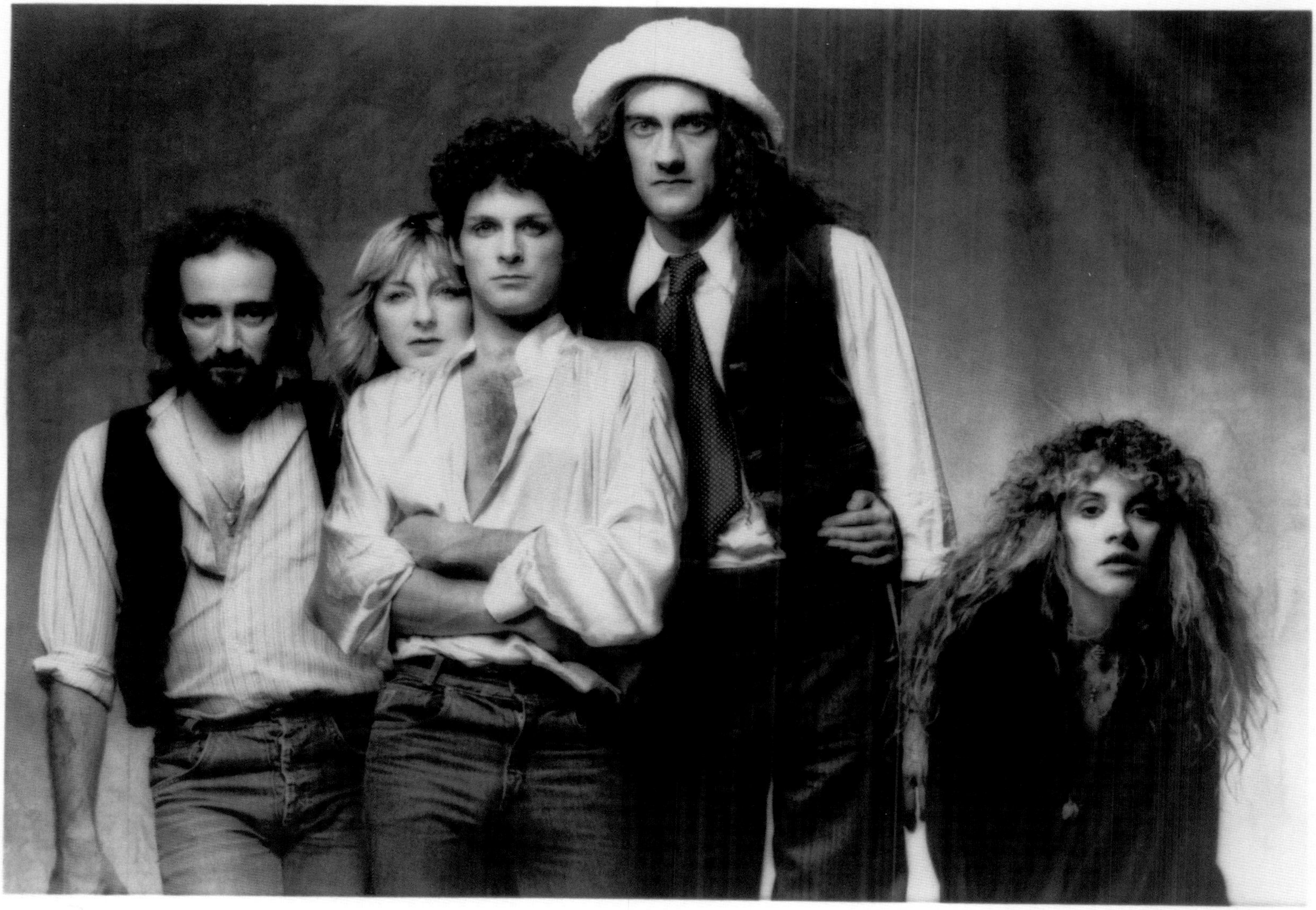

OCTOBER 1979

FLEETWOOD MAC

WARNER BROS.

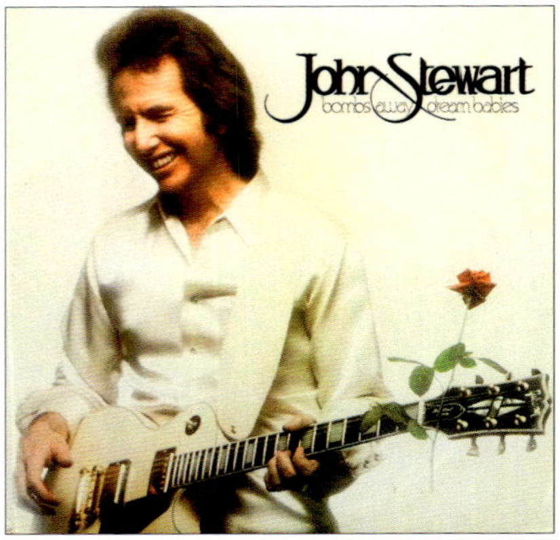

Billboard 200: *Bombs Away Dream Babies* (#10)
Billboard Hot 100: "Gold" (#5); "Midnight Wind" (#28); "Lost Her in the Sun" (#34)

John Stewart joined up with Fleetwood Mac's Lindsey Buckingham and delivered *Bombs Away Dream Babies*.

JOHN STEWART'S career had had its share of ups and downs—contributing to the folk music movement in the early Sixties with the Kingston Trio, then the largest-selling group in the world; big royalty checks from the Monkees and Anne Murray for writing "Daydream Believer"; and a slew of critically acclaimed and commercially snubbed albums (notably *California Bloodlines*) in the early Seventies filed under "folk," "country," "folk rock" or "pop" in record stores.

"Things are very tight in the record business—it's tough on everybody, not just ol' John," Stewart said. "See, I've been through this so many times that it's nothing new to me. If I wasn't optimistic, I wouldn't be doing it. It's just a matter of finding the one guy who likes what I'm doing."

Lindsey Buckingham from Fleetwood Mac, still riding high on the success of *Rumours*, played a substantial role in the success of Stewart's *Bombs Away Dream Babies* album. Buckingham, who sang, played guitar and co-produced, and Stevie Nicks (who sang background vocals), were ardent Stewart fans who had once played the grooves off old Kingston Trio recordings.

"The man is a genius, and I don't say that lightly," Stewart enthused about Buckingham. "I've worked with a lot of people and he is blessed, absolutely the most innovative, creative guy I've ever known. We've been gigging around Southern California, and I haven't had so much fun onstage since the Kingston Trio."'

Everything fell into place for Stewart when *Bombs Away Dream Babies* spawned three hits and made him an "overnight sensation" at the age of 40. The music was more aggressive and assertive.

"I know now that it's very easy to hear a hit record—after it's a hit. When I went in to do *Bombs Away*, I had three songs—'Lost Her in the Sun,' 'Midnight Wind' and 'Gold'—and I was told by the record company that they weren't hits, and that I couldn't do the album until I came up with some hits. And then, in the final analysis, they were the three hits. I know what a guessing game this really is."

The music-business veteran saw dealing with record labels was just another step in promoting his work. "It's a marriage," he explained. "The problem is that it's a marriage made before you date—there's no wooing process there, so you don't know if you're going to get along." ■

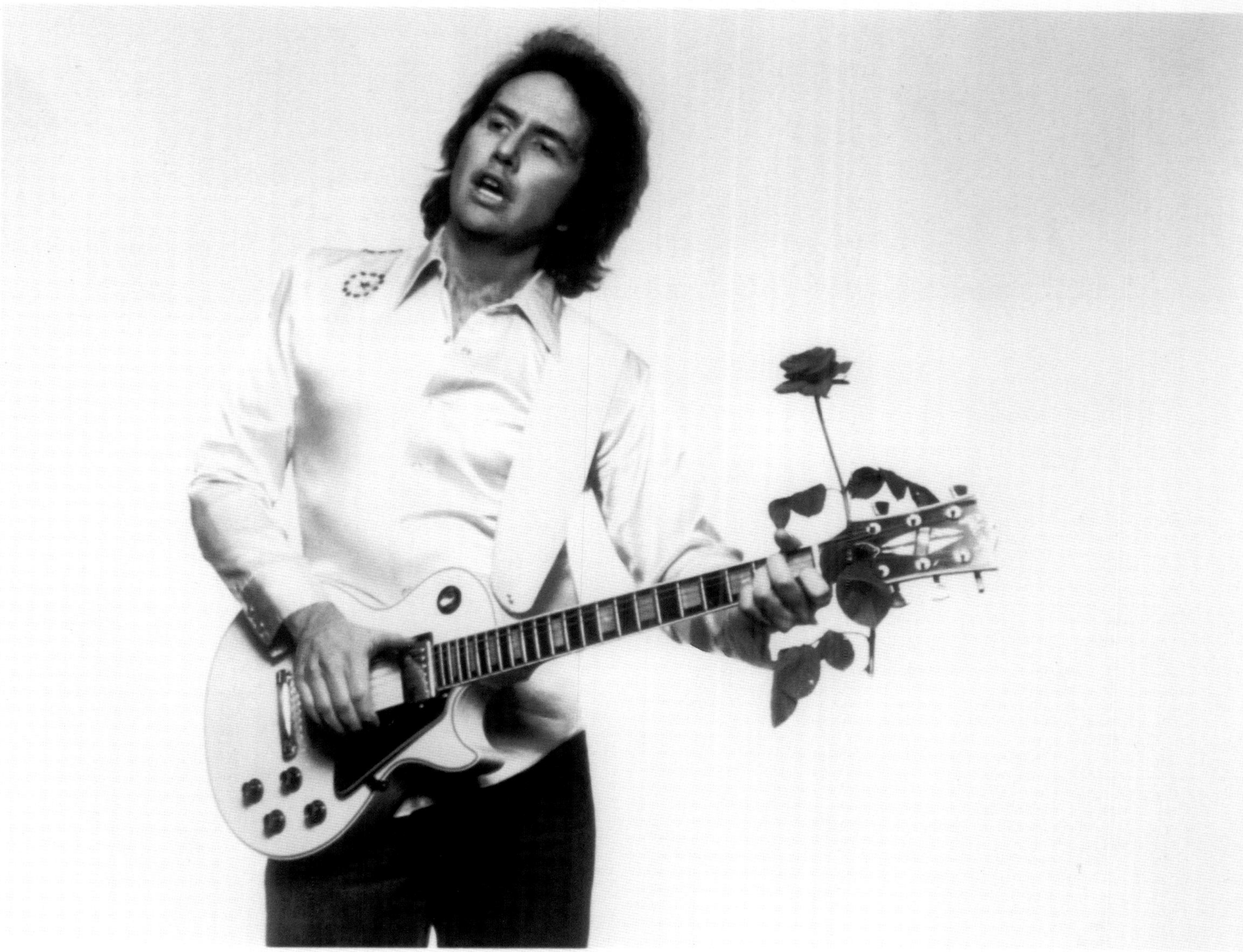

JOHN STEWART

RSO Records, Inc.

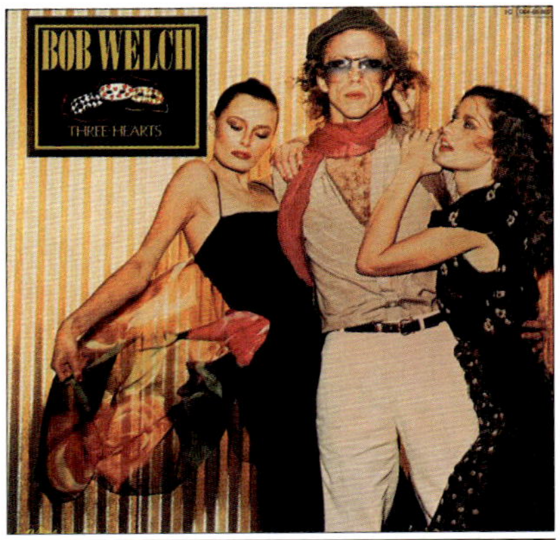

Billboard 200: *Three Hearts* (#20)
Billboard Hot 100: "Precious Love" (#19); "Church" (#73)

On *Three Hearts*, his second solo release, Bob Welch replicated the platinum precepts of the hit *French Kiss*.

WHEN HE left Fleetwood Mac just prior to that band's explosive success, Bob Welch's sense of timing took a beating, but the guitarist turned those circumstances into a successful career on his own.

A Los Angeles native, Welch had begun his musical path working with the Seven Souls, a seven-piece showband. "All my earliest playing experience had to do with jazz and R&B," he said. "It was the style of playing that groups like Earth, Wind & Fire were later to refine and perfect. But the music we played then was not the blues. We always played with a certain degree of slickness—in fact, as far as *blues* blues goes, I don't think that I even learned to bend a string until I got into Fleetwood Mac."

In 1971, Welch was approached to fill the guitarist slot vacated by Jeremy Spencer in that British-based blues band. "I had been writing some things, one of which was 'Future Games,'" he noted. "It turned out that everybody wanted me to contribute." Welch became one of Fleetwood Mac's main singers and songwriters through four years and five albums. "In a way, I had too much freedom, and I remember wondering sometimes if it would be easier if we had a real label, like 'hard-rock band' or 'jazz group' or whatever. But there we were, stuck with all this horrendous originality."

Welch left the group in 1975 and formed Paris. With the demise of that hard rock trio, he then became a solo act, and *French Kiss* established him as both a recording artist and concert attraction. A new version of the Fleetwood Mac song "Sentimental Lady," featuring Mac members Christine McVie and Lindsey Buckingham playing and producing, gave the album its initial attention. The hard-driving "Ebony Eyes" became Welch's signature song, with "Hot Love, Cold World" following in its wake.

With *Three Hearts*, Welsh generated another an infectious rocker in "Precious Love," a vibrant, bouncy Top 20 smash, and a minor hit in "Church."

"I relaxed and did what I could do best, which is write songs that I, myself, would like to hear on the radio, rather than songs that would impress my friends with my obscure and moody brilliance—and I'm only half-kidding. There's a great tendency for musicians to write for other musicians who will automatically know when a D minor 9 flat 5 chord is played—much rehearsal and no song."

Welch was never a stranger to the successes and frustrations of the entertainment business. His father, Robert L. Welch, produced a string of hit films at Paramount with Bob Hope and Lucille Ball, and produced the first Academy Awards television broadcast and *The Thin Man* episodes for NBC.

"My father always told me that, especially in show business, there are those moments when everything comes together exactly as the artist feels it," Welch said. "Those are the times every creative person lives for." ■

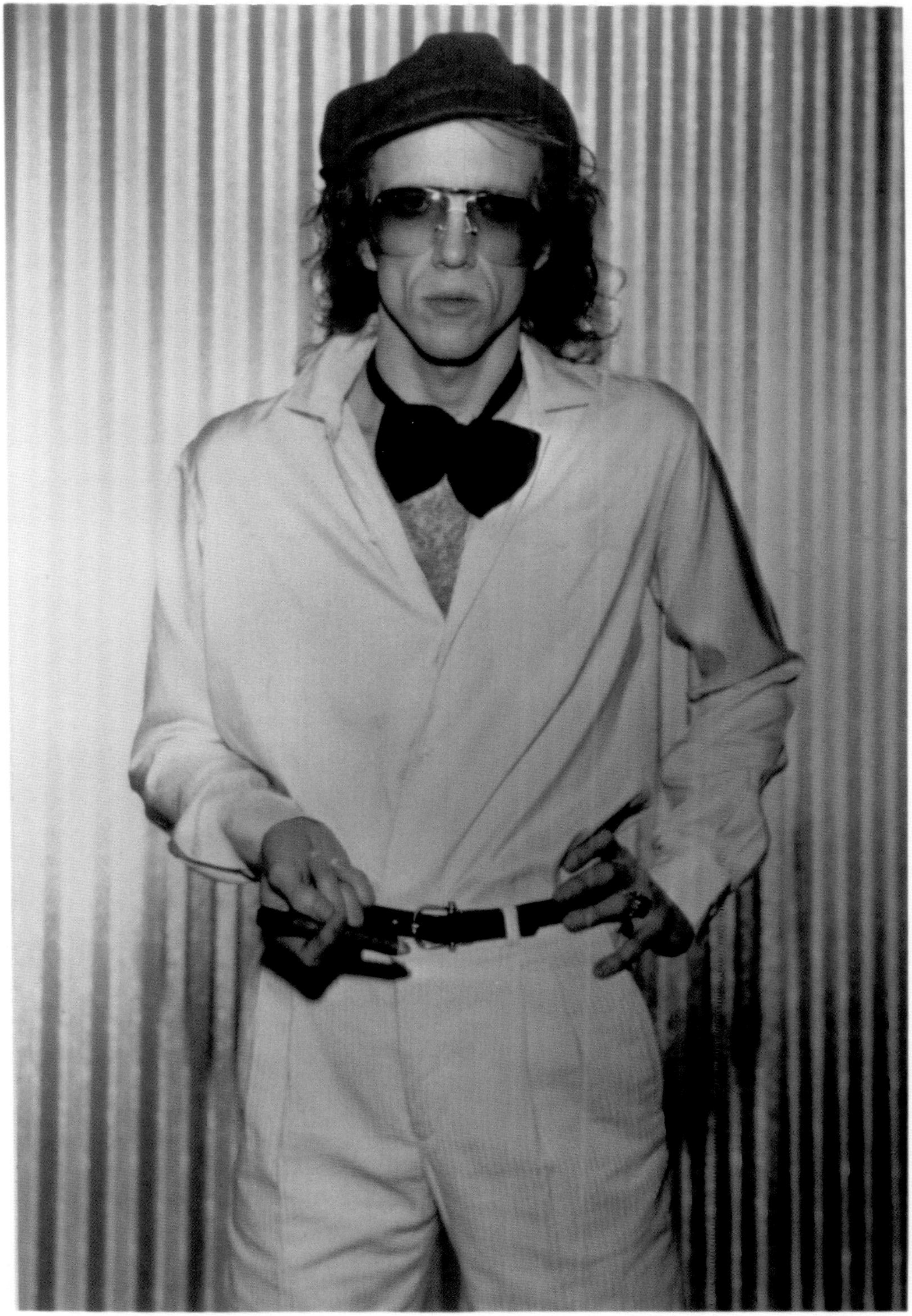

BOB WELCH

Photo: Olivier Ferrand

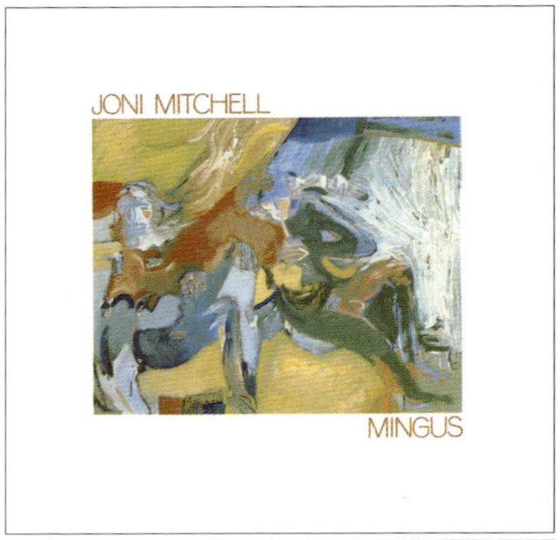

Billboard 200: *Mingus* (#17)

Canadian singer-songwriter Joni Mitchell declined to be diminished by the restrictions of gender and genre.

A POET who explored deep feelings and personal experiences—music she referred to as "confessional"—Joni Mitchell typified the singer-songwriter movement. Her total originality as a female artist was on display with 1971's *Blue*, shown in emotional and insightful lyrics and her piano and open-tuned guitar compositions. 1974's *Court and Spark*, recorded with Tom Scott and the L.A. Express, saw her adapt to an upbeat rock milieu with a funky, jazzy flavor.

"Pigeonholes all seem funny to me," she said. "I feel like one of those lifer-educational types that just keeps going for letters after their name. I want the full hyphenate—folk-rock-country-jazz-classics. So finally, when you get all the hyphens in, maybe they'll drop them all—and get down to just some American music."

In her pursuit of newer, more sophisticated modes of expression, Mitchell explored working with noted jazz musicians. She was contacted by Charles Mingus, the esteemed composer and bassist who was suffering from Lou Gehrig's Disease. He had liked some music of hers played to him by a friend and wanted her to write lyrics to some of his melodies. They began a collaboration, but he died before the resulting album, *Mingus*, was completed.

The experimental work had jazz elements, but it was not a jazz album in the strict, traditional sense. The main musicians were Herbie Hancock (keyboards), Wayne Shorter (saxophone), Jaco Pastorius (bass) and Peter Erskine (drums).

"The Dry Cleaner from Des Moines" was one of four songs where the lyrics were by Mitchell, while the music was composed by Mingus. Fans were confused over such a major change in Mitchell's overall sound.

"If I have any expectations or hope, it would be that people would find it accessible," she mused. "I'm talking about the context of the pop field. I would be surprised if it wasn't accepted in the jazz world, because it contains all the best elements of that music. It's very spontaneous, creative and fresh. You can't really say it's jazz or pop. It's not an obviously classified sound, and that will give it a better chance to be explored." ■

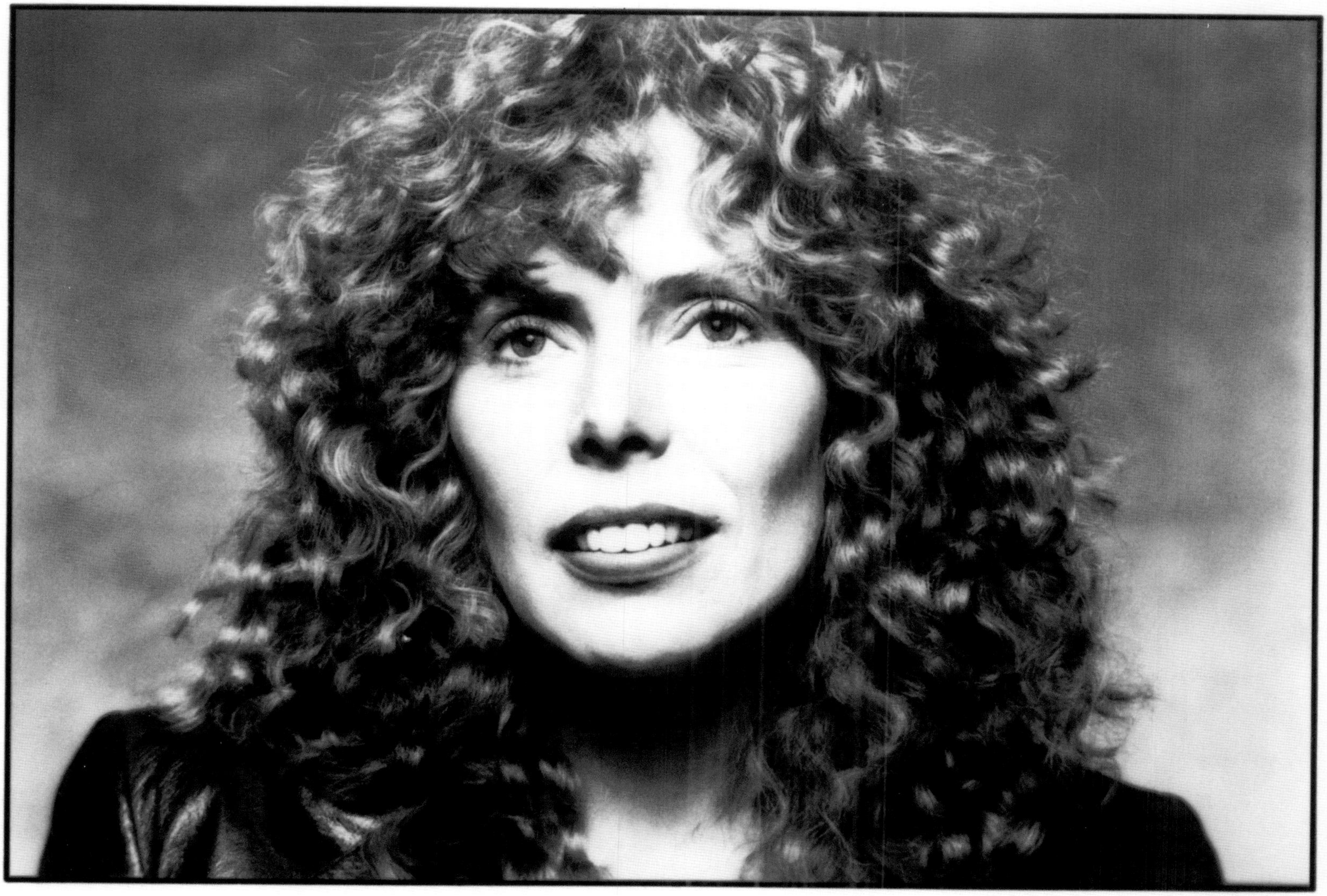

Photo Credit: NORMAN SEEFF

JONI MITCHELL

asylum

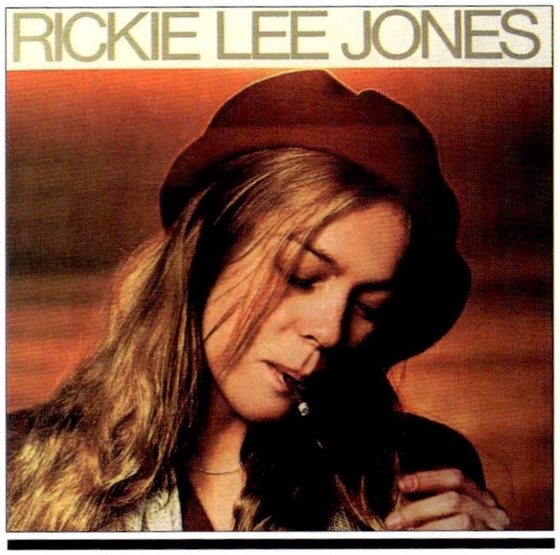

Billboard 200: *Rickie Lee Jones* (#3)
Billboard Hot 100: "Chuck E's in Love" (#4); "Young Blood" (#40)

Arriving on the scene with a vivid set of tunes, Rickie Lee Jones won the Grammy Award for Best New Artist.

BEFORE SHE made a splash with her self-titled debut, an album full of memorable characters and bohemian cool, Rickie Lee Jones played in dives and little bars in Los Angeles for $10 per four sets. She scored a Top 5 hit with the snazzy "Chuck E's in Love," a radio staple that made Jones the reigning queen of street life to an adoring audience.

"My songs are pretty eclectic," Jones observed. "They're written on an acoustic guitar and some of them have an R&B feel. Others have a jazz base, and it's kind of young; it's kid, but it's really sensitive in a lot of ways. Wait, I'll give it to you in colors—it's very dark red and blacks and browns. That's much better."

Jones' image—the wise wild waif with the red beret and beatnik airs—was endearing, but her artistry was steadfast. *Rickie Lee Jones* weaved jazz, folk and R&B into distinct pop compositions, enlisting outstanding musicianship from a host of top session masters. She rendered her lyrics in an expressive, smoky vocal style—an engaging stream of sweetly slurred syllables and purposely languid phrasings, soaring from deep baritone to lilting soprano.

"Most girls—most artists, for that matter—aren't real secure," she commented. "They walk into a situation and they don't really direct; the producers direct. So you don't have that collaboration, that involvement. It's very unusual for someone to get this much support. Now that I know I won't have to fight to make these songs heard, I can feel a lot more confident about writing and performing my music."

Jones' poetic imagination and streetwise swagger led to comparisons to everyone from Joni Mitchell to Tom Waits, her sometime beau.

"When people start comparing me to other singers and writers, I just ignore it," Jones asserted. "I've gotta laugh. My music is real personal. I think that's what—if anything—will make it noticed." ■

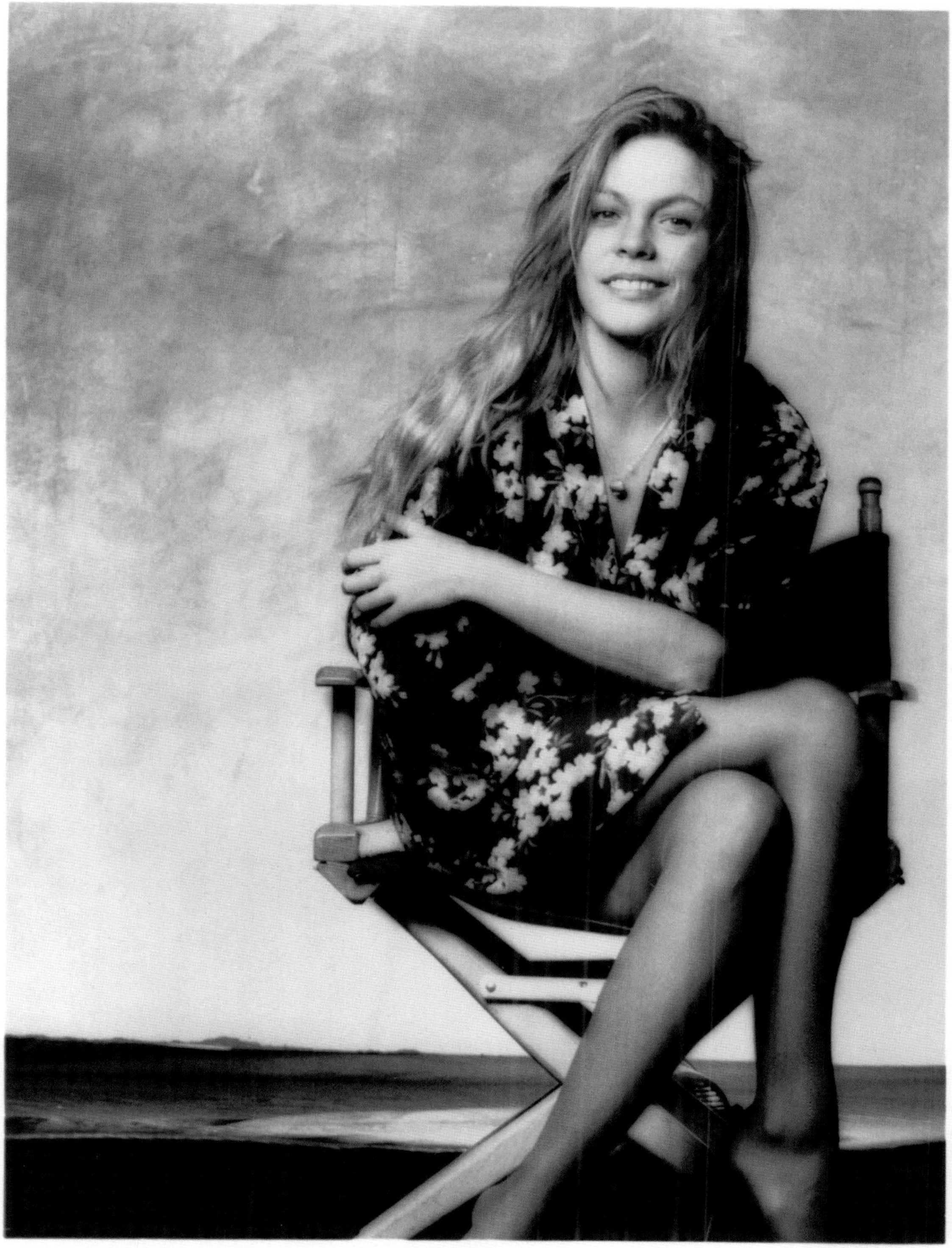

RICKIE LEE JONES

WARNER/REPRISE

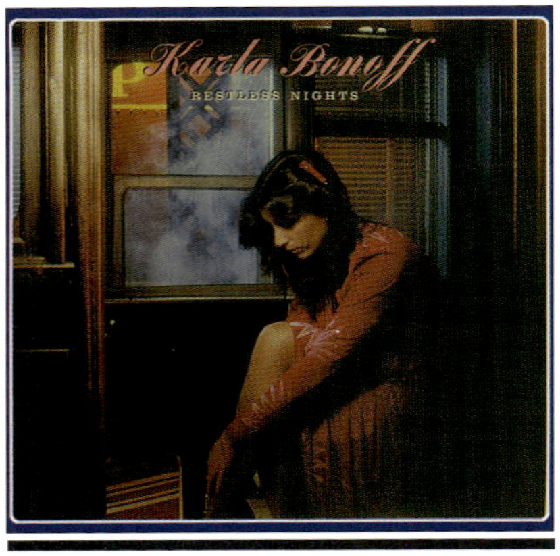

Billboard 200: *Restless Nights* (#31)
Billboard Hot 100: "Baby Don't Go" (#69)

After reaping critical raves for her debut release, Los Angeles native Karla Bonoff proffered *Restless Nights*.

BY PERFORMING at L.A.'s notorious Troubadour club, Karla Bonoff had been discovered as a solo act, but her notoriety was linked to three of her songs included on Linda Ronstadt's 1976 album *Hasten Down the Wind*—"Lose Again," "Someone to Lay Down Beside Me" and "If He's Ever Near." Bonoff's fine voice and sweet-heartache songs showed enormous potential—some people expected a work on the scale of Carole King's *Tapestry* someday.

The album *Restless Nights* followed two years after Bonoff's debut recording."I had a good idea that it was gonna take me some time. It took me seven years to put together the songs for the first album," she said. "And I knew how I write—which is not fast." But Bonoff insisted on her standards. "The record company said people would forget about me, and I've come to find out that's a bunch of bull. People haven't forgotten at all. And what good would it have done to put out a crummy album?"

Despite the excellence of her recorded output, Bonoff still suffered from classification, especially from East Coast critical cliques. She had the perfect credentials for the "Los Angeles sound"—born and raised, the Ronstadt connection, the similar sopranos, the Troubadour days, touring with Jackson Browne, the same session players.

"A lot of people back East misinterpret that so much. I know very few people who grew up in L.A. who are considered part of the 'sound' except for Jackson. The Eagles, Wendy Waldman and Linda all came from somewhere else—they just spent the last 10 years growing together musically. I grew up in L.A., so I have no perspective when people pay attention to the 'laid-back and mellow' end of it. I have no idea what it means."

In recording *Restless Nights*, Bonoff defended her use of Ronstadt's band. With her endearing attention to craft, she beat her mentor at her own game by effortlessly tossing off songs such as "Baby Don't Go."

"I'd have a hard time finding people as good," she said. "I knew the session people and cared about them, and the first thing I did was go into a situation I could count on, with people who understand my songs and that kind of music. Sure, it's a safe way to go—when I make a record, I'm not into taking chances." ■

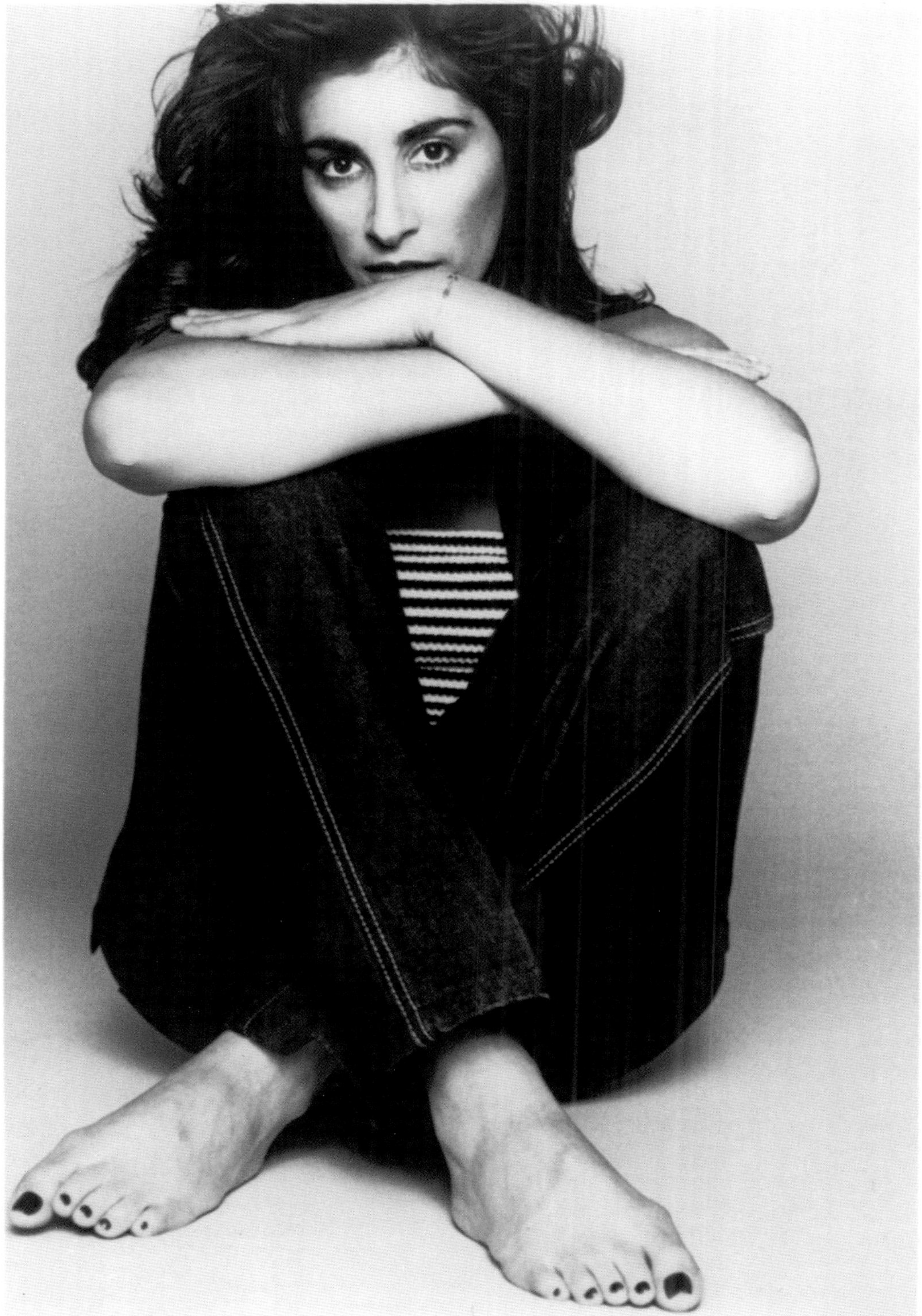

KARLA BONOFF

COLUMBIA

7908

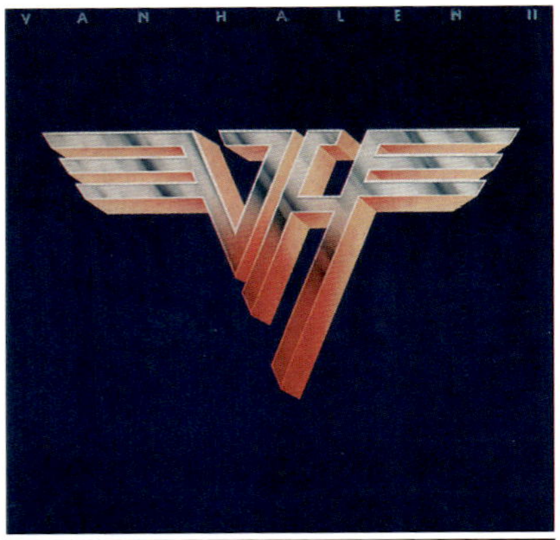

Billboard 200: *Van Halen II* (#6)
Billboard Hot 100: "Dance the Night Away" (#15);
"Beautiful Girls" (#84)

"Dance the Night Away" was a propitious pop change-of-pace from Van Halen's notorious hard-rock style.

THE KIDS who were too young to remember Deep Purple or vintage Led Zeppelin needed some new hard-rock detonations to scramble their frontal lobes. Van Halen's music reflected the power that came from four years of playing small clubs, beer bars, backyard parties and dance contests in and around the Los Angeles area.

Lead singer David Lee Roth assessed Van Halen's feel-good appeal. "We make music that the crowds enjoy 'cause we're the crowd ourselves. I might be out there dressed a little fancier since I'm on the stage, but we're just there to party down like everyone else."

Van Halen II, the group's second album, featured the same crisply engineered thunder that catapulted the band's debut into the million-seller category. The expanded repertoire was reinforced with Eddie Van Halen's flashy guitar pyrotechnics and Roth's street-smart shuck and jive.

"We do it all," the excitable vocalist crowed. "The one thing we wanted when we started out was control, and now we've got that bottom line. Everything you see or hear—the sound, the album covers—is designed or approved by the four of us. And we've been pretty successful with that approach so far."

The last bastion of acceptance for the group, AM radio airplay, crumbled with the release of the track "Dance the Night Away," a terrific power-pop single. "Beautiful Girls" embodied the band's confident swagger.

"The reaction has been real good to those tunes," Roth insisted. "We're always confident, thinking one step ahead to our next move. We're always writing new material—we can't be stopped. We all stand in a circle and hum at each other, and that's how we get new songs. And even if we hum it wrong, Eddie plays it right. Then it's just, 'To the mics!'" ■

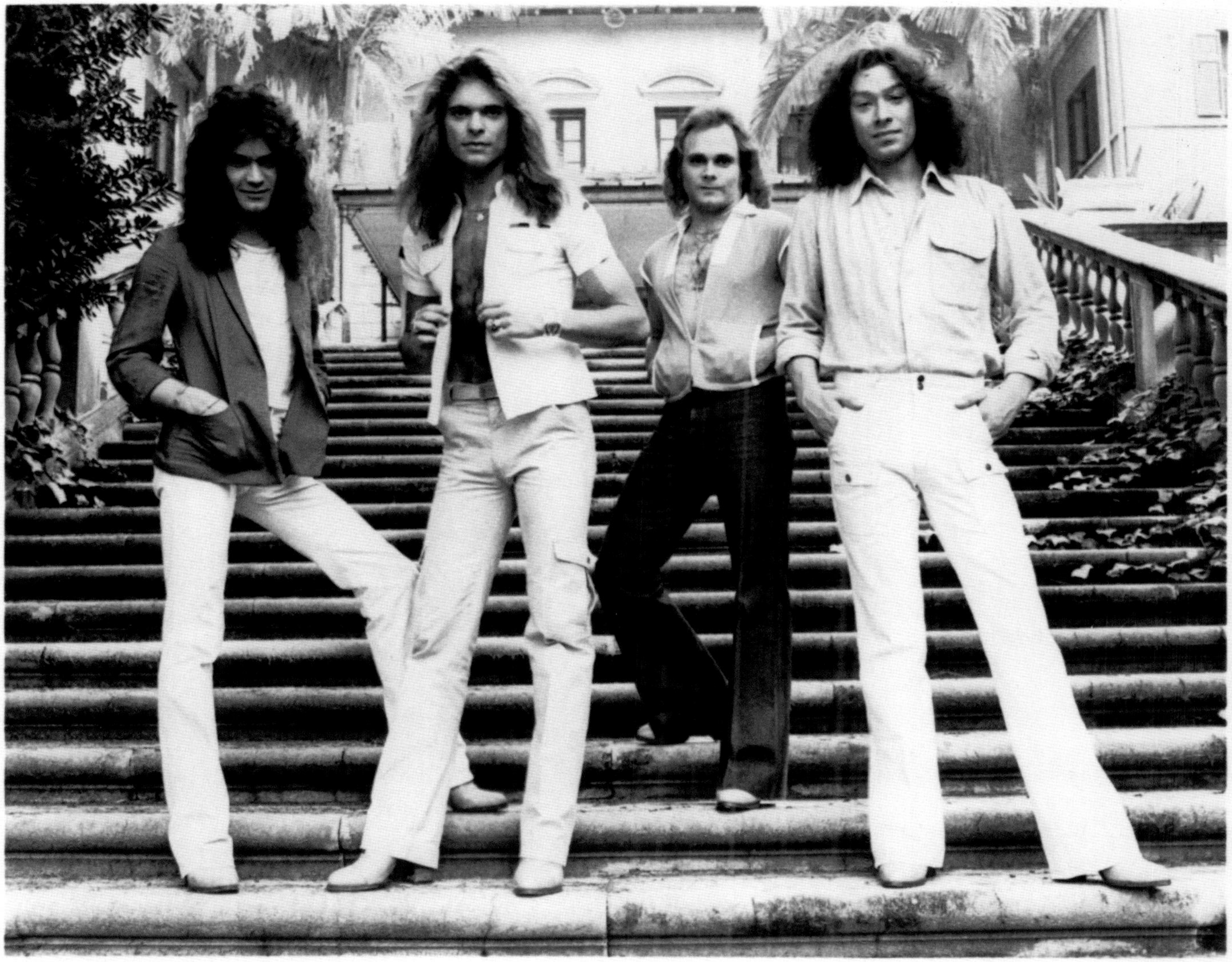

WARNER / REPRISE

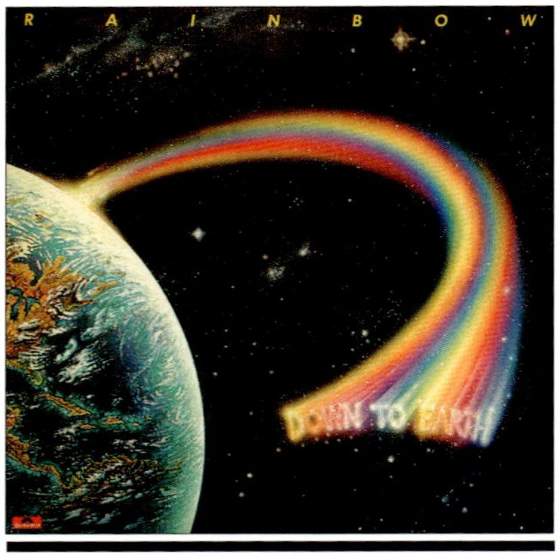

Billboard 200: *Down to Earth* (#66)
Billboard Hot 100: "Since You Been Gone" (#57)

Rainbow reached a zenith with the presence of Roger Glover, a pillar throughout Deep Purple's halcyon years.

THE EARLY Seventies were the years of the guitar hero, and in the realm of heavy metal rock, no one was more notorious than Ritchie Blackmore. During his tenure with Deep Purple, he virtually wrote the book on sledgehammer riffing and speed-of-light solos. Through it all, his musical anchor was bassist Roger Glover.

"I left Purple in '73, a year before Ritchie left," Glover explained. "I wanted to produce records independently, write more songs than being in the Purple would allow, and get off the road. I had produced an album for Nazareth that was in the Top 10 in England when I left, so I was okay. I was lucky that I had another career to fall into."

Blackmore left Deep Purple as the band entered a period of creative stagnation. He started a solo album that turned into a permanent entity as Rainbow. He recruited lead singer Ronnie James Dio from Elf, a band Deep Purple had toured with and Glover had produced. Rainbow's personnel fluctuated over the years but kept Blackmore, Dio and ace drummer Cozy Powell as a nucleus. Mystical lyrics and epic compositions were the cornerstones of the band's repertoire.

Then Rainbow needed a new producer and approached Glover. "I said fine, but the band split after a few months because of the usual musical unrest. Ritchie and Cozy were left, and they went into the studio without a bass player or singer. They asked if I'd play bass for the session and help them out. I really enjoyed it—I hadn't picked up the bass guitar much in six years. It was inevitable that they would ask me to join the group. It felt good to work with Ritchie again."

Graham Bonnet, whose outstanding voice was first heard in the English pop duo the Marbles, auditioned as lead singer and won the job. Keyboardist Don Airey rounded out the Rainbow lineup. *Down to Earth* showcased a much different musical perspective than the heavy-handedness of past Rainbow albums. It was a smash in Europe and Japan, where the band was one of the top concert attractions.

The single "Since You Been Gone" gave Rainbow its breakthrough in the US market. Much of the credit went to Glover, who tempered Blackmore's guitar attack with more commercial trappings, such as vocal harmonies and lyrics based on boy-girl relationships. "The States is where we've struggled," Glover admitted. "That was the reason for the change in production. We weren't getting any airplay, and my job as producer was to get an American hit for the band."

The prickly Blackmore embraced the new pop-rock direction. "He's got a lot of confidence in himself," Glover noted of his friend. "He pushes himself very hard instead of resting on his laurels. He's a dedicated musician, and I appreciate that. I stand next to him in the studio and my jaw falls open at the magnificent stuff he plays just relaxing." ■

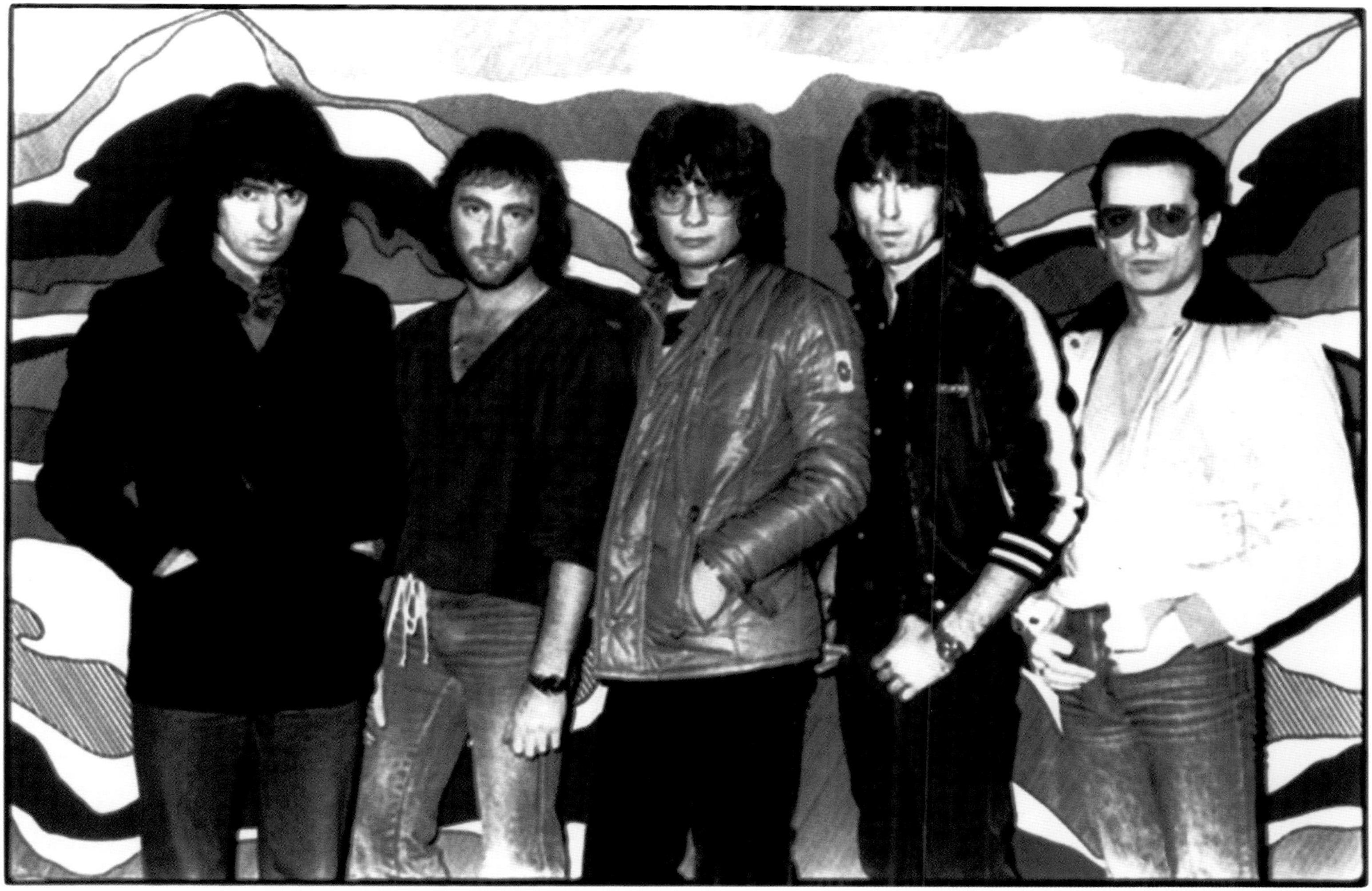

RAINBOW

Polydor

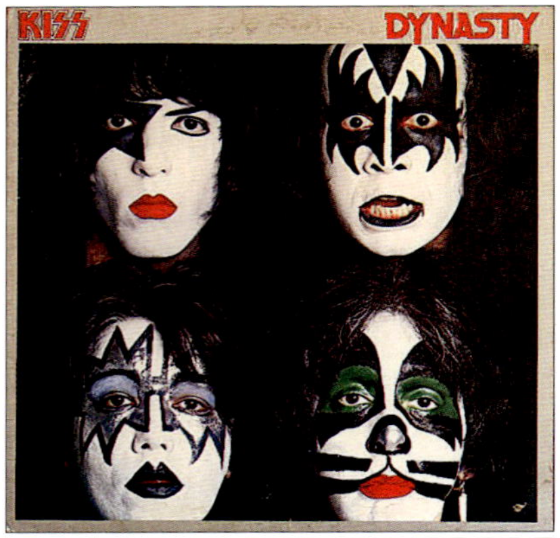

Billboard 200: *Dynasty* (#9)
Billboard Hot 100: "I Was Made for Lovin' You" (#11); "Sure Know Something" (#47)

The categorically danceable "I Was Made for Loving You" marked a change of direction in Kiss' heavy sound.

KNOWN FOR their flamboyant costumes and makeup, Kiss had risen to prominence with anthemic, fist-pounding hard rock. For the *Dynasty* album, the band dropped engineer Eddie Kramer as a producer and linked up with Vini Poncia, whose credits included such strange musical bedfellows as Barbra Streisand and Ringo Starr.

Dynasty turned into a worldwide smash thanks to the single "I Was Made for Loving You." The song's subtle disco beat brought cries of "sellout" upon its release in the US, but it became a No. 1 hit from Canada and Belgium to the Netherlands and New Zealand.

"It's by far the biggest record we've ever had," bassist Gene Simmons gloated. "We wanted to change a bit and take in some new influences, and that's where Vini came in—his input was obviously strongest on 'I Was Made for Loving You.' We were interested in him because he didn't come from a rock 'n' roll background. We knew we could get that end of it ourselves—we just wanted someone to bounce ideas off."

On tour, Kiss continued to work hard at giving its devotees the most outrageous stage shows their adolescent minds could handle. Simmons gleefully recounted some of the tidbits in the Kiss onstage arsenal.

"I can't wait to melt their faces," Simmons said. "I fly 40 feet in the air to the top of the lighting truss that holds 500 airplane lights to blind the first 50 rows. I'm zipping along at six feet per second—that's not Peter Pan, that's flying. Ace Frehley's guitar does everything but talk—it lights up in patterns and then flies out of his hands, and another one appears in his hands and then explodes. Peter (Criss) goes up with his drum kit 35 feet in the air and does a 360 turn. There's a 21-gun salute, and it rains fire."

Simmons couldn't wait for the global tour, getting to the countries that *Dynasty* had just introduced to Kissmania.

"We had a 17-month layoff before recording *Dynasty*, and everyone thought Kiss went away to the south of France to bask in the sunshine and do other things. In fact, we were working on tons of stuff that people are only beginning to see." He mentioned film projects, a television special, a publishing company for comics and books, and even an amusement park. "It sounds a bit like K-Mart," he admitted sheepishly.

Due to Kiss' cartoonish image and merchandising, fans who were parents started to attend concerts with their kids in tow. But the band still hadn't captured everyone's imagination. "Some religious fanatic in Texas is doing the record-burning bit again," Simmons related. "The last time he got excited was over the Beatles, and before that it was Elvis. If that's 'devil's music,' I guess we're in pretty good company." ■

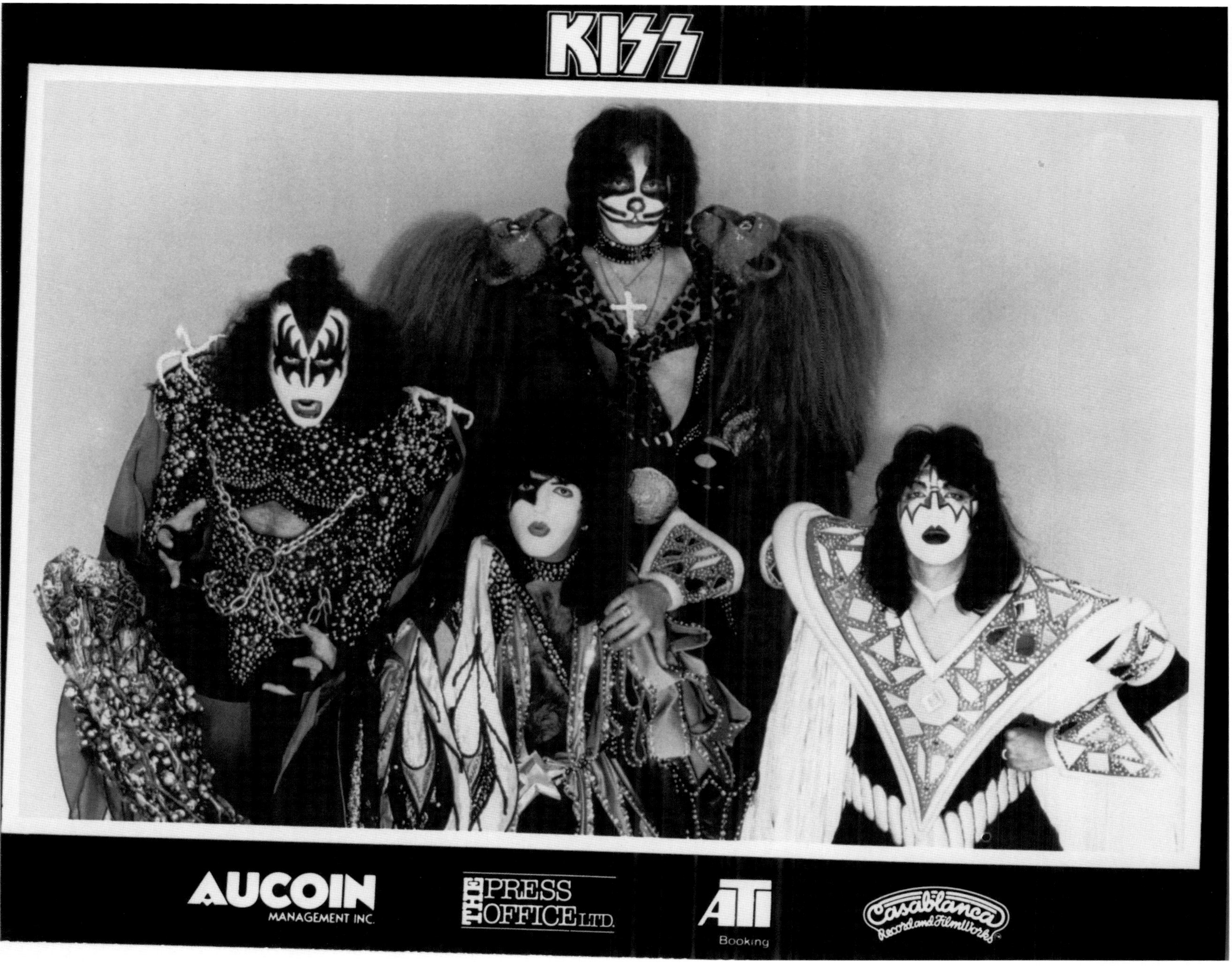
KISS
AUCOIN
MANAGEMENT INC.
THE PRESS OFFICE LTD.
ATI
Booking
Casablanca
Record and FilmWorks

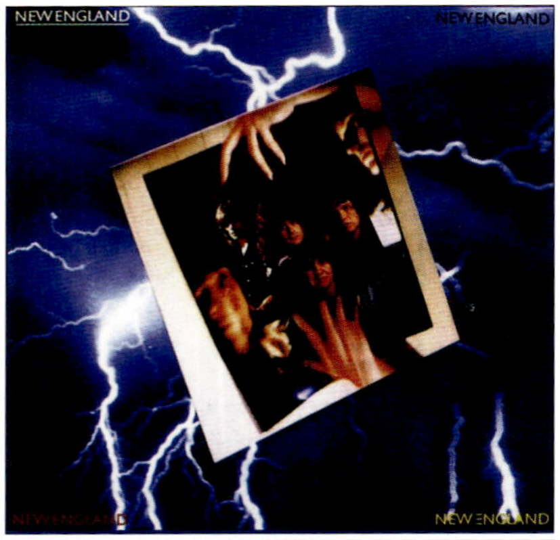

Billboard 200: *New England* (#50)
Billboard Hot 100: "Don't Ever Wanna Lose Ya" (#40); "Hello, Hello, Hello" (#69)

Guided by John Fannon, the group New England had its moment of glory with "Don't Ever Wanna Lose Ya."

AN AUSPICIOUS new band, New England's popularity was due mainly to the hit "Don't Ever Wanna Lose Ya," but guitarist and vocalist John Fannon's affinity for all modes of English rock extended beyond the melodic bombast of the band's charting single. *New England*, the debut album, tracked like a textbook of classic Anglo influences. The opening "Hello, Hello, Hello" could have been lifted from any ELO album, while "P.U.N.K. (Puny Undernourished Kid)" resurrected the sound of early Sweet singles.

The band's derivative stance might not have been so charming if Fannon and his cohorts (Jimmy Waldo on keyboards, Hirsh Gardner on drums, Gary Shea on bass) weren't upfront about their influences.

"Sure, that's always been our favorite kind of music," Fannon allowed. "From the Beatles on, we've gone through every phase—Pink Floyd, King Crimson, 10cc, Supertramp. We like to think we've developed a New England sound, but our debts are too obvious to ignore."

The group's potpourri of British rock stylings and experience—"We've been at it quite a while," Fannon admitted—had paid off handsomely. Aucoin Management, the firm that guided the fortunes of Kiss, was handling the same duty for New England. Paul Stanley of Kiss, a Brit-rock fanatic himself, produced the group's album, which ensured them some notoriety. "This couldn't be a better time for New England," Fannon said.

However, New England fell through the cracks with Starz and Piper, two other Aucoin projects, and the band's label Infinity Records was absorbed by parent company MCA. ■

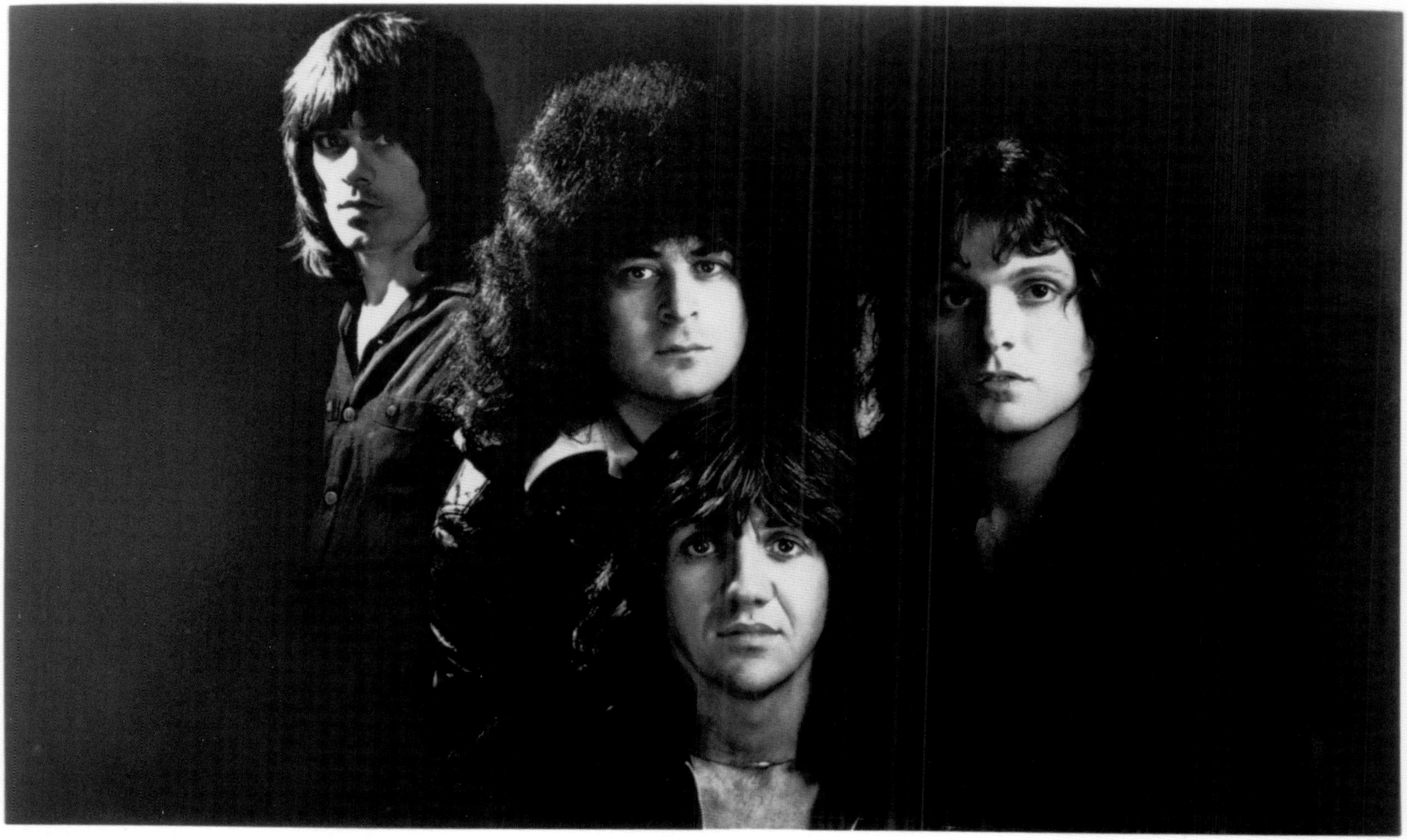

AUCOIN
MANAGEMENT INC

ATI
Booking

NEW ENGLAND

INFINITY RECORDS

10 East 53rd Street
New York, New York 10022
(212) 888-9700

100 Universal City Plaza
Universal City, California 91608
(213) 763-8283

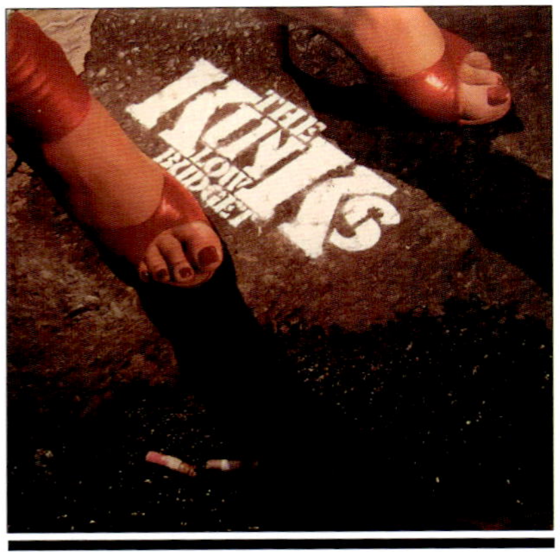

Billboard 200: *Low Budget* (#11)
Billboard Hot 100: "(Wish I Could Fly Like) Superman" (#41)

The Kinks, tending to the economic problems America was enduring, pocketed a gold record for *Low Budget*.

ONE OF the most influential rock bands of the British Invasion of the Sixties, the Kinks were experiencing a revival. Savvy songwriter Ray Davies had built a reputation for commenting acerbically on English culture, but the Kinks abandoned the concept albums and nostalgic sounds created during most of the Seventies and refashioned themselves as a hard-rocking arena act.

Low Budget, the Kinks' first studio release made primarily in the US rather than London, testified to Davies' wittily observational style, addressing the mood behind contemporary themes—ingratitude, lowered expectations, imposed frugality, nervous tension and bad attitude. "A Gallon of Gas" satirized the oil crisis, and "Catch Me Now I'm Falling," summed up America's tumultuous time of need. The album yielded a chart hit, the disco-influenced, topically pertinent "(Wish I Could Fly Like) Superman."

"Ray came up with the song, which was obviously inspired by the success of Christopher Reeve's first *Superman* movie," lead guitarist and brother Dave Davies said.

"The song is really about how weak, clumsy and awkward human beings are, muddling on from one day to the next. At first, I thought it was a bit corny, but some of the lyrics are actually very funny. Ray was looking for a kind of disco-ish drum sound. I simply hated the disco explosion—it was horrible. I suggested putting a heavy guitar riff over the rhythm track to veer it away from that dance vibe, making it more of a rock 'n' roll record."

With a bunch of rock upstarts like the Pretenders, Van Halen and others adding Kinks tunes to their repertoires, an audience of longtime admirers and new converts cheered the band on, and *Low Budget* was the Kinks highest-charting original album in America. "And as is so typical of the Kinks," Davies mused, "it's become a hit during a recession." ■

THE KINKS LOW BUDGET

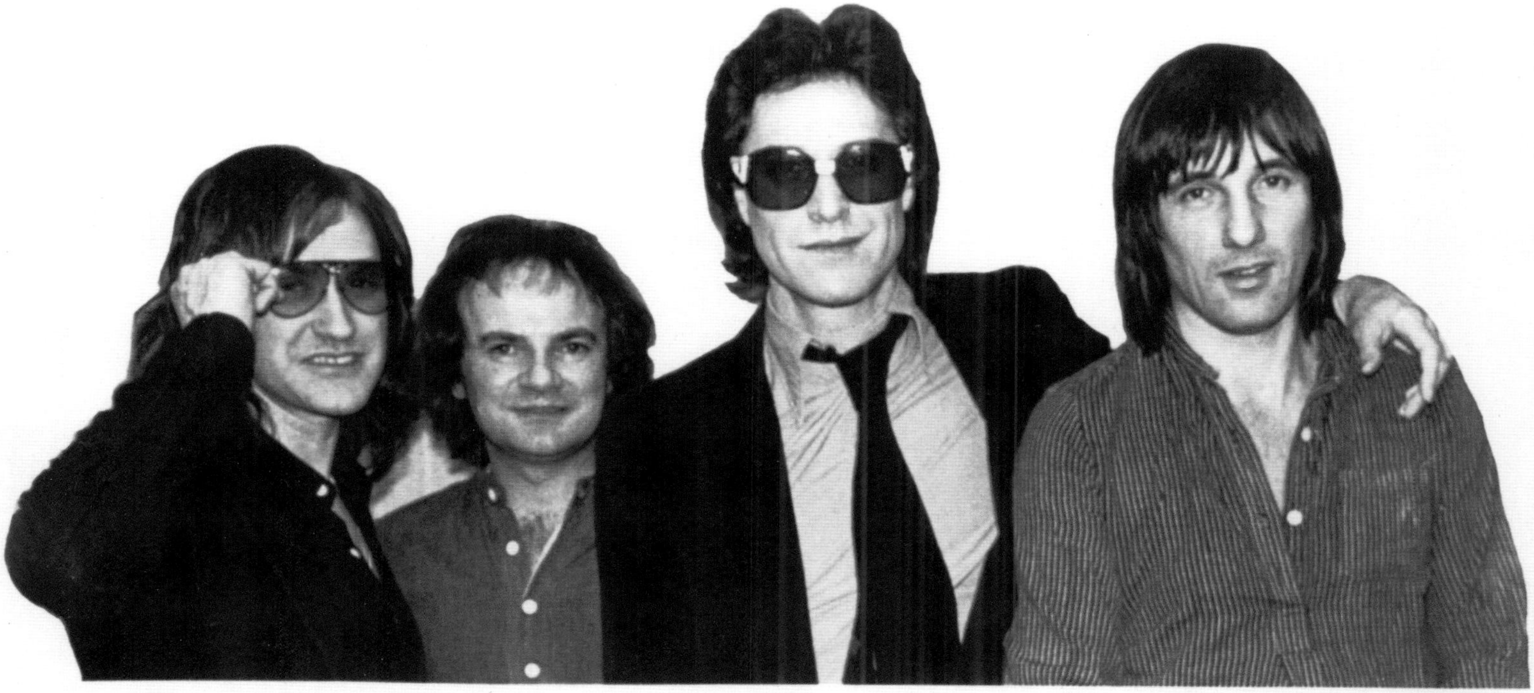

Renaissance Management
433 North Camden Drive
Beverly Hills, CA 90210
213-273-4162

ARISTA™

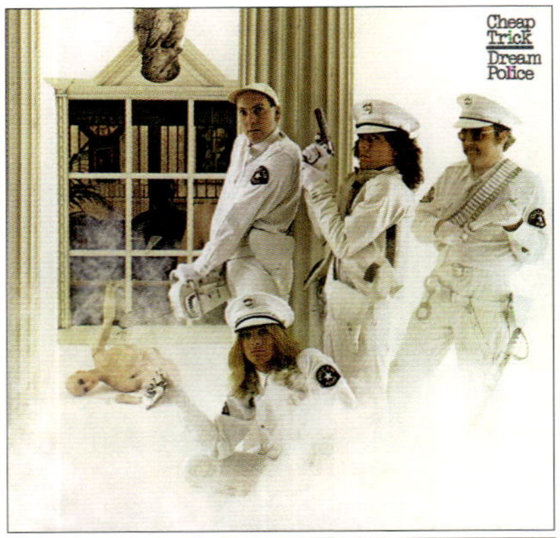

Billboard 200: *Dream Police* (#6)
Billboard Hot 100: "Dream Police" (#26); "Voices" (#32)

The fluke commercial certification of an import-only live album held up Cheap Trick's slated *Dream Police*.

THE CARTOONISH guitarist for Cheap Trick, Rick Nielsen was a little miffed about his band's fortunes in early 1979. The group had just finished work on its fourth studio album, entitled *Dream Police*, but the record company had other ideas. *Cheap Trick at Budokan*, a live album that the band had released in Japan, was selling as an import for up to $25 in America, and the clamor for stateside release was overwhelming. The release of *Dream Police* was postponed.

But by the fall, Nielsen had grown to like the idea. *Cheap Trick at Budokan* went on to become the biggest live album of the year, hitting the Top 5 and spawning the group's first Top 10 hit in "I Want You to Want Me." *Dream Police* remained in the can until *Budokan* sales tapered off. For a band that had charted carefully many aspects of its career, from a well-crafted sound to extraordinary visual appeal, the success of the live record had to be considered a surprising but welcome aberration from their plans.

For three excellent studio albums, Cheap Trick had tried to win the affections of the record-buying public. *Cheap Trick*, the debut offering, captured the raw sound of the band. *In Color* was produced by Tom Werman, an Epic Records staff producer, and the fusion of Nielsen's pop sense and Werman's sympathetic studio work made the album an eclectic masterpiece. *Heaven Tonight* refined the concept further and spawned one of the decade's most anthemic singles in "Surrender."

But the big time barely eluded the band, and *Cheap Trick at Budokan* changed all that, making the group the latest superstars. With *Dream Police*, the band was poised to challenge their listeners with another studio album.

"This is a big change," Nielsen related. "We've written strings into the stuff—we've gotten more diverse than ever." The paranoid title track and the classic pop of "Voices" showcased hook-laden melodies in a progressive setting that was simply breathtaking. "Gonna Raise Hell," which catered to a disco audience, understandably drew attention.

"Don't worry, it's got real nasty lyrics and sloppy guitar–it's interesting, real teenage stuff," Nielsen offered. "It's disco in that the beat is close, but it's still the way Bun E. (Carlos, drummer) plays. It's got a hook, but it's nowhere near something Donna Summer is ever gonna sing. It's got lyrics, but it's not like 'Le Freak.' But we did it on purpose. People say, 'Disco sucks.' Well, 99 percent of rock 'n' roll, country and classical sucks, but one percent is still valid music. We don't expect people to come to us—we feel we have to educate an audience. So we bridge the gap."

Nielsen was aware of the band's capabilities, but he never let on to the considerable smarts behind the Cheap Trick operation. "We've changed our name to the Cee Tees," he deadpanned. "Actually, I'm the fifth Gibb brother and I don't want to rest on my brothers' laurels. Also, my second cousin is John Travolta. And I'm an only child, but if I had a sister she would have been married to John Lennon. It's stuff like that I don't want everyone to know. It could have helped our career, but I wanted to do it the tough way." ■

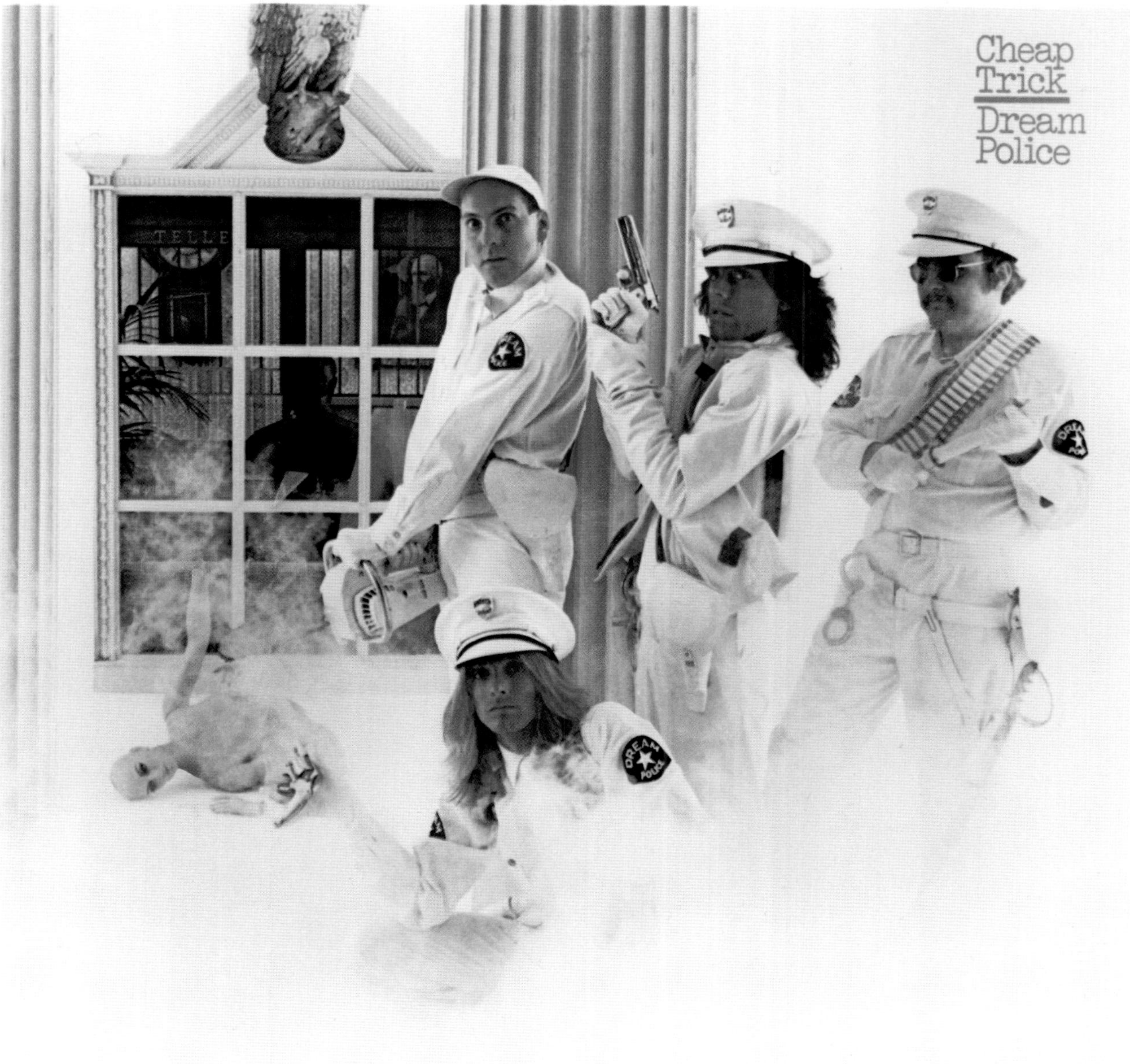

Cheap Trick
Cheap Trick

Rick Nielsen   Tom Petersson   Bun E Carlos

Robin Zander

Epic

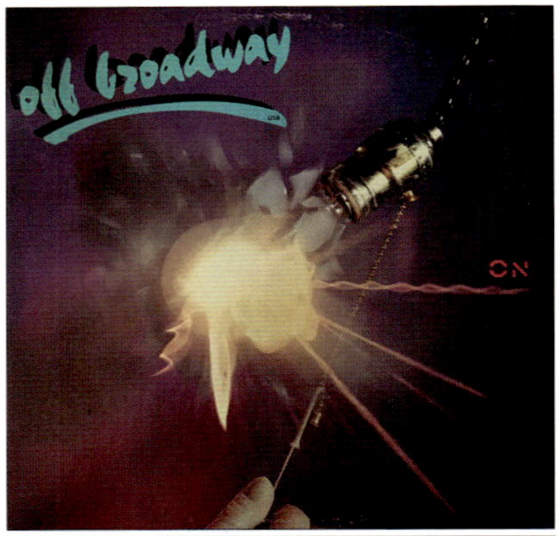

Billboard 200: *On* (#101)
Billboard Hot 100: "Stay in Time" (#51)

Off Broadway was brought to market by some of the same people who developed Cheap Trick's career path.

SOME INSIDERS predicted Off Broadway's considerable charms would soon make an impact in the rock world. The Chicago-based band was led by singer Cliff Johnson, who met up with Cheap Trick management as a member of Pezband.

"The Trick was playing in Illinois, and Rick Nielsen asked me up on stage to sing," he recalled. "I got a little too excited and ended up getting thrown off the stage. That's how our relationship began."

Johnson killed several years singing with a heavy-metal band—"big hair, bigger amplifiers, and a 'let's maim and cripple' attitude"—as the new wave and modern pop axis defined itself. When the time was right, he turned to answering phones in his dad's travel agency to finance his songwriting and robbing area bands of their personnel to form his own group.

Cheap Trick manager Ken Adamany took the finished lineup under his wing, and Atlantic Records signed the band on the basis of a concert in Chicago, bypassing the let's-make-a-demo-and-move-to-the-coast syndrome. The band followed the Cheap Trick axiom for success—tour until you drop dead. "It's okay, though," Johnson admitted. "We'd rather be sled dogs for rock 'n' roll than found face down in a Corvette with hypoglycemia."

On, Off Broadway's debut album, featured a sophisticated brand of melodic power pop that wasn't expected from the Midwest boogie belt. Produced by Tom Werman (who had worked with Cheap Trick), the record included a sleeper single, "Stay in Time," and offered evidence that Johnson was one of the more innovative new singers on the scene.

"We have a strong United States consciousness," Johnson said of his band, whose name fully appeared as "Off Broadway usa." "For so many years, American bands tried to act like the Beatles—cross your legs like John and so on. We don't feel like anybody but us. The light bulbs that we hang onstage are our way of being intimate. We're bringing our wide-load garage to your amphitheater. We're off the big productions. Let's keep a low profile and be pals instead of stars and fans." ■

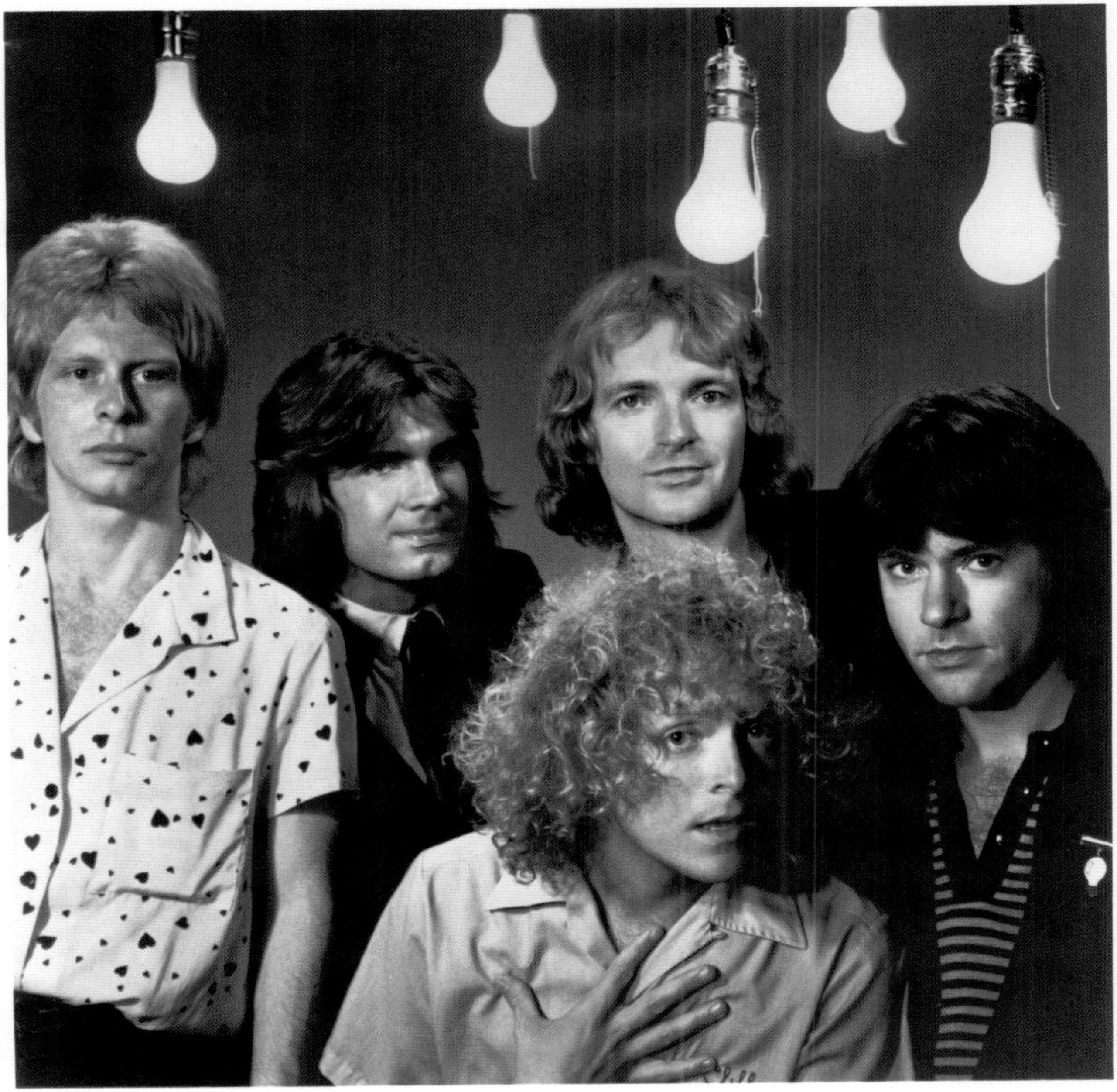

off broadway T.M

usa

ATLANTIC

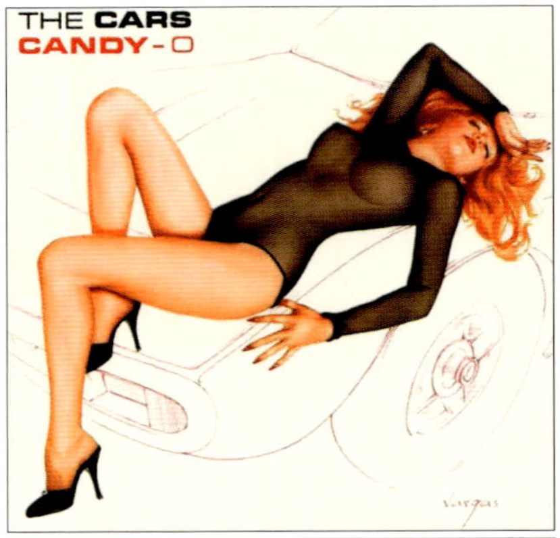

Billboard 200: *Candy-O* (#3)
Billboard Hot 100: "Let's Go" (#14); "It's All I Can Do" (#41)

The Cars' *Candy-O* and the smash "Let's Go" broadened the group's polished, detached new wave sensibility.

SOME PEOPLE viewed *Candy-O,* the follow-up to the Cars' arresting double-platinum debut album, as a test concerning the members' ability to cope with pressure. Would the band forget what had made them million-sellers in the first place? Leader Ric Ocasek had a good laugh about that rhetorical question, since he had a demo that included every one of the new tunes a year earlier.

"All of the songs were stockpiled, some of them even longer than the songs on the first album," he smiled. "We just went into the studio and played our demo and told Roy (Thomas Baker, their producer who had also worked Queen, Foreigner and Journey) that he'd better learn, too. He has wonderful sympathy with people and electronics, but we knew what we were doing."

Candy-O featured an album cover created by the famed *Playboy* pin-up artist Alberto Vargas, depicting a body-stockinged babe draped across the hood of a Ferrari. The 83-year-old Vargas, saddened by the death of his wife, hadn't picked up a paintbrush for four years. He painted the *Candy-O* piece at the behest of Cars drummer David Robinson, a collector of pin-up art.

"Let's Go," a magnificent summer single, was the Cars' first Top 20 hit. The band unanimously described *Candy-O* as "punchier" than the first album.

"Everything is more up front instrumentally, and vocally it's better as well—it's not as heavy on harmonies," Ocasek said "I think it shows us having progressed as much as we could have in a year's time." ■

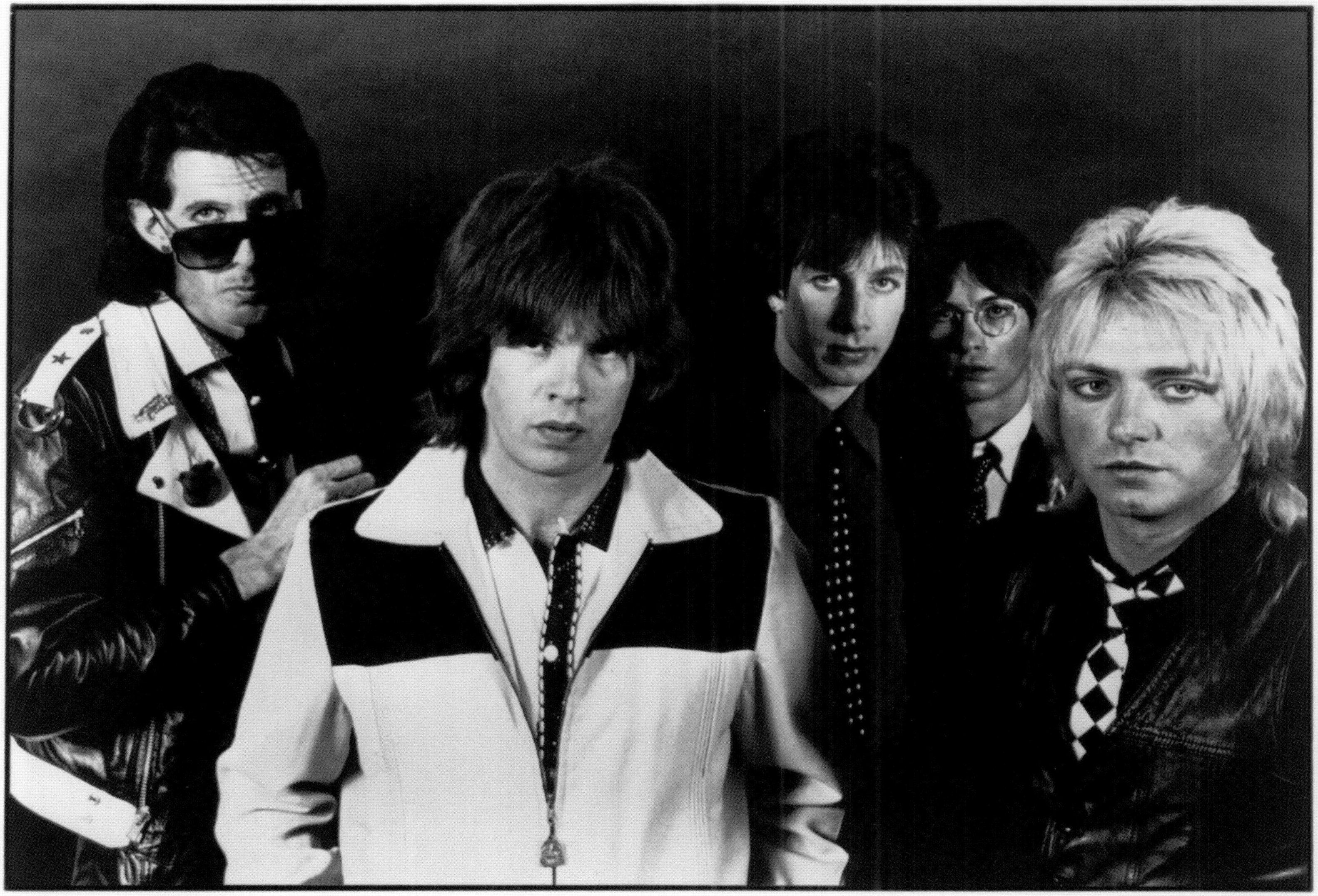

Photo Credit: JEFF ALBERTSON

Ric Ocasek Elliot Easton David Robinson Greg Hawkes Benjamin Orr

THE CARS

elektra

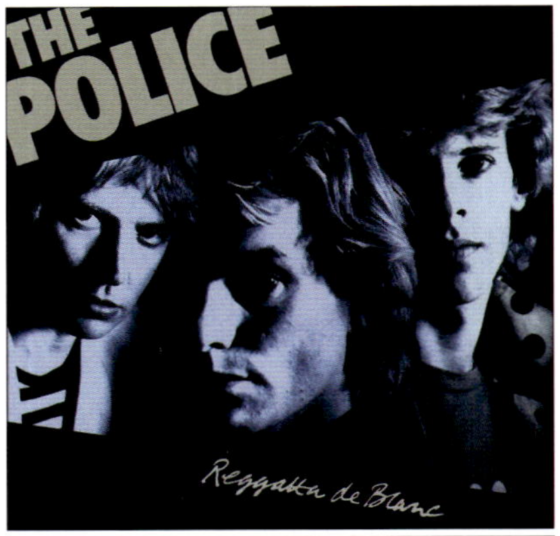

Billboard 200: *Reggatta de Blanc* (#25)
Billboard Hot 100: "Message in a Bottle" (#74)

The Police, with "Message in a Bottle" and "Walking on the Moon," stepped forward as a high-powered act.

SINCE THE recording of a debut album and its smash hit "Roxanne," the Police had been riding the crest of new-wave music. The trio's status as radio sensations continued with the *Reggatta de Blanc* album and two particularly fine singles, "Message in a Bottle" and "Walking on the Moon," a testament to the band's charisma and instrumental proficiency.

Sting, the Police's bassist, singer and songwriter, found himself courted by the likes of *People* magazine, who had followed him around for the better part of a day. "I've read it. It's weird. Better than *Rolling Stone,* though," he laughed. "We'll talk to anybody. Hopefully the best part will come through. We're not an elitist group. We don't like to be unattainable."

When asked about the most promising new groups, rock's more established bands invariably mentioned the Police in glowing terms. "It's largely because we're one of the few new bands they can relate to," Sting explained. "Whereas the Sex Pistols and the Stranglers are a bit abrasive, we're actually an interface between old-style rock music and some of the new stuff."

The band's philosophies were also a blend of attitudes. "Absolutely, we're out to make a bundle," Sting allowed. "We like making money and making records that sell a lot. But the lucky thing is that we haven't compromised anything musically. These days, to make money you must obey certain marketing rules and listen to what the record company says. And we don't. It just happens that we're in a position where the music that we enjoy making is commercial, happening at this place in history or time."

As if being a top new band wasn't enough to occupy the Police's time, the group was active in other endeavors. Sting had a role in the Who's *Quadrophenia* movie, which concerned the struggles of English youth in the mid-Sixties. He played the Ace, the striking chief Mod. "My role is fairly small, but it's crucial to the plot," he noted. "The film is an excellent production, but it's very English—the dialogue is in a broad Cockney accent."

Another pastime of the band was I.R.S. Records, an independent label formed by manager Miles Copeland, who also happened to be the older brother of Police drummer Stewart Copeland. "We're all part of it," Sting enthused. "We use the distribution of A&M Records (the Police's label), but we're like a separate A&R department—we all have a hand in spotting bands. It's definitely a new thing happening, and we want to be at the forefront—and control it." ■

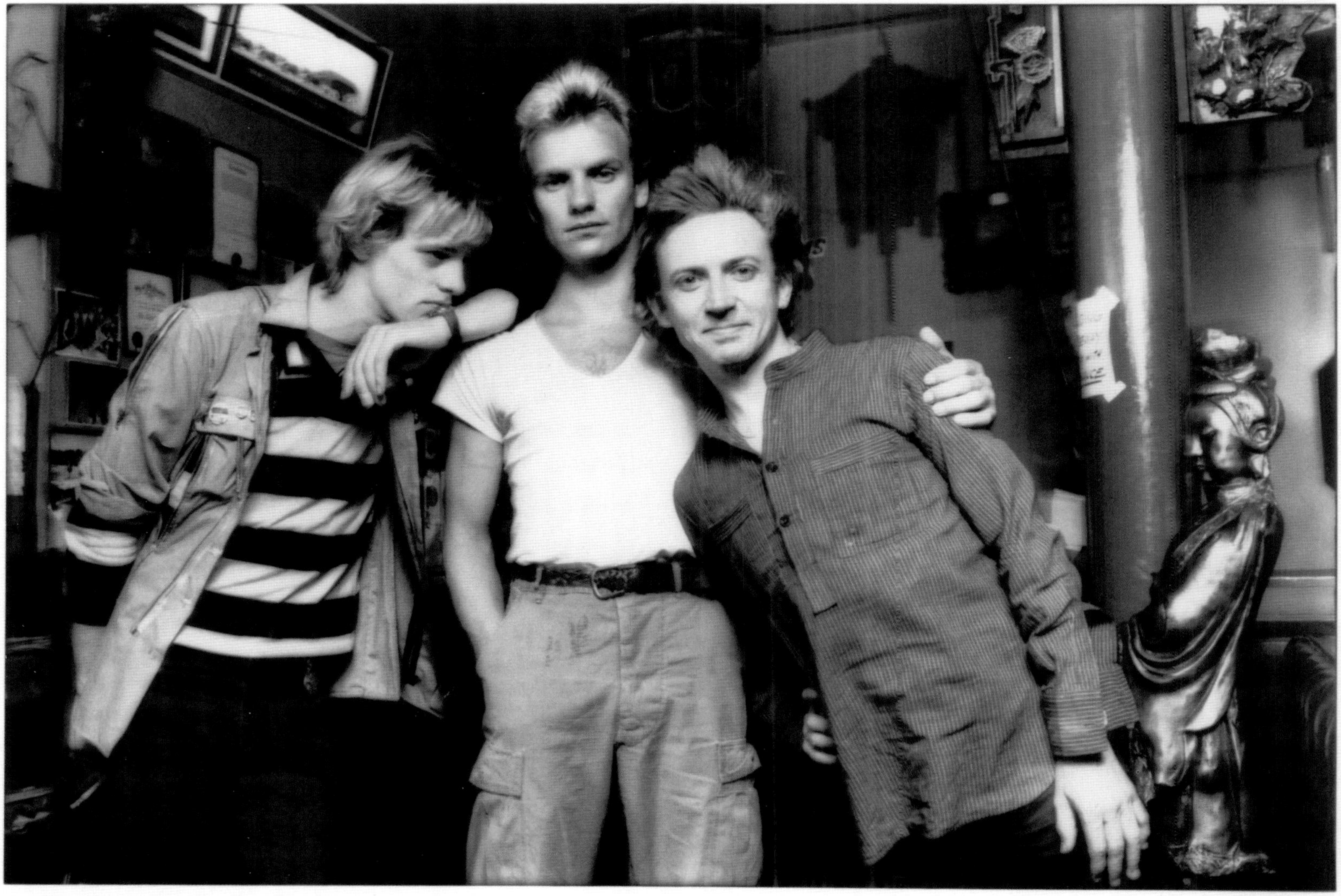

THE POLICE

L-R: STEWART COPELAND, STING, ANDY SUMMERS

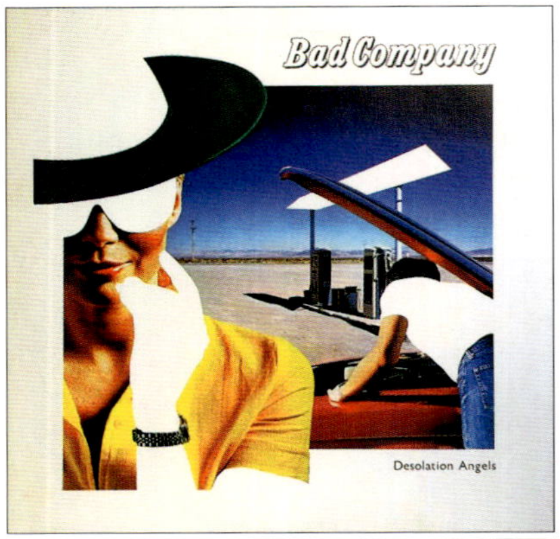

Billboard 200: *Desolation Angels* (#3)
Billboard Hot 100: "Rock 'n' Roll Fantasy" (#13); "Gone, Gone, Gone" (#56)

During their Seventies heyday, the Bad Company members defined the conviction of a hard-rock supergroup.

BY THE time Bad Company took form in 1973, all four players were experienced. The frontman, Paul Rodgers of the band Free, was one of the scene's richest, most passionate singers, able to deliver lyrics with sharp phrasing and control.

"I went through the usual thing that a musician goes through—you're influenced by what's on the charts, then you look a little deeper," he said. "In Free, we thought we were grown up, but we were 17, 18. We saw that the bands that were being successful, like Jethro Tull, were writing their own material—that seemed to be key. Free was a blues band, originally—that's all we played—so we made an effort to emphasize that aspect when we started writing."

It all coalesced on Free's biggest hit, the enduring "All Right Now," a classic three-chord stomp, but Rogers and drummer Simon Kirke dismantled the group and convened Bad Company. Guitarist Mick Ralphs had been with Mott the Hoople, a band that had the help of David Bowie as producer and scored big with "All the Young Dudes," but Ralphs disliked its glam direction. Bassist Boz Burrell had played in King Crimson.

Sharing a record label and manager with Led Zeppelin, Bad Company took the popular British blues-rock sound of the time and stripped it down to a sparse, no-nonsense attack. The band achieved instant recognition as a top attraction in the American market, producing such standards as "Can't Get Enough," "Ready for Love," "Bad Company," "Feel Like Makin' Love," "Good Lovin' Gone Bad," "Shooting Star" and "Silver, Blue and Gold." Compared to his shrieking competition, Rodgers was a remarkably musical vocalist, smooth but powerful and aggressive, epitomizing the group's swaggering macho-rock approach. Ralphs' power chording was rock steady, as was the thumping Kirke/Burrell rhythm section.

According to Rodgers, they shared a love of American R&B and blues."We had an immediate rapport musically. The whole approach was simplistic—Mick leaned more toward the style of Steve Cropper, who was the guitar player for Otis Redding. There was a connection there."

Desolation Angels, Bad Company's fifth album, added synthesizers and some minor string work to the tracks. "Rock 'n' Roll Fantasy" became the band's best-selling single, another staple on album-rock radio. The band went back on the road to support the album.

"We've always loved touring, but it's definitely getting a bit unreal—we're on another planet, from the limousines to the private jets with beds and TVs and no seats," Rodgers said. "I've done all the nasty, excessive things that everybody else does, and I'm coming to the conclusion that they don't lead anywhere. I survive because the music is always the most important thing—that's where the excitement and the buzz really exists. If you make yourself physically unable to do it, it's self-defeating." ■

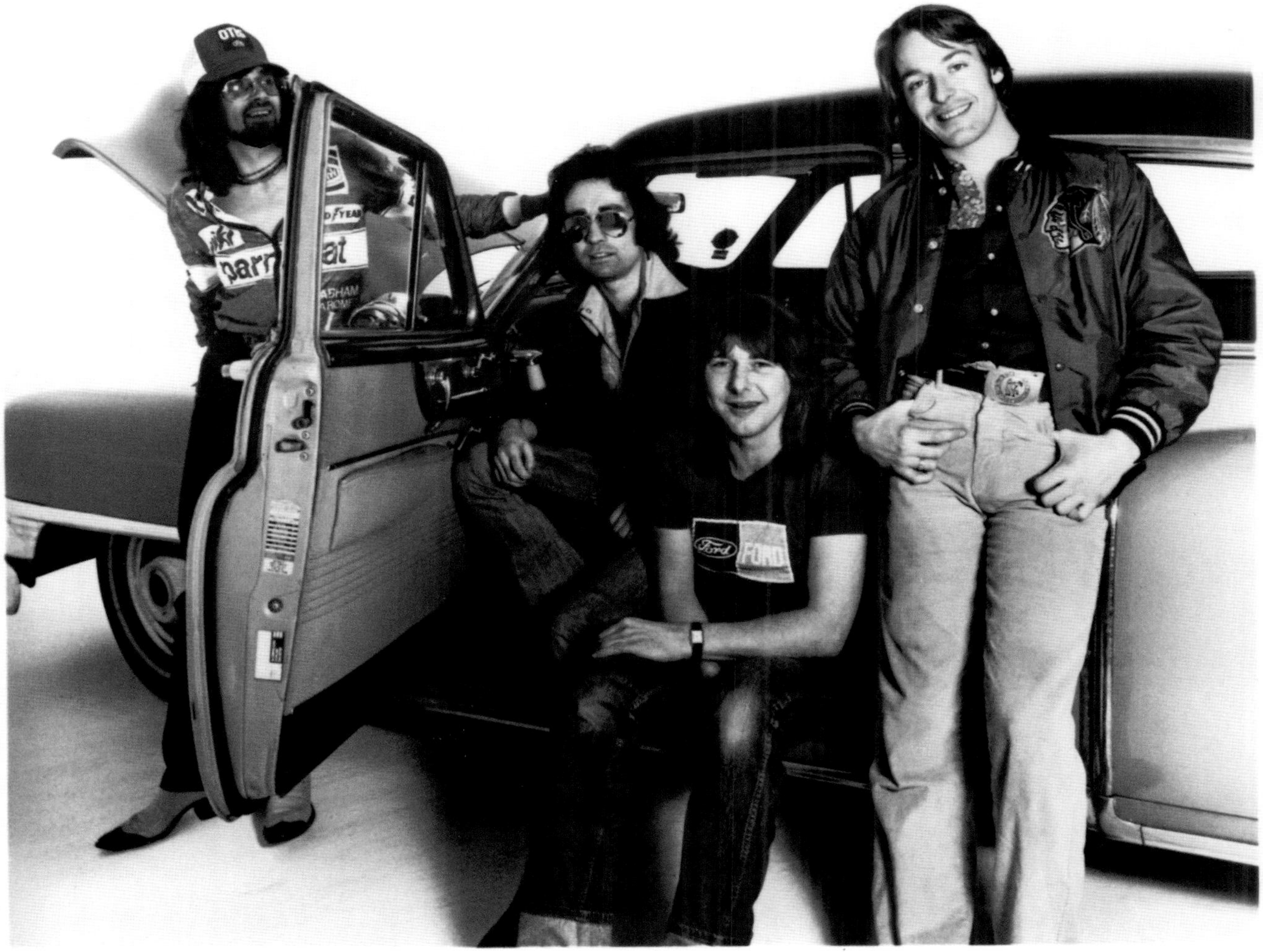

BAD COMPANY

Boz Burrell   Paul Rodgers   Mick Ralphs   Simon Kirke

SWAN SONG

Distributed by ATCO Records
A Division of Atlantic Recording
Corporation.

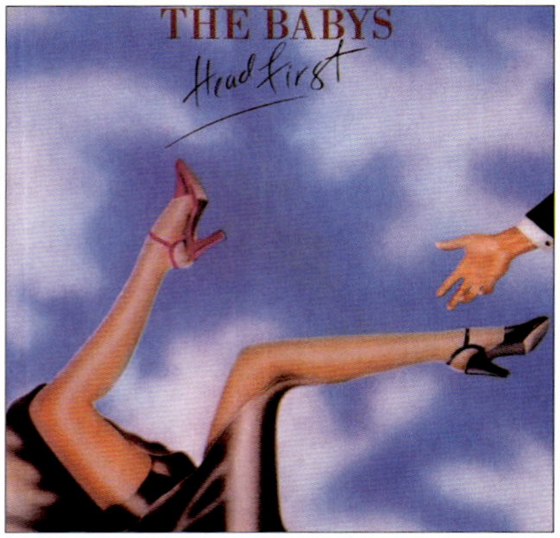

Billboard 200: *Head First* (#22)
Billboard Hot 100: "Every Time I Think of You" (#13);
"Head First" (#77)

The Babys transmuted into a British-American rock band and birthed a hit ballad, "Every Time I Think of You."

THE BABYS had been the subject of record industry derision since their first days as a recording entity. Chrysalis Records signed the group out of England on the strength of a novel videotape performance, coughing up a huge advance to go all out to break the band.

From day one, the publicity ploy was overkill. Everything from satin jackets to mylar posters heralded the Babys as the biggest English rock act since Led Zeppelin. The debut album was enjoyable albeit derivative, showcasing the heavy riffs on which the band's songwriting relied. The second album, *Broken Heart,* balanced frontman John Waite's vocals with Ron Nevison's classy production to good effect.

Yet controversies ensued. The *Broken Heart* album cover featured a soft-focus *Vogue*-ish portrait of the band, hardly the needed hook to grab a macho hard-rock audience. Chrysalis hoped that the band could bridge the audience between the Bay City Rollers and Aerosmith and ended up satisfying neither faction totally. And band member Mike Corby worked his way right out of the band with his penchant for gaudy jewelry and desire to be a teen idol first and musician second.

Head First served as a transitional album as the remaining Babys—Waite, guitarist Wally Stocker and drummer Tony Brock—shuffled the songs around Corby's absence.

They agreed to delay the release to straighten out the personnel situation, adding two new members—Jonathan Cain (keyboards) and Ricky Phillips (bass)—to flesh out the sound and free Waite from his bass-playing duties.

The recruits, both Americans, immediately went from auditioning to touring, finding themselves in what had previously been a quintessential English rock band. "The first tour was a trying time in the band's maturity," Phillips noted. "The five of us had to decide whether we did the right thing." The chemistry apparently worked, and Nevison's big production gave the band a classy hit single, "Every Time I Think of You," with Waite's heartfelt vocal augmented by prominent female vocals.

"A lot of people are still out to get us because of a hype—not put on by the band, but by the record company," Phillips reflected. "The early push was an unfair thing to do, because the group was just a rock 'n' roll band with maybe something unique. But to come out and overstate the case just so the company can sell records and immediately recoup its investment—you can't anticipate anything too much. What's happening now could have happened a lot sooner." ■

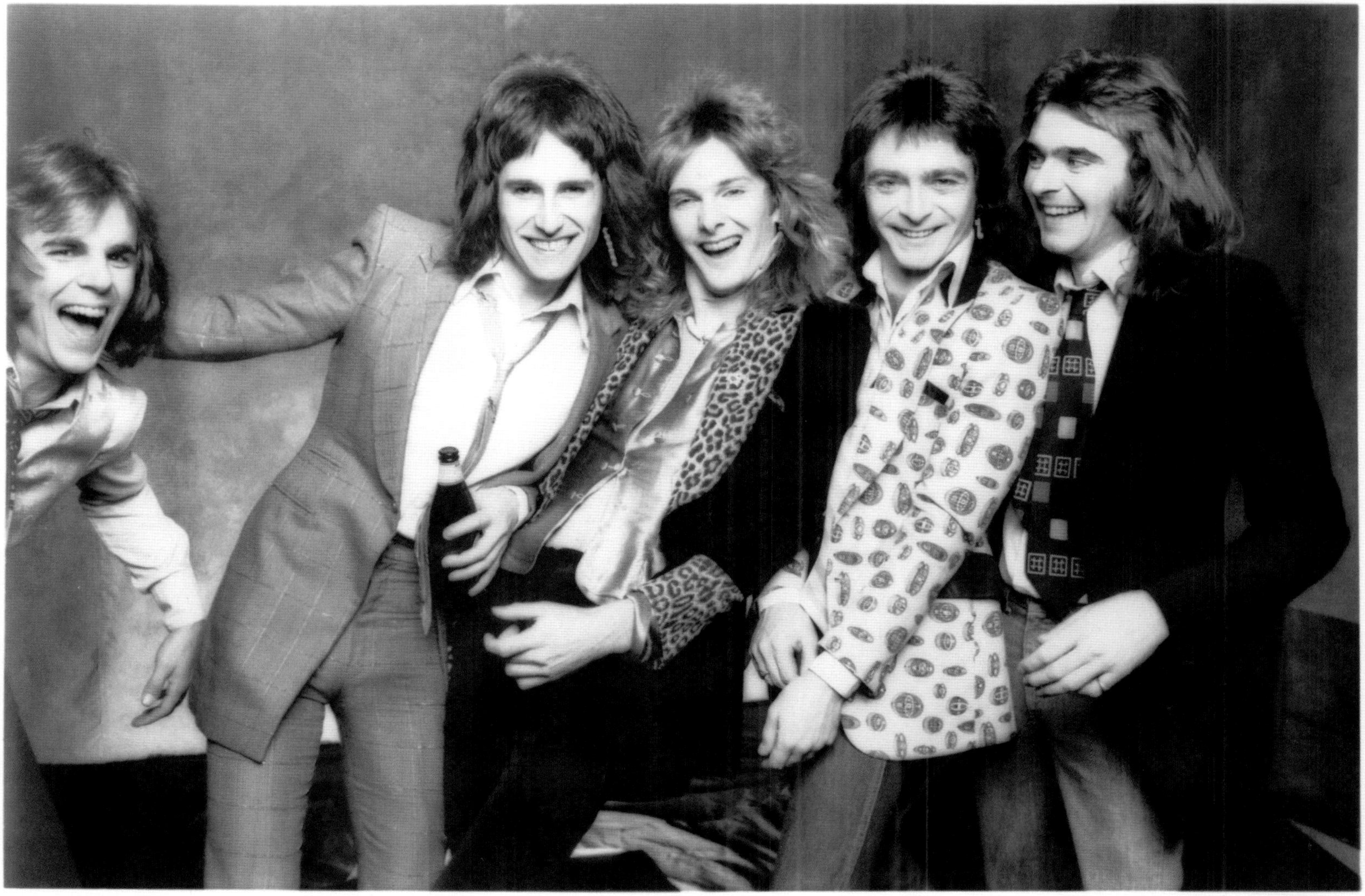

The Babys

Chrysalis™

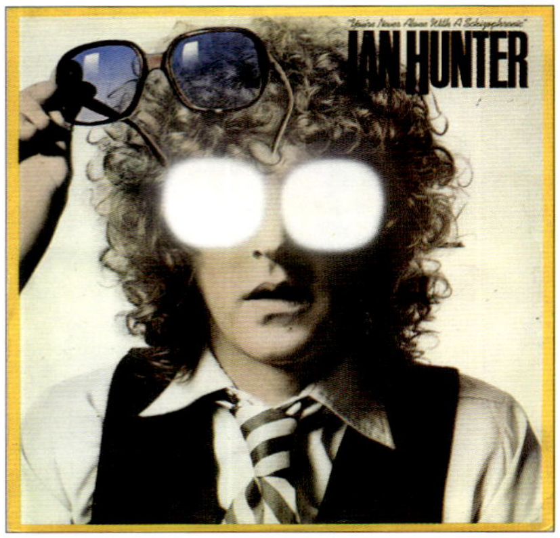

Billboard 200: *You're Never Alone with a Schizophrenic* (#35)
Billboard Hot 100: "Just Another Night" (#68)

Aided by ace guitarist Mick Ronson, Ian Hunter reached a peak with *You're Never Alone with a Schizophrenic.*

IAN HUNTER'S popularity stemmed primarily from his years as frontman of Mott the Hoople. With corkscrew hair and dark glasses that became a trademark, he established himself as one of the smartest hard-rock songwriters of the early Seventies. But it was admirer David Bowie who wrote "All the Young Dudes," which became the British band's only American Top 40 hit in 1972—an anthem for the glam-rock era.

Mick Ronson, formerly the leading member of the Spiders from Mars, Bowie's backing band, produced *You're Never Alone with a Schizophrenic*, Hunter's fourth solo album. Hunter's accompaniment was provided by members of Bruce Springsteen's E Street Band—Garry Tallent (bass), Max Weinberg (drums) and Roy Bittan (keyboards).

"I wanted to use a rhythm section that was used to each other," Hunter noted. "We worked at the Power Station in New York City, and Max was in for months learning how to tune his drums for this studio. After we started recording, in two hours I was hearing things that made my hair curl."

The album contained "Cleveland Rocks," which became a de facto anthem in Cleveland, Ohio, where mayor Dennis Kucinich gave Hunter the key to the city. "There's only one thing lacking in rock 'n' roll these days, and that's corn," Hunter said. "Everyone's like ice now, you've gotta be cool. But corniness was a big part of rock 'n' roll, and I miss it. Mott the Hoople had that commitment, but I think we lost it after the first album."

"Ships," a Hunter-penned ballad on *You're Never Alone...*, became an adult contemporary hit for Barry Manilow in late 1979. "Everybody types me as a guy that writes hard-rock songs, but I've always liked the slow stuff," Hunter said. "I'm fully aware of the need to be commercial, but I've never quite understood American commercial taste. I listen to the radio, but it doesn't tell me anything. I have my ups and downs with songwriting—it's difficult for me because I don't sit down and write one unless I'm desperate, on a deadline. The best ones just come out of the air—you're like a transmitter, you just catch it. You've got to be truthful."

Hunter, an Englishman, kept close tabs on his homeland. "British politics have been going around in my mind," he said. "America and England were founded on different principles. America pretty much remains true to what it was founded on. In England, we have all these grand traditions and vocations—cricket and the Empire and all that. It's the infrastructure of morale that's being whittled away at. I don't enjoy that." ■

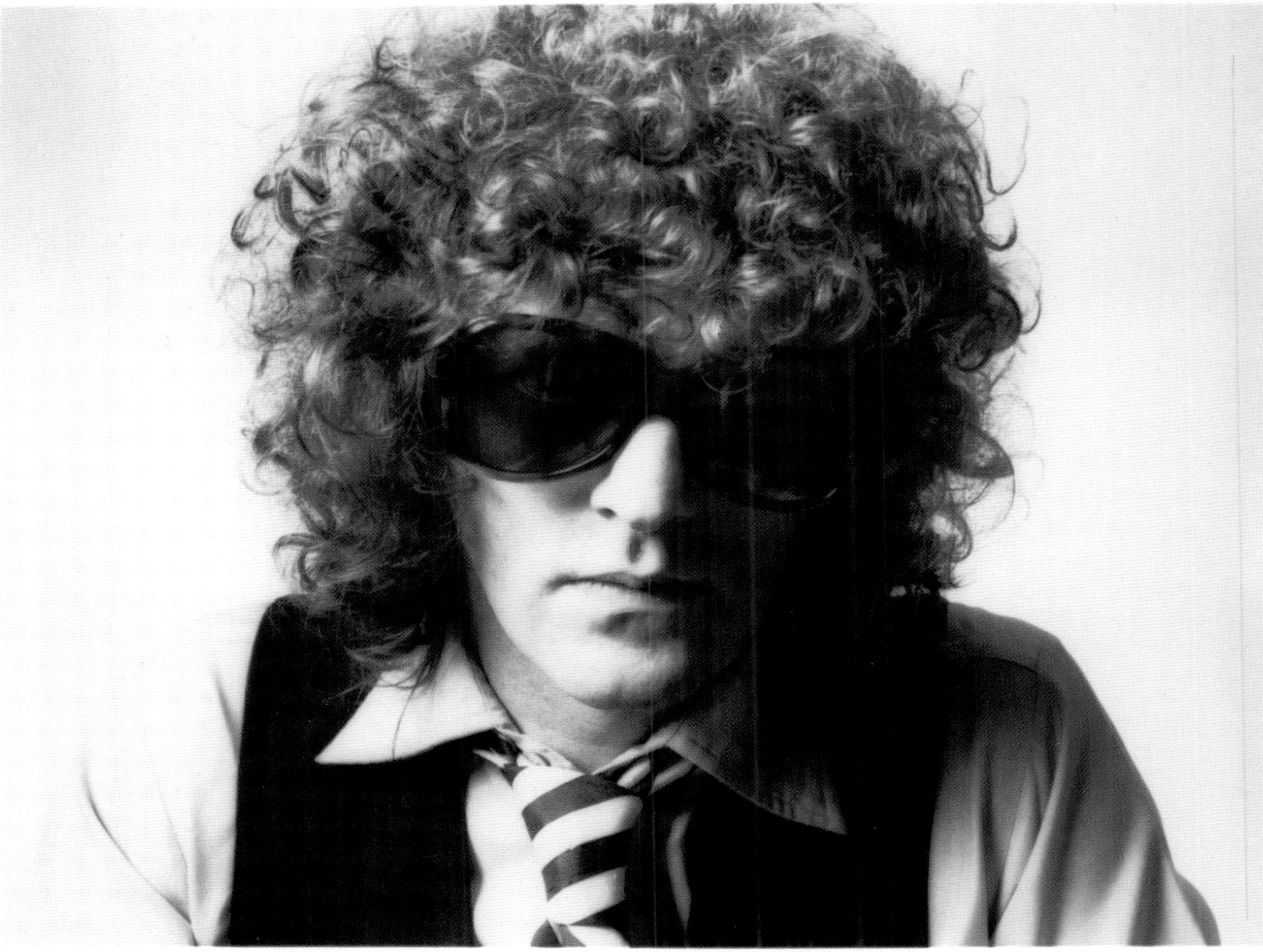

Ian Hunter

Chrysalis™

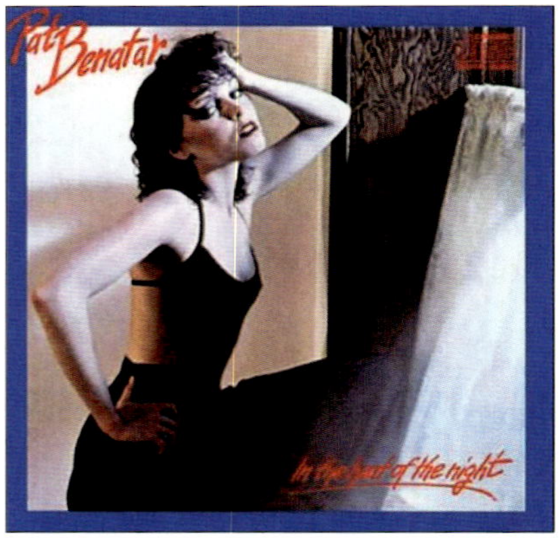

Billboard 200: *In the Heat of the Night* (#12)
Billboard Hot 100: "Heartbreaker" (#23); "We Live for Love" (#27)

Out of a few newcomers, Pat Benatar was the most riveting entrant in a competitive field of female rockers.

HER DYNAMIC performances on vinyl and onstage had made Pat Benatar head of a new class dispe ling—with disdain—the notion that no woman could rock out, keep her femininity and be accepted. And to think, she almost abandoned power chords for Verdi.

"My mom was an opera singer, so I studied opera until I was 17 and planned to go into it," she explained. "I always wanted to sing rock 'n' roll, but I had this real clean voice which didn't suit it very well. When I turned 21, I decided to see if I could change."

The New York born-and-reared Benatar moved to Virginia in 1974 and started her professional career by singing "cabaret and lounge music." Finding no hope there, she returned to the Big Apple and became a fixture at Catch a Rising Star, a club where she spent three years making the changeover to hard rock. Her break came in late 1978 when she signed a contract with Chrysalis Records.

A bigger opportunity occurrec when Mike Chapman agreed to produce her album. Chapman was the hottest producer in the business (12 charting singles in 1979), and he had a particular knack for handling female singers (Blondie, Suzi Quatro). He had vowed not to work with any new artists, but he made time after hearing a tape of Benatar over a casual lunch one day. The resulting debut, *In the Heat of the Night,* showed off her voice in a convincing rock context. "I still sing kinda dramatically," she admitted. "Anc I can't get rid of that, even though I try sometimes. It still comes out a little, um, flamboyant."

Several cover versions were included, as well as eclectic musical styles. "Calling it 'new wave' is semantics—I just call it Eighties-sounding rock," Benatar explained. "I covered 'I Need a Lover' (written by John Mellencamp), not to come across as a man-hater, but to show that women go through other things than always getting dumped on and crying. 'My Clone Sleeps Alone' started as a joke, but I really felt that last verse. I mean, there *is* something that bothers me about cloning."

Benatar's "Heartbreaker" was all over the radio, and Ellen Foley, Carolyne Mas and Ellen Shipley had also released their first albums. All were from New York, and Benatar knew each of them.

"We were all born around the same time, no matter how much they lie," she laughed, admitting to being "27 and proud of it. We had the same family backgrounds, we were all tomboys, we studied classical voice and we grew up with the Ronettes. It's interesting that we've all ended up with the same interest at the same time. Some people think we started doing music because of women's liberation. Hey, we were always liberated."

And Benatar could rock with the best. "I hate being categorized as a woman first and a rock 'n' roller second. Most people are cool about it, but some idiots say, 'Are you selling music or sex?' Well, that's their problem—if we look good, it's not our fault." ■

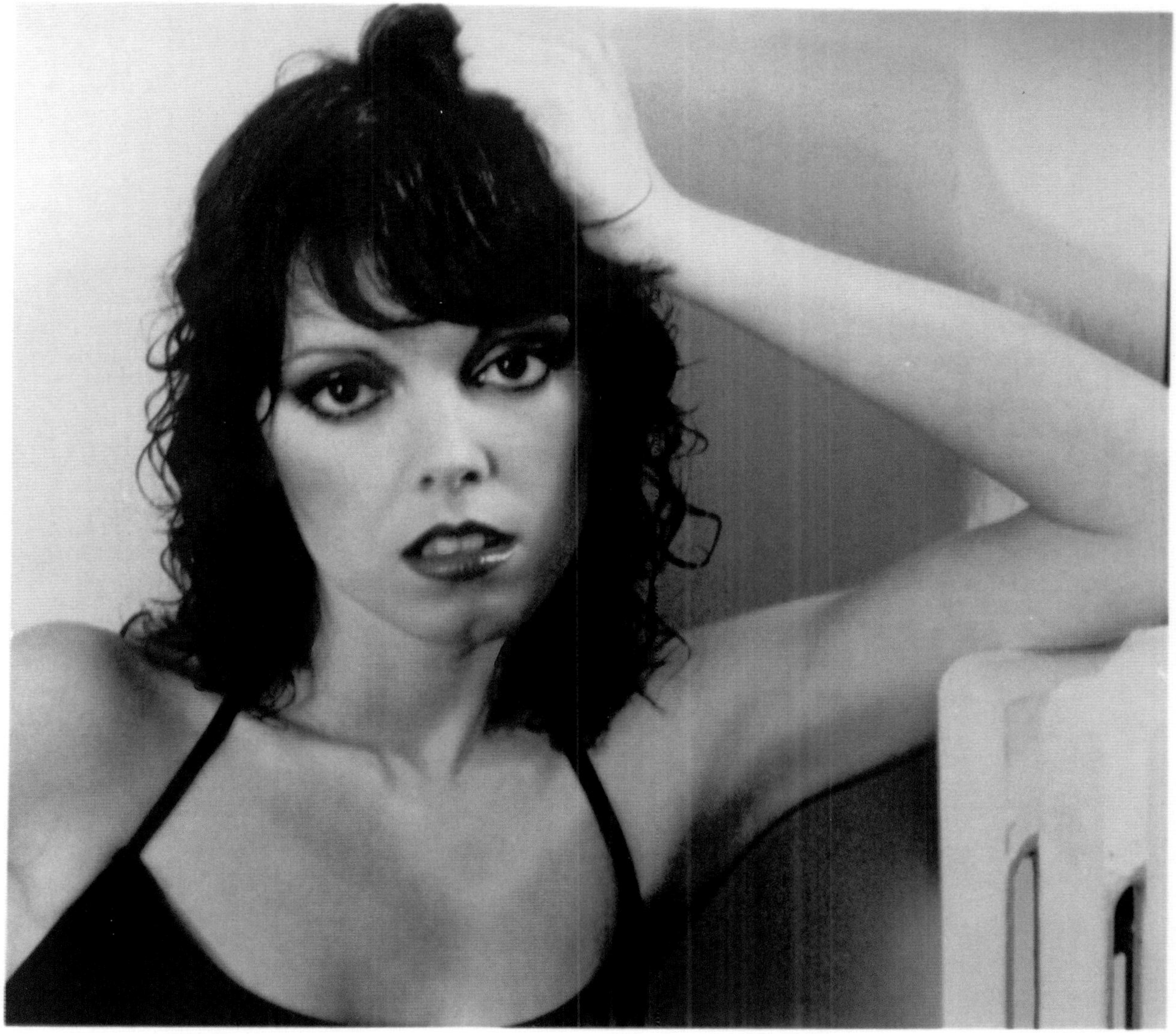

Pat Benatar

Chrysalis ™

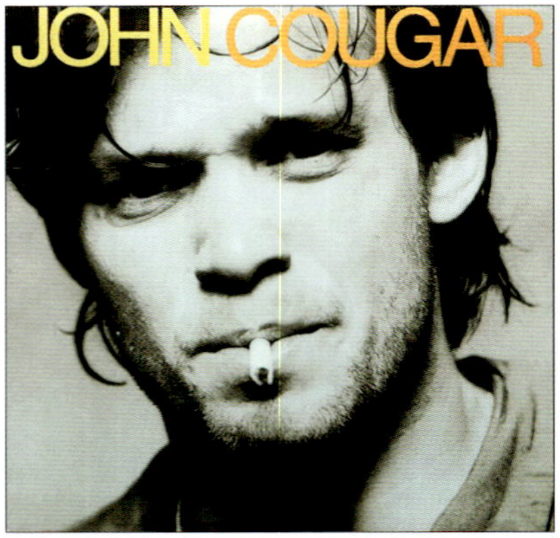

Billboard 200: *John Cougar* (#64)
Billboard Hot 100: "I Need a Lover" (#28); "Small Paradise" (#87)

Growing up in public wasn't an easy path to take, but small-town kid John Cougar emerged nearly unscathed.

THE EVENTS of the last four years had been enough to send anyone else packing, but John Cougar figured he was the luckiest guy on earth to be making records.

"Yeah, getting into this business was a real fluke," he admitted. "I had just gotten out of college and been fired from my job and was collecting unemployment. I had a whim that I wanted to try and make records. I'm from a real small town in Indiana, and everybody said, 'Hey man, why don't you use your degree and act like you've got some sense in your head?' I told my old man that I was going to New York to make records and he just laughed—'Go ahead, there's people running into each other trying to do that.'"

Cougar took off and dropped off a tape of the three songs he'd written with Tony DeFries of MainMan Management, a firm managing David Bowie. "I had to leave after a couple of weeks when I ran out of money, but a phone call beat me home. I flew back out the next day and got signed—and I spent the next few years learning about the record business in front of the American public.

Cougar—his real name was John Mellencamp, but DeFries insisted that his German surname was too discordant to market—recorded *Chestnut Street Incident* and the never-released *The Kid Inside*.

"*Chestnut* was an honest record—ignorance is bliss," Cougar admitted. "Some people say I should have been credited with the whole punk rock movement, because I came out with that record in 1975 with a garage-band sound and weird haircut when no one else was even thinking about it. I'm not a real smart guy in that I don't think things out. I just act impulsively on them. Heck, I'm from Indiana—I don't know shit. I came in believing that hippies ran the record business and found out it's an illusion."

When the approaches used to market Cougar's music failed, he knew he was in too deep, but he didn't know how to extricate himself from MainMan. Cougar finally met Billy Gaff, who had managed Rod Stewart to the top of the rock star heap.

"He just said, 'Great, I'd like to meet this guy DeFries in court.' That was his attitude, and you know what? He stood up to him and we settled out of court, no problem!"

Gaff got Cougar out of the States to England to figure out what he wanted to do. *The Biography* was released virtually everywhere in the free world except North America, but Cougar found his second wind with "I Need A Lover," added to his *John Cougar* album and released in the US, where it became his first Top 40 hit. Pat Benatar covered the song on her debut album *In the Heat of the Night*.

Cougar was feeling feisty. "You can't write totally from experience because no one pumping gas at the 76 station can relate to the things I've done. But they can't be contrived emotion, either—they've got to be somewhat traditional. Something like, 'I need a lover that won't drive me crazy'!" ■

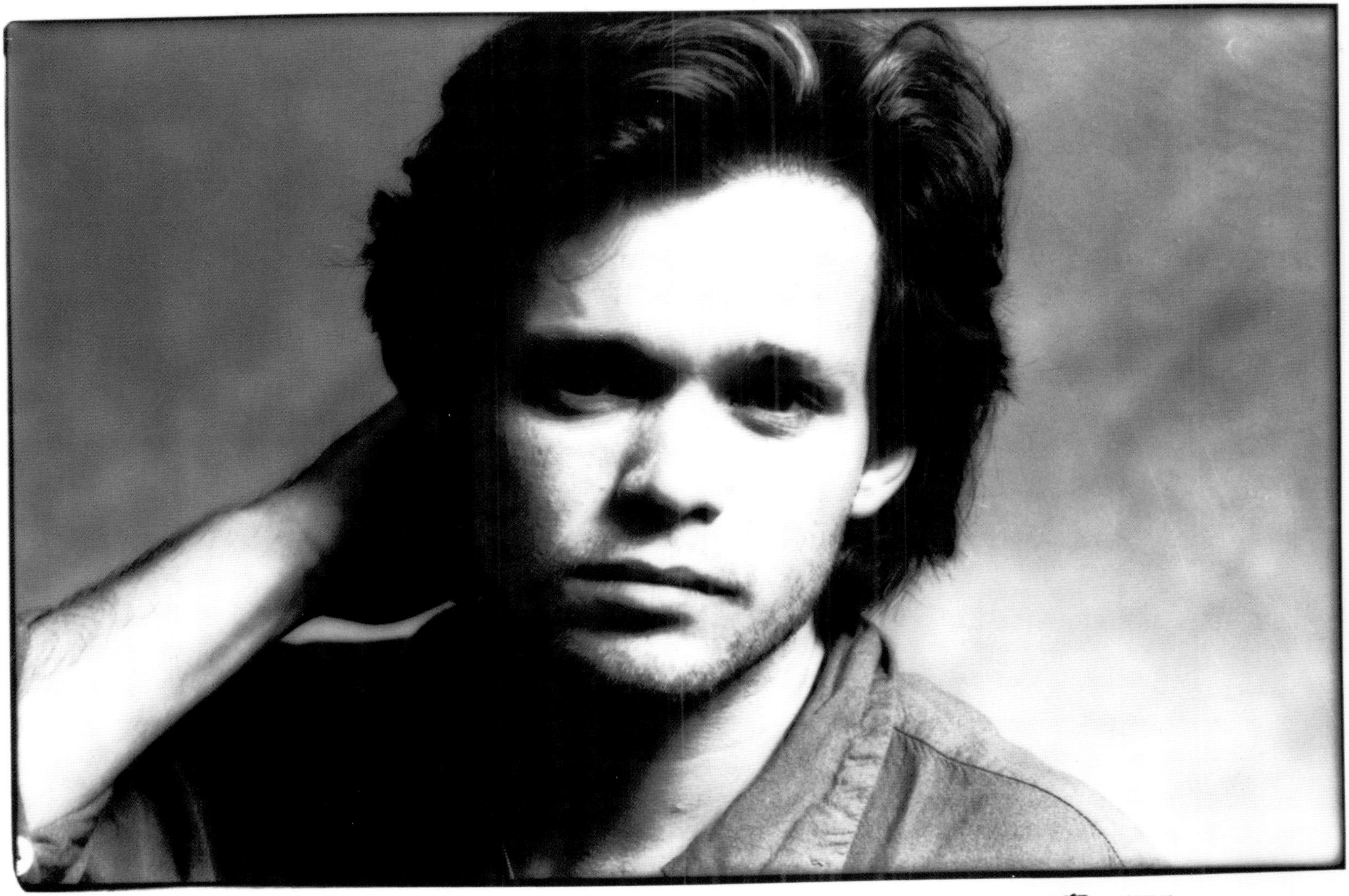

JOHN COUGAR

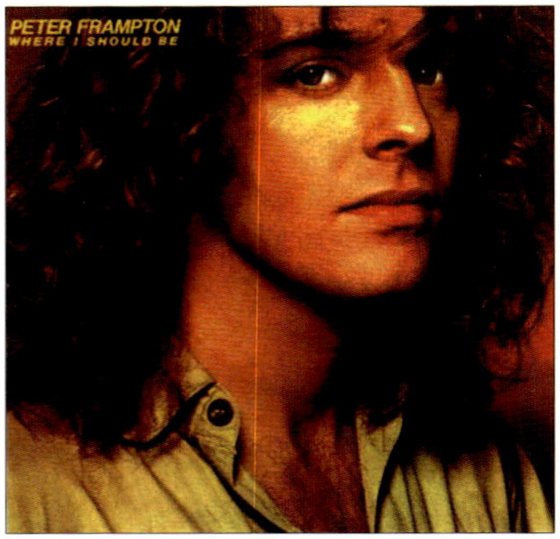

Billboard 200: *Where I Should Be* (#19)
Billboard Hot 100: "I Can't Stand It No More" (#14)

After falling from commercial favor, Peter Frampton regained public interest with "I Can't Stand It No More."

FOLLOWING APPRENTICESHIPS with the Herd and Humble Pie as well as years on the road opening for other acts, Peter Frampton blew up in the summer of 1976 with *Frampton Comes Alive*. The two-record set became the most successful live album in rock history, an astonishing success. Playing stadiums, armed with a pretty baby face, long, curly blond hair and a seductive electric guitar style, there was no bigger international star on the rock music scene.

Yet Frampton soon felt a backlash. His manager coerced him into releasing *I'm in You*, a wimpy follow-up album that catered to teenyboppers rather than to his rock following. *I'm in You* was, by Frampton's admission, one of the hardest albums he'd ever had to work on because he knew it would be under critical scrutiny of almost impossible standards.

"While I was making *I'm in You*, all I could feel was that I was in a fog," he said. "I knew three million people had already ordered the album before I set foot in the studio. It was scary."

His appearance in the turgid musical film version of *Sgt. Pepper Lonely Hearts Club Band* cemented his fate—in his own words, Frampton had come to be perceived as a "pop music cartoon." Then he was involved in an automobile accident in the Bahamas that left him hospitalized for several weeks with multiple broken bones, a concussion and muscle damage.

"I can't completely straighten my right arm out," he admitted. "It's something probably only I'd notice, but I wondered about my guitar playing at first. It was something I had to prove."

Frampton returned to the studio to record the album *Where I Should Be*, which earned a respectable chart placing on the strength of the single "I Can't Stand It No More."

"I didn't think people were taking me seriously," the guitarist said. "The press and the public thought I had let them down—and on face value, they were right. But they didn't know what was going on behind the scenes. The image came about through mistakes I made." ■

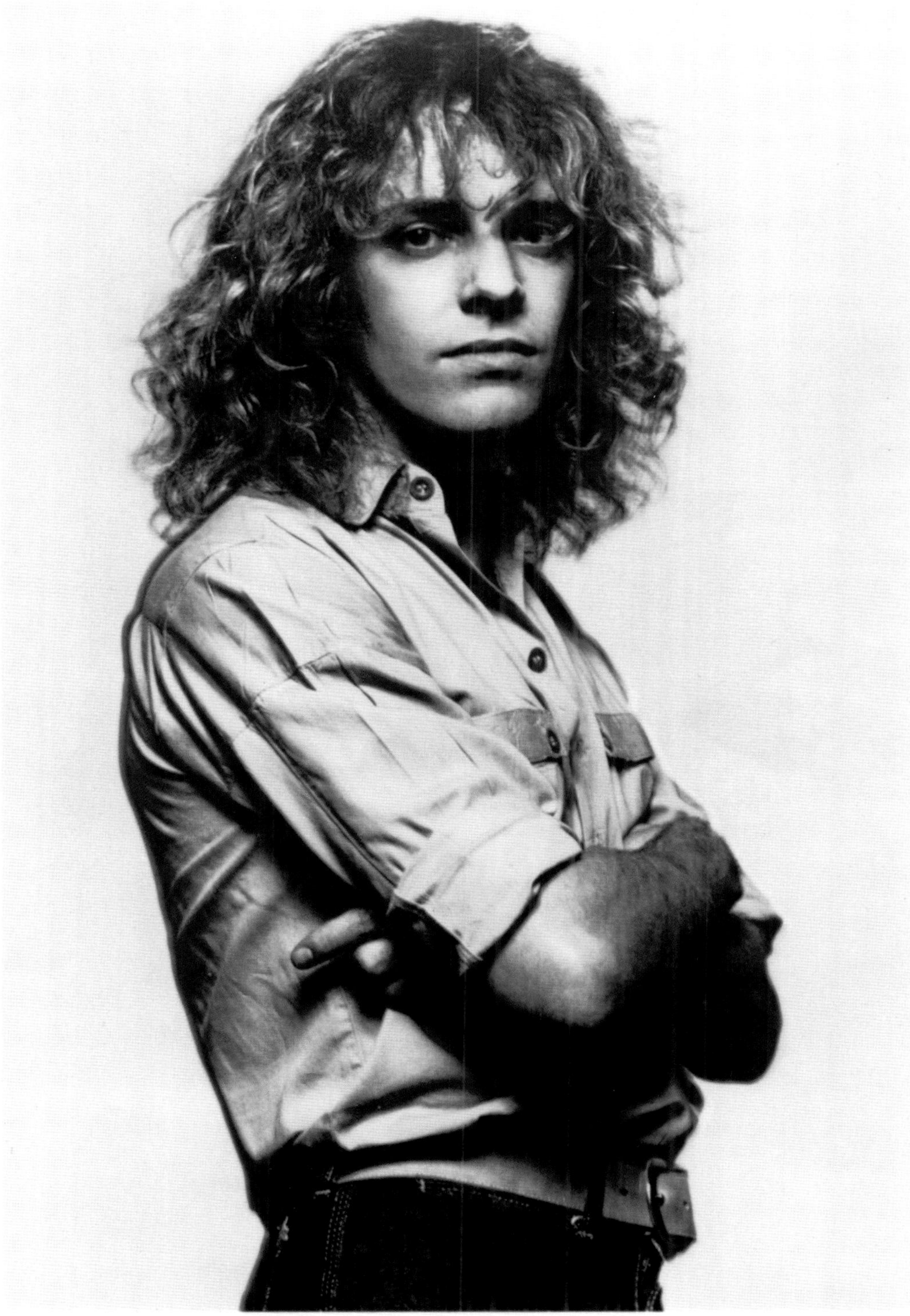

Peter Frampton

Direction : Dee Anthony Organisation

A&M RECORDS

Printed U.S.A.

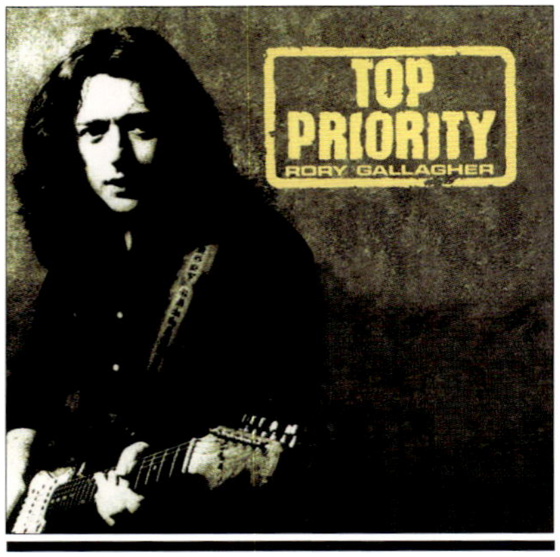

Billboard 200: *Top Priority* (#140)

A rocker with a genuine sense for blues-based work, Rory Gallagher had no boogie skeletons in his closet.

SAY THE words "guitar hero" and an image came to mind—gold lamé jumpsuit, Z-shaped guitar, maybe a flashpot or two. Say "Rory Gallagher" and things got a little less pretentious—flannel shirt, blue jeans, an ancient Stratocaster with chipped paint and fingers that moved faster than the eye could follow.

Gallagher's straight-ahead approach had never brought him his commercial due, but few could approach him as a live performer. He and his rhythm section easily could have been considered an anachronistic power trio except for his fiery and frenetic fretwork.

The Irish guitarist's career began inauspiciously. In the late Sixties, Gallagher fronted a trio called Taste, which earned a small but loyal cult following. Following the group's demise, he went solo and had been grinding away ever since, recording the yearly album and touring his brains out.

Accordingly, Gallagher's best-selling releases were his live albums, but *Top Priority* came close to being a breakthrough. The tune "Follow Me" proved his worth with a roaring opening and meaty chording. On "Philby," a Gaelic-tinged electric sitar allowed an esoteric flourish in his playing. Most guitarists relied on a bank of effects to alter their sound, but Gallagher used naught but his fingers to control his tones. His gruff, whiskey-soaked vocals were competent enough, part of his no-nonsense approach.

"I like to keep things exciting and lean," he admitted. "That's why I got rid of my keyboard player a while back. Keyboards let you explore mellower avenues, but I wanted to get the band back into more aggressive things. If I was more laid-back, it would work, but the way I play is more open-ended."

Gallagher's underproduced sound had yet to give him a hit, but the musician had no worries on that level. "I have a clear-cut idea of what I want in the studio. In the Eighties, I don't think kids will be fooled as easily anymore. They're gonna want meat-and-potatoes stuff from people who can deliver. And I think my music fits into that category." ■

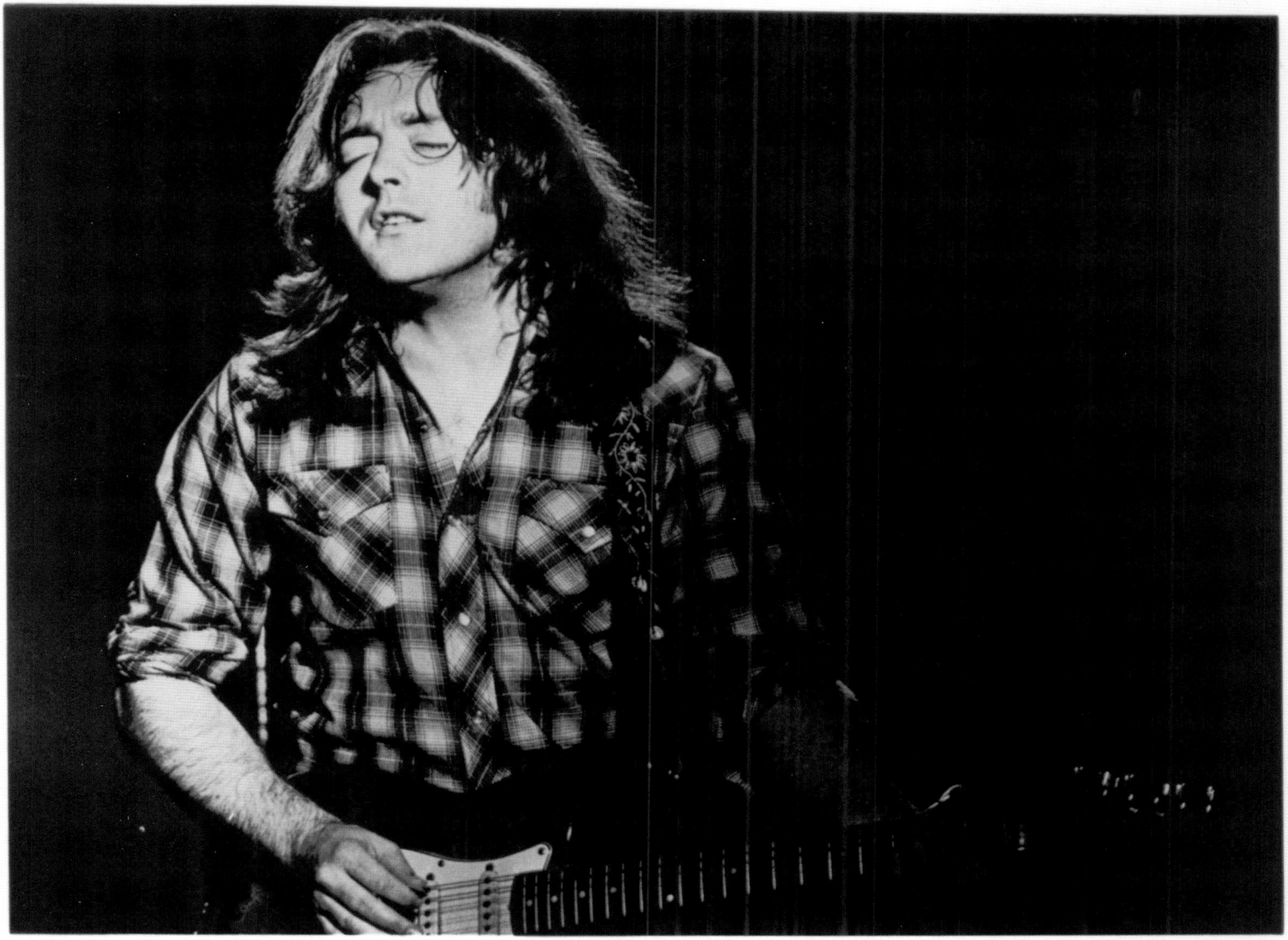

Rory Gallagher

Chrysalis™

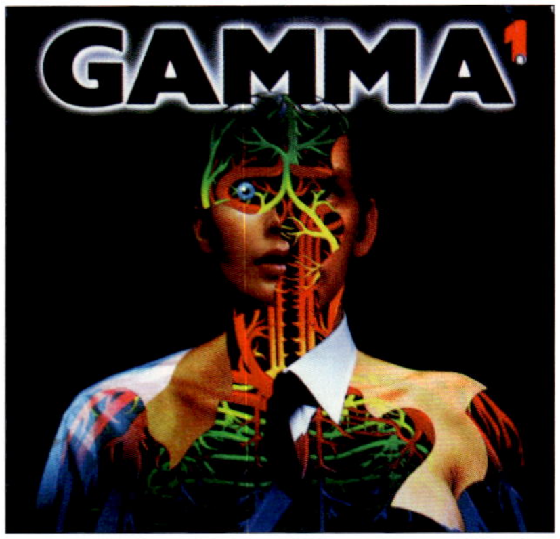

Billboard 200: *Gamma 1* (#131)
Billboard Hot 100: "I'm Alive" (#60)

Guitar star Ronnie Montrose's probing of synthesizers and vocoders was realized on Gamma's debut album.

HE MIGHT have sounded just happy to survive, but Ronnie Montrose was convinced that his best music lay ahead of him. Gamma, his new group, had renewed his musical focus, and the right-place-wrong-time days of his career appeared to be over.

"My old record company told me, 'Rock 'n' roll is old hat.' Rock 'n' roll will never be old hat. People will always want that jolt, and that's why I'm still grinding away."

Montrose started making a name for himself as a session musician in the early Seventies, contributing some lovely acoustic guitar work on Van Morrison albums. He found himself joining the Edgar Winter Group, where his monster riffing on electric guitar transformed "Frankenstein" and "Free Ride" into hit singles.

The next logical step was his own band, imaginatively named Montrose, and he set out to conquer America. The ingredients were there—young Sammy Hagar was an exuberant, throaty vocalist, and Montrose took Jeff Beck's style one step further with his speed-of-light solos—but the band never met with the expected success. After a brilliant debut album (*Montrose*) and a decent follow-up, Hagar left to go solo. Two albums later, the band disintegrated in 1976.

Montrose found himself wanting to express his eclectic tastes. "I got the reputation of being a heavy-metal guitarist, but I've got many other kinds of music in me. There was no way to get away from the categorization except to dramatically make a change."

Open Fire, his first solo album, featured all instrumentals and some unexpected forays into experimental and acoustic music. The record brought Montrose peer recognition, but his old fans didn't buy it. "I went out on tour, and the kids weren't ready for anything but rock 'n' roll," he said. "It became really uncomfortable."

Drawing a hard line between his solo career and a group endeavor, Montrose formed Gamma. "It's a clear-cut way not to compromise either trip," he said. "Now I can continue my solo albums recording different styles and then pursue the full-blown, high-energy rock 'n' roll with Gamma."

Jim Alcivar, Montrose's keyboard player for many years, dabbled in electronic design, and Montrose was interested in its practical application on the *Gamma 1* album. The effect was most notably heard on the hit "I'm Alive," the old Hollies song that the band thoroughly reworked via electronically treated vocals. Producer Ken Scott lent the band his considerable engineering skills, resulting in a dynamic sound that recent albums had lacked. Montrose even recruited his finest vocalist since Hagar in Davey Pattison.

The best track, "Fight to the Finish," closed the record with some patented guitar fury and dynamic synthesizer work. Montrose promised that the band would continue from there. "We're working hard, touring hard and talking it up," he said. "I've learned how to do those things over the years. This time I've got a bit of an edge." ■

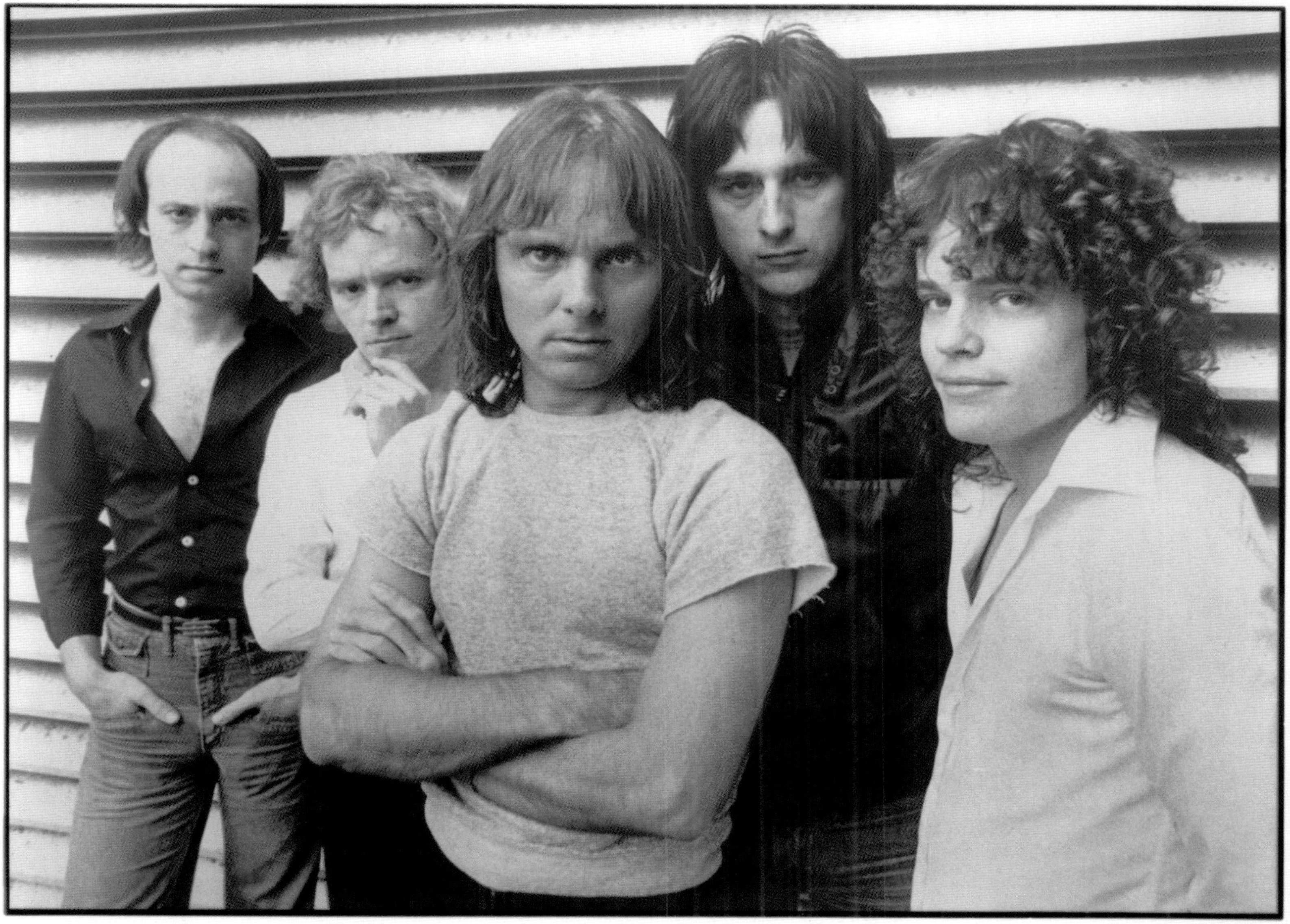

Photo Credit: BRUCE STEINBERG/1979

Alan Fitzgerald Davey Pattison Ronnie Montrose Skip Gillette Jim Alcivar

GAMMA

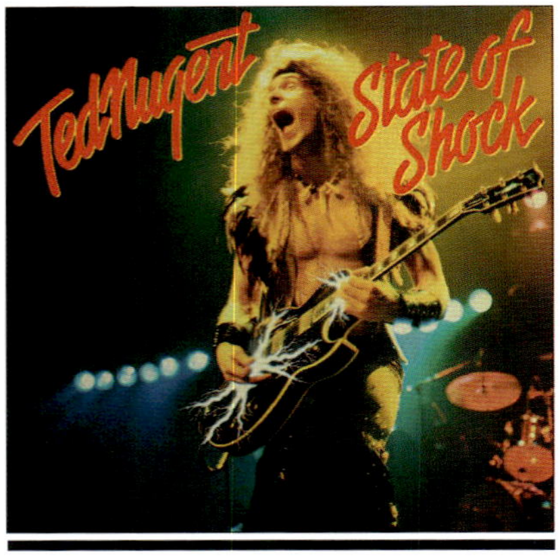

Billboard 200: *State of Shock* (#18)

Looking to keep his hot streak going, unreserved rocker Ted Nugent hit a speed bump with *State of Shock*.

CLOSING A decade in which he took his wild-man persona to the top of the charts, Ted Nugent showed a bit of musical maturation on *State of Shock*, his fifth solo studio album. "Paralyzed" was an electrifying opening track; "I Want to Tell You," the old George Harrison chestnut, received hit-single treatment; and there was even a ballad, "Alone," that could have fooled anybody.

"And I've got tons of new songs. There's 'Bushwacker,' 'Detroit Magical Lip Lock Tour' and 'The Five-Knuckle Shuffle.' No one writes better songs than me," Nugget explained in a typical fit of modesty.

But *State of Shock* was Nugent's first solo album not to attain platinum certification. Before the recording, his right-hand man and lead singer, Derek St. Holmes, had defected along with bassist Rob Grange to form their own band, St. Paradise. Did they leave with Nugent's blessing?

"You mean before I gave them the boot?" Nugent bellowed. "Listen, they just couldn't keep up with me anymore." Yet "Turn It Up," co-written by Nugent, was the best song on the *St. Paradise* album. "Of course it is!" he roared. ■

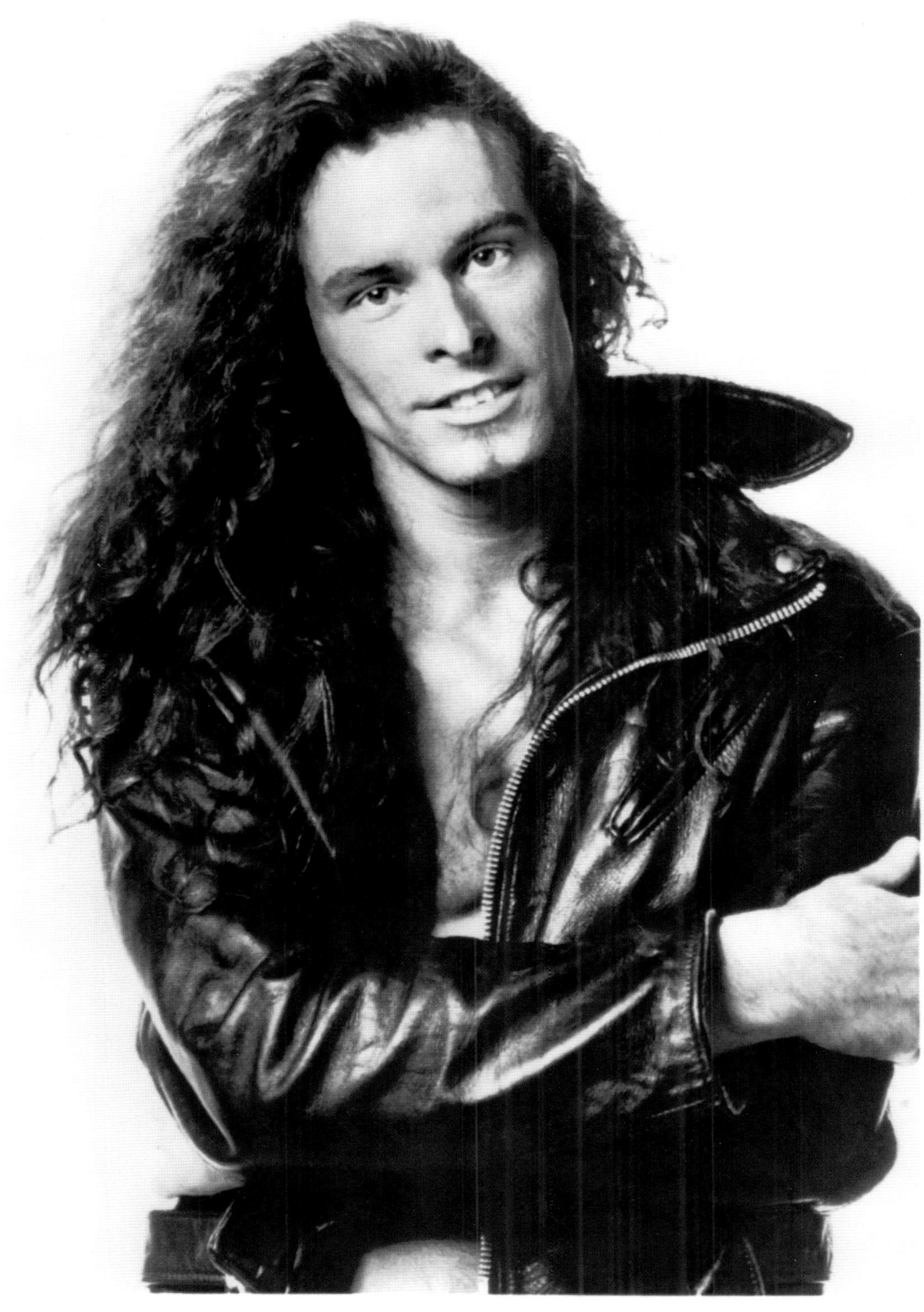

DMA
DIVERSIFIED MANAGEMENT AGENCY

LEBER–KREBS INC.

TED NUGENT

Epic

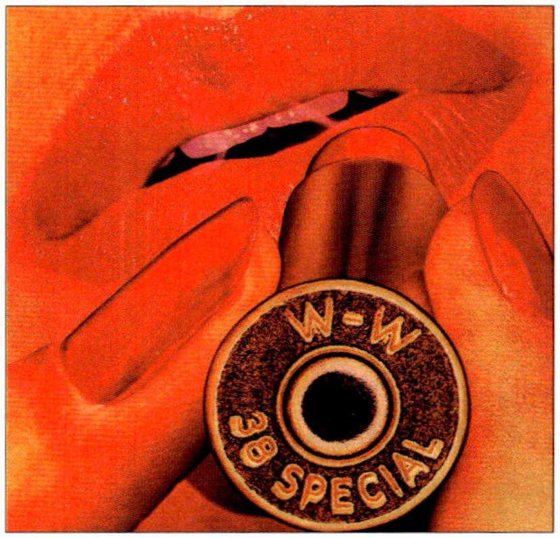

Billboard 200: *Rockin' into the Night* (#57)
Billboard Hot 100: "Rockin' into the Night" (#43)

38 Special fully matured from a soft-focus Lynyrd Skynyrd into one of Southern rock's hottest commodities.

OUT OF the Southern-rock tradition, Jacksonville-based 38 Special came into its first hit single, "Rockin' into the Night," without sacrificing credibility or integrity—a situation the members ascribed to their mentors in Lynyrd Skynyrd. After an airplane carrying that seminal rock group crashed in 1977, killing leader Ronnie Van Zant and several others, it fell to guitarist and neighborhood friend Don Barnes to keep the legacy alive in 38 Special with Donnie Van Zant, Ronnie's younger brother.

"It's tough to talk about—I was probably influenced more by Ronnie than anyone," Barnes reflected. "He always took control and was tougher than the toughest. The guys in Skynyrd were such underdogs, and they went out and won every show over the headliner. Coming from the wrong side of the tracks as someone who never had a dime to his name, Ronnie made the whole world listen to him—he found his chance to compete in this business, and he wasn't going to be satisfied with that. He was going to win at it.

"I was in awe of him at a distance, intimidated in his presence. He believed in me enough to co-sign on an amplifier when I was still broke and living in a rat-infested shack. And I was one of the last people to see him—I took his father to the funeral home before the closed-casket burial. Things like that hit home with you. That plane crash snapped me out of things and made me serious. At that point I realized I was only using 80 percent of my talent—singing background, trying to write these clichéd rock songs that weren't me, following what everybody else was doing. Ronnie helped me along, and when he was no longer there, I was going to give 100 percent from that moment on. That was the turning point—I wasn't going to bother with anybody else's influences, only what I heard on that little radio in *my* head."

Barnes convinced a devastated Donnie Van Zant that they could make it as a team, and 38 Special established an identity with "Rockin' into the Night," one of the best arena-ready singles out of the Southern band camp competition. The Henry Paul Band, Blackfoot, Point Blank—all of them were gentlemanly, sincere musicians willing to tour until they dropped, sensing their chance to assume the vacated throne.

"Hey, Skynyrd was the peak, the top," Barnes admitted. "They were the best, and since the crash, a lot of us folks have tried to fill the void. Ronnie used to tell us to be true to ourselves and let our own influences creep in, and I think we do that successfully. But no group will ever replace Skynyrd. We're all just out there filling the space that they left." ■

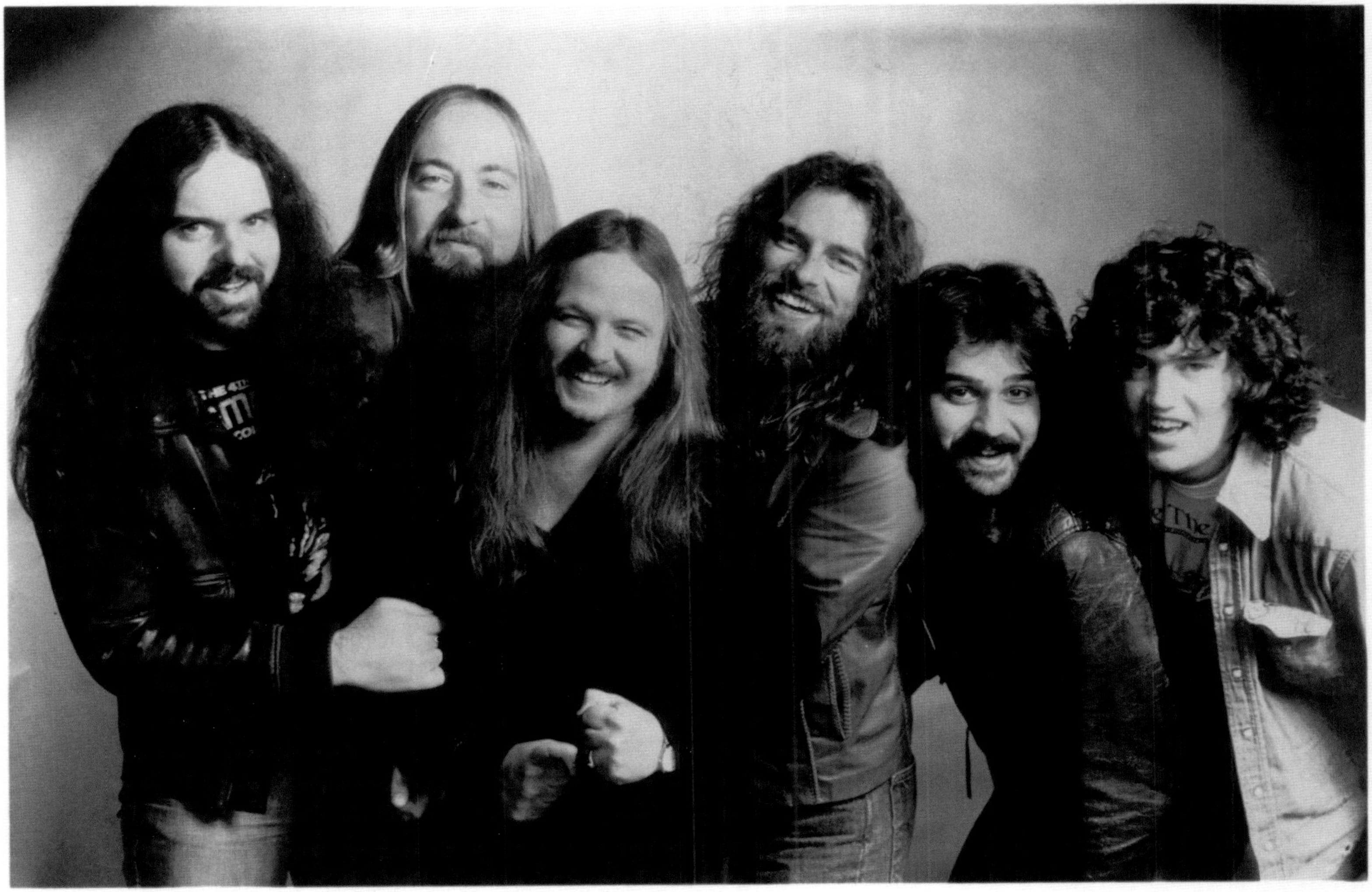

DON BARNES LARRY JUNSTROM DONNIE VAN ZANT JACK GRONDIN JEFF CARLISI STEVE BROOKINS

.38 SPECIAL

MANAGEMENT
MARK SPECTOR
(212) 308-1110

Printed in U.S.A.

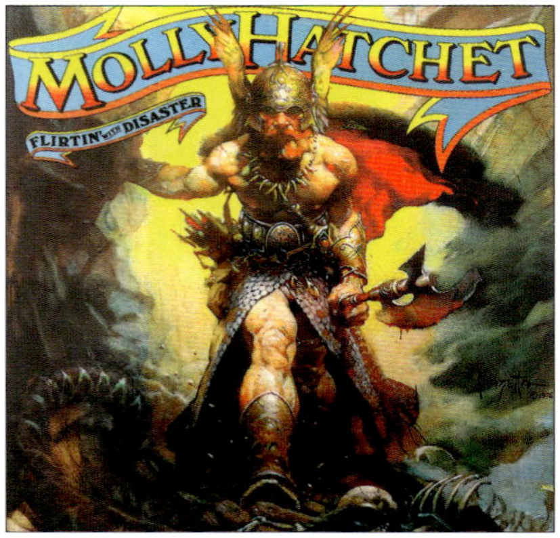

Billboard 200: *Flirtin' with Disaster* (#19)
Billboard Hot 100: "Flirtin' with Disaster" (#42)

The title track of Molly Hatchet's *Flirtin' with Disaster* gave the basic gist of the band's Southern stamped fury.

THERE WAS no dearth of bands ready to step into the Southern boogie shoes vacated by Lynyrd Skynyrd with a pat formula—gutsy guitar-based jamming, a hardcore boogie beat and a hoarse-voiced singer to complete the brawn-over-brains equation.

Flirtin' with Disaster, Molly Hatchet's second album, followed a year of hard work for the Jacksonville band. It drew a generation of rowdies ready to boogie at the drop of a Jack Daniel's cap, smitten with the fantasy-art album cover (a painting by Frank Frazetta). Power-chord aficionados basked in the delight of Molly Hatchet's triple lead-guitar attack, and the growl of lead singer Danny Joe Brown served the band well.

"Danny is always good with moves and stage presence, and he's a shouter," bassist Banner Thomas noted. "But he's a diabetic, and it's to the point where he's having to pump insulin twice a day intravenously. It's very hard to maintain the strict dietary regulations when you're on the road ordering from a Holiday Inn room service menu. We're having to do shows only on the weekends—Danny will be in the hospital all week and get released against doctor's orders to fly in and do the show with us."

The material on *Flirtin' with Disaster* was credited to the entire group. "When we're rehearsing, maybe two of us will have an idea we came up with on the road six months before, and somebody will come in with a lyric that they scribbled down from last night, and somebody might even surprise everyone with a completed song that he's secretly worked up over the past year," Thomas explained of Molly Hatchet's writing procedure. "And if one of us hasn't contributed anything, maybe he has to run out to the liquor store that day. Everybody contributes—and that last part has priority!" ■

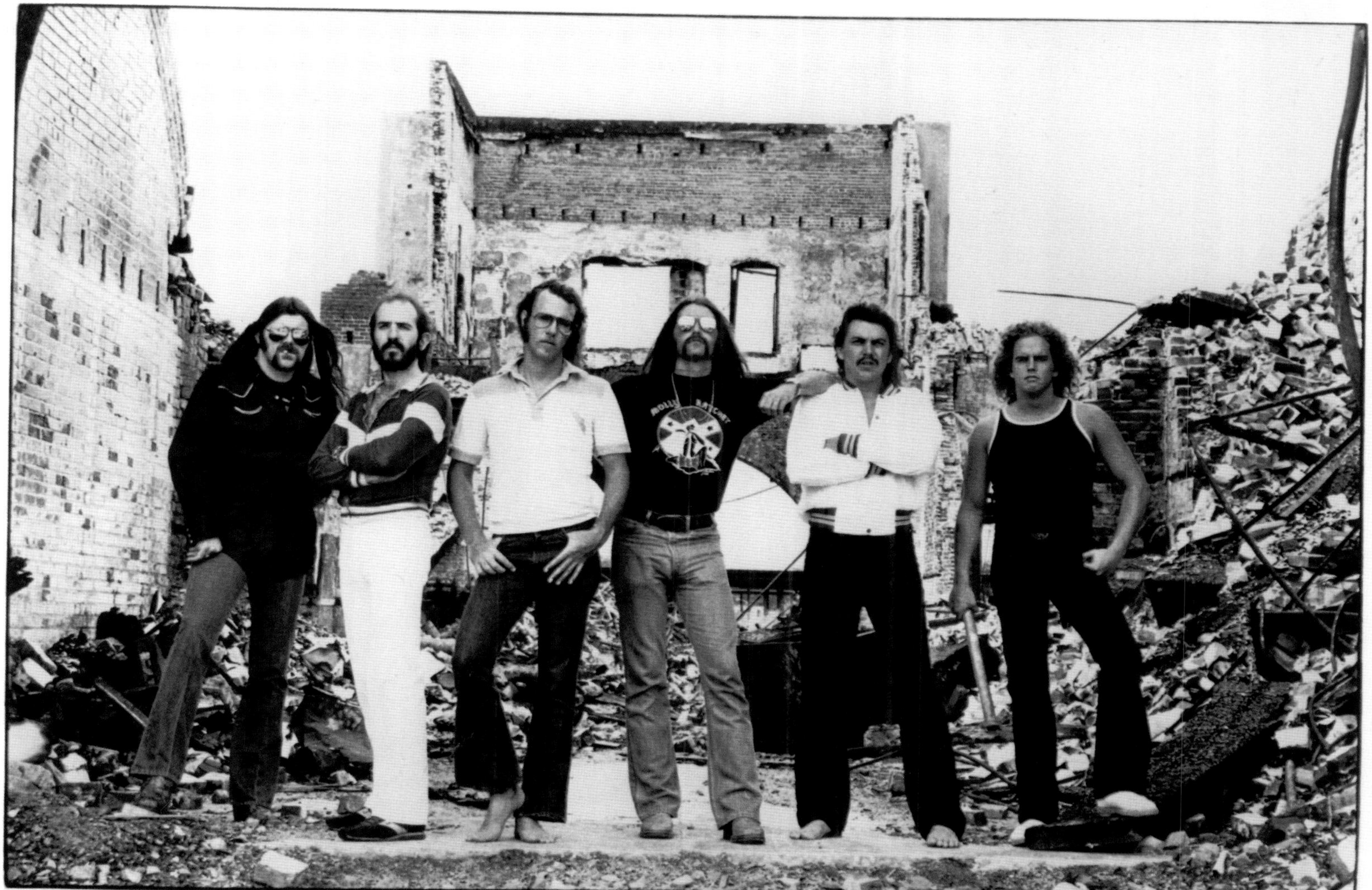

Dave Hlubek, Banner Thomas, Steve Holland, Duane Roland, Danny Joe Brown, Bruce Crump

MOLLY HATCHET

Flirtin' With Disaster

photo David Gahr

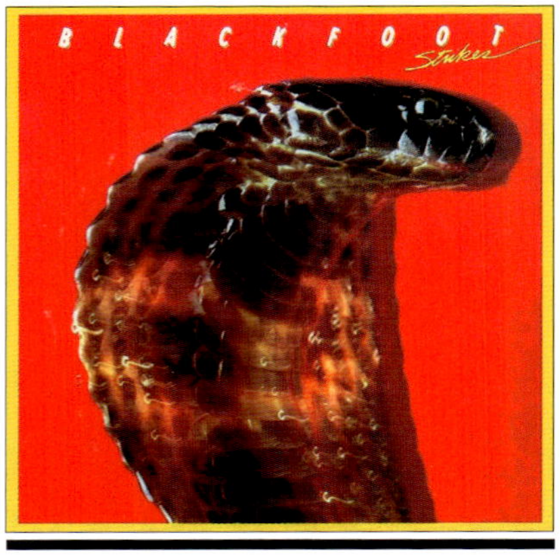

Billboard 200: *Strikes* (#42)
Billboard Hot 100: "Highway Song" (#26); "Train, Train" (#38)

Southern rock band Blackfoot finally made its mark, racking up the hits "Highway Song" and "Train, Train."

RICK MEDLOCKE was brought up in Jacksonville, Florida by his grandfather, Shorty Medlocke, a former sharecropper and a well-known local musician. Shorty had Rick playing banjo when the boy was only three years old. At the age of eight, Rick began playing drums, and at ten, he picked up the guitar. Along with neighborhood friends Jackson Spires and Greg Walker, Medlocke formed his first rock 'n' roll band.

The three remained together as Blackfoot, the last of the Southern bands to emerge from the musical activity centering around Jacksonville in the late Sixties. Fusing the blues technique of their Southern heritage with the fiery sounds of British blues-rock acts, many of the groups—the Allman Brothers, Lynyrd Skynyrd, Atlanta Rhythm Section—went on to greater things. A joint called the Comic Book Club provided gigs and a meeting place for musicians.

"Before one o'clock in the morning, the bands would play their sets for an audience mostly of kids," Medlocke explained. "Then about three o'clock, it would turn into a blues club—all of these great blues players would come in and it was mostly a Black audience. But some of the musicians from the rock bands would stick around to jam. I remember watching Duane Allman in there, playing amazing stuff all night long, and everyone would be just knocked out by it."

Medlocke contributed to the nucleus of Lynyrd Skynyrd (playing drums early on), but decided to reform Blackfoot in 1972, paying dues in bars and nighteries across the nation. Two records weren't successful, but finally, *Strikes* captured the band's explosive brand of hard rock. The seven-minute "Highway Song," a high point of live performances, became a pop hit.

And Medlocke's cover of his grandfather's "Train, Train," with Shorty himself providing a churning harmonica intro, was one of the album's hottest moments. Medlocke laughed when he recalled how much the studio confused Shorty. "He couldn't believe you could record one thing and then record something else along with it—he thought everything had to be done at the same time." ■

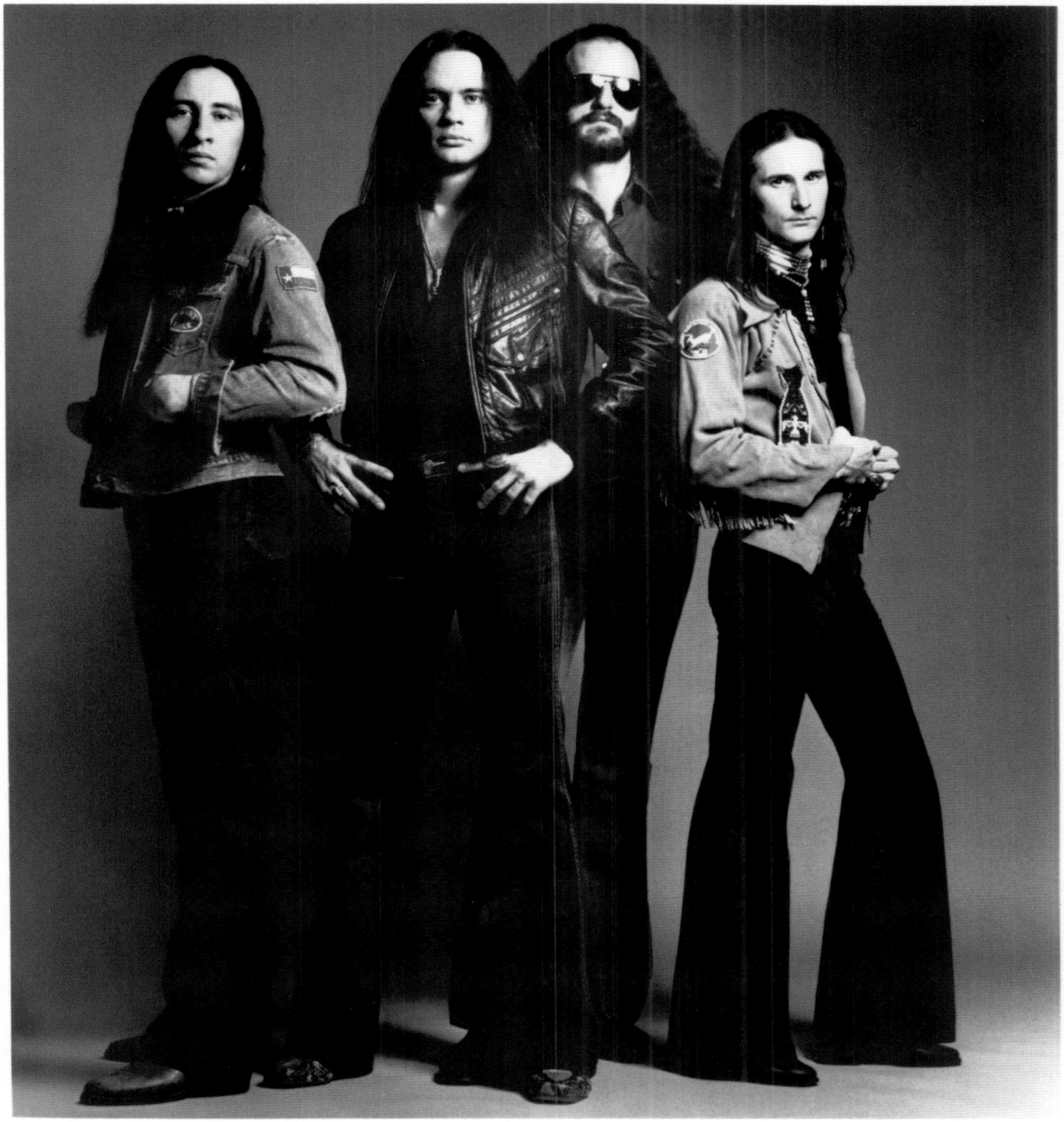

BLACKFOOT

ATCO

312 S. Ashley Street
Ann Arbor, Michigan
313-769-5454

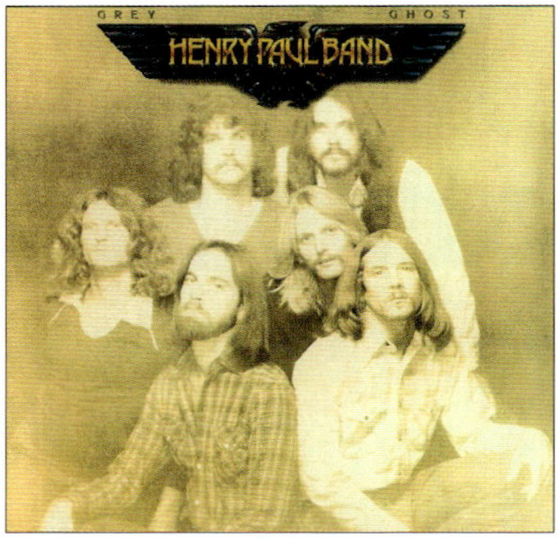

Billboard 200: *Grey Ghost* (#107)

Grey Ghost by Henry Paul Band made plain its leader's input, which had been played out on Outlaws records.

FOR EACH of the first three Outlaws album, Henry Paul served as the lead singer for the Southern-rock band, but 1977's *Hurry Sundown* marked his last. "The decision to leave the band was mine," he explained. *"Hurry Sundown* was what I considered a well-developed album for the Outlaws, and I wanted to stick with that. The rest of the band wanted to get into a hard-rock sound. So rather than fight, I moved into a situation where I could pursue what I wanted."

Grey Ghost, the Henry Paul Band's debut album, was much more song-oriented than the mostly instrumental fare served up by the Outlaws. The title track, the album's showcase, paid tribute to Lynyrd Skynyrd's Ronnie Van Zant and highlighted the lyrical subtleties Paul was striving for. The group featured the same three-guitar lineup that made the Outlaws such a powerful live unit, and Paul promised to maintain that part of his performing heritage.

"We still attract a lot of human battering rams at our shows—lots of young male aspiring guitarists," he laughed in reference to the enthusiasm of fans. "But the potential for this band to do different things is far greater than it was in the Outlaws. There aren't any dragged-out instrumental sections—I understand the Outlaws do a 29-minute version of 'Green Grass and High Tides' now. We'll never sacrifice the power and drive of the music, but with this group, there's even a chance we might have a hit!" ■

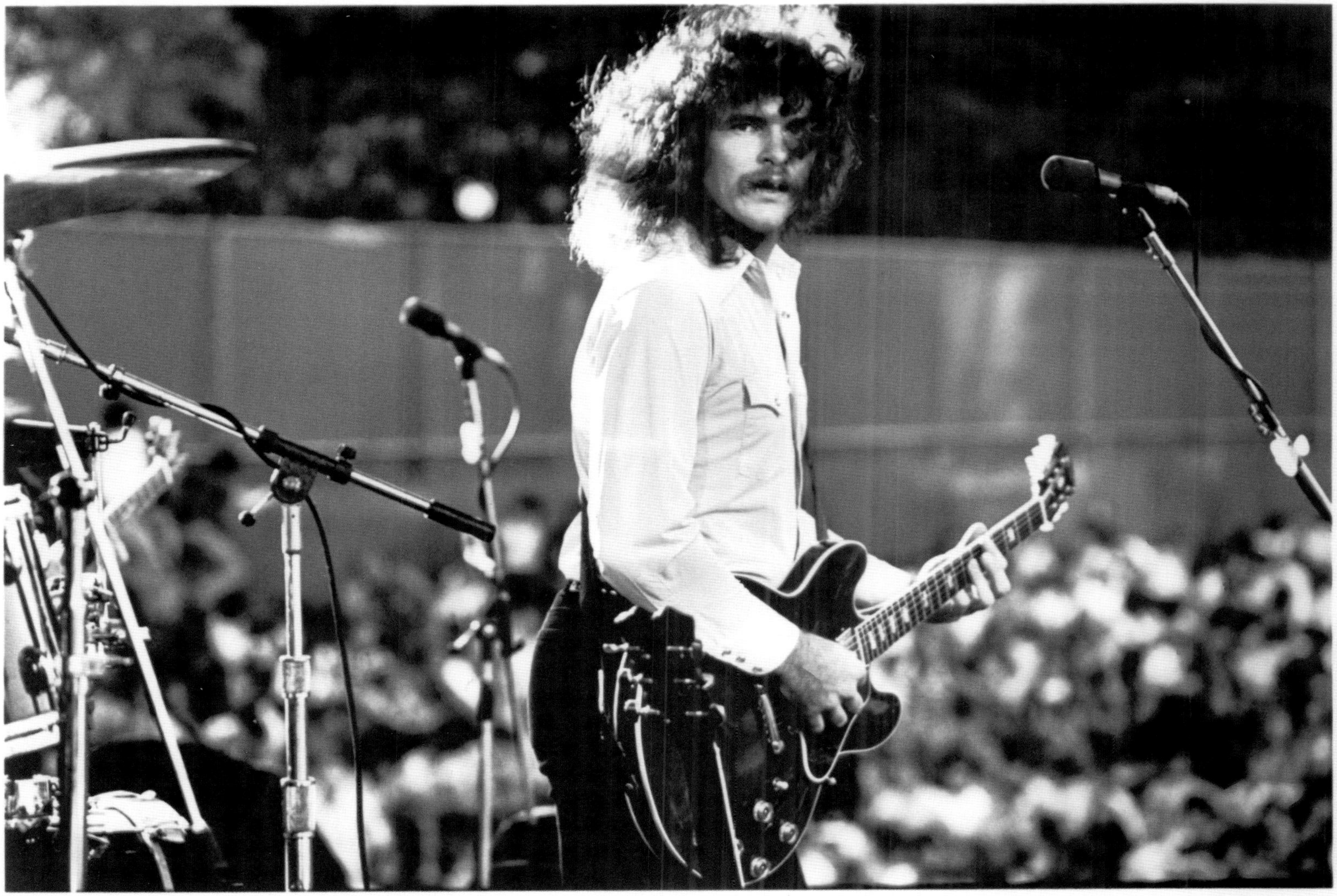

HENRY PAUL BAND

ATLANTIC

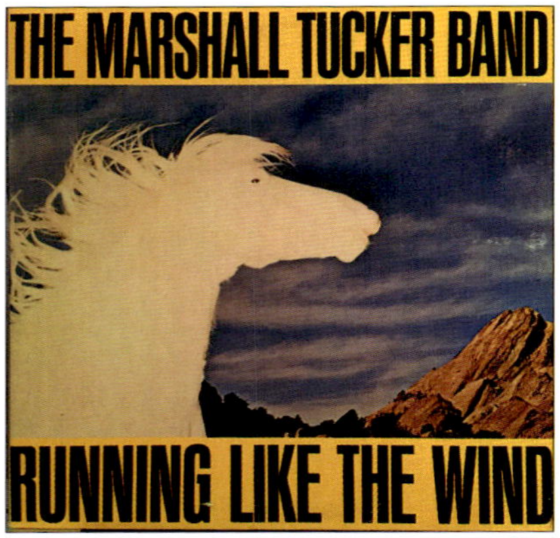

Billboard 200: *Running Like the Wind* (#30)
Billboard Hot 100: "Last of the Singing Cowboys" (#42)

The Marshall Tucker Band's *Running Like the Wind* secured a hearty reception among dyed-in-the-wool fans.

ALL SIX of the Marshall Tucker Band's members lived within a few miles of Spartanburg, South Carolina, a foothills community where they'd grown up together. Singer Doug Gray attributed the group's longevity to that closeness.

"We're all real comfortable with each other," Gray admitted. "We know each other's likes and dislikes, and it helps us take the same tone. We know what it's like to be real poor. Now it's different, of course, but we still maintain a lifestyle that you'd expect from us. That's what has kept us together for more than 10 years."

The Marshall Tucker Band—Gray, Toy Caldwell (lead guitar), Tommy Caldwell (bass), George McCorkle (rhythm Guitar), Paul Riddle (drums) and Jerry Eubanks (sax, flute)—made an immediate splash in the music scene with a 1972 debut album, which contained such standards as "Can't You See" and "Take the Highway."

Many gold and platinum albums later, *Running Like the Wind* represented a departure for the act. It was the Marshall Tucker Band's first release on Warner Bros. Records after years on Capricorn Records, which had gone bankrupt, and the production by Stewart Levine (famed for his work with the Crusaders) incorporated horns and some jazzy overtones into the Southern-rock group's sound, designating the music as "country-jazz."

"It's kind of scary," Gray allowed. "You figure you have a new record on a new label, and you've worked hard to improve your old sound, and you think, 'Maybe we're going the wrong way with it and maybe we should have stayed where we were.' It's hard to change. You can't please yourself on a record—you've got to please everybody. But all of Stewart's records are understandable, and he wanted to do this kind of record. You can hear the jazz influences coming out. I hope we use more horns."

"Running Like the Wind" garnered some radio airplay, and "The Last of the Singing Cowboys" became a substantial hit.

"We know we're going to be playing music for the rest of our lives, because we all enjoy playing together," Gray said. "I know it sounds corny, but if there's an argument, it's all forgotten when we get onstage. We're taking people away from everyday life. We all get off on a cut like 'Running Like the Wind.' I get into listening onstage and I forget we're playing it. I end up getting lost, and everybody has to play a couple more bars before I wake up!" ■

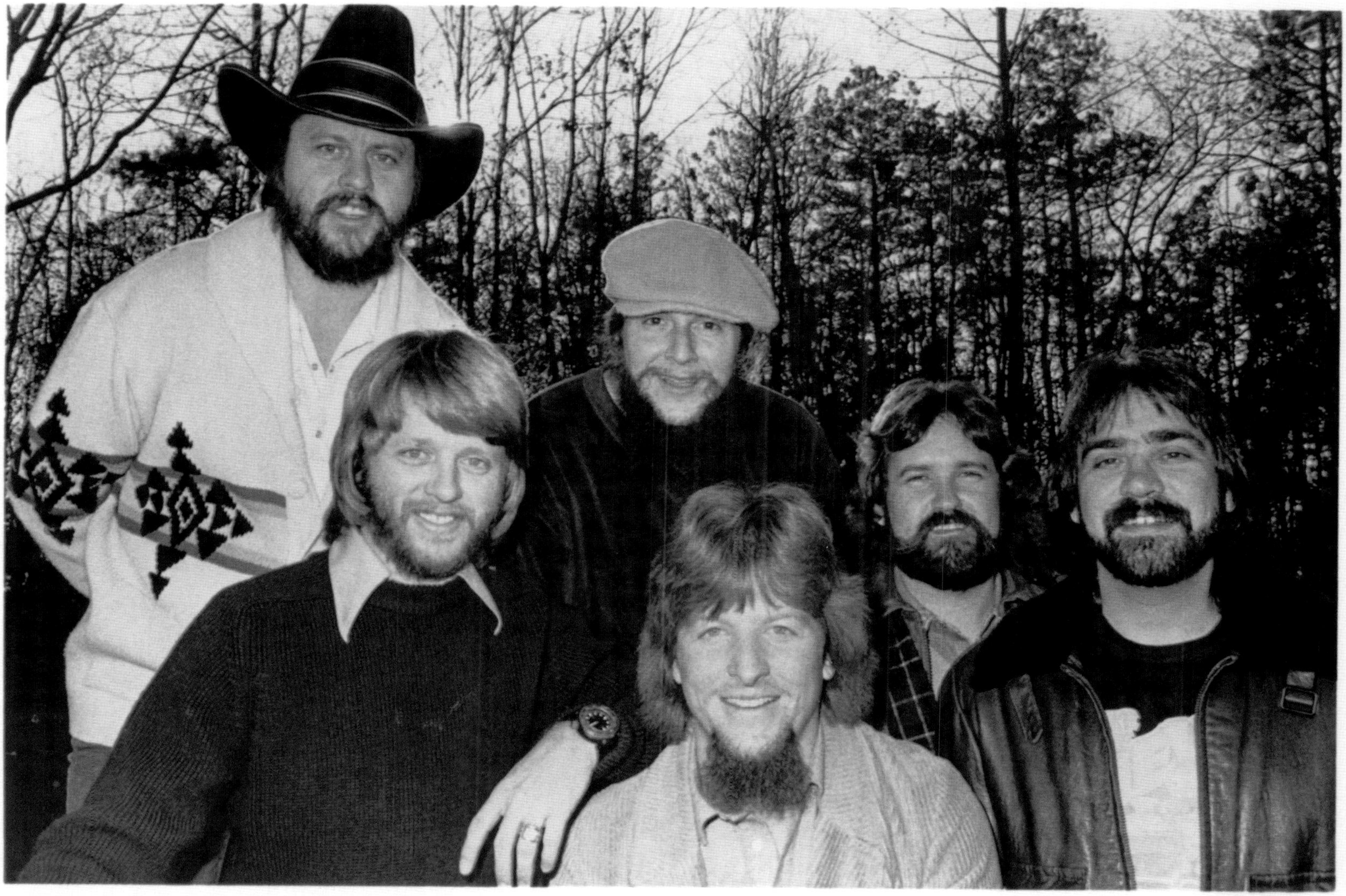

THE MARSHALL TUCKER BAND

WARNER / REPRISE

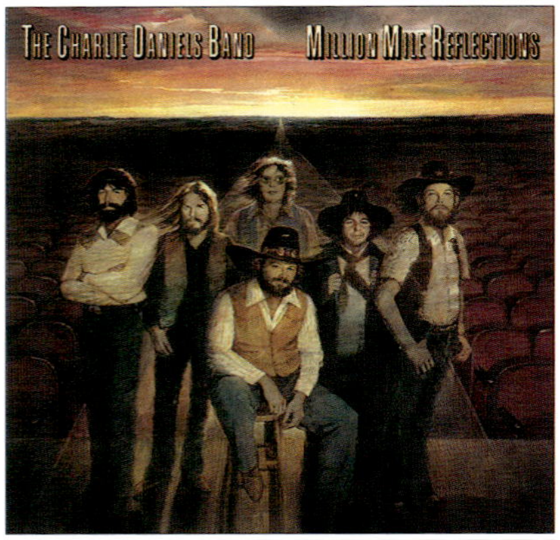

Billboard 200: *Million Mile Reflections* (#5)
Billboard Hot 100: "The Devil Went Down to Georgia" (#3)

The Charlie Daniels Band's "The Devil Went Down to Georgia" drove a worldwide following with its narrative.

IT HAD been a long haul from the tobacco fields and lumber mills of North Carolina to the top of the charts, but Charlie Daniels made the leap from session musician to a Southern country-rock star. He'd played sessions for Bob Dylan (including the landmark *Nashville Skyline* album) and cut his eyeteeth in notoriously raucous juke joints.

"I come from a real rural part of North Carolina, and I never saw a picture on a television set until I was about 15 years old—everything that happened, happened last in that part of the country. I used to listen to my granddaddy swap stories with my dad and my uncles and my aunts when I was a kid. When we went out coon hunting, we used to sit around fires and trade stories back and forth—some were old stories you'd hear 15 times. I've heard some great storytellers in my time."

Daniels brought his yarn-spinning skills and fiery fiddle to "The Devil Went Down to Georgia," a rollicking Dixie allegory which told the tale of a fiddling contest between the Devil and a good ol' boy named Johnny.

"Songwriting is a gift, and I'm good at telling a story, but I go about it a little differently. Once I get a melody, I lie in bed and run it over and over again through my mind, kind of like a tape loop in my head, coming up with different rhyming schemes and trying out combinations of words. I keep doing that until it becomes a song."

Released on the album *Million Mile Reflections,* "The Devil Went Down to Georgia" made Daniels famous, soaring to the top of both the country and the pop charts at the height of disco fever. The song won a Grammy for Best Country Vocal Performance and was included on the soundtrack to the hit movie *Urban Cowboy*.

Daniels wasn't exactly a Las Vegas kind of entertainer, but the man-mountain headlined in a casino shortly after "The Devil Went Down to Georgia" became a hit.

"Up until then, I always thought casinos were the domain of Frank Sinatra, Tony Bennett, Sammy Davis, Jr.—people of that generation. But my friend Willie Nelson was asked to headline Harrah's in Lake Tahoe for seven nights, filling in because Sinatra had cancelled. Willie could only do four nights, so he asked me to headline the other three. They sold out in advance—I had no idea we would get that kind of reception. I played in Vegas soon after that, at the Sands. There were a lot of cowboy hats there!" ■

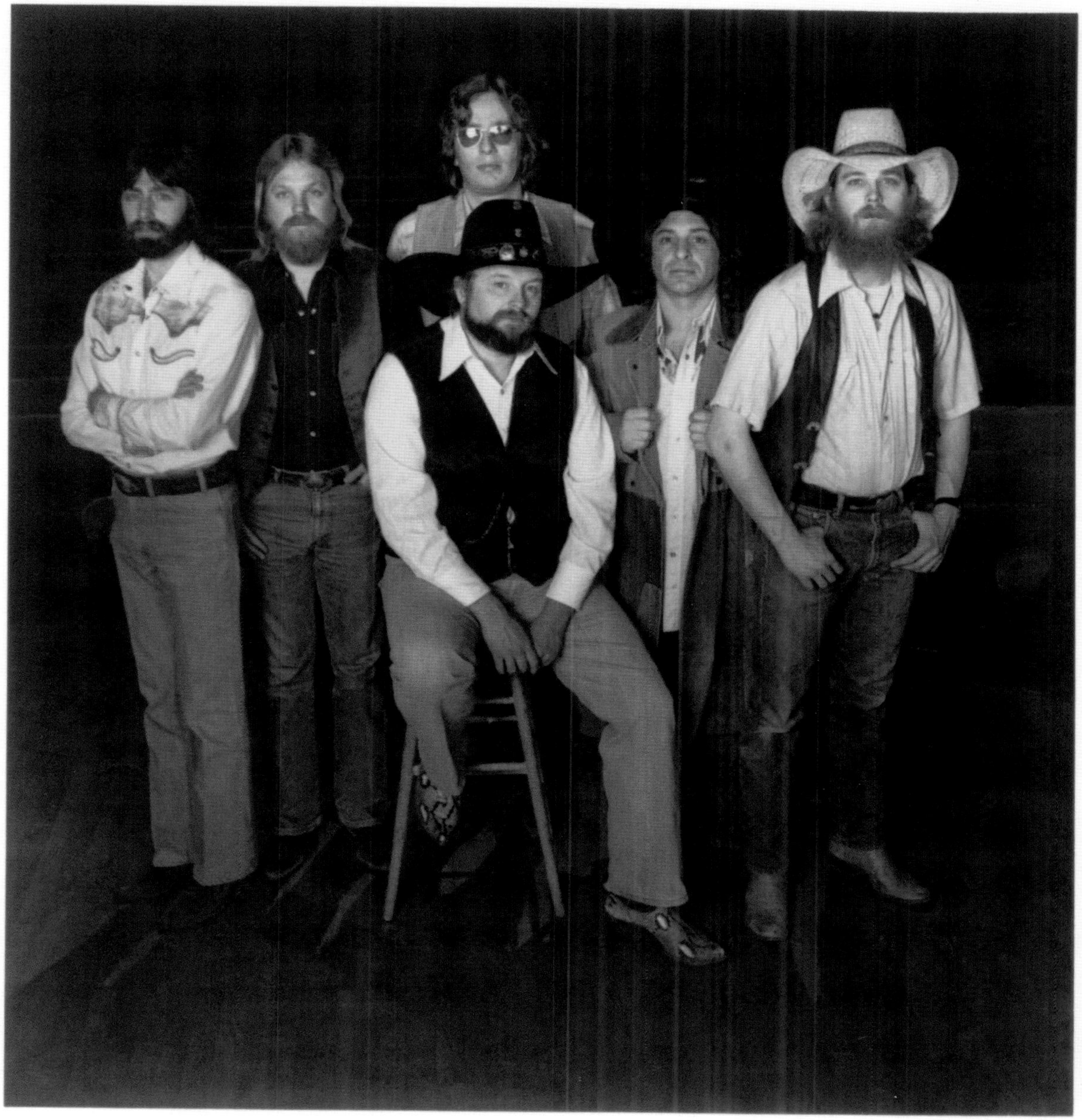

THE CHARLIE DANIELS BAND

Epic

SOUND SEVENTY MANAGEMENT INC.

210 25TH AVE. N./THE SOUND SEVENTY SUITE/NASHVILLE, TN. 37203/615-327-1711

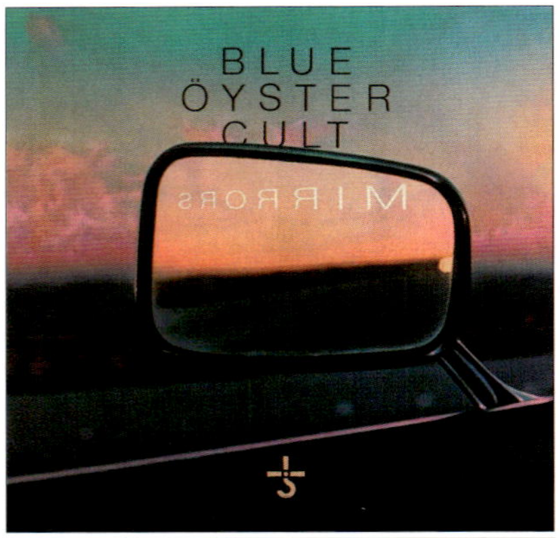

Billboard 200: *Mirrors* (#44)
Billboard Hot 100: "In Thee" (#74)

Blue Öyster Cult readily chose to put aside the ominous and offbeat for a pop-friendly approach on *Mirrors*.

WITH BARELY a pause, Blue Öyster Cult had been plying its trade through the Seventies. On the band's early albums, an undefined metaphysical thread ran through the material, combining off-the-wall lyrics with some rousing rhythms to reach some then-new heights of image mongering.

"We were even called 'the thinking man's Black Sabbath,'" guitarist Eric Bloom reflected. "Sandy (Pearlman, the producer and manager of Blue Öyster Cult) really thought we could be the biggest band in the world doing that sort of stuff. The group liked doing that music, but it became apparent that if we didn't take on another angle, we would never make much of a living."

The "anti-reaction" of the band was the *Agents of Fortune* album, which racked up double the sales of the previous efforts and spawned the stunning single "(Don't Fear) the Reaper," which stood as one of the quintessential Seventies rock songs. But the subsequent release of *Spectres*—which had the FM radio hit "Godzilla" and the well-known songs "I Love the Night" and "Goin' Through the Motions"—and a live album failed to generate the same enthusiasm.

"We were all disappointed," Bloom admitted. "I mean, they were gold records, but these days gold isn't enough."

"I have no more ideas," Pearlman said. "I thought that *Spectres* was the finest commercial album the Cult could ever make. Obviously, the public didn't think so."

The public then got to judge *Mirrors,* an album produced by Tom Werman of Cheap Trick and Ted Nugent fame. For the first time, the New York-based band traveled to California to record. Werman's expertise showed in the tight arrangements and snappy sound, but it was the songwriting of the Cult that stood out. The acoustic ballad "In Thee" was a tribute by keyboardist Allen Lanier to his lady, Patti Smith. Lead guitarist and vocalist Donald "Buck Dharma" Roeser took the lead on the title track, his composition propelled by clever lyrics and some tasty female vocal accompaniment. Part of BÖC's knack for fresh material came from a willingness to collaborate with sources outside the group—"The Great Sun Jester" featured lyrics by British sci-fi writer Michael Moorcock coupled with Bloom's music.

The band's gift for arranging never let things get too heavy or too mellow. "Light metal" might have defined BÖC's style, but Bloom merely classified it as "Cult-ivated." Yet the approach of straddling pop and hard rock appeared to displease metal-oriented enthusiasts, and the record's glossy production led to disappointing sales.

"We've never abandoned our original fans—we've always kept the cynicism and humor and heaviness, no matter what kind of music we've played," Bloom insisted. "You just can't say yet whether *Mirrors* is a punctuation in the band's career, because we don't know how much impact it will have. You can only judge that from a historical viewpoint." ■

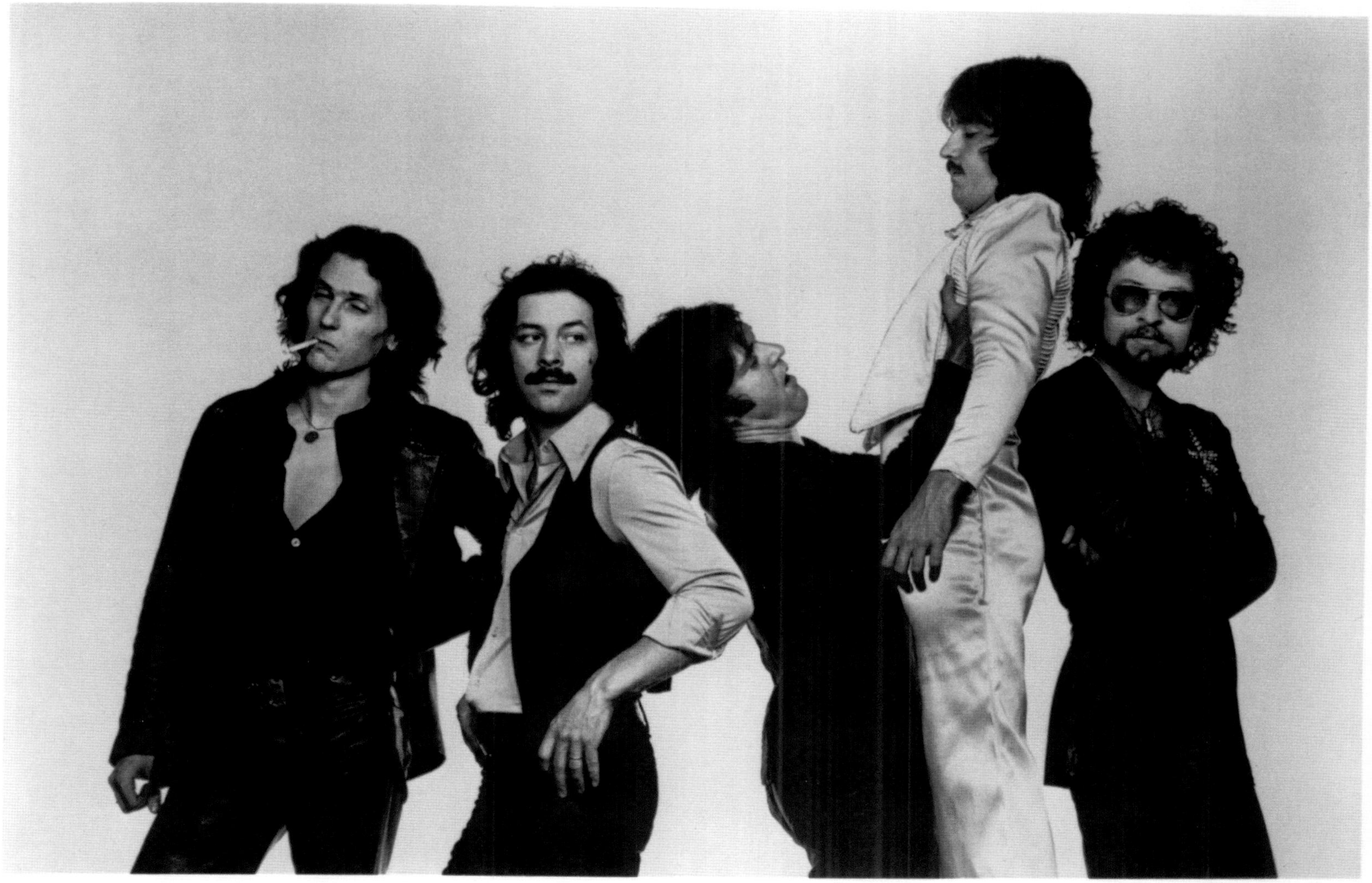

BLUE ÖYSTER CULT

COLUMBIA

PHOTO CREDIT ERIC MEOLA

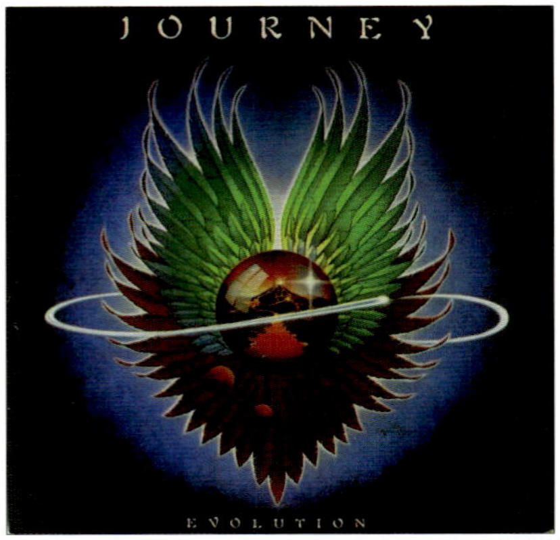

Billboard 200: *Evolution* (#20)
Billboard Hot 100: "Just the Same Way" (#58);
"Lovin', Touchin', Squeezin'" (#16); "Too Late" (#70)

The members of Journey continued their heady musical odyssey with the appropriately titled *Evolution* album.

WITH 1978'S *Infinity* album—a million-selling recording that finally captured the dynamics of the group's instrumental attack while introducing the soaring vocals of Steve Perry—Journey ascended to national prominence. For the three albums prior to *Infinity*, Gregg Rolie (keyboards, vocals), Neal Schon (guitar) and Ross Valory (bass) had toured incessantly and made sure that success would come on their terms.

They intended *Evolution* as an extension of the *Infinity* style in every way, from the adjunct cover design and layout to the butt-to-butt tracking of some songs. But some important decisions had occurred. The group had reservations about again using Roy Thomas Baker as a producer after his work on *Infinity*. That album was one of Baker's first notable successes (the others came with the Cars and Queen), but the astonishing music on record wasn't matched by compatibility in the studio.

"We weren't too sure about using him again because he flaked out on us and we had to finish *Infinity* ourselves," Rolie explained. "He went back to England and we were left with an unmastered recording that was all sloshy. Steve Perry and I stayed up two nights resequencing and mastering that album ourselves."

The matter was resolved before the band entered the studio to record *Evolution*. "This time Roy was a much more open human being to what we wanted to do. We had all of the arrangements down before we went in together, and his engineer Geoff Workman was involved from the beginning."

Longtime Journey fans were shocked when the group fired highly regarded drummer Aynsley Dunbar. Dunbar's contribution to Journey's sound was considerable, and he spoke uncharitably about his former bandmates after the separation. Rolie and the other Journey members steadfastly refused to badmouth Dunbar, citing the musical differences at the root of the confrontation. "Aynsley played in a style that was more progressive and a little busier," Rolie said.

Ironically, Dunbar was one of the band's more vocal proponents of the simpler and more commercially successful style of *Infinity*, but when the band toured seven months in support of the album, the controversies arose. Dunbar's replacement on *Evolution* was Steve Smith, who had kept time for Jean-Luc Ponty and Montrose.

Evolution put more emphasis on Neal Schon's economic guitar work, rocking rhythms and the shimmering pop textures that Steve Perry had introduced to the band. "Lovin', Touchin', Squeezin'" became Journey's first single to crack the Top 20.

"Things are great," Rolie admitted. "Steve (Perry) has turned out to be a good frontman, Steve Smith worked right in as a drummer—and Neal and Ross are as goofed up as ever." ■

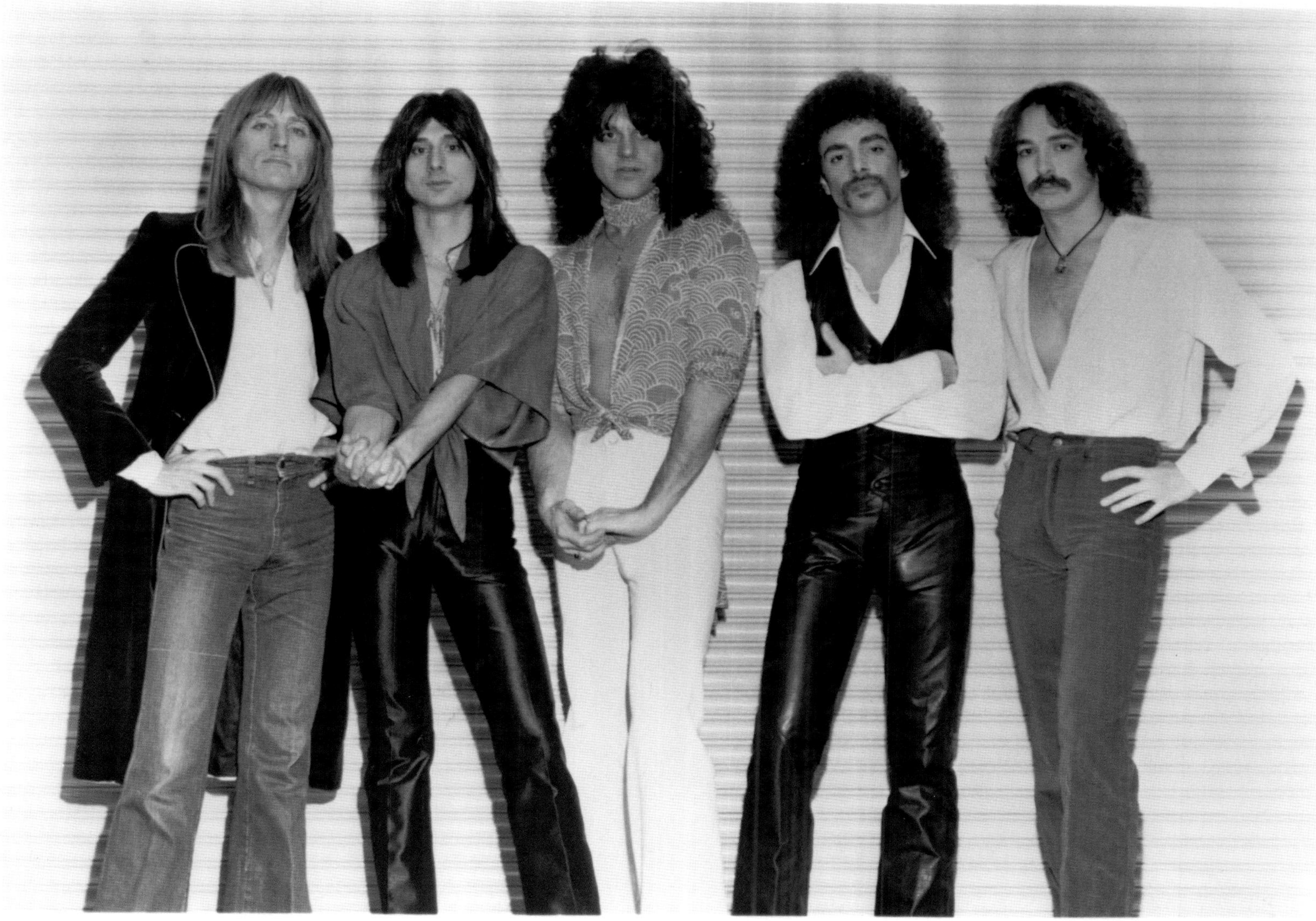

MANAGEMENT: HERBIE HERBERT
NIGHTMARE, INC
SAN FRANCISCO, CA

JOURNEY

Columbia

7902

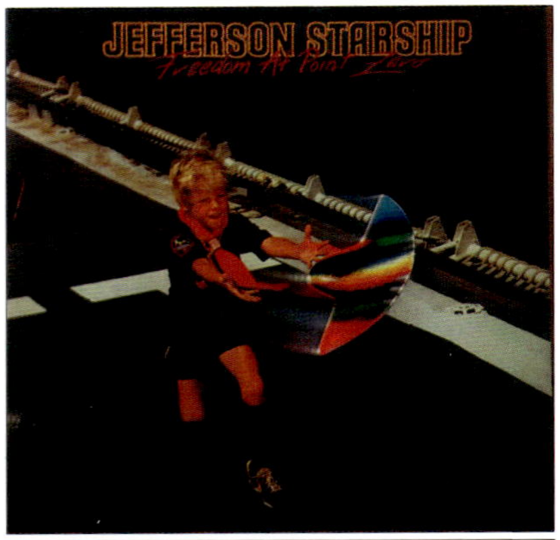

Billboard 200: *Freedom at Point Zero* (#10)
Billboard Hot 100: "Jane" (#14); "Girl with the Hungry Eyes" (#55)

The hard-rocking "Jane" propelled a reconfigured Jefferson Starship to yet another plane of pop puissance.

PAUL KANTNER of Jefferson Starship had a bigger recruiting job ahead of him than any college coach. Two of the band's principals since the Jefferson Airplane days, singers Grace Slick and Marty Balin, once again had decided to leave the group, leaving Kantner in need of some blue-chip prospects.

The band wound up with singer Mickey Thomas and powerhouse drummer Aynsley Dunbar.

The results on *Freedom at Point Zero* and the single "Jane" showcased a harder sound than other traditionally melodic Starship releases. Kantner shrugged off his do-nothing talent-acquisition genius. "We were heading in that direction while we were recording *Earth,* and since we had that tentative resolve, we looked for people who could help us out," he explained.

Thomas lived in Sausalito, California, where his manager put him in touch with the Starship management. He had signed with Elektra Records as a solo act a month before being contacted, and after some trying negotiations he was cleared to join.

"I really didn't know him—we just sort of went through our heads, 'Hey, who's around that sings? Paul Rodgers? Robert Plant?'" Kantner laughed. "We thought Mickey was a cute little pop singer from his 'Fooled Around and Fell in Love' days with Elvin Bishop. But we heard a tape, got in touch and said, 'We like what you do—we think—so why don't we do it?'"

Dunbar, acknowledged as one of rock's best timekeepers, was an even bigger coup. Kantner had been at odds with John Barbata over his mercenary commercial attitude before the drummer was seriously injured in a car accident. Dunbar had just left Journey, and when the vacancy appeared, he fit right in. Either bashing away or delicately fleshing out arrangements, he shone throughout the record.

"We're a new group, basically," Kantner admitted. "Realistically, we're not gonna go out and sell out coliseums, but I get embarrassed playing in pits like that." ■

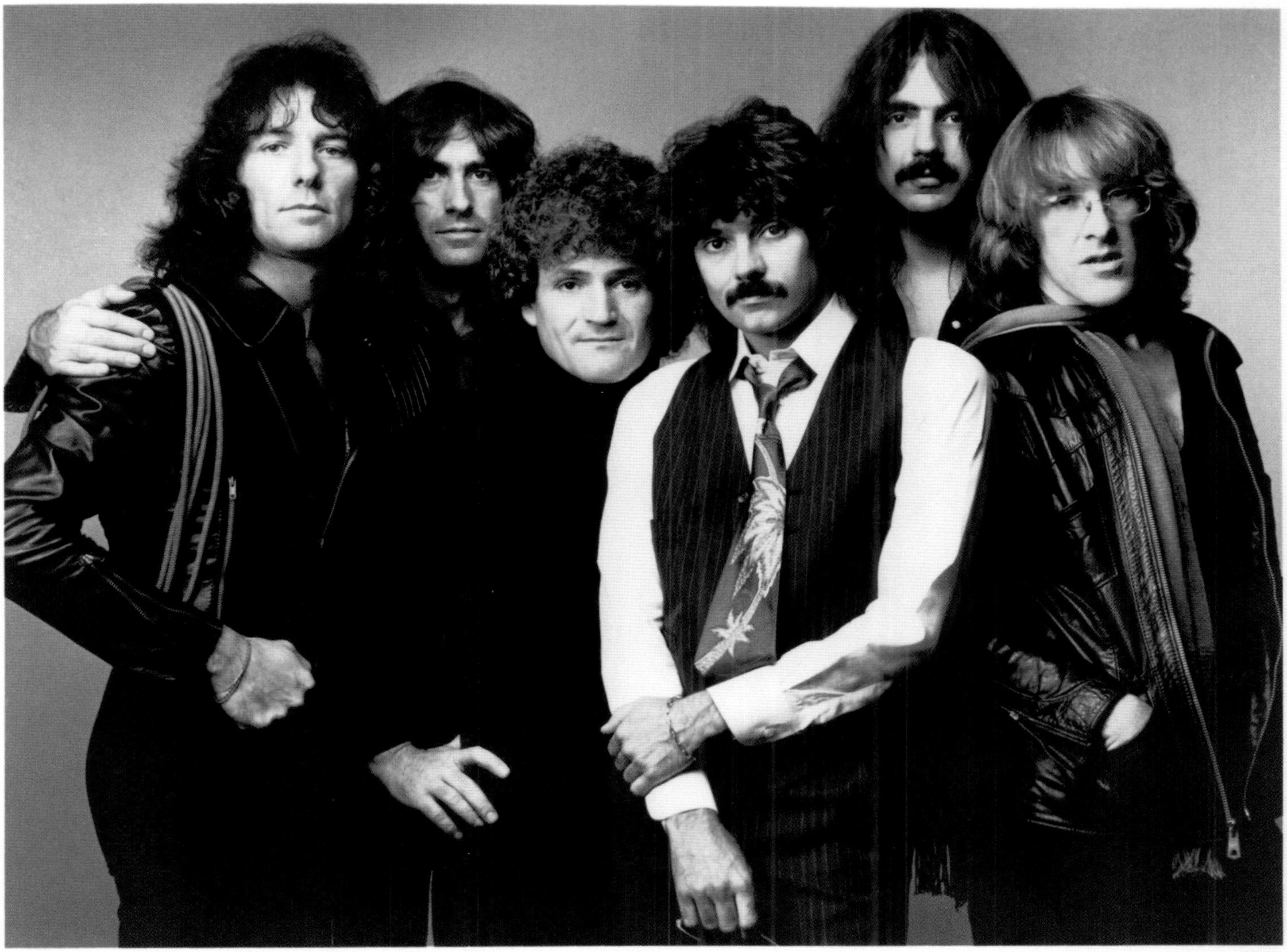

Photo Credit: GARY REGOSTER

AYNSLEY DUNBAR PETE SEARS DAVID FREIBERG MICKEY THOMAS CRAIG CHAQUICO PAUL KANTNER

JEFFERSON STARSHIP

GRUNT RECORDS

Manufactured and Distributed by RCA Records

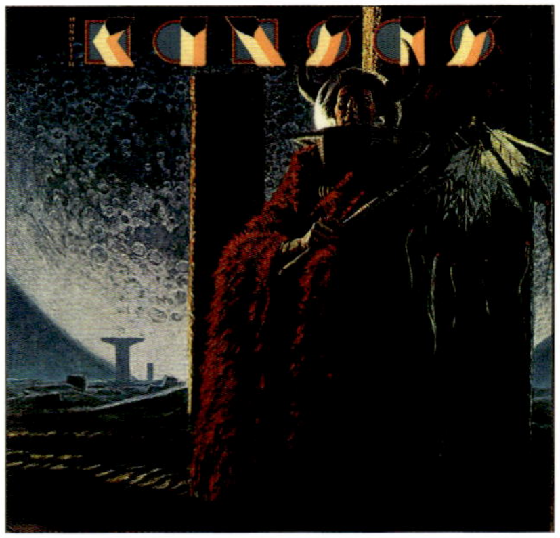

Billboard 200: *Monolith* (#10)
Billboard Hot 100: "People of the South Wind" (#23); "Reason to Be" (#52)

Now a major headlining act, the prog-rock outfit Kansas formulated its first self-produced endeavor, *Monolith*.

AFTER SETTING the bar for adventurous American rock, Kansas had become popular on album-oriented rock charts with hit singles such as "Carry On Wayward Son," "Dust in the Wind" and "Point of No Return." The band's follow-up studio album to two multiplatinum releases was *Monolith.*

"Everybody's involved in all the decisions, from whether a song should go on an album to how it's arranged and produced," drummer Phil Ehart insisted. "Steve (Walsh, singer) and Kerry (Livgren, guitarist) get a bit more recognition since they write most of the songs, and both are also at work on solo projects. But everybody has a role, and everybody cares. There are really no flaming egos in this band. We're pretty much a bunch of bar musicians that have picked a different style of music to play."

Yet Walsh had quit Kansas twice before, once in the middle of recording the *Point of Know Return* album and again in the mixing stages of *Two for the Show,* the group's live album. He was coaxed into returning on both occasions.

Monolith generated a Top 40 single in "People of the South Wind," a tuneful Livgren original that was the album's best bet for radio airplay.

"We've been getting more commercial in the last few years, and the more mainstream we get, the more we just blend into the surroundings," Livgren said. "In my mind, the songs are like the difference between a painting and a billboard—and we've been making a lot of billboards." ■

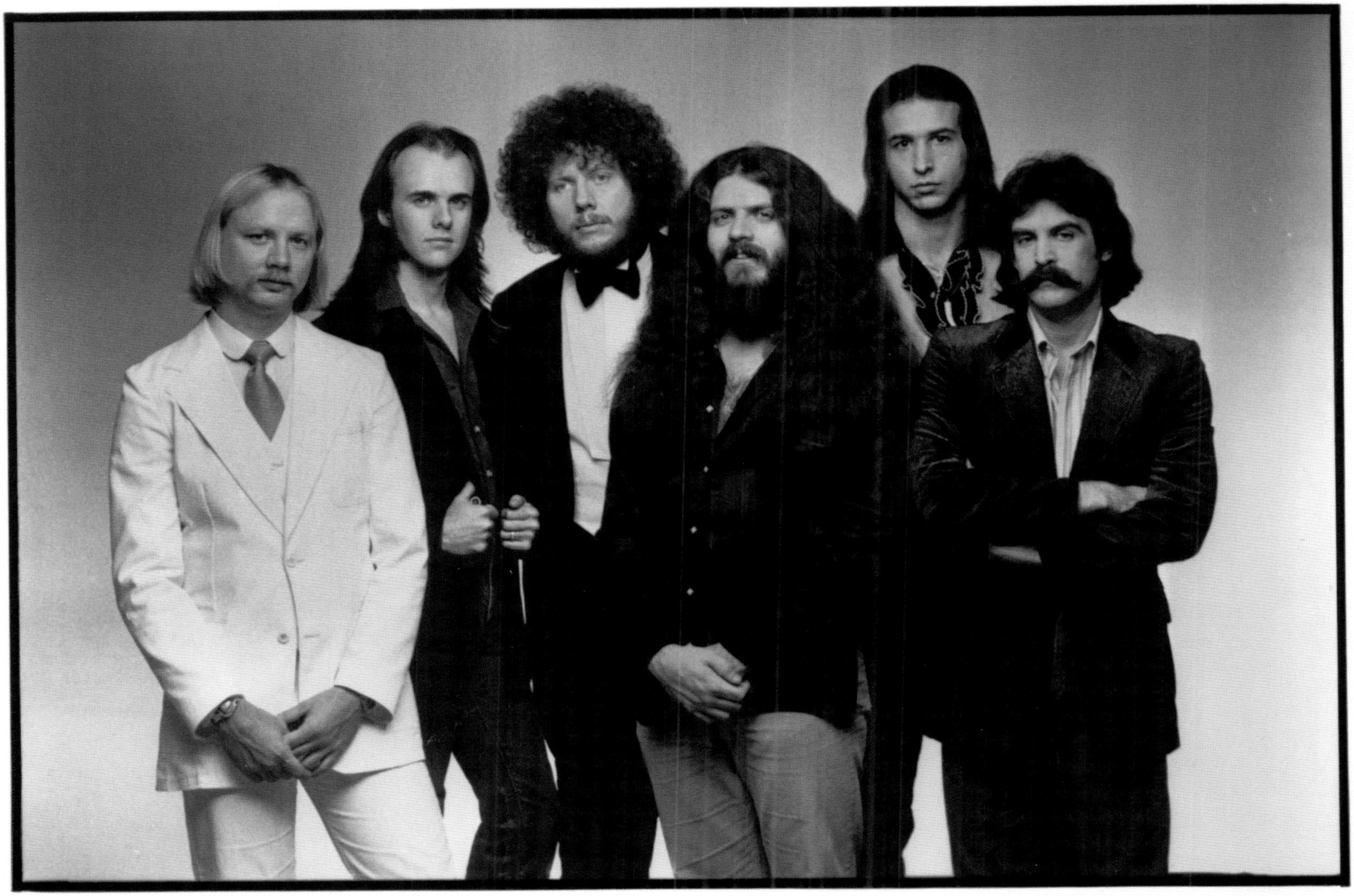

KERRY LIVGREN PHIL EHART RICH WILLIAMS ROBBY STEINHART STEVE WALSH DAVE HOPE

KIRSHNER

KANSAS®

EPIC PORTRAIT ASSOCIATED

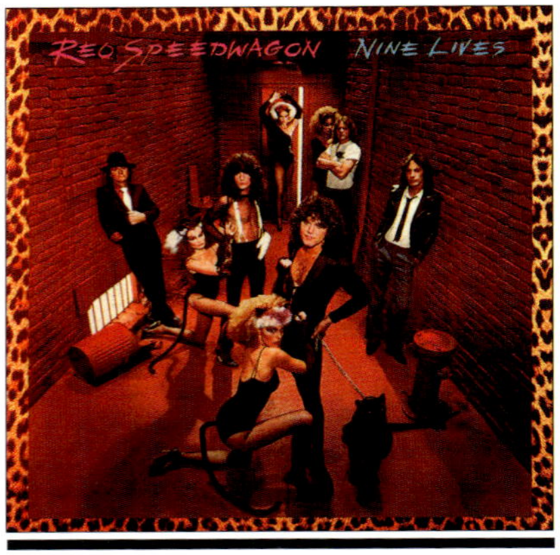

Billboard 200: *Nine Lives* (#33)

Making songwriting strides on *Nine Lives*, REO Speedwagon's album sales remained in a persistent pattern.

YEARS OF touring had paid off—REO Speedwagon was doing booming concert business as other rock bands couldn't draw. The record business was another matter, and the band tried to sustain a commercial breakthrough with *Nine Lives*, the follow-up to *You Can Tune a Piano but You Can't Tune a Fish*, REO's first album to make the Top 40.

"We used to tour all year and record for one month, and the records used to suffer," guitarist Gary Richrath said. "Now, we tour for six and record for six, and everything is better."

Richrath's new tunes were the strongest he'd ever written, with "Only the Strong Survive" standing out. The challenge was to get the message to the fans.

"It's hard, because we've got the reputation of being a good live act, and when kids see a live album, that's the one they want to pick up," Richrath explained. *You Get What You Play For,* REO's live testament released in 1977, had outsold previous studio releases by 200,000 copies.

A publicity clipping making the rounds described Richrath was one of rock music's most underrated guitarists. "Of course, I agree with them," he laughed. "I listen to every record that comes out, and I know I can play everything I hear. Jeff Beck is the only one who even starts to boggle me." ■

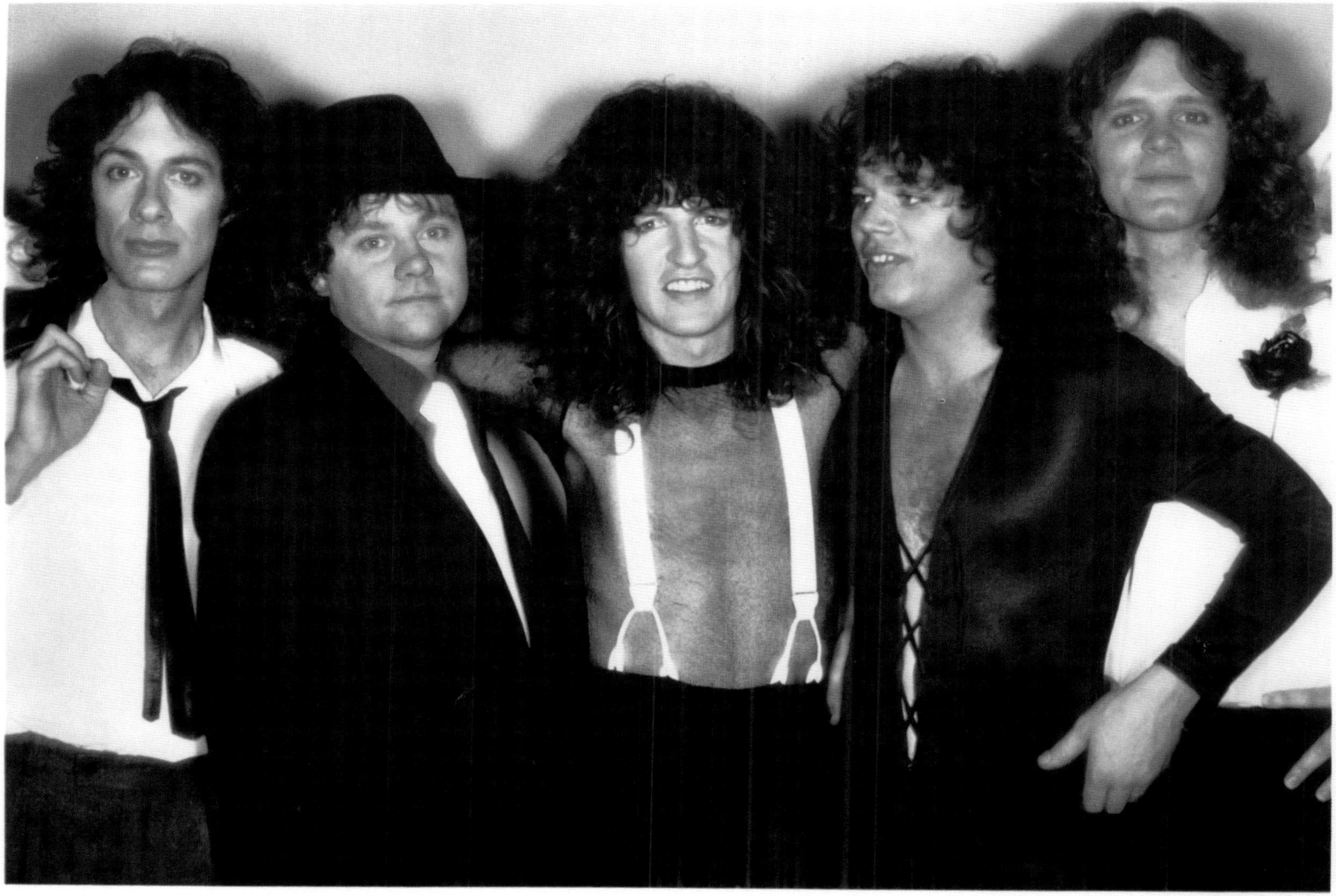

Left to right Alan Gratzer, Neil Doughty, Kevin Cronin, Gary Richrath, Bruce Hall

REO SPEEDWAGON

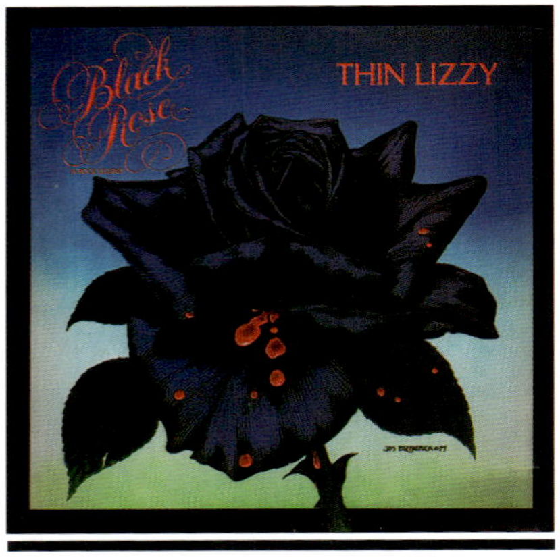

Billboard 200: *Black Rose: A Rock Legend* (#81)

Phil Lynott, Thin Lizzy's creative force, refocused the Irish hard-rock act to make *Black Rose: A Rock Legend.*

PHIL LYNOTT was imbued with a fighting spirit. Growing up in Dublin as the biracial son of an Irish mother and a West Indian father he never knew, he stood out in any crowd, and his special energy shone through in his insightful, intelligent songwriting.

Lynott and his school friend, drummer Brian Downey, formed Thin Lizzy in 1969. Success was far from immediate, but the unfertile period did spawn one hit, "Whiskey in the Jar," a version of a traditional Irish ballad. With the 1976 album *Jailbreak* and the classic single "The Boys Are Back in Town," Thin Lizzy's career took off in earnest. Lengthy spells of touring with first-rate live shows established the band in the major leagues.

Though *Jailbreak* went as high as #11 in the US, Thin Lizzy's subsequent success had been erratic. The band claimed that its former record company didn't know how to steer its career to the best advantage. Singer and bassist Lynott felt certain that his group would solidify its popularity in America.

"We know how to make it there now—how to combat all the problems like the music business being just totally stagnant because of the extent to which the media is controlled," Lynott said. "I mean, there's even computerized radio with preset programs coming in over there now."

Thin Lizzy had used the twin-guitar lineup to great effect, and the band featured several guitarists over the years. Gary Moore had brief stints with Thin Lizzy in 1974 and 1977, but *Black Rose: A Rock Legend* marked the first time he remained in the band long enough to record an album. Moore then walked out in the middle of the band's US tour.

The album reached #2 in the UK, and "Waiting for an Alibi" and "Do Anything You Want To" were successful singles. "Sarah," a song about Lynott's newborn daughter, featured harmonica parts by "Bluesy Hughie"—Huey Lewis, an American musician who had been a member of Clover, a band that supported Thin Lizzy on previous tours.

Thin Lizzy was one of the few established outfits not to be attacked verbally by ambitious punk bands. "The worst thing the press ever did was to turn us musicians against each other," Lynott said. "We all have the same hopes and fears." ■

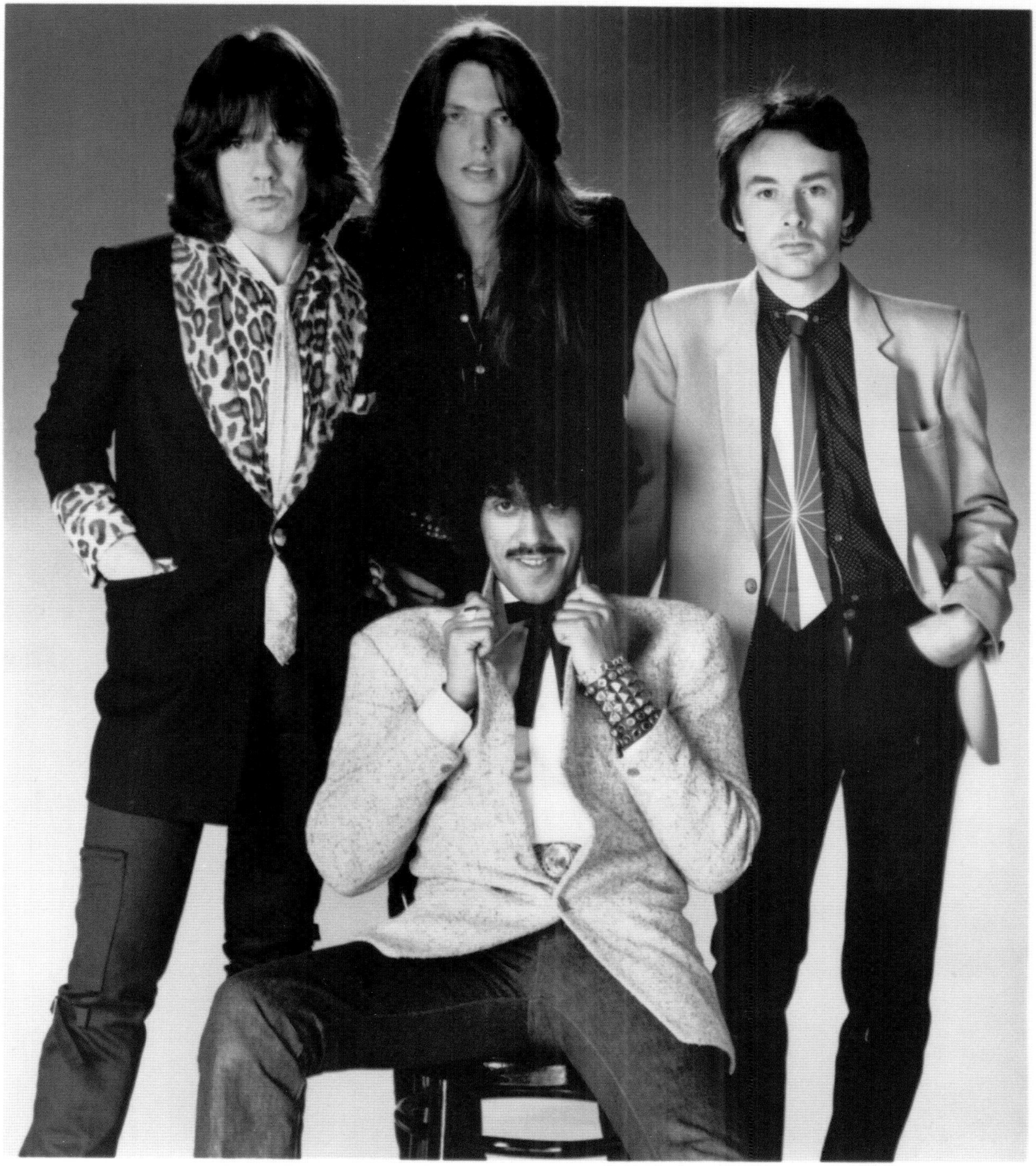

MAY 1979

THIN LIZZY

WARNER / REPRISE

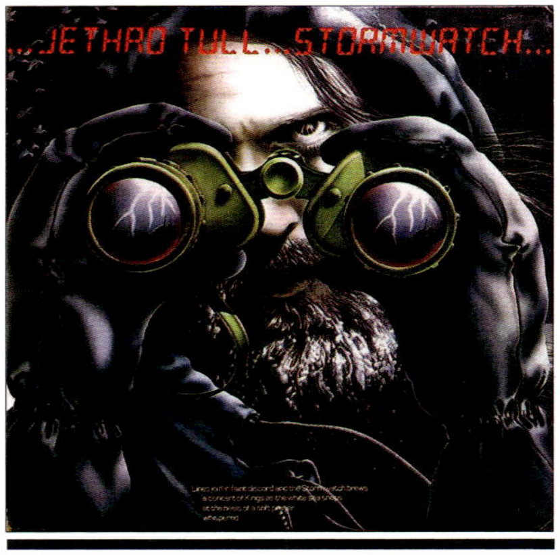

Billboard 200: *Stormwatch* (#22)

Circumstances prevented *Stormwatch* from being the triumphant turnaround Jethro Tull had counted upon.

IN 1978, Jethro Tull marked its 10-year anniversary with a live album, *Bursting Out*, that served to encapsulate the group's first decade of music. Ian Anderson, the band's outspoken mentor, promised at the time that the next year would bring some changes in the Tull repertoire. "We're looking to achieve a harder-edged sound, away from the English folk influences we've experimented with recently," he explained.

But problems arose. Foremost among them was the ill health of bassist John Glascock, an excellent musician who underwent open heart surgery. Unable to convalesce properly amidst the strains of rehearsal, he left the band before it went into the studio to record *Stormwatch*. Anderson ended up playing bass on most of the tracks, a matter of "having sympathy for the lower end of the spectrum." Glascock died from heart complications a few weeks after the album's release.

"We ended up getting close to the sound I wanted on the record, but we didn't succeed in the way I'd hoped," Anderson admitted. "It was inevitable with the upheaval resulting from John leaving the group. We lost about a month of recording time. Rather than developing that hard edge to the material, we had to settle for the most expedient manner—shaping songs in the studio rather than fully rehearsing them."

Many rock bands that had lasted as long as Jethro Tull had entered a state of semi-retirement, releasing albums every few years and touring only when the mood struck. Tull had always maintained a closer rapport with fans, however.

"If we recorded once every three years, goodness knows what we'd do for the other two—we'd have to call ourselves something other than musicians on our passports," Anderson mused. "We record and tour every year because of a desire to present new material. We are the wandering minstrels of a contemporary age, albeit jet-powered. There are some bands with the same outlook, I'm sure, but upon reaching success they only go out on the road when the bank account is getting low—whereas we don't let the bank account get low!"

Anderson claimed that there was pressure to do something with his money. "I'd be unhappy with only 14 Rolls-Royces and seven swimming pools and other material trappings to show for my success, but it's immoral to just leave it in the bank. In England's economy, in particular, it needs to be recycled. So I am involved in modern farming pursuits—salmon farming in Scotland and deer farming in England. I have no interest in putting my money back into the record industry. Making sure people can eat is of more concern." ■

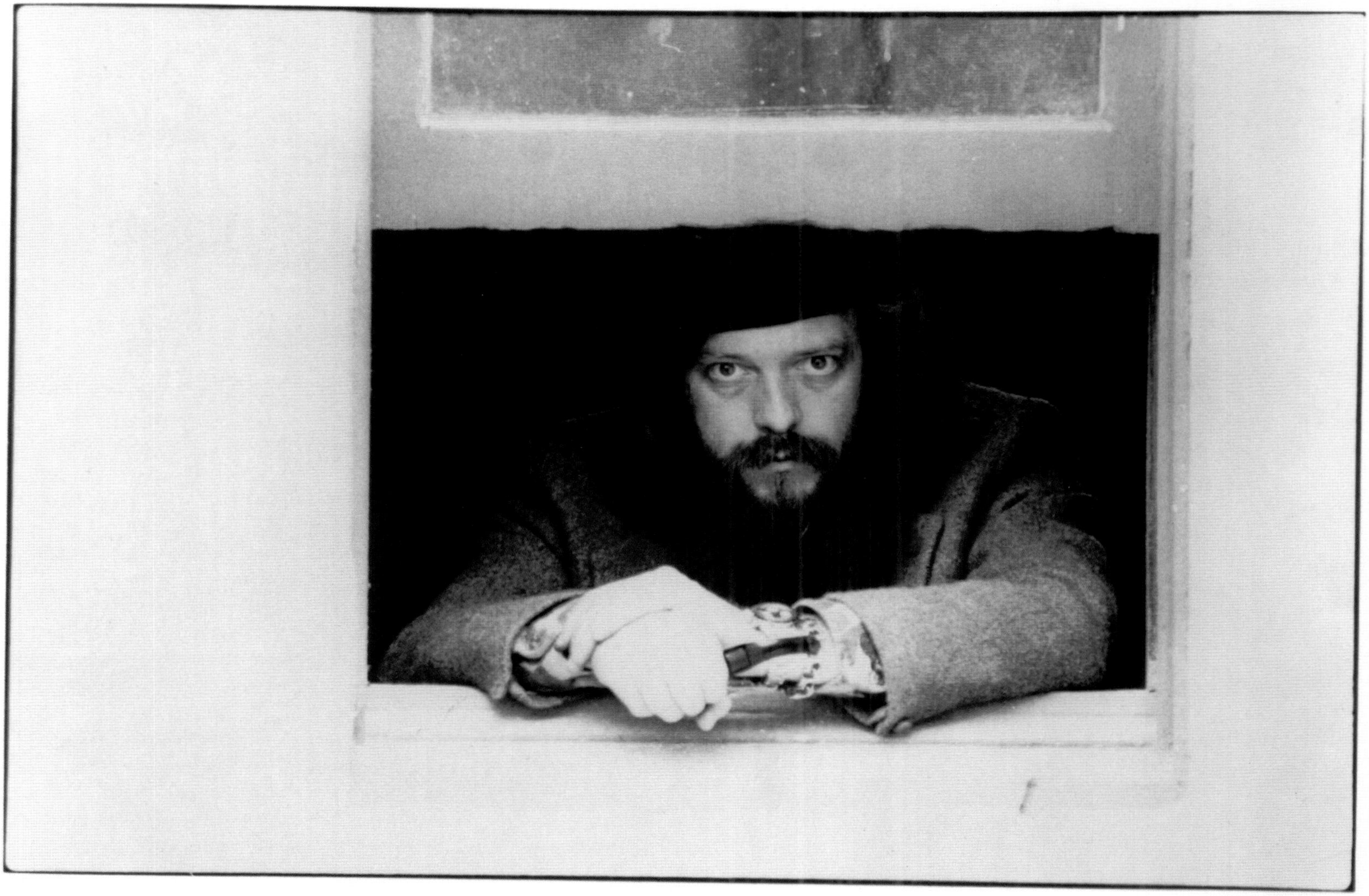

Jethro Tull

Chrysalis

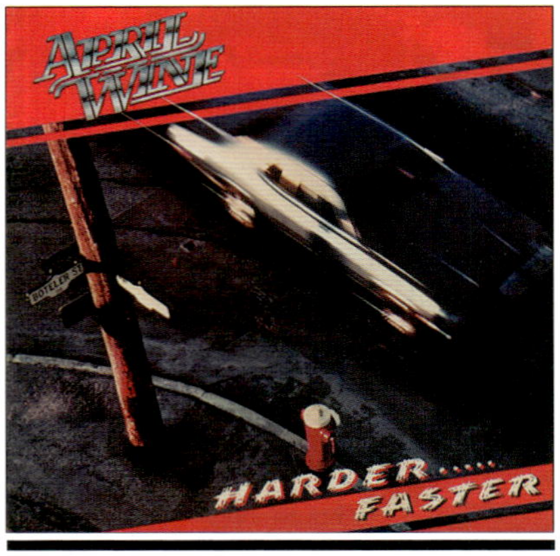

Billboard 200: *Harder...Faster* (#64)
Billboard Hot 100: "I Like to Rock" (#86)

Canada's distinguished April Wine picked up an even bigger bloc of support in America with *Harder...Faster*.

AS A precocious 18-year-old from the Canadian province of New Brunswick, Myles Goodwyn helped found April Wine in 1970 and moved the quartet to Montreal, where he talked his way into a recording contract. A year later, April Wine had a Top 20 hit, "You Could've Been a Lady." Amid many lineup changes, the band became a veritable institution north of the border, with several platinum albums and sold-out tours of concert halls. In 1977, April Wine recorded an album at Toronto's El Macombo Club the same nights as the Rolling Stones.

But the US market remained frustratingly elusive. The band went through a process of "refocusing"—toughening the sound, simplifying the arrangements, taking the music to another loud, flashy level.

"We've experimented in the past with different kinds of songs that sounded good on an album, but didn't do anything for our show—in Canada, especially, we've always been known for our ballads," Goodwyn said.

Things began to break open with 1978's "Roller," a Top 40 and album rock hit. The success meant extensive touring through America. Goodwyn, April Wine's lead vocalist, guitarist and producer, gave himself one thing to think about when writing the songs for *Harder...Faster*.

"We've done enough touring to know that a great album and a great show go hand in hand," he said. "We're seasoned. Although people think we're new to the scene, we've been around. We have our thing pretty much worked out, and we can contend with almost any situation—from headlining to being third on a bill."

"I Like to Rock" was arguably the band's signature song—sung from the character's perspective about his love for rock music, playing to big crowds in concert and late-night partying. "Say Hello" became another popular hit on both sides of the border, and *Harder...Faster* achieved gold status in America.

"We had to break through in the US to be taken seriously—maybe we took the formula too literally, just to be accepted, but you have to pay that price," Goodwyn mused. "The essential notion in the industry is communication, so the larger your audience, the more interesting it is to communicate. I suppose we could play the 'offended sensibilities' bit and not accept any compromises, but rock is really an art form that was born of a compromise between mass culture and music. You can't escape the fact that your efficiency is measured by your success." ■

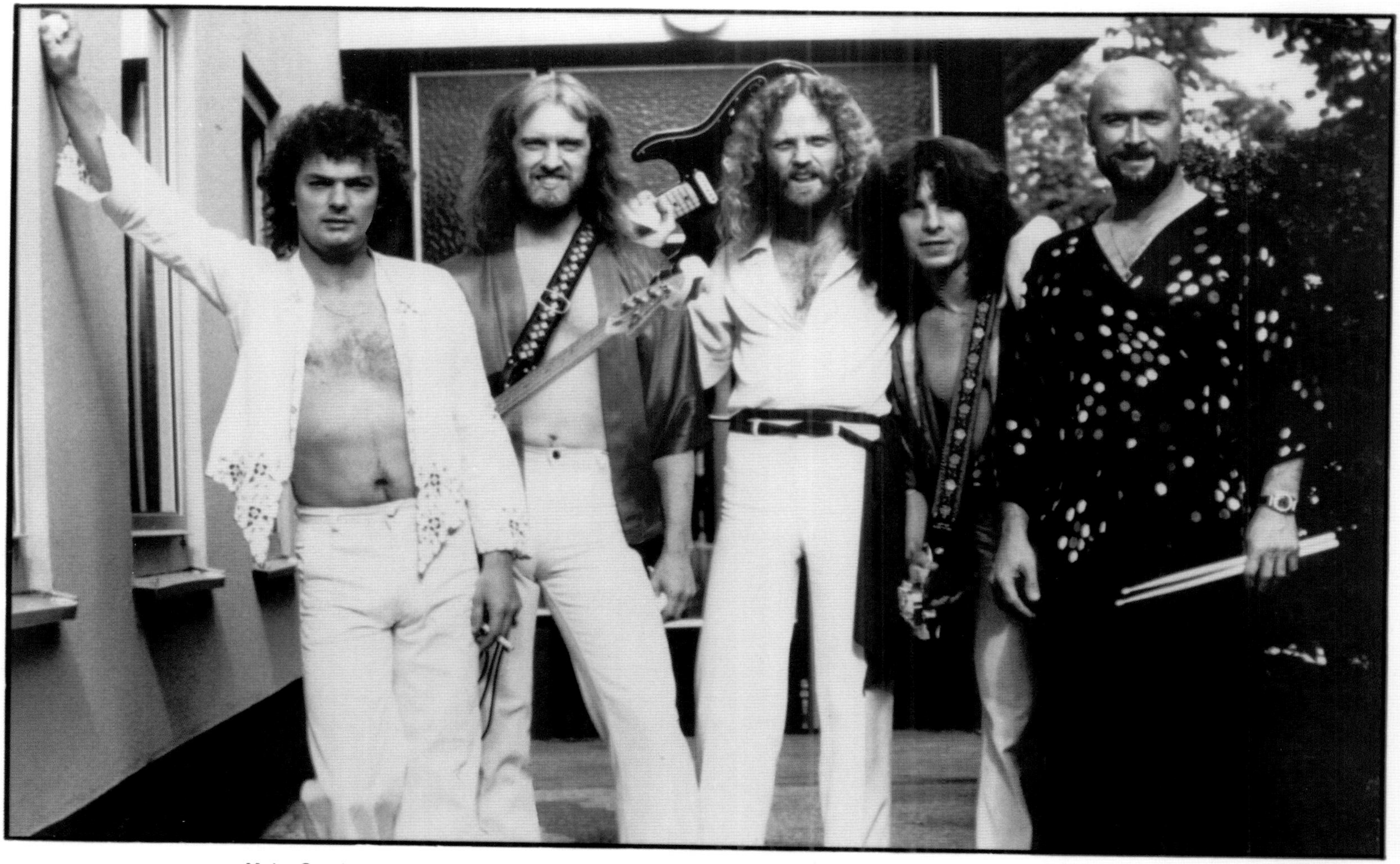

Photo: EMI Electrola/Prange

Myles Goodwyn Steve Lang Gary Moffet Brian Greenway Jerry Mercer

ICM

APRIL WINE

Capitol Records

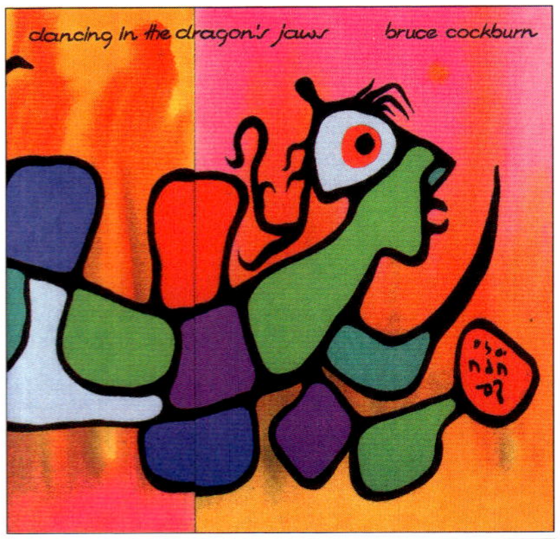

Billboard 200: *Dancing in the Dragon's Jaws* (#45)
Billboard Hot 100: "Wondering Where the Lions Are" (#21)

Touted as "Canada's best-kept secret," Bruce Cockburn was primed for his chance in the US after a long wait.

BRUCE COCKBURN recorded his first Canadian album in early 1970, acclaimed enough to launch a career that gained momentum throughout the decade and garnered him numerous awards in his homeland.

"I had written a lot of songs and felt choked up by them," the soft-spoken artist recalled. "I wanted to get rid of them so I could write more and yet not lose those songs. I discovered after I put the album out that it didn't work that way—you put the songs on record and you just have to sing them more."

Cockburn eventually built up a concert audience throughout Canada, but he was not as widely accepted as his "nine gold albums" publicity campaign suggested—he pointed out that he only had two, with the first taking five years to accrue enough sales. However, Cockburn had made no impression in the American market. Two records picked up for distribution by a major label in the mid-Seventies never surfaced, and three releases on Island Records only allowed him a small tour of folk clubs in the northeast US.

But *Dancing in the Dragon's Jaws* changed things, and with the excellent single "Wondering Where the Lions Are" finding its way onto American airwaves, Cockburn had a major hit to his credit. Acceptance of his album led to his first extensive US tour. Cockburn admitted to being more prolific than ever, writing many more songs in the lyrical style that his new listeners found appealing.

"I guess people are hungry for something to be optimistic about these days," he explained of his music. "I'm not that optimistic by nature—I'm prepared for the worst without expecting it. There's a lot of garbage around, and it's not new—just the face it puts on is new. We live under the same degree of threat as all the generations before us have, but it just comes in a different form. That's part of the human condition. It's an artist's job to reflect upon and portray aspects of that.

"There is a current of optimism in my music, which I get from God and my belief in God. Other people find it in different areas, but you can't sidestep the different heavies out there. If you don't look at the crap, then it's just a Pollyanna trip."

Cockburn's considerable guitar style incorporated influences from jazz to blues to rock with good effect.

"Music is a vehicle for words that come to me, but it's also something to have fun with," he said. "I don't know what to expect in America—it's not something I've been through before—but at the same time it's the ideal time for this to be happening, because I've done it for 10 years and nothing overwhelms me at this point. I already make a living, so I don't have to scuffle and lick boots to get notoriety. I can just play for people without getting hung up on those other questions. At least I hope I don't—and since it's up to me, I won't." ■

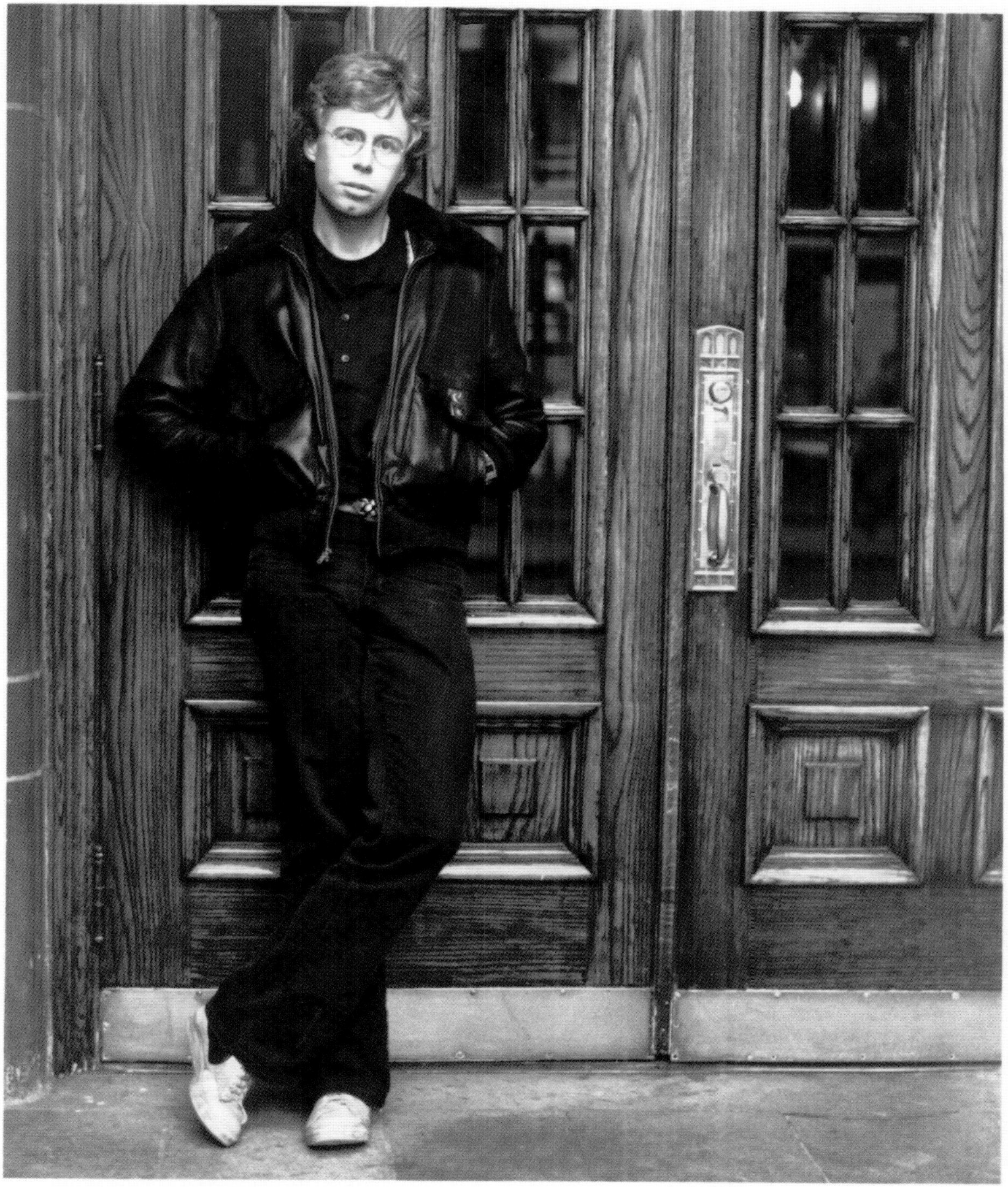

BRUCE COCKBURN

Direction: the finkelstein fiedler company

Millennium RECORDS

Manufactured and Distributed by RCA Records

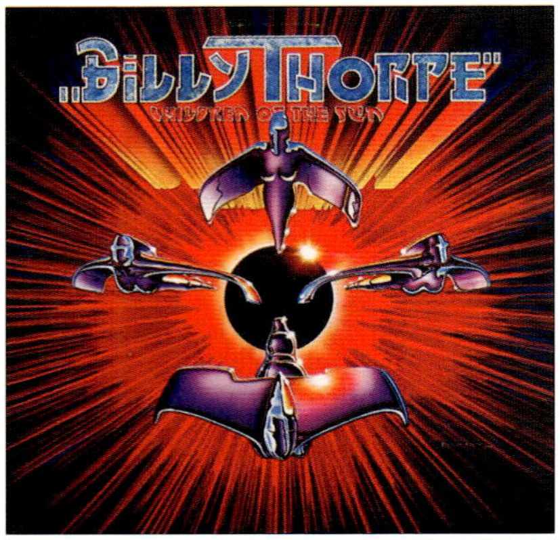

Billboard 200: *Children of the Sun* (#39)
Billboard Hot 100: "Children of the Sun" (#41)

Australian guitar hero Billy Thorpe gained a footing in the American marketplace with "Children of the Sun."

IN AUSTRALIA, with more than a dozen platinum albums to his credit, Billy Thorpe had attained superstar status. As a teenager, he formed the Aztecs, a rock band which enjoyed considerable success in the late Sixties. Early in the next decade, Thorpe turned to acoustic work, performing almost exclusively solo. Reforming the Aztecs in the mid-Seventies, Thorpe again attained stardom and scored big at the era's Australian rock festival.

"I made my first record when I was 16, and it turned into a situation where you're part of an ambience, a musical evolution of an entire country," he said. "See, I made 16 or so albums, and we had something like ten No. 1 records down there—we were an institution like the Grateful Dead."

But when Thorpe arrived in Los Angeles in 1976, nobody knew him from Adam—hence the sci-fi "visionary rock" found on *Children of the Sun*, an invasion-from-outer-space concept album centering around alien beings who visit Earth and urge its inhabitants to leave with them. The conceptual "space visitation" theme took up an entire side of the album.

Children of the Sun represented a drastic departure for Thorpe, who considered himself "primarily a rock 'n' roll artist." As he explained, "When I got here, the whole disco scene was huge. I had people tell me point blank, 'If you're gonna do rock 'n' roll, go back to Australia—we're not interested.' At the same time, the incredible thing with *Star Wars* and *Close Encounters of the Third Kind* was going on. Plus I was starting to write in a late-Sixties direction, with Queen, King Crimson, Yes and early Pink Floyd influences."

Artists Kelley & Mouse of San Francisco, noted for their form-of-reality work, were commissioned for the cover art. The title track of *Children of the Sun* peaked in the Top 40 and made enough of a dent on the airwaves for the album to garner a cult following. The space opera was purported to be the first record in a trilogy.

"I'm feeling my way through this, chasing my own ass dealing with concepts all the time," Thorpe admitted. "You start turning into a space cadet yourself, y'know?" ■

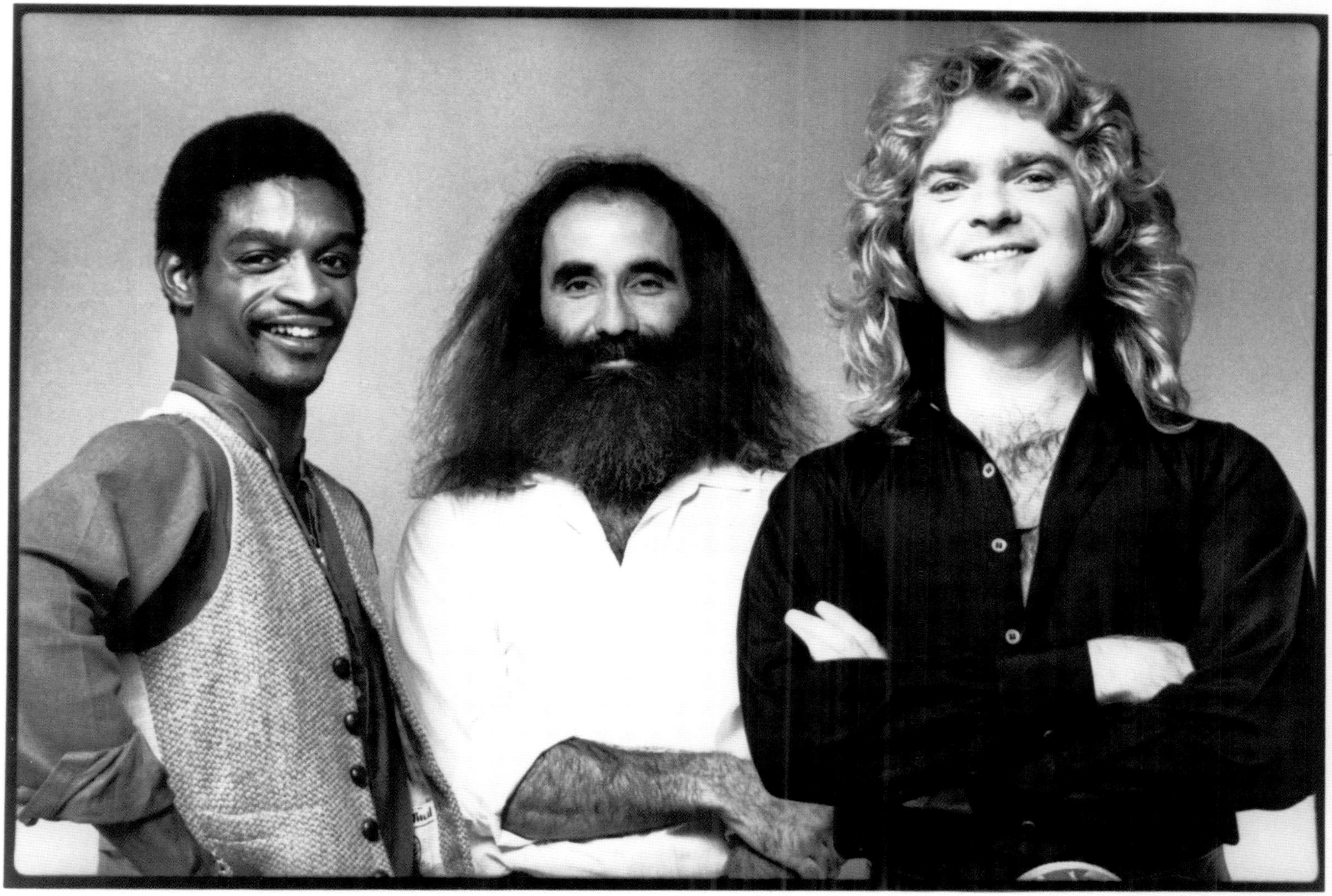

THE BILLY THORPE BAND

Left to right: Alvin Taylor, Lee Sklar, and Billy Thorpe.

CAPRICORN RECORDS.

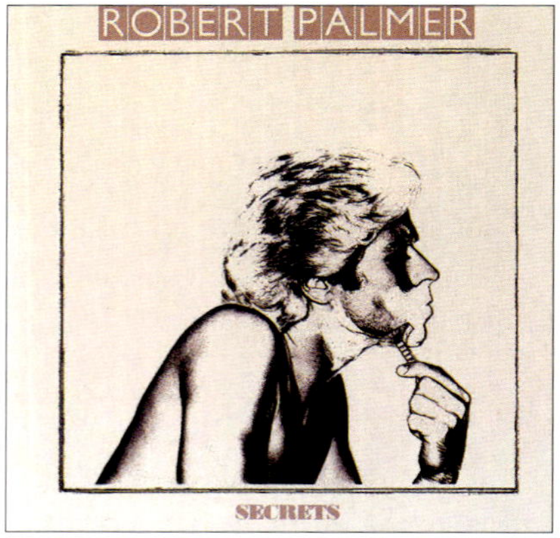

Billboard 200: *Secrets* (#19)
Billboard Hot 100: "Bad Case of Loving You (Doctor, Doctor)" (#14); "Can We Still Be Friends" (#52)

A rollicking rendering of "Bad Case of Loving You (Doctor, Doctor)" became a decisive hit for Robert Palmer.

THE SOFT-SPOKEN Englishman behind the hit "Every Kinda People," Robert Palmer endured a portrayal as a polished, good-looking charmer, tackling R&B and reggae. The *Secrets* album concentrated on the uptempo side of his repertoire and his knack for choosing cover versions. The strategy was evident on his second Top 20 single, a reading of Moon Martin's "Bad Case of Loving You (Doctor, Doctor)."

"I'll hear a song and it will occur to me to do it a different way—I can only write within a certain width myself," he admitted. "When there's a style of song I want to do, rather than fake it, I take an existing song and maneuver it to fit my attitude. Then, next time, I have a better idea of what I'm trying to accomplish."

Palmer remained sanguine about unveiling of the rocking side of his music. "It's intriguing to watch acts emerge," he noted. "If the media describes them strongly enough in one direction, they tend to strike that pose as realistic—Boz Scaggs, for instance. I've found it confusing that some people's conception of me has nothing to do with my inspiration—I'm not into fashion or style or sex like they said. I never was or said I was. It's ironic now that I'm trying to do something else, but I insist it was misconstrued in the first place." ■

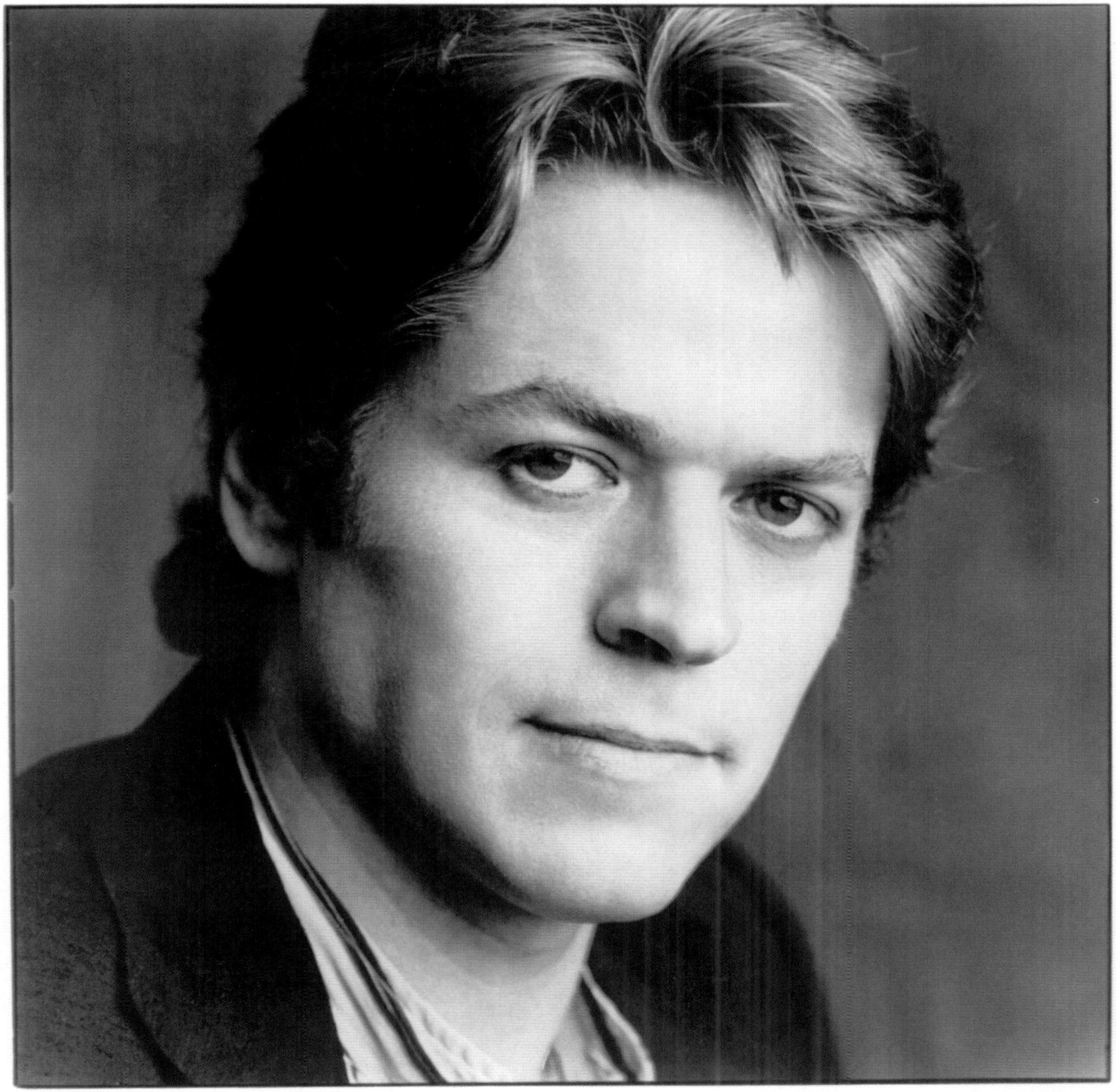

JUNE 1979

ROBERT PALMER

ISLAND

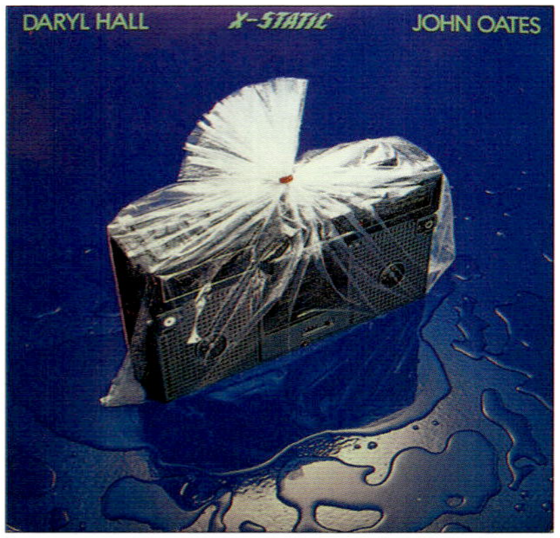

Billboard 200: *X-Static* (#33)
Billboard Hot 100: "Wait for Me" (#18)

Daryl Hall & John Oates relayed the pang of separation in another Top 20 hit, the touching "Wait for Me."

DARYL HALL & John Oates were in the midst of a middling recording streak. 1978's *Along the Red Ledge* album was an eclectic pop masterpiece, but the duo hadn't benefited from a pervasive hit single like "Sara Smile" or "Rich Girl" for a while. *X-Static* concentrated on merging what some people might have termed mutually exclusive musical styles.

"On some songs, I took modern beats and put them to rock 'n' roll," Hall said. "By doing so, we've transcended at least some of the artificial barriers that separate people into factions, in addition to creating music you can move your head and body to. This is dance music."

A centerpiece of *X-Static* was "Portable Radio," which enacted the stylistic synthesis Hall & Oates had worked to achieve with a big beat and a thoughtful lyric. "It's a positive song, a real simple idea," Hall explained. "Radio is so immediate—it reflects the true nature of what's going on around the country. Not even television is as true to that. I don't like the radio now any more or less than I ever did. It's just part of my life. People get the government they deserve, and people get the radio they deserve."

Hall & Oates' idea of what people deserved were the songs "Who Said the World Was Fair"—topical and easy to listen to, a tough combination to pull off—and "Intravino," an ode to fermented grapes that Hall insisted he researched thoroughly himself.

And "Wait for Me," the smash single, showcased the pair's trademark sound and Hall's diabolically perfect singing. "The truth is, I could sing before I could talk," he said of his knack for phrasing and delivery. "I can't ever remember not singing."

Hall & Oates had enjoyed the considerable skill of Elton John's old band, but various demands on everyone's time kept them from continuing as a unit. *X-Static* featured such top-flight musicians as Jerry Marotta, G.E. Smith, John Siegler and Charlie DeChant.

"Our new band is great—it's people we've known for a long time, so we didn't have to audition anyone," Hall admitted. "But we're still looking for the ultimate combination." ■

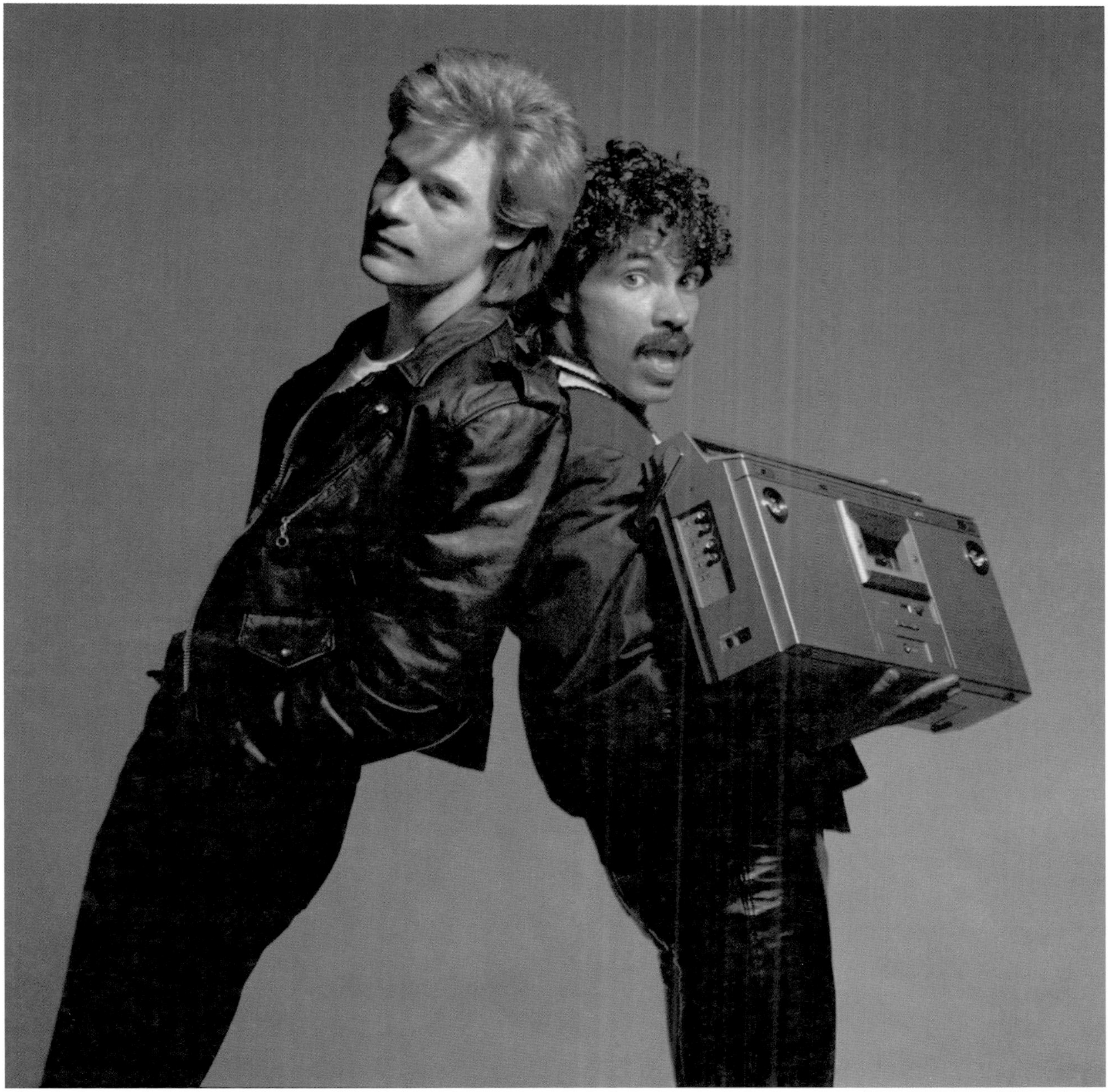

DARYL HALL

JOHN OATES

RCA Records and Tapes

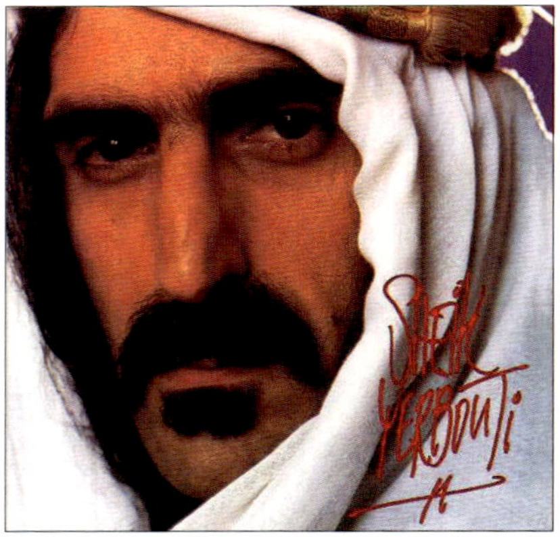

Billboard 200: *Sheik Yerbouti* (#21)
Billboard Hot 100: "Dancin' Fool" (#45)

Frank Zappa, who once developed the title *No Commercial Potential*, scored a hit single with "Dancin' Fool."

MAINTAINING A low profile during the early and mid-Seventies, Frank Zappa had released the occasional album on his own Discreet Records—a company made possible by shrewd investments from his iconoclastic, radical Sixties reputation and his satirical, humorous and otherwise offensive material.

But Zappa fell out with Warner Bros. Records, which distributed Discreet products. He steamed while the label released albums of studio jams that were never intended for public consumption. Zappa finally signed another deal with Phonogram Records, which also gave him his own call-your-own-shots label—dubbed Zappa Records.

Sheik Yerbouti, the initial album from Zappa, garnered him the most attention he'd had in years. It featured a fairly satisfying disco parody in "Dancin' Fool," and "Rat Tomago" got a Grammy nomination for Best Rock Instrumental Performance. But Zappa had never been more outrageous lyrically, especially "Bobby Brown"—a smash in Europe, but in the US, the sexually explicit song was banned from airplay—and a song called "Jewish Princess," which got him accused of anti-Semitism.

"I have this problem," he said. "The people who write about me have always done so in a very crude manner, without much skill. So there are all sorts of misconceptions as to what I do. There is no such thing as obscene. That is a myth perpetuated by stupid people. There is no word, no sound that can come out of a human being's mouth so powerful that it will send you to hell. The whole concept is primitive and irrelevant to the 20th century. I don't write obscene songs because obscenity doesn't exist.

"The only fun in this business for me is playing guitar and doing a show. The rest of it is all work. It's almost a shame people want to hear songs. If I could get away with it, I'd just go out there and play guitar all night." ■

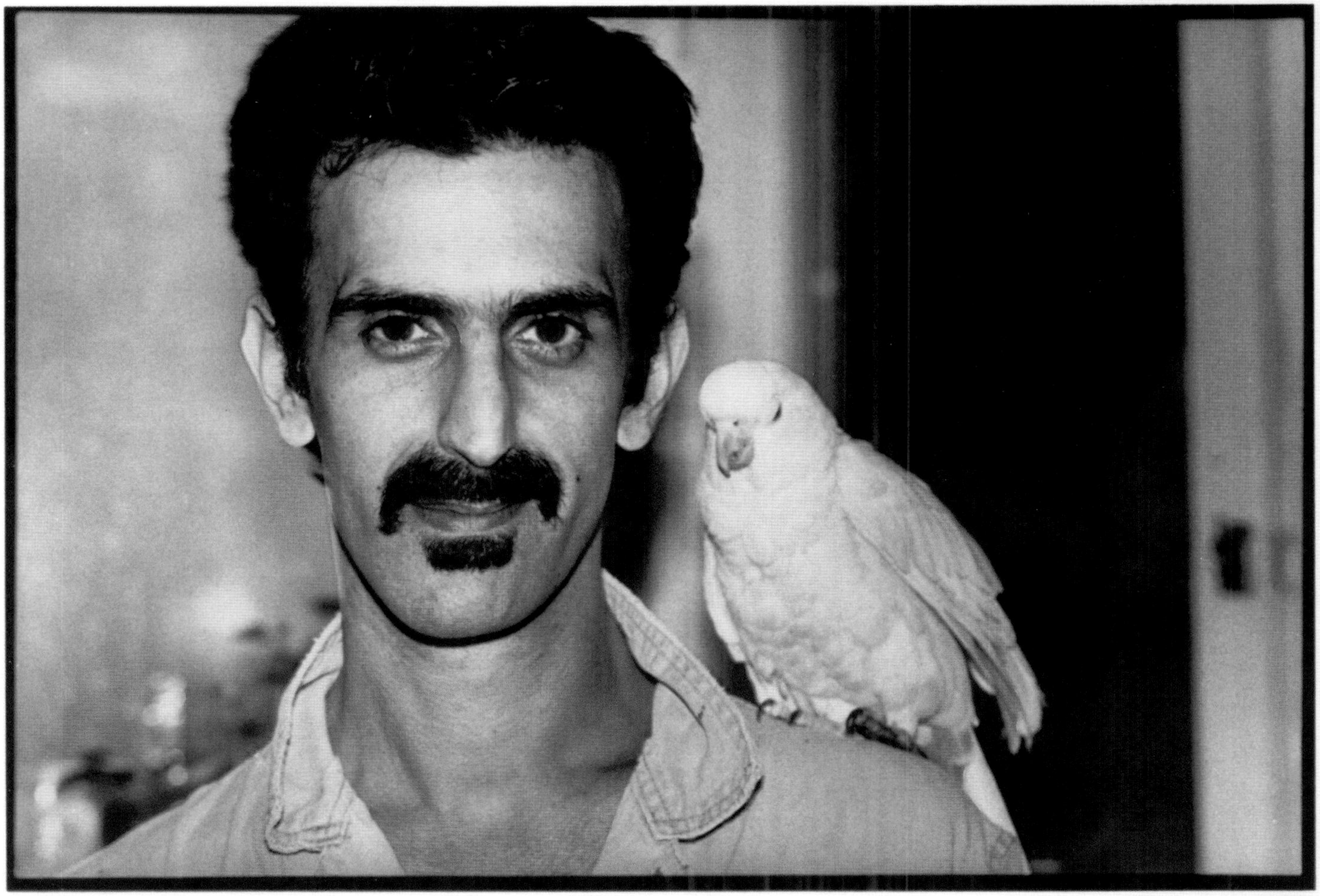

FRANK ZAPPA

Photo by: Lynn Goldsmith, Inc

Recording Exclusively for

ZAPPA RECORDS

Marketed by Phonogram, Inc

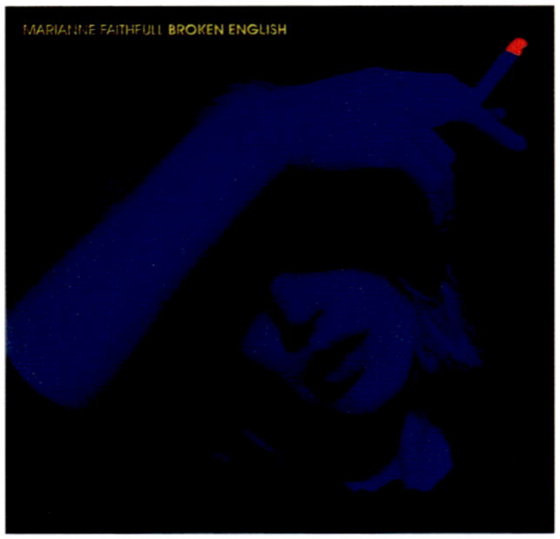

Billboard 200: *Broken English* (#82)

Considered a creative, vital artist, Marianne Faithfull had survived a stormy personal life and aura of fatalism.

IN THE Sixties, Marianne Faithful appeared on the pop scene as the sweet-voiced singer of her first recording, "As Tears Go By," a hit written by Rolling Stones Mick Jagger and Keith Richards—at 17, her girlish voice far from actual tears. But she became better known for her turbulent romance with Jagger in the days before Brian Jones' death.

As Jagger's beautiful, blonde, teenaged party companion, Faithfull ensured her place in the headlines that followed the Stones wherever they went. She was found semi-clad—infamous as the "girl in the fur rug"—subsequent to Jagger and Keith Richards getting busted for drug possession at the latter's country home in Sussex; she rocked the "establishment" by preaching free love in interviews. She found a proper expression for her talents when she co-wrote "Sister Morphine" with Jagger, supplying the lyrics.

But in late 1969, the relationship began to fall apart. By her own admission, Faithfull lived on pills and made several suicide bids, and one of the most ravishing icons of the Sixties became one of rock's most celebrated casualties. Most of the Seventies were spent battling personal trauma and heroin addiction.

Yet Faithfull staged an astonishing comeback with *Broken English,* an album marked by venomous and ofttimes pornographic lyrics about guilt and personal violence. Her raspy, cracked voice was full of experience—harsh, nicotine-encrusted and capable of frightening aggression, speaking volumes about her state of mind. Critics wrote that the songs were "a cry from the gutter" and "telegrams from hell."

"It was a breakthrough—I learned how to put emotional intensity into my work where I hadn't before," Faithful said. "I sing about my feelings and my truth."

The title track flaunted edgy, brittle punk sounds. "I had read a book called *Hitler's Children*, about the Baader-Meinhof Gang (a far-left militant organization that had terrorized West Germany), and the theme was crystalized one day when I was watching television, and on the screen came the subtitles 'spoken English…broken English.' I wrote the phrase down immediately."

And the aggressive "Why D'Ya Do It?," adapted from a poem by the playwright Heathcote Williams, was a caustic, graphic rant of a woman reacting to her lover's infidelity. "He showed me some of his poetry, and one poem in particular appealed to me because of its theme—sexual jealousy." ■

Marianne Faithfull

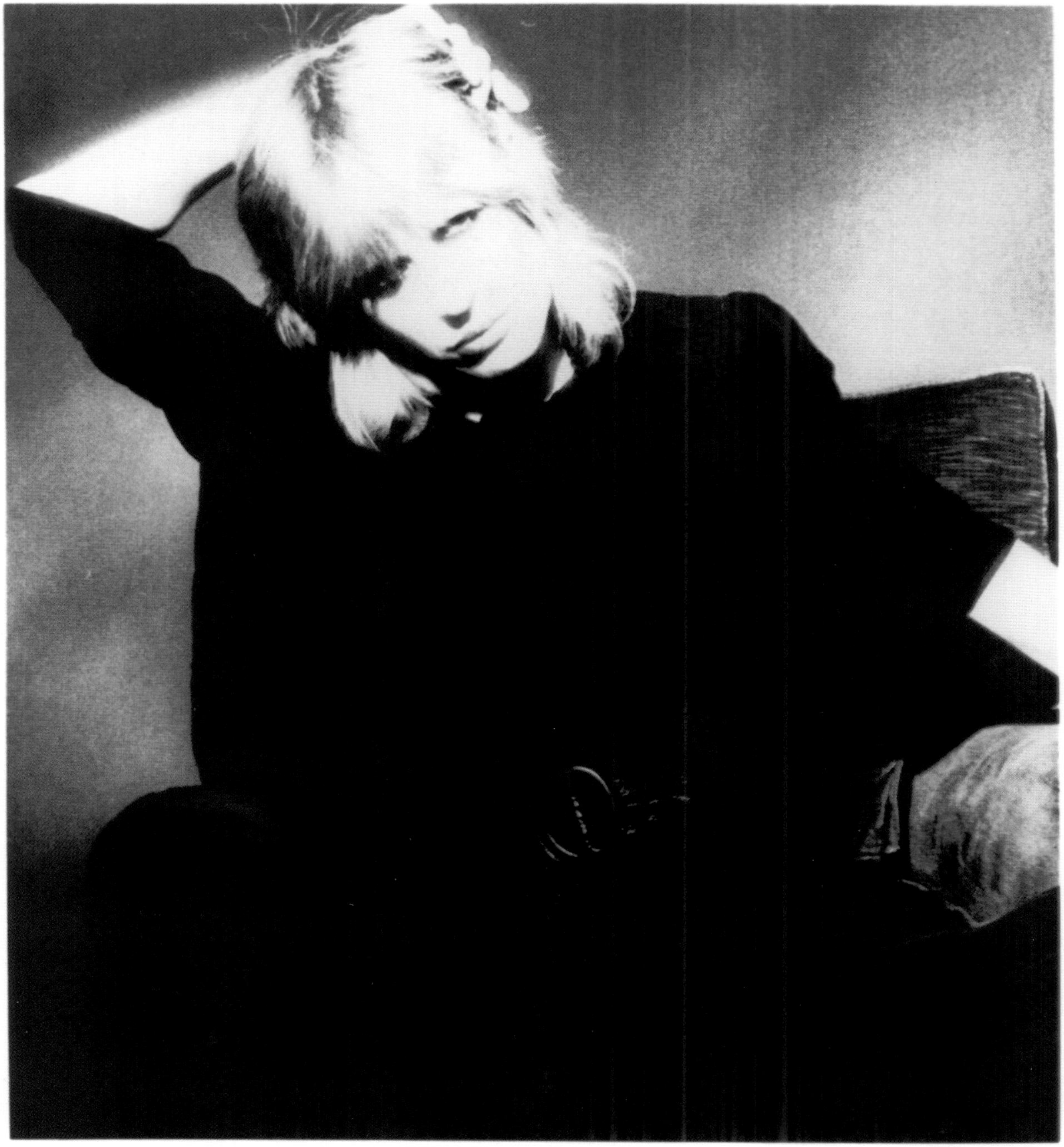

Photo Credit Dennis Morris September 1979

ISLAND

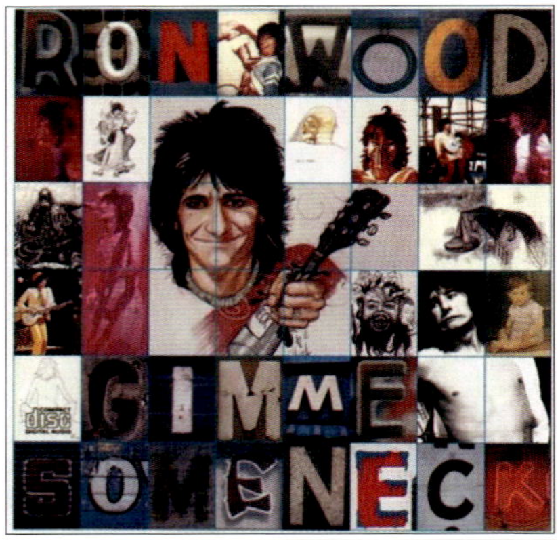

Billboard 200: *Gimme Some Neck* (#45)

Guitarist Ron Wood drew attention for the bawdy *Gimme Some Neck*, his first solo project as a Rolling Stone.

RON WOOD recorded two albums between 1974 and 1975 that sold poorly, despite his efforts to promote them. The ultimate ignominy came when the art department put his name on the first as "Ron Woods" (he crossed out the "s" and left it on). But Wood had become friends with Rolling Stones guitarist Keith Richards, and when Mick Taylor left the Stones in late 1974, Wood became the temporary guitarist for their summer tour.

The Faces, the good-time English rock group that launched Wood and Rod Stewart, broke up in 1975, but there was never an official notice of Wood joining the Stones. It was only when his picture appeared on the cover of the *Black and Blue* album ("the worst picture I've ever had taken") that his role was set. The Stones came through with their best work in years with 1978's *Some Girls*, and Wood played a large part in the band's revitalization.

But, as he explained, "Mick (Jagger) and Keith have so many songs that it takes forever for one of mine to come to light." As an outlet for his music, Wood found the time to record *Gimme Some Neck* (the title referred to his affinity for any stringed instrument). "The Stones have a mature attitude about that," he explained. "In the Faces, it would have been, 'What's Woody doing, recording a solo album?' Whereas the Stones say, 'Okay, he's doing it, so let's give him as much advice as we can."

Wood wanted a producer for direction and advice. He ended up using the services of Roy Thomas Baker (the Cars, Journey, Queen), who was known for a polished studio sound—although the record suggested that Wood got Baker to make compromises. "We had this standing joke," Wood explained good-naturedly. "If it was getting too slick, Roy would say, 'Is this too 10cc for you?'"

"Seven Days," written by Bob Dylan when he and Wood were present at a recording session for Eric Clapton in 1976, featured Wood's astonishing imitation of Dylan's hoarse vocal style. The other standout track, "Buried Alive," was "done with the Faces and Clapton, but they never got around to using it. That's a perfect example of why I do solo albums, to let things like that see the light of day."

The happy-go-lucky Wood, a graduate of an art school in England, took the opportunity to display some of his drawings on the album jacket. Most of them were self-portraits, drawings of his friends, or extensions of the Stones' fetish for wacky layouts of the female anatomy. "I'm glad I thought of it on this third record rather than the others, because my artwork would have been just as overlooked as the albums," he laughed.

Wood's friends got together on a moment's notice for a US tour to promote Gimme Some Neck—Richards on guitar, saxophonist Bobby Keys (a Stones confederate), bassist extraordinaire Stanley Clarke, drummer "Ziggy" Modeliste of the Meters and former Faces keyboardist Ian McLagan. They called themselves the New Barbarians, and after the outing the group split up as quickly as they banded together. ■

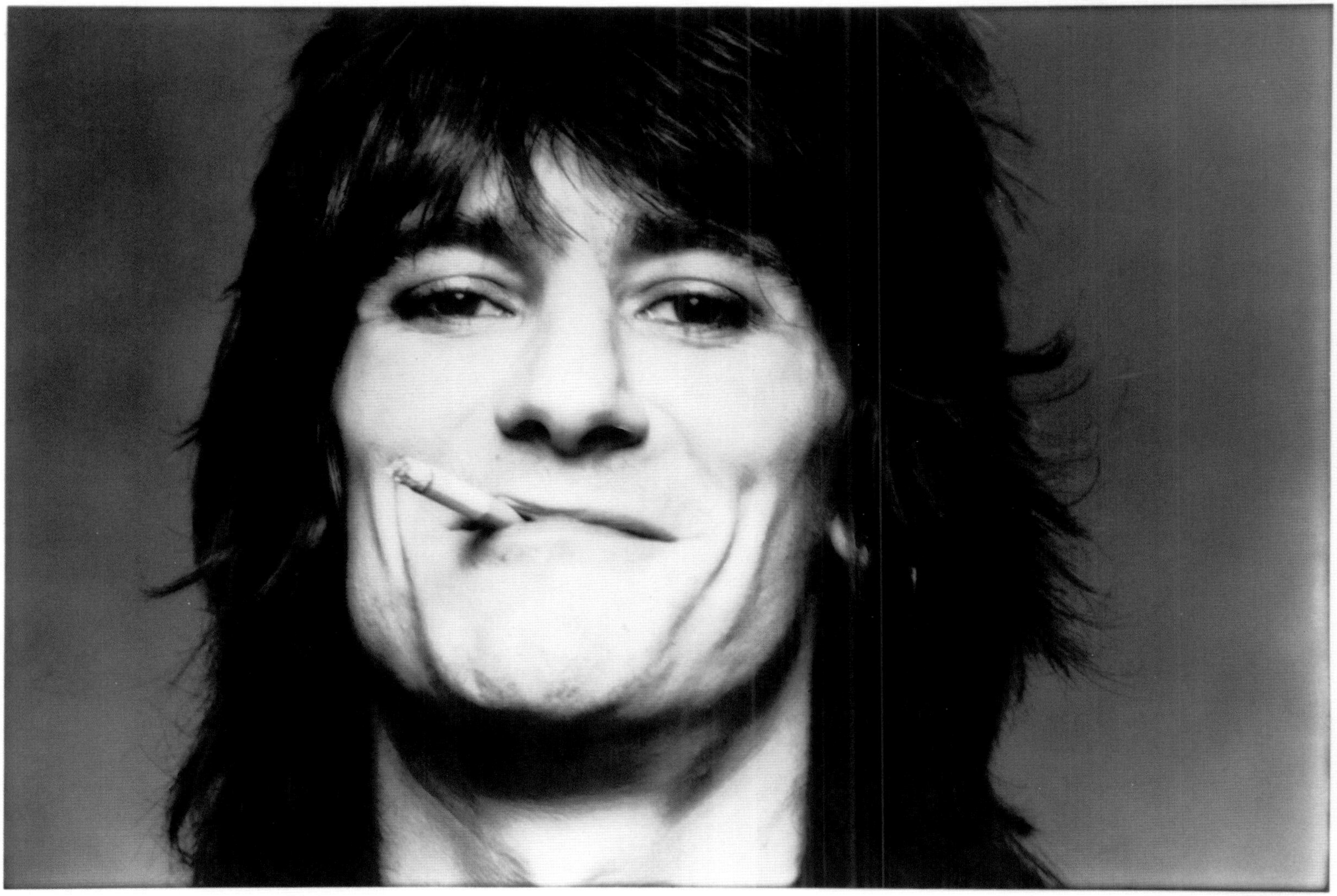

RON WOOD

Columbia

7903

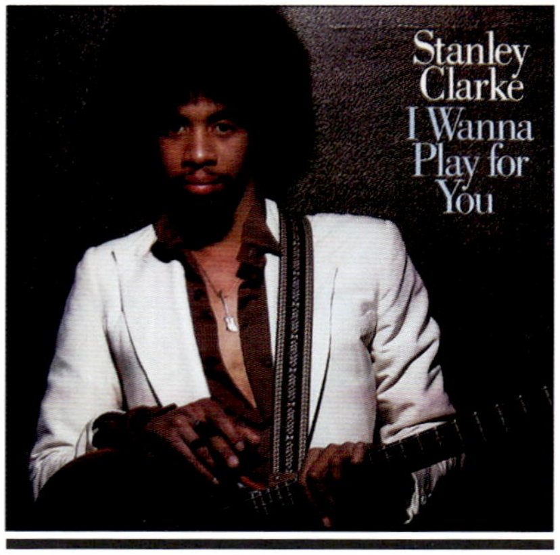

Billboard 200: *I Wanna Play for You* (#62)

Eminent bassist Stanley Clarke staked out untried musical territory for himself with *I Wanna Play for You*.

IN THE course of the Seventies, Stanley Clarke had transcended the traditional role of the bass guitar in contemporary music. He first rose to international prominence as a founding member of the seminal Return to Forever band with jazz pianist Chick Corea. He had since emerged on his own albums and in concert as a distinctive and powerful musical personality, closing the gap between mainstream jazz, progressive jazz and jazz rock fusion.

Clarke maintained a firm hold as "Top Electric Bassist" in virtually every major music publication's annual poll. With *I Wanna Play for You*, his sixth solo album, Clarke was making his bid for across-the-boards acceptance. His two-record set was a varied selection, including live tracks, disco mixes, instrumental and vocal cuts, hard rock as well as jazz.

"I can hang with anybody or anything—I intended to play in the Philadelphia Orchestra until I met Chick Corea," Clarke said. "I just try to do a lot of things well. I don't want to be the jack-of-all-trades and master of none."

The leadoff live version of his composition "Rock 'n' Roll Jelly" effectively captured the energy Clarke generated in concert. Jeff Beck added some ferocious guitar work on "Jamaican Boy," a reggae tune that transcended the genre with Clarke's inventive bass line. "Blues for Mingus," an acoustic piece, featured Michael Garson's piano stylings.

Listeners were ready for such an eclectic approach. Clarke also found the time to go on the road with the Ron Wood supergroup, the New Barbarians.

"I'll go to where the good players are," Clarke said. "I don't care what kind of music they play." ■

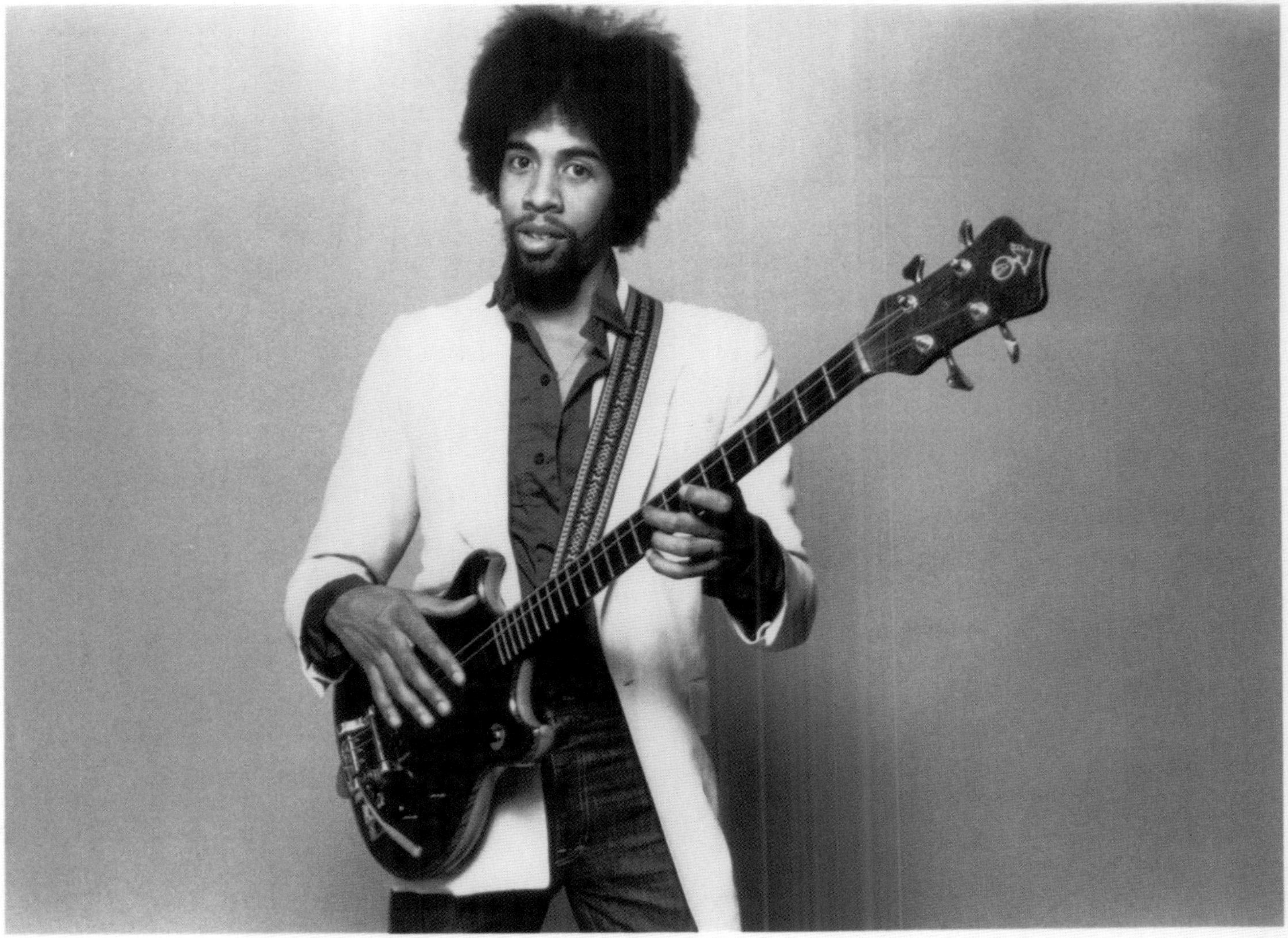

NEMPEROR RECORDS

STANLEY CLARKE

CONTEMPORARY ARTIST ENTERPRISES, INC.

8500 WILSHIRE BOULEVARD · SUITE 829 · BEVERLY HILLS, CALIFORNIA 90211

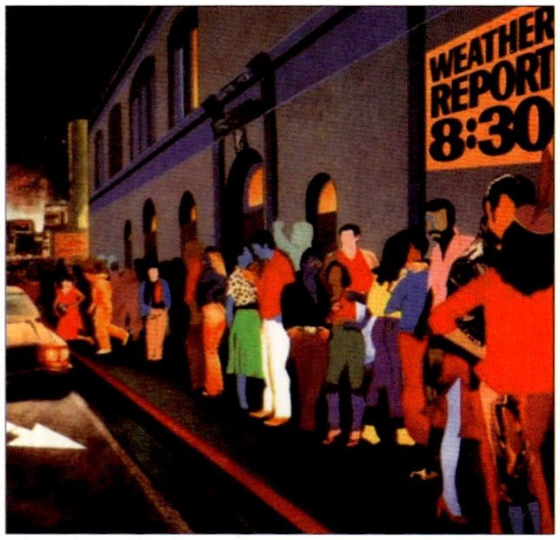

Billboard 200: *8:30* (#47)

Nailing Weather Report's verve and influence, *8:30* won a Grammy Award for Best Jazz Fusion Performance.

WEATHER REPORT'S 1971 debut album had caused a sensation in the jazz world, beginning a significant era of improvisational music. Formed by keyboardist Joe Zawinul and saxophonist Wayne Shorter, the group became a leading institution in the realm of jazz fusion. Now, under the creative direction of its co-leaders, Weather Report was unique for surviving the seven-year itch as well.

"We knew our collaboration would last so long," Shorter said. "We were aware that it would take a while for our kind of music to make its way into the public network in the first place."

Weather Report came together as an outgrowth of Zawinul and Shorter's work together on the Miles Davis albums *In a Silent Way* and *Bitches Brew*. The two had first met in 1959 at a small coffee shop near Birdland in New York. Later that same year they worked together in Maynard Ferguson's band. After that, each man went on to win notoriety as a sideman—Zawinul with Cannonball Adderley, Shorter with Art Blakey and then Davis.

With Weather Report's emergence came its innovative assimilation of rock and funk elements with those of jazz and classical, as well as the influences of varied African, Asian and Latin American styles. Refusing to be categorized, Shorter allowed only that his band was open to all new ideas.

"I don't call our kind of music anything," he insisted. "You know, it's difficult—how would you explain the differences in yourself from the time you were five years old to the time you became 25? There's too much to assimilate. This group is something I've spent every moment of this decade with—I'm too close to it to analyze it."

The first three sides of the *8:30* album, a two-record set, offered a slightly abridged version of the group's live show, recorded at a variety of locations. Side four consisted of four new compositions. The lineup was a quartet of Zawinul and Shorter with drummer Peter Erskine and Jaco Pastorius, a talented young bassist who had become the band's focal point onstage. *8:30* rose to #3 on the *Billboard* Jazz Albums chart.

Shorter, who had been named *DownBeat* magazine's Best Soprano Saxophonist for nine consecutive years, noted the number of musicians who had benefitted from their associations with Weather Report, including drummers Alejandro Acuna and Chester Thompson and bassist Alphonso Johnson.

"It's not really important why people leave," Shorter mused. "What's the saying—at the end of a five-year cycle, a particle takes off and makes its own axis? Change is healthy. It's a chance to go out and spread your wings from the family. It's all by mutual agreement when the time comes." ■

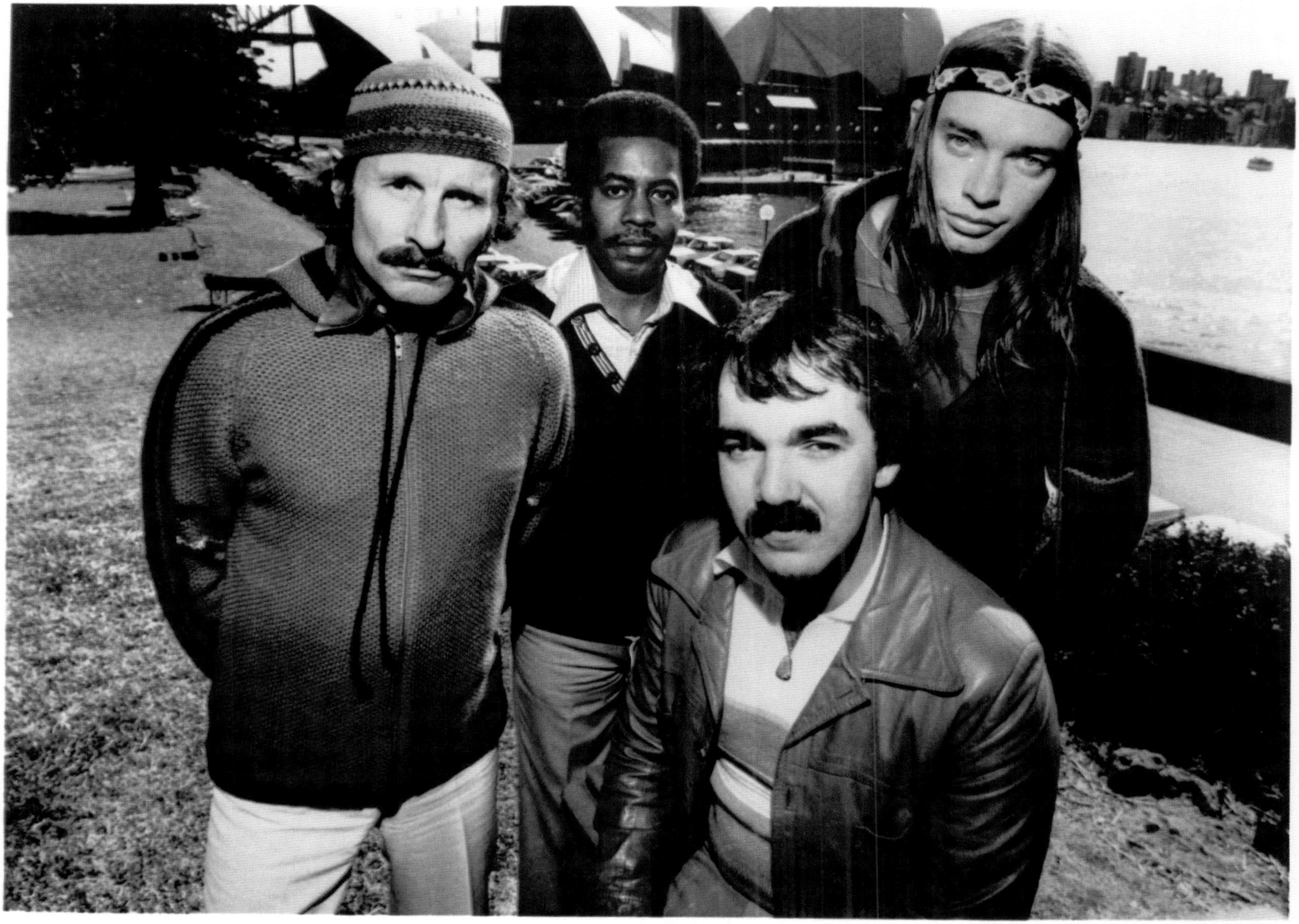

WEATHER REPORT

Columbia

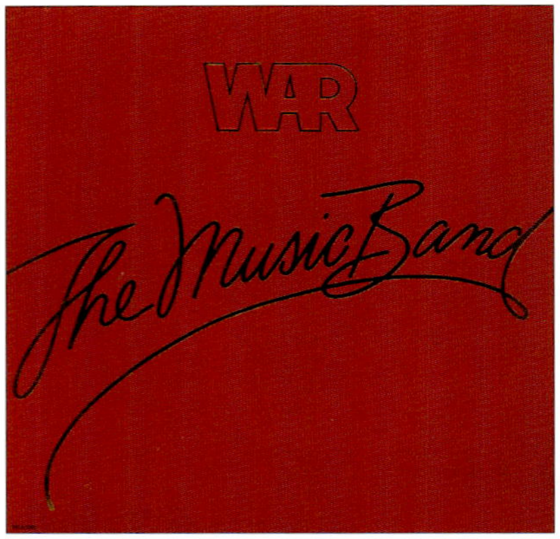

Billboard 200: *The Music Band* (#41)

The core members of War made personnel valuations and embarked on a new chapter with *The Music Band*.

WAR WAS America's great unacknowledged supergroup. When the music trade magazine *Record World* reviewed the first album, the act was called an "Afro-Cuban, jazz, rock, blues band," but War defied every truism of music marketing by appealing to Blacks, whites and Hispanics in almost equal proportion.

War had never known anything but success. Formed in 1969, the band originally served as ex-Animals frontman Eric Burdon's backing group on his global smash "Spill the Wine"—the first group ever to earn a gold record without having a label (War wasn't under contract to Burdon's company). The members set out on their own and went on to sell more than 25 million albums with such hits as "Slippin' into Darkness," "The Cisco Kid," "The World Is a Ghetto," "Low Rider," "Summer" and "Why Can't We Be Friends?"

"We never had any musical direction—we didn't know where we were going," founder and keyboardist Lonnie Jordan said. "We couldn't read music as well as Bach or Debussy. We usually bounced off the people. But we were influenced by everybody from Ray Charles to Hank Snow to Tito Puente to Harry Belafonte—the list goes on. We put a mixture of all that into our music, in one salad bowl. We ended up creating our own style from thinking that we were emulating everyone else."

Changes started with the admittance of female vocalist Tweed Smyth and Luther Rabb, who took over on bass. The band considered changing their name to the Music Band but decided to continue as War and use *The Music Band* as the title of an album. The new additions expanded the multi-ethnic lineup's sound.

"We're coming into a new ear for War—for 10 years, we were the same seven members, but as the music scene hanged, the group grew until we now have a nine-piece band," Jordan explained. "Now we've got a girl singer and the added rhythmic pattern from two drummers."

The Music Band led off with the title track, a tribute to fans. "Staying together hasn't always been easy—we're individuals with different tastes," Jordan said. "But we're also a family devoted to our music, which keeps us together. The main thing for us is to have fun and to make people happy." ■

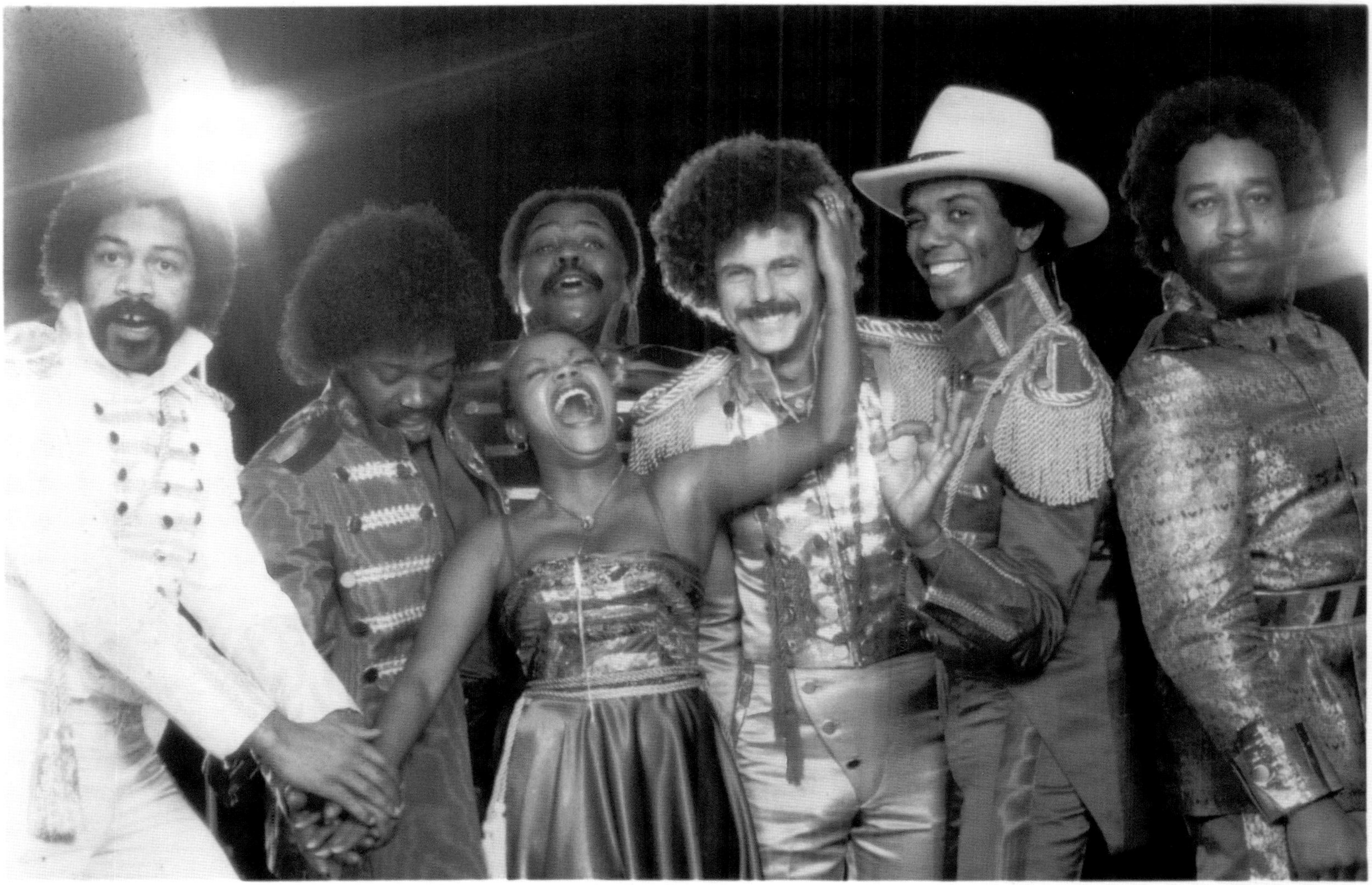

Lonnie Jordan | Luther Rabb | Dee Allen | Lee Oskar | Harold Brown | Howard Scott

Twee Smith

WAR

Exclusively On

FAR OUT™

MCA RECORDS

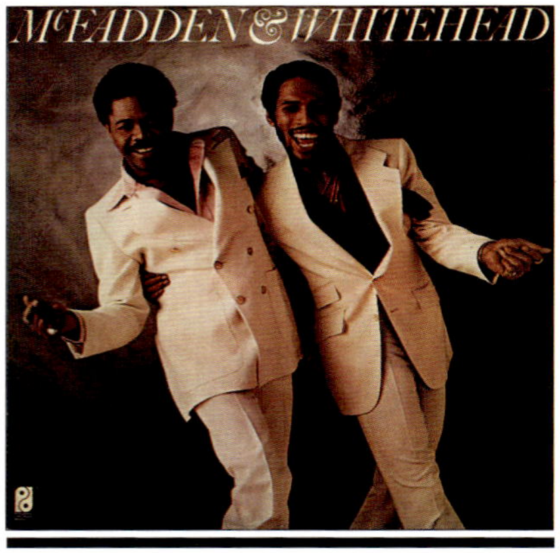

Billboard 200: *McFadden & Whitehead* (#23)
Billboard Hot 100: "Ain't No Stoppin' Us Now" (#13)

The zippy hit "Ain't No Stoppin' Us Now" garnered the R&B team of McFadden & Whitehead proper notoriety.

HAVING WRITTEN and produced some of the most powerful hits of the Seventies, partners Gene McFadden and John Whitehead finally fulfilled a lifelong dream, stepping out front as performing artists and making a mark with "Ain't No Stoppin' Us Now."

"We've been anxious to record since we first teamed up years ago as kids in the streets of Philly," Whitehead said. "You can trace our beginnings all the way back to the tenth grade when we formed a group called the Epsilons." The Epsilons found moderate success as part of the famed Otis Redding Revue. After tiring of the road, the two young men eventually returned to Philadelphia and signed as recording artists with Philly International, the soul music label mentored by Kenny Gamble and Leon Huff.

The venture didn't jump off as quickly as anticipated, reflecting their inexperience and lack of a track record. Whitehead even took on assorted odd jobs within the company. They finally sat down in McFadden's kitchen one night, determined to create their first "official" song, and "Backstabbers" became a No. 1 across-the-board smash for the O'Jays.

"It was hard getting Mr. Huff to listen to our lyrics, because we were literally following him down the hallway reading the words to him," Whitehead laughed. "But we finally got to him because, before we even finished, he stopped by his office, turned to us and said, 'Come on in here.'"

McFadden & Whitehead's R&B credits included "I'll Always Love My Mama" for the Intruders, "Let's Groove" and "Strategy" for Archie Bell & the Drells, and "Bad Luck" and "Wake Up Everybody" for Harold Melvin & the Blue Notes.

"For years we've poured our all into making things happen for other artists while all the time saying to ourselves, 'Hey, that could be us doing our tunes,'" Whitehead said. "Despite the enormous success we've had as composers and producers, our hearts were really into being, or at least attempting to be, performers."

The debut album *McFadden & Whitehead* weaved its way through funk to disco to romantic ballads, and the infectious, uptempo "Ain't No Stoppin' Us Now" stated the inspirational motto that made the two men click. The single soared to No 1 on the R&B charts, peaked on the pop and disco charts and earned them a Grammy nomination. The duo received many fan letters about how their song inspired people, especially the African American community.

"We couldn't write a song stronger than 'Ain't No Stoppin' Us Now," Whitehead explained. "We like being an information center for the public, writing about anything positive and good." ■

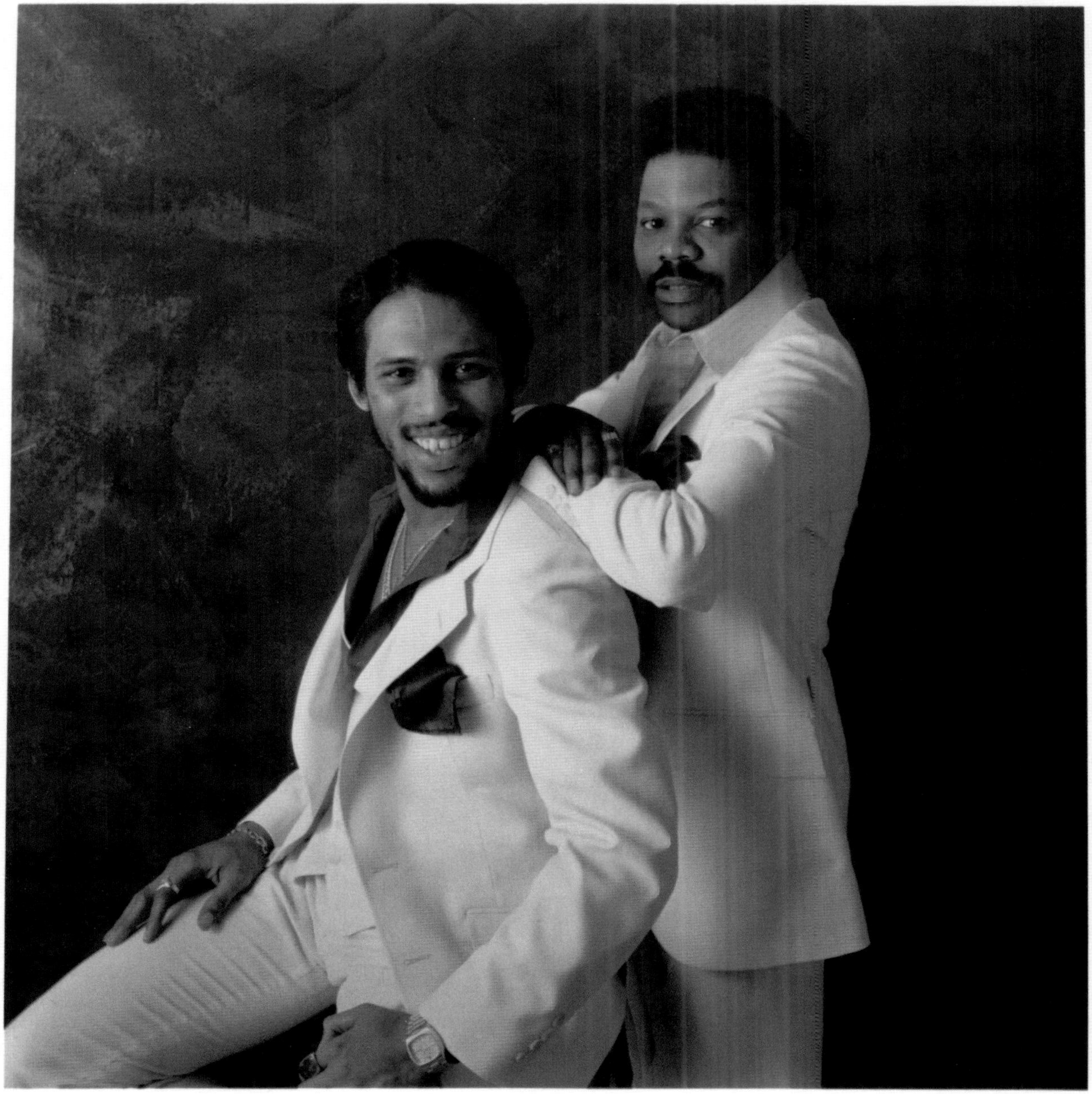

MCFADDEN & WHITEHEAD

Philadelphia International Records

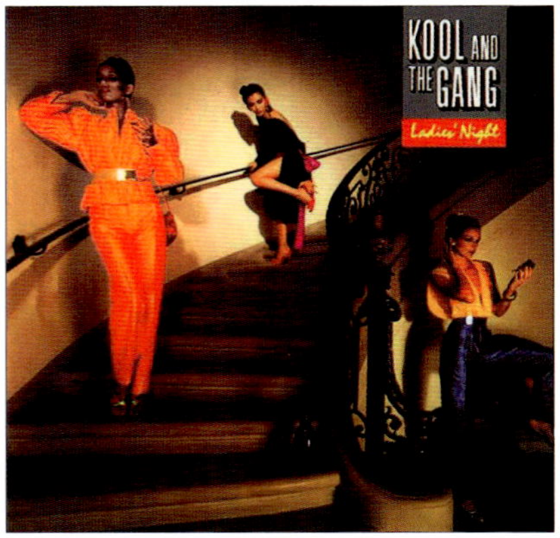

Billboard 200: *Ladies' Night* (#13)
Billboard Hot 100: "Ladies' Night" (#8); "Too Hot" (#5)

The right alliance of group and producer steered Kool & the Gang to their first major success, *Ladies' Night.*

WITH THE Top 10 hits "Ladies' Night" and "Too Hot," the group's biggest songs since "Jungle Boogie" and "Hollywood Swinging," Kool & the Gang could be heard all over the radio airwaves. While past singles had fit neatly into the disco mold that the group pioneered, the *Ladies' Night* album featured a slicker, jazz-tinged sound courtesy of Brazilian producer Eumir Deodato.

Deodato, a successful recording artist on his own—he won a Grammy award for "Also Sprach Zarathustra (2001)," his 1973 instrumental—was recruited by the band when they met each other at a studio.

"We were starting to get slightly overcreative, putting in extra horn lines because that's what we're known for," group leader Robert "Kool" Bell admitted. "He kept us from going too much in that direction, just saying, 'I've been through that, and it's not the route to go.' He moved us towards a more mainstream commercial sound."

Kool & the Gang also were celebrating their 10-year anniversary, marking the days they played the East Coast bar circuit as the Jazziacs in the Sixties. In the Seventies, the nine-piece aggregation had been adding funkier trademarks to their jazz-rooted sound "because we had to live," Bell laughed. "So we had to learn to adjust our musical ideas. We had to make sure our jazz roots didn't overpower the funk."

Ladies Night also marked the debut of singer James "J.T." Taylor, who became a focal point to the music—notably "Too Hot," a hit ballad of lost love—and he inspired the band's performances as well. "We've always strived for a straight-forward, laid-back, choreographed show," Bell said. "And we're likely to get into some improvisation—we just love to stretch out and jam a bit." ■

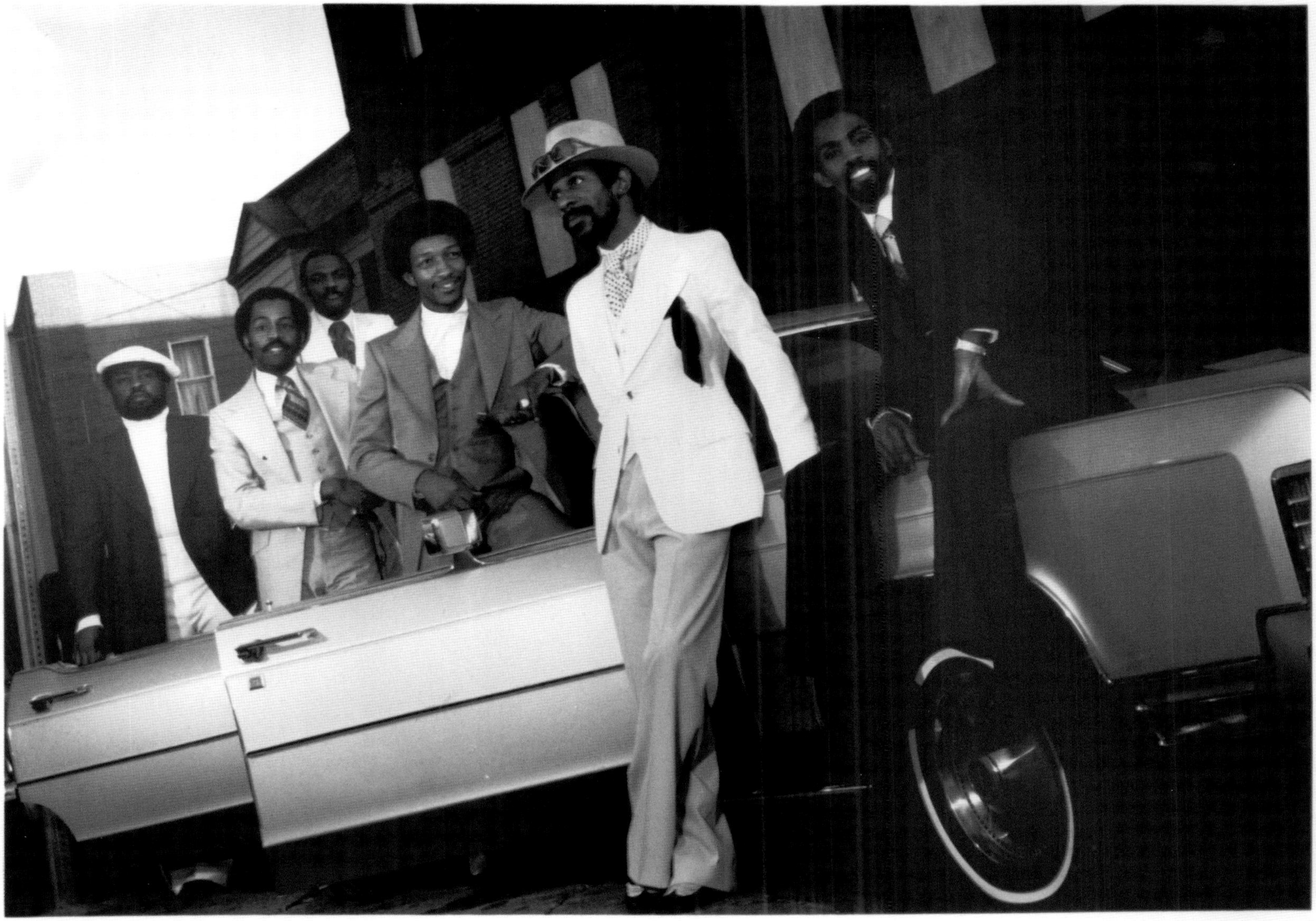

KOOL & THE GANG

Recording Exclusively For
De-Lite RECORDS
Marketed By Phonogram Inc.

Billboard 200: *Injoy* (#35)
Billboard Hot 100: "Move Your Boogie Body" (#57);
"Today Is the Day" (#60)

Featuring the Top 5 R&B smash "Move Your Boogie Body," *Injoy* was the biggest-selling Bar-Kays recording.

THE BAR-KAYS had been knocking around the Black music scene since the mid-Sixties, when Stax Records in Memphis signed the band as the house group to back singer Otis Redding. In addition, the act recorded its own records, such as the smash "Soul Finger" in 1967. Tragedy struck that year when a plane carrying Redding and all but one of the Bar-Kays crashed into a Wisconsin lake. James Alexander, who flew on another flight that day, and trumpeter Ben Cauley, who survived the crash, were the only members left of the original Bar-Kays.

"It all happened so fast," Alexander recalled. "I didn't really have much time to think. I was only 17 years old, and I inherited it all. I was asked if I was going to continue the Bar-Kays, and I just said, 'Yes.'"

The reformed Bar-Kays continued recording for Stax—under their own name and backing Isaac Hayes on *Hot Buttered Soul,* as well as the Staple Singers, Albert King, Carla Thomas and Johnnie Taylor—until the company declared a cataclysmic bankruptcy. The Bar-Kays were caught up in litigation for much of the early Seventies, but a new contract with a new label finally enabled them to resume their hit-making status as a funk ensemble. "Shake Your Rump to the Funk," "Too Hot to Stop," "Let's Have Some Fun," "Attitudes," "I'll Dance" and "Shine" all topped the soul charts.

The single released from the *Injoy* album was "Move Your Boogie Body," another dance floor gem.

"The cheering and applause of the audiences and the chart-topping success of our recordings is its own reward," the warm, reserved Alexander said. "All the original members were like brothers to me, and I thought they'd truly want me to take the name further. I'm doing it." ■

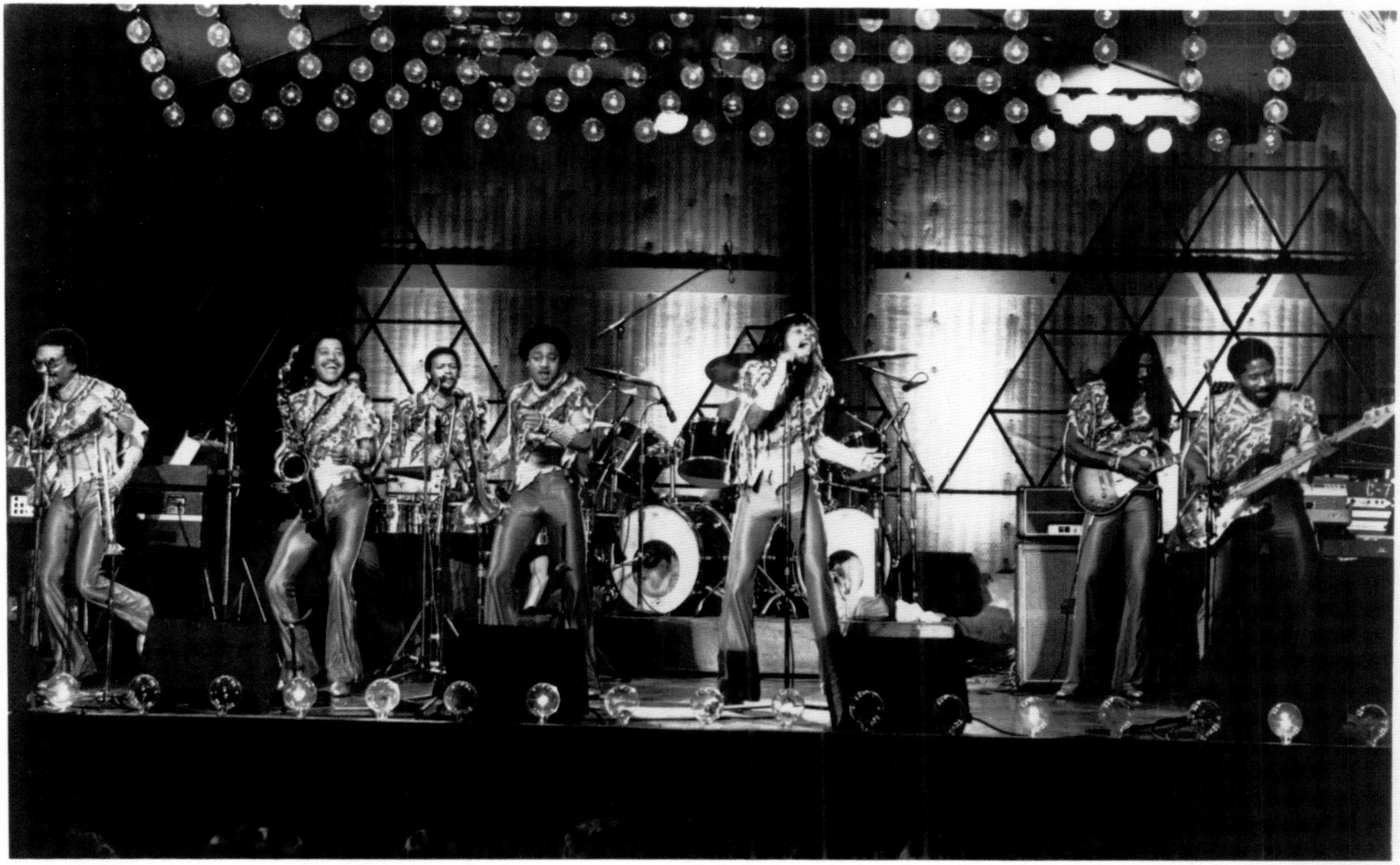

BAR-KAYS

Recording Exclusively For

mercury

A product of Phonogram, Inc.

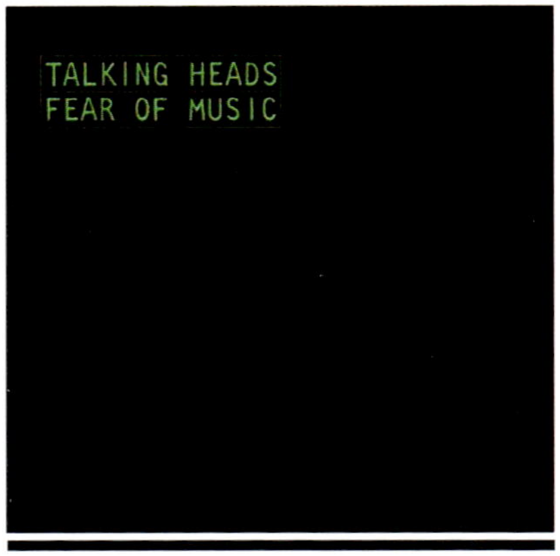

Billboard 200: *Fear of Music* (#21)
Billboard Hot 100: "Life During Wartime" (#80)

Talking Heads' third album, the riveting *Fear of Music*, popularized leader David Byrne's singular sensibility.

LISTENERS WERE kept on their toes with Talking Heads' *Fear of Music*, a record full of provocative sonic shifts courtesy of producer Brian Eno. David Byrne, the leader of the band, had perfected his vocal idiosyncrasies to where his endearing yelping perfectly projected his anxious demeanor.

Byrne approached the recording of *Fear of Music* as "an experiment. I didn't have the material finished because I wanted to try working different ways on the songs. I wanted to start with lyrics on one and come up with the music, and then have a riff and improvise words on another. I wouldn't want to get into a rut or formula writing songs."

Despite the progressive nature and unconventional rhythms of his songs, Byrne didn't consider himself a musical pioneer. "Stretching boundaries is only a by-product of getting bored with what you've done before. If I'm working on something that I don't understand, I get more excited than I would just relying on technical expertise."

Fear of Music contained some compelling and rewarding music. "Life During Wartime" was a sensible tour of Byrne's neurosis, producing the catchphrase "This ain't no party, this ain't no disco, this ain't no foolin around." High points also included the mesmerizing "I Zimbra," an African-influenced track enhanced by guitarist Robert Fripp, and the jittery "Cities." The other Heads—Jerry Harrison (keyboards), Tina Weymouth (bass) and Chris Frantz (drums)—contributed stellar ensemble playing.

"The one song that I thought might be melodic and accessible enough for radio play was 'Heaven,'" Byrne said. "So I specifically withdrew embellishments so that the arrangement wouldn't work that way."

Using mobile recording equipment, the tracks were recorded in part at a loft space in Long Island City owned by Frantz and Weymouth, and Byrne was enamored of the results. "Regular studios don't sound exciting—there's too much baffling. We perform better when we're just playing around, anyway."

Eccentric? Bryne knew what he wanted. "I tried being a normal musician in high school. I don't know what it sounded like, but I gave up on it right after that." ■

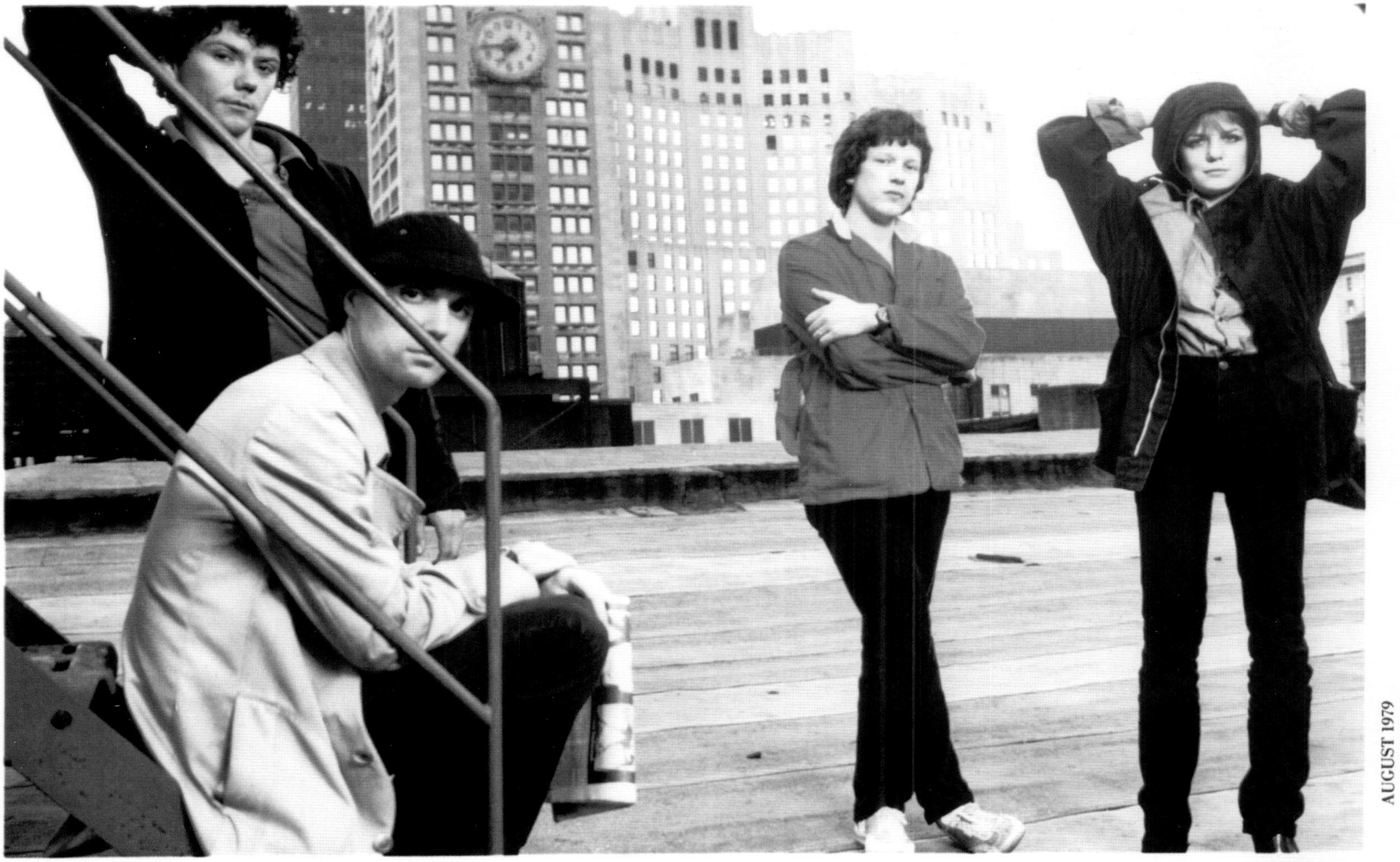

TALKING HEADS

SIRE RECORDS

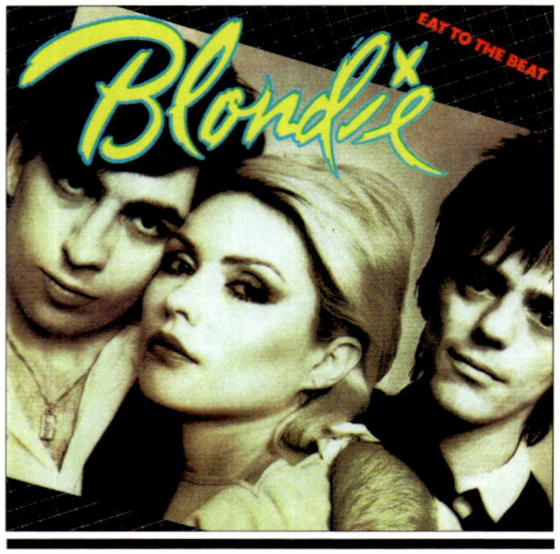

Billboard 200: *Eat to the Beat* (#17)
Billboard Hot 100: "Dreaming" (#27); "The Hardest Part" (#84); "Atomic" (#39)

The group Blondie sprang up from the late Seventies punk scene as New York's most highly marketable band.

LIKE THE Ramones and many New York-area peers, Blondie had gradually released several excellent singles, all of which made the band famous worldwide and none of which became a hit at home. It wasn't until the disco-fied track "Heart of Glass" appeared in a seven-inch format that American radio got behind the band. The single's crossover appeal owed to singer Debbie Harry's comic-book impersonation of Donna Summer and drummer Clem Burke's rock-solid backbeat.

Blondie offered Harry's considerable photogenic allure, yet the basis of the group's fortunes had always been the carefully crafted pop rock served up by the five male musicians. Chris Stein, Blondie's guitarist, was known by insiders as the mastermind behind the music. When asked questions, Harry usually put on disinterested airs and let Stein do the talking.

Stein always wore his influences on his sleeve, and much of the charm of Blondie's music had derived from his love of pop culture, from the one-hit groups of the Sixties to every B-movie ever made. He expounded on *Eat to the Beat*, the group's fourth album. "It's a smorgasbord of sound—very eclectic, with lots of different kinds of music once again."

Longtime fans who feared that "Heart of Glass" would trap Blondie in a 132-beats-per-minute framework were assured that the band remained a rock-oriented outfit. Blondie once again used the talents of producer Mike Chapman, who started his domination of the singles charts (Suzi Quatro, the Knack, Nick Gilder) with "Heart of Glass." "Dreaming" became a staple of Blondie's live shows.

"Actually, some of the stuff is a little weirder than the last one, I would think," Stein noted of the patent "platinum pressure" to follow up a hit. "I don't use any E-bow guitar (his favorite guitar device), but I do use a Gizmo—Lol Creme and Kevin Godley (formerly of 10cc and inventors of the Gizmo) make it sound like strings, but one single string sounds like a mandolin trill. Neat stuff."

Success had given Blondie a chance to indulge its enthusiasm for celebrity. "We recorded at the Power Station in New York, the studio that Chic uses," Stein enthused. "Bruce Springsteen and the Kinks were in there recording at the same time we were. Lorna Luft, Liza Minnelli's sister, sings on a track. We were going to get Brooke Shields, but she was out of town." ■

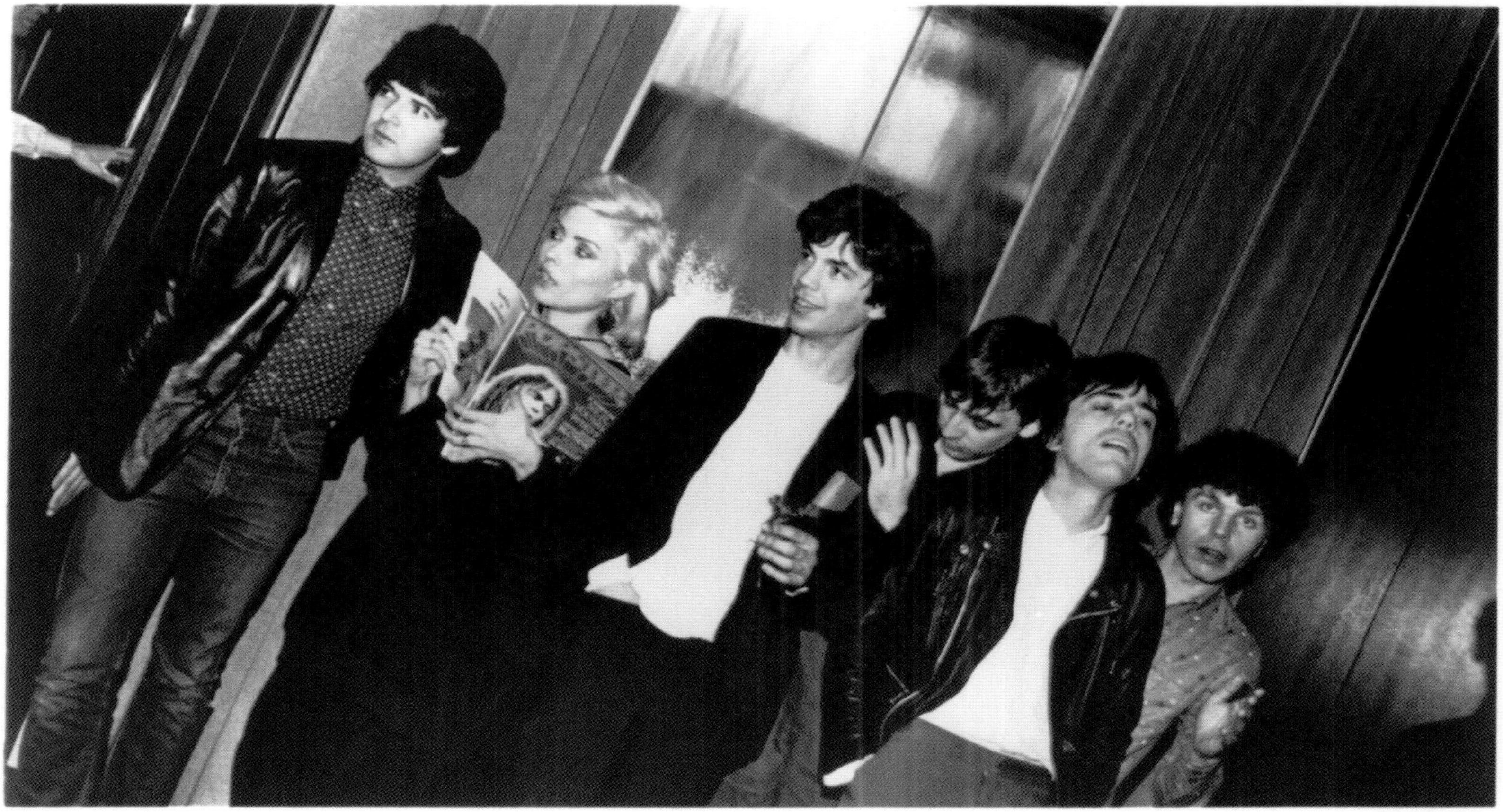

Blondie

Clement Burke Deborah Harry James Destri Chris Stein Frank Infante Nigel Harrison

Chrysalis™

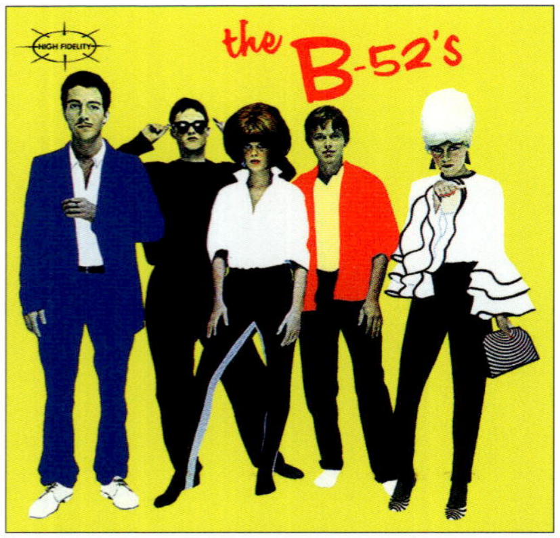

Billboard 200: *The B-52's* (#59)
Billboard Hot 100: "Rock Lobster" (#56)

The B-52's added the vivacious camp classic "Rock Lobster" to the underground music scene's bill of fare.

TRADING ON an encyclopedic knowledge of junk culture and kitsch, the B-52's began as a low-rent lark in Athens, Georgia—and the outlandish, fun-loving band soon became a central part of the new wave movement.

"We first started one night in October 1976 when, after tropical drinks at a Chinese restaurant, we went to a friend's house and jammed," vocalist and keyboardist Cindy Wilson said. "We had to play parties in Georgia. What was going on down there was cowboy rock and folkie stuff, almost coming out of the hippie era. Definitely, we were trying to be shocking to sorority and fraternity types. We had a bit of a punk ethic, even though we were so different from everybody else."

In their garish thrift-shop polyester garb and tacky wigs ("B-52" was Southern slang for a bouffant hairdo), the Georgia bohemians revved up the scene.

"We had to go to New York to get an audience," Wilson explained. "It was such an amazing, incredible place. We played the legendary clubs, Max's Kansas City and CBGB. They heard us and said to come on back, so we started building a following by word of mouth. You didn't make any money—you actually had to pay to play. We put out 'Rock Lobster' as an independent single, and the next time we played New York there was a line all the way around the block. So we knew something was happening."

The members immersed themselves in an eccentric musical style, pitting B-grade sci-fi electronic effects and surreal, upper-register harmonies with echoey guitar and beach-blanket movie soundtrack melodies, devising their own highly danceable formula. The goofy joy of the re-recorded version of "Rock Lobster" panned out to be the zany band's biggest hit on *The B-52's*, the irrepressible debut album that launched their success. "Dance This Mess Around" and "Planet Claire" were equally infectious.

"Our music is a novelty in that it's not Top 40 schlock, what you normally hear," singer Fred Schneider admitted. "We started out as a party band with humor, and people are wigging out dressing for our shows. We're just following our own path." ■

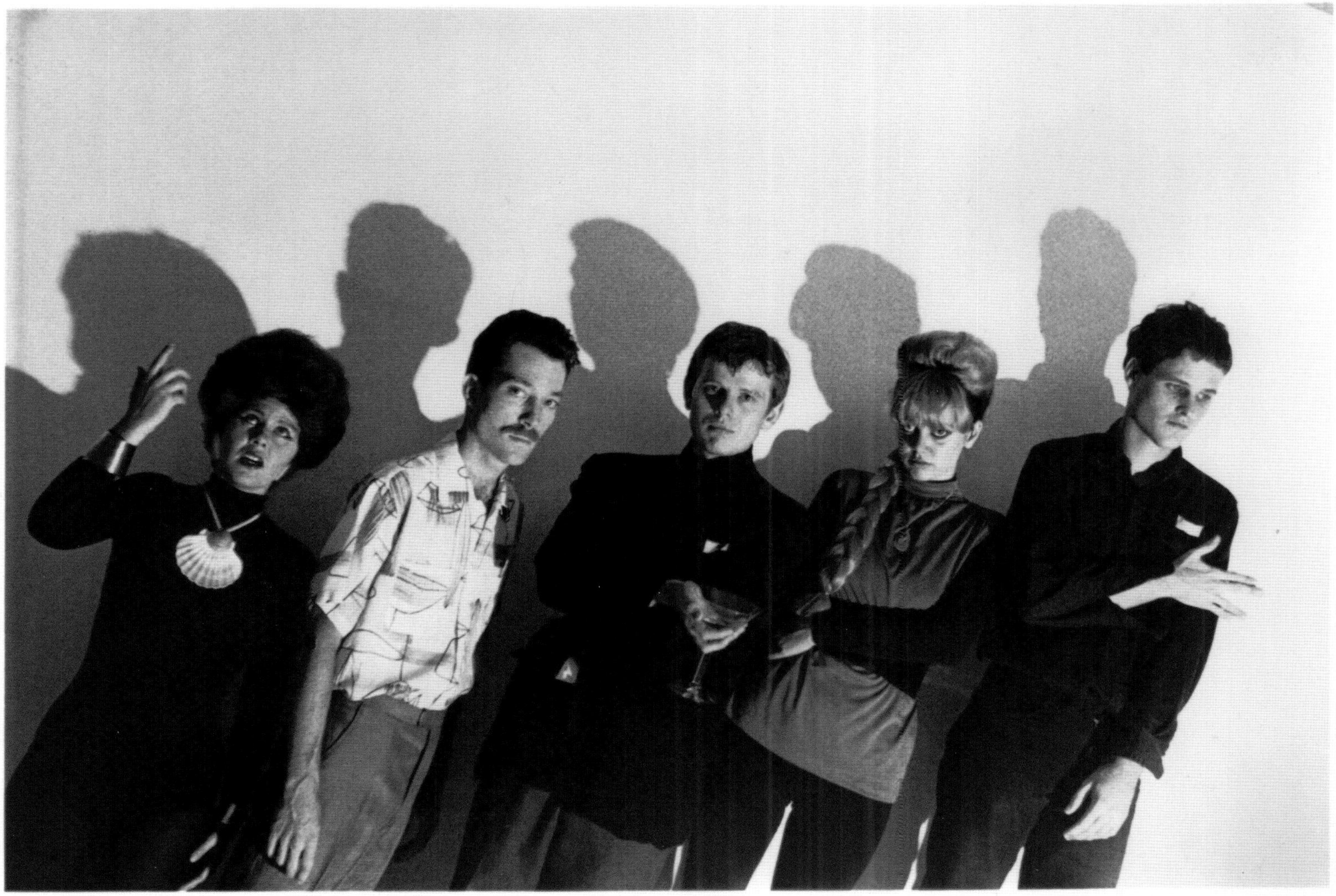

PHOTO CREDIT: GEORGE DUBOSE

JULY 1979

the B-52's

WARNER / REPRISE

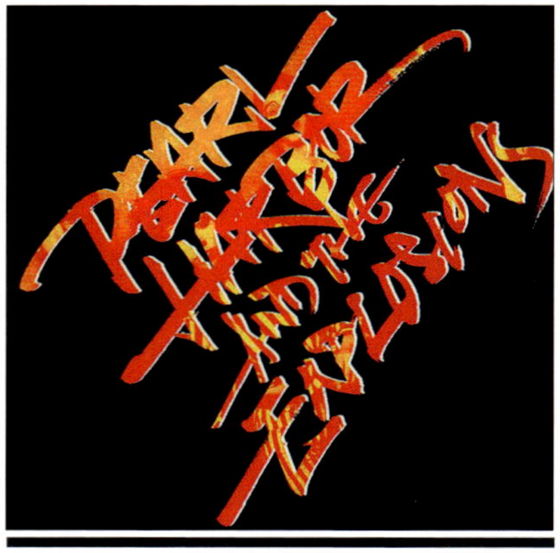

Billboard 200: *Pearl Harbor & the Explosions* (#107)

With a primo debut, Pearl Harbor & the Explosions were hailed as San Francisco's hottest musical export.

FRONTED BY vocalist Pearl E. Gates, Pearl Harbor & the Explosions had been together a little more than a year before they were heading up an entire San Francisco area scene.

"At that time the real heavy punk thing had come and gone," Gates explained. "That had a lot to do with why we were so readily accepted in the beginning—the old story of everyone looking for something new. We were the first people in the area to take that genre and make it into something that you didn't have to be afraid to listen to."

The group started receiving attention outside of the Bay Area when an independently produced single, "Drivin'," became an underground smash across the US and in England. Warner Bros. Records signed the group and allowed them to continue working with David Kahne, a producer without a significant track record but with a superb knowledge of the band's strengths. A re-recorded "Drivin'" and the striking single "You Got It (Release It)" were the high points of the group's self-titled debut album.

"At this point there are a lot of local bands that have potential, and new clubs are opening, too," Gates noted. "We did break it open in terms of bringing less mainstream rock into the clubs. Now no one wants to go see a regular rock band anymore. It's all new wave or whatever."

"Most people like labels so they can immediately identify what you're doing," bassist Hilary Stench added. "New wave is really the closest thing to what we do. Now I've heard about this other label that's just starting—'dance-oriented rock.' I understand we're getting shuffled into that category, so DOR is the new thing."

That brand of pop, referred to in the song "Shut Up and Dance," had evolved as a matter of necessity. "We had to get on the club scene immediately for financial reasons when we started," Gates explained. "So we did a bunch of cover tunes—R&B and rockabilly. Everybody likes that stuff, and no one else was doing it. If nothing else, people come to dance." ■

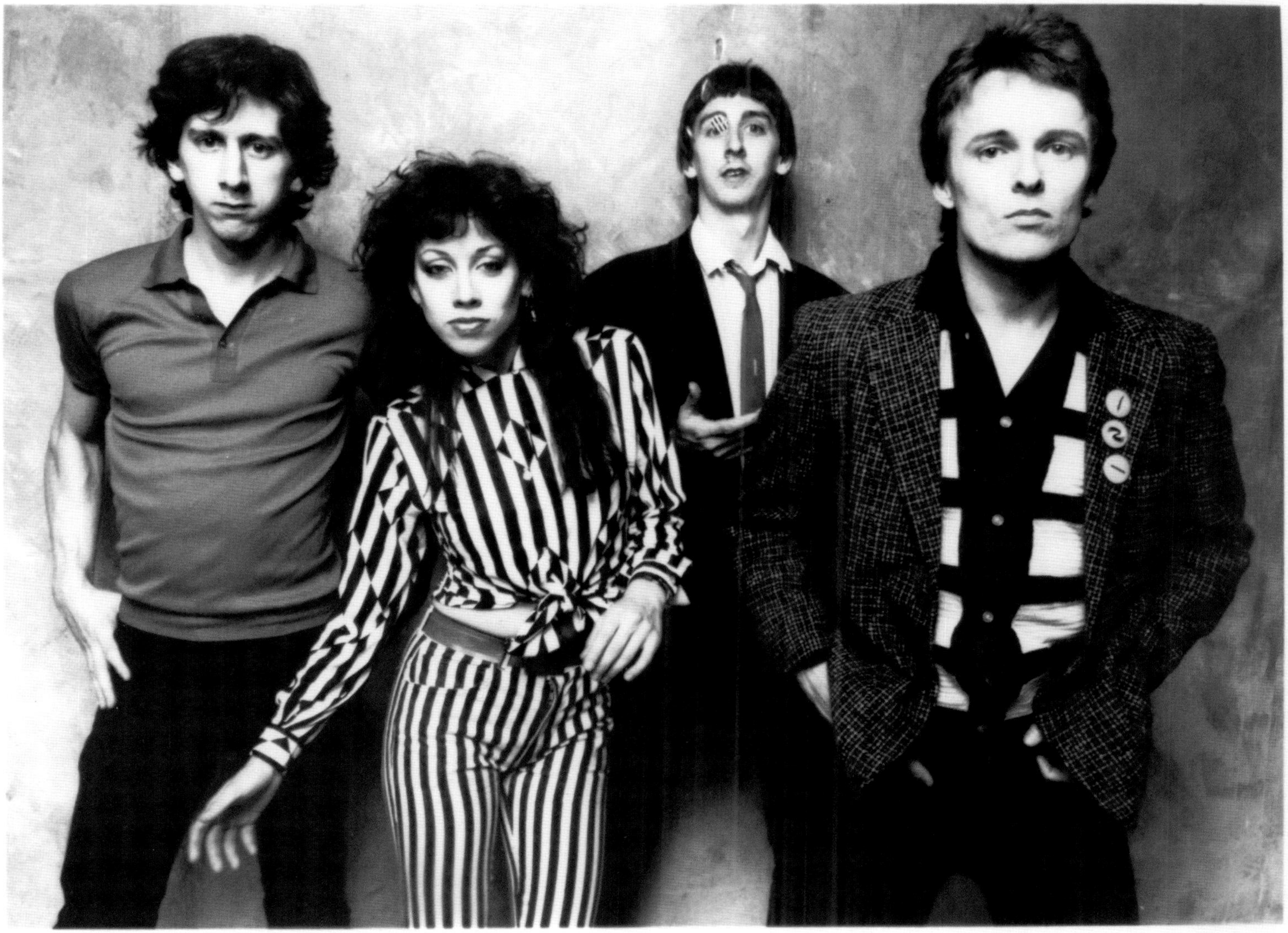

Photography by: *Michael Jang* DECEMBER 1979

JOHN STENCH PEARL E GATES HILARY STENCH PETER BILT

PEARL HARBOR AND THE EXPLOSIONS

WARNER BROS.

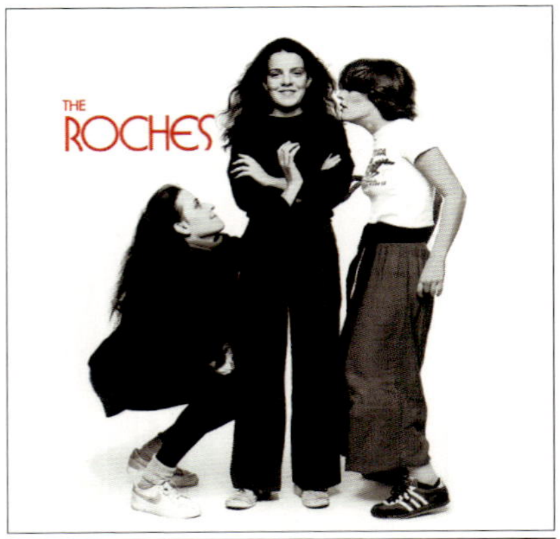

Billboard 200: *The Roches* (#58)

The Roches' self-titled release celebrated rather than camouflaged the eccentricities in the sister act's music.

FOR AS long as they could remember, the Roche sisters had been vocalizing—asked where their music began, Suzzy Roche said, "in the back seat of our parents' car." Bolstered by singing Christmas carols around their home in Park Ridge, New Jersey and helping their father compose and perform songs to support local Democratic candidates, Suzzy's older siblings, Terre and Maggie, had hit the folk circuit while still in their teens.

Paul Simon brought them into the studio for backing vocals on his 1974 album *There Goes Rhymin' Simon*. The following year, he co-produced their debut as a duo, *Seductive Reasoning*. Suzzy, a drama major at SUNY Purchase, graduated a year later and joined the other two for some caroling on New York City streets, and the Roches began performing as a threesome.

"A lot of our arrangements come from those years of singing carols together," Terre said. "In the culture I grew up in, it's the closest thing I can think of to traditional roots music—that is, music everybody knows the tune to."

Robert Fripp from King Crimson took production reins for *The Roches*, an intriguing initiation to the trio's slightly whacked-out approach to both lyrics and traditional folk influences. The album, which included such live favorites as "Hammond Song," "Pretty & High" and "The Troubles," made a number of year-end "best of" lists including that of *The New York Times*, while word spread about the magic of their harmonies and the charm of their live show.

The sisters' harmonies, acoustic playing and are-we-hip-or-too-dumb-to-notice posturing endeared them to a sizable cult following. "Whenever you're in the public eye, whatever you're like becomes a badge," Terre admitted. "In that sense, we've always kind of stuck out." ■

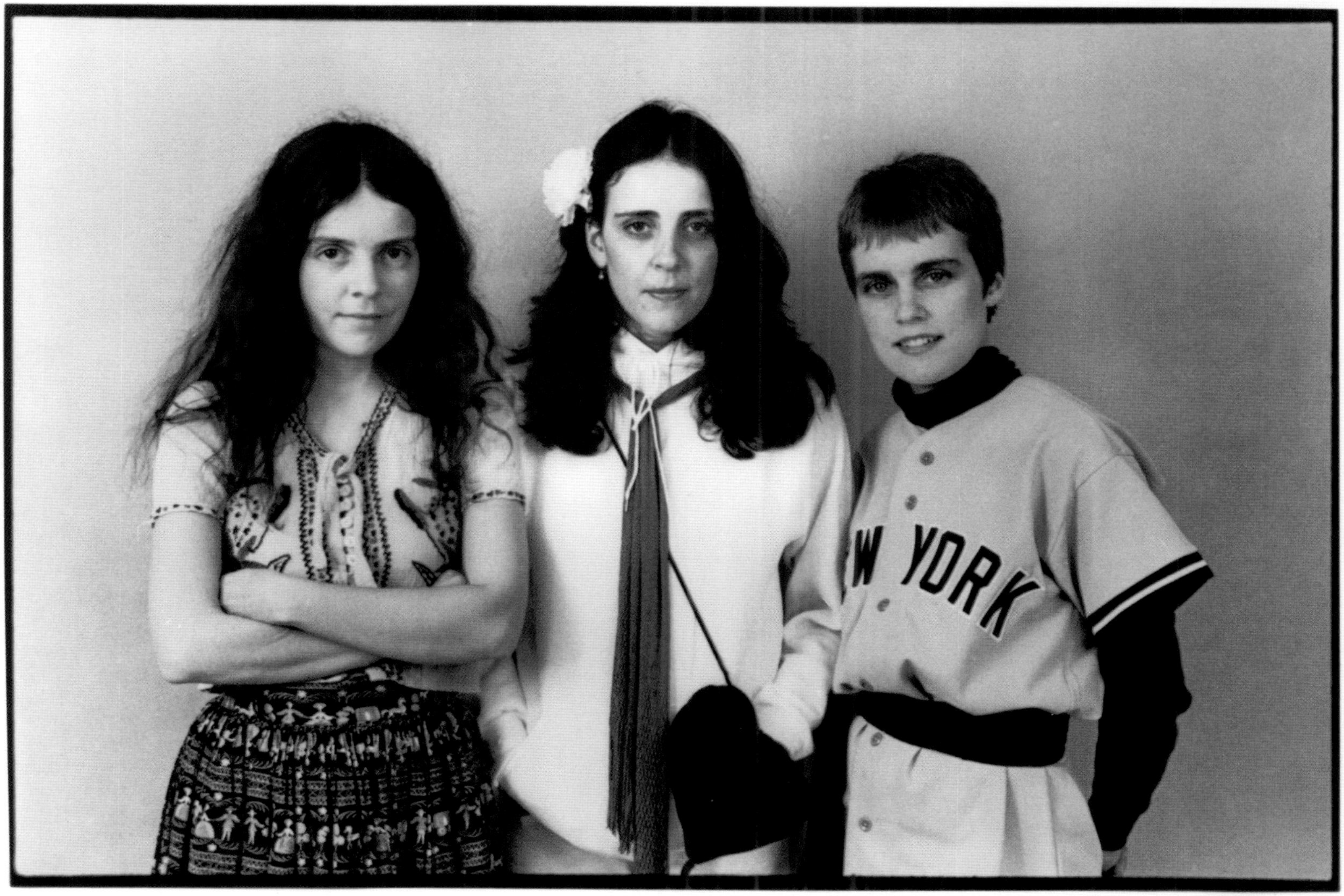

THE ROCHES

WARNER / REPRISE

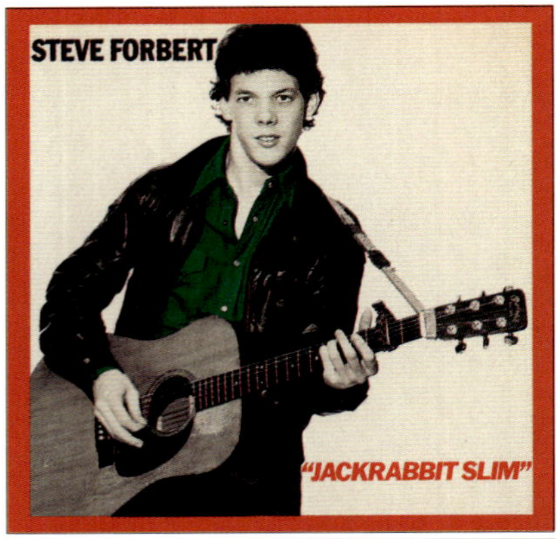

Billboard 200: *Jackrabbit Slim* (#20)
Billboard Hot 100: "Romeo's Tune" (#11);
"Say Goodbye to Little Jo" (#85)

The hit "Romeo's Tune," a song of giddy passion, put Steve Forbert on the map as a singer and songwriter.

UPON THE release of *Alive on Arrival,* his 1978 debut, Steve Forbert's following burgeoned. The songs were brilliant and Forbert's folksy evocation—a kid from Mississippi bringing his music to the big time—invited the inevitable Dylan-esque comparisons. In concert, he proved equally endearing with his inclusion of such rock classics as "Wooly Bully."

Jackrabbit Slim was a little more controversial, a more adventurous album than its predecessor, the main factor being the production of John Simon, who had worked with the Band. Some listeners found the addition of horns and background vocals an unforgivable intrusion on Forbert's songs. Forbert disagreed.

"He was my choice, and he helped me get what I wanted—if you want to 'blame' anybody about the record, it's me," he insisted. "But I couldn't put out a record I didn't like. I can only honestly express myself. There may be some people who wanted my second album to sound like my first, but I certainly didn't feel like it."

Forbert's compositions stood up under the varied arrangements, and "Romeo's Tune" became his signature song, a major charting single with a memorable piano melody. "Wait" and "The Sweet Love That You Give (Sure Goes a Long, Long Way)" were strong examples of his talent, though the material was not as autobiographical as *Alive on Arrival.* "I told the story of 'the kid comes to New York' on the first record—that was sort of a loose theme—and I just wanted to do something different."

"The Oil Song," a nifty tune about spillage and waste available as a bonus single, gave an indication that Forbert's future held some important songs.

"I don't read the newspapers that much," he said, "but now and then something will happen that I have a particular feeling about. Then I'm bound to write about it." ■

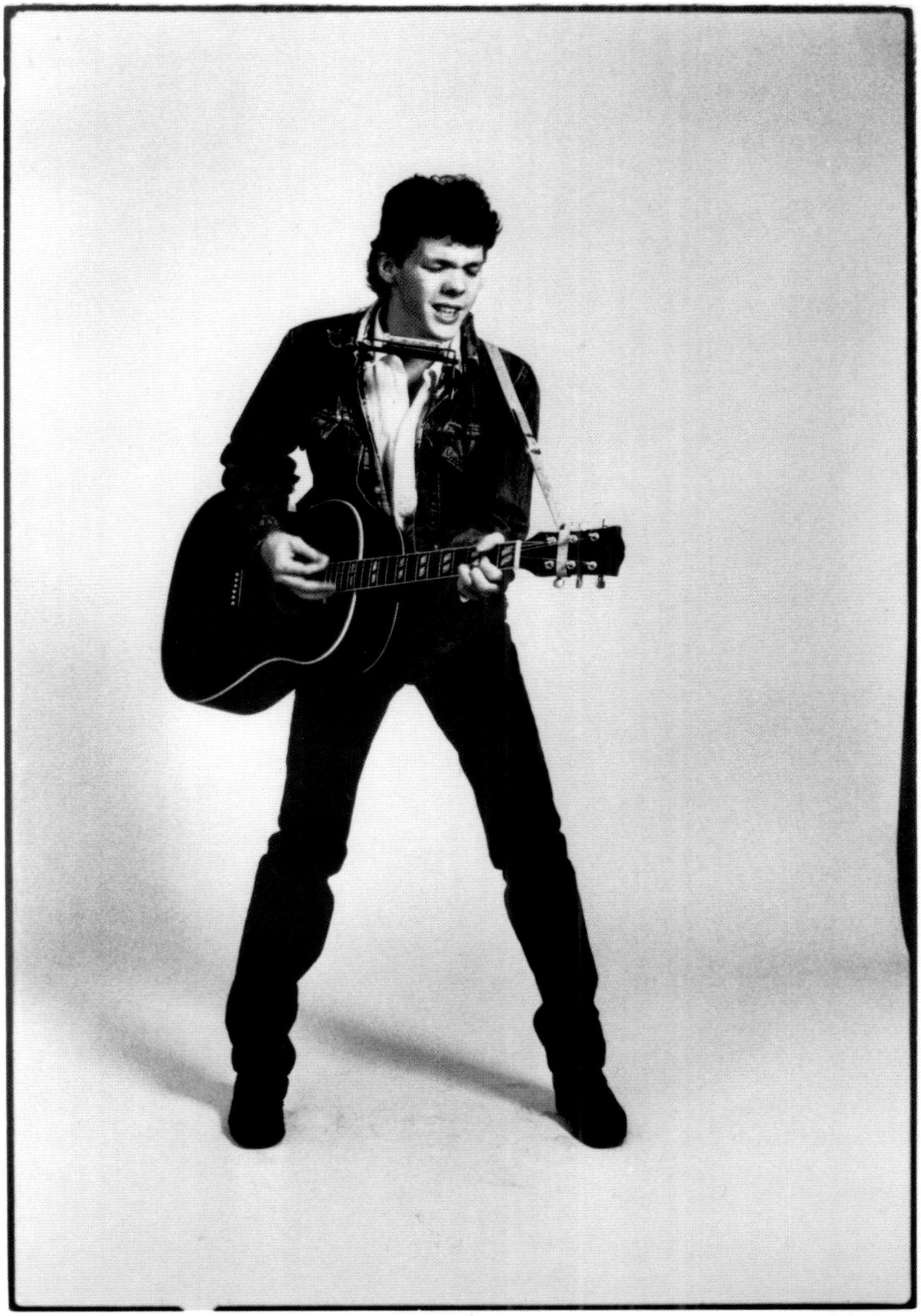

photo credit: David Gahr

NEMPEROR

STEVE FORBERT

EPIC PORTRAIT ASSOCIATED

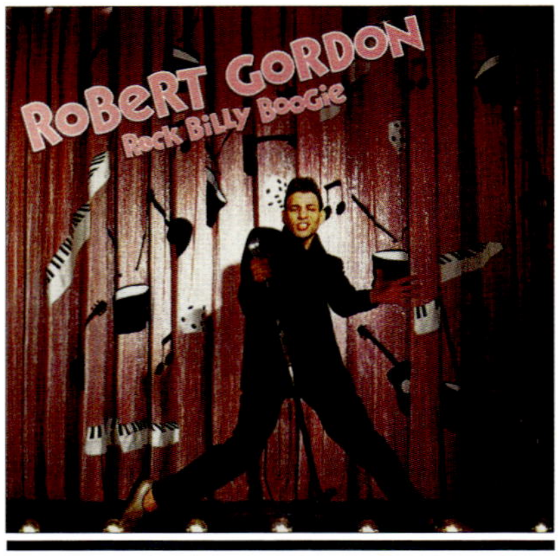

Billboard 200: *Rock Billy Boogie* (#106)

A pillar of the NYC downtown club scene, Robert Gordon revitalized the style and commitment to rockabilly.

AT THE age of nine, Robert Gordon heard Elvis Presley's debut RCA single, "Heartbreak Hotel." "I remember really flipping out," he said. "Ever since I was twelve or thirteen, I knew I was going to pursue a musical career. It occupied just about all my time, except for cars and motorcycles. My family didn't dig my black pegged pants, but I went through it, all through junior high and high school."

Influenced by rock 'n' roll, R&B and rockabilly, Gordon gained his first performing experience in his teens with school mates and pickup bands around Bethesda, Maryland, making his recording debut fronting a group called the Confidentials. One of his favorite spots was the Glen Echo Amusement Park, where he picked up stylistic influences from seeing Little Richard, guitar legend Link Wray and other big-name rockers.

"That's where I saw the rebel types—these cats with motorcycle boots and these chicks with beehive hairdos," he recalled. "Not that I emulated them, but it definitely left an impression. It was something different."

Moving to New York in 1970, Gordon spent several years as a normal citizen. He was introduced to the city's burgeoning rock scene, making his vinyl debut fronting Tuff Darts on the *Live at CBGB's* compilation album. His time with the punk band brought him together with producer Richard Gottehrer and resulted in his debut album and the single "Red Hot" in 1977, working with Wray. *Fresh Fish Special,* his second album, premiered "Fire," written by Bruce Springsteen.

Gordon then signed with RCA Records, the company that had helped make Presley a star, and released *Rock Billy Boogie,* which teamed him with ace London guitarist Chris Spedding. The album featured a rendition of Conway Twitty's "It's Only Make Believe" alongside a wild version of "Black Slacks" (rescuing a classic originally performed by Joe Bennett & the Sparkletones in 1957) and "The Catman," Gordon's evocative tribute to another early idol, Gene Vincent.

The mixing of styles garnered Gordon a following with rock, country and new music audiences. "Ultimately, I gravitated to the music I do best, which I guess you could call updated rockabilly," Gordon said. "I don't mind comparisons—that's flattering in a way—but some people think anyone who does this music is a Presley imitator, and that's just people who are uneducated. Vocally, I don't sound like Presley—it's just a feeling. I live this music. It's a part of me." ■

1

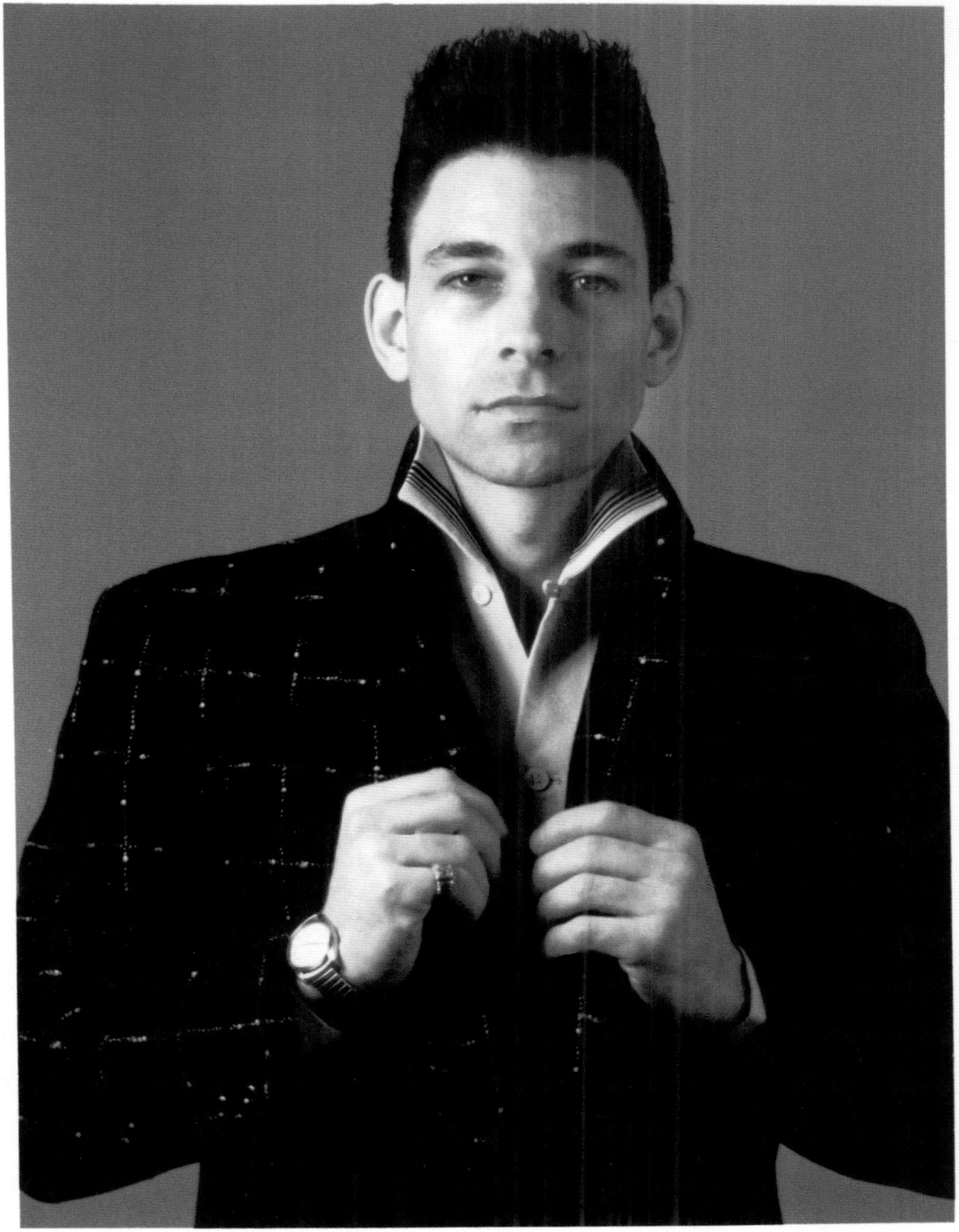

PHOTO BY:DAVID GAHR

ROBERT GORDON

RCA Records

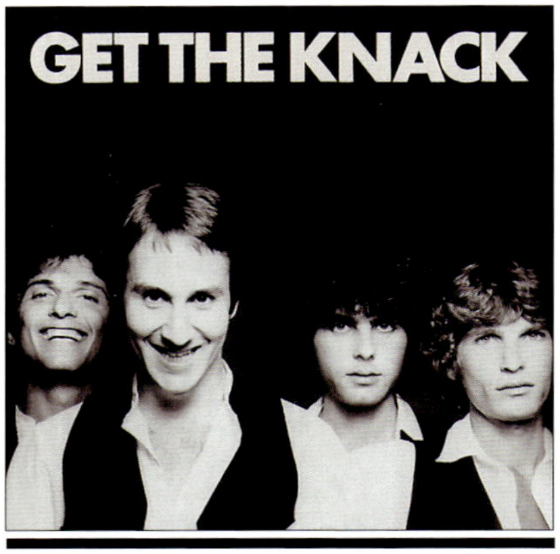

Billboard 200: *Get the Knack* (No. 1)
Billboard Hot 100: "My Sharona" (No. 1); "Good Girls Don't" (#11)

The Knack's rise to fame with "My Sharona," a worldwide No. 1 hit, also precipitated an immense backlash.

THE DISCO movement had a lock on the charts, but with the instant success of *Get the Knack* and the single "My Sharona," the Knack took power pop to the world, reviving the sturdy sense of songcraft rooted in the original British invasion of the mid-Sixties.

Yet the quartet generated a fair amount of controversy—detractors massed as quickly as supporters, and one disgruntled San Francisco artist invented a "Knuke the Knack" kit. All the negative feeling somehow caught up to the Knack.

"It's the end of the punk era," lead vocalist Doug Fieger observed. "You're not loved if you're not making a thumb-your-nose-at-somebody political statement, and everybody has to have a *raison d'etre*. Ours is, 'Enjoy pop music, have fun.'"

It was difficult for Fieger to appreciate on how many levels the Knack offended people. Musicians resented the group for its meteoric rise to the pinnacle of pop success—gold certification for *Get the Knack* took 13 days, platinum less than a month and final sales topped 4 million. "My Sharona" was *Billboard*'s No. 1 single of 1979.

The magnitude of the chart-climbing speed also shocked its creators—Fieger, lead guitarist Berton Averre, drummer Bruce Gary and bassist Prescott Niles. *Get the Knack* was famous within the record industry for its astounding economics. The album took just 11 days from start to final mix, costing a total of $18,000.

"Before we had our record deal, we were the darlings of the hip L.A. scene—they wrote about us, said we were great," Fieger said. "We went in the studio (with Blondie producer Mike Chapman) and recorded our live show for the first album, and the very same people listening to the very same music are slamming it because it sells."

Beatles lovers hated the *Meet the Beatles* imagery used to sell the Knack as a new Fab Four. For the photography on the back of *Get the Knack,* the foursome posed before television cameras in what looked like an outtake from *A Hard Day's Night.*

"We wanted to look different than the punk bands, but we had no money," Fieger said. "We couldn't afford anything but black pants and white shirts. The drummer's girlfriend had these skinny black ties that she said were hip, so we put those on. And that's literally as much thought as went into it. The rest was the record company's thing."

Feminists loathed the Knack's young-girls-as-objects bent. "Our album is filthy," Fieger allowed. "But it's done in fun. Some people say we're misogynous, which is absurd. Go listen to the Stones' 'Under My Thumb'—I've never written anything like that."

And the press perceived an edge of sleazy cynicism. "Some people feel that because we're clever, we couldn't possibly like the music that we play, that it's too simple. The reality is that we love it, we make it for ourselves. When I hear a hit on the radio, I respond. I don't care who it's by." ■

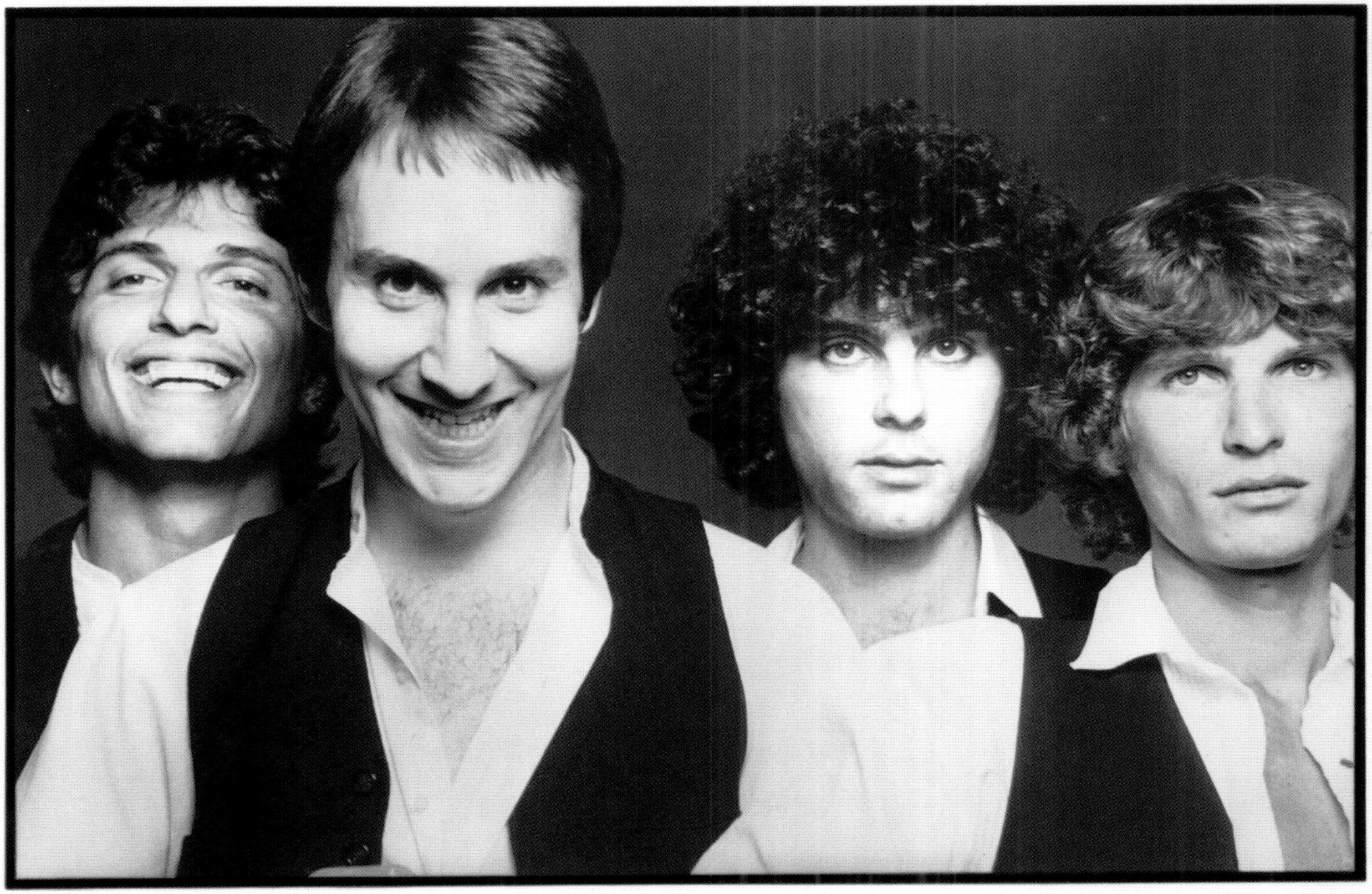

THE KNACK

PHOTO: RANDEE ST. NICHOLAS

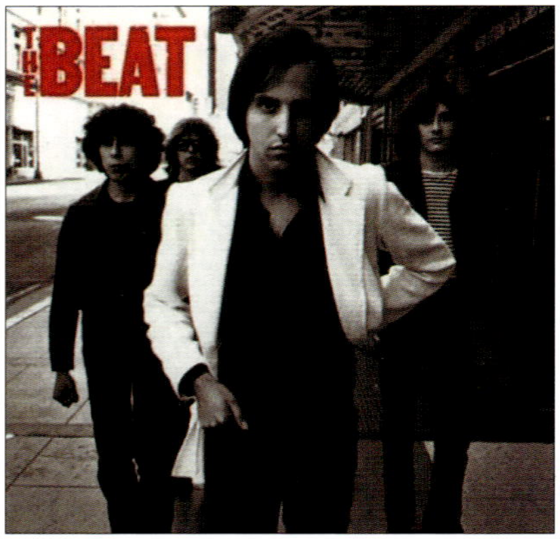

The Beat, led by Paul Collins, bowed with a superb self-titled album, a neglected gem of the power-pop genre.

WITH THE Eighties looming, new bands were emerging with a brand of rock that was unpretentious, wary of studio gimmickry and direct—energetic three-minute melodic odes to girls, alienation and frustration performed by the classic four-piece lineup. The Knack had the most influence and a rapid rise on the charts, but the Beat's underappreciated debut album was the power-pop pacesetter.

"What we're doing is not big deal to us—we're doing what comes naturally," singer, songwriter and rhythm guitarist Paul Collins said. "The difference is that we're not trying to be the stuff that's going on now. We think we are what should be now."

Collins formed the California quartet from the ashes of the Nerves (a band with Jack Lee and Peter Case—"Hanging on the Telephone," later a hit for Blondie, was included in their repertoire). Sharing the stage with bassist Steven Huff, guitarist Larry Whitman and drummer Mike Ruiz, Collins was a determined young frontman.

"Bands do showcases, and a vice president of a record company came to see us at a punk club that stunk of piss and beer," Collins said. "We had a crude P.A., and we wailed through a dozen songs. The audience was less than four feet from us. The guy turned to his lieutenant and said, 'Sign 'em.' The next thing we knew we were recording our album."

The Beat was produced by Bruce Botnick (of Doors, Rolling Stones and Buffalo Springfield renown) who oversaw the band's efficient recording sessions—five days for basic tracks and out. Whitman, a veteran of the L.A. scene at the age of 23, was proud that four tunes on the album were first takes.

Things looked good for the Beat. The band was on Columbia Records and managed by the legendary concert promoter Bill Graham. And the enthusiastic pulse of *The Beat* was impossible to resist on a cranked car radio. "Rock N Roll Girl," "Different Kind of Girl" and the vibrant "Don't Wait Up for Me" were instant classics—hard and fast, simple and satisfying. "The guys think the drummer can't keep good time, so Steve keeps the time with his bass, and that's how we get our sound," Collins cracked. "Who's to say what's good and what's bad?"

But the Knack's hype and arrogance was already getting under people's skin, and the backlash caught up with the Beat and other groups essaying the revved-up skinny-tie style (Shoes, 20/20, the Plimsouls). *The Beat* wasn't properly promoted, and the band was never able to crack the Top 40, but the album stood as an inspirational chapter of pop-rock history. ■

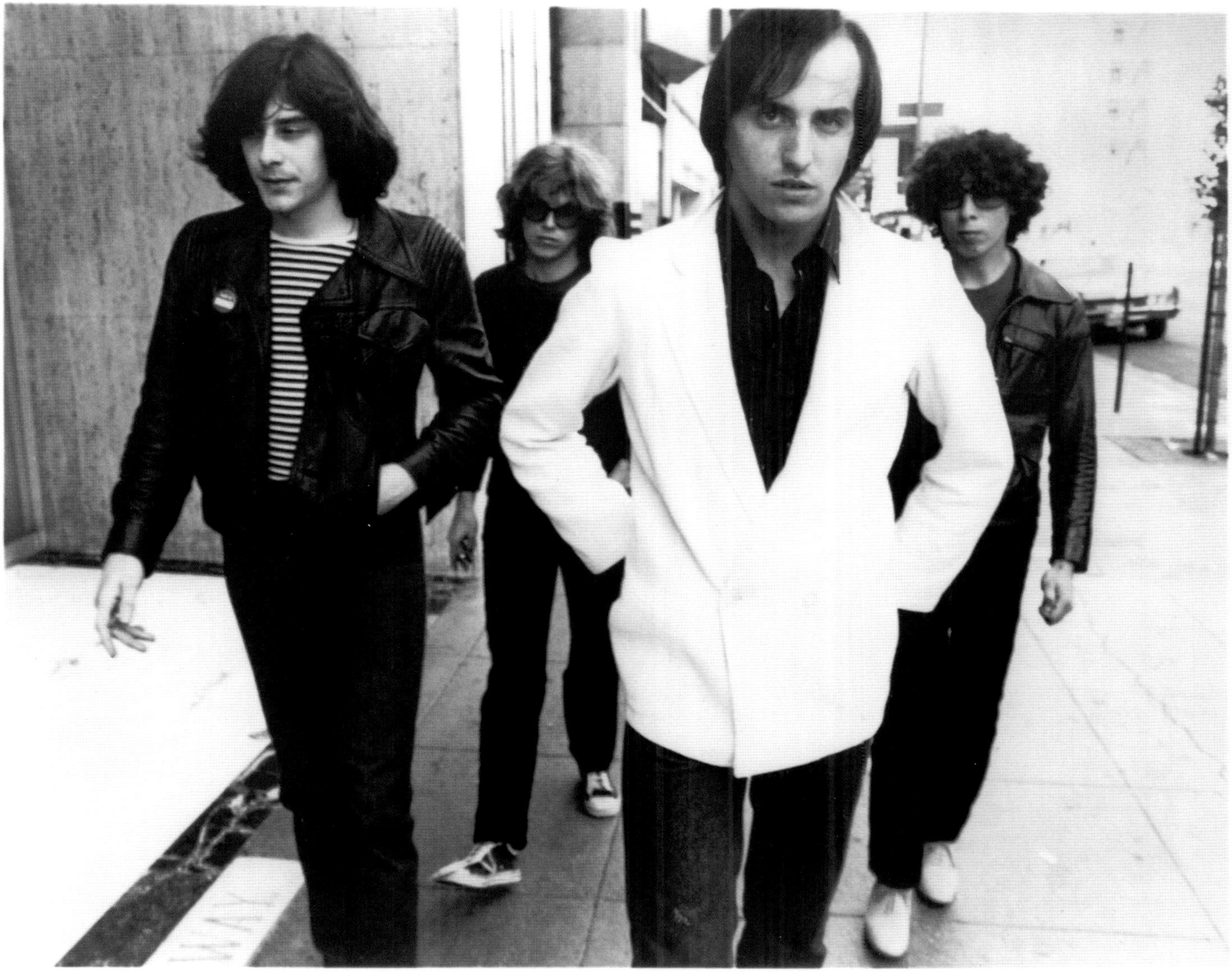

BILL GRAHAM MANAGEMENT

wolfgang

THE BEAT

Columbia

7909

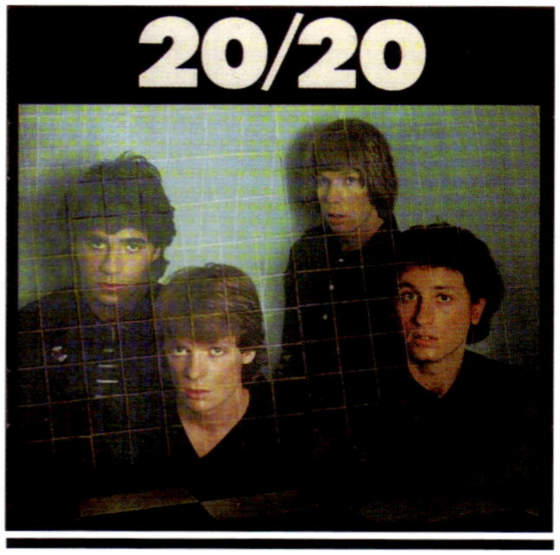

Billboard 200: *20/20* (#138)

"Yellow Pills" emerged as the prime track from 20/20's first album, a casual anthem of the power-pop scene.

A NEW energy was emanating from the Los Angeles music community, as a lively club scene accommodated an abundance of weariless local bands—including 20/20, a quartet delivering forthright, tightly constructed songs.

Bassist Ron Flynt and guitarist Steve Allen, boyhood friends from Tulsa, had been cultivating their skills in a spate of Top 40 cover bands.

"We played all the teen deals, 'Gloria' and 'Louie, Louie,' and during the college years, whatever the frats would buy, from ZZ Top and Yes to Deep Purple and the Doobie Brothers," Allen recalled. "In Oklahoma, it's not like you are a band playing your own original material. You're just a musician who plays at a club."

"The scene there was really discouraging," Flynt agreed. "The bars didn't believe a band could come in and make a crowd like original stuff because it just never happened. Nobody even thought about it. For us to see it happen in L.A. was astounding."

Inspired by the success of Dwight Twilley and Phil Seymour, similarly minded Oklahomans who had scored big in 1975 with "I'm On Fire," Allen headed for Hollywood in early 1977 and struck up a friendship with drummer Mike Gallo. Flynt made the journey west six months later, and 20/20 was born.

"We had a definite concept of what we wanted to do from the beginning," Gallo remembered. "We wanted the energy of a punk band, but the songs which the punk bands at the time didn't have. We were definitely influenced by the melodies of the Sixties."

Chris Silagyi joined the band as a rhythm guitarist and keyboardist for 1979's *20/20*, which decisively demonstrated the lean propulsion of the group's three-minute pop-rock material. The album, ably produced by Earle Mankey, starred the single "Cheri," the brilliantly straightfoward "Remember the Lightning" and the signature "Yellow Pills."

"We all write, but we're coming from the same approach," Gallo noted. "We're all different, but we're all trying for the same thing—which I guess is why it's worked."

Gallo was let go by the band not long after the release of the album. ■

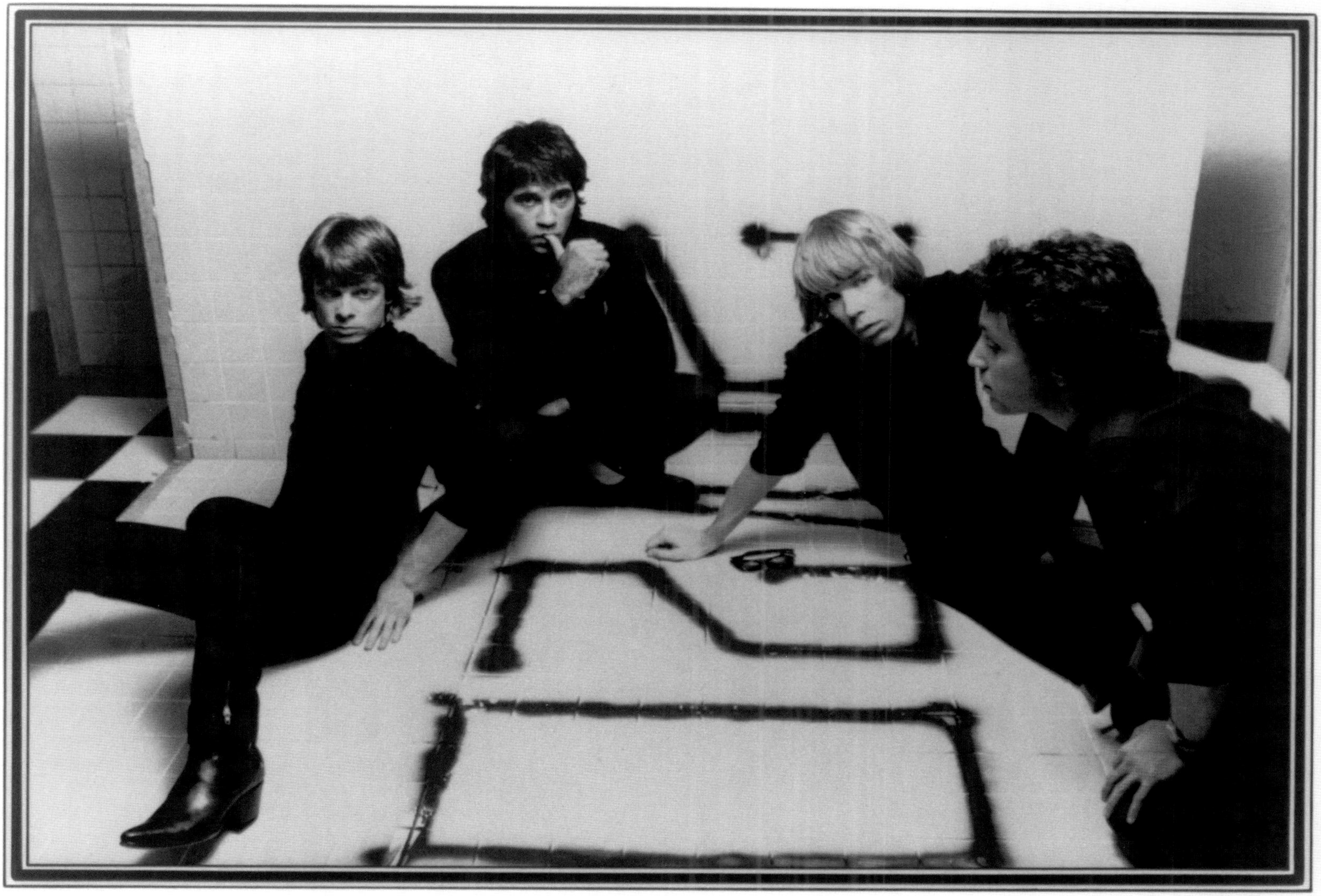

STEVE ALLEN MIKE GALLO RON FLYNT CHRIS SILAGYI

20/20

EPA
EPIC PORTRAIT ASSOCIATED

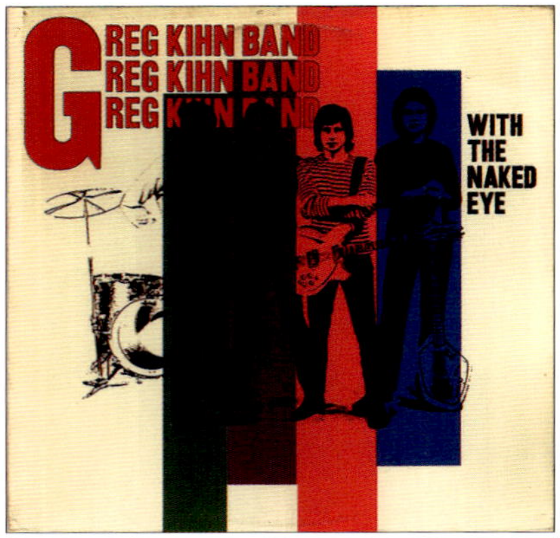

Billboard 200: *With the Naked Eye* (#114)

Greg Kihn Band's *With the Naked Eye* album upheld the frontman's infectious enthusiasm for music and life.

BASED IN Berkeley, California, the Greg Kihn Band had built a reputation in Europe as being America's best "West Coast band"—that, even though Kihn was reared in Baltimore.

"It's heavy industrial back there—you want to get out so bad that you'll even sing to get away," he said. "Kids are getting tired of foreign bands—they're ready for some homegrown heroes."

Kihn aspired for the group to be accepted in the tradition of great American bands like Creedence Clearwater Revival. Many observers thought he would be a star if he signed with a major label. But he continued to record for Berserkley Records, a small independent company that took pride in its unorthodox methods.

"We're like the Ma & Pa drug store that's competing with Safeway," Kihn said. "But we don't care. Matthew Kaufman isn't even called the president of the label—he's the 'reigning looney.' All of our success has come from going against the grain and being blatantly maverick. All of our fans are totally honest, because we've never had an ad campaign or a lot of hype."

The material on *With the Naked Eye* was inspired, notably Bruce Springsteen's "Rendezvous," written especially for Kihn ("He taught me about gargling with salt water—it's the best thing for your throat"), and a cover of Jonathan Richman's classic ode to driving "Roadrunner." Despite some tinny production, the record glimmered with Kihn's conviction.

"All of our albums sound like demos, but people can listen to them and get a sense of our history, hear what we've done and what we're doing now. We're going to be recording for a decade, so it's good for people to know that we've got plenty of room to grow. With bands like the Knack and Tom Petty coming up, there's a real scene starting to happen again. And I want to be on top of it—I don't want to be the Blues Magoos of the Eighties." ■

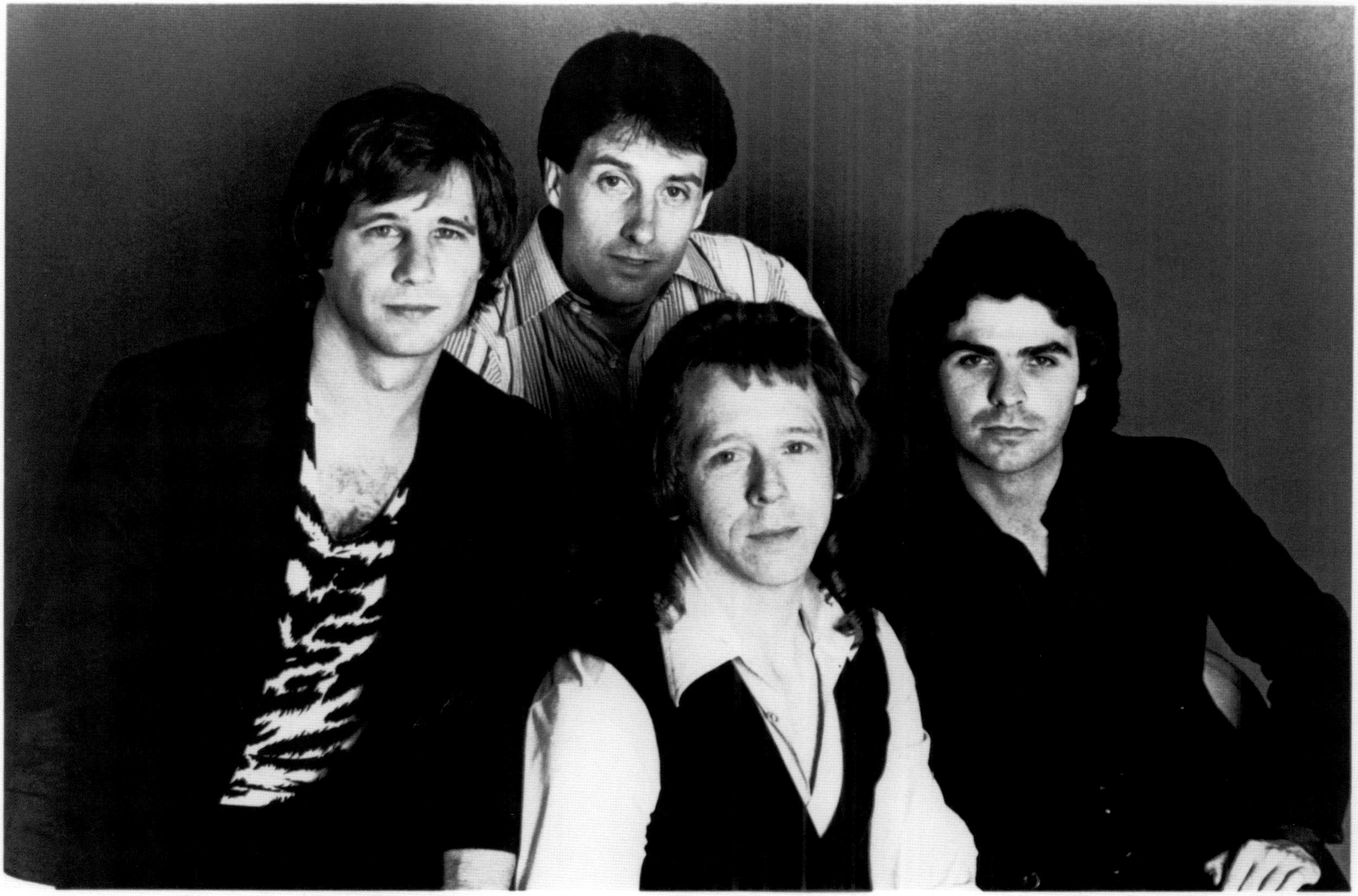

THE GREG KIHN BAND

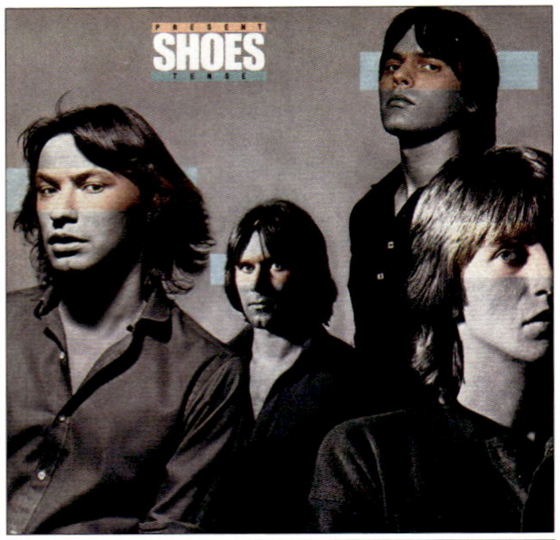

Billboard 200: *Present Tense* (#50)
Billboard Hot 100: "Too Late" (#75)

A DIY ethic and a cult following were the catalysts in getting Shoes signed to a major-label record contract.

MUCH OF the Seventies had been spent in adulation of old musical heroes instead of seeking new ones. But 1979 brought a commitment to young groups, and the exciting atmosphere gave record companies the desire to take chances on some intriguing bands. Shoes had gained attention with *Black Vinyl Shoes,* a homemade record that garnered rave reviews and fan letters from across the world.

Surprisingly, the Beatles-esque youthful pop on the album had been recorded on a four-track machine in vocalist and guitarist Jeff Murphy's living room. The four members of Shoes had no idea that a market existed for their music outside of Zion, Illinois, a religious "dry town" with no theaters or pool halls.

"Our only input was the radio," Murphy explained. "Our influences were middle-class stuff—Beatles, Stones, Who. We didn't know about any underground or new wave movement. We'd just always wanted to make music, so we started making tapes."

Shoes' proclivity for pop stemmed from the youth of its members at the time the Beatles first crossed the Atlantic. "I was in elementary school," Murphy allowed, "but that's why we were so heavily influenced—they were like the gospel." That type of song style got lost in the late Sixties and early Seventies, however. "Shoes was formed as a reaction against that—nobody was doing the music we liked," Murphy recalled. "Everything on the radio was crap. Heavy metal came in and destroyed melody. It was depressing."

The pipe dream started with Murphy's brother, John, and school chum Gary Klebe, who sank money from their jobs to sink into hi-fi equipment and stereo components. In 1974 they started making tapes. "Nobody played an instrument, so we just borrowed—saxes, autoharps, anything we could get our hands on, just to make noise. We bought rummage-sale guitars and did everything piecemeal, learning each part as we went along. If you knew two chords, you wrote a song that had two chords."

Drummer Skip Meyer joined up and the band grew more adept at its homemade recordings. Shoes disdained the Chicago-area live-music circuit—Murphy put the total number of Shoes concerts at a mere 30. "Why should we have played in a club where people were trying to pick each other up when we could spend the same amount of time making a tape, trying to get it on the radio and reaching hundreds more people?"

The tapes finally paid off. The group packaged *Black Vinyl Shoes* with a lyric sheet, photos and a t-shirt transfer and distributed it independently, tapping them into the expanding underground market. Shoes figured the press response would land them a record deal, but nothing happened. The band recorded more demos with no response.

Then Elektra Records came calling with a contract in hand—ironically, having just heard *Black Vinyl Shoes.* Producer Mike Stone, the engineer on most Queen albums, holed the band up in England to record *Present Tense.* The album yielded the minor hit single "Too Late," and Shoes rode the rollercoaster of big-time record management. "At least we're not stale," Murphy insisted. "We're *scared*—but that's what makes it fun." ■

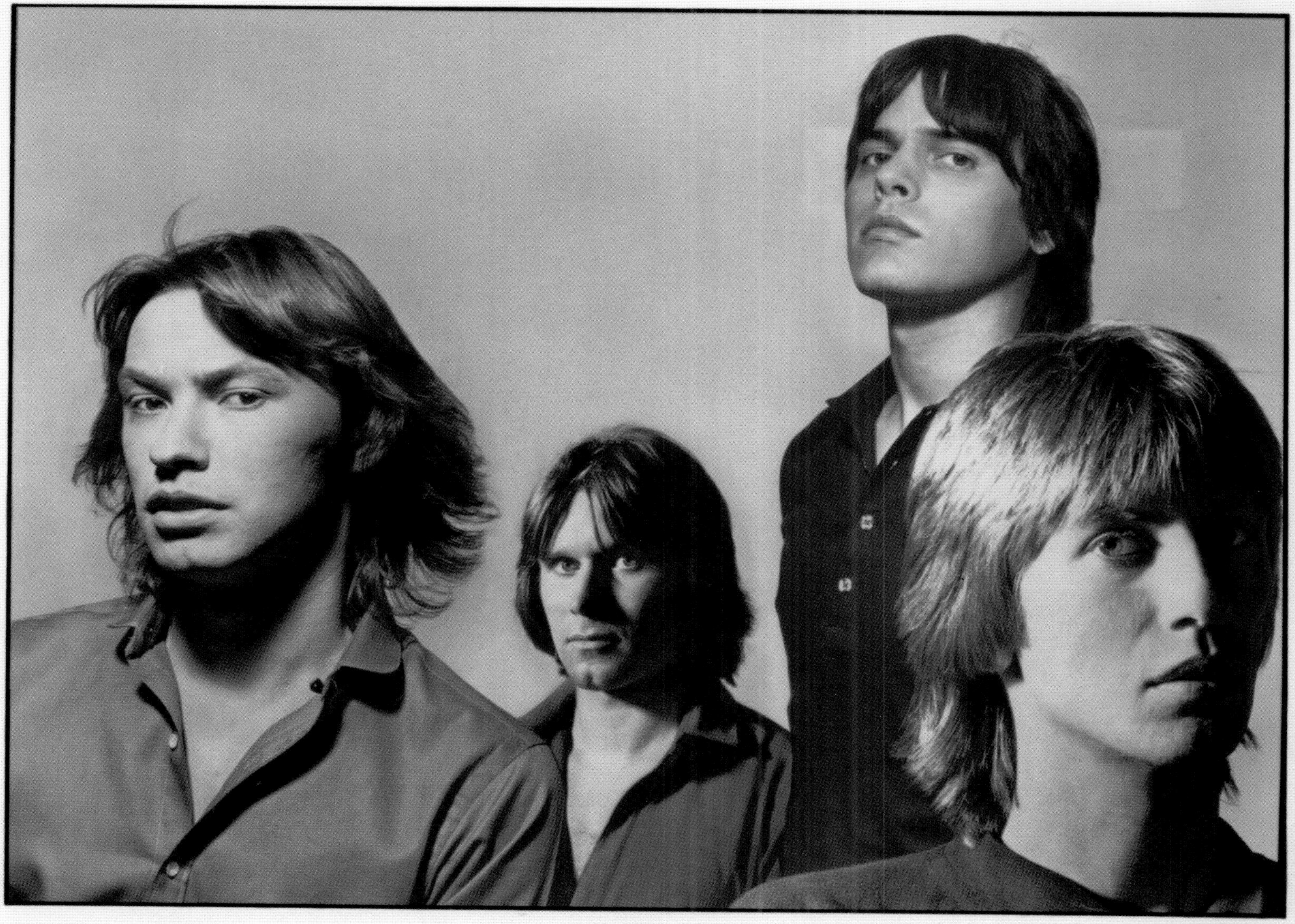

Photo Credit: ELLIOT GILBERT/1979

Jeff Murphy Skip Meyer Gary Klebe John Murphy

SHOES

elektra

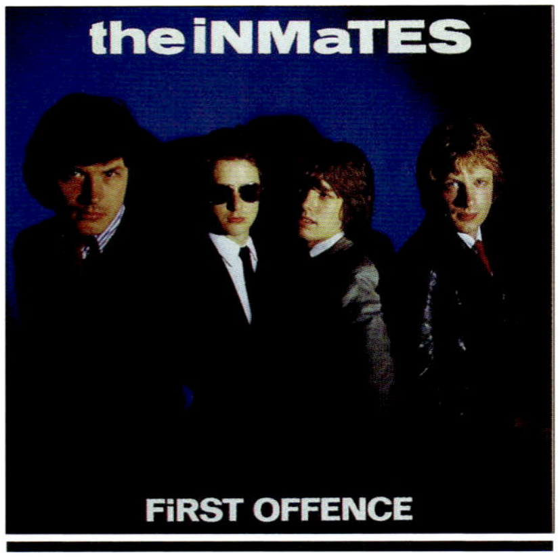

Billboard 200: *First Offence* (#49)
Billboard Hot 100: "Dirty Water" (#51)

The Inmates broke out in the US with their version of the Standells' "Dirty Water," a garage-rock hit in 1965.

IT MIGHT have been a new wave, but it was the same old ocean. The Inmates were the latest act from England to make a splash in America, but despite the newness of the product, the band members' roots—the R&B music of the Fifties and early Sixties—were as old as they were.

"It's funny that we're not so well-known in England," lead singer Bill Hurley stated. "It's more difficult there—there are so many different types of bands playing all sorts of music that it's harder to break through. That's especially true for a basic R&B band—now you've got a Mod revival, the usual heavy-metal bands and the ska and reggae comeback. We're sort of in a minority."

In America, acceptance had come easier. *First Offense,* the Inmates' debut album, began a buzz as a cover version of the Standells' classic "Dirty Water" garnered heavy radio airplay, challenging the raw, urgent sound of the early Rolling Stones with Hurley's perfect Jagger-esque vocal. Not too shabby for a group composed of guys in their mid-20s who had never been in a studio before.

"We just played in pubs starting around March of 1978," Hurley explained. "We found each other through ads in the music papers—no one was interested in doing R&B. We all shared an infatuation with that music since we were growing up. 'Dirty Water' is only one of the types of stuff we like. I'm particularly fond of Stax/Volt Black music and Elvis Presley and Eddie Cochran types of singing."

Record companies in England started showing up at gigs, and "Dirty Water" was released on an independent label. The lineup—Hurley, Ben Donelly (bass), Peter Gunn (lead guitar), Tony Oliver (rhythm guitar) and Jim Russell (drums)—stabilized after the sessions. The band toured the States and drummed up interest in "Dirty Water."

"It's surprising that America has welcomed us so quickly," Hurley noted. "But there's no question in our minds—whether or not we're successful, we'd still be playing R&B." ■

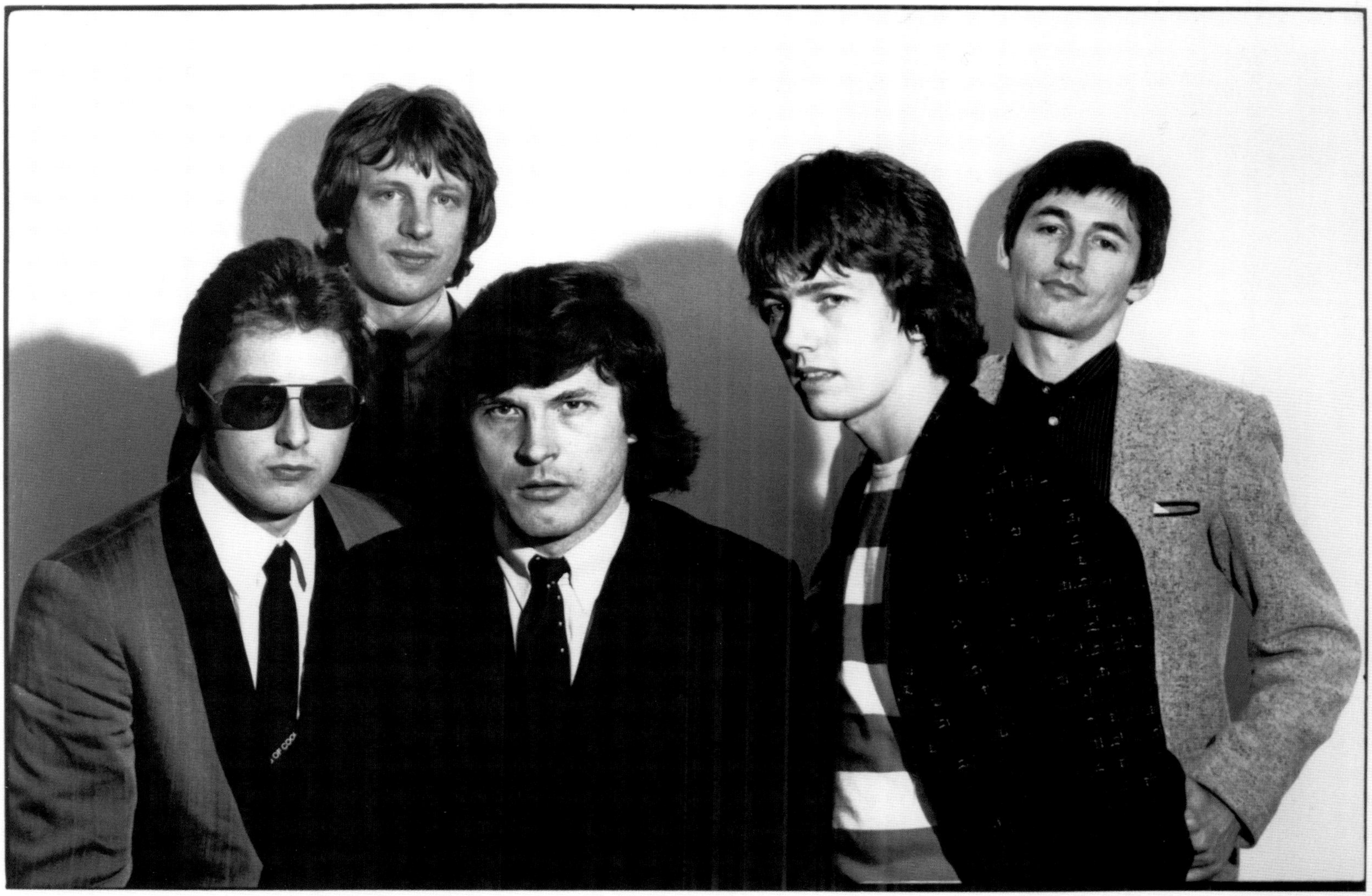

BEN DONELLY PETER GUNN BILL HURLEY TONY OLIVER JIM RUSSELL

THE INMATES

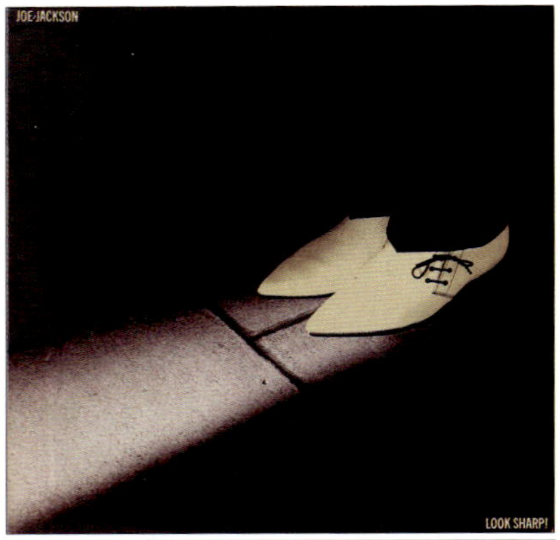

Billboard 200: *Look Sharp!* (#20)
Billboard Hot 100: "Is She Really Going Out with Him?" (#21)

The singular hit "Is She Really Going Out with Him?" smartly established Joe Jackson in the angry-young-Brit camp.

FALLING IN love with music as a child, Joe Jackson taught himself piano. At 18 he won a scholarship and undertook formal musical training at the Royal Academy of Music in London. By the time he graduated, he'd become disillusioned with the prospects for a "serious" composer and plunged into the rock world, seeking a suitable direction for his abilities.

Alongside Elvis Costello and Graham Parker, Jackson was designated a member of England's new wave explosion, making a name with his debut album, *Look Sharp!* Energy and exactness characterized such catchy classics as "One More Time," "Got the Time" and "Sunday Papers." The derisive "Is She Really Going Out with Him?" made an impact on the charts.

Jackson called his music "spiv rock"—a *spiv* defined as "a shady character who avoids honest work and lives by his wits"—reflecting his self-seriousness. Skinny and balding, favoring pin-striped suits and polka-dot ties, he came off as a brash, gifted, surly, inquisitive sad sack.

"If I didn't make music, I don't know what I'd do—I'm not good at anything else," he explained cheerlessly. "Anyway, whatever I'd be doing, it probably wouldn't be anything legal. It should be possible to write a song about absolutely anything—I'm surprised at how relatively few people see it that way. People have said that I'm bitter about relationships in my songs. That's not true. I just try to look at things from different angles, to find out what really goes on between people instead of just using clichés." ■

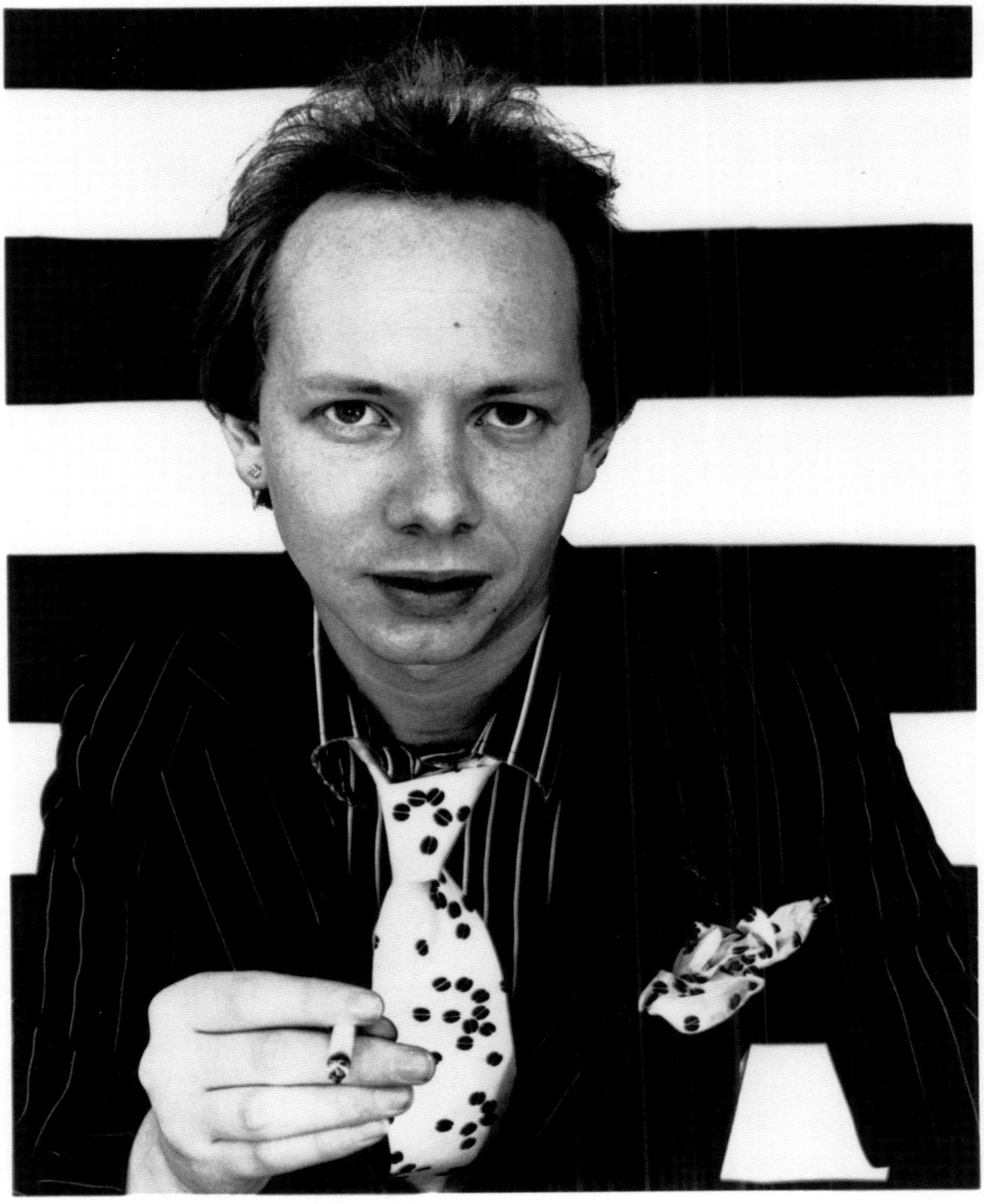

JOE JACKSON

A&M RECORDS

Printed in U.S.A.

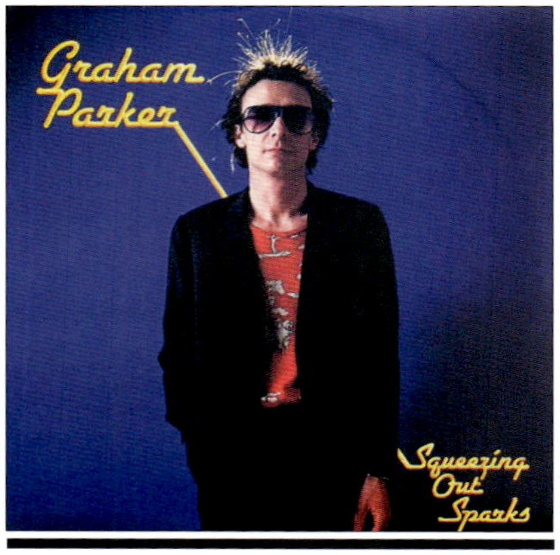

Billboard 200: *Squeezing Out Sparks* (#40)

Graham Parker coalesced the working-class tensions of punk to the emotion of R&B on *Squeezing Out Sparks*.

WITH 1976'S *Howlin' Wind*, a pre-punk album that laid the angry-young-man groundwork for Elvis Costello and Joe Jackson, Britain's Graham Parker had exploded on to the rock scene.

"At 25, the eventfulness of that year was amazing," the former gas-station attendant said. "My thought was, 'What can I do now? Every song seems so precious and hard-earned.' I thought it was all like a stored-up energy that would be released and then dissipated."

Parker delivered another of the era's most praised albums, *Heat Treatment*. Unfortunately, no record company saw fit to promote his passionate, urgent vision in the US. He left his former label with a pointed swan song—"Mercury Poisoning."

And then came the classic. The wiry singer and songwriter fronted the Rumour, a razor-sharp band of pub-rock all-stars headed by guitarist Brinsley Schwarz. That unit recorded the exhilarating *Squeezing Out Sparks,* acclaimed as the most intense pairing since Bob Dylan teamed up with the Band. The raw edge and drive of "Local Girls" and "Discovering Japan" made Parker a hit with critics and won him a wider audience in the US. Some tracks—the strongly stated "You Can't Be Too Strong," about abortion—dealt with universal matters. "To me, it is like desperation to make music," Parker said. "It's life and death." ■

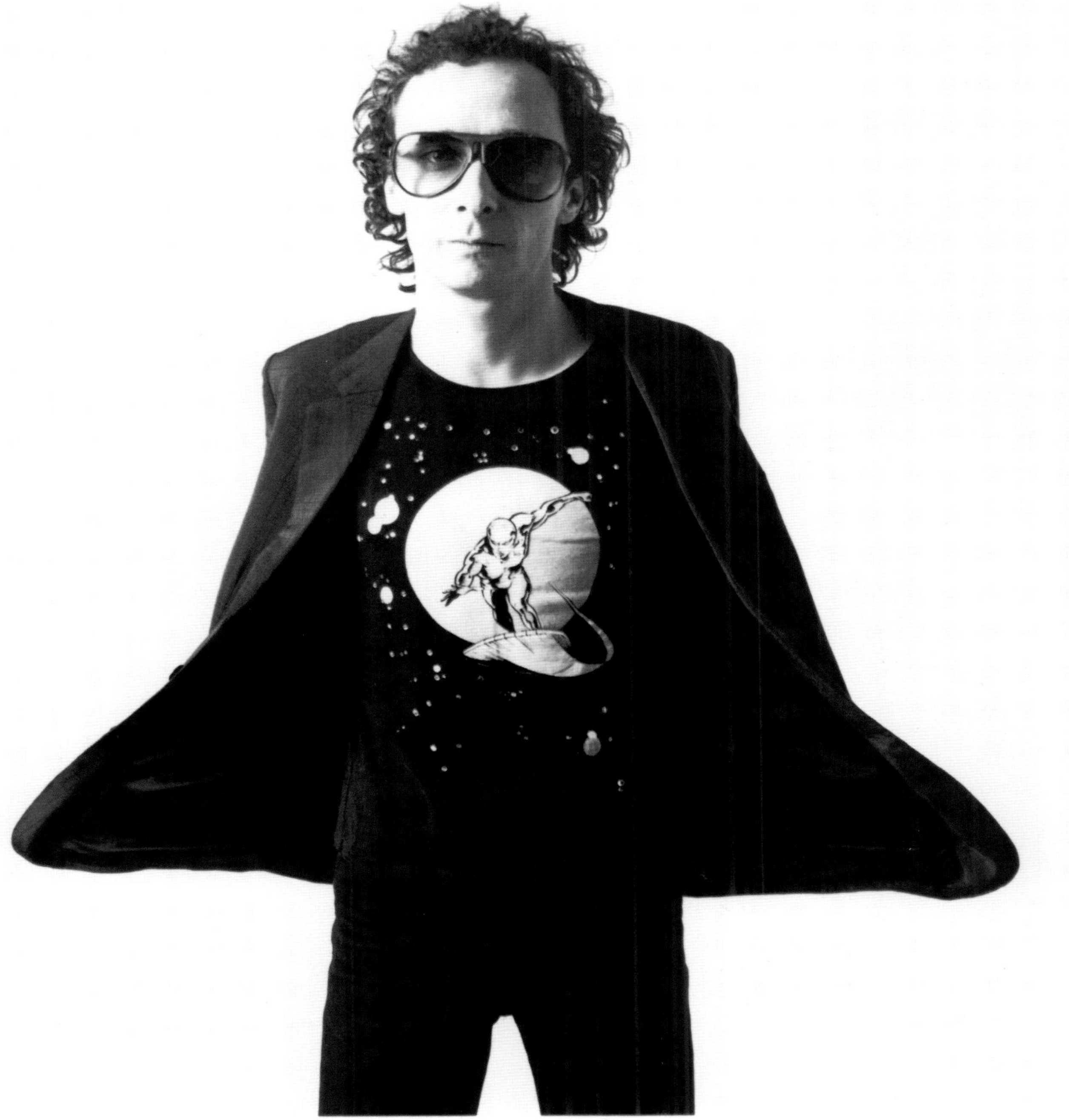

A.R.S.E.
MANAGEMENT INC.
157 WEST 57

Graham Parker

ARISTA™

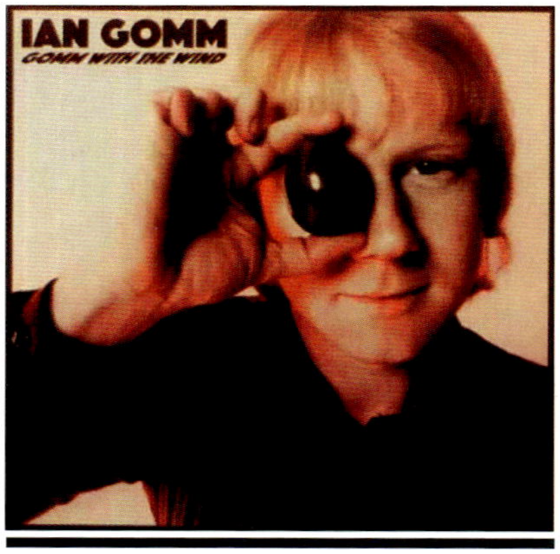

Billboard 200: *Gomm with the Wind* (#104)
Billboard Hot 100: "Hold On" (#18)

Ian Gomm's effortless "Hold On," a full-sounding British production, served to bring his career up to date.

IAN GOMM got his start as the singer and rhythm guitarist with the seminal English pub-rock band Brinsley Schwarz, a group that boasted as alumni new wave pioneer Nick Lowe (Gomm co-wrote Lowe's hit "Cruel to Be Kind") and guitarist Brinsley Schwarz and keyboardist Bob Andrews of the Rumour. The band blended rock, country and music-hall exuberance to become one of the hottest cult favorites of the early Seventies.

"The pub-rock scene was quite the thing in London for a couple of years," Gomm explained. "It was a mini-training ground—even Elvis Costello played in a pub-rock band. The idea was that you'd go into a pub and play all night. Everybody went to have a look and it seemed to work well. The band just got paid from the drinks sold at the bar. The pub owners saw that their places were filling up, and they were making more money. Within a year there were 20 or 30 pubs around London doing it."

Yet none of the pub-rock groups were able to transcend the local scene and make successful records. "At the time, the record companies were more into Uriah Heep," Gomm said with a laugh. Brinsley Schwarz had attempted to crack a bigger market with an East Coast tour of America, which turned out to be a disastrously overhyped fiasco. Gomm joined the group following the debacle. "I am completely guiltless," he chuckled. "I just had to share the consequences."

Brinsley Schwarz served as a vehicle for Lowe's tunes, and Gomm's material didn't surface. The band broke up in 1975, and Gomm retreated to the Cambrian Mountains of Wales, where he found work as a studio engineer. It turned out to be the turning point of his career. "I did it just to learn that side of the business, really," he explained. "But luckily, not many people came up there in the mountains. I had a lot of time on my hands to muck around and make demos. It got me back playing again."

Gomm signed with Albion Records in England and released his album (entitled *Summer Holiday* there), which didn't sell well. But Albion signed an American distribution deal with Stiff Records, and the retitled *Gomm with the Wind* blew into the US. Stiff was the most notorious of the new wave companies. Elvis Costello was the first act signed (he had left), and such charming eccentrics as Ian Dury & the Blockheads and Lene Lovich had sustained the label in its native England.

Of course, Gomm's mainstream sound shared little with the English-style humor of the other Stiff artists. Yet he didn't find his association with the label incongruous. "'Melodious' is a good way to describe my music," he explained. "I was Stiff's insurance policy."

With "Hold On" climbing the charts, Gomm found the perfect antidote to any image problems—a song that sounded irresistible over the airwaves. He was content to see his career finally taking shape, supporting Dire Straits on that band's tour. "It's better than it has been in the last few years," he admitted. "Now I could have a gripe at everybody, eh? No—I just want a dishwasher." ■

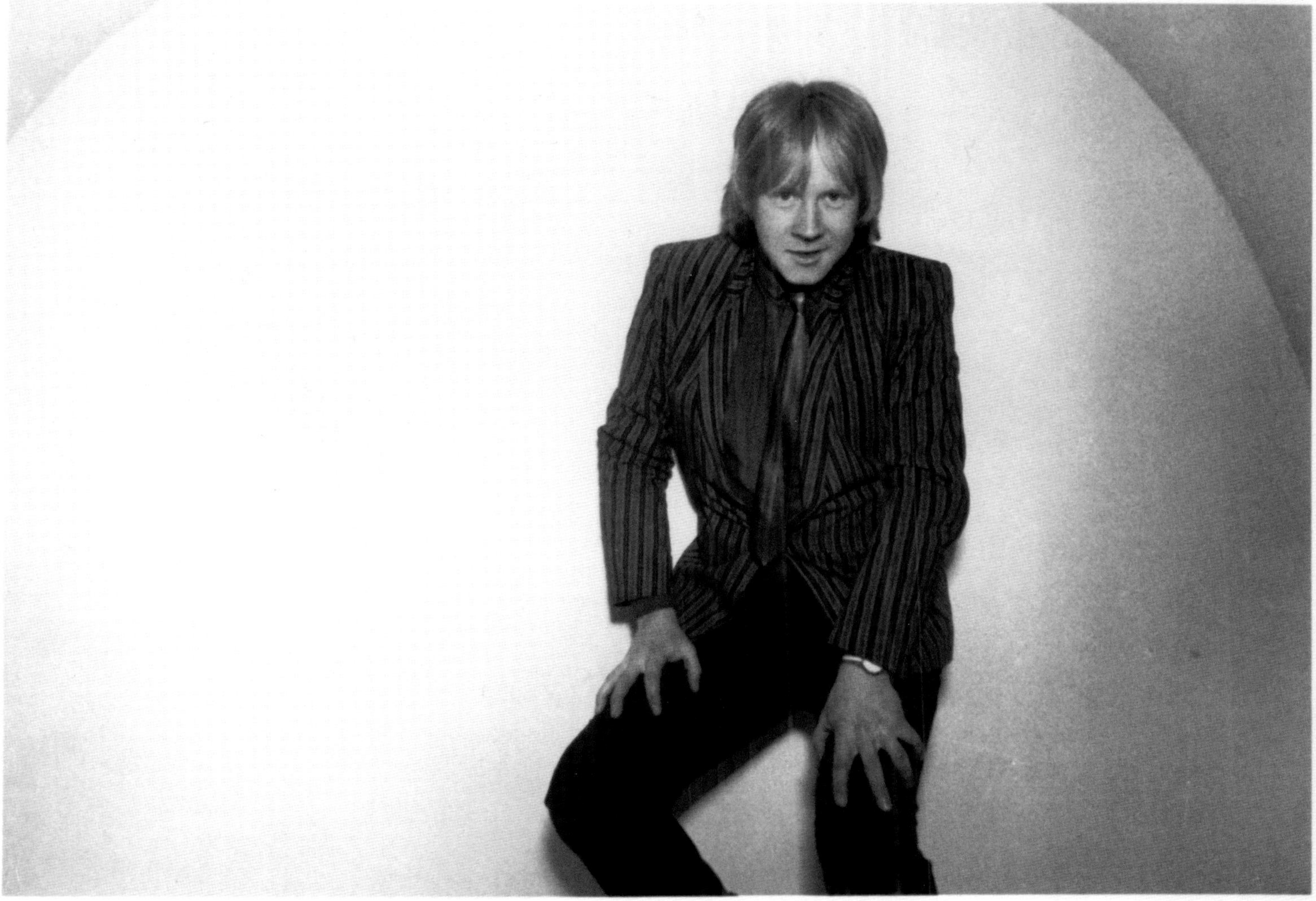

IAN GOMM

GOMM WITH THE WIND

STIFF · Epic

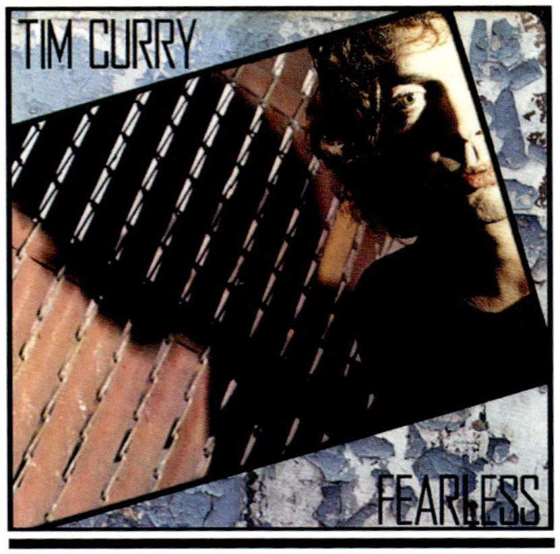

Billboard 200: *Fearless* (#53)
Billboard Hot 100: "I Do the Rock" (#91)

On the cheeky "I Do the Rock," protean performer **Tim Curry** played pop star and garnered rotation on MTV.

SOME ARTISTS approached the rock 'n' roll creative process from the outside, using the form as a vehicle for their own peculiar vision. Tim Curry's major successes had been as an actor—the garter-belted Dr. Frank-N-Furter in the 1972 cult movie sensation *The Rocky Horror Picture Show*, as well as creating the title role in a six-part BBC production on the life of Shakespeare. But he had been bitten by the rock 'n' roll bug.

"It's always been a matter of singing or acting for me," he explained. "I just waited for control of my singing career before pursuing it seriously, and the acting parts came naturally in the meantime. But I've got the fever bad now, I'm afraid. I wouldn't miss going out on the road. I get terrible stage withdrawal, anyway."

The London-based Curry had surrounded himself with some stellar musical talent. The co-producers of *Fearless* were Michael Kamen and Dick Wagner. Kamen had directed the fortunes of the New York Rock Ensemble and worked with David Bowie as musical director. Wagner had made a name as one of rock's premiere session guitarists via his work with Alice Cooper. Together they gave credence to Curry's excursion into rock music.

The trio met during the recording of Curry's debut release, *Read My Lips*. Curry remembered it as "confusing—it was a very expensive album that changed style from song to song. It was so diverse that I think it discouraged people."

Yet a subsequent tour changed Curry's outlook and convinced him to start writing material as opposed to covering other people's songs. *Fearless* was the result, a more accessible and intriguing recording than its predecessor. David Sanborn's saxophone danced over the single "I Do the Rock," an excellent example of Curry's ability to incorporate wit and intelligence into a melodic statement.

"It's definitely a New York album," he stated. "It's about America and money—cheap shots at expensive targets, I'm fond of saying."

The considerable *Rocky Horror* following had given Curry some built-in support, but he maintained that his concerts reflected none of the campy outrageousness of his 1972 film performance.

"Nobody comes expecting to see Frank-N-Furter, and if they do, they're going to be disappointed. I've turned down a lot of acting offers to work on this, and it is starting to pay off." He laughed after hearing the seriousness of his words. "I behave quite badly out there, however. No sense standing behind a microphone with a gardenia in your hair, right?" ■

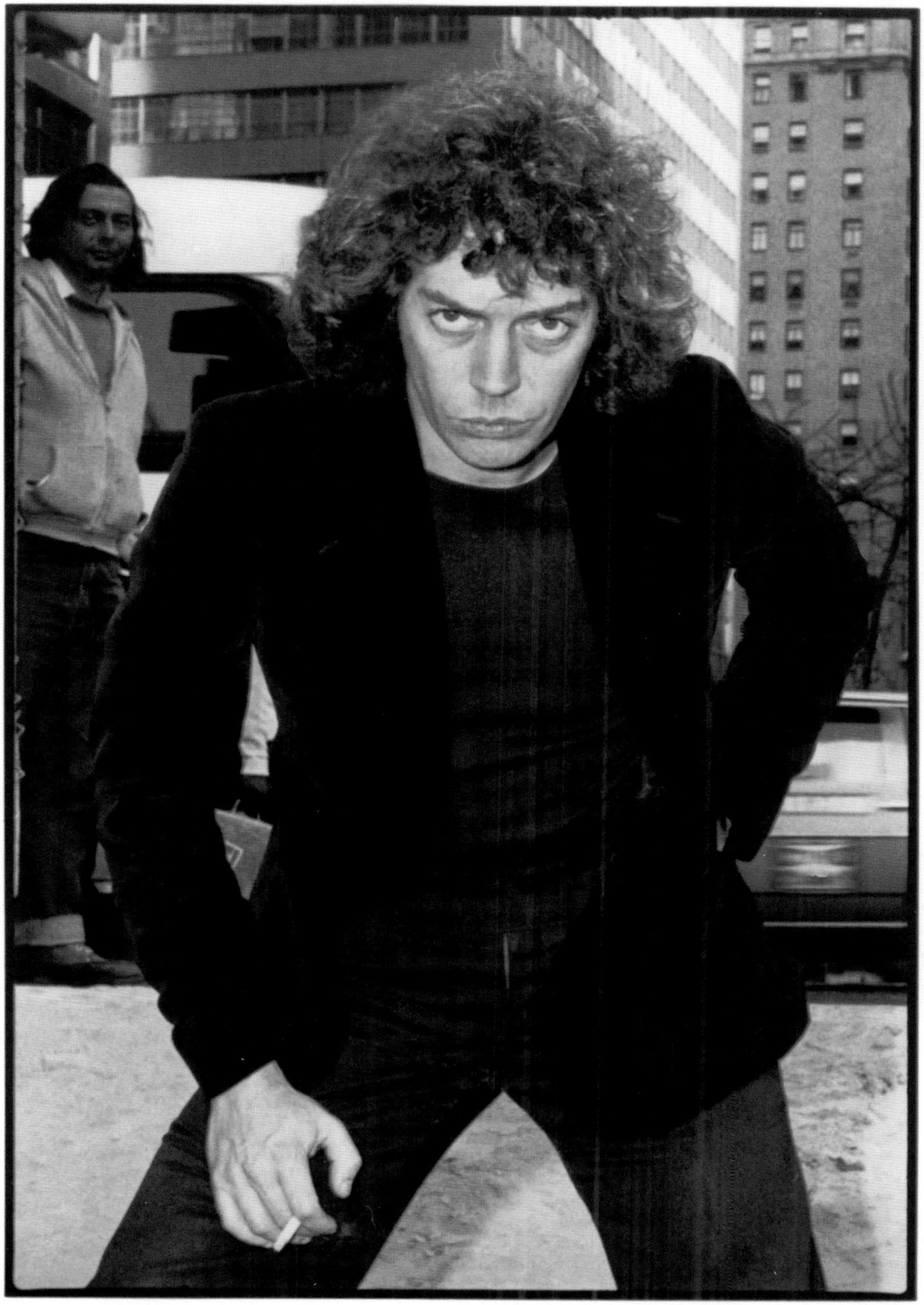

TIM CURRY

MANAGEMENT:
CLODAGH WALLACE
LORD NAPIER PLACE, NO. 3
LONDON, W6, ENGLAND

PREMIER TALENT ASSOCIATES, INC. THREE EAST 54TH ST., NEW YORK, N.Y. 10022

Premier

A&M RECORDS

Printed in U.S.A.

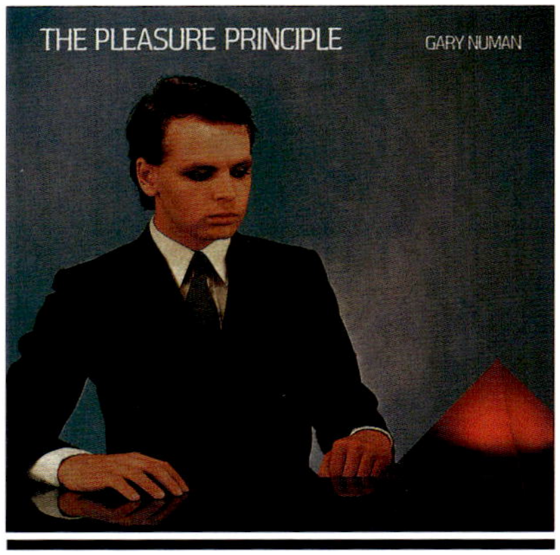

Billboard 200: *The Pleasure Principle* (#16)
Billboard Hot 100: "Cars" (#9)

The Pleasure Principle contained Gary Numan's unordinary track—"Cars," a No. 1 hit in several countries.

LIKE A lot of young British musicians in the late Seventies, Gary Numan started out spewing nihilistic lyrics in a punk-rock band—in his case, Tubeway Army. Then he discovered synthesizers and began creating the techno-pop that put him ahead of the curve.

On the *Replicas* album, Numan contributed all lyrics and music, creating soundscapes of synthesizer and guitar laid over a pulsing rhythmic base, with his clipped vocal style telling tales of future shock, machines and aliens—the cover art depicted Numan made up in android fashion. The attraction to electronics created a sensation in the UK, where his single "Are Friends Electric" hit the No. 1 spot.

Under the influence of such groups as Kraftwerk and Ultravox, the enigmatic Numan went solo, releasing his debut album *The Pleasure Principle*, and the appropriately steely tune "Cars"—a Top 10 hit—broke him in America. But Numan's tour, with a pyramid-shaped set and an all-electronic band, proved a bit too futuristic for Stateside tastes, whereupon the new wave robo-boy retired from performing at the ripe old age of 24.

"It dawned on me that I had been going down a misguided musical path, writing songs simply to keep from slipping," he said. "That's not the same thing as writing songs that you love and care about, that come from the heart. It was soulless, an empty attempt at commercialism, simply because I was in a terrible state financially. All I could think about was surviving."

Numan remained known to American audiences for "Cars."

"I don't want to put it down—I'm really proud to have written something like that. But undeniably, there have been times when it's created the wrong impression, cementing me in a nostalgic era. It's almost like a protective parent—most of the time it's looked after me really well, but there are times you think, 'Get out of the way—let me grow!'" ■

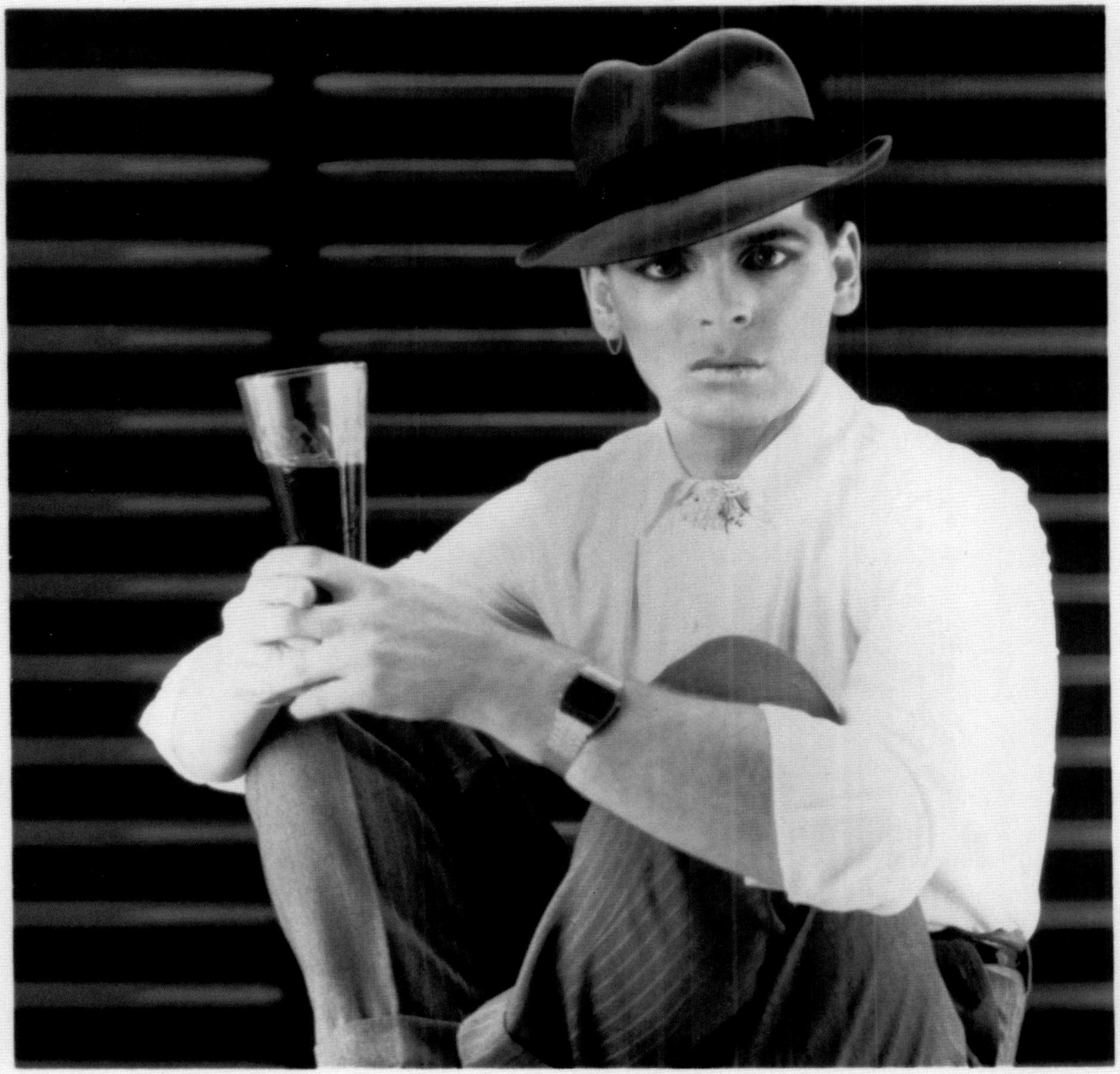

GARY NUMAN

ATCO

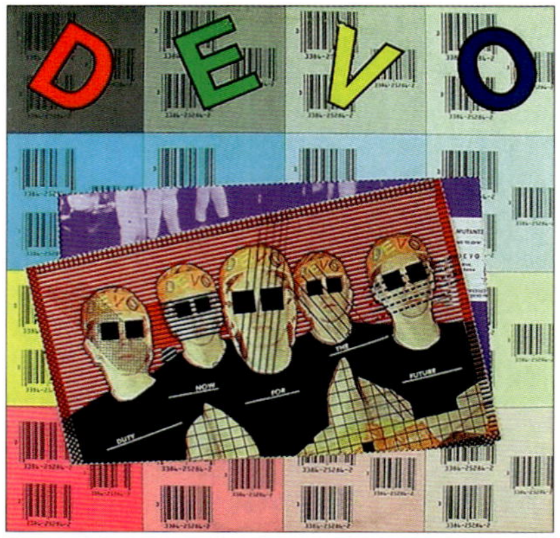

Billboard 200: *Duty Now for the Future* (#73)

Devo intended to provoke consumers with *Duty Now for the Future*, the band's second mission statement.

THE BOYS in Devo formed in 1973 and hadn't stopped spreading the word. And the word was that their school of thought was, well, different. The Ohio quintet dressed in yellow radiation suits, moved around like a bunch of twisted R2D2s and played a brand of music described as "regressive rock." They could counter any question with a mouthful of verbiage concerning the importance of devolution.

"We looked around us and saw the reaming of the environment, the decay of the human condition, and realized that man wasn't evolving, he is devolving," keyboardist and bassist Gerald Casale explained.

The members couldn't get away with their act if it wasn't honed to perfection. Offstage, they still looked like the wimpy bookworms who always got beat up in study hall. At the same time, they knew that a rock band was probably the least important existence imaginable. But for a bunch of guys who couldn't possibly pass for Mick Jaggers, they were getting their share of attention with all the wrinkles they had devised for their avocation.

"We don't feel any allegiance to any particular country—we feel a part of a multinational state of rational intelligence," Casale explained stone-faced. "We celebrate our holiday on September 17 to commemorate the day when man created the universe. Man will survive the holocaust. He'll just learn to eat radioactive vegetables and mutate."

1978's *Q: Are We Not Men? A: We Are Devo!* presented the joys of the band's off-the-wall approach. Devo's sophomore album, *Duty Now for the Future*, was a much denser work, moving towards electronic instrumentation as produced by Ken Scott (David Bowie, Supertramp). The herky-jerky rhythmic patterns of the band were applied to the almost-commercial "The Day My Baby Gave Me a Surprize" and another insane cover version, this time of Johnny Rivers' 1965 hit "Secret Agent Man."

A short clip of the band standing at attention and then saluting was filmed to accompany "Devo Corporate Anthem" and was used in concert performance. In converting crowds to the precepts of devolution, the possibility existed that Devo's fame wouldn't come from acceptance of their doctrines as opposed to people falling in love with their bizarreness.

"That's okay, too," Casale insisted. "The information has to start somewhere. If our appeal starts with beautiful mutants seeing us perform and feeling better about themselves in comparison, that is acceptable. That is truly Devo. And remember, we're *all* Devo." ■

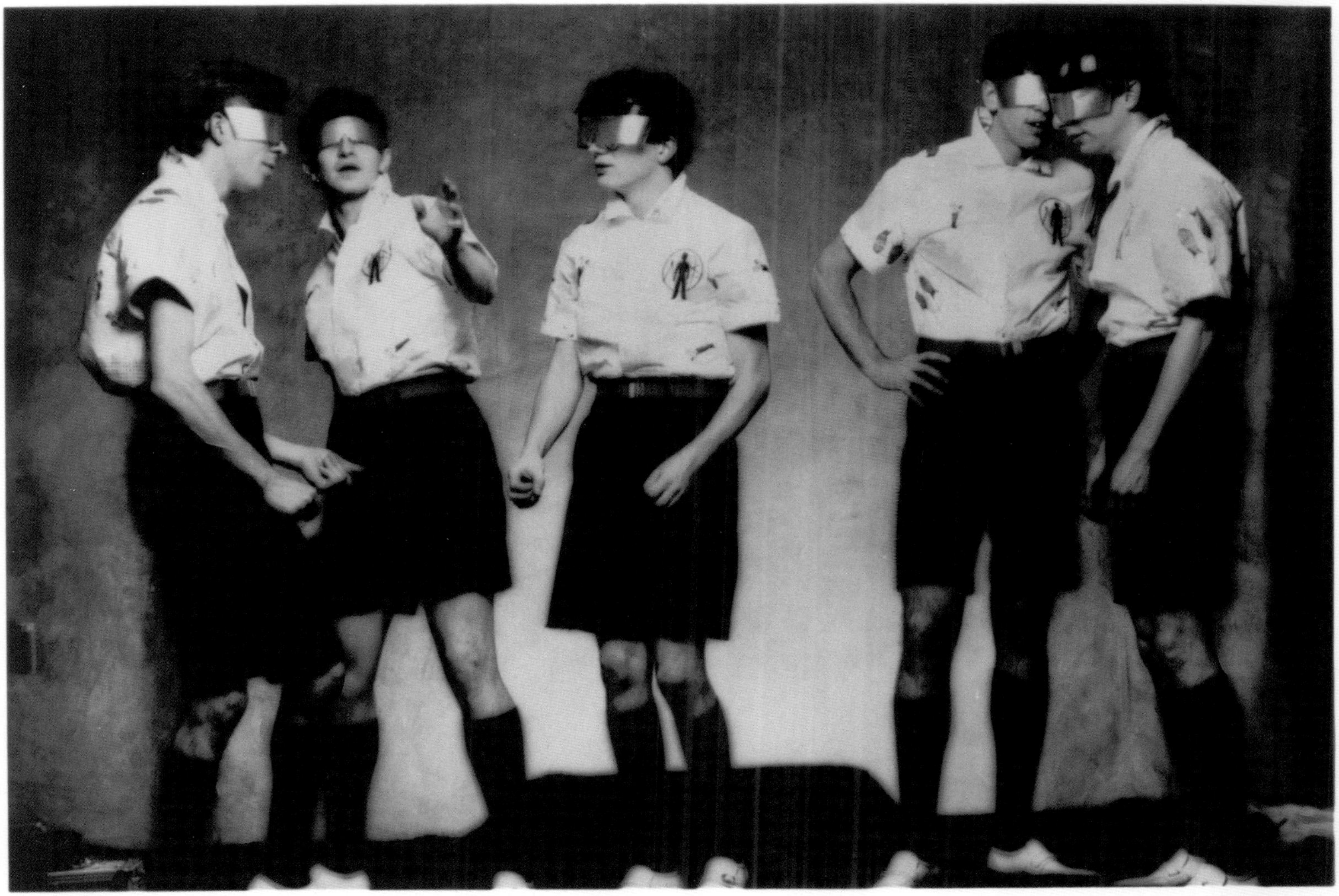

JUNE 1979

DEVO

WARNER / REPRISE

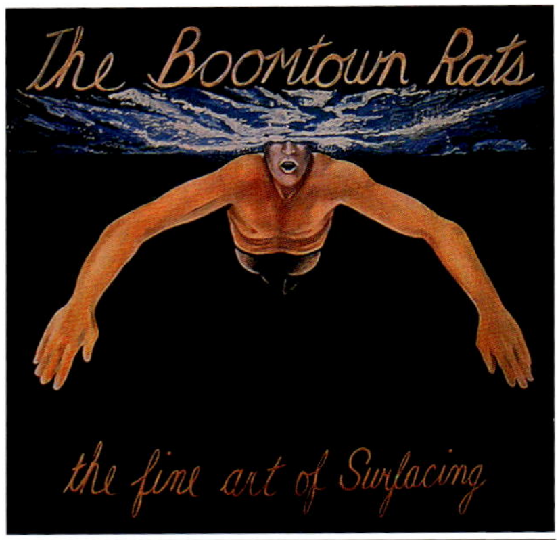

Billboard 200: *The Fine Art of Surfacing* (#103)
Billboard Hot 100: "I Don't Like Mondays" (#73)

The Boomtown Rats, the aural equivalent of a UK pop encyclopedia, enlivened the American rock perspective.

BOB GELDOF, the mastermind and lead singer of the Boomtown Rats, got involved in the music scene when he lied about his experience to land a job as music editor for an alternative Canadian weekly circa 1974. In 1975, he returned to his native Ireland to realign himself with his old school chums—Pete Briquette (bass), Simon Crowe (drums), Gerry Colt (guitar), Gary Roberts (guitar) and the pajama-clad Johnny Fingers (keyboards). They took their name from a gang mentioned in Woody Guthrie's autobiography *Bound for Glory*.

The Boomtown Rats moved to England and immediately established themselves as one of the leading singles machines in Europe. Every tune was cleverly arranged—handclaps, cascading harmonies, drum rolls, call-and-response vocals and other hooks were thrown at the listener every three seconds. The result was witty, engaging music that had translated into five gold singles in 13 months in England.

Yet America remained uninformed of the Rats' charms due to record company problems. Typical of the band's treatment was a publicist's idea (thankfully overruled) to send out dead rats sealed in Baggies to media people. But the UK success brought other labels running to the band's aid, and Columbia Records was chosen to get "someone with enough clout to make up for a year."

A Tonic for the Troops was the band's second album but the first real exposure for the group in the US. Robert "Mutt" Lange's intricate production jibed perfectly with the songs that had inundated airwaves outside of the States—with its cold neurotic tone,"Like Clockwork" was the consummate European single, and "Rat Trap" rode a warm Springsteen-ish sax riff to drive home its British *West Side Story* point (the song reached No. 1 in England, no small feat for a new band).

But the fun began on tour. In the US, Geldof bought a copy of every local newspaper the moment he arrived in a town so he could relate to each audience in a unique way. He talked his associates into putting up the $2 million insurance to allow the band to play at slice-of-America venues—a Coca-Cola plant in Atlanta, a Ford Motor plant in Detroit, a steel mill in Pittsburgh, and Frederick's of Hollywood in Los Angeles.

"America exports its cultural images through TV and movies, right?" he asked. "I find it without doubt the most refreshing place we've been to yet. Here, I don't feel guilty about being in a rock 'n' roll band. The English think it's more morally correct if you live in a slum. They don't realize that most kids start bands to escape that."

The Fine Art of Surfacing featured tunes about Geldof's time in America. The title of "I Don't Like Mondays" came from the glib line uttered by a 16-year-old San Diego girl when asked about her motive for shooting students and killing a teacher and custodian at an elementary school. "The record's content was leaked to America, and her lawyers attempted to injunct its release, fearing it might prejudice her case," Geldof explained. "I Don't Like Mondays" was a worldwide hit—except in the US. ■

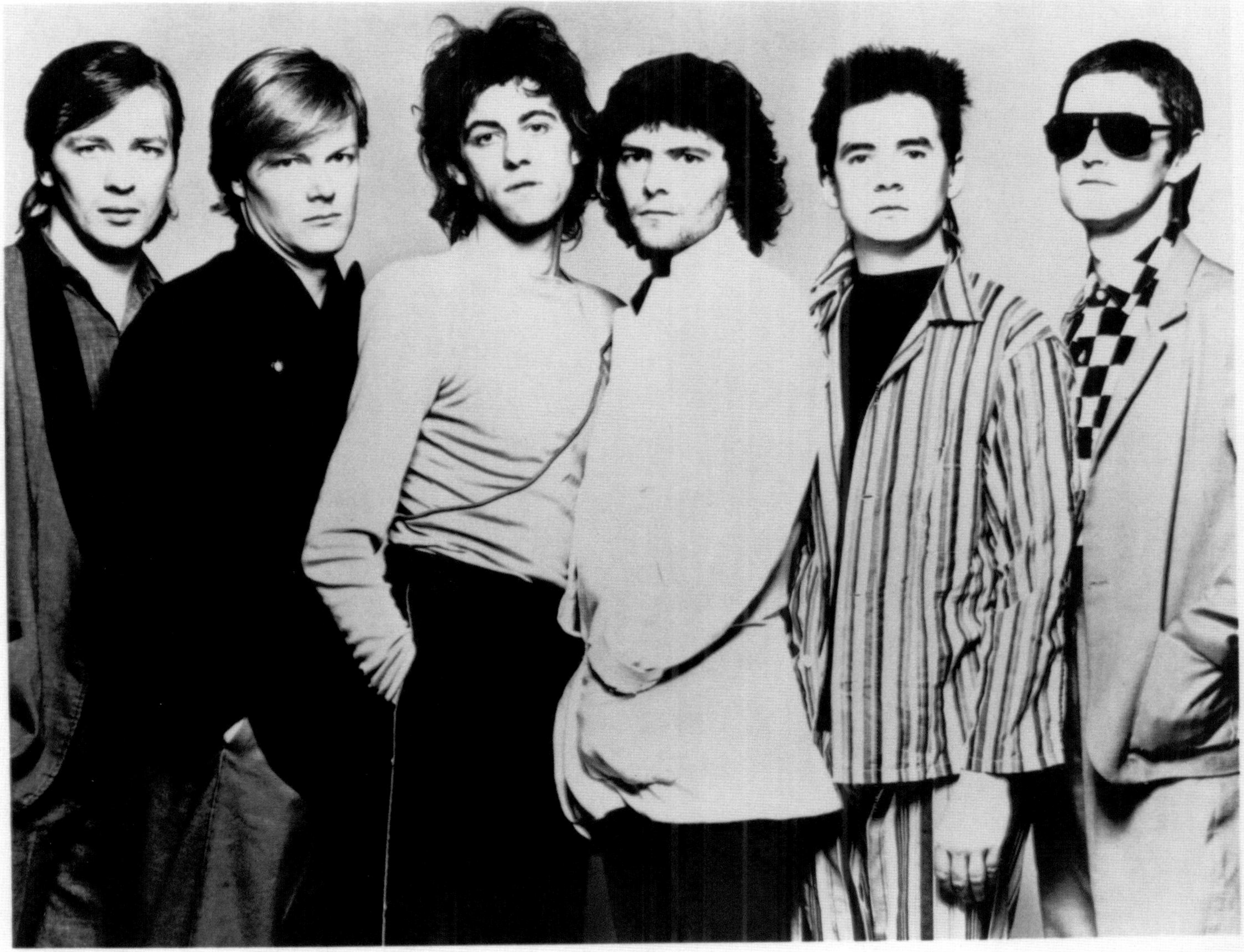

Boomtown Rats

7910

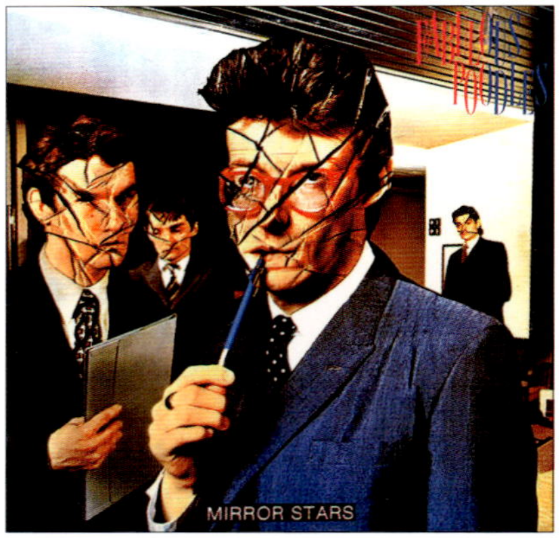

Billboard 200: *Mirror Stars* (#61)
Billboard Hot 100: "Mirror Star" (#81)

With the droll *Mirror Stars,* England's Fabulous Poodles made some inroads toward American acceptance.

IF A wry sense of humor was a requisite for charming British bands, listeners had to contend with the Fabulous Poodles.

Guitarist and vocalist Tony de Meur fronted the band in pink Buddy Holly specs and some rude clothes, combining the nerd posturing of Elvis Costello with the spastic antics of Cheap Trick's Rick Nielsen. Bobby Valentino, who was blessed with Clark Gable matinee-idol looks, added interesting textures to the band's rock framework with his violin and mandolin playing. Bassist Richie C. Robertson and diminutive drummer Bryn B. Burrows combined for an anarchic rhythm section.

If the four Poodles were merely poseurs concerned with constructing a crazy image, they would have been immediately forgettable. The excellent tunes on their debut American album *Mirror Stars* (a compilation of the first two British records) belied their whimsical appeal, given the sardonic treatment of mundane subjects (bad haircuts in "Chicago Boxcars," late night television in "B Movies"). "Mirror Star" became a geek-rock anthem.

"We've been compared to everyone from the Kinks to Frank Zappa," Valentino admitted. "People make it hard to work it out to be yourself. But our stage show developed gradually—it wasn't forced. We've always worn striped clothes and had short hair even back when everyone wanted to look like Rick Wakeman. When we were going to gigs back in '74, we were being called a new Bonzo Doo-Dah Dog Band, and that was hard to change."

The Poodles survived what de Meur described as "the great punk rock scare" to benefit from the energy of the new wave movement, giving them a unique musical brand.

"At one point, in October of '77, we were the only non-punk band in England playing clubs," Valentino enthused. "Which was ironic, because we satirized the punk scene before it ever took off—I'd be crooning 'On the Street Where You Live' and Tony would jump me and start a spitting war. Now it's a good time to be a young band. Punk is dead, but a lot of changes have stemmed from that kick in the pants. It's just taken a while to see. Except for the Bee Gees, the English charts are dominated by new acts."

To crack the American market, touring was a necessity, and the Fabulous Poodles' witty presentation—a country version of the Sex Pistols' "Anarchy in the U.K." (which they swore they performed at the Grand Ole Opry) and a new dance dedicated to self-gratification dubbed "The Wrist"—elicited big reactions. Yet, this was also a band whose members had been known to list their likes, dislikes and favorite colors in true *Tiger Beat* fashion. But the Fabulous Poodles knew how to keep their satiric edge finely honed.

"We've always had a weird bent," Valentino chuckled, "but we also play good music, so I think people are ready for us. We'll get the teens at some point, but for now, we're content to let the more mature people see how twisted we really are." ■

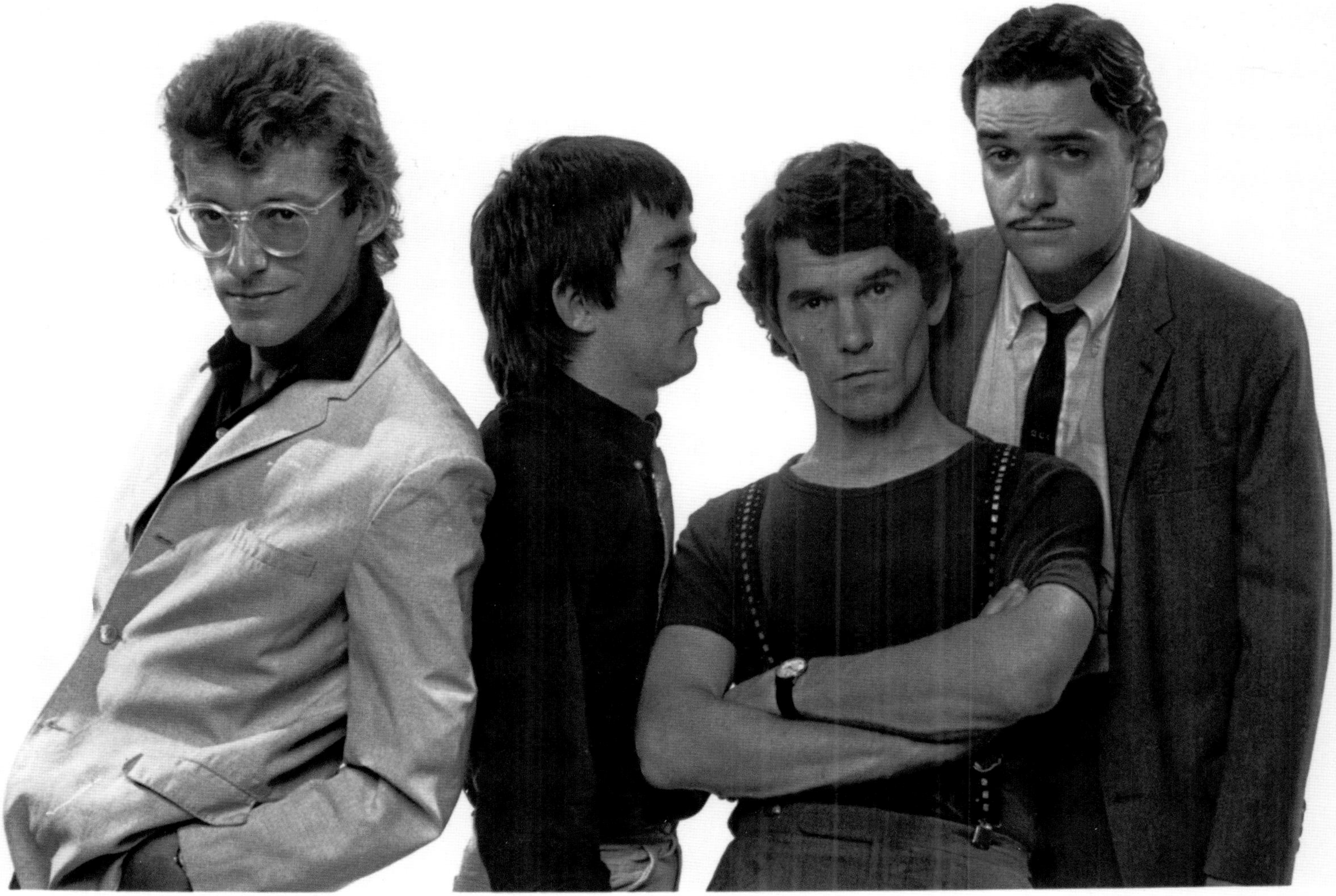

Tony deMeur Bryn Burrows Richie Robertson Bobby Valentino

PARK LANE RECORDS

THE FABULOUS POODLES

Epic

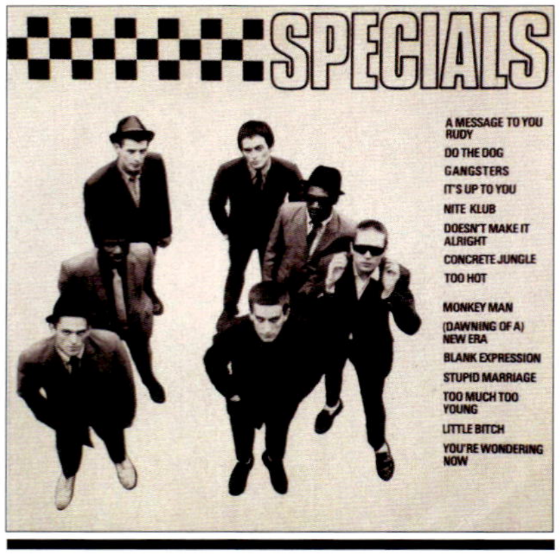

Billboard 200: *The Specials* (#84)

The Specials burst upon the British music scene meshing the zest of ska and the pugnaciousness of punk.

THE SPECIALS epitomized the rapidly changing social, racial and economic forces that were striking a chord with unemployed youth in England. The band offered a revival of ska (pre-reggae Jamaican pop) that was more danceable and melodic yet no less politically charged than punk.

Catalyzed by keyboardist Jerry Dammers, the nucleus of the seven-man band was formed in and around Coventry in 1977. The summer of 1978 saw the Specials supporting the Clash on tour, incentivizing the band to take over its own management with the financial backing of a local businessman and set up the 2-Tone label. "Gangsters" soon reached the top of the charts in England, and record-company A&R reps were keen to ink the group a contract.

But the Specials insisted on the freedom to continue the 2-Tone label as an outlet for bands they wanted to sign. Chrysalis granted the unusual deal and released *The Specials*, a debut album produced by Elvis Costello. A cover of "A Message to You, Rudy," a Dandy Livingstone single in 1967, featured trombonist Rico Rodriguez, a former member of Jamaica's Skatalites who performed on the original recording. "Too Much Too Young" disdained teen pregnancy, based on the 1969 song "Birth Control" by Lloyd Charmers.

"The album was the result of the material we had been playing for two years," bassist Horace Panter explained. "It was a matter of just putting them down, trying and get a live sound in the studio."

The racially integrated band wore Sixties-period rude boy outfits, showing the way for the burgeoning 2-Tone movement and groups like Madness and the English Beat. "We stick to our energy, ideals and motivation, try to live life the way we've planned to," guitarist Roddy Byers (aka Roddy Radiation) said. "We wear skinny ties and porkpie hats and wraparound shades, but it's just too hot to wear a suit onstage—you're lucky to get through two songs before you take your jacket off."

Breaking in America, where audiences were just beginning to accept reggae and ska-flavored music, presented a challenge. "We don't view it in those terms—if you crack it, you have to live over there because you can't afford to live in Britain," Panter said. "And we don't want that." ■

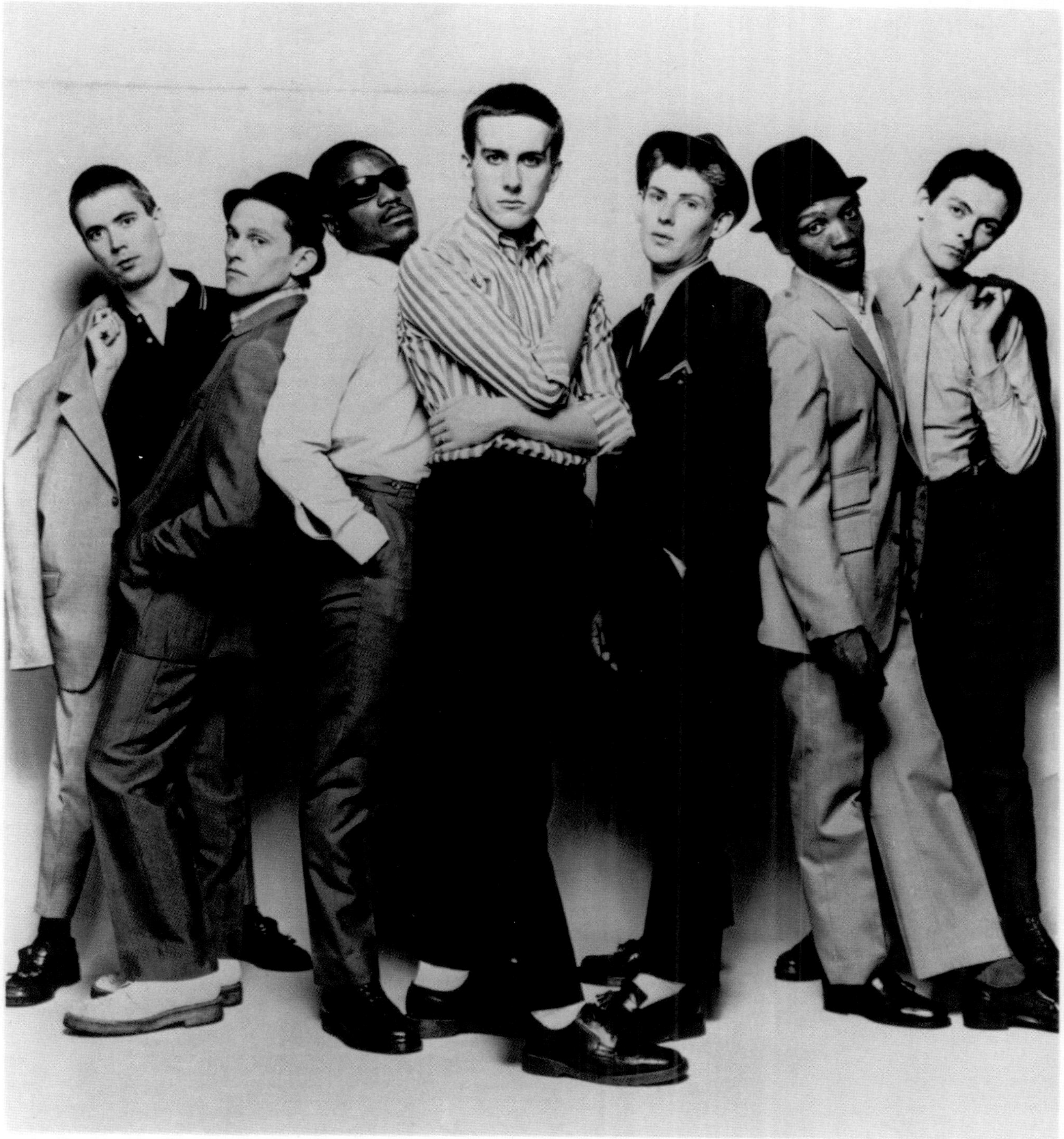

The Specials

Chrysalis

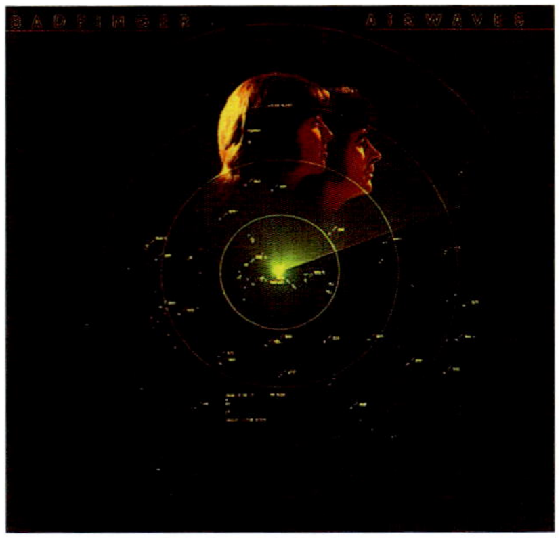

Billboard 200: *Airwaves* (#125)
Billboard Hot 100: "Love Is Gonna Come at Last" (#69)

Badfinger's history of musical attainment marred by frustration and tragedy showed no signs of stopping.

BADFINGER EVOLVED out of a band in South Wales called the Iveys, signed by the Beatles' Apple label in 1968. Under Paul McCartney's direction, the renamed group recorded the debut album *Magic Christian Music* and topped the charts with "Come and Get It." Two highly successful albums followed—1970's *No Dice* and 1971's *Straight Up*, including such hits as "No Matter What," "Day After Day" (produced by George Harrison) and "Baby Blue" (produced by Todd Rundgren), evoking, without imitating, the Beatles. "Without You" became a No. 1 song for Harry Nilsson.

"The best part of being associated with the Beatles was the quality of players you could work with," guitarist and pianist Joey Molland noted. Badfinger shared the stage with the likes of Leon Russell, Bob Dylan and Eric Clapton at George Harrison's historic Concert for Bangladesh. Guest players on Harrison's *All Things Must Pass* and John Lennon's *Imagine* album, the members of Badfinger also played along with Clapton, Russell, Klaus Voorman and Billy Preston on Ringo Starr's hit "It Don't Come Easy."

But then various management, legal and financial problems began to set in. A switch to another label yielded several more albums, the last being *Wish You Were Here* in 1974, but the band's difficulties continued to mount. Finally, original member Pete Ham took his own life out of frustration and despair. The remaining members joined various other groups or dropped out of music.

After two years, Badfinger started up again—Molland formed a new group in Los Angeles and enticed founding member Tom Evans (vocals, bass) to join. Discovering they would have more marketing power if they revived the Badfinger name, they teamed with producer David Malloy, best known for his work with Eddie Rabbitt, for their "comeback" album, *Airwaves*. The single "Love Is Gonna Come at Last" was the first Badfinger chart hit in seven years.

"It's a song about hope," Molland said. "I think this one sounds the most like the things we did in the past, brought up to date."

Molland and Evans toured in support of the album, but hopes weren't realized, and sales figures failed to impress the band's label. ■

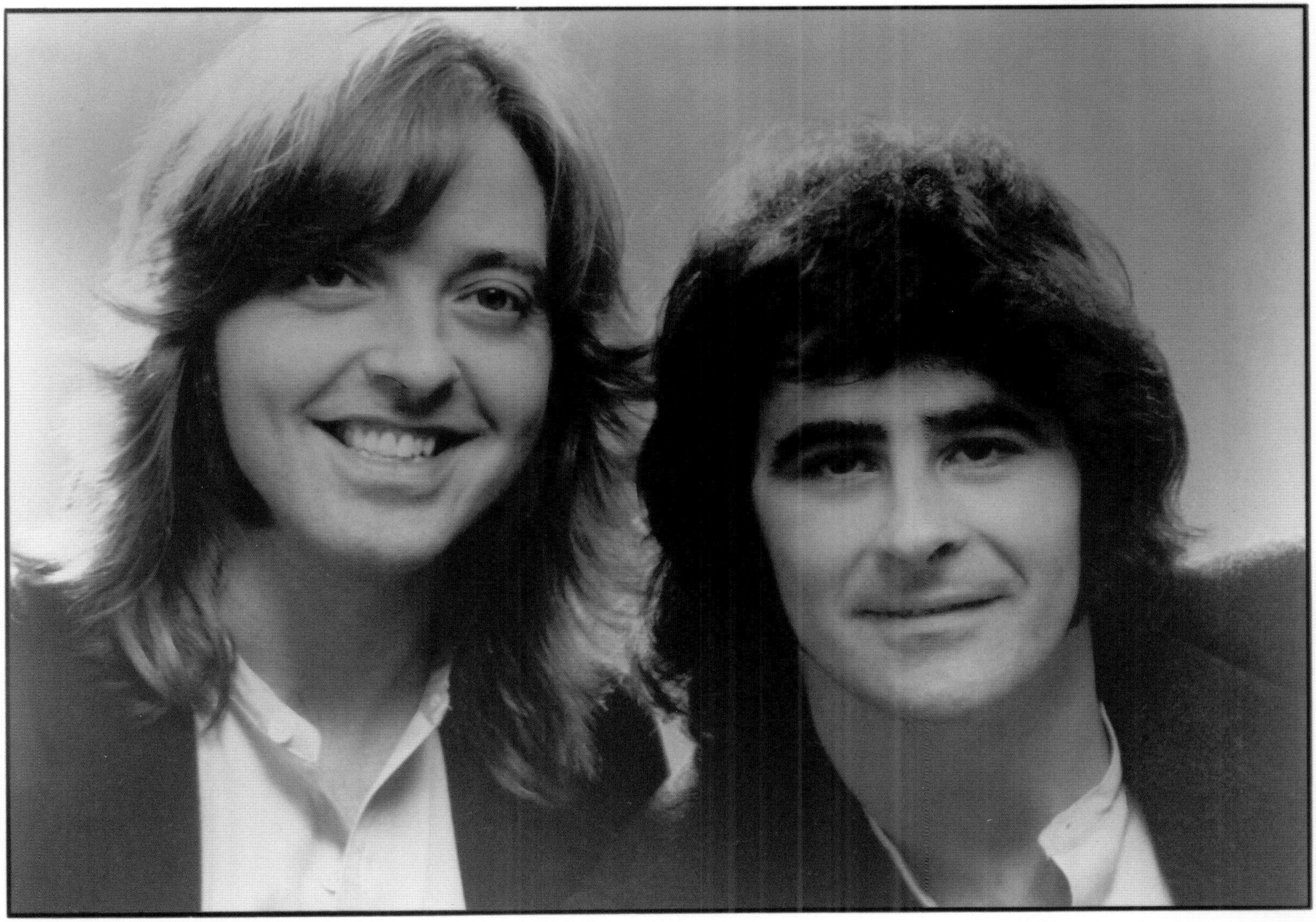

Photo Credit: JIM SHEA

Joey Molland Tom Evans

BADFINGER

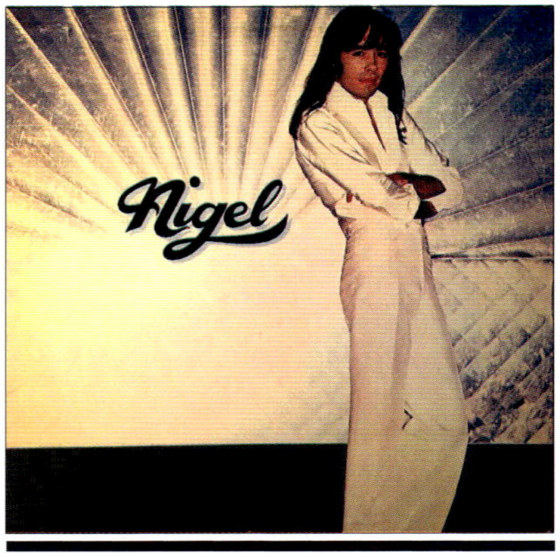

Billboard 200: *Nigel* (#140)
Billboard Hot 100: "Dancin' Shoes" (#18); "Little Bit of Soap" (#34)

Elton John fans recognized Nigel Olsson, whose audience had been determined to be predominantly female.

AS THE black-gloved and head-geared basher who was engulfed behind his mammoth drum orchestra on Elton John's early tours, Nigel Olsson had kept the beat from the early days of "Border Song" through *Captain Fantastic and the Brown Dirt Cowboy*. Only an occasional flip of his waist-length black hair gave a clue to his presence on stage. John had dismissed Olsson along with the rest of his band in 1975 when the Rocketman started tampering with his own success.

"Five years of my life was dedicated to someone else," Olsson reflected. "The first four years were totally devoted to getting the EJ thing off the ground, and the last year—well, I'd always had it in the back of my mind that I'd really like to record on my own."

Without a band, Olsson decided he wanted to be accepted as a singer-songwriter on his own merits. He recorded an album that wasn't promoted properly, and then bought the rights and re-released *Nigel* with two singles added. "Dancin' Shoes" and an outstanding ballad arrangement of the Jarmels' 1961 R&B hit "Little Bit of Soap" went on to reach the pop charts.

Olsson's appeal was marketed primarily to women. "Elton gave me the push to get me out there and said, 'Now's the time for you to make it,'" he said. "I haven't been on a stage in four years—drumming is hard work, in case anyone wondered. Now to be singing as well is a real backbreaker, but I welcome the chance to do my songs." ■

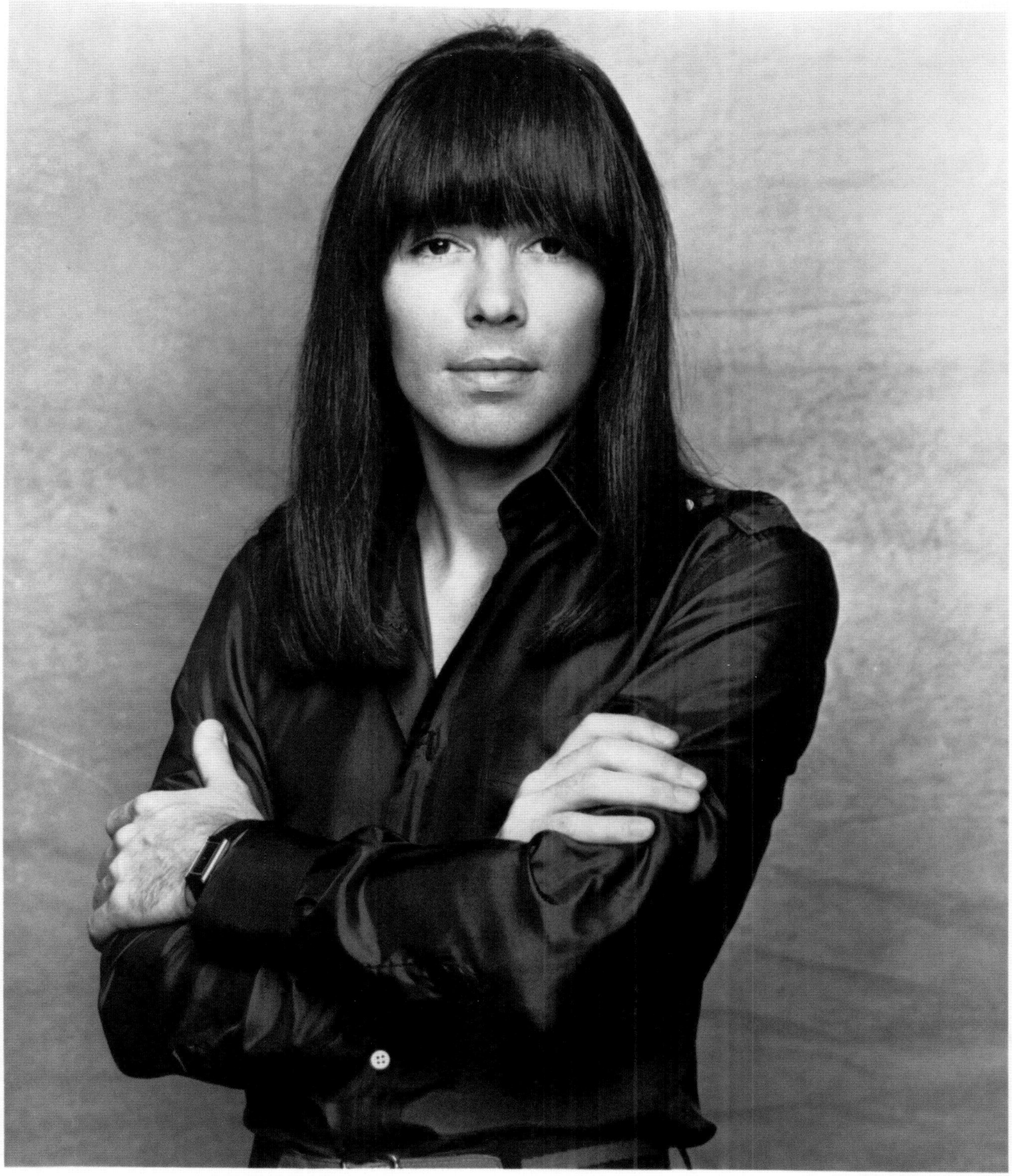

NIGEL OLSSON

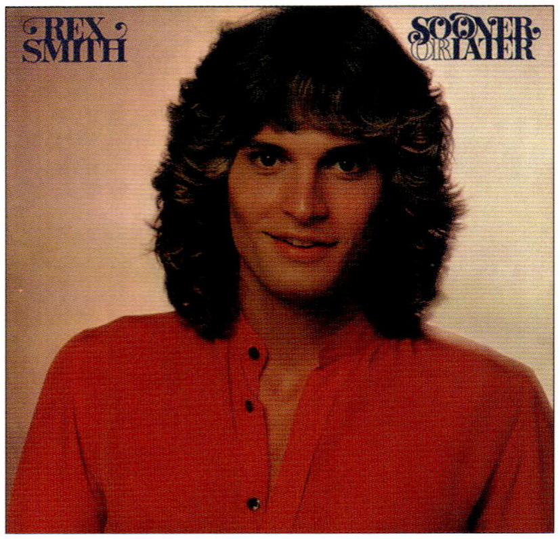

Billboard 200: *Sooner or Later* (#19)
Billboard Hot 100: "You Take My Breath Away" (#10)

Cognizant of losing credibility with his "Sexy Rex" image, Rex Smith crooned "You Take My Breath Away."

REX SMITH was doing his part to change the public's limited perception of teen idols. "I get it all the time—people come up and say, 'What beach were you sitting on when the producer discovered you and asked you to do a poster?' Hey, I'll grin and bear it—I know what I'm doing. I've lived three or four lives between the ages of 19 and 24. People will find out that I can do different things."

Smith had been around the block a few times. He first gained notoriety fronting a rock band called Rex, a dreadful group that nevertheless found itself opening shows for such heavyweights as Ted Nugent at Madison Square Garden.

But Smith's dreams of becoming the next Mick Jagger soon gave way to other opportunities. A producer saw him perform and asked him to do a made-for-television movie. "Sometimes you fall back and punt," he said of the move. "The band thing was shaky, and I had to pay the rent."

Sooner or Later catapulted Smith to fame on the cover of *16 Magazine, Tiger Beat* and every other teen-oriented magazine in America. He recorded a gold-selling piece of fluff, "You Take My Breath Away," that solidified his new image as the boy whose chiseled good looks placed him on the bedroom walls of prepubescent girls everywhere. The hit was featured on the album *Sooner or Later,* named for the movie. All signs pointed for Smith to follow in the hallowed and lucrative footsteps of David and Shaun Cassidy.

But he kept on moving. Smith's record company was unfamiliar in dealing with the teenybopper market, so he shunned further recording to take the role of Danny Zuko in the Broadway production of *Grease.*

"I just learn as I go along," he insisted. "I had never been in a play before *Grease*, but they just taught me how to do the hand-jive and dance. I had a good sense of rhythm and performing from playing in rock bands for so long. Now I'd like to think that I can do well in anything—singing, acting, whatever—but my next projects won't have anything to do with my being a 'teen idol.' Face it, though—those girls are nice fans to have. They'll go see one of my movies five or six times to make up for no one else going." ■

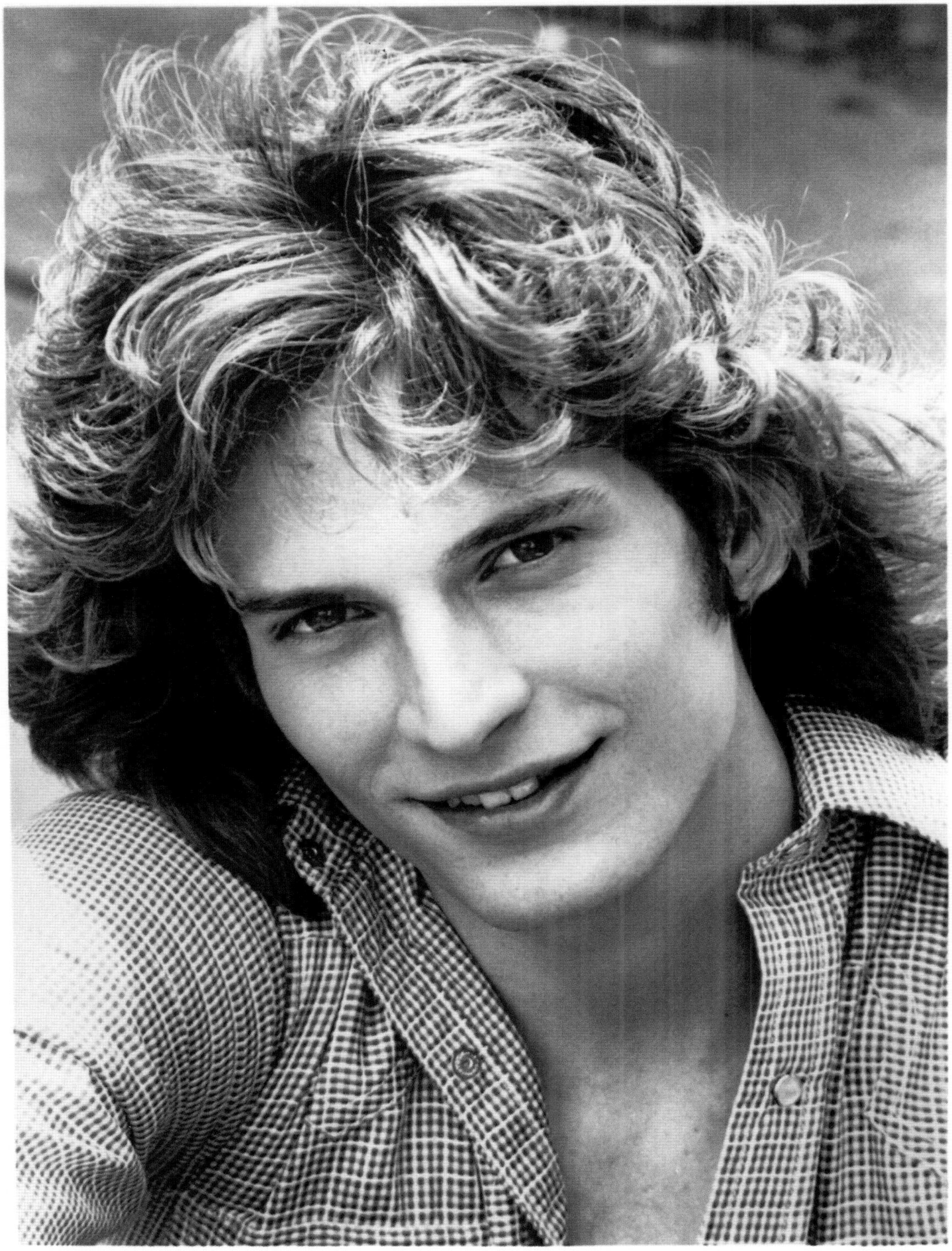

Rex Smith

Columbia

7903

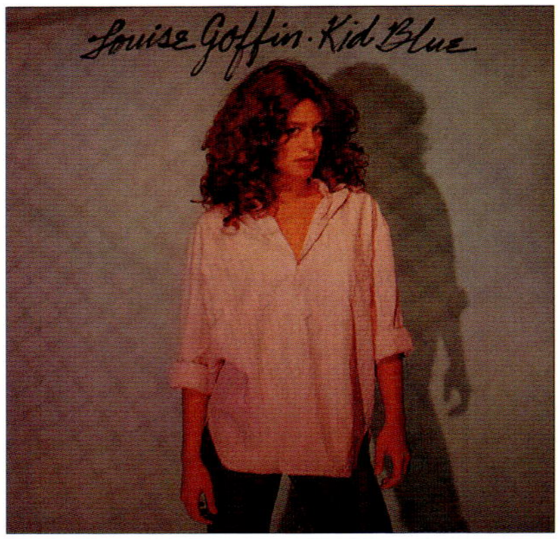

Billboard 200: *Kid Blue* (#87)
Billboard Hot 100: "Remember (Walking in the Sand)" (#43)

With *Kid Blue* in the marketplace, young Louise Goffin found herself navigating a career in the making.

MOST OF the attention showered upon Louise Goffin could be attributed to her genes. The 19-year-old was the offspring of Carole King and her ex-husband Gerry Goffin, who dominated the airwaves in the early and middle Sixties with an unbroken streak of hits recorded by groups like the Shirelles and the Drifters. But Miss Goffin's musical sensibilities were a far cry from her parents' Brill Building output.

"Songwriting was something my parents always did, so as a child I identified it with an adult role," she said. "But I can remember writing a song when I was 12 and just knowing what my mom would do in a certain spot, and there was no way I was going to do the same things. I came up on real contemporary music—the Beatles, Jackson Browne, the Eagles. Then came Led Zeppelin and the Who, and I started getting into Elvis Costello—rock and more rock."

Professional opportunities presented themselves, and Goffin opened for Browne at the Troubadour. Her rich-kid bitchiness translated on record to a beguiling spunkiness, and her debut album, *Kid Blue*, showed a knack for fictionalizing events and characters into interesting song forms. The Shangri-Las' cover "Remember (Walking in the Sand)" gave her some notoriety, an indication of her way with a torchy ballad.

"I used to try and put adult feelings into my songs, but now I'm doing more things that make sense for me to sing about," she said. "I mean, I'm a teenager for another year yet." ■

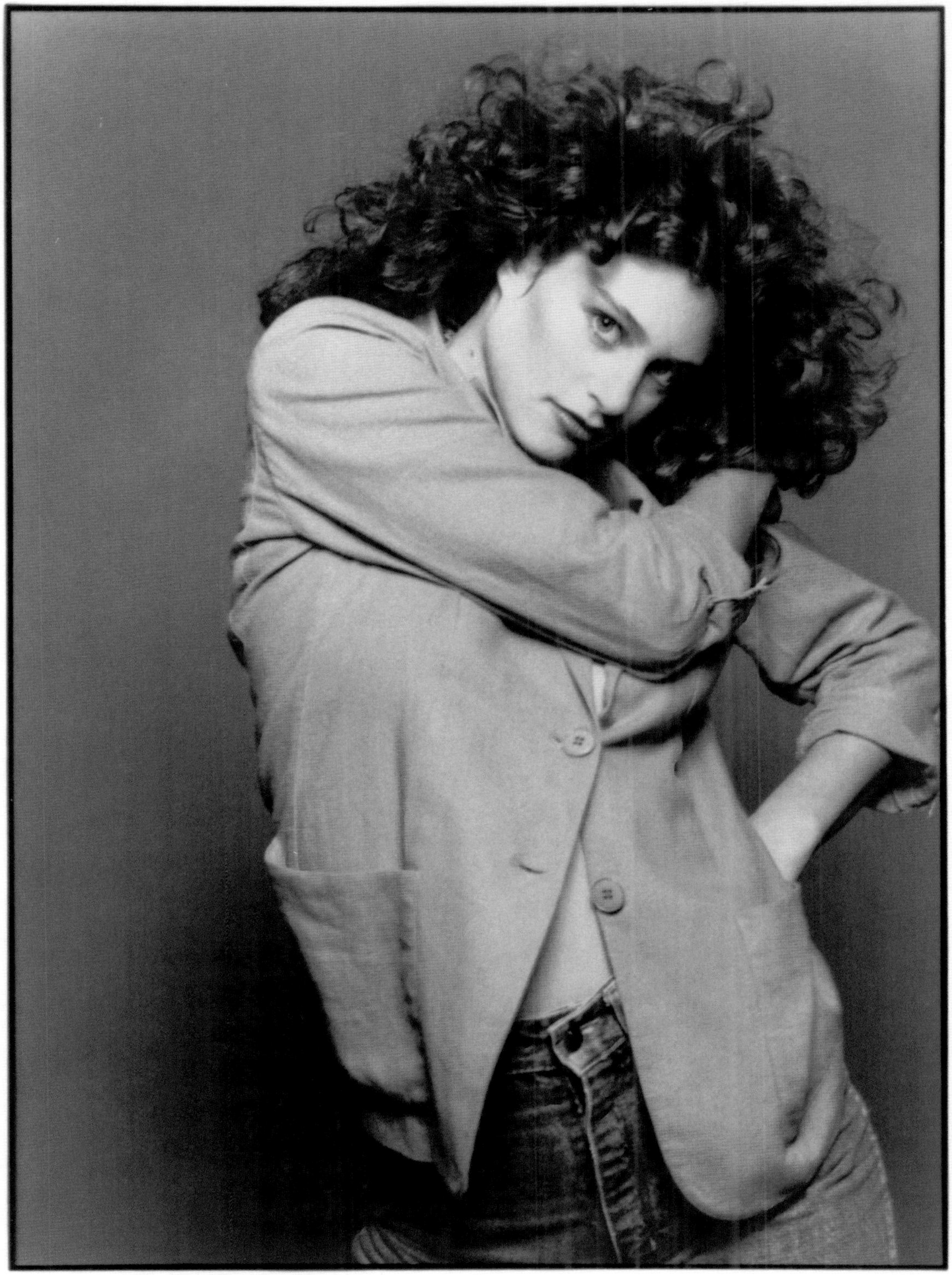

Photo Credit: RANDEE ST. NICHOLAS

Louise Goffin

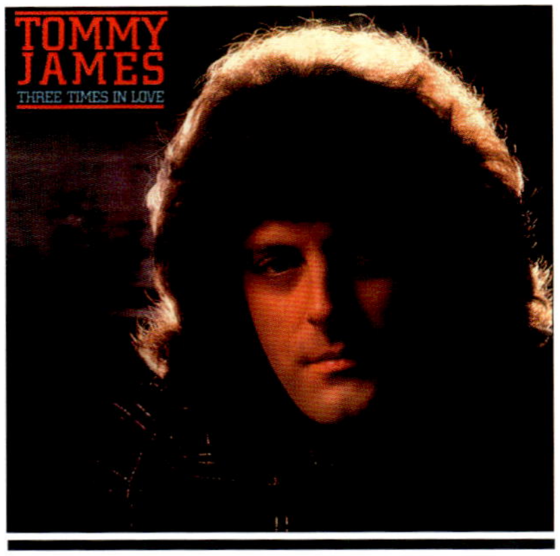

Billboard 200: *Three Times in Love* (#134)
Billboard Hot 100: "Three Times in Love" (#19)

A decade after his fine chart run with the Shondells, Tommy James delivered the hit "Three Times in Love."

THE LEADER of Tommy James & the Shondells, Tommy James had some of the biggest pop-oriented rock hits of the Sixties—"Hanky Panky," "Mony Mony," "I Think We're Alone Now," "Crimson and Clover" and "Crystal Blue Persuasion" among them.

"I've been doing the same job since I was 12," James said of his show-business saga. "That's like being a 32-year-old paperboy."

In 1964, James was fronting his own rock band in Michigan and was asked by a local DJ to record a few songs for a small local label. One of those, an obscurity titled "Hanky Panky," became a minor regional hit, but for lack of wider distribution, soon faded and was quickly forgotten.

Four years later, "Hanky Panky" resurfaced when a Pittsburgh disc jockey found the record in a stack of oldies and started playing it, prompting a wild response from his audience. "The switchboard lit up—everybody wanted to know what that record was," James recalled. "It was a Cinderella story."

The disc jockey traced James to his hometown to tell him that he had the No. 1 record in Pittsburgh. By this time, the original Shondells had disbanded, and James was forced to hire a bar band to back him. A week later, James was in New York, with every record mogul in the city pursuing him and the group. He sold the original master of "Hanky Panky" to Morris Levy at Roulette Records, which needed a hit. A month later, the record went to No. 1 nationwide.

Though the success of "Hanky Panky" may have at first appeared to be a fluke, subsequent chart busters were proof that James was no one-shot wonder. Between 1965 and 1972, he scored 11 gold and three platinum singles, and four gold and two platinum albums.

The hit machine shifted into neutral in late 1970 when James escaped the imposing demands of the record business, retiring to his upstate New York farm. He returned to the studio to co-write and produce Alive 'N Kicking's "Tighter, Tighter," another gold record. James went solo and charted a hit with "Draggin' the Line" in 1971, then recorded albums that sold poorly.

Three Times in Love appeared in 1979, and the album's title track was James' first hit in eight years, reaching No. 1 on the adult contemporary chart and reaching the pop and country charts. It contained the essence of his classic sound—soaring harmonies, an addictive hook and sweet-sounding guitars. James termed the music's maturation "complex simplicity."

"My music has changed to the extent that I've grown up," he said. "It's not the money anymore, or all the things I wanted a long time ago. There are important things to me that need to be said. I want to have that access to people through my music." ■

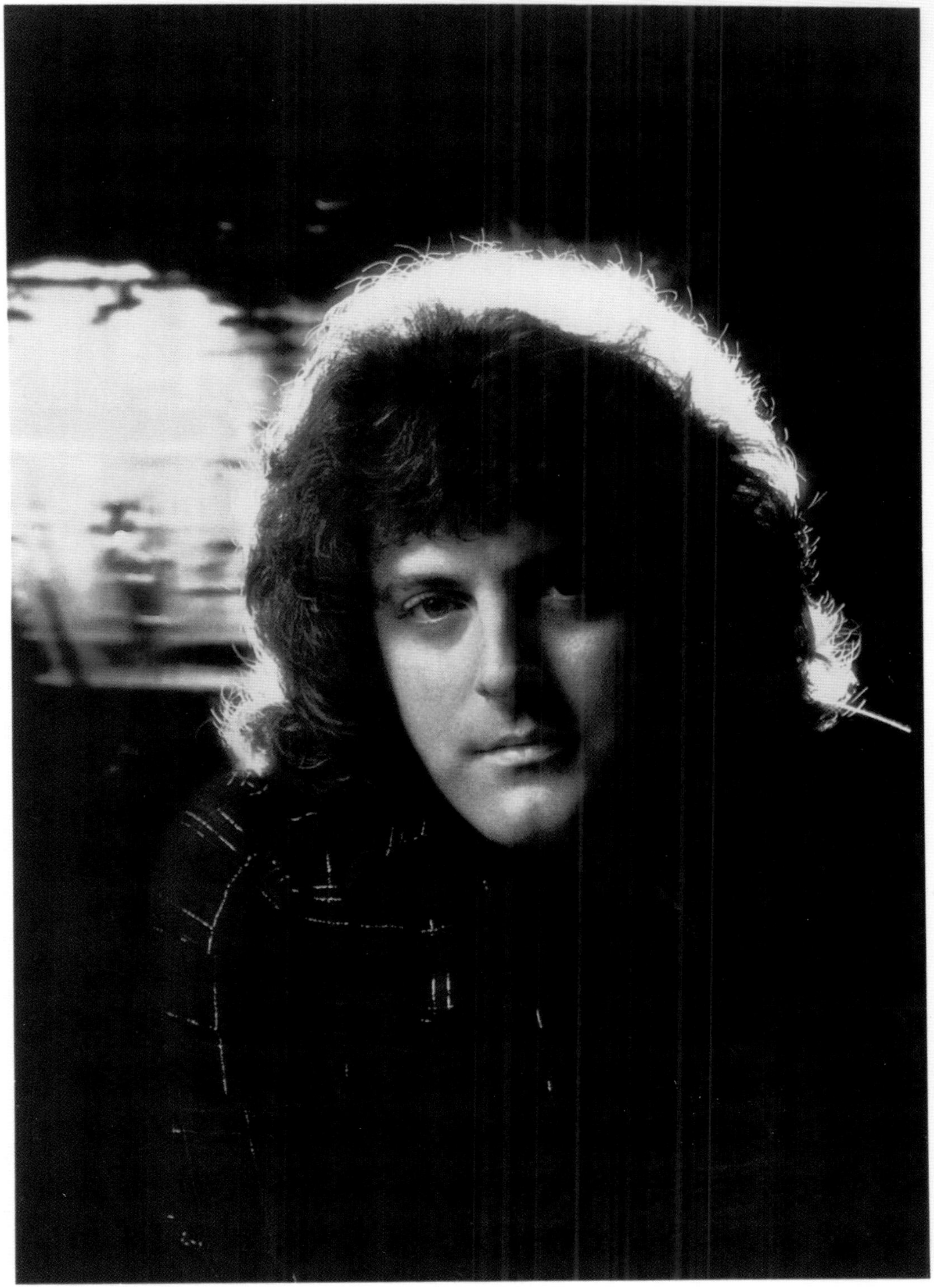

TOMMY JAMES

Millennium Records

Manufactured and Distributed by RCA Records

I

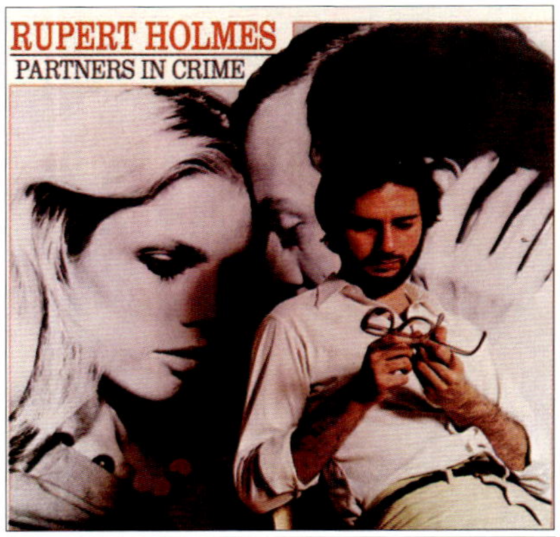

Billboard 200: *Partners in Crime* (#33)
Billboard Hot 100: "Escape (The Piña Colada Song)" (No. 1); "Him" (#6); "Answering Machine" (#32)

Per the beachy "Escape (The Piña Colada Song)," singer-songwriter Rupert Holmes got a career-making hit.

BORN IN England and raised just north of New York City, Rupert Holmes had gradually established himself since his early songwriting days while attending the Manhattan School of Music. He wrote the 1971 hit "Timothy" for the Buoys—a willfully controversial tale about two survivors of a mining disaster who cannibalize the third—and tunes for the Partridge Family. He also composed and arranged for the Drifters, the Platters and Gene Pitney.

Barbra Streisand recognized Holmes' 1974 debut release, *Widescreen*, and asked him to arrange and produce her *Lazy Afternoon* album. She recorded more of his songs, including two for her remake of *A Star Is Born.* He also produced albums for Sparks and the UK-based band Sailor.

Songwriting was no trivial enterprise to Holmes, a worldly wordsmith who delivered clever, relevant bulletins. "I don't have any answers—I've just got millions of questions," he allowed. "I'm not evangelical, but I do want people to be sensitive to other people's feelings, their pain, their fears, their dreams. It's time we all owned up to our vulnerabilities—I'm going out on a limb, and I have to believe that there are other people who will get out there with me until we outnumber those who play it safe on the ground."

Holmes fashioned three Top 40 hits for *Partners in Crime,* his fifth album and commercial quantum leap—"Him," "Answering Machine" and the No. 1 "Escape (The Piña Colada Song)." With its surprise ending, the latter was a testimony to Holmes' flair. It told the story of a man so bored with his girlfriend that he answers a personal placed by a woman who likes piña coladas and getting caught in the rain. He responds with a personal of his own and they plan to meet the next day in a bar. When she arrives, he instantly recognizes her—his girlfriend.

"I'm happiest writing about what two people do with each other, for each other, against each other and despite each other," Holmes stated. "As long as there's to be life on this planet, and until cloning is perfected, there has to be a future for men and women. Many times, relationships don't work—but neither does the phone company. And yet we continue with the phone company—and relationships." ■

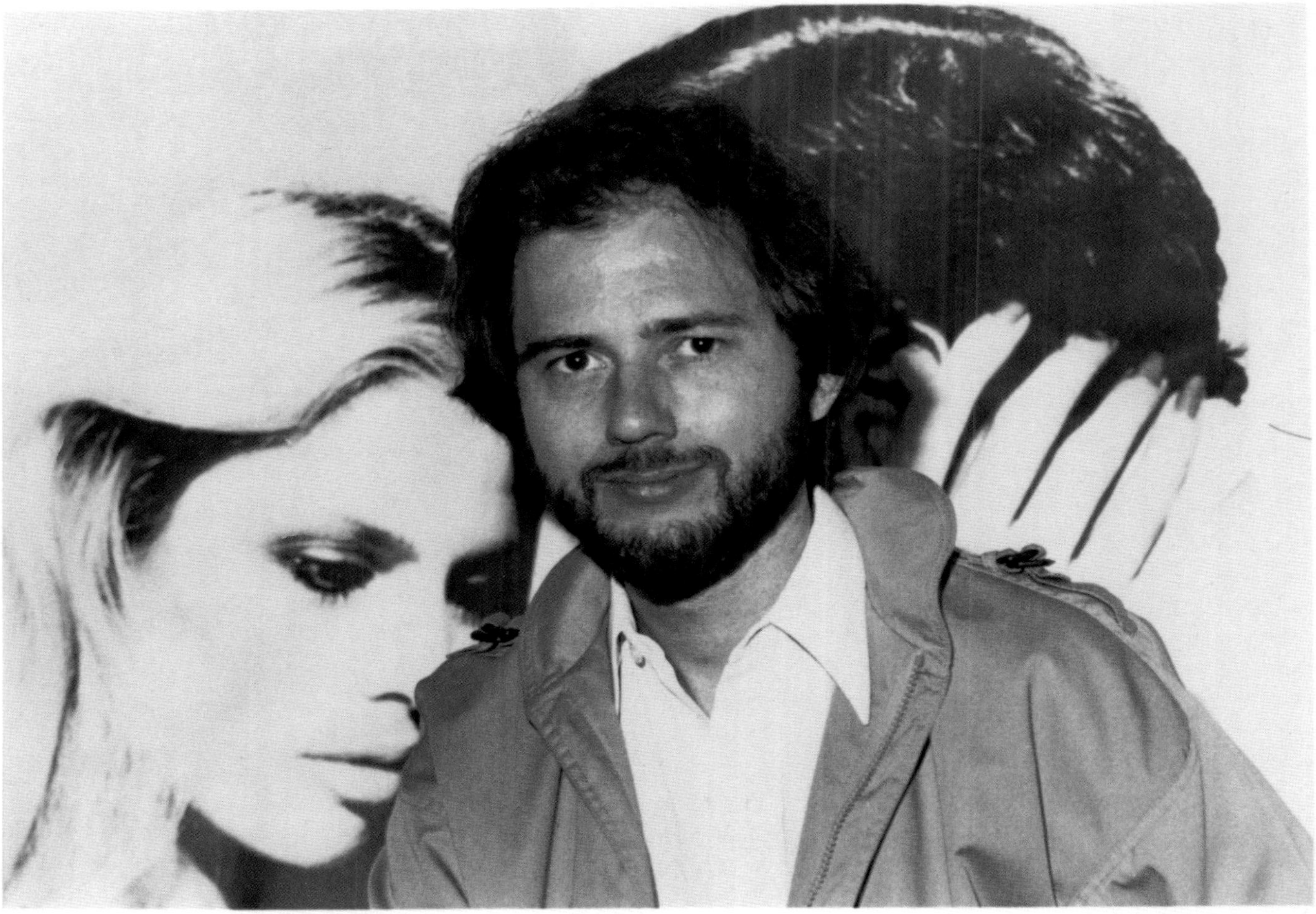

RUPERT HOLMES

THE HOLMES LINE

MANAGER:
Normand Kurtz
712 Fifth Avenue
New York, NY 10019
(212) 765-3850

INFINITY RECORDS

10 East 53rd Street
New York, New York 10022
(212) 888-9700

100 Universal City Plaza
Universal City, California 91608
(213) 763-8283

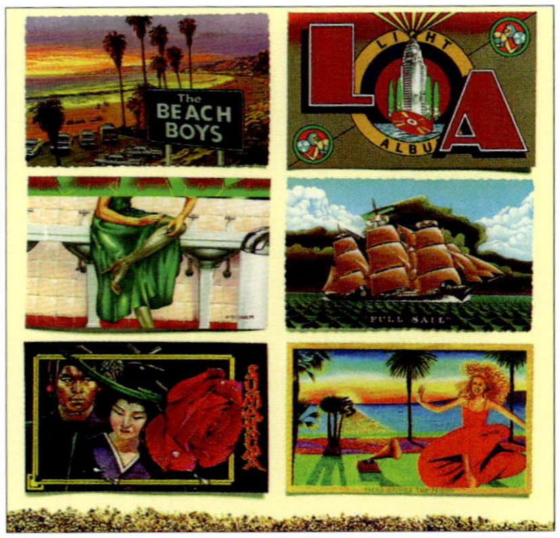

Billboard 200: *L.A. (Light Album)* (#100)
Billboard Hot 100: "Here Comes the Night" (#44); "Good Timin'" (#40)

The Beach Boys' Bruce Johnston, an official member again, focused his attention on rejuvenating the group.

EVERY SUMMER, there was a rekindled interest in the music of the Beach Boys. Early on in their recorded history, they defined the sun-and-fun ethic of the "California sound," and for that they were still mightily revered—even in the hearts of kids who weren't even born when the band's first album was released in 1962.

But it had been hard for the Beach Boys to break out of the confines of a nostalgia tag. The beginning of the Seventies found them acting as musical spokesmen for TM and ecology without much commercial success, due to the public's preoccupation with leader Brian Wilson's absence. When Wilson returned to the group in 1976, the huge "Brian's Back" hype put immense pressure on the composer of the group's classic material.

15 Big Ones did become the Beach Boys best-selling album in years, mainly on the strength of the single "Rock and Roll Music," but the record consisted entirely of covers of old material. Wilson was exposed in the press as a drug casualty who had lost confidence in his legendary composing and producing skills. The following albums, *The Beach Boys Love You* and *M.I.U. Album*, found the group floundering again commercially, although yearly tours continued to keep them in the public eye.

Wilson and the other longtime Boys—brothers Dennis and Carl, cousin Mike Love and friend Al Jardine—decided to switch to Caribou Records, former Chicago producer James William Guercio's label, for a fresh start. Bruce Johnston, who had become the sixth Beach Boy back in 1965 when Brian had decided not to tour with the group, was called in halfway during the recording of a new album to act as producer. "I'm a Beach Boys alumnus, and I love what they taught me," he said. "I just want to give back something."

The result, *L.A. (Light Album),* didn't turn out to be the classic that the band intended. The record was a hodgepodge of the individual members' songs, with minimal input from Brian Wilson. "Good Timin'" showcased the group's classic harmonies, but the song was merely a fragment when compared to past vocal excursions. The first single, "Here Comes the Night," aroused much controversy. Originally a synthesized delight found on the *Wild Honey* album, the song was restored in an 11-minute disco version.

Dance music lovers yawned, while old Beach Boys fans were disgusted. Johnston's love for the band hadn't endeared him accordingly—there was a shroud of doubt concerning the musical intent of someone who wrote "I Write the Songs," which had become Barry Manilow's biggest hit, and then convinced the Beach Boys to do a disco song in his first move as producer. But Johnston wasn't fazed.

"I really don't see how people can be so narrow-minded," Johnston said. "The Beach Boys are not an instrumental group, they're a vocal group. That disco tune has some amazing singing on it. Everyone harped for years about how the Beach Boys were stagnating, and then they try something new and get nothing but trouble for it. I'm hoping that 'Here Comes the Night' will be a prototype for things to come, in terms of all the intricate production and vocal things going on. On that level, I think it's in the spirit of what Brian does." ■

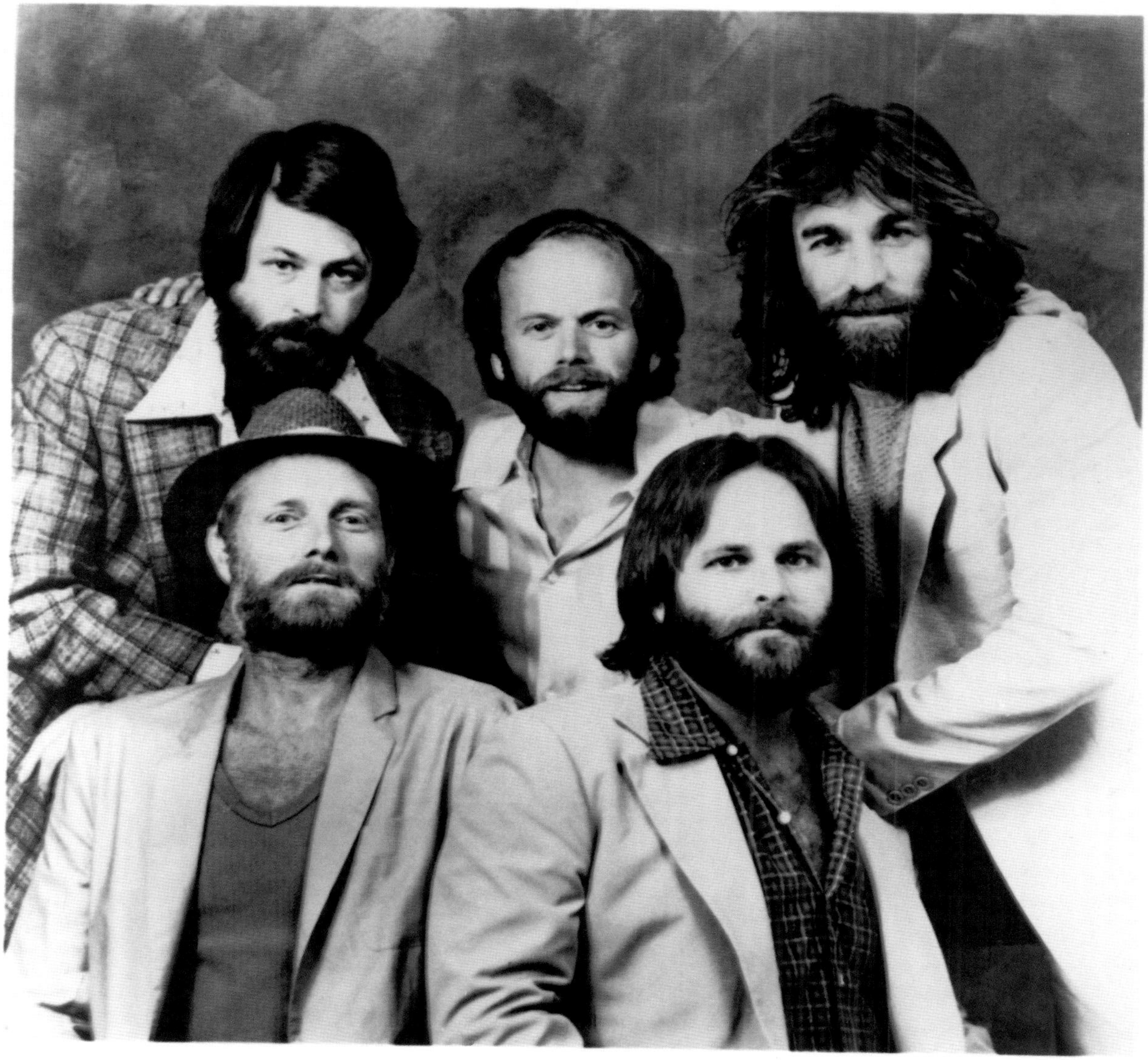

THE BEACH BOYS

Brian Wilson — Al Jardine — Dennis Wilson

Mike Love — Carl Wilson

Caribou Records

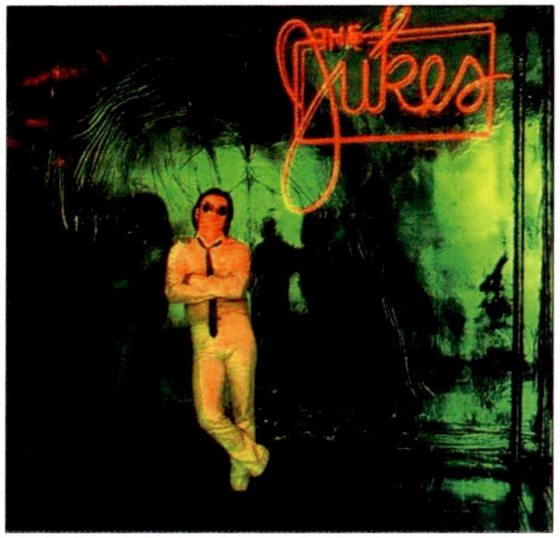

Billboard 200: *The Jukes* (#48)
Billboard Hot 100: "I'm So Anxious" (#71)

The Jukes, a rallying of Southside Johnny & the Asbury Jukes, gave a total group effort due to circumstance.

SOUTHSIDE JOHNNY & the Asbury Jukes had battled the odds since their bar-band days. *I Don't Want to Go Home*, the 10-man group's first record released in 1976, harnessed the chops that had been refined during years in the New Jersey shore rock scene. The title cut made the band's strengths obvious—a terrific horn section, the vocals of Southside Johnny Lyon, and a solid grasp on classic R&B and soul music.

Some of Lyon's pals shared the same passion, namely Bruce Springsteen and his guitarist Miami Steve Van Zandt. The friendship with Springsteen garnered the band some media attention, but more important was the collaboration with Van Zandt, whose songs provided perfect vehicles for Southside Johnny's voice and the passionate, hard-driving backup provided by the Jukes.

"When we started out, Steve and I thought about all of the ramifications," Lyon related. "I decided that this is the music that I like to do, and it obviously worked to some degree because we were packing our home club, the Stone Pony in Asbury Park, three nights a week, five sets a night. If we bomb, at least we bomb with the music we love."

This Time It's for Real, the group's second album, furthered the relationship. On the third record, *Hearts of Stone*, a breakthrough seemed imminent. But the release never received any push from the label, and the band was dropped shortly afterward. Around that time, Lyon cut his hand on a piece of glass while performing at a Sacramento club, an accident that forced the cancellation of the remaining tour dates.

Thankfully, the band linked up with Mercury Records and solid management, relieving Van Zandt of having to oversee the band's dealings from his hotel room. However, Mercury wanted a record right away, and with Miami Steve busy with his gig in Springsteen's E Street Band, the Jukes were forced into recording on their own. The group used Barry Beckett as a producer, the famed Muscle Shoals studio veteran who had recently produced Bob Dylan and Dire Straits.

Lyon and guitarist Billy Rush composed most of the material. "God, we didn't know," the frontman laughed. "It was, 'Well, here we are, we need 10 songs, so let's start writing.' The pressure brought out a lot. Everybody was contributing, the personalities came through—and that's why the album is called *The Jukes*."

The dynamic appeal of the minor hit "I'm So Anxious" and the blistering opening cut "All I Want Is Everything" portended the thrust of the band's self-penned material. Lyon attributed the solid collection to his painstaking research in the matter of music collecting.

"I've been through all of the pawn shops and thrift stores looking for records and guitars—everybody back east puts outrageous prices on things, but in the Midwest they're more realistic," he chuckled. "I found an old Gibson Gospel guitar in Omaha, but the price the guy wanted was a little steep. I'll have to go back there and threaten his life." ■

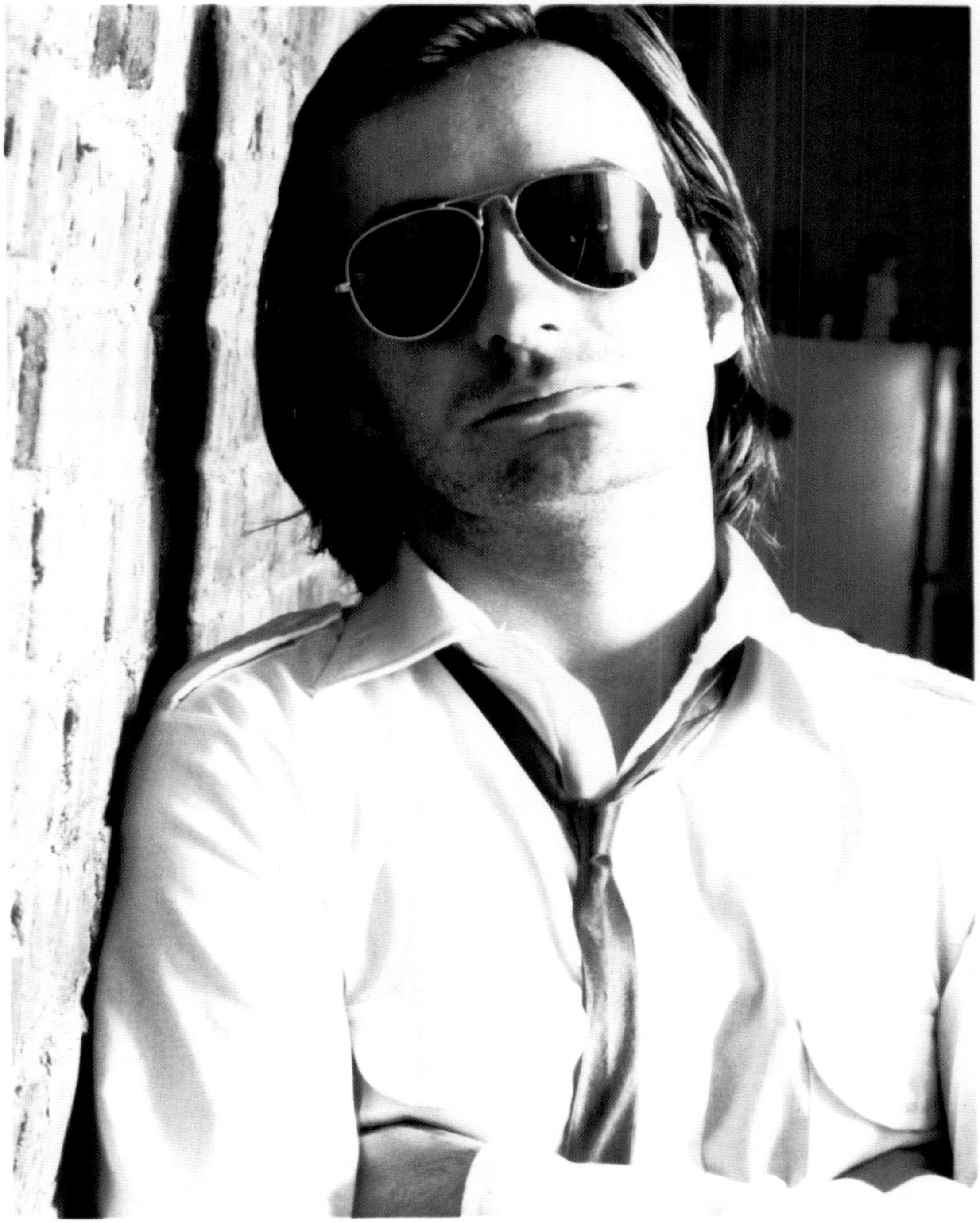

SOUTHSIDE JOHNNY

MANAGEMENT/DIRECTION:
Amundo Ent Inc
P O Box 177
Park Ridge, N J. 07656
Phone: 914/735-9334

THE Jukes

Recording Exclusively For
Mercury
A product of Phonogram, Inc.

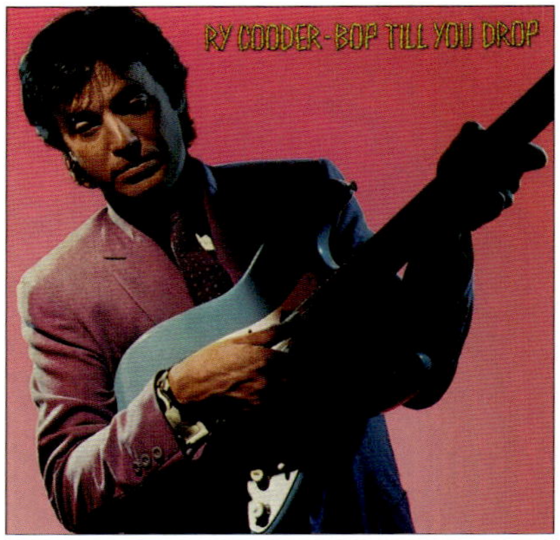

Billboard 200: *Bop Till You Drop* (#62)

Ry Cooder's *Bop Till You Drop* was perceived as the first major-label rock release to be recorded digitally.

ACUTELY ATTUNED to the richness of American musical tradition, Ry Cooder had created a celebrated body of work with his collective experience as a guitarist and arranger.

Born and raised in Los Angeles, Cooder spent his youth slouched over a Martin guitar that he got from his father. As an adolescent student of fingerpicking, he hung out at the Ash Grove, a Los Angeles folk club. He worked briefly in the Rising Sons, a band with Taj Mahal, before becoming a fixture on the L.A. session scene. By the time his first solo album was released in 1970, Cooder's reputation as a rural country blues devotee had spread.

Bop Till You Drop, his eighth album, returned to some of the stylistic elements mapped out on his earlier releases, particularly in his use of male background vocals and his experiments in Hawaiian and Tex-Mex blends. The repertoire consisted almost entirely of R&B classics, including Elvis Presley's "Little Sister," which became Cooder's biggest hit, and "Don't Mess Up a Good Thing," a duet with Chaka Khan.

"It's the form of the songs—to make albums that don't have horns, strings, synthesizers, that don't use a lot of outside help," Cooder explained. "I've tried to enrich this music as much as I could, this R&B thing—the small band, the guitar band—using instruments in an expressive way, rather than just a guy who plays a solo all the time."

An interesting production note to *Bop Till You Drop* involved the employment of digital recording technology rather than typical analog methods.

"Little nuances, things that I've been after for years, are suddenly there," Cooder enthused. "Digital gives range—any musician would be knocked out by the fullness of it. It's very dramatic, say, on drums, because of the peaks, the highs and lows. For guitars, the textures come out—you get that real 'finger chord skin' sound, that brush feel. On vocals, you can really get the edge. For the first time we are hearing back exactly what we played." ■

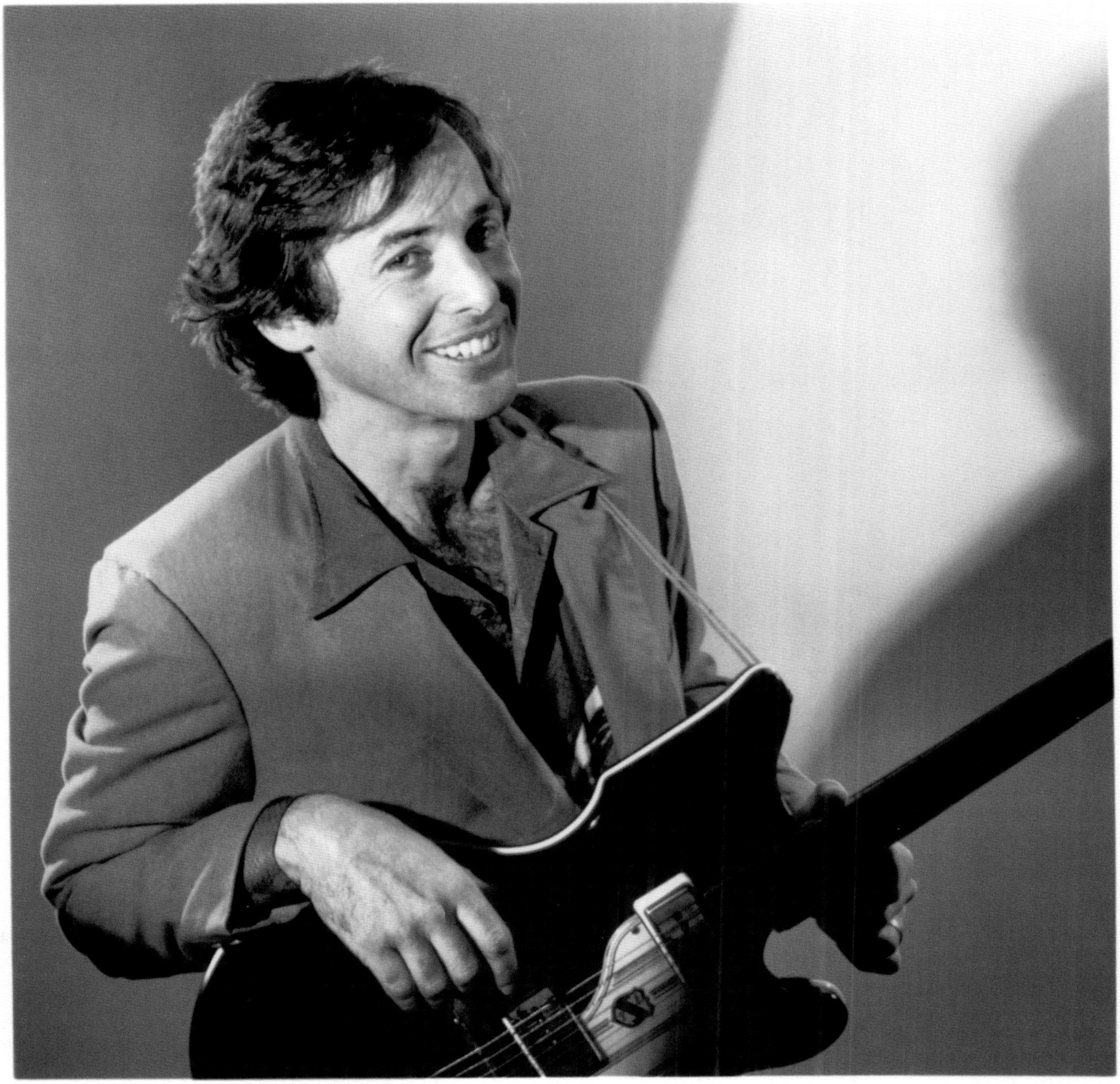

RY COODER

WARNER / REPRISE

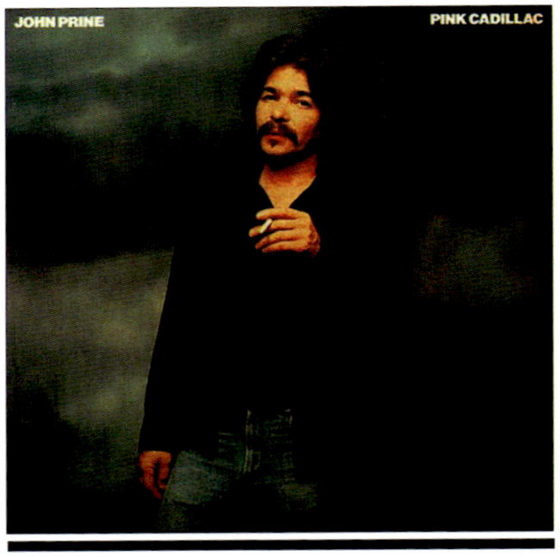

Billboard 200: *Pink Cadillac* (#152)

John Prine decamped to Memphis to put together the *Pink Cadillac* album and access the Sun Records sound.

STEADILY AND decisively, John Prine had established himself during the Seventies as one of America's most talented singer-songwriters. Born in 1946 in Maywood, Illinois, a working-class Chicago suburb, he developed an early interest in music, particularly country and rock 'n' roll. His older brother Dave taught him to play the guitar.

"He showed me how to play a chord, and when I finally played that chord without muffing it—well, I just sat there with my ear on the wood, even after the sound died, just feeling the vibrations," Prine said. "From then on, it was me sitting alone in a room, singing to a wall. The wall seemed to like it."

Prine struggled through high school and took a variety of jobs before going to work as a mailman. After a short, involuntary trip to Germany, courtesy of the US Army, he briefly returned to Chicago and the post office before actively devoting himself to songwriting. In 1970, Prine stepped onstage for the first time at the Fifth Peg during an open-mic night. He soon started playing the Earl of Old Town, another Chicago club, on a regular basis.

"John Belushi used to work right across the street with Second City back then," Prine remembered. "When he was off the stage, on a break, he'd come over to Earl's to listen, and when we were between sets, we'd go over to see him. I'll never forget the way he used to do his impression of Marlon Brando singing 'Angel from Montgomery.'"

Since then, Prine's songs had been recorded by many top country, folk and rock performers, notably Bonnie Raitt's cover of "Angel from Montgomery" and Bette Midler's version of "Hello In There." He'd developed a widespread, loyal audience through club and concert tours and television appearances.

To record *Pink Cadillac,* his sixth album, Prine traveled to Sam Phillips Studios in Memphis—"the cradle of rock 'n' roll." By then, Phillips—the Sun Records founder and producer of music by Elvis Presley, James Cotton and other rock and blues legends—rarely did any studio work, but he produced two songs on the album (his sons Knox and Jerry produced the others). Leading a full-size band through an easeful electric session with the sound of Fifties rockabilly, Prine mixed original tunes and covers of rock 'n' roll classics that he had loved as a kid.

Of the songs he wrote, "Automobile" resonated—"It's a song I started long ago one February morning when I called in sick to the post office, because my car wouldn't start." Fans were charmed, but the album received mostly negative reviews. Prine remained reflective and gratified.

"In a way, things ain't really that much different than the way they were when I was six or 16—just different people and I travel a lot more," he said. "I'd like to grow into the kind of good man my grandfather was, somebody that they'd want to say a few words over their dead body. So if I take care and live to be 50 or 60, I should be feeling pretty good by then, rather than remorseful or regretful." ■

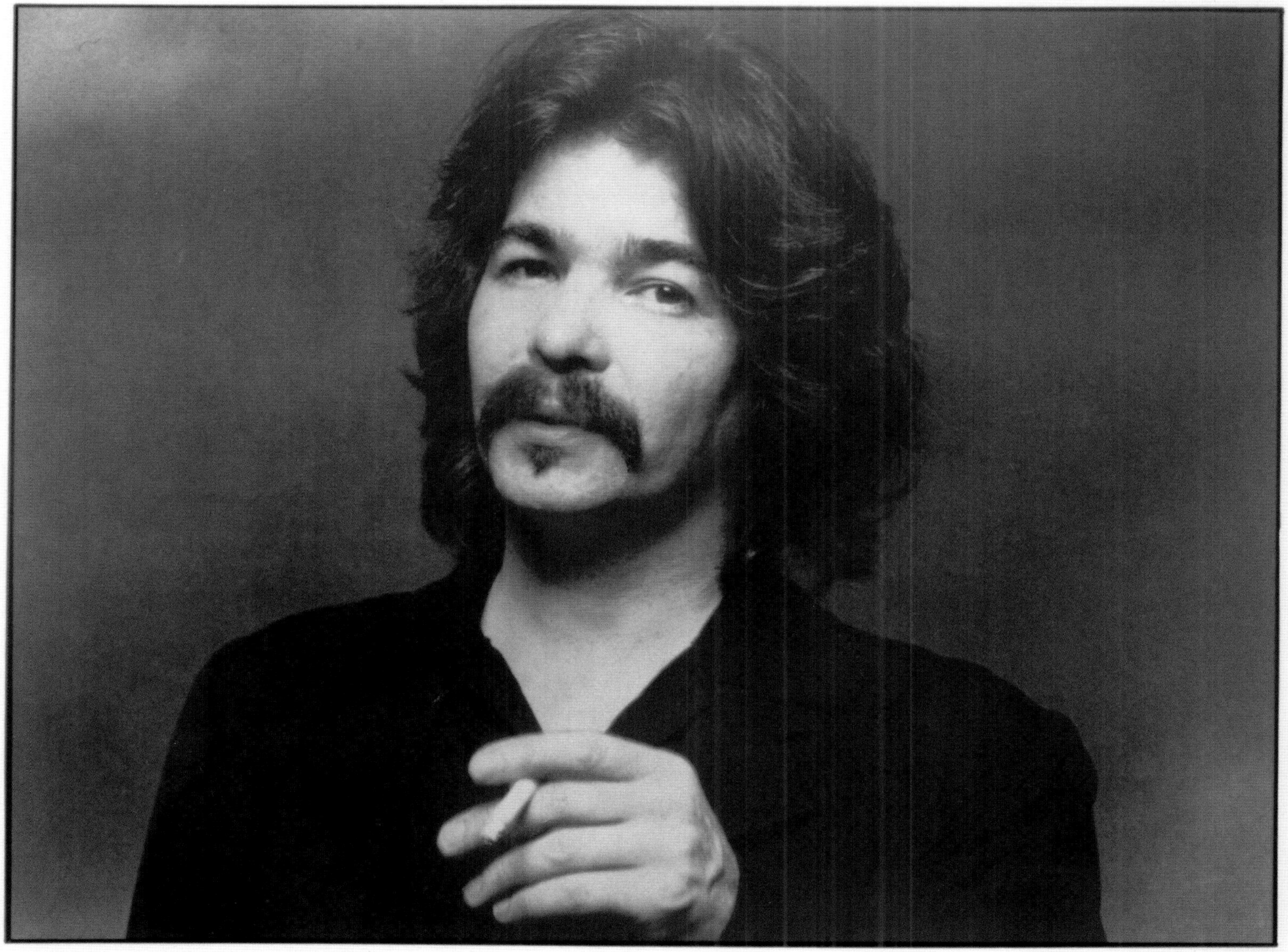

Photo Credit: GARY HEERY/1979

JOHN PRINE

asylum

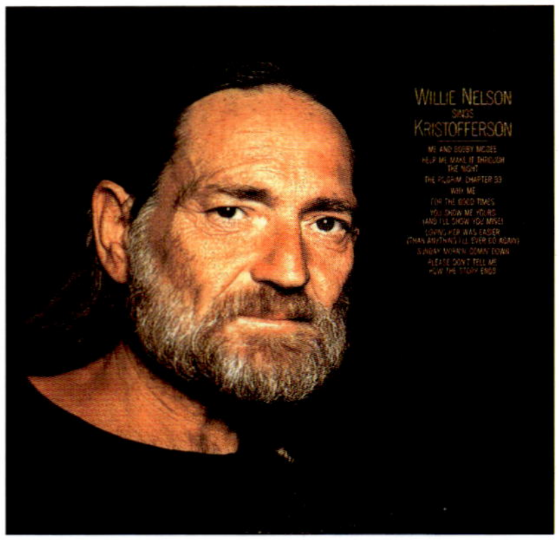

Billboard 200: *Willie Nelson Sings Kristofferson* (#42)

As a notable figure in country music and entertainment in general, Willie Nelson's time had finally arrived.

WILLIE NELSON'S rise in popularity as a performer and recording artist arched a few executive eyebrows in Nashville. For years, the Texas troubadour had been turning out hit songs of a high quality, still singing his heart out in the clubs and honky-tonks around Austin, Texas. The powers-that-be along Music Row advised Nelson to concentrate on songwriting and forget about trying to make it as a singer. His singing was peculiar, they insisted, and that unusual style held him back.

"Actually, the way I sing isn't all that hard," Nelson explained. "It's phrasing. Sinatra's been phrasing for years—a lot of pop singers have. It's just that nobody in country music in those days was doing it—but I couldn't imitate anybody else!"

Nelson moved back to Texas in 1972, and his singing began to draw the acclaim it deserved. "I found a lot of young people who had been into rock 'n' roll or whatever and all of a sudden they became interested in country music," he recalled. "And I also knew that they didn't have any place to go to listen to country music—their hair was too long to get into some of those places without getting into trouble. But I knew there was an audience there, so I went down to the Armadillo World Headquarters and told them I wanted to play for their audiences and see if what I was thinking was right."

The experiment worked—Nelson's cult-like following in the Southwest burgeoned into national superstardom. In 1976, *Wanted! The Outlaws*, a compilation of songs recorded by Nelson, Waylon Jennings, Jessi Colter (Mrs. Jennings) and Tompall Glaser, became the first country album ever to be certified platinum for sales exceeding a million copies. Nelson received a Grammy Award for "Blue Eyes Cryin' in the Rain," and his albums attracted a steadily widening audience.

"There was a whole wave of new energy behind country music," he said. "People started listening to the lyrics, and country music is where you find the most prolific and simple lyrics. That's where all the poets are these days—country music songwriters like Kris Kristofferson."

Willie Nelson Sings Kristofferson was the proof of two artists' mutual admiration over the years. Nelson interpreted nine songs written by Kristofferson—notably "Me and Bobby McGee," "Help Me Make It Through the Night" and "The Pilgrim, Chapter 33"—with Kristofferson singing harmony vocals. In 1979, Nelson also made his motion picture debut in *The Electric Horseman*, starring Robert Redford and Jane Fonda.

"I went to see Kris and Rita (Coolidge, his soon-to-be wife) when they were down in Durango, Mexico, doing the *Pat Garrett and Billy the Kid* movie (released in 1973). Sam Peckinpah was directing that movie, and he told me to hang around and he'd put me in a scene. I didn't have the time—I was in a hurry, so I left. But Kris was instrumental in my wanting to get interested in the movies because he was doing okay at it. He's pretty good at things like that." ■

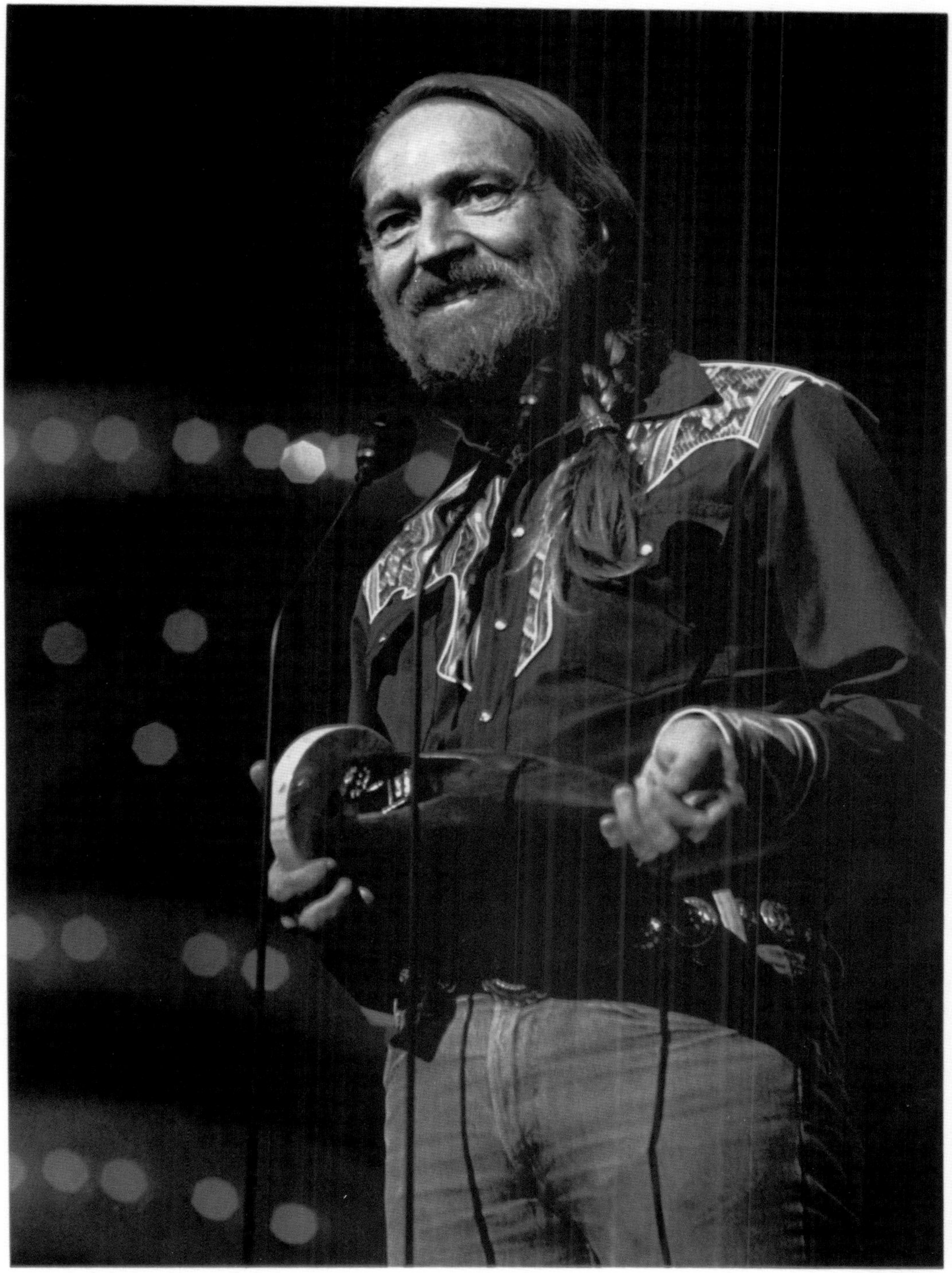

WILLIE NELSON

Columbia

7910

CMA "ENTERTAINER OF THE YEAR" AWARD 1979

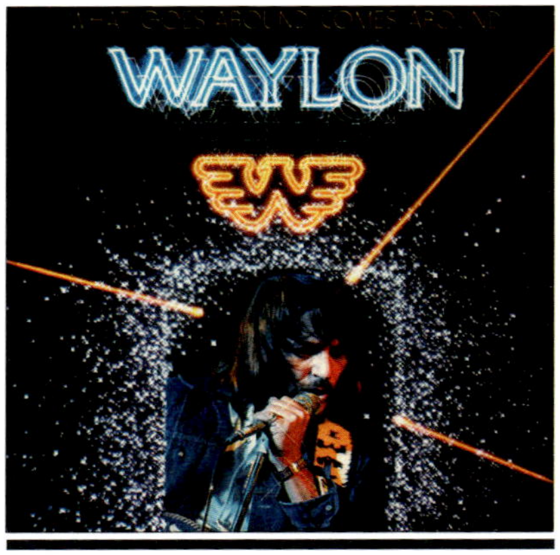

Billboard 200: *What Goes Around Comes Around* (#49)

What Goes Around Comes Around kept Waylon Jennings at the fore of music referred to as "outlaw country."

WAYLON JENNINGS had risen above involuntary and self-imposed adversity to the pinnacle of commercial success. He first cracked the music business as a DJ on West Texas radio stations. Striking up a friendship with another Lubbock boy, Buddy Holly, he gained his first real playing experience as Holly's bass player on his 1959 tour—abruptly interrupted by the tragic plane crash claiming Holly, Richie Valens and J.P. Richardson, "the Big Bopper." Jennings sacrificed his seat on the plane to the latter at the last minute and rode to the next town.

Depressed and confused, Jennings pieced his life and career together again, settling in Phoenix where he scrutinized his musical mentors. Under the guidance of Chet Atkins, he was signed to RCA and moved to Nashville. But after years of laboring in and out of the limelight, all he had to show for his time were lines on his face and a seemingly insurmountable debt because of mismanagement.

Jennings was at the end of his rope when he convinced RCA to give him artistic control. The musician set out in search of contemporary cowboy music—tunes and titles like Lee Clayton's "Ladies Love Outlaws," Steve Young's "Lonesome, On'ry and Mean" and Billy Joe Shaver's "Honky Tonk Heroes."

"Honesty is something you can't wear out," he said. "Being yourself—that's what you have to do. Look that fellow in the mirror in the eye." Soon Jennings could do no wrong, the acknowledged leader of a new music which blew a rock 'n' roll attitude and creative freedom right into Music Row, with 12 Top 10 country hits since 1973, four straight No. 1 country albums and a stream of concert promoters clamoring for his time. *What Goes Around Comes Around* included two No.1 country singles—"Come with Me," where a more contemplative side emerged, and a "kicker" by Rodney Crowell, "I Ain't Living Long Like This."

"I'm an interpreter, a fan of writers—I like to take another man's song and make it sound like I wrote it," Jennings stated. "People always go into all that macho crap when they write about me. They make it sound like my main interest in life is tearing things apart. They forget I'm a musician—that's what I've always been."

In 1979, Jennings also wrote and sang "Theme from *The Dukes of Hazzard* (Good Ol' Boys)," a song for the CBS television series, which would become the biggest hit of his career. ■

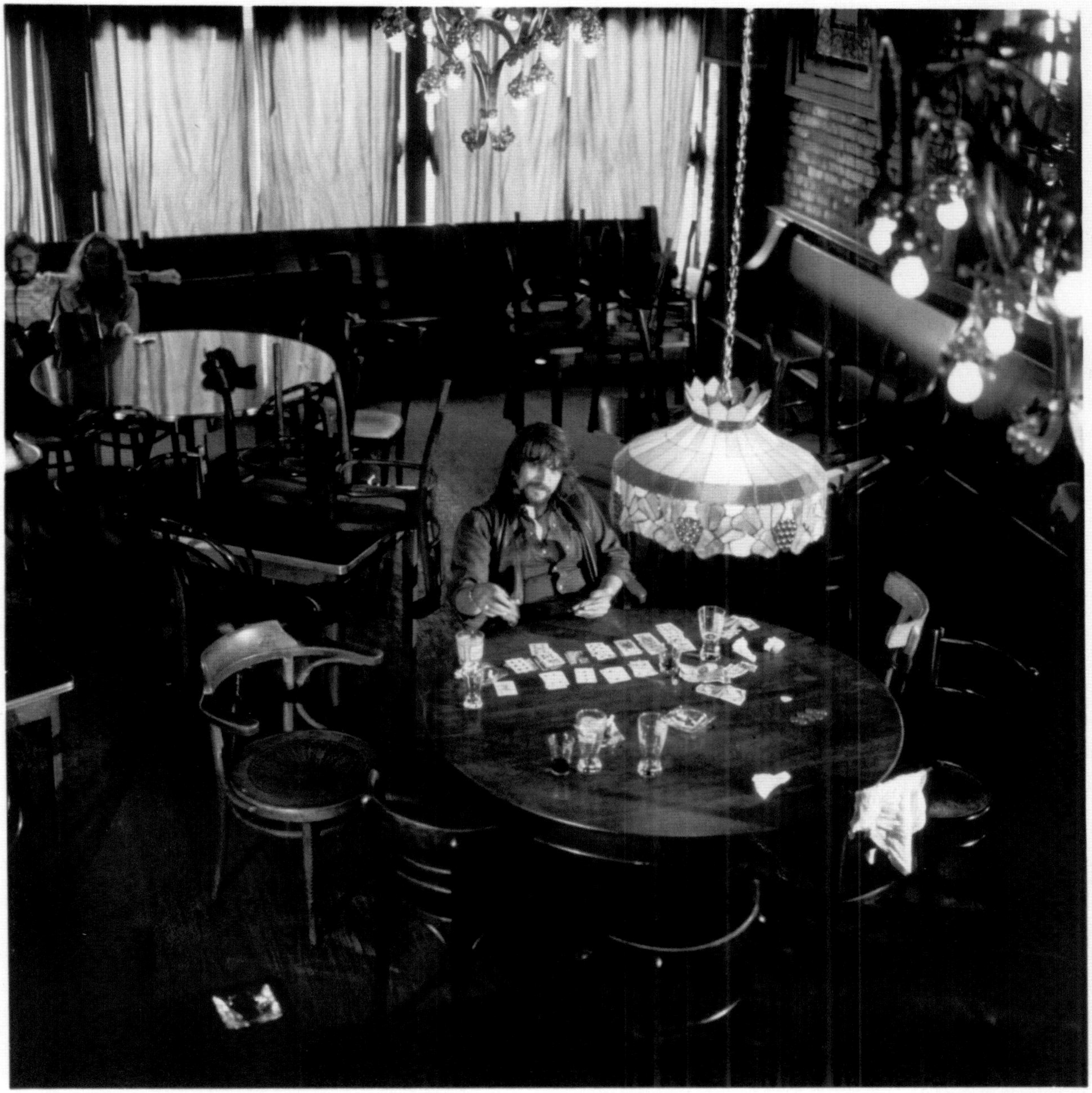

Waylon JENNINGS

Exclusively on RCA

RCA Records and Tapes

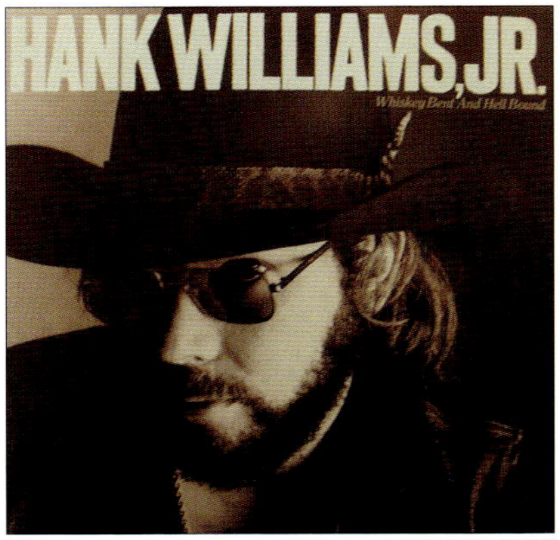

For country music's Hank Williams, Jr., the hardest way to get to the top turned out to be starting from the top.

THE SON of a country music legend, Hank Williams Jr. began his career at the tender age of eight, following in his famed father's footsteps. His own style evolved slowly as he struggled to find his own voice and place.

"Those were polarized times, and the music was the cutting edge of the times," he explained. "If you listened to country music, you were a redneck, and if you listened to rock 'n' roll, you were a hippie freak. So what happened to the Allman Brothers in Macon, Georgia, was of no concern to the pickers in Nashville, Tennessee, a couple of hundred miles up the road. But it was important to me, because those Georgia boys were trying to tell me something."

In 1975, just when it seemed like he was about to make Nashville shut up and listen, he headed for Montana for one last fling before hitting the road to introduce the "new" Hank Williams Jr. While hiking along the Continental Divide, a snowfield collapsed underneath him, and he fell more than 500 feet, most of it in the air, and crashed into a boulder. He survived, but his skull was split and his face was crushed.

After extensive reconstructive cosmetic surgery, he had to relearn how to speak and sing, a recovery period lasting a full two years. When he re-emerged, he challenged the country music establishment with a blend of country, rock and blues, positioning himself as a rowdy redneck. *Whiskey Bent and Hell Bound* launched a streak of hits that ran for a decade.

He said the title track, a moody Southern-rock ballad, was "Hank Williams Jr.'s life from about 1971 to 1975. A true story—and I still like to pour one now and then." The notorious "Women I've Never Had" veered between macho culture and benevolent sexism. "Puts me in a great mood—better than Columbian," Williams said. "This song should be the national anthem of the cowboy." ■

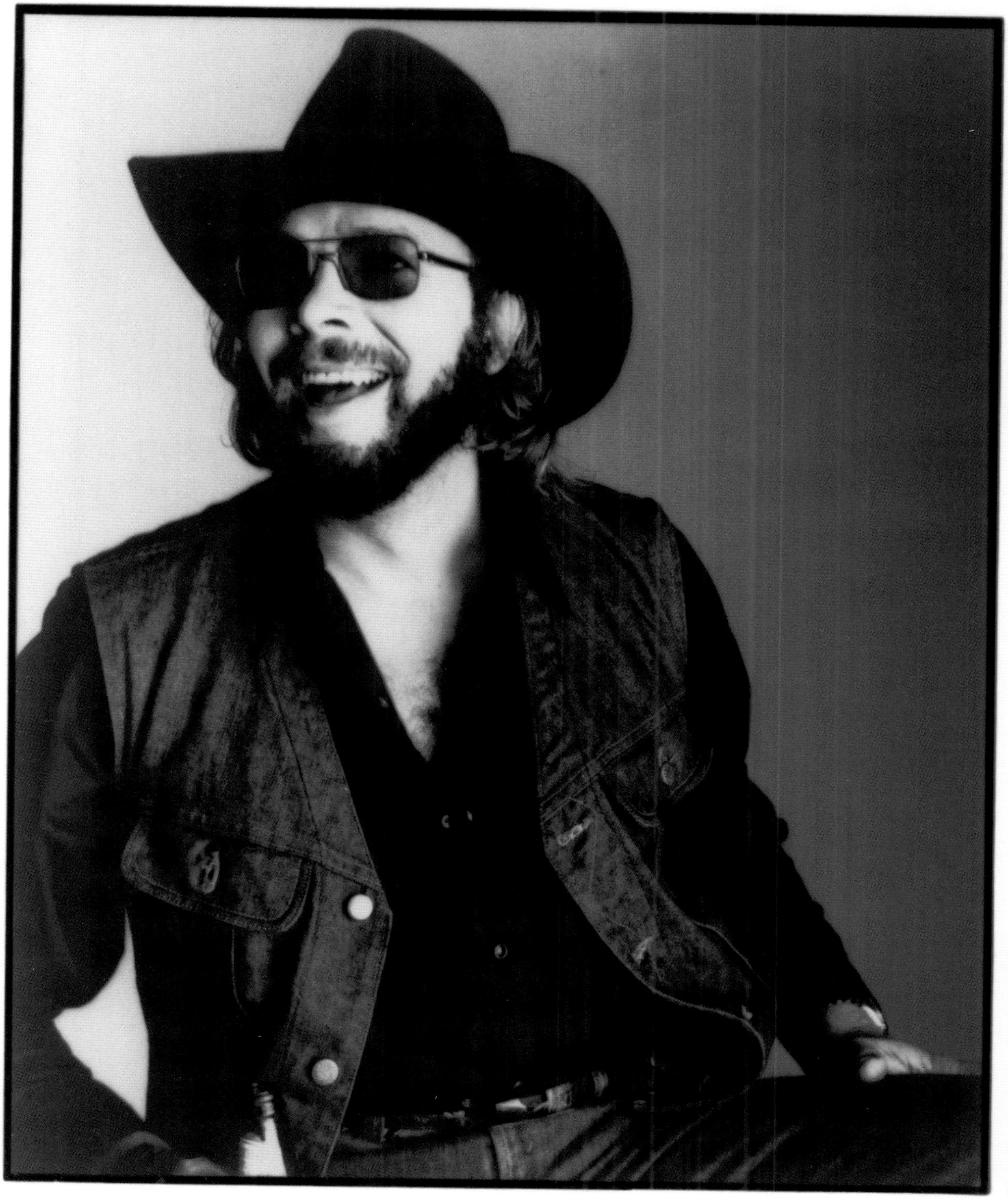

Photo Credit: ETHAN RUSSELL /1979

HANK WILLIAMS, JR.

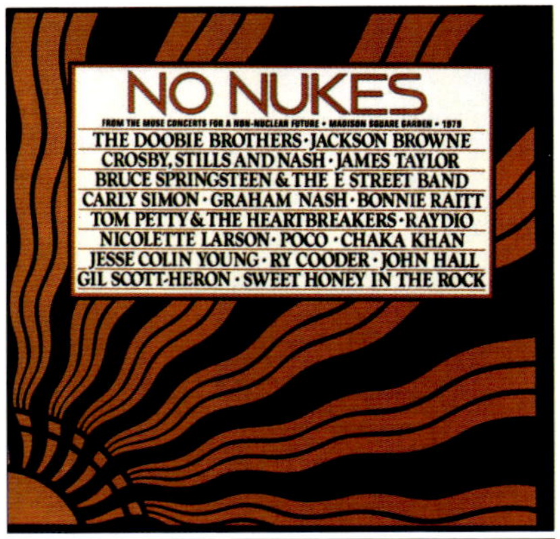

Billboard 200: *No Nukes: The MUSE Concerts for a Non-Nuclear Future* (#19)

The No Nukes live album drew attention for an efficient and fruitful integration of music and social activism.

TWENTY ACTS appeared in late September 1979 at New York's Madison Square Garden for five nights of concerts to raise money for MUSE—an acronym for Musicians United for Safe Energy. The shows were organized and headlined by MUSE board members Jackson Browne, Graham Nash, Bonnie Raitt and John Hall, and featured such stars as Bruce Springsteen, James Taylor and Carly Simon, the Doobie Brothers, Jesse Colin Young and others.

Nash and Browne stayed up for seven straight days putting the final touches on *No Nukes,* a three-record set chronicling the concerts. "I've been in rock 'n' roll about 20 years now, and I have never worked so hard or been up so long continuously," Nash wearily noted of the weeklong marathon. "But the 'high' was in the completion, the sense of history, and the fact that if we could get it out before Christmas it would be a much more powerful missile on behalf of the movement."

There was no question that the $17.95 *No Nukes* set was capable of generating considerable sums of money to MUSE to distribute to various anti-nuclear groups.

"MUSE is setting up to counter the incredible financing that the opposition has," Nash explained. "When Proposition 15 (an anti-nuclear initiative) was viable in California, we were outspent 10 to 1. We decided that the only way we could make a dent is by being a catalyst for people to initiate their own investigations. We figure once you find out the pros and cons of nuclear power, it will be an unequal equation."

The political, corporate and musical ramifications of the entire project were staggering, but the cause had proved to be bigger than the usual petty differences. Joe Smith, the head of Asylum Records, put $500,000 into the MUSE bank account when no contracts or releases were signed for any of the artists, a prodigious display of good faith.

The usual "you can't put his name at the top of the credits" business went by the boards. In fact, Columbia Records allowed MUSE to include Bruce Springsteen & the E Street Band's powerful "Detroit Medley" ("Devil with the Blue Dress," "Good Golly, Miss Molly" and "Jenny Take a Ride"), despite the fact that it was Springsteen's first authorized live recording—and hence a commercial goldmine.

Much of the music contained on the album fell into a "greatest hits" category than songs addressing the nuclear power controversy directly. When musicians entered into the realm of politics and proved capable of generating such financial clout, they had to make assurances that they were making responsible decisions in lieu of their public image. Nash and his cohorts weren't about to be denied.

"It's an incredible feeling—the kids realize they do have a voice and a say in which way their future goes. Trying to pull off this entire project has been crazy, but I'm personally honored that I'm in a position to strike such a blow against nuclear power. I feel like we've stabbed a monster in the side, and although we might not kill it, I can feel it bleeding to death." ■

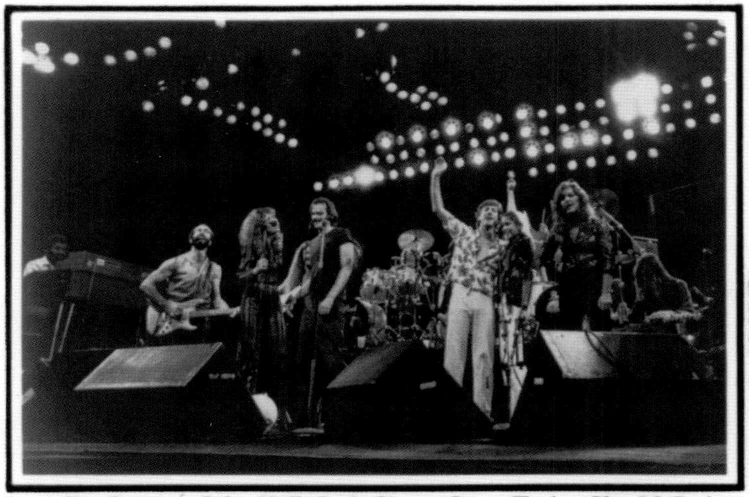

Photo Credit: LYNN GOLDSMITH

Cornelius Bumpus, John Hall, Carly Simon, James Taylor, Chet McCraken, Graham Nash, Nicolette Larson, Bonnie Raitt, David Lindley

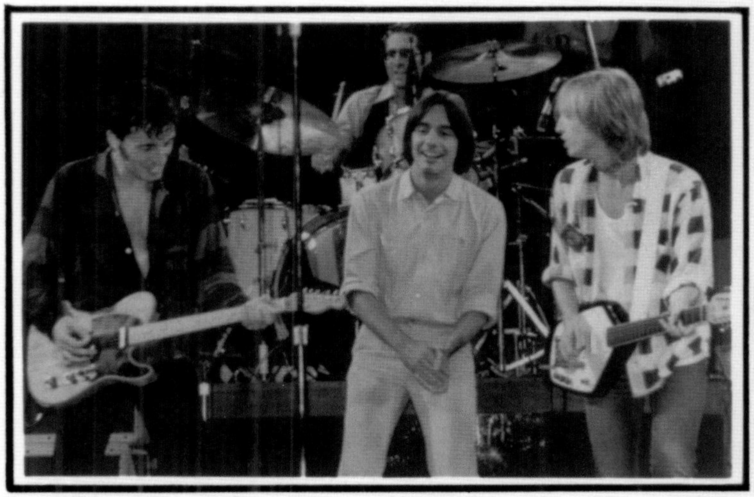

Photo Credit: LYNN GOLDSMITH

Bruce Springsteen, Jackson Browne, Tom Petty

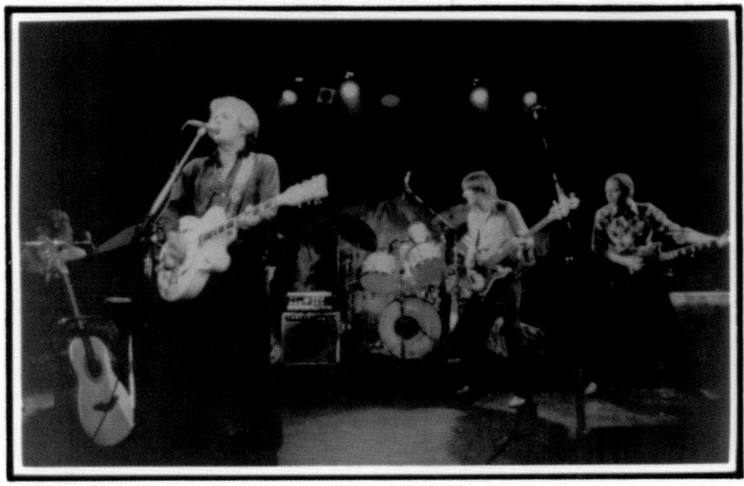

Photo Credit: BRIAN D. MCLAUGHLIN

Poco

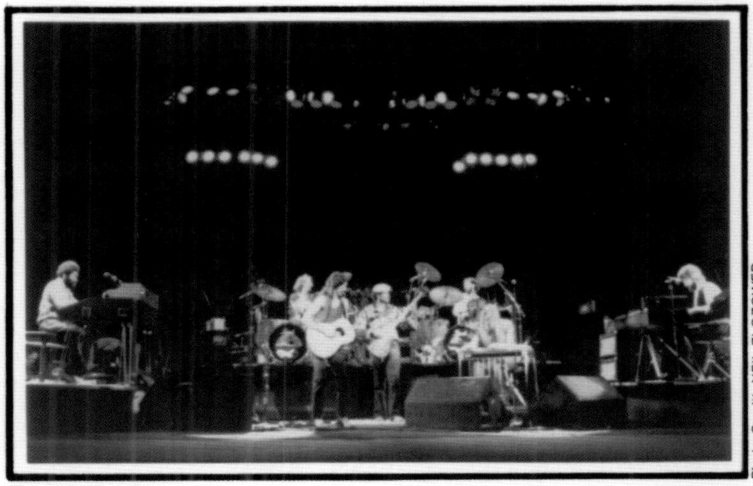

Photo Credit: NEIL ZLOZOWER

Doobie Brothers

NO NUKES

asylum

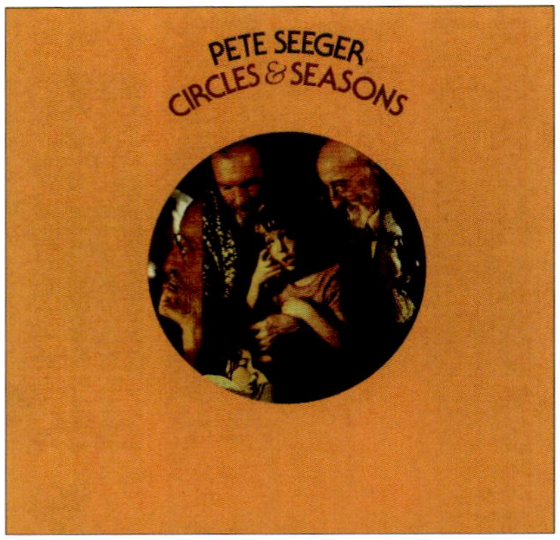

Folk music still elated Pete Seeger, who found another measure of his worth per the *Circles & Seasons* album.

AT 60 years old, Pete Seeger had remained at the forefront of the folk music scene for more than four decades, starting with his initial inspiration during the late Thirties.

"What got me started was the fight against fascism—Hitler was trying to drag the world into war," the venerable singer and activist explained. "The older I get, the leerier I get of trying to accomplish things with a few words, but I guess that's why I'm a musician. All problems—safe energy, toxic chemicals, unemployment—are related. That's what an artist should try to do, tie all these things together."

In the course of his career, Seeger had recorded more than 30 albums for a variety of labels and remained involved with many causes, although his low profile in the late Seventies suggested his most active period was over. "TV could be the answer if we weren't in a commercial straitjacket," Seeger noted, referring to a PBS broadcast pairing him and Arlo Guthrie that generated the most coverage of his career.

"But I've got nothing to complain about personally. I just want people to reconsider the definition of 'folk' music. People think you play it on guitar and banjo, but there are as many kinds of folk music as there are folks—played on bagpipes, bongo drums, accordions. We not only have strains from Ireland and Scotland, France and Germany, but Africa and Mexico and a hundred other countries.

"I date the biggest change in music back to the Twenties, when every town had its own musicians. Then music became automated, and radio and records took over. As soon as someone starts performing professionally, they leave the boundaries of folk music. They become pop performers—which I am, too, in a sense."

Seeger blurred the distinction further on his *Circles & Seasons* album, which dressed up several of his songs in contemporary trappings. Yet in the liner notes, Seeger urged his audience to join in on any instrument available. "People that like my music don't really listen to records. I don't sell many. They're just for people to pick up ideas from. I want to play to people directly."

Seger had always been a captivating performer, although in the old days he concentrated on motivating people through his lyrics. With rock music replacing folk music in leading causes (MUSE), Seeger was more than happy to rely on his charisma.

"I just try to get the crowd singing with me," he explained. "When they're singing well, the message still comes across—there are many things you can do if you get together. And I'm an old hand at getting a crowd singing—been doing it for 40 years." ■

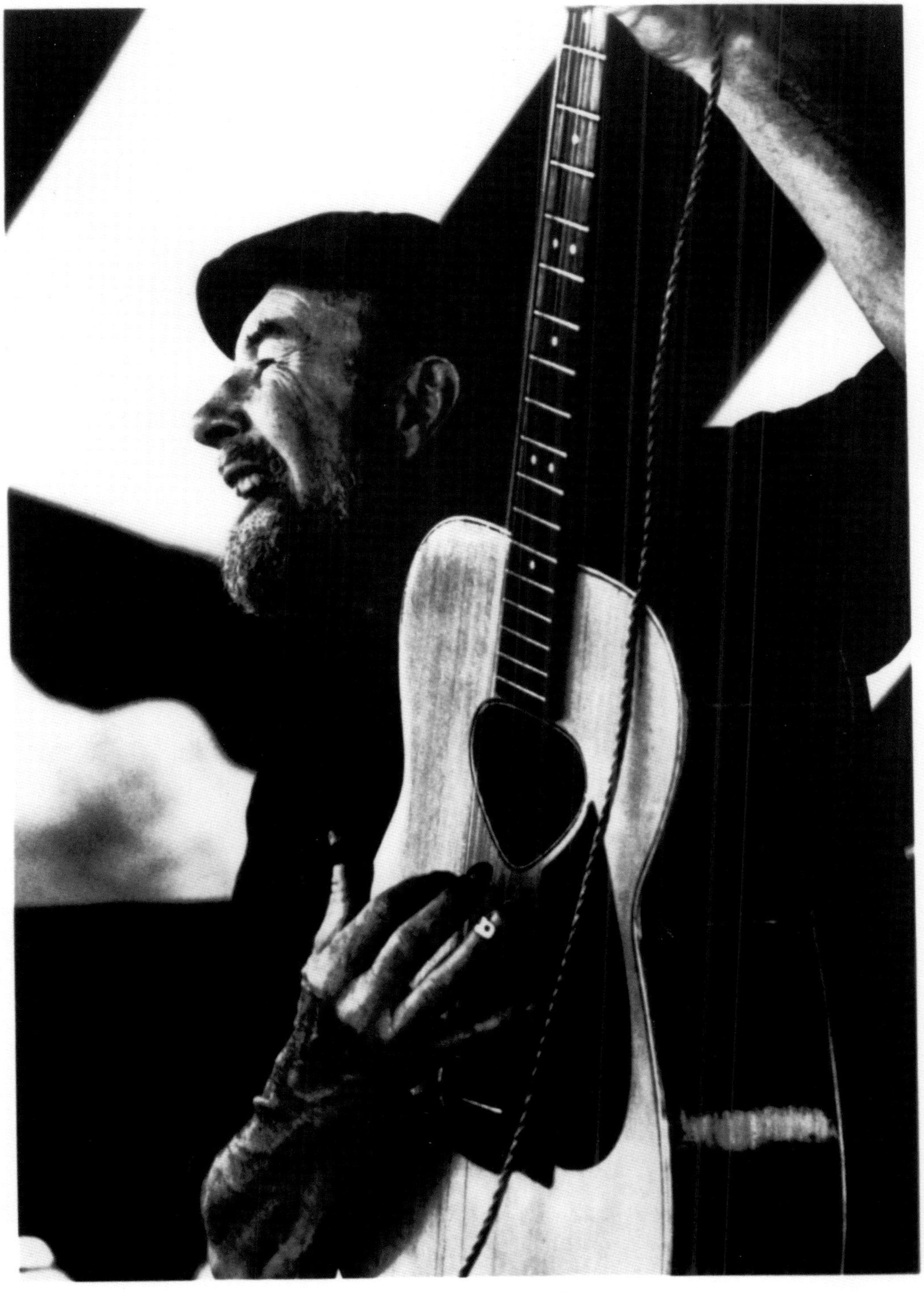

Photo by: Charles Porter JULY 1979

PETE SEEGER

WARNER/REPRISE

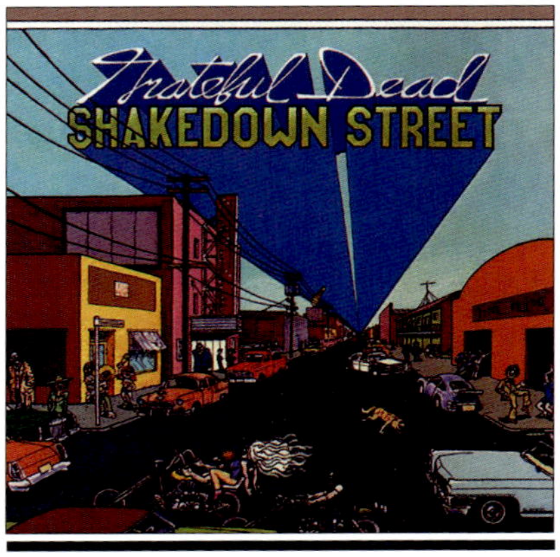

Billboard 200: *Shakedown Street* (#41)

Shakedown Street, produced by Little Feat's Lowell George, was yet another tame Grateful Dead studio album.

HAVING REHEARSED a solo project at a warehouse in San Rafael, California, Jerry Garcia liked the room's ambience so much that the Grateful Dead decided to install studio equipment. The cartoon-like cover of *Shakedown Street*—depicted by Gilbert Shelton, creator of the Fabulous Furry Freak Brothers—evoked the feeling of the scene on Front Street.

The Dead brought in Little Feat's Lowell George as a producer, partly on the premise that he "understood band mechanics," Garcia said. Unfortunately, George contributed very little besides supervising the recording of the basic tracks. *Shakedown Street* was a notoriously awkward effort that didn't convey the group's dynamism.

"There's always something to be learned from working with other people," Garcia allowed. "Whether or not working with producers has been in any way helpful for us as a recording band is maybe doubtful. The sales were about steady, just like our other records. It didn't create any change."

"It's frustrating to me that we don't make better records than we do," guitarist Bob Weir added. "One of the reasons, generally, is because we don't know the material when we're doing it. We don't know the material until years later. We should make a blanket policy of not recording anything that we haven't played onstage."

"Shakedown Street," a disco-boogie dalliance, emerged as a performance staple for years to come (and become the name for the vendors' markets outside Dead shows). "Fire on the Mountain" was later reworked in concert, and the group performed its cover of the Young Rascals' hit "Good Lovin'" on *Saturday Night Live*. *Shakedown Street* peaked on the *Billboard* charts in February 1979, but the album failed to reach the Top 40, the first time that had happened since 1969's *Aoxomoxoa*.

A few months later, pianist Keith Godchaux and singer Donna Jean Godchaux, members since the early Seventies, were eased out of the group..

According to bassist Phil Lesh, "By the first week of the winter '79 tour, it was apparent that Keith and Donna were melting down. Keith's playing had degenerated to the point that most of us were simply trying to 'lose him onstage,' in Bob's eloquent phrase. When we put their increasingly overt self-destructive behavior together with that, we knew it was finally time for a change." ■

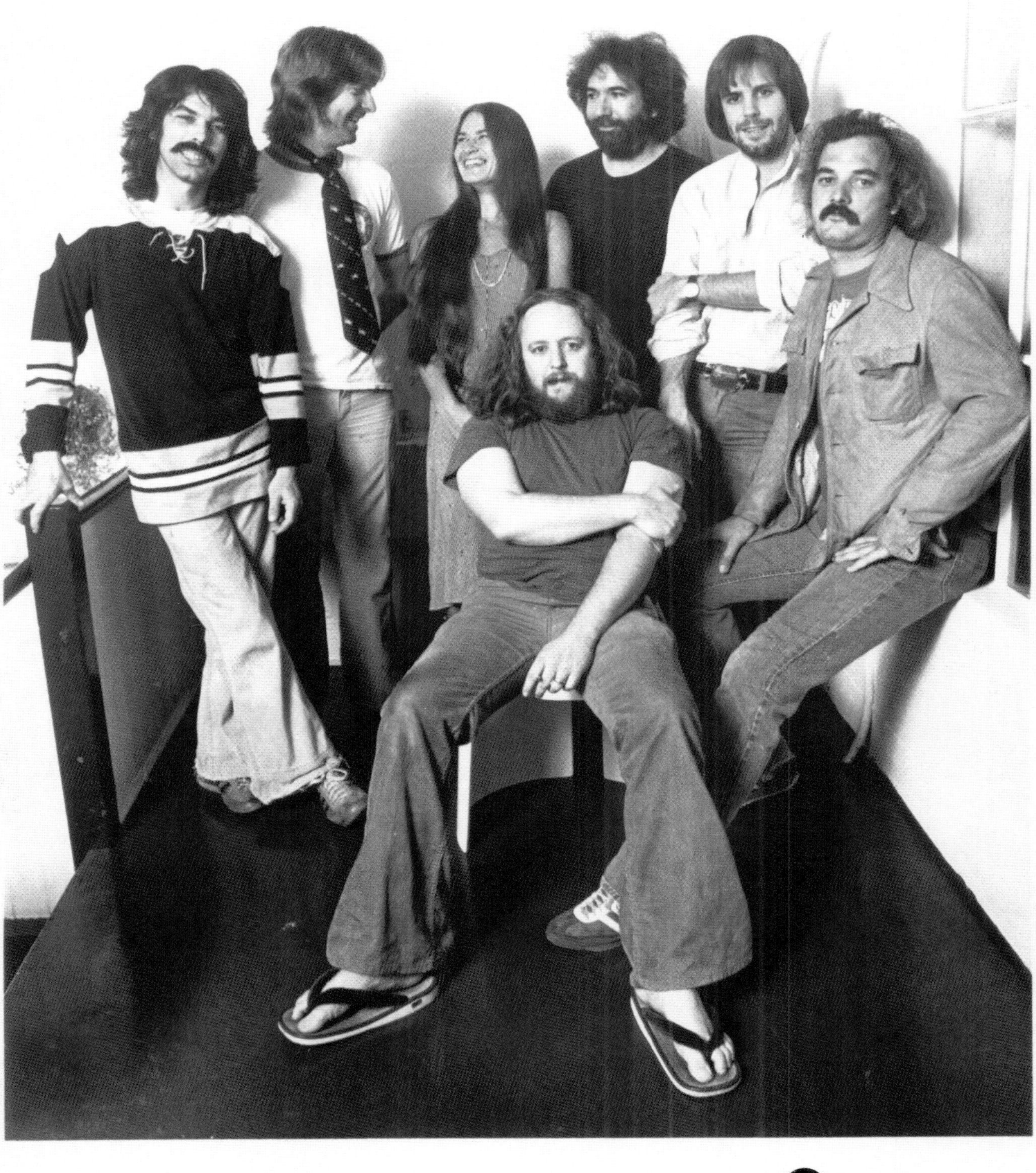

GRATEFUL DEAD

ARISTA RECORDS

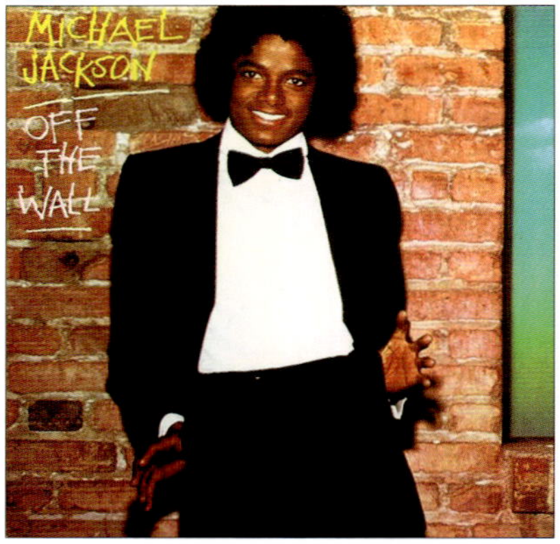

Michael Jackson rose to solo stardom with the mammoth success of *Off the Wall*, produced by Quincy Jones, yielding four singles that made the Top 10.

Billboard 200: *Off the Wall* (#3)
Billboard Hot 100: "Don't Stop 'Til You Get Enough" (No. 1); "Rock with You" (No. 1); "Off the Wall" (#10); "She's Out of My Life" (#10)

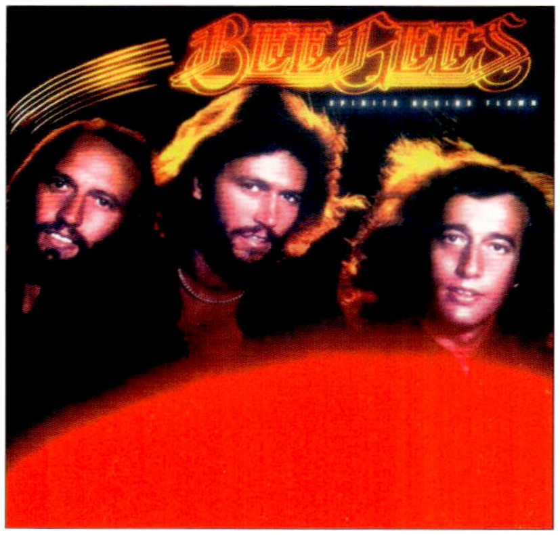

The **Bee Gees** album *Spirits Having Flown* bore three more consecutive No. 1 hits for the trio—"Too Much Heaven," "Tragedy" and "Love You Inside Out."

Billboard 200: *Spirits Having Flown* (No. 1)
Billboard Hot 100: "Too Much Heaven" (No. 1); "Tragedy" (No. 1); "Love You Inside Out" (No. 1)

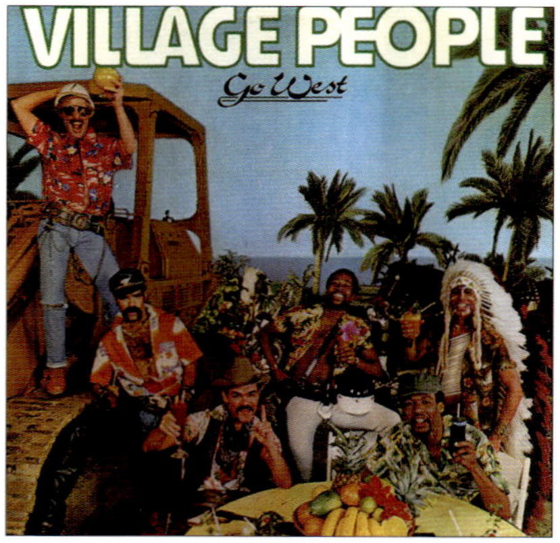

After the colossal success of "Y.M.C.A.," the campy **Village People** capitalized on another institution and scored a worldwide smash with "In the Navy."

Billboard 200: *Go West* (#8)
Billboard Hot 100: "In the Navy" (#3); "Go West" (#45)

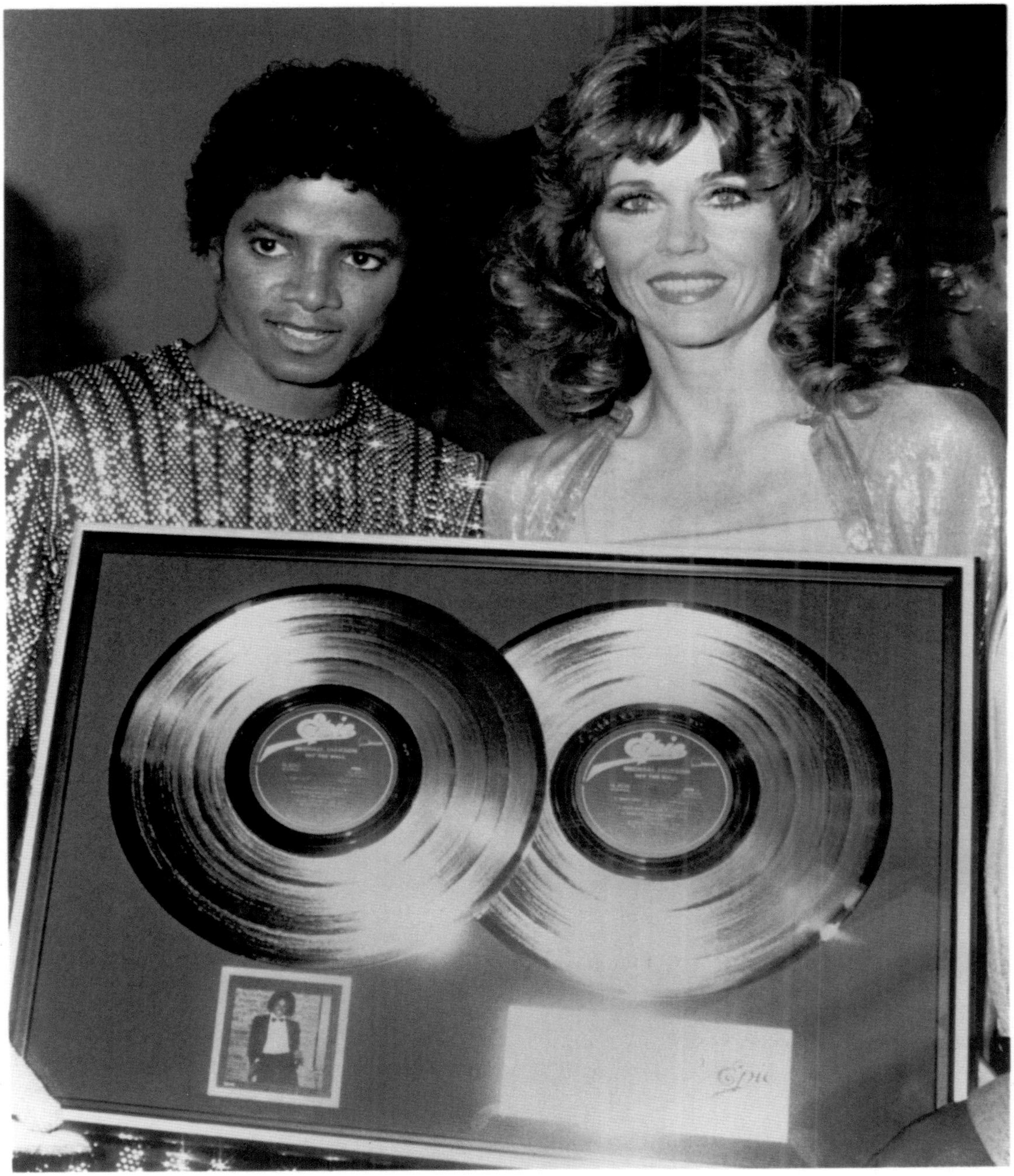

Picture caption: Epic recording artist Michael Jackson and Jane Fonda at a recent platinum record award ceremony for Michael Jackson's OFF THE WALL LP.

MICHAEL JACKSON

Epic

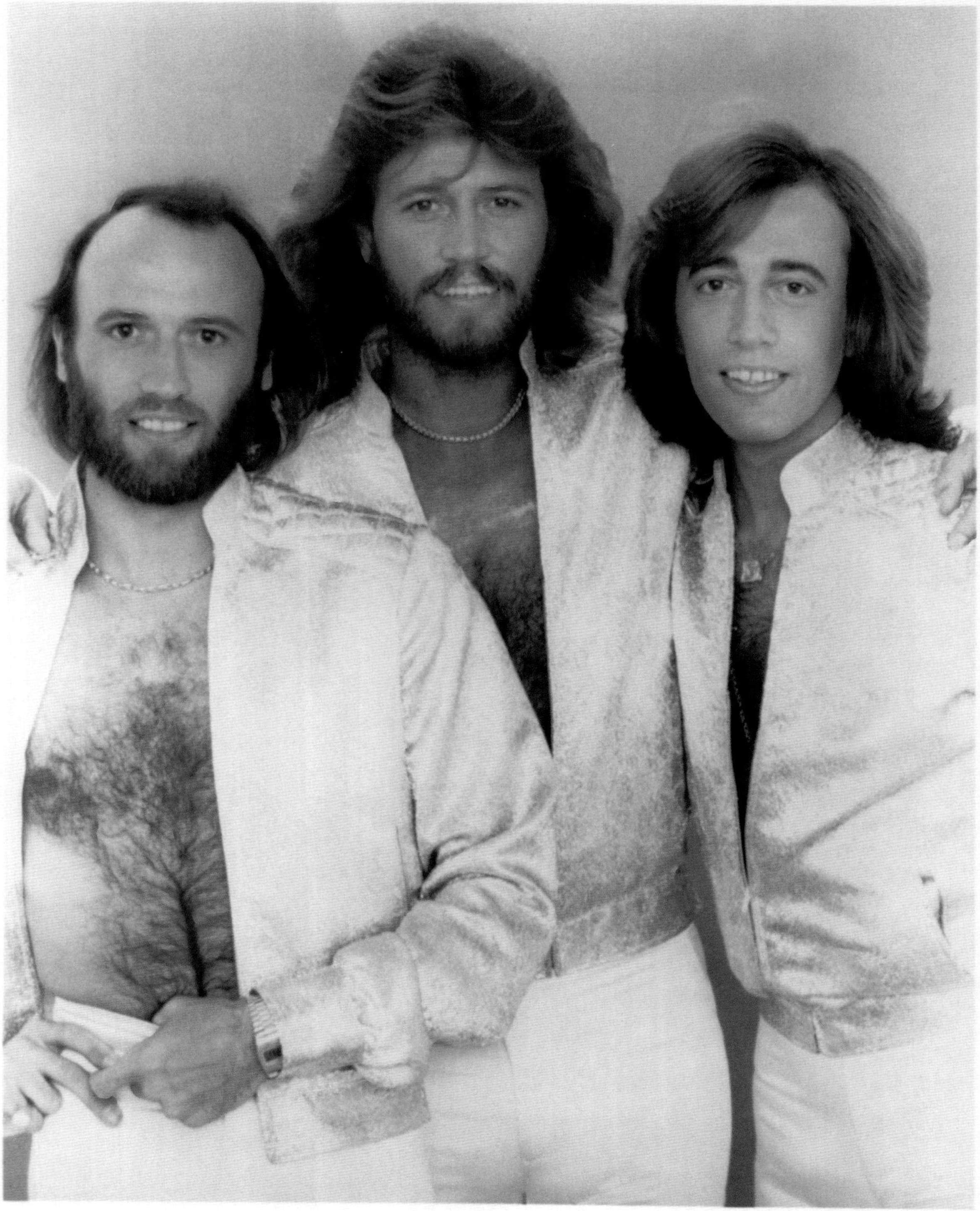

BEE GEES™

RSO Records, Inc.

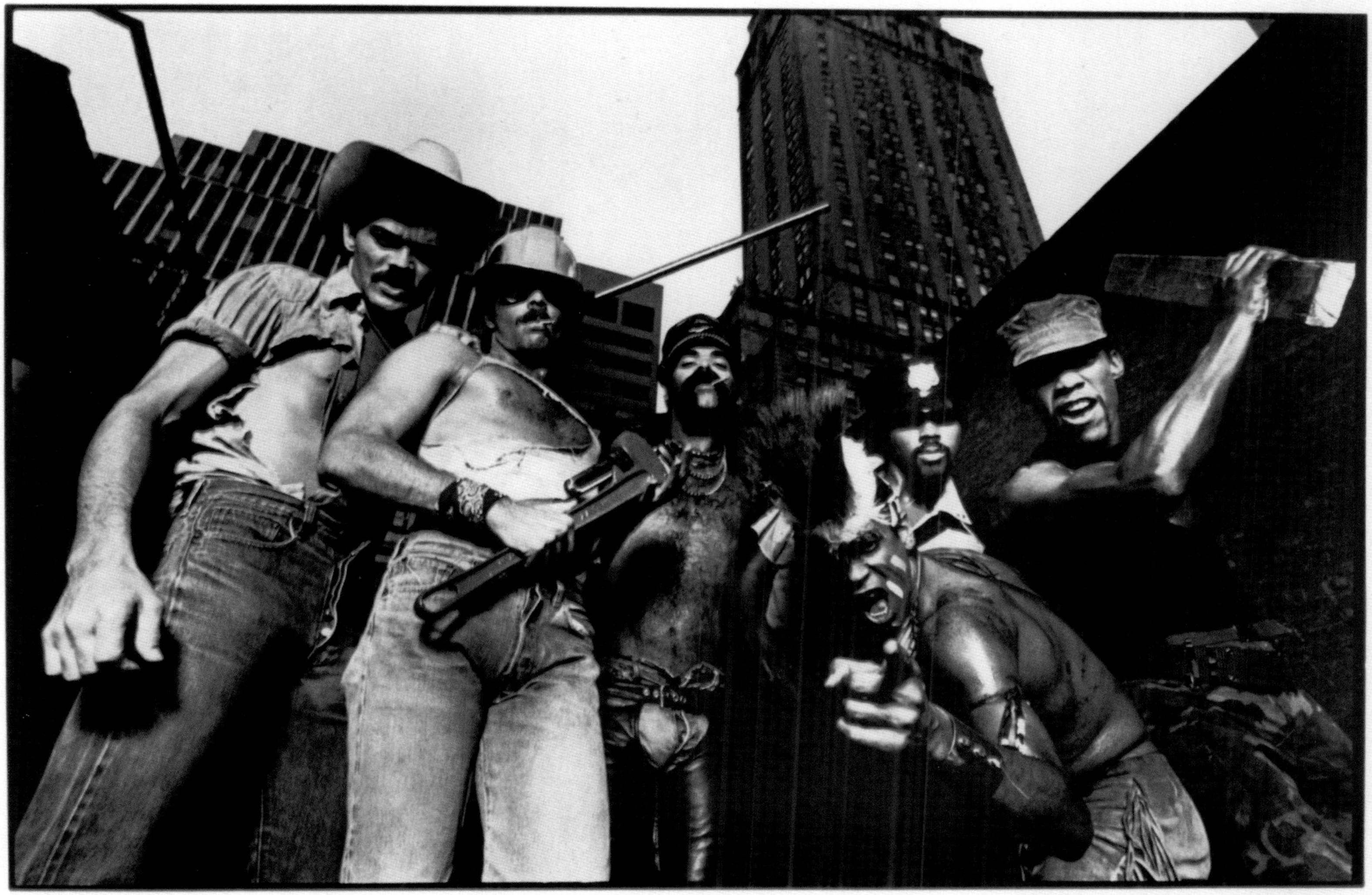

PHOTO: LYNN GOLDSMITH

Casablanca Record and FilmWorks

VILLAGE PEOPLE

CAN'T STOP PRODUCTION INC.
65 EAST 55TH
NEW YORK, NEW YORK 10022
(212) 751-6177
688-6470

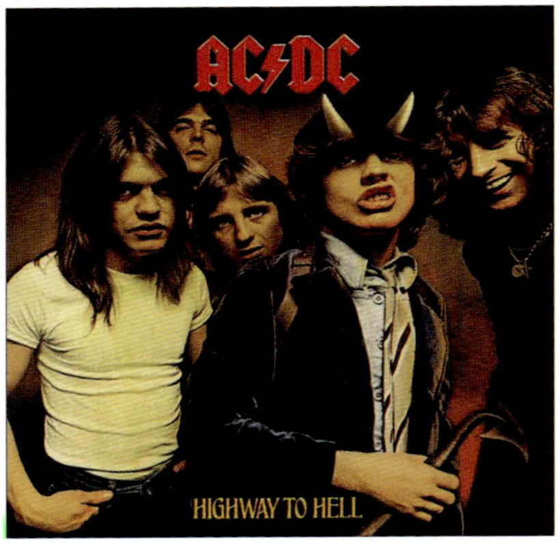

Hailing from Australia, **AC/DC** advanced into the top ranks of hard-rock acts with *Highway to Hell* and the mammoth power-chord roar of the title song.

Billboard 200: *Highway to Hell* (#17)
Billboard Hot 100: "Highway to Hell" (#47)

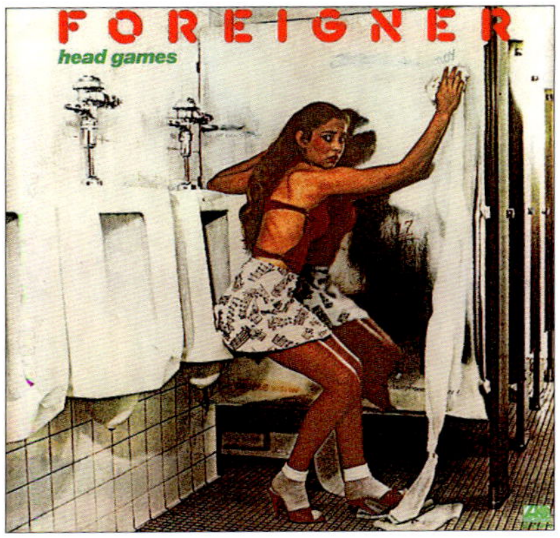

Marked by a lineup adjustment, *Head Games* kept **Foreigner** atop the arena-rock pecking order with the title track and the boisterous "Dirty White Boy."

Billboard 200: *Head Games* (#5)
Billboard Hot 100: "Dirty White Boy" (#12); "Head Games" (#14); "Women" (#41)

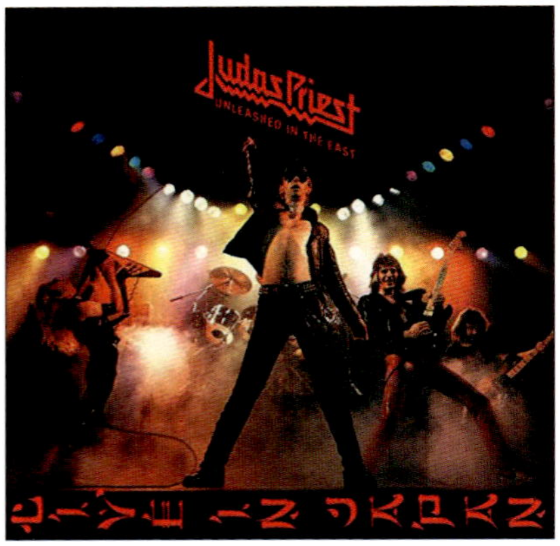

Unleashed in the East, **Judas Priest**'s first live album, was recorded on stops along the UK heavy metal band's tour of Japan, then enhanced in the studio.

Billboard 200: *Unleashed in the East* (#70)

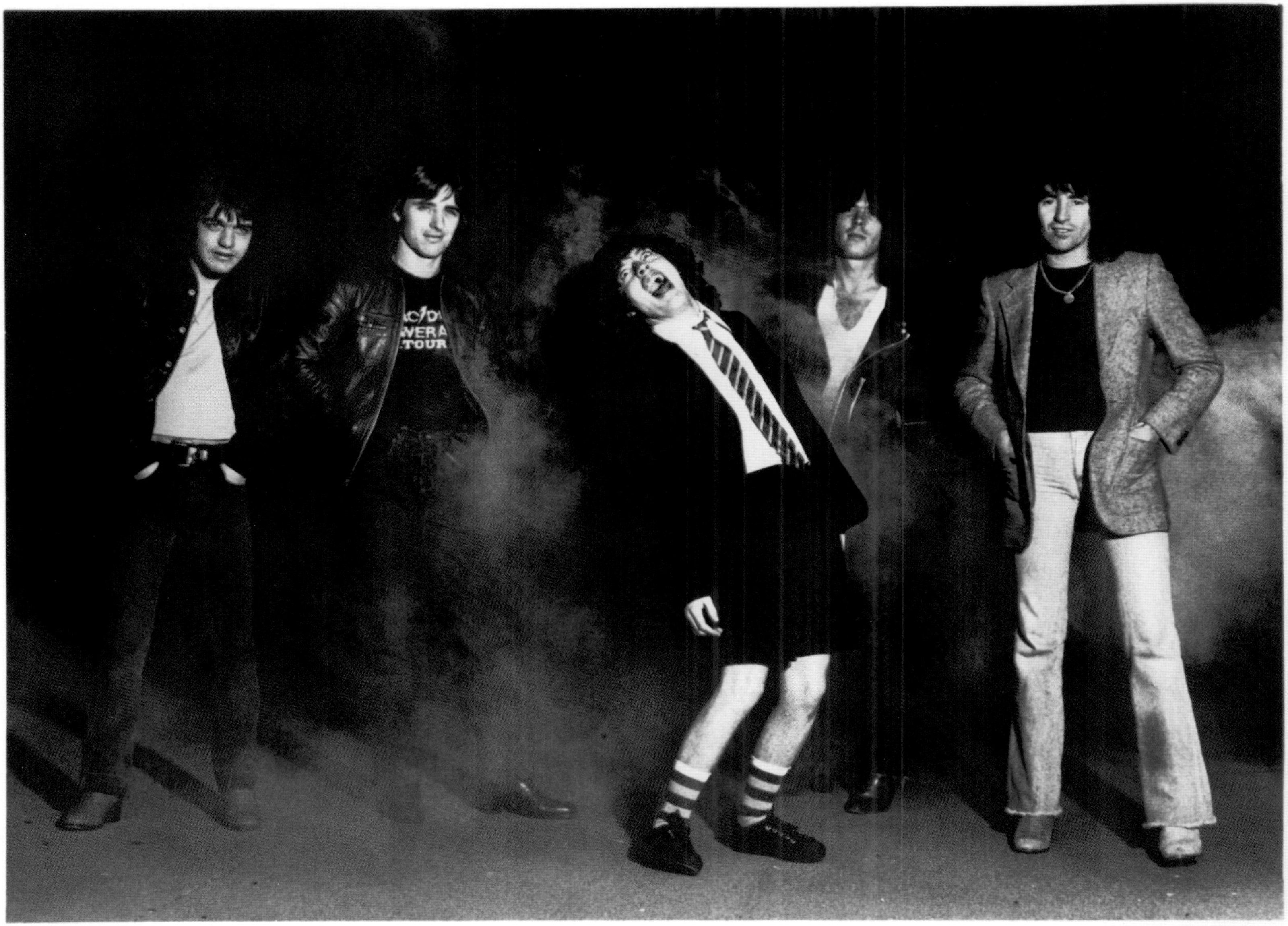

AC/DC

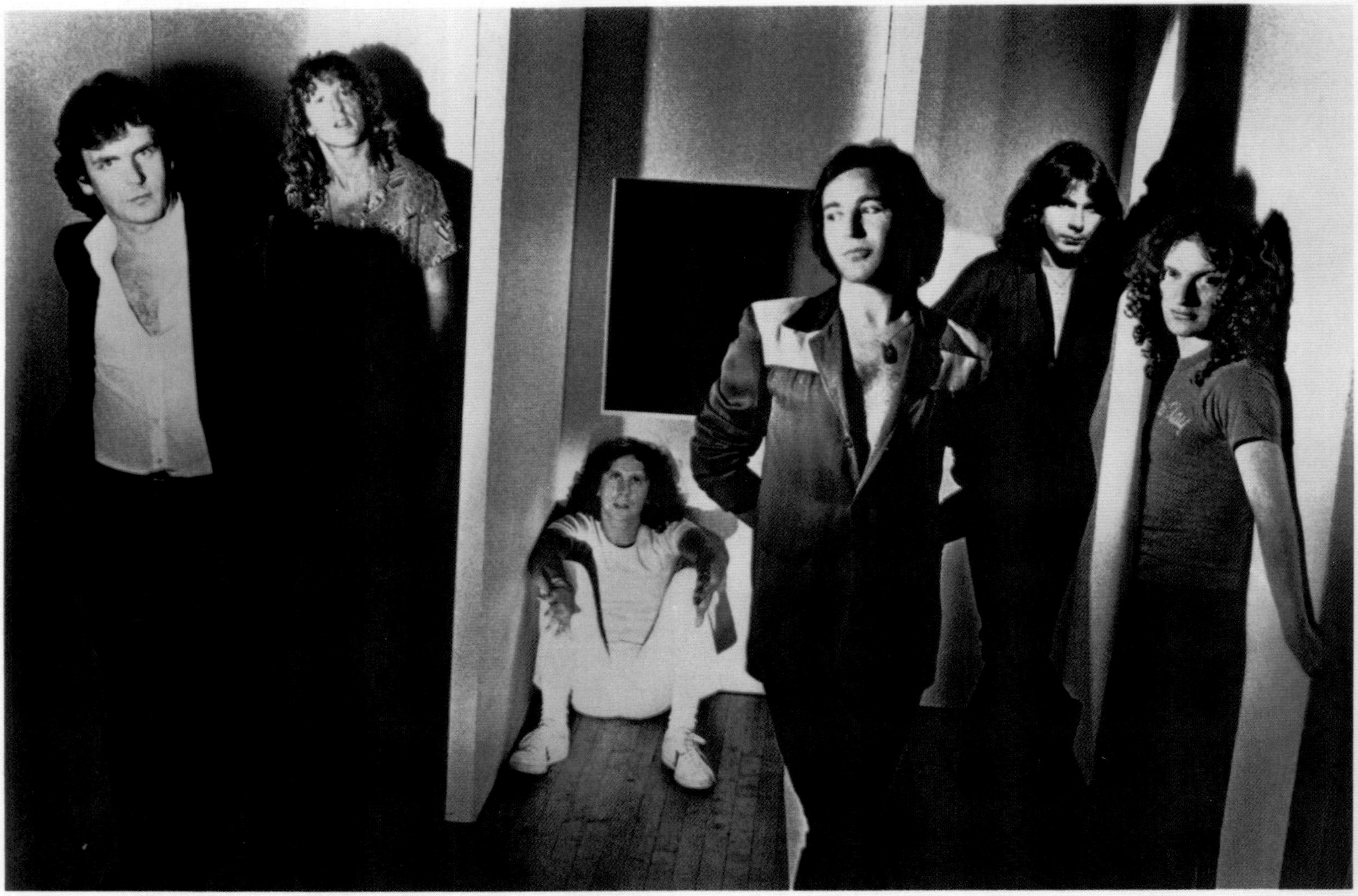

Ian McDonald Rick Wills Dennis Elliott Mick Jones Al Greenwood Lou Gramm

FOREIGNER

ATLANTIC

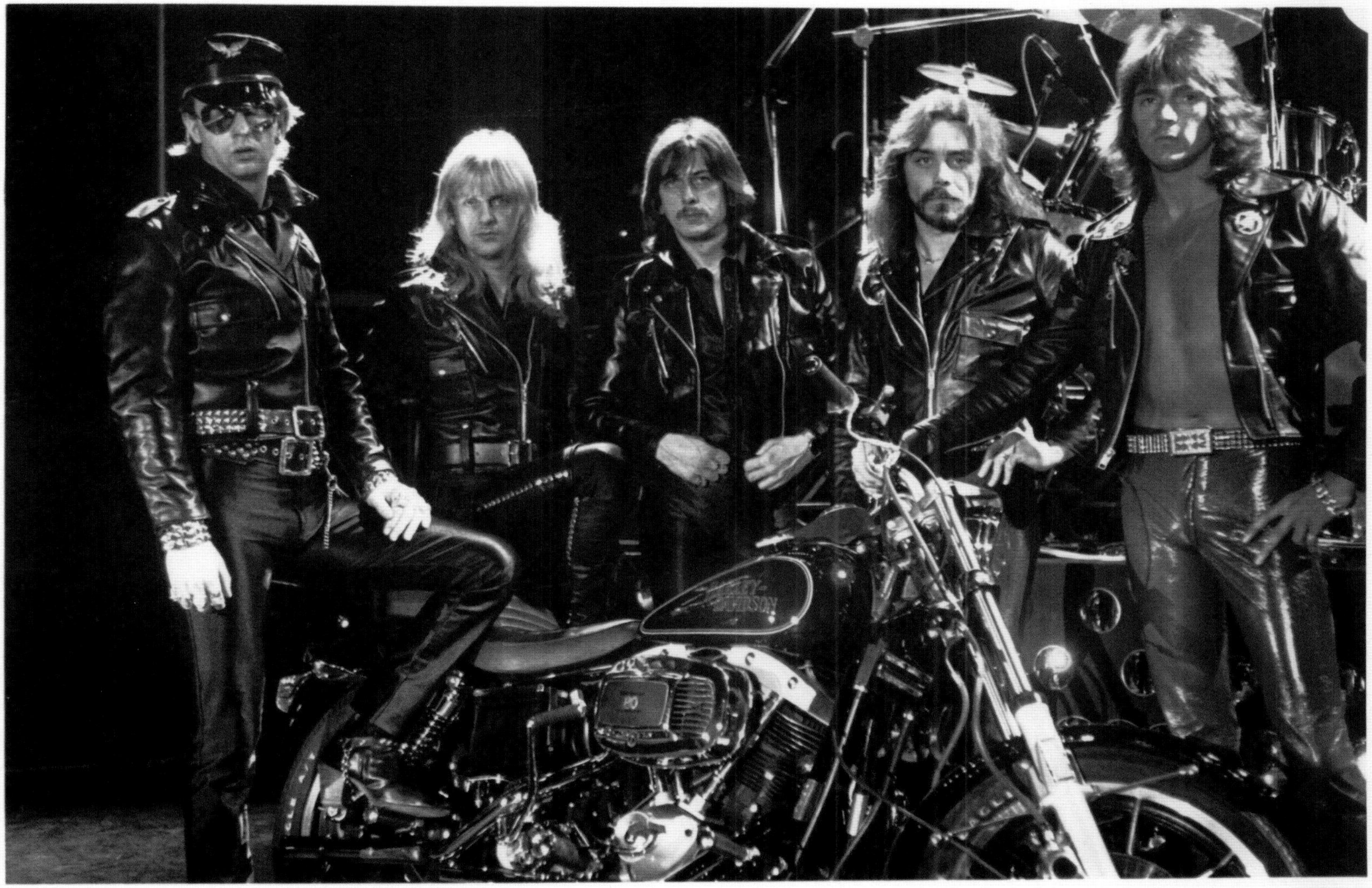

Columbia

1179

JUDAS PRIEST

& Harley-Davidson "Low Rider"

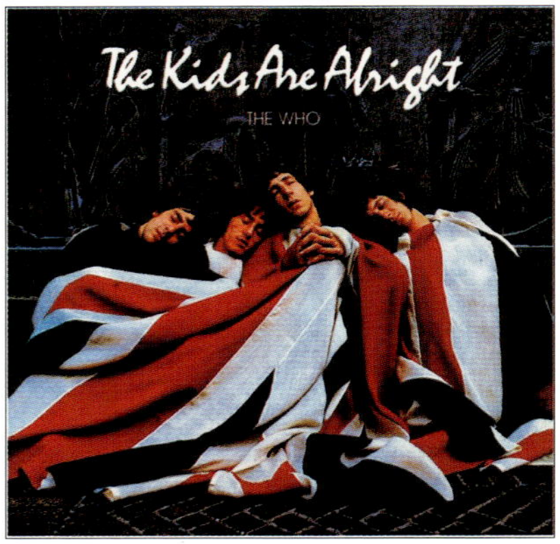

The Who's history was explored in *The Kids Are Alright*, a documentary film, with a soundtrack album of the same name culling live rarities and studio cuts.

Billboard 200: *The Kids Are Alright* (#8)
Billboard Hot 100: "Long Live Rock" (#54)

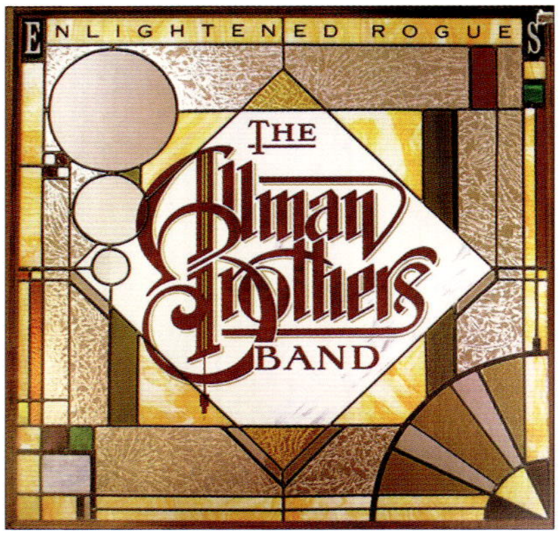

The Allman Brothers Band attempted to reclaim past glory with *Enlightened Rogues*, a reunion effort titled after Duane Allman's description of the group.

Billboard 200: *Enlightened Rogues* (#9)
Billboard Hot 100: "Crazy Love" (#29)

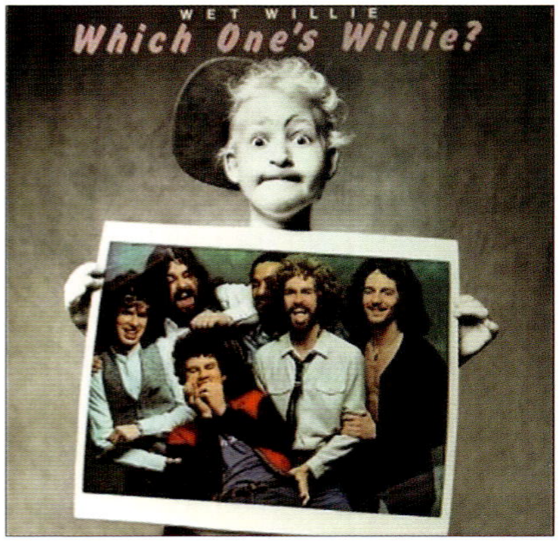

Fronted by singer Jimmy Hall, **Wet Willie** hit the charts with the summertime song "Weekend," adding a dose of pop sheen to its soulful Southern rock.

Billboard 200: *Which One's Willie?* (#172)
Billboard Hot 100: "Weekend" (#29)

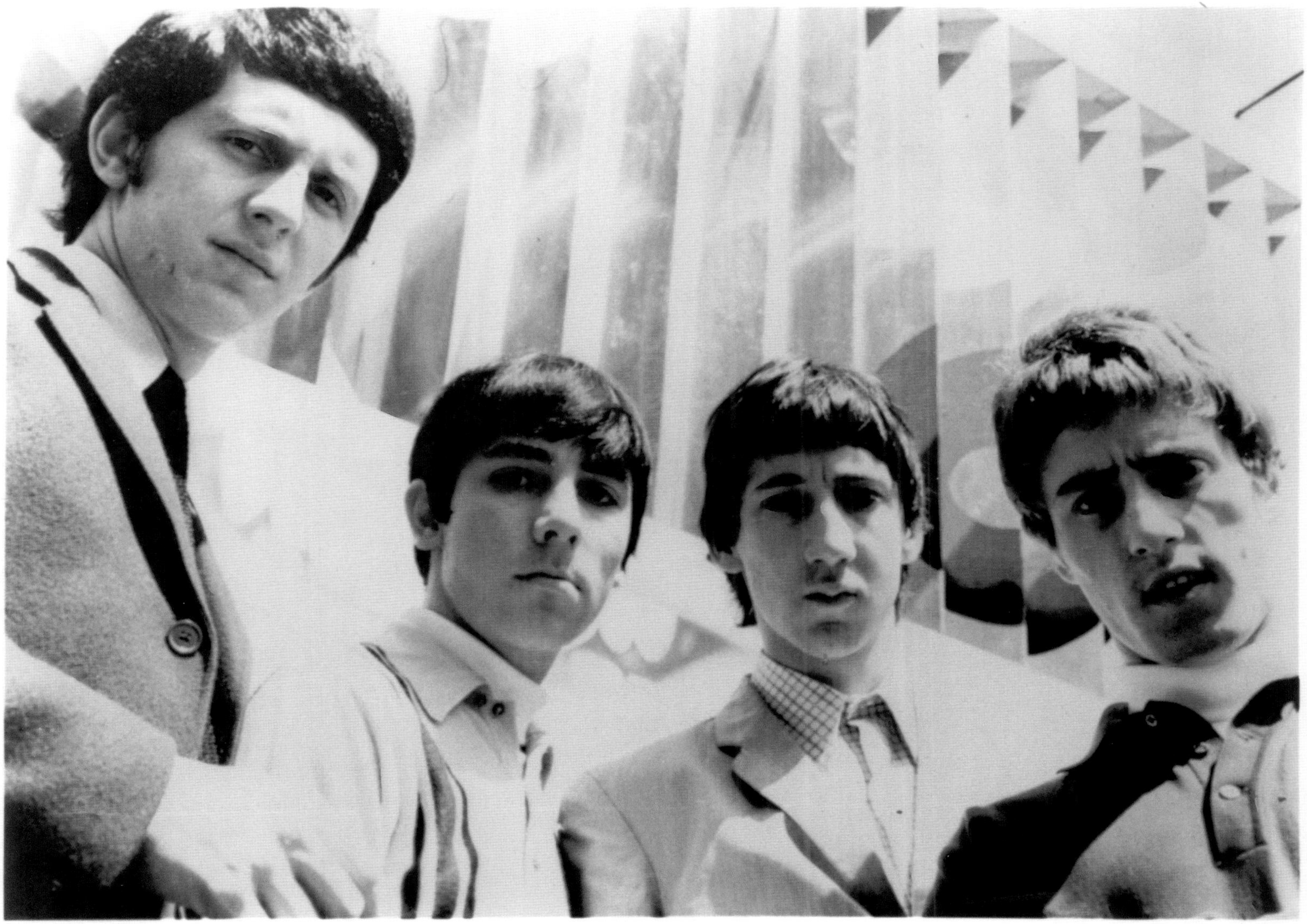

The Who
(circa 1965)

The Kids Are Alright

Exclusively On
MCA RECORDS

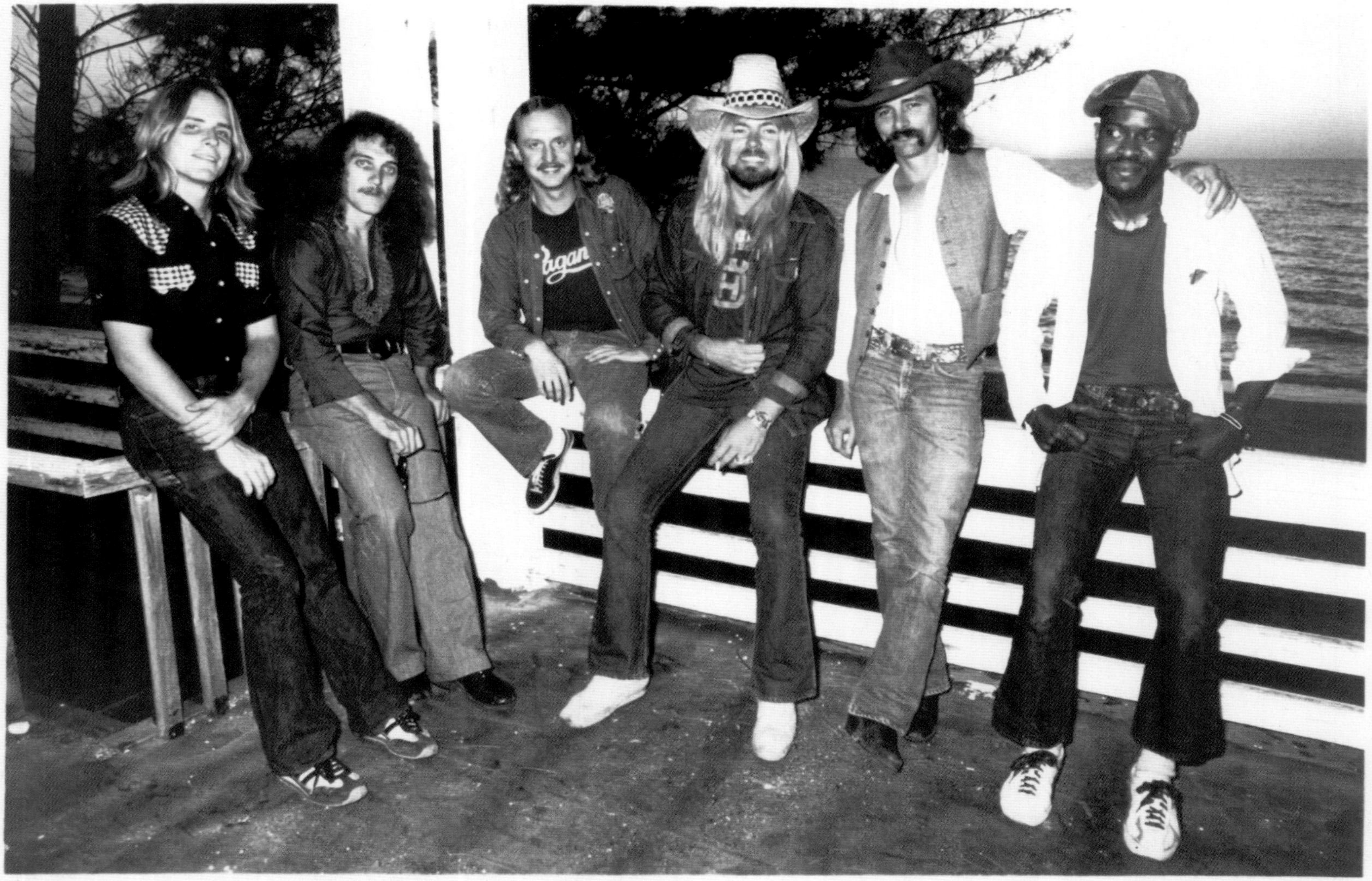

THE ALLMAN BROTHERS BAND

David "Rook" Goldflies, "Dangerous" Dan Toler, Butch Trucks, Gregg Allman, Dickey Betts, & Jaimoe Johanny Johanson.

CAPRICORN RECORDS.

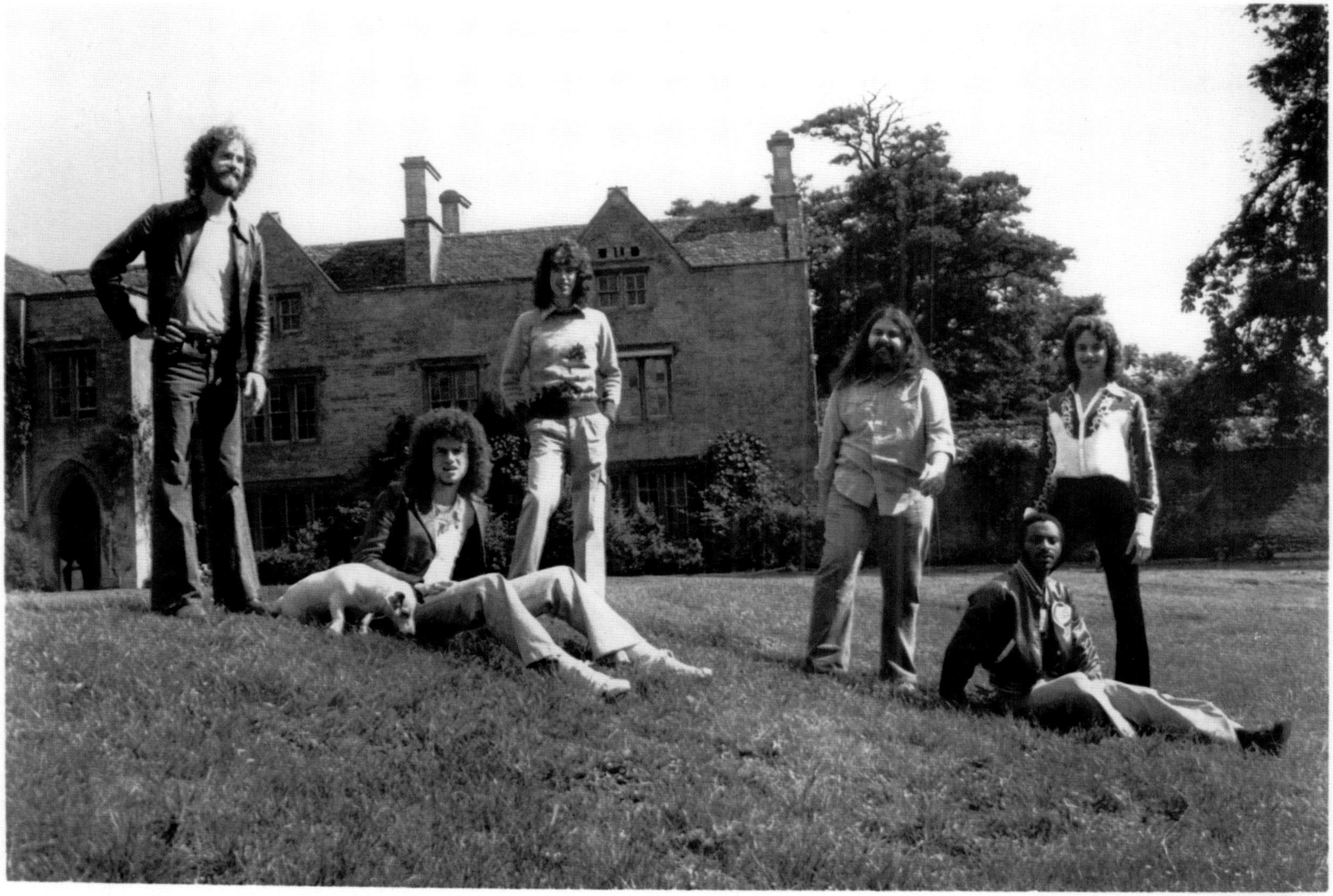

WET WILLIE

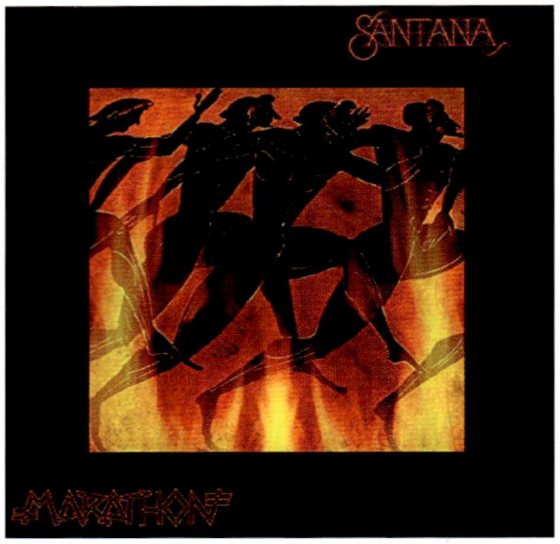

Marathon and the Top 40 hit "You Know That I Love You" denoted a transition from **Santana**'s Latin rock roots to more commercially oriented overtones.

Billboard 200: *Marathon* (#25)
Billboard Hot 100: "You Know That I Love You" (#35)

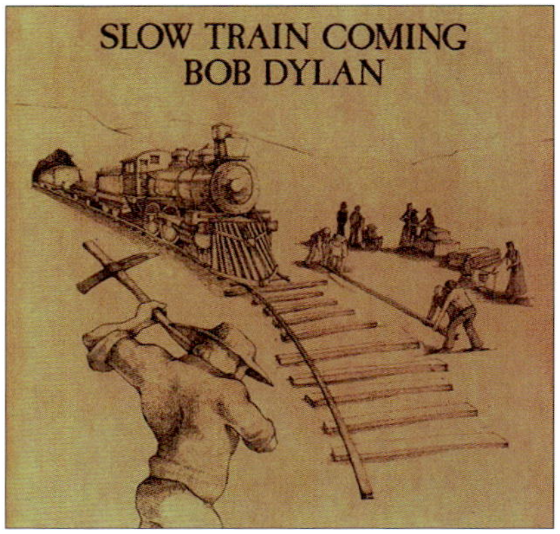

Having converted to Christianity, **Bob Dylan** released *Slow Train Coming*, an album of modern gospel music spurred by the hit "Gotta Serve Somebody."

Billboard 200: *Slow Train Coming* (#3)
Billboard Hot 100: "Gotta Serve Somebody" (#24)

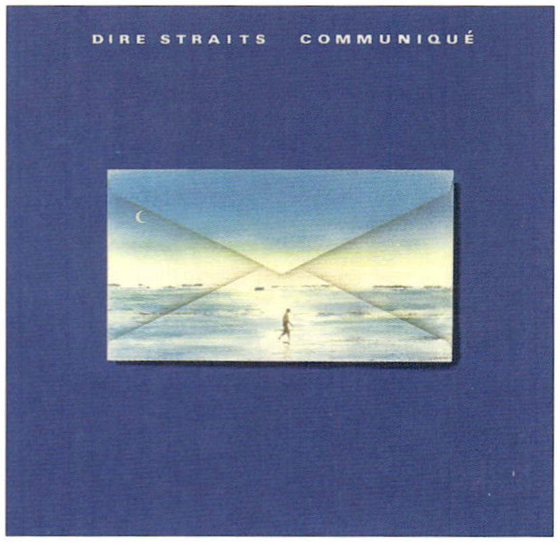

Dire Straits' *Communiqué* built on a sound shaped by Mark Knopfler's guitar work, especially on "Lady Writer" and "Once Upon a Time in the West."

Billboard 200: *Communiqué* (#11)
Billboard Hot 100: "Lady Writer" (#45)

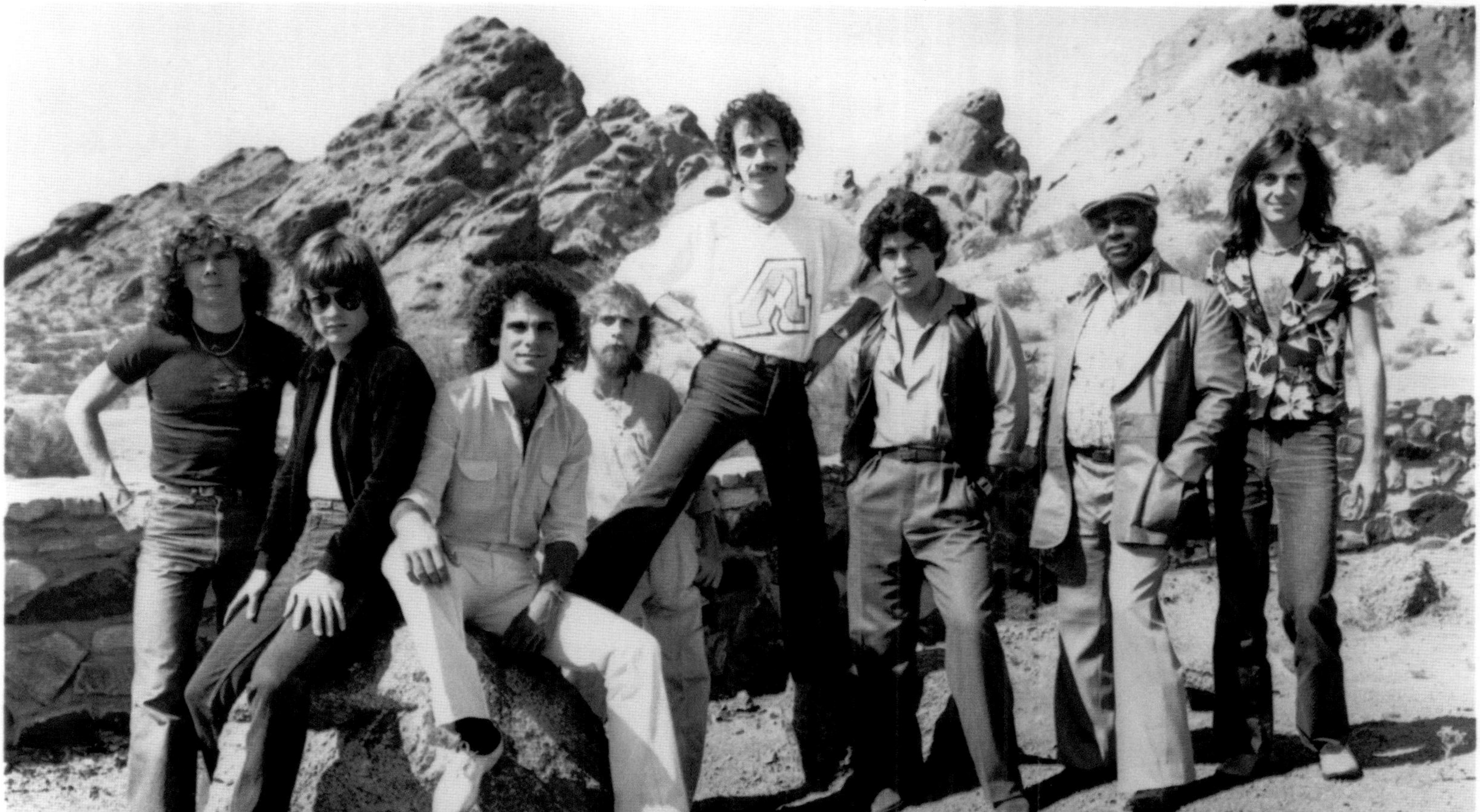

SANTANA

Columbia

7910

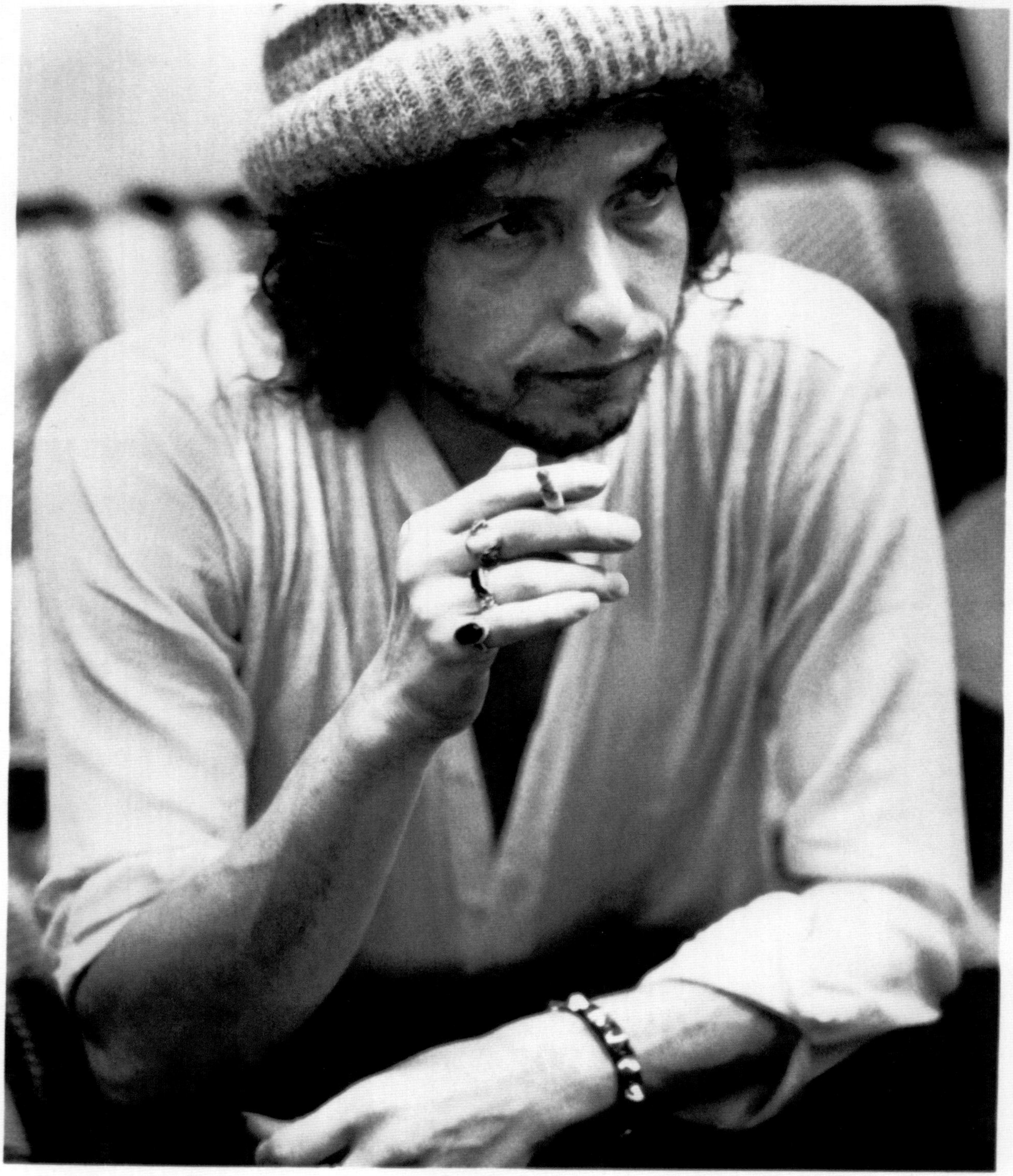

BOB DYLAN

Columbia

7910

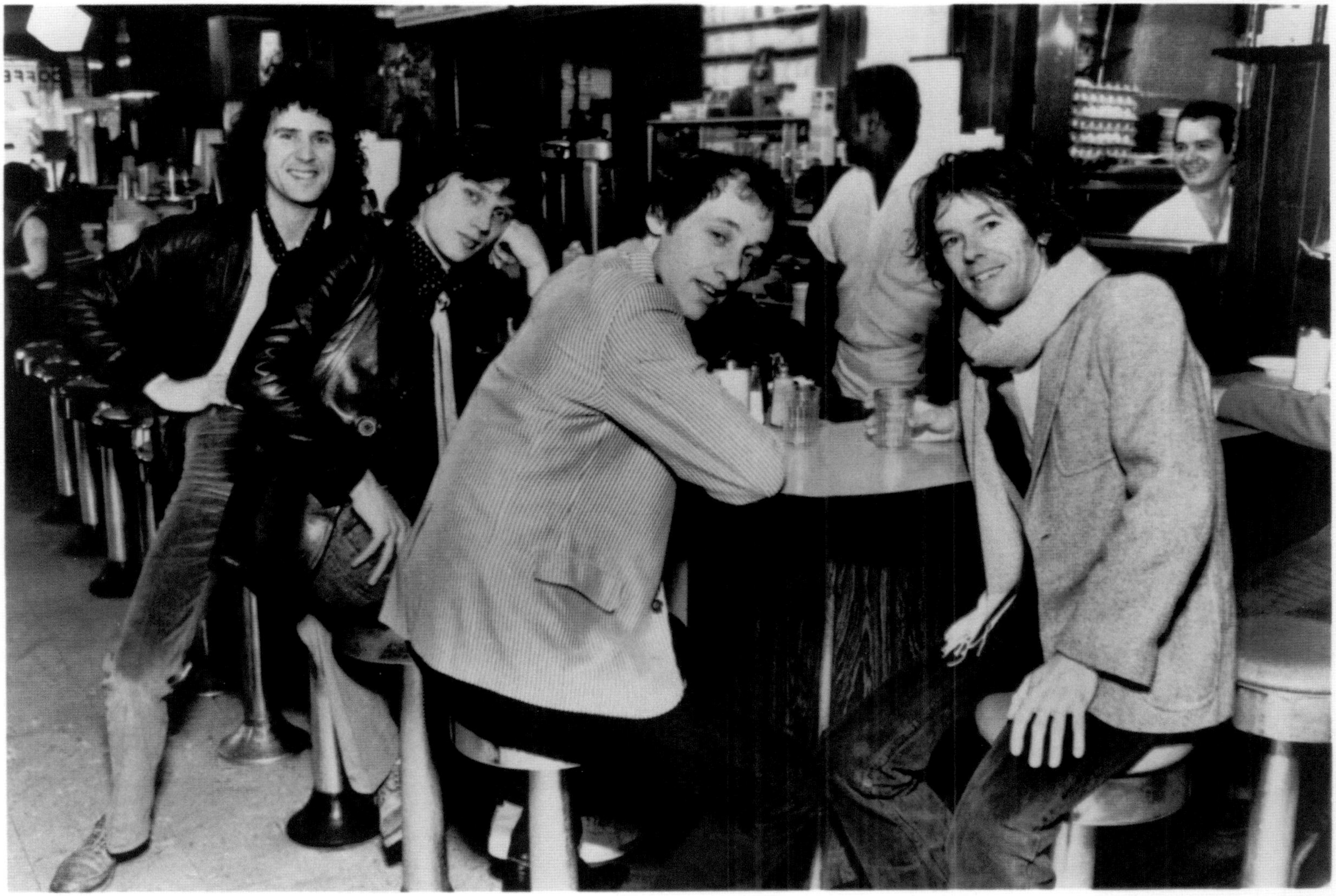

JUNE 1979

Dire Straits

WARNER / REPRISE

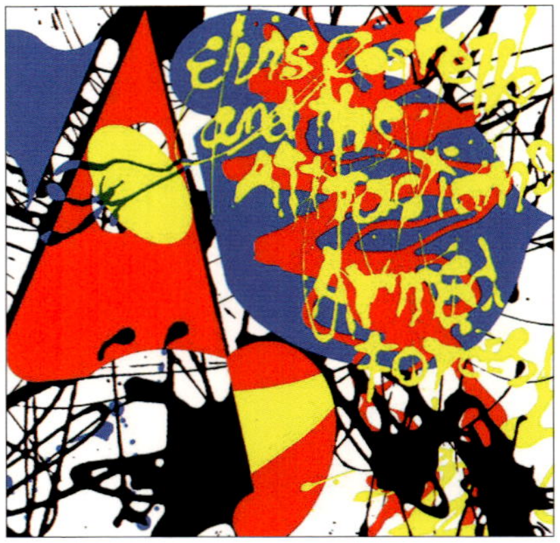

"Accidents Will Happen," "(What's So Funny 'Bout) Peace, Love and Understanding" and "Oliver's Army" marked **Elvis Costello & the Attractions**' *Armed Forces.*

Billboard 200: *Armed Forces* (#10)

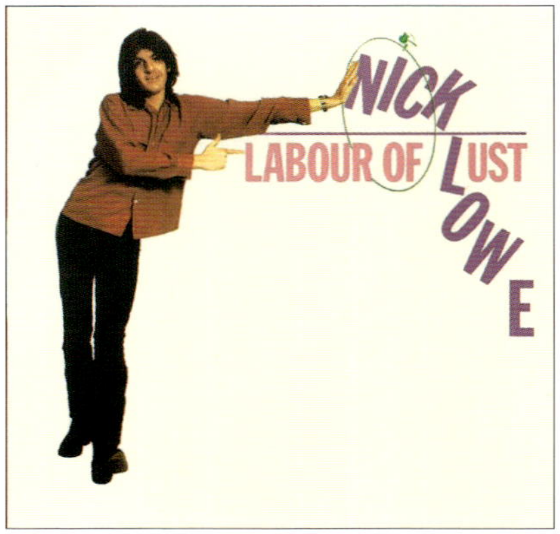

The splendid "Cruel to Be Kind" turned into British rocker **Nick Lowe**'s biggest US hit, supported by Rockpile, the tireless band he formed with Dave Edmunds.

Billboard 200: *Labour of Lust* (#31)
Billboard Hot 100: "Cruel to Be Kind" (#12)

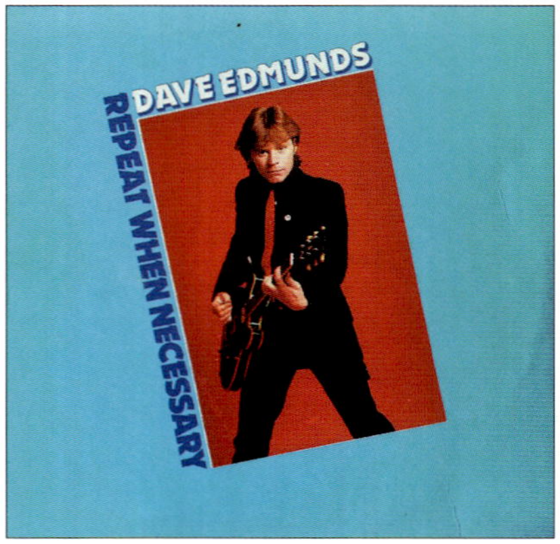

Recorded with Rockpile, Welsh revivalist **Dave Edmunds**' *Repeat When Necessary* was highlighted by a cover of "Girls Talk," written by Elvis Costello.

Billboard 200: *Repeat When Necessary* (#54)
Billboard Hot 100: "Girls Talk" (#65)

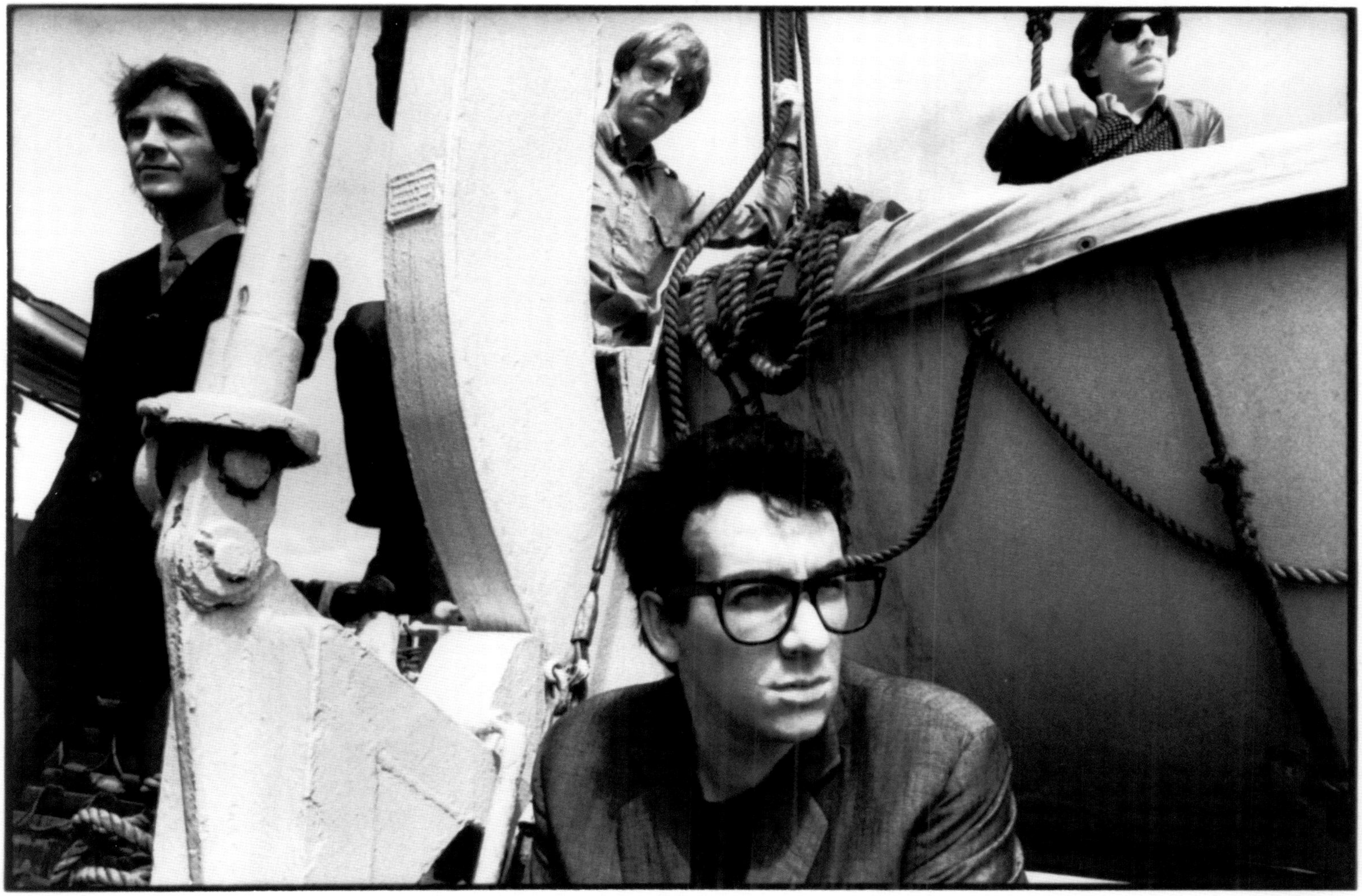

ELVIS COSTELLO & THE ATTRACTIONS

Columbia

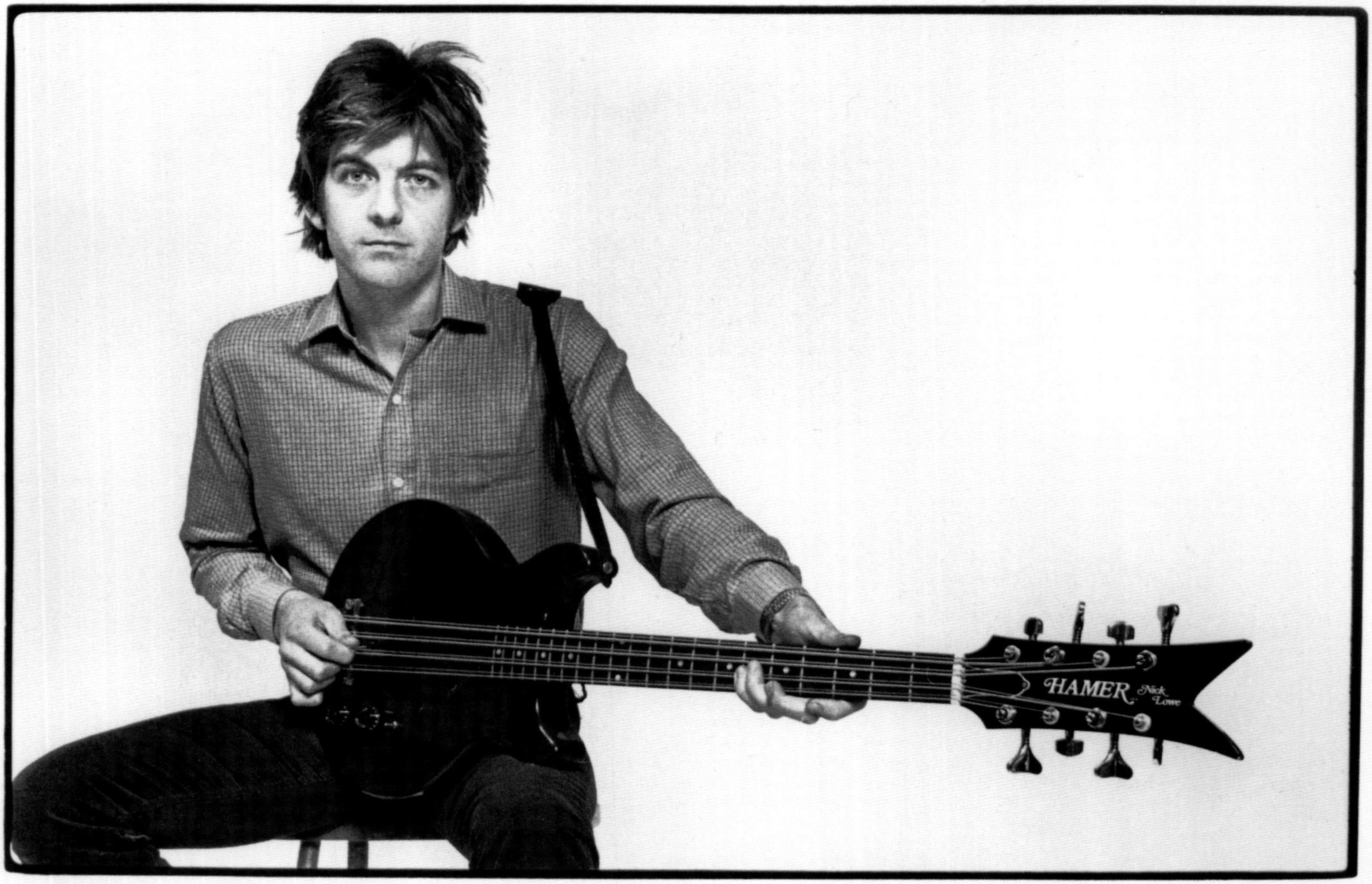

NICK LOWE

Columbia

7906

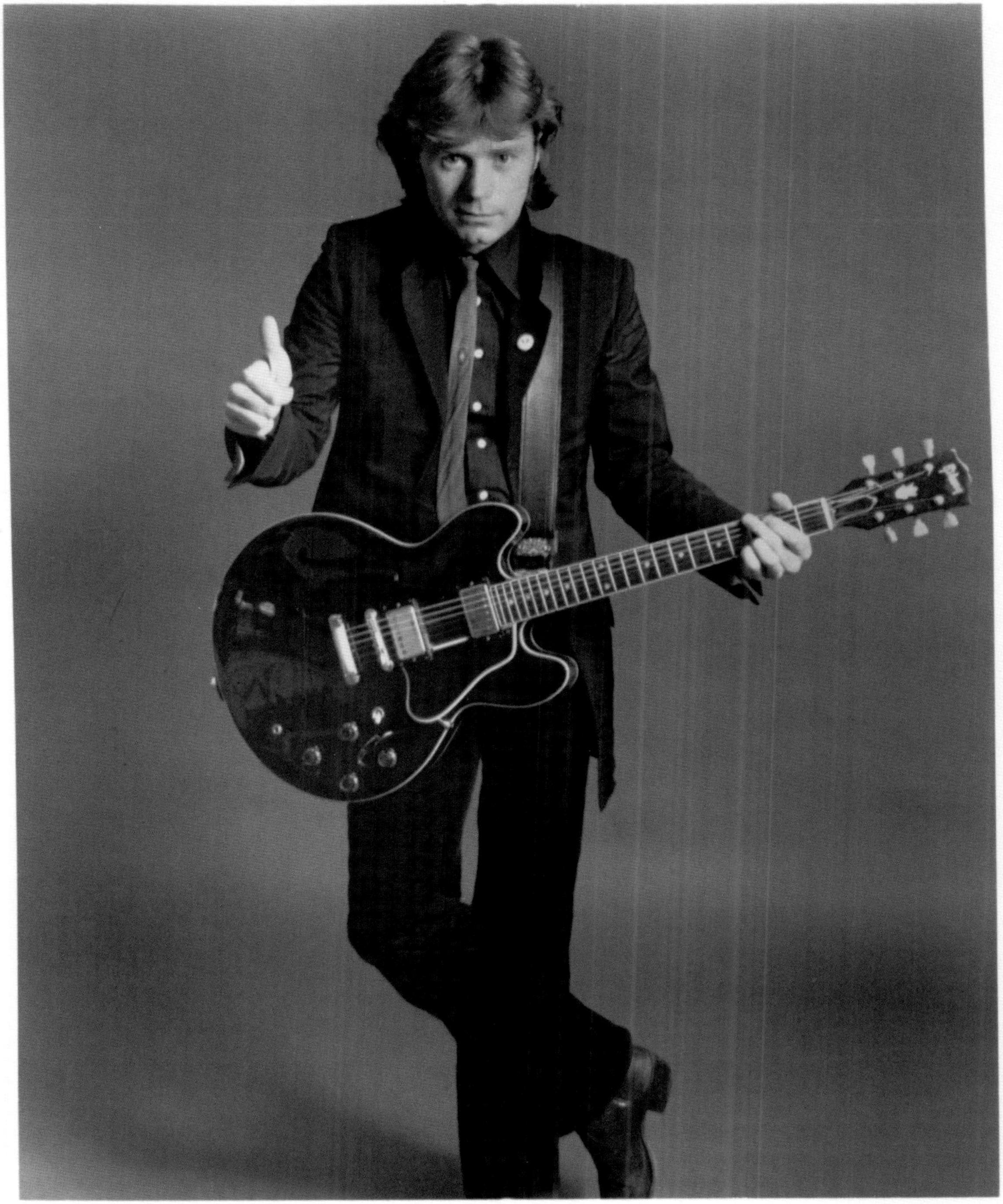

DAVE EDMUNDS

Swan Song

Distributed by Atlantic Recording Corp.

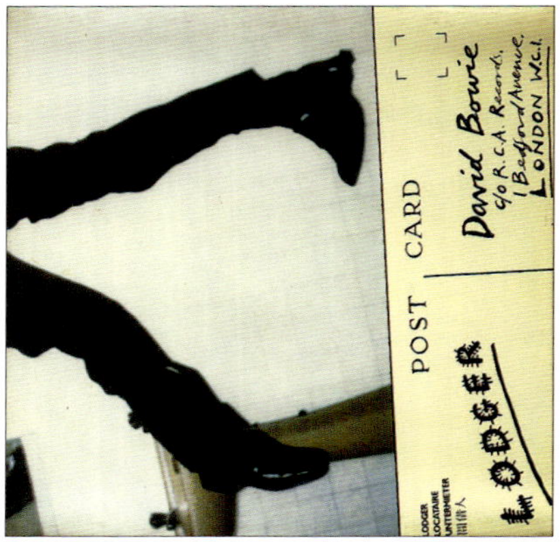

Concluding the Berlin-era trilogy of collaborations with Brian Eno that began with the *Low* and *"Heroes"* albums, the mercurial **David Bowie** issued *Lodger*.

Billboard 200: *Lodger* (#20)

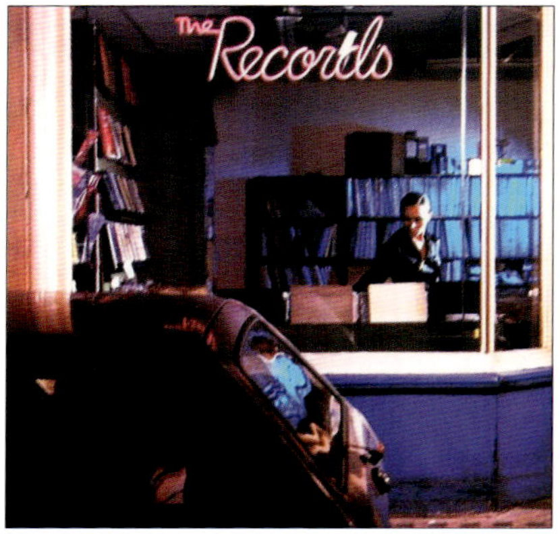

The Records, formed when the Kursaal Flyers disbanded in Britain, struck it big with the US single "Starry Eyes," revered as a near-ideal power-pop song.

Billboard 200: *The Records* (#41)
Billboard Hot 100: "Starry Eyes" (#56)

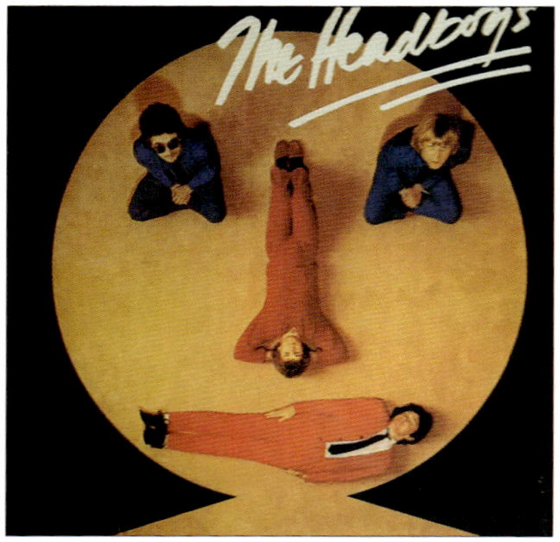

The Headboys put every spare shilling into making demo tapes, culminating in a charting US hit for the Scottish outfit, "The Shape of Things to Come."

Billboard 200: *The Headboys* (#113)
Billboard Hot 100: "The Shape of Things to Come" (#67)

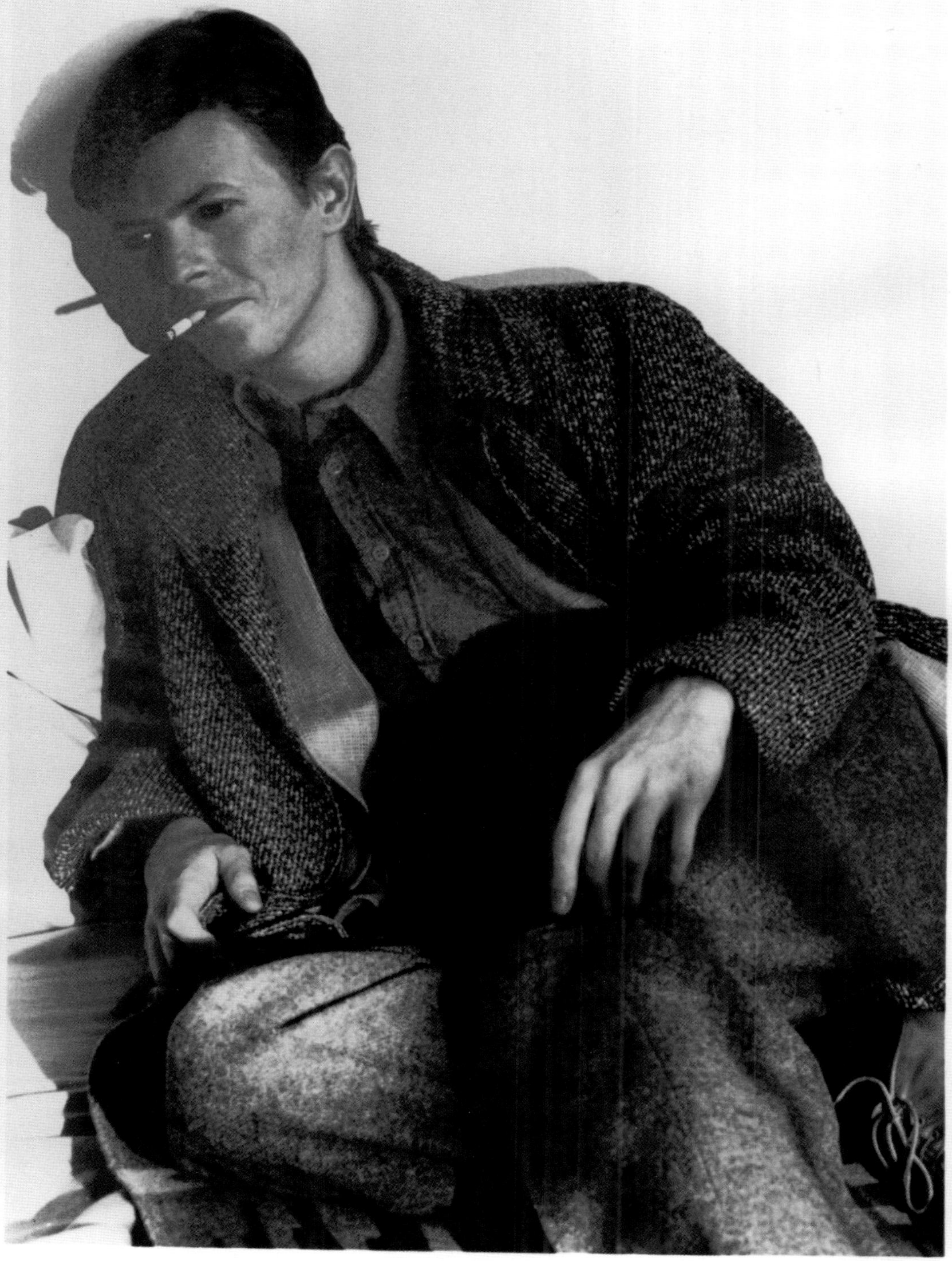

DAVID BOWIE

RCA Records

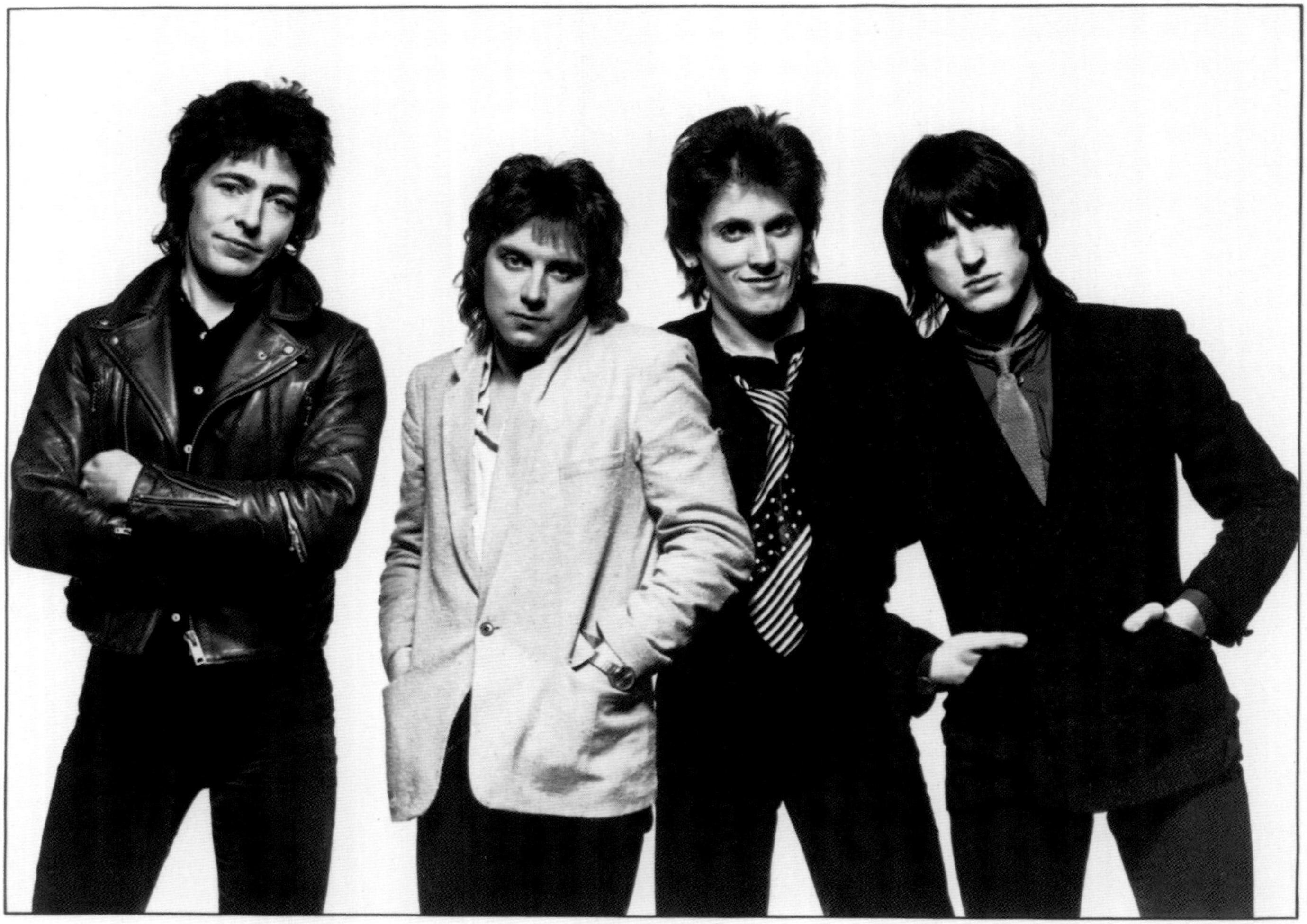

THE RECORDS

(Left to right) **HUW GOWER, JOHN WICKS, PHIL BROWN and WILL BIRCH**

RECORDS

THE HEADBOYS

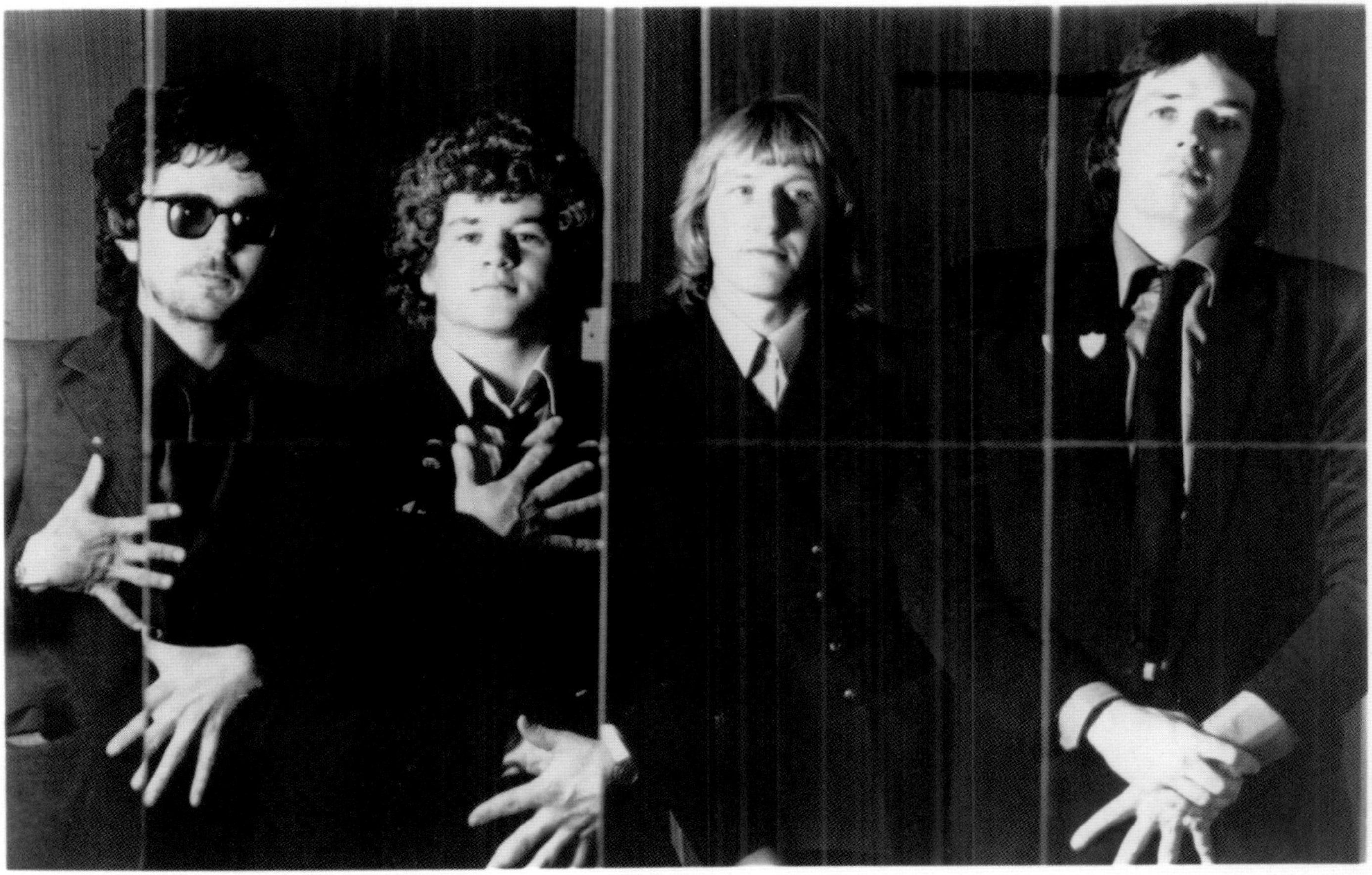

BRIAN LEWIS DAVEY ROSS GEORGE BOYTER CALUM MALCOLM

RSO RECORDS AND TAPES

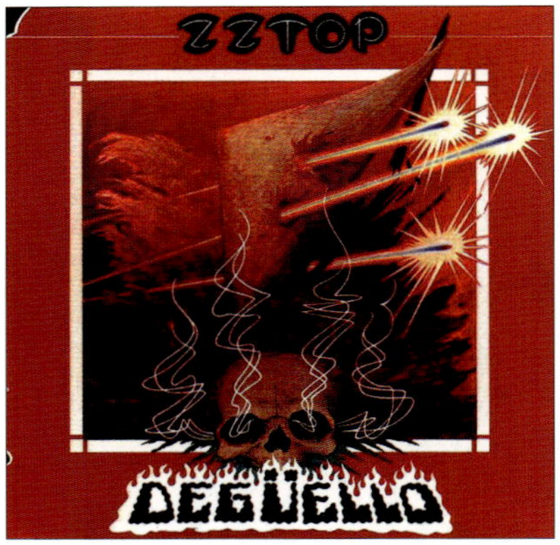

ZZ Top's *Degüello* housed the Texas trio's cover of "I Thank You," a soul hit initially recorded by Sam & Dave, and the scruffy boogie of "Cheap Sunglasses."

Billboard 200: *Degüello* (#24)
Billboard Hot 100: "Cheap Sunglasses" (#89); "I Thank You" (#34)

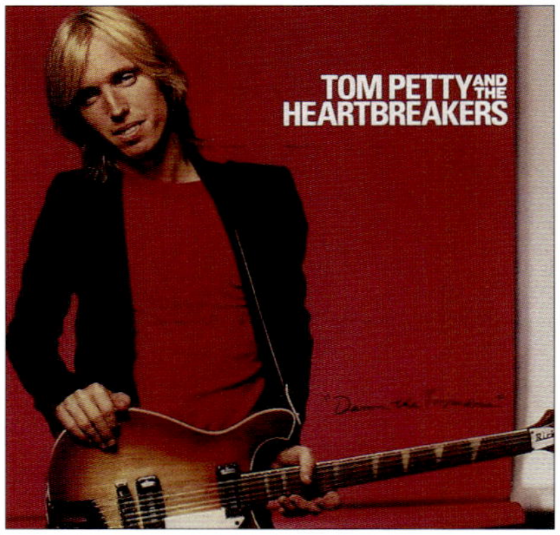

The rock songcraft of **Tom Petty & the Heartbreakers** crested on their third album, *Damn the Torpedoes,* led by "Don't Do Me Like That" and "Refugee."

Billboard 200: *Damn the Torpedoes* (#2)
Billboard Hot 100: "Don't Do Me Like That" (#10); "Refugee" (#15); "Here Comes My Girl" (#59)

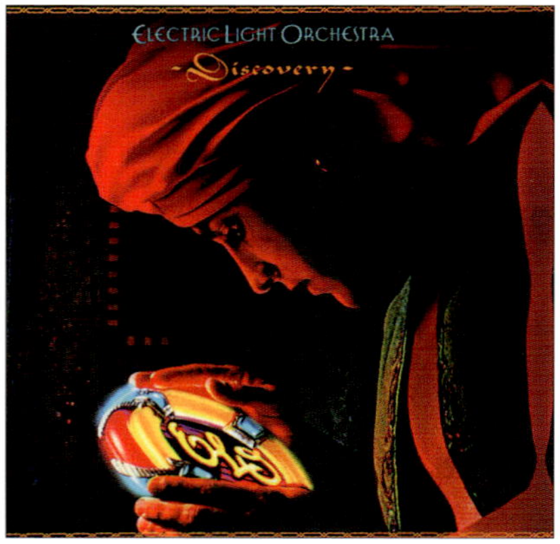

The stringless "Don't Bring Me Down" and "high-class disco" of "Shine a Little Love" stood out as the Top 10 hits from **Electric Light Orchestra**'s *Discovery.*

Billboard 200: *Discovery* (#5)
Billboard Hot 100: "Shine a Little Love" (#8); "Don't Bring Me Down" (#4); "Confusion" (#37); "Last Train to London" (#39)

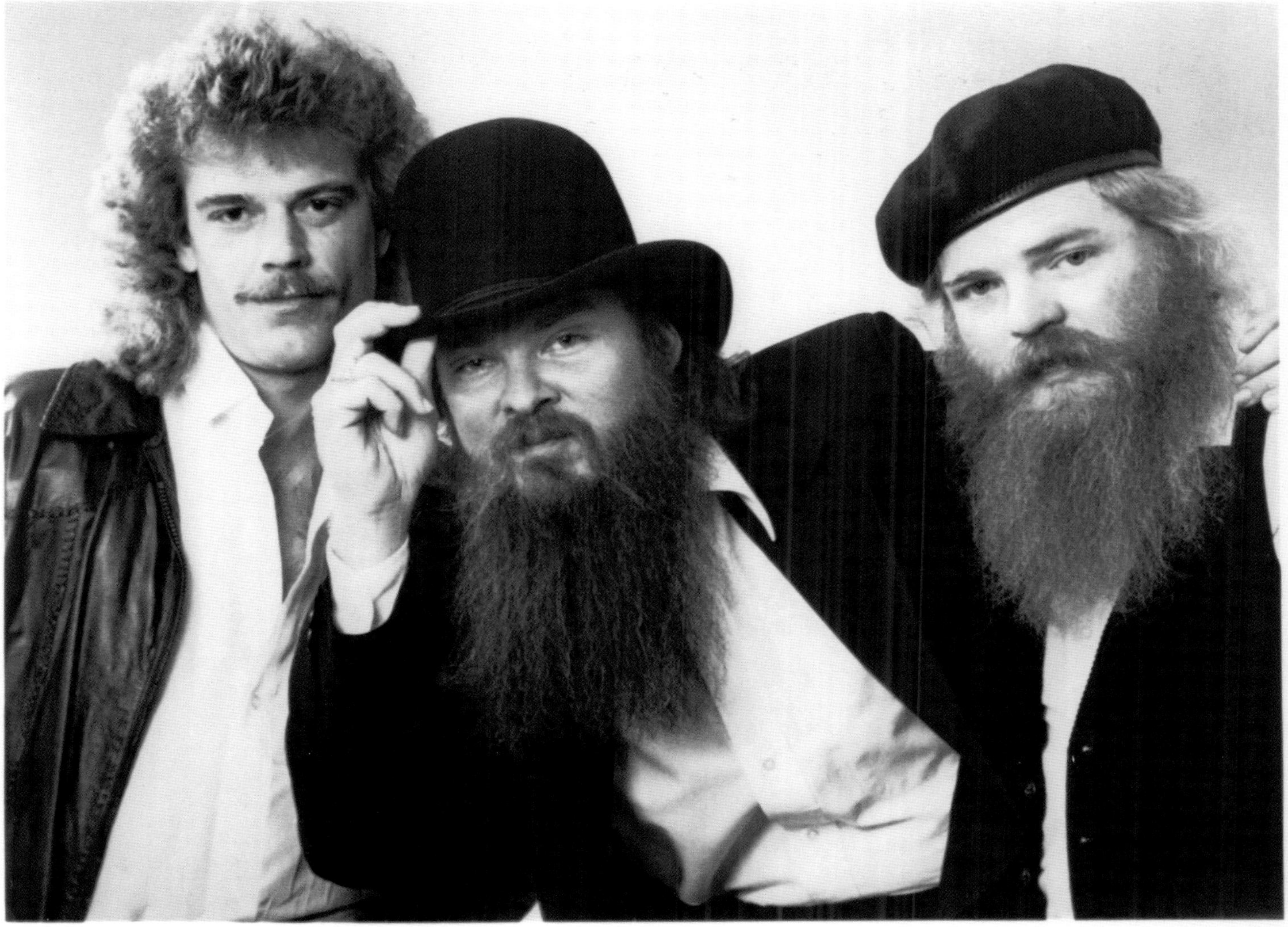

NOVEMBER 1979

ZZ TOP

WARNER BROS.

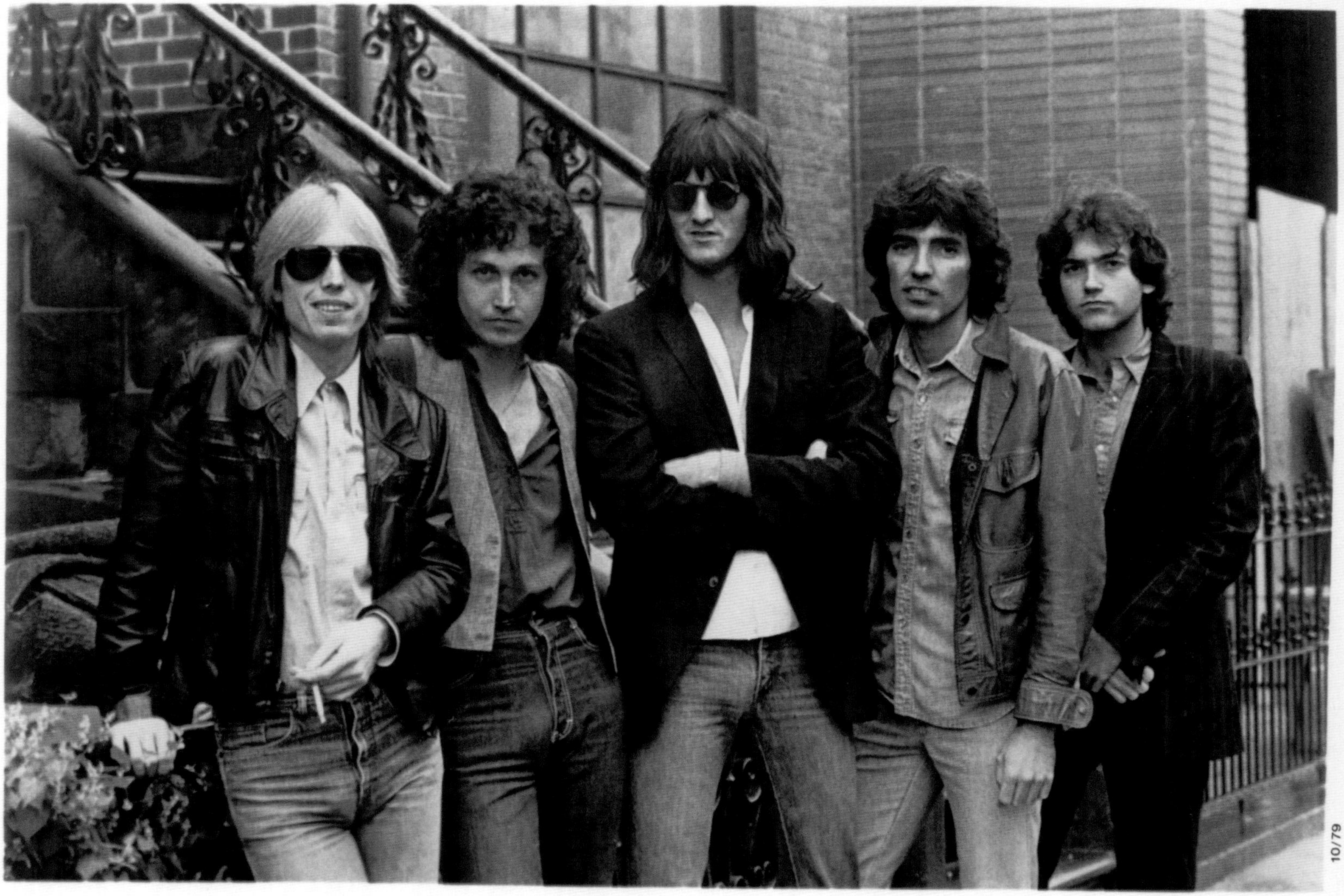

T. P. Mike Campbell Stan Lynch Ron Blair Benmont Tench

Backstreet
MCA RECORDS

TOM PETTY AND THE HEARTBREAKERS

Management: Lookout Management

MAHONEY/WASSERMAN & ASSOCIATES
PUBLIC RELATIONS
117 N. Robertson Blvd., Los Angeles, California 90048
(213) 550-3922
510 Madison Avenue, New York, New York 10022
(212) 751-2060

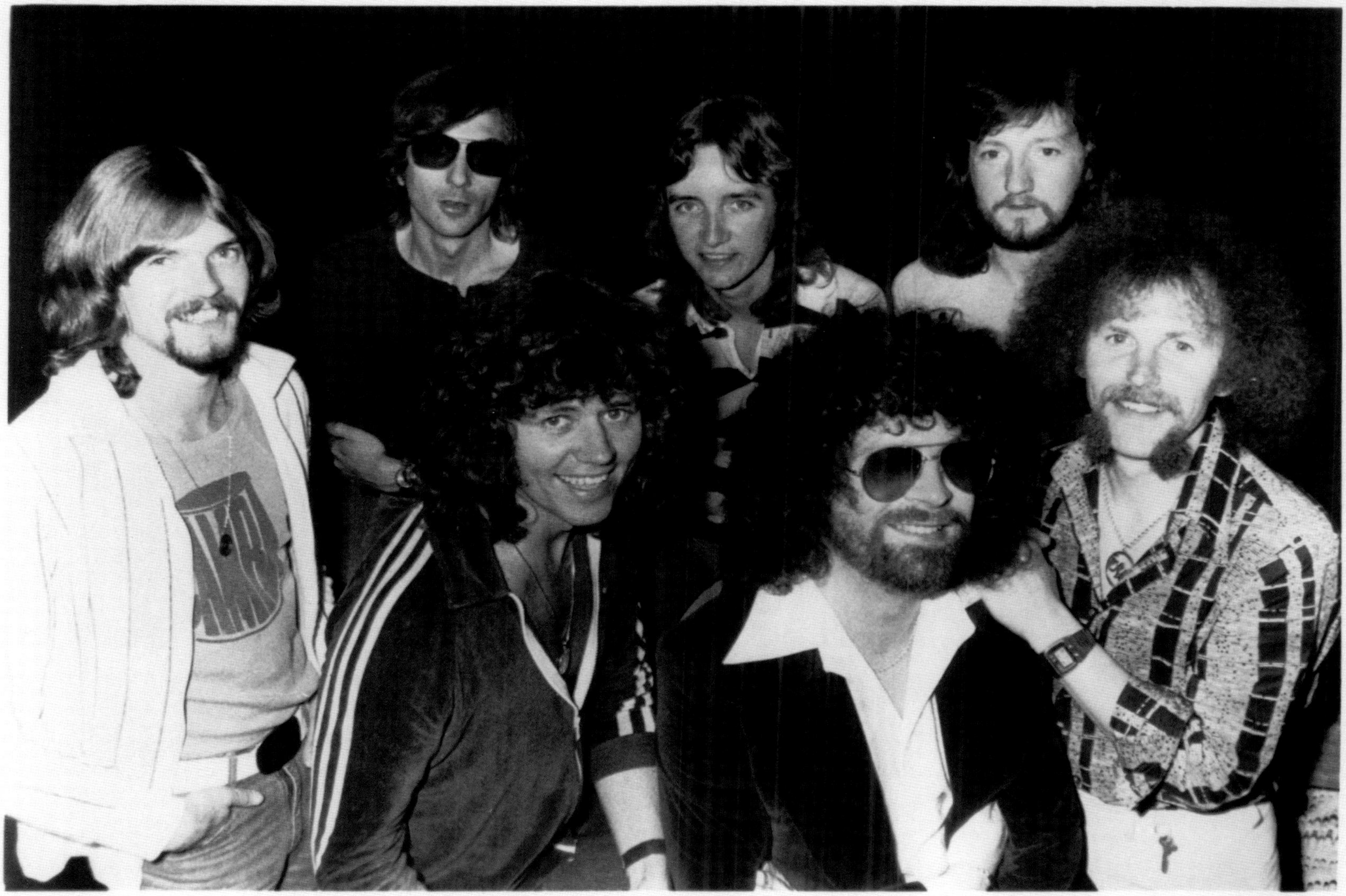

ELECTRIC LIGHT ORCHESTRA

-Discovery-

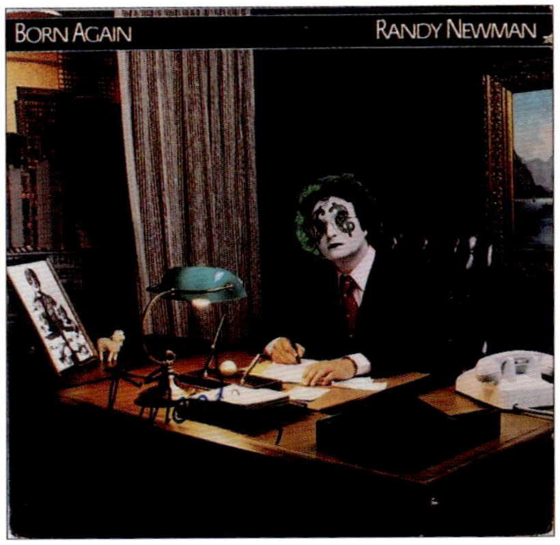

Randy Newman's *Born Again* album featured "The Story of a Rock and Roll Band," a farcical sendup of Electric Light Orchestra's origin and approach.

Billboard 200: *Born Again* (#41)

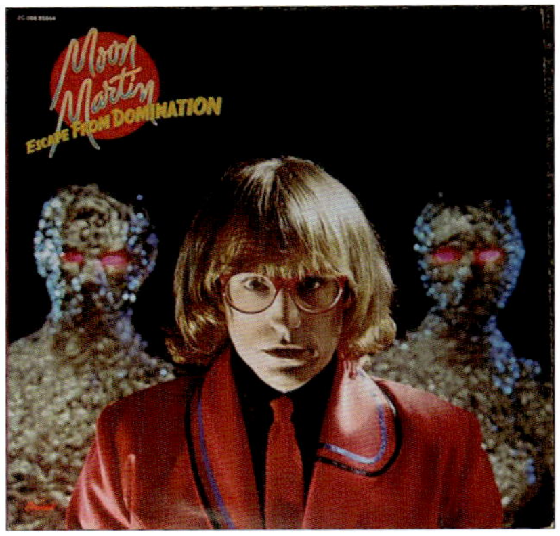

Enjoying repute as a crafty composer ("Bad Case of Loving You," "Cadillac Walk"), **Moon Martin** scored hits of his own with "Rolene" and "No Chance."

Billboard 200: *Escape from Domination* (#80)
Billboard Hot 100: "Rolene" (#30); "No Chance" (#50)

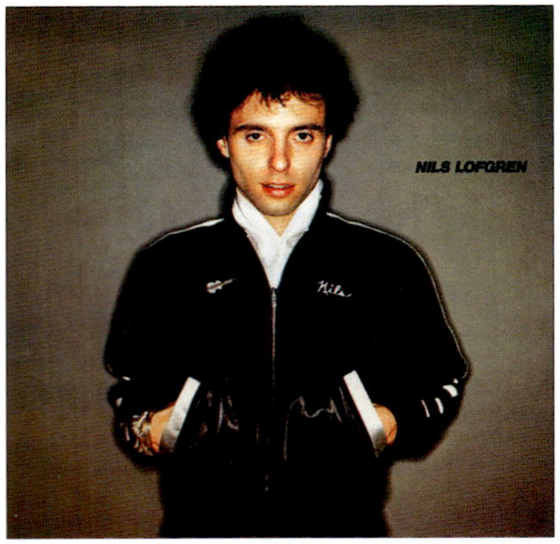

After four albums with Grin and four albums as a solo artist, **Nils Lofgren** felt *Nils* would be a turning point and the understated "Shine Silently" a hit.

Billboard 200: *Nils* (#54)

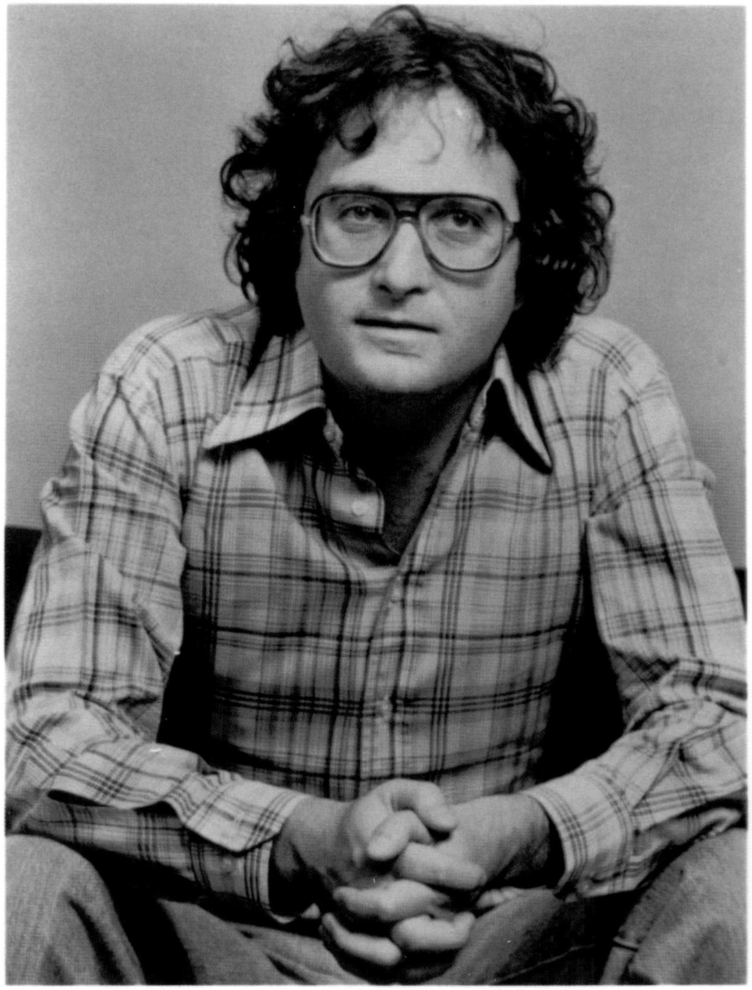

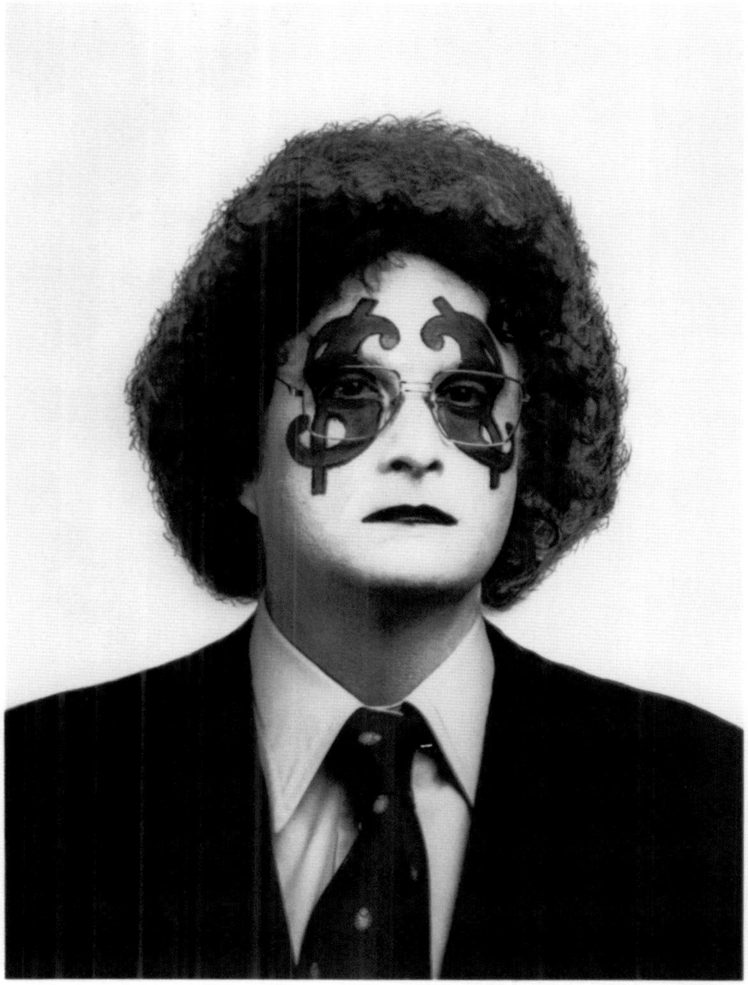

AUGUST 1979

RANDY NEWMAN

BORN AGAIN

WARNER BROS.

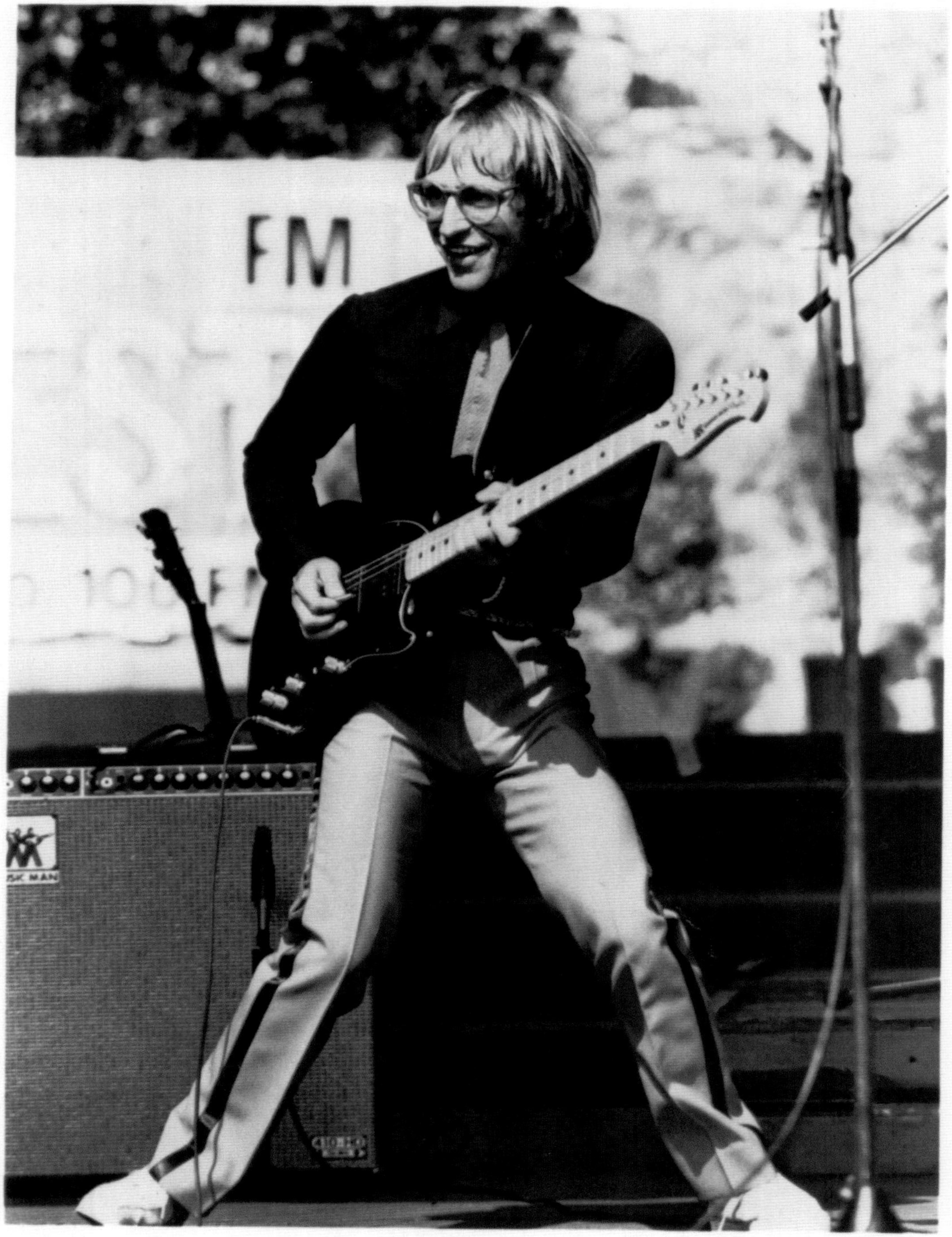

ICM

Moon Martin

Capitol Records

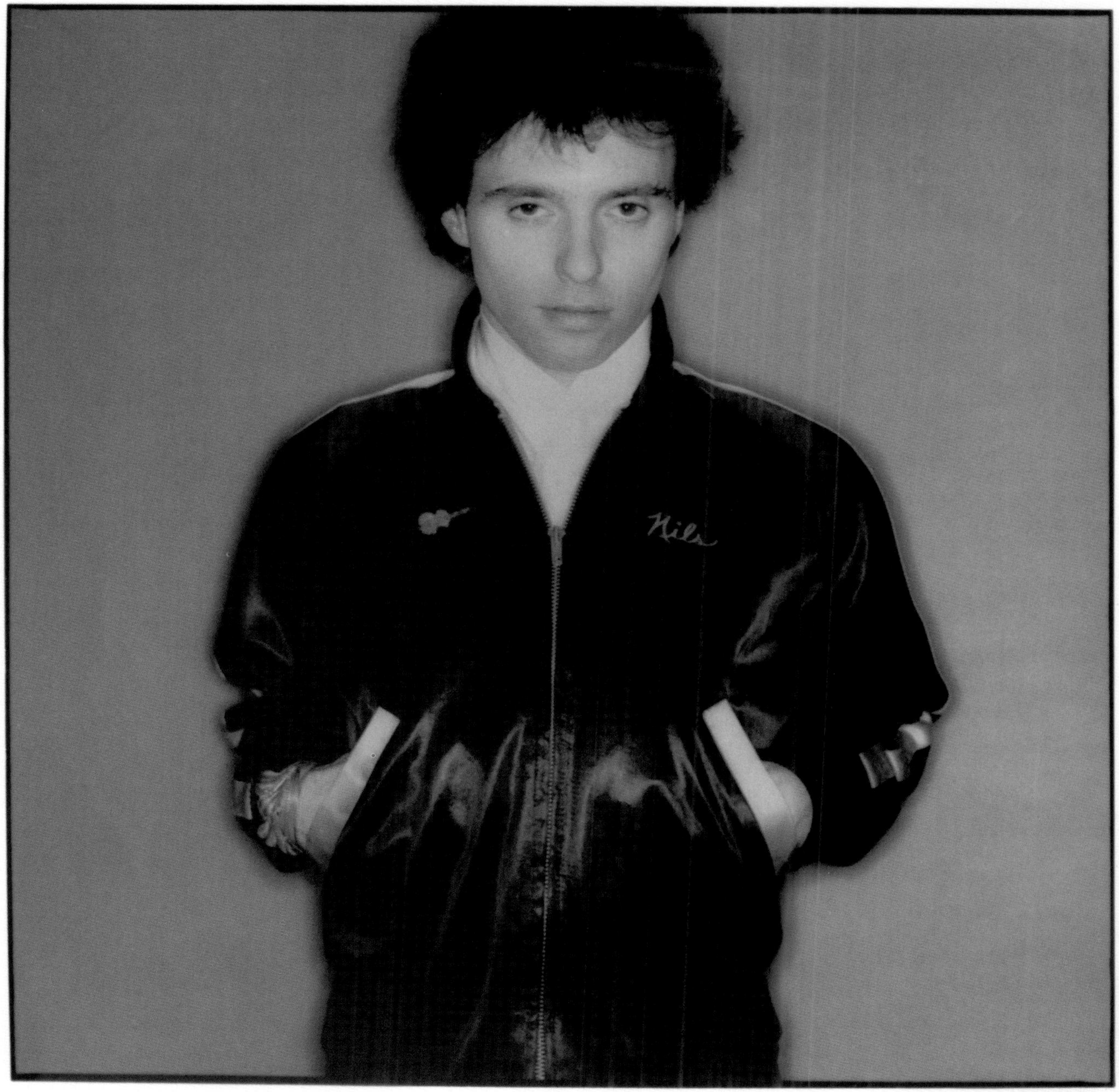

NILS LOFGREN

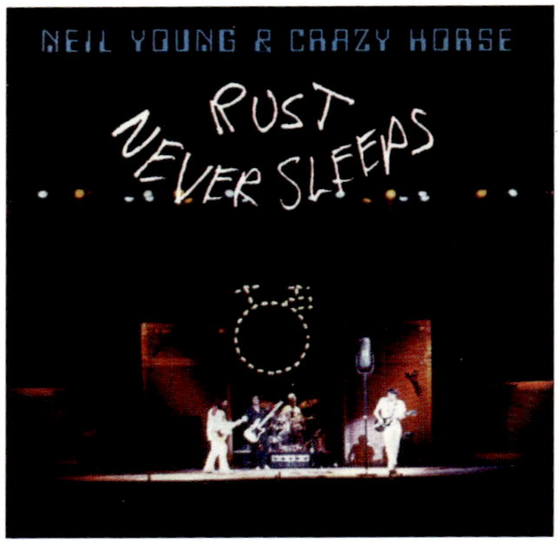

The acoustic "My My, Hey Hey (Out of the Blue)" and the electric "Hey Hey, My My (Into the Black)" framed **Neil Young & Crazy Horse**'s *Rust Never Sleeps*.

Billboard 200: *Rust Never Sleeps* (#8)
Billboard Hot 100: "Hey Hey, My My (Into the Black)" (#79)

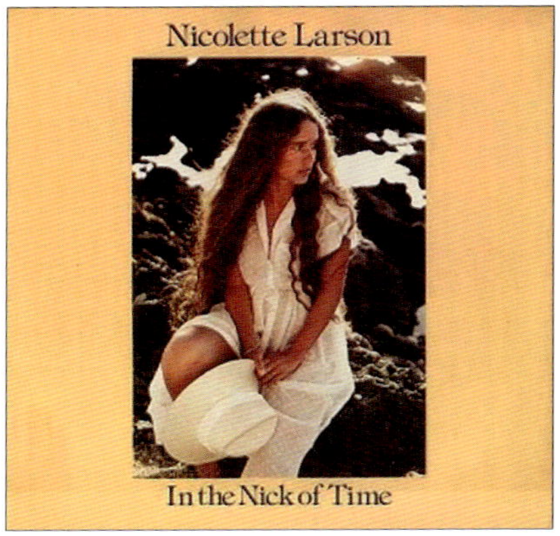

Nicolette Larson followed the accomplishment of "Lotta Love" with *In the Nick of Time*, her second album, and "Let Me Go, Love," a duet with Michael McDonald.

Billboard 200: *In the Nick of Time* (#47)
Billboard Hot 100: "Let Me Go, Love" (#35)

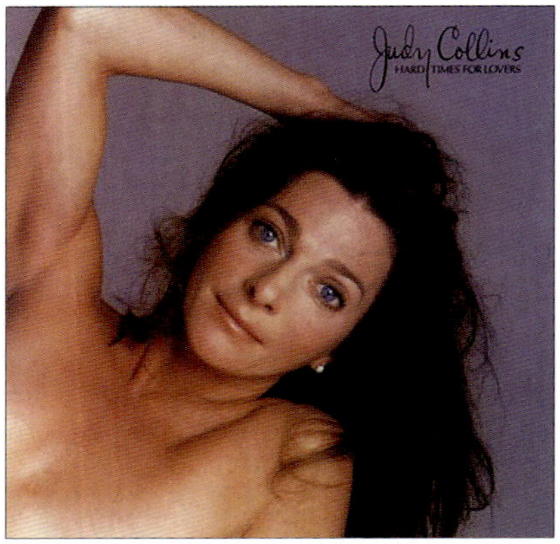

With cover art photographed by Francesco Scavullo depicting the singer in the nude, **Judy Collins**' *Hard Times for Lovers* gained some additional publicity.

Billboard 200: *Hard Times for Lovers* (#54)
Billboard Hot 100: "Hard Times for Lovers" (#66)

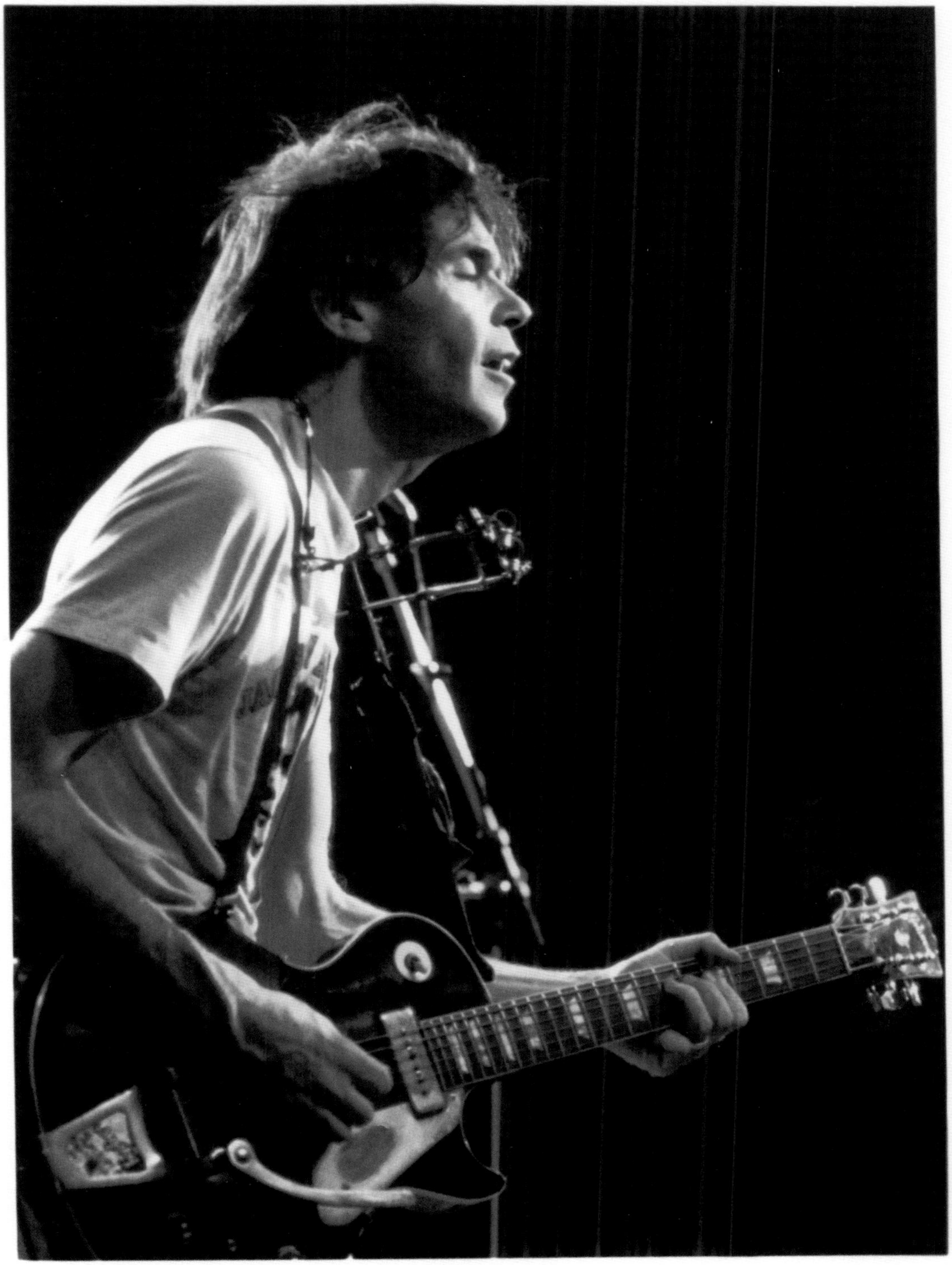

JUNE 1979

NEIL YOUNG

RUST NEVER SLEEPS

WARNER / REPRISE

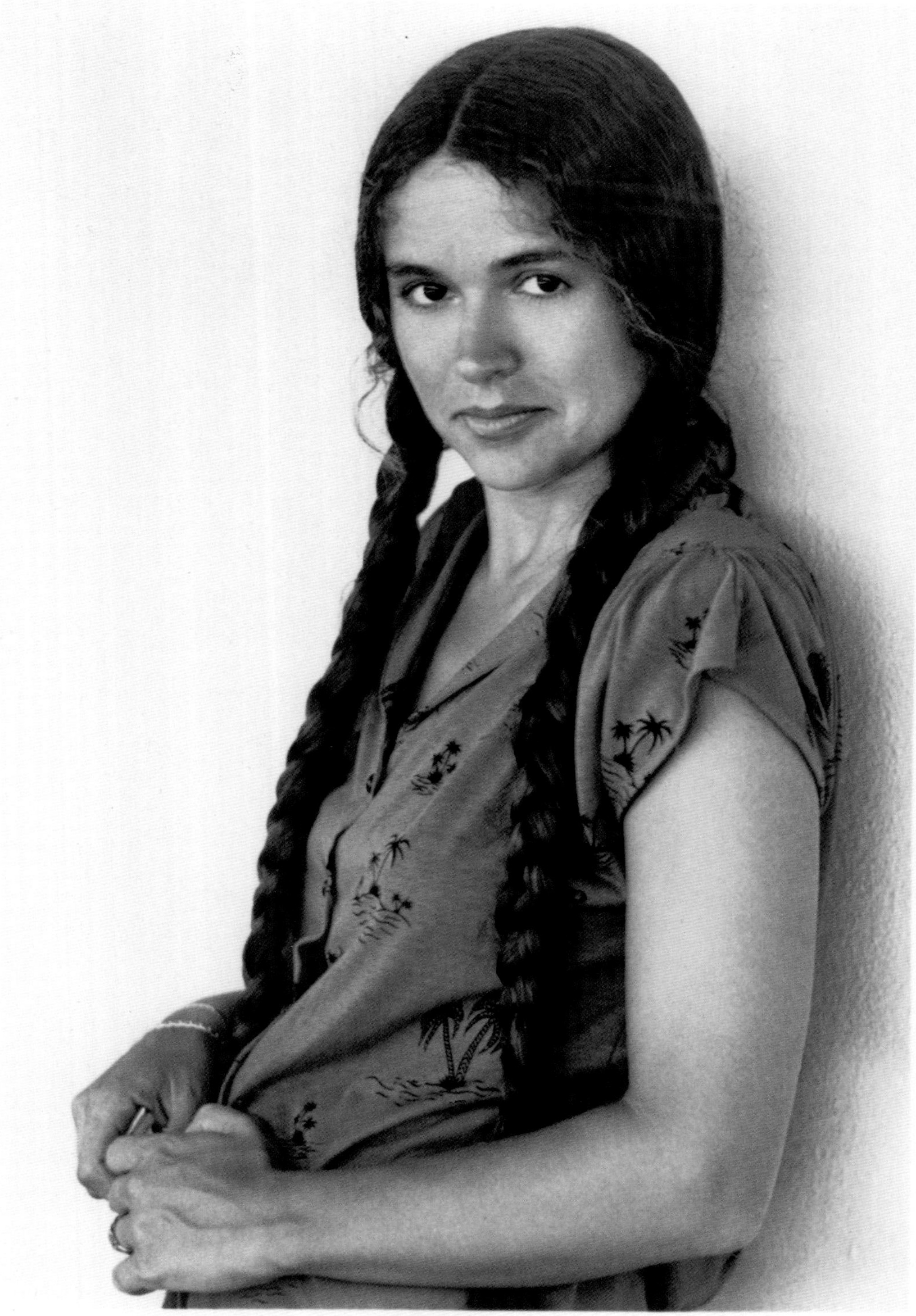

OCTOBER 1979

NICOLETTE LARSON

WARNER BROS.

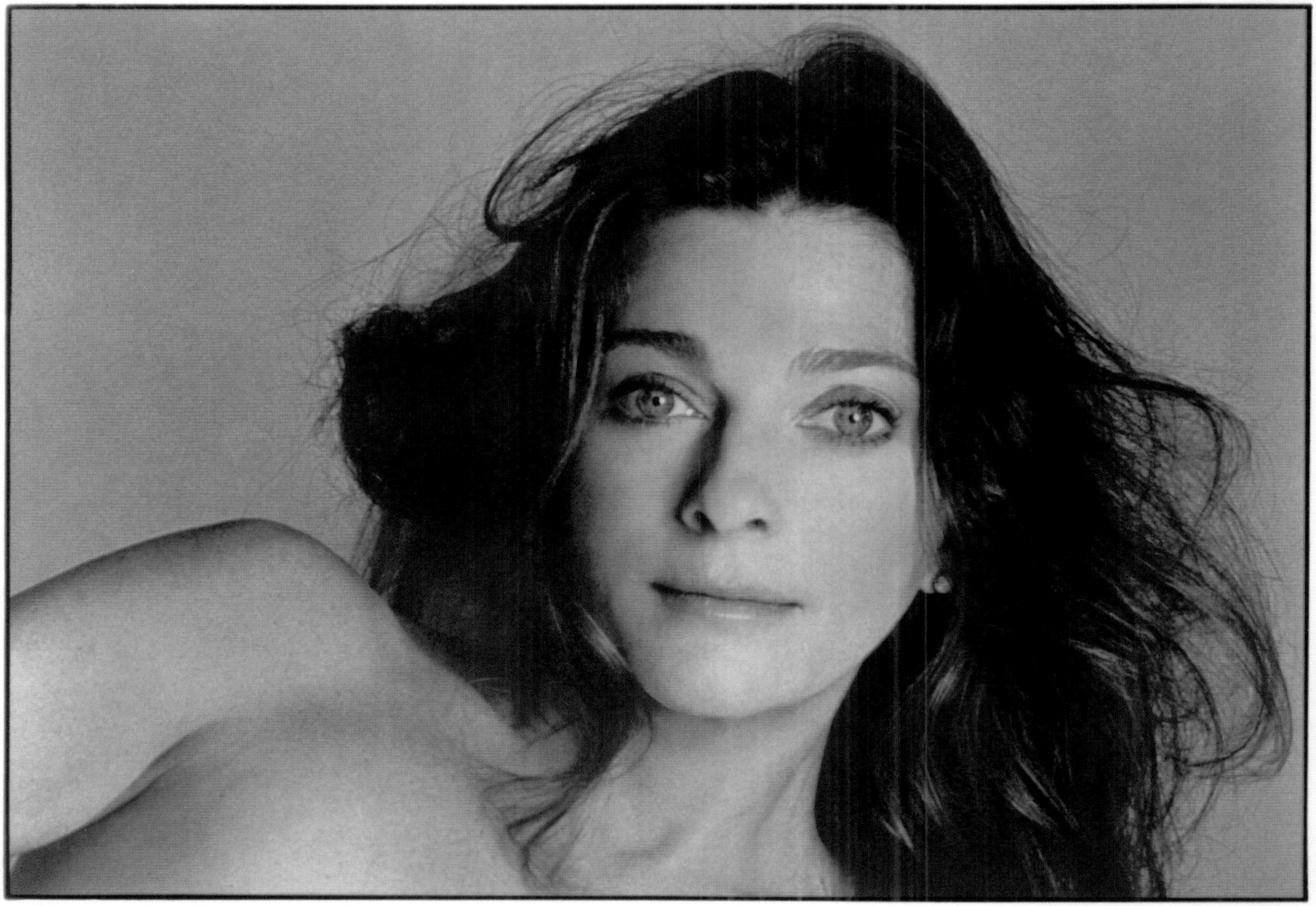

Photo Credit: FRANCESCO SCAVULLO

Judy Collins

elektra

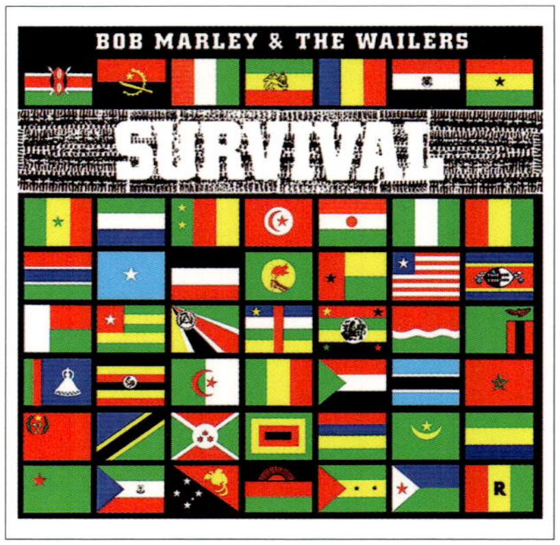

Bob Marley & the Wailers released the politically charged *Survival* album, reflecting the reggae icon's message of unity for Black people around the world.

Billboard 200: *Survival* (#70)

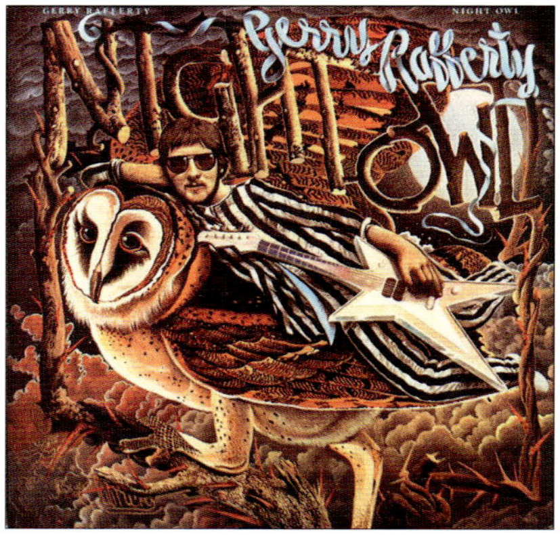

After scoring a major triumph with "Baker Street," **Gerry Rafferty** offered *Night Owl* and the hit tunes "Days Gone Down" and "Get It Right Next Time."

Billboard 200: *Night Owl* (#29)
Billboard Hot 100: "Days Gone Down" (#17);
"Get It Right Next Time" (#21)

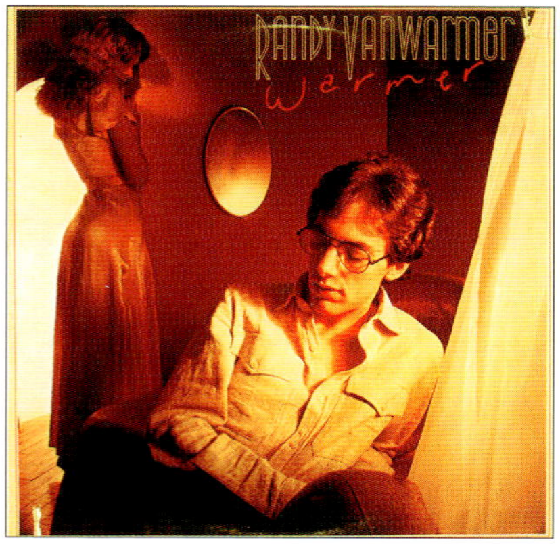

Singer-songwriter **Randy VanWarmer** impressed with a No. 1 adult contemporary hit, "Just When I Needed You Most," a simple expression of heartbreak.

Billboard 200: *Warmer* (#81)
Billboard Hot 100: "Just When I Needed You Most" (#4)

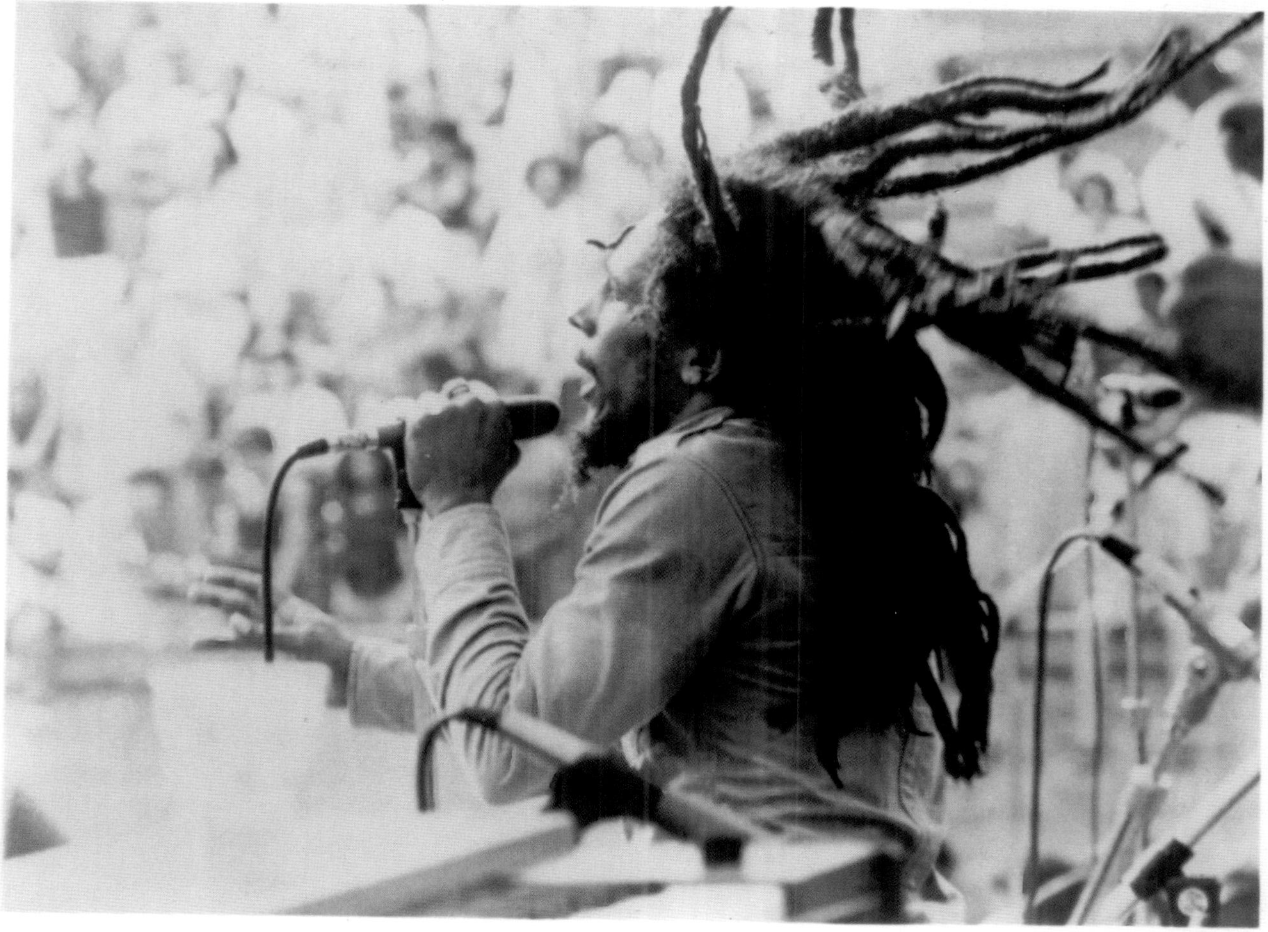

OCTOBER 1979

BOB MARLEY

ISLAND

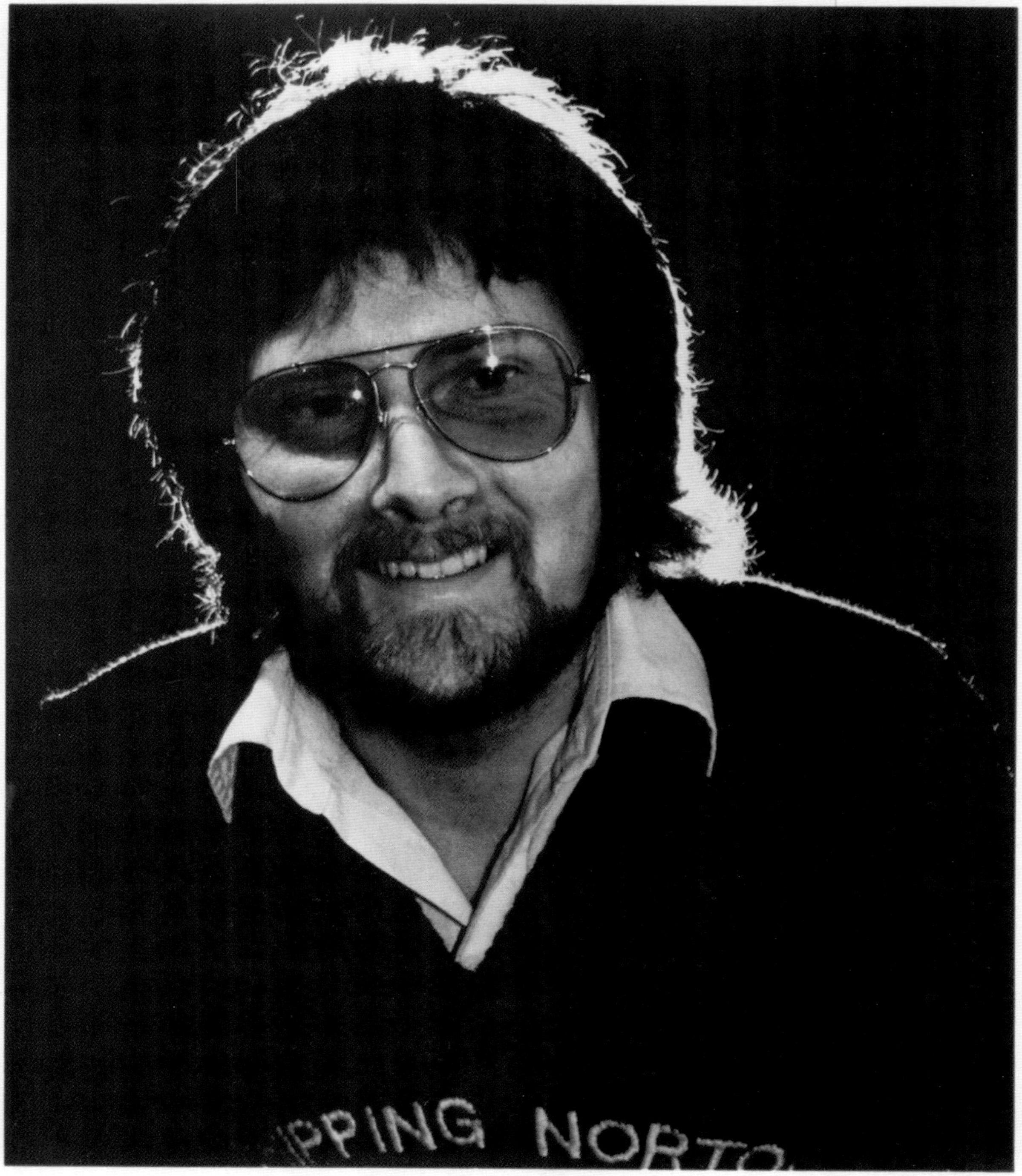

Gerry Rafferty

UNITED ARTISTS RECORDS

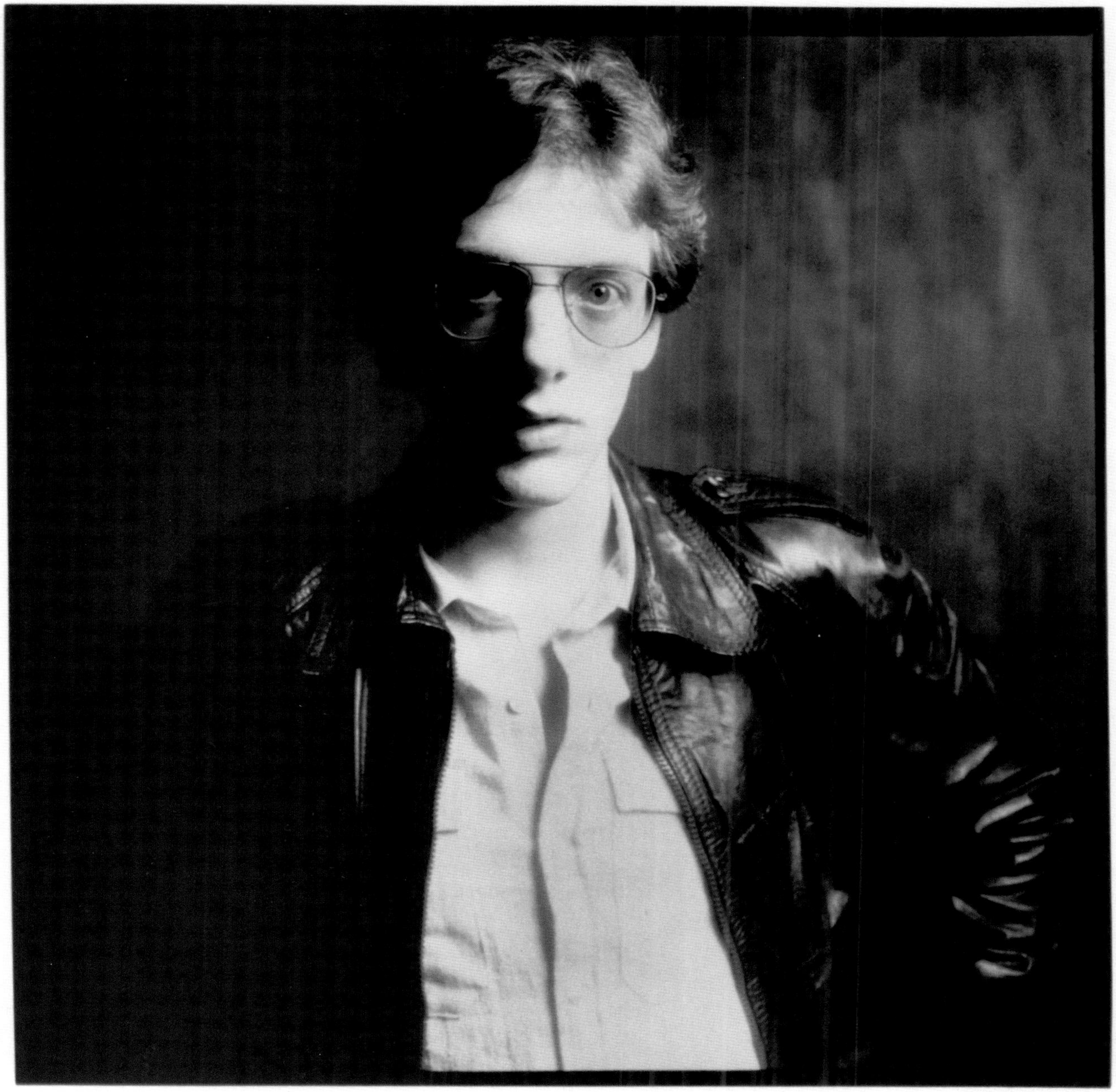

RANDY VANWARMER

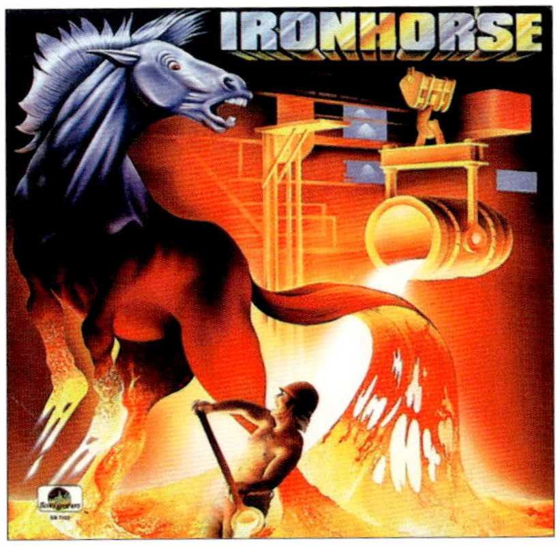

Led by former Guess Who and Bachman-Turner Overdrive guitarist Randy Bachman, **Ironhorse** invoked the best of BTO with "Sweet Lui-Louise," a Top 40 hit.

Billboard 200: *Ironhorse* (#153)
Billboard Hot 100: "Sweet Lui-Louise" (#36)

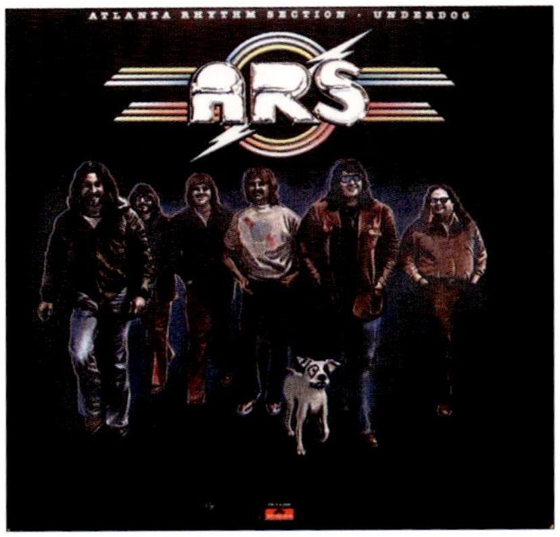

Atlanta Rhythm Section progressed with "Do It or Die" and "Spooky," a cover of the 1968 smash by Classics IV, whose lineup had included ARS members.

Billboard 200: *Underdog* (#26)
Billboard Hot 100: "Do It or Die" (#19); "Spooky" (#17)

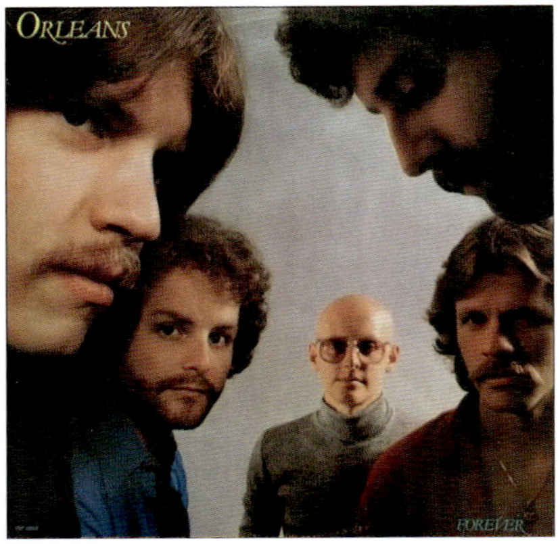

Persevering through personnel changes without founder and lead singer John Hall, a new lineup of **Orleans** produced another big hit, "Love Takes Time."

Billboard 200: *Forever* (#76)
Billboard Hot 100: "Love Takes Time" (#11)

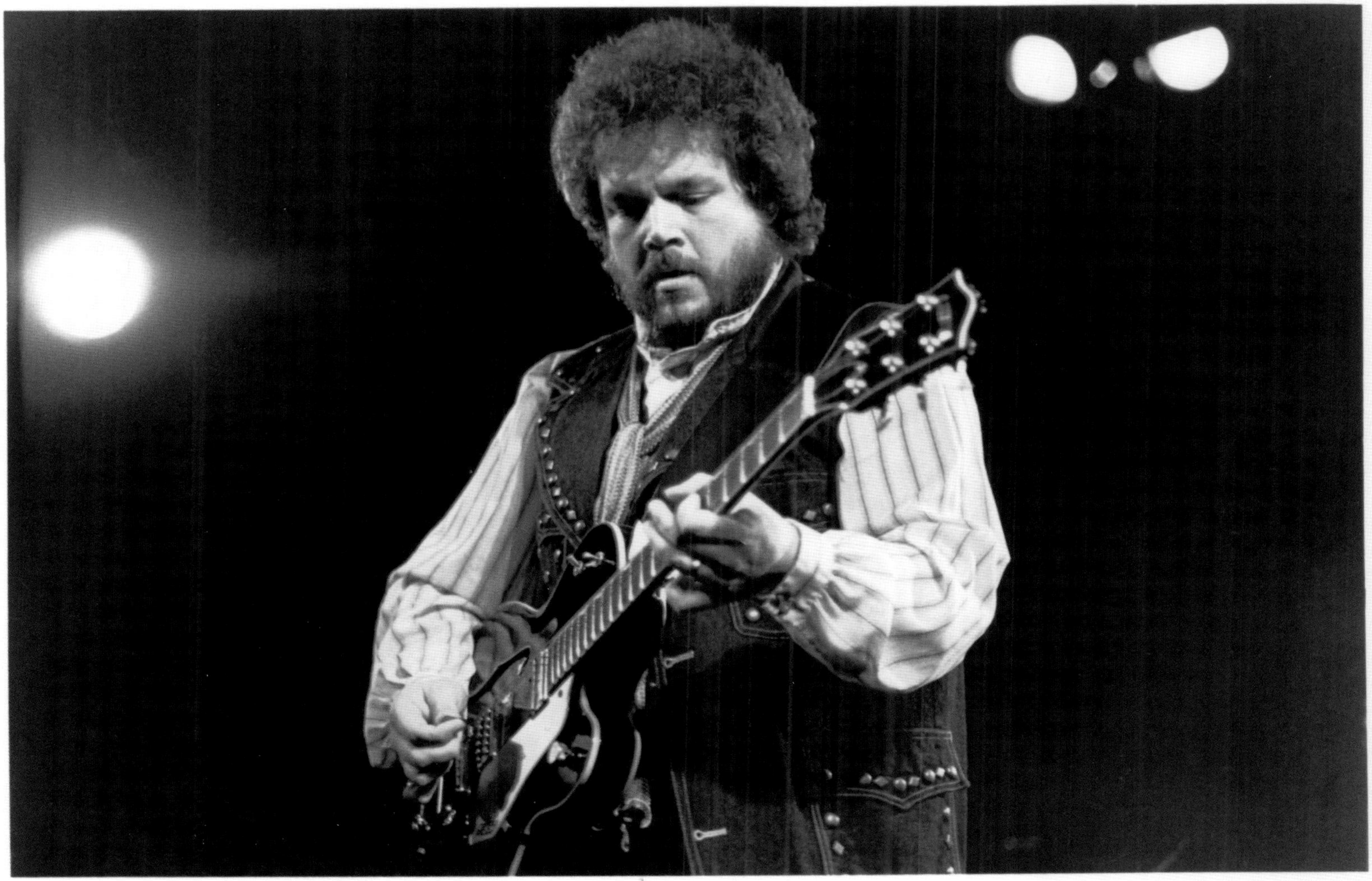

IRONHORSE

Randy Bachman

Scotti Brothers Records ™
Distributed by Atlantic Records

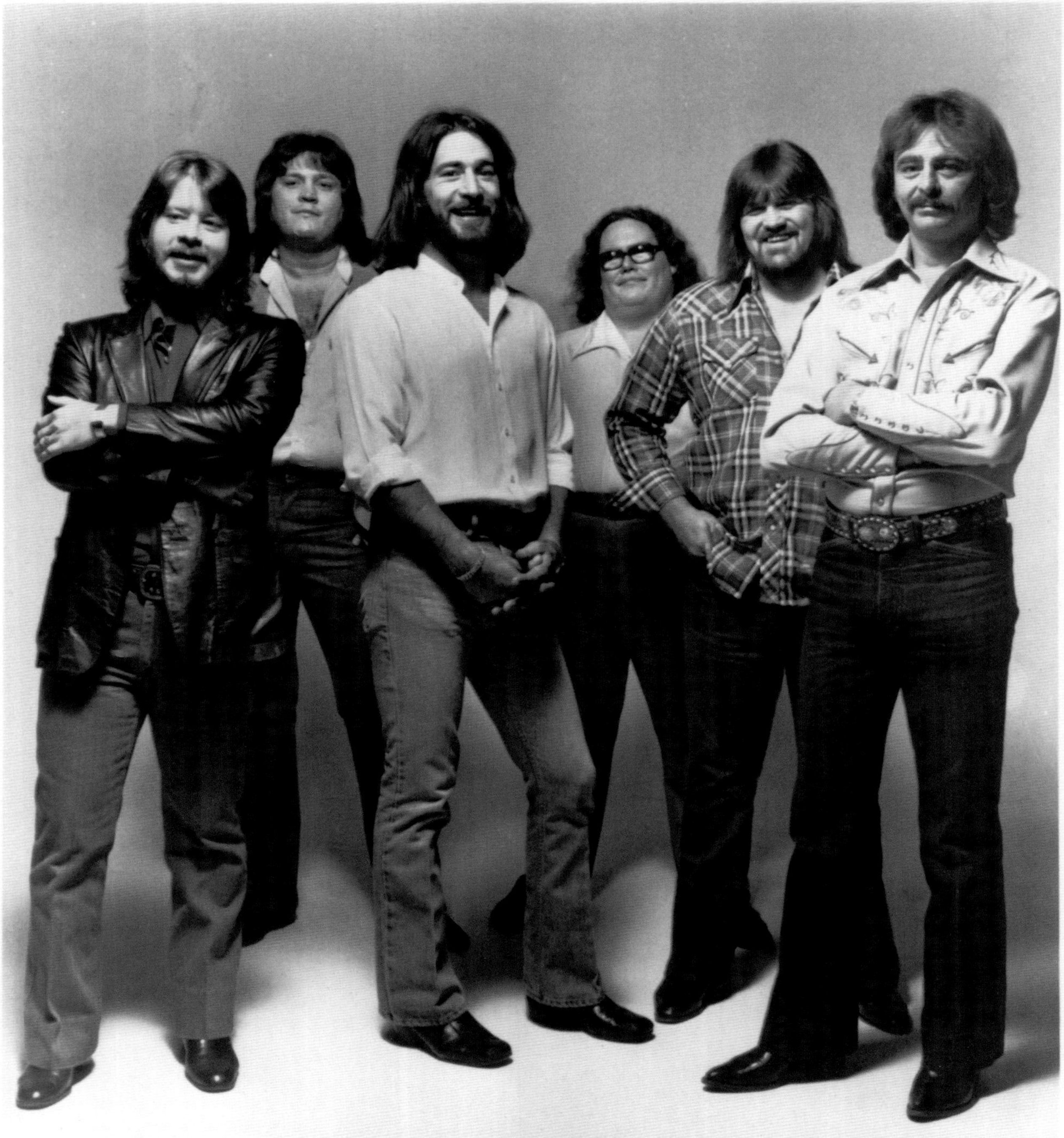

ATLANTA RHYTHM SECTION

polydor

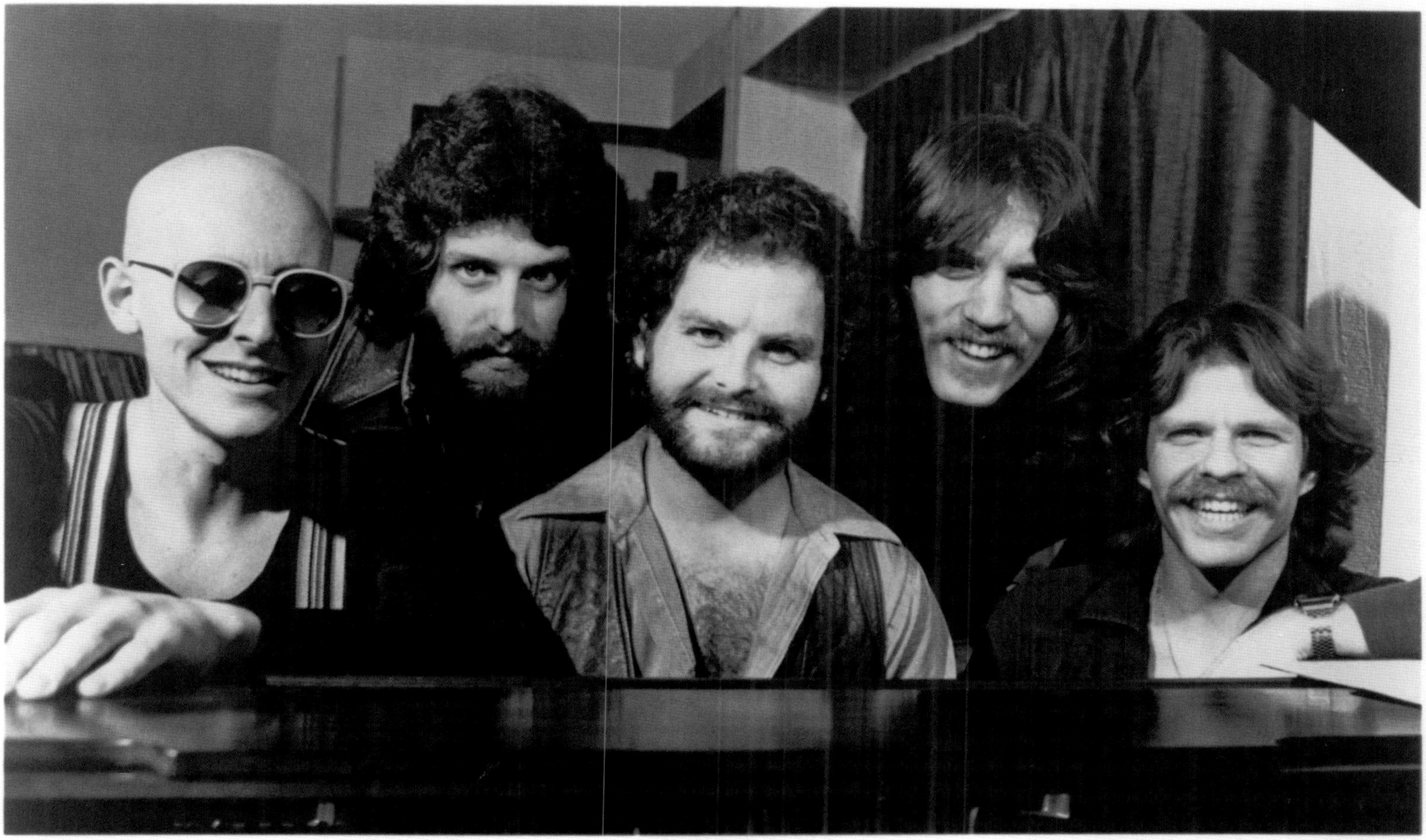

ORLEANS

Direction:
Bob Schwaid
Sight & Sound Management Ltd.
Suite 901
119 W 57th Street
New York, New York 10019

INFINITY RECORDS

10 East 53rd Street
New York, New York 10022
(212) 888-9700

100 Universal City Plaza
Universal City, California 91608
(213) 763-8283

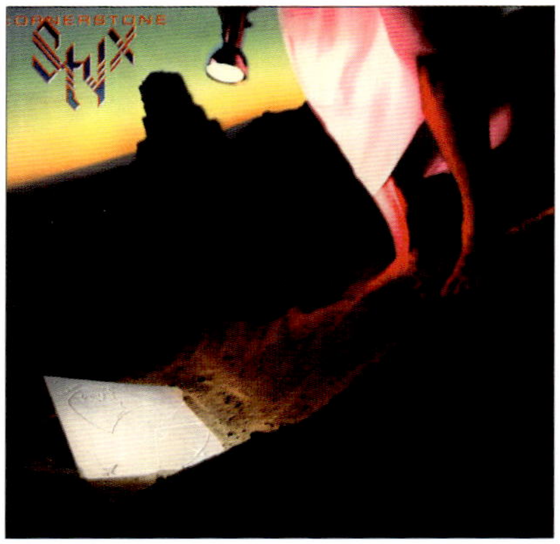

The triple-platinum *Cornerstone* yielded **Styx**'s first No. 1 hit, "Babe," a heartfelt power ballad written by singer and keyboard player Dennis DeYoung.

Billboard 200: *Cornerstone* (#2)
Billboard Hot 100: "Babe" (No. 1); "Why Me" (#26); "Borrowed Time" (#63)

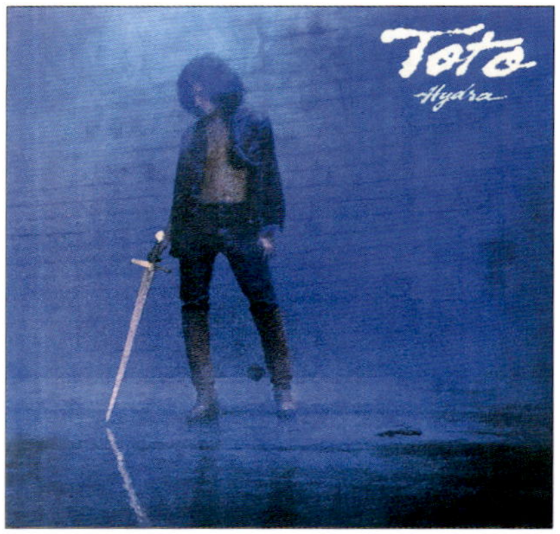

For *Hydra*, its second album, **Toto** produced some of the first conceptual rock videos, in particular "99," written in tribute to the sci-fi movie *THX 1138*.

Billboard 200: *Hydra* (#37)
Billboard Hot 100: "99" (#26)

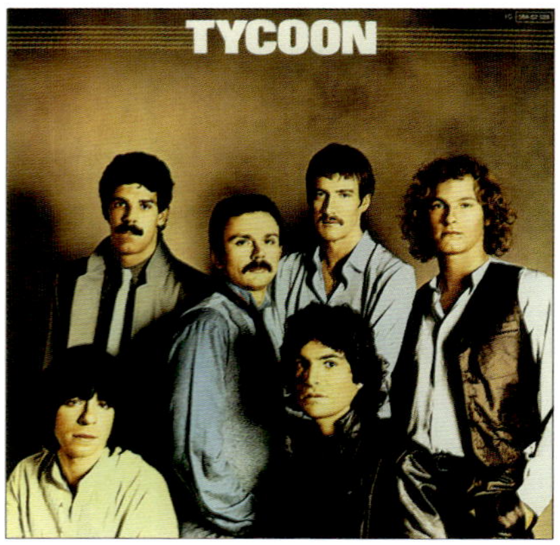

Tycoon's demo tape gained the New York City session players a recording contract—and a debut album with a polished Top 40 hit, "Such a Woman."

Billboard 200: *Tycoon* (#41)
Billboard Hot 100: "Such a Woman" (#26)

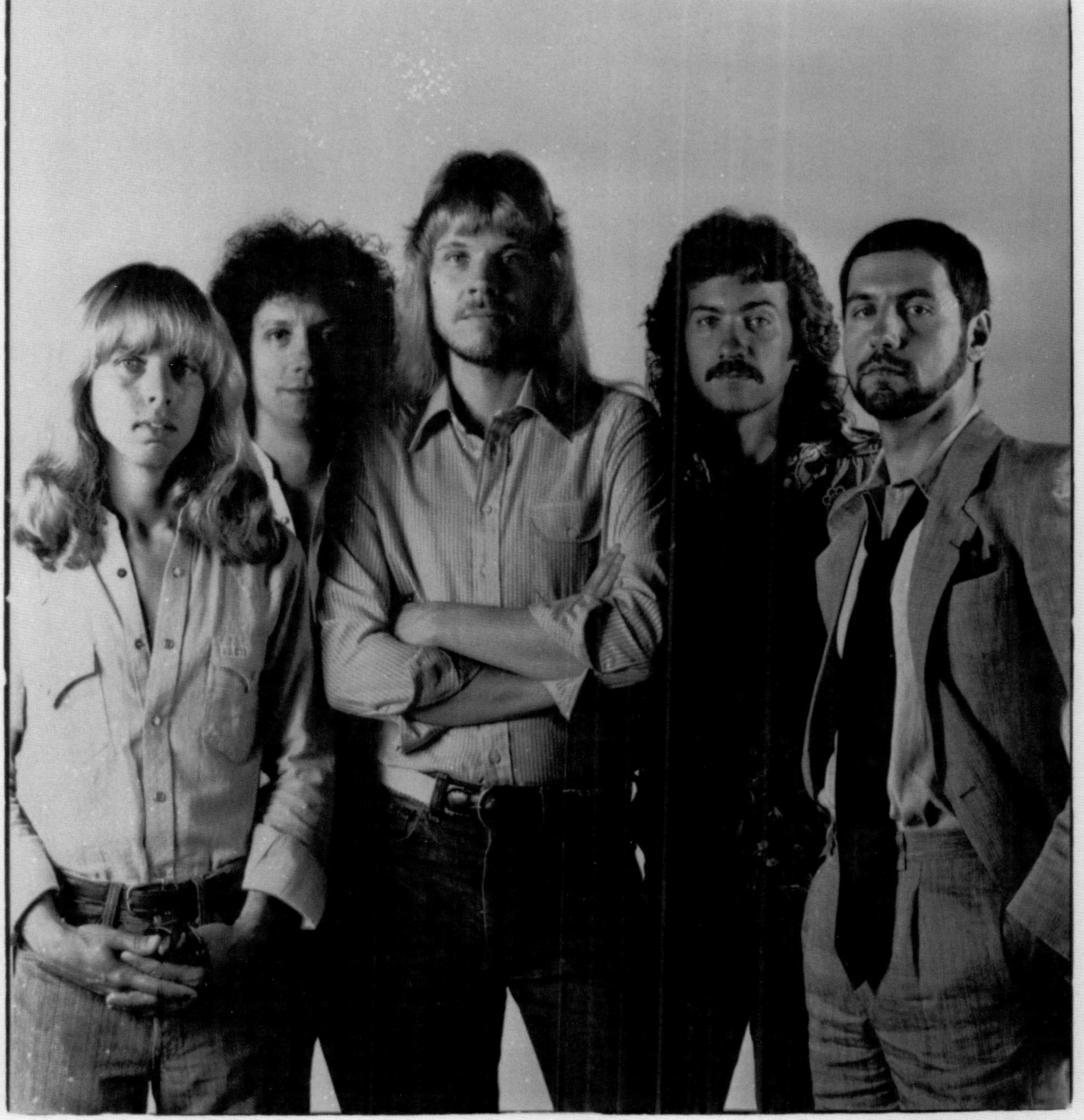

Styx

L to R: TOMMY SHAW, JOHN PANOZZO
JAMES YOUNG, DENNIS DE YOUNG, CHUCK PANOZZO,

A&M RECORDS
Printed in U.S.A.

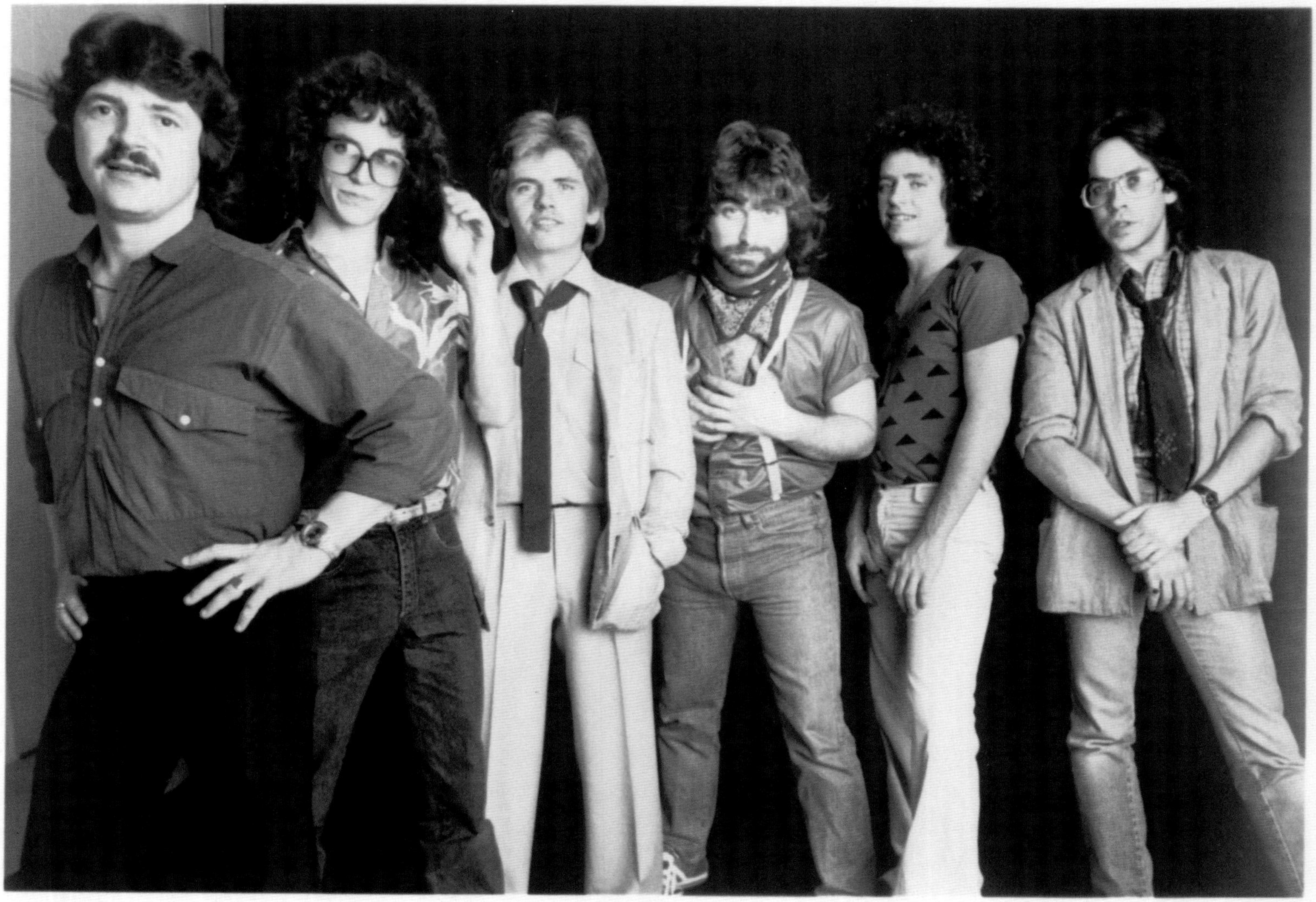

Direction:

The FITZGERALD HARTLEY Co

7250 Beverly, Los Angeles Ca.
(213)934-8002

TOTO

GAIL ROBERTS PUBLIC RELATIONS
7250 BEVERLY BOULEVARD LOS ANGELES, CA 90036 (213) 934-7765

Columbia

7910

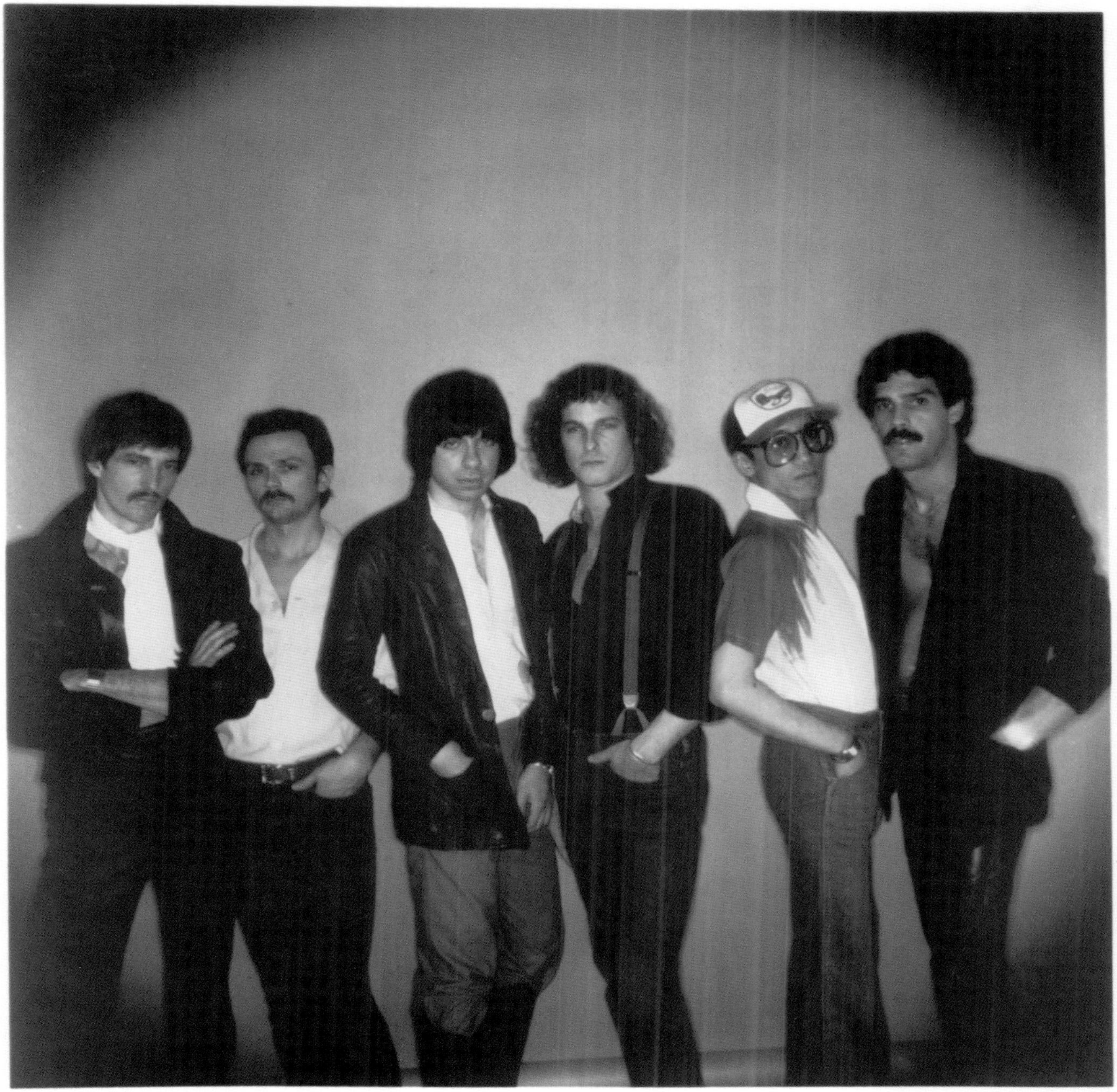

Management Jim Sullivan
330 W 58 Street
N Y N Y 10019
Suite 7-J
212-265-2520

TYCOON

ARISTA™

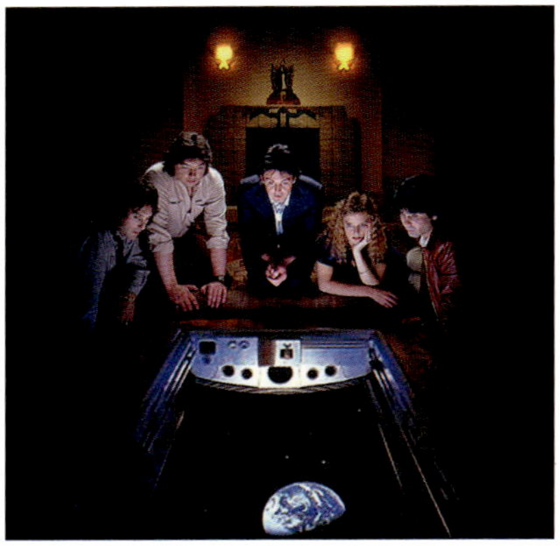

Paul McCartney maintained his group **Wings**, recruiting new members and recording *Back to the Egg*, but the album fell short of commercial expectations.

Billboard 200: *Back to the Egg* (#8)
Billboard Hot 100: "Getting Closer" (#20); "Arrow Through Me" (#29)

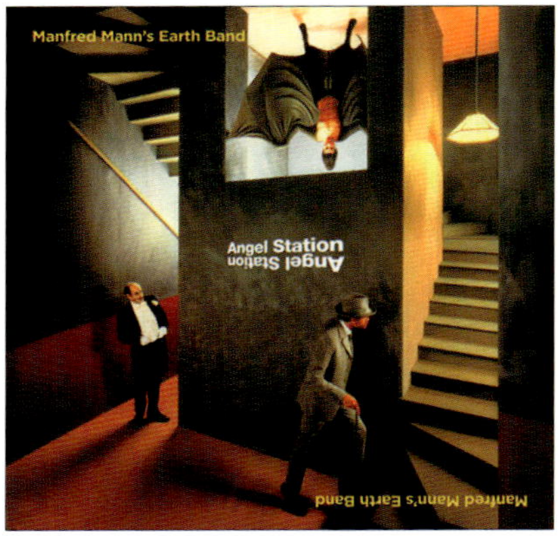

Manfred Mann's Earth Band, once celebrated for a version of Bruce Springsteen's "Blinded by the Light," dressed up "You Angel You," a Bob Dylan work.

Billboard 200: *Angel Station* (#144)
Billboard Hot 100: "You Angel You" (#58)

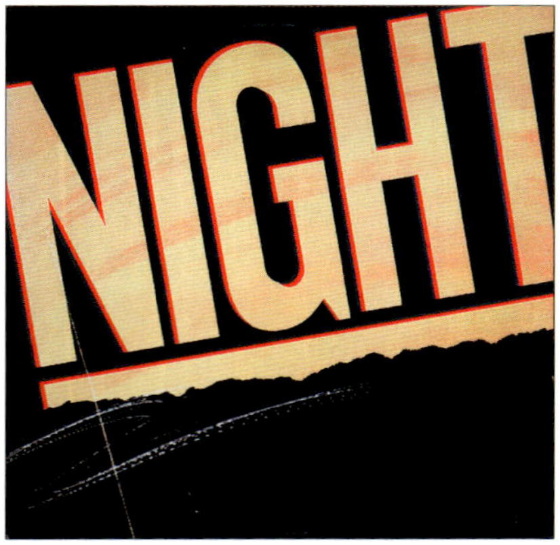

Borne out of the distinctive voices of Stevie Lange and Chris Thompson, **Night**'s debut provided two hits, "Hot Summer Nights" and "If You Remember Me."

Billboard 200: *Night* (#113)
Billboard Hot 100: "Hot Summer Nights" (#18);
"If You Remember Me" (#17)

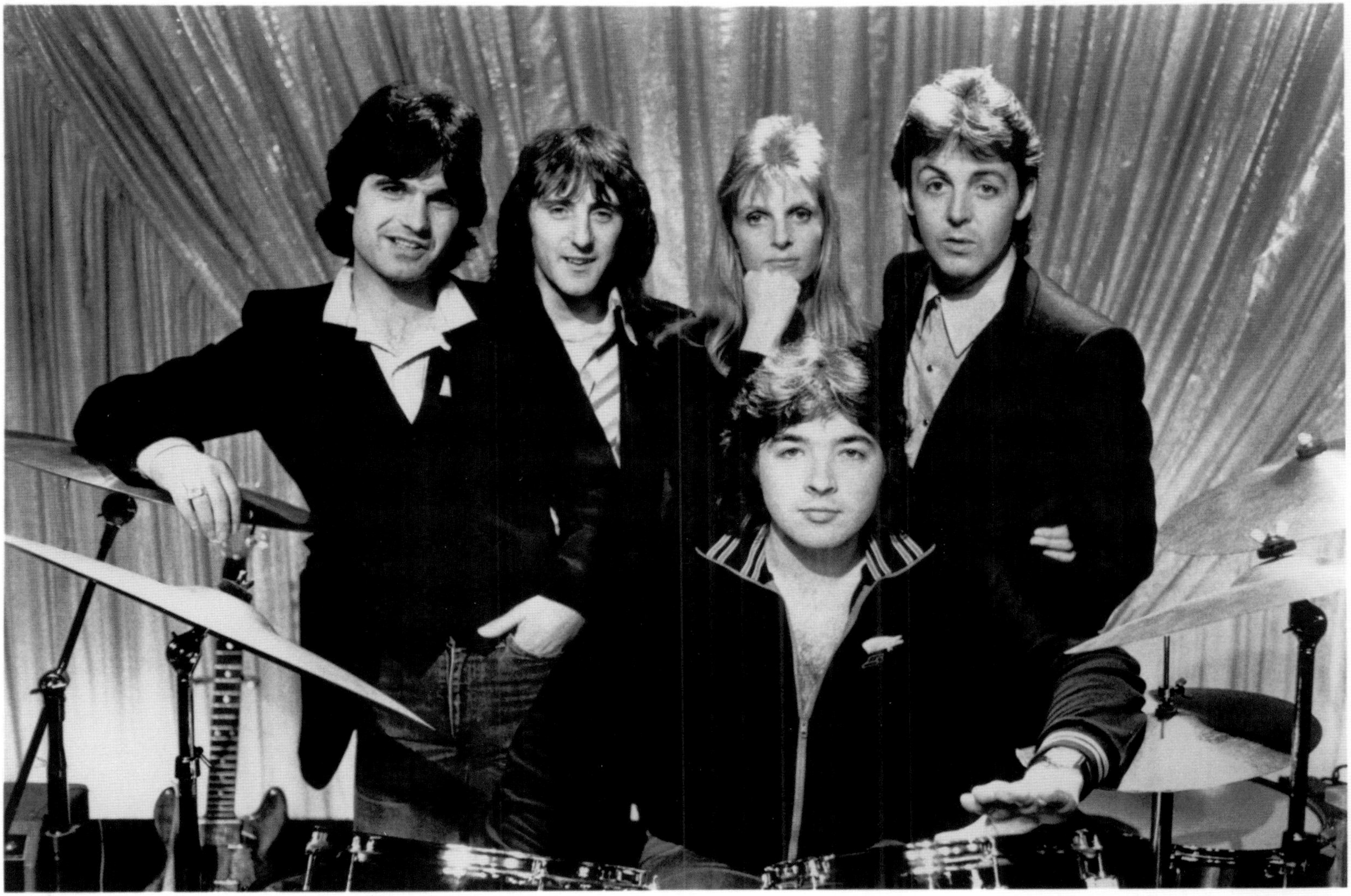

Columbia

7906

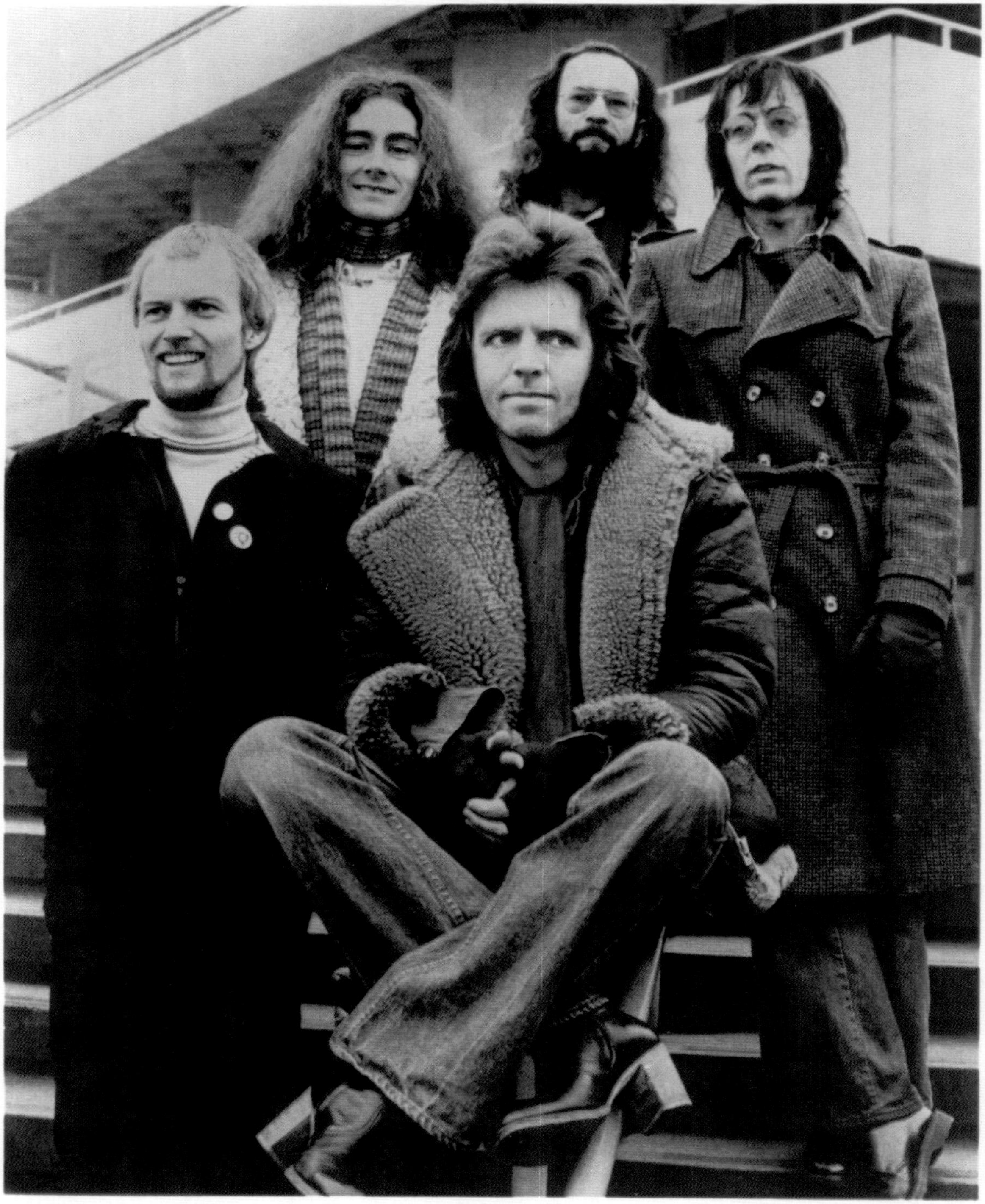

MANFRED MANN'S EARTH BAND

WARNER / REPRISE

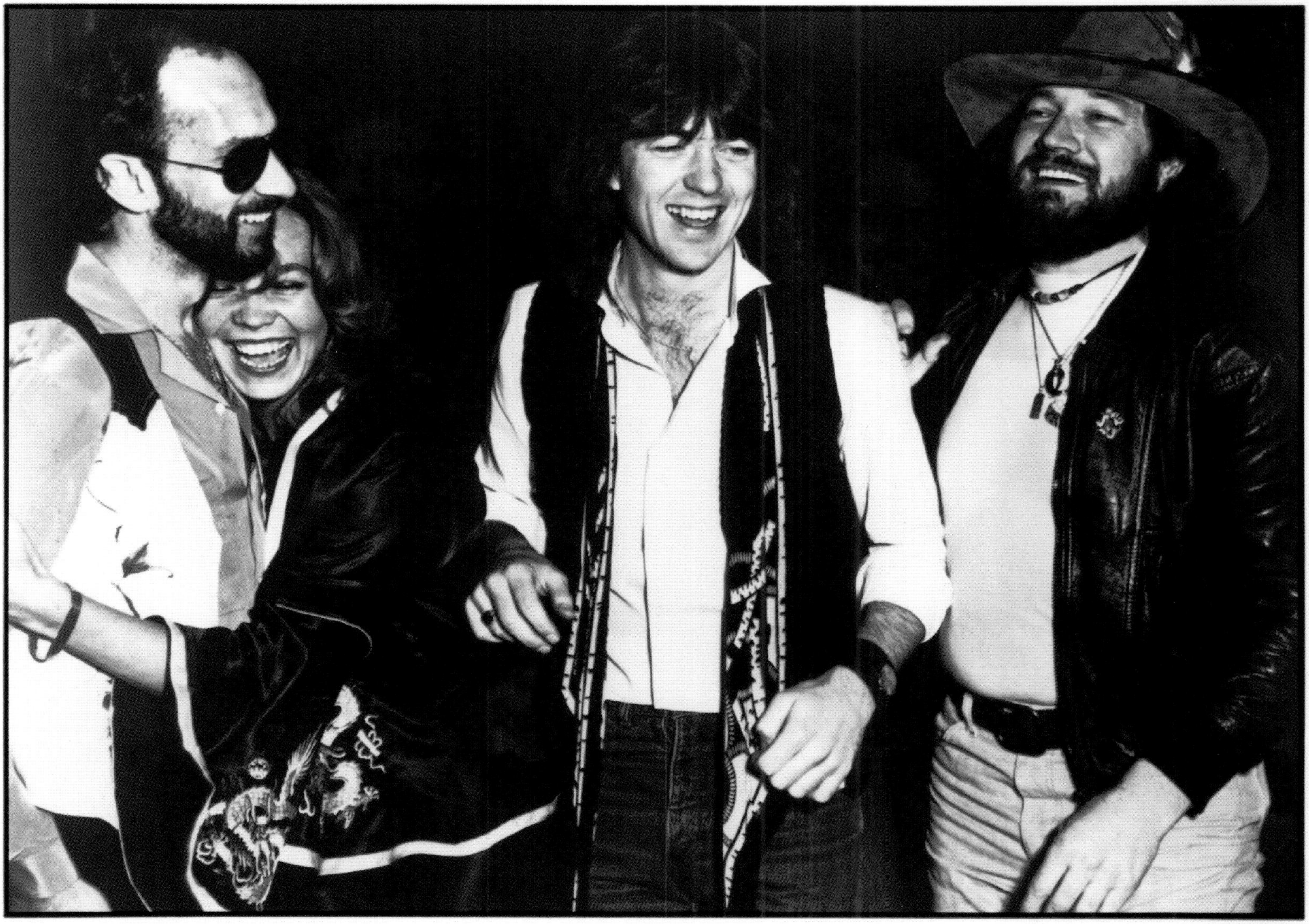

Photo Credit: JIM SHEA

Chris Thompson Stevie Lange Robbie McIntosh Billy Kristian

NIGHT

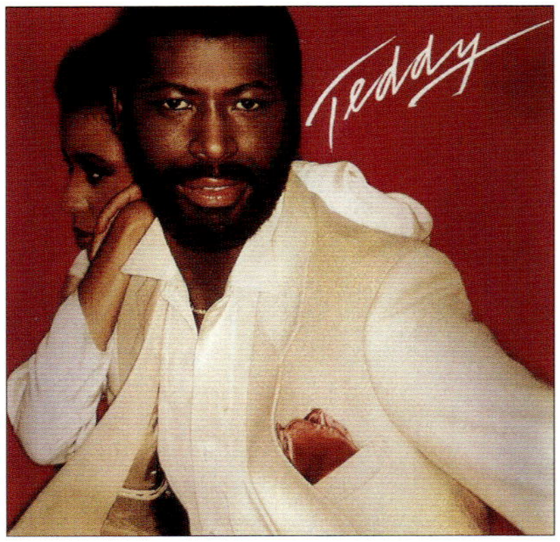

A No. 1 R&B album for eight weeks, seductive soul singer **Teddy Pendergrass**' *Teddy* showcased the erotic "Turn Off the Lights," a seminal "bedroom ballad."

Billboard 200: *Teddy* (#5)
Billboard Hot 100: "Turn Off the Lights" (#48)

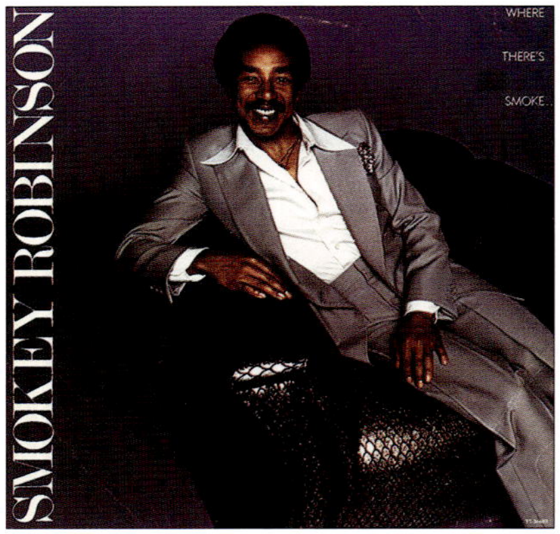

Former lead singer and co-founder of the Miracles, Motown legend **Smokey Robinson** circled back with the sensuous "Cruisin'," his first solo Top Ten single.

Billboard 200: *Where There's Smoke…* (#17)
Billboard Hot 100: "Cruisin'" (#4)

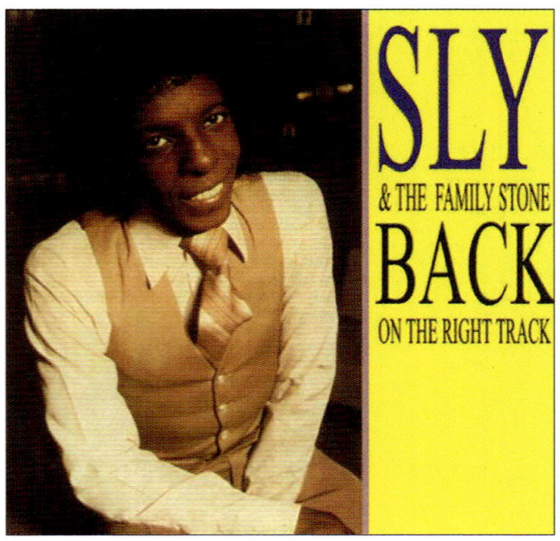

Sly & the Family Stone frontman Sly Stone's drug misuse and erratic behavior forced the pioneering band into recording an unsuccessful comeback album.

Billboard 200: *Back on the Right Track* (#152)

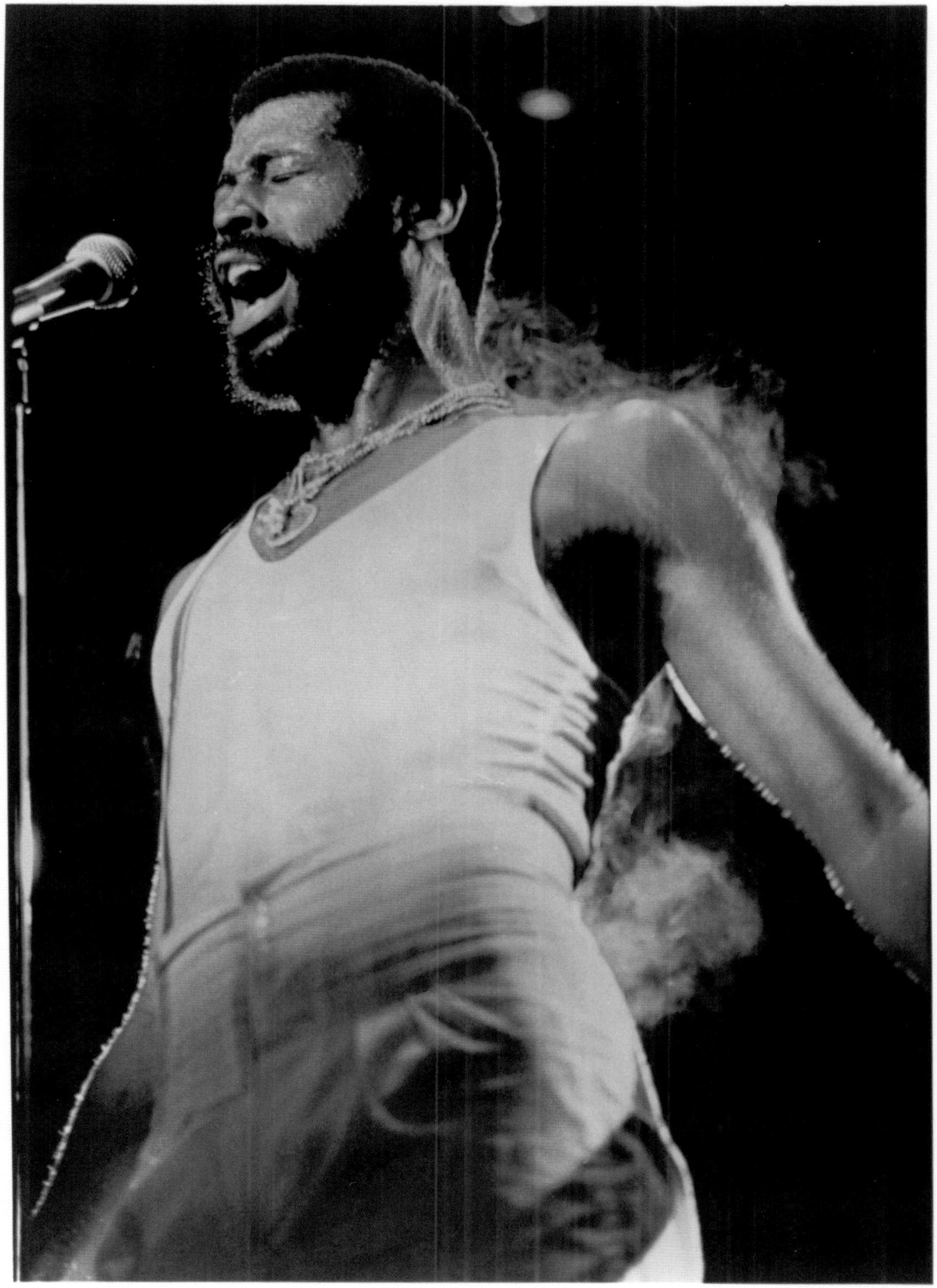

Teddy Pendergrass

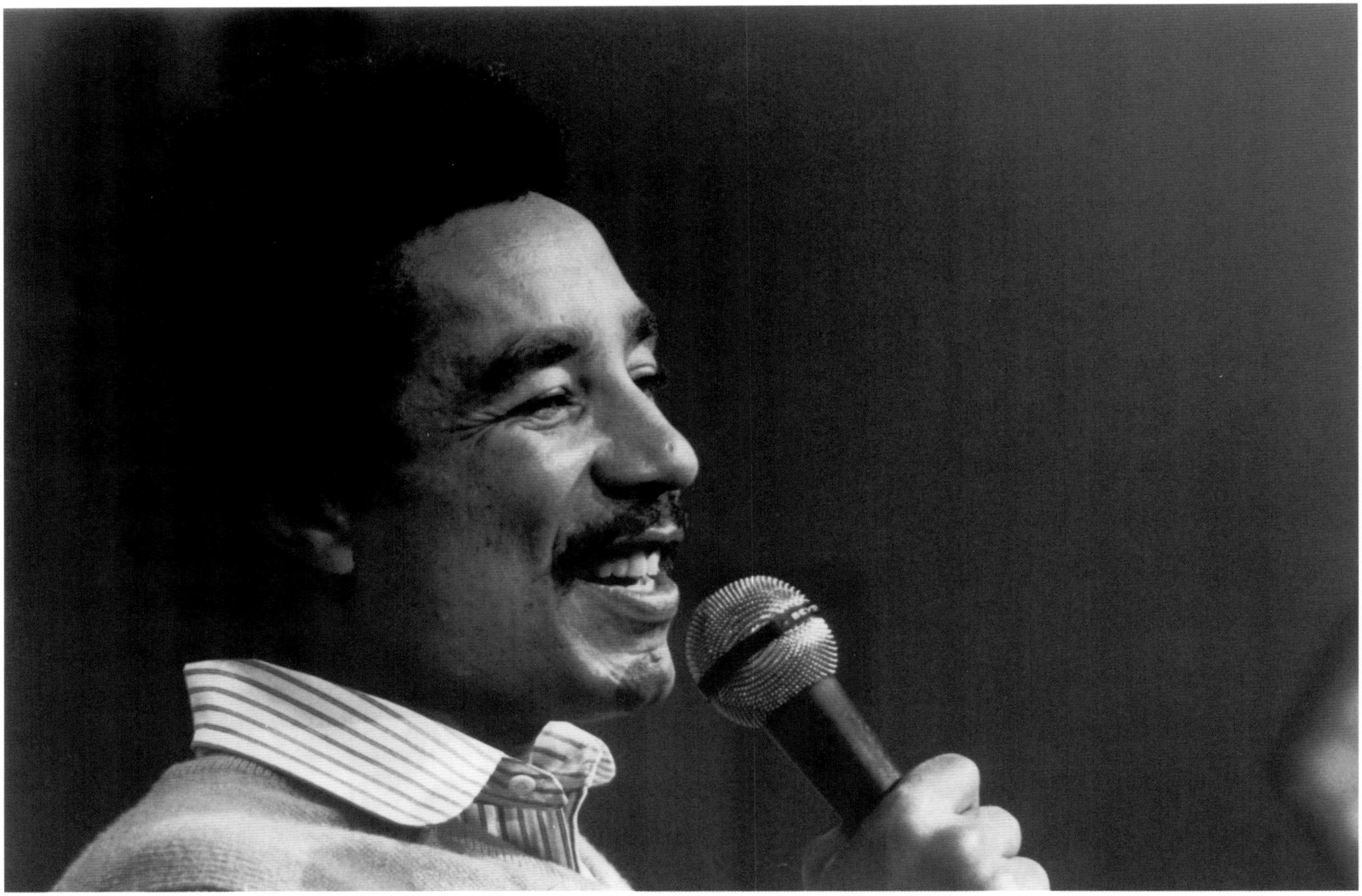

SMOKEY ROBINSON

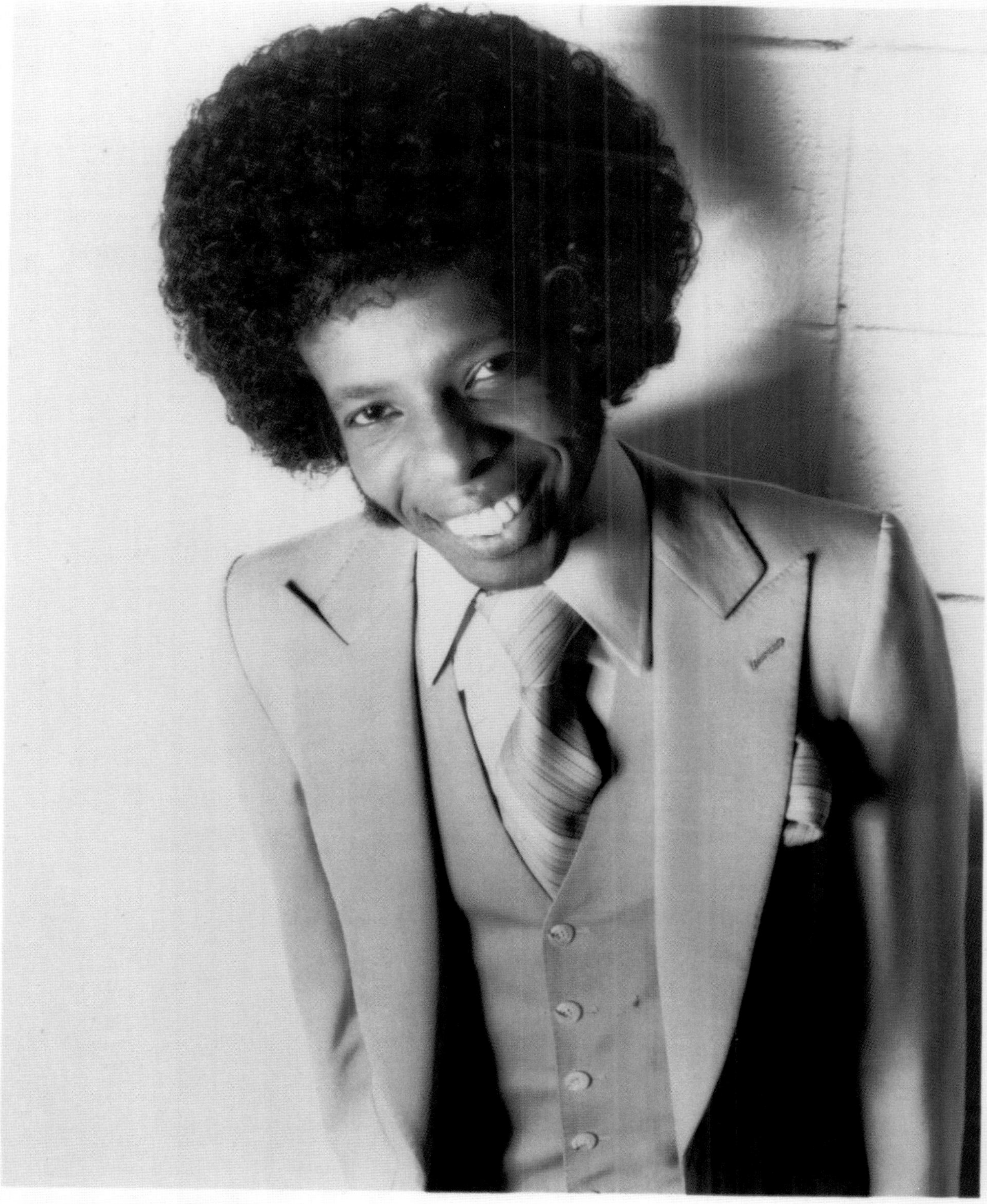

OCTOBER 1979

SLY STONE

WARNER BROS.

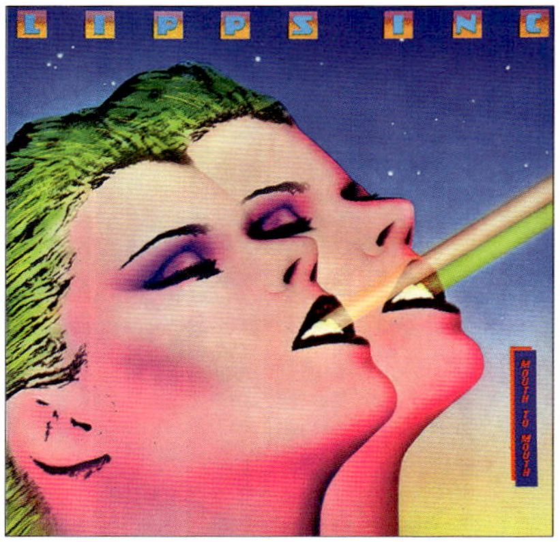

The alliance of writer and producer Steven Greenberg and singer Cynthia Johnson, disco act **Lipps, Inc.** broke out with "Funkytown," a global No. 1 smash.

Billboard 200: *Mouth to Mouth* (#5)
Billboard Hot 100: "Funkytown" (No. 1); "Rock It" (#64)

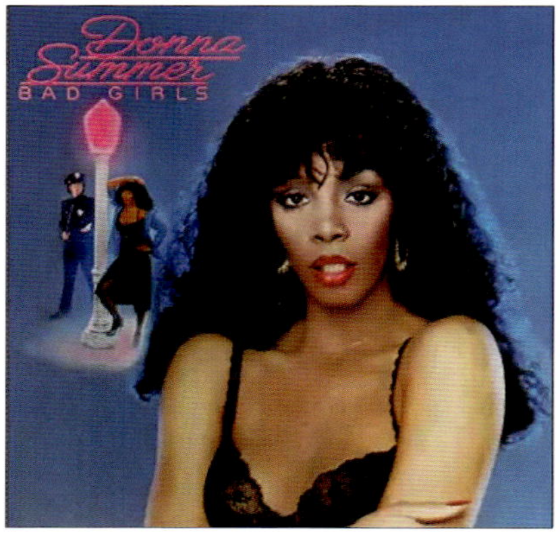

Bad Girls became the creative and commercial pinnacle of **Donna Summer**'s career, bearing the mega hits "Hot Stuff," "Bad Girls" and "Dim All the Lights."

Billboard 200: *Bad Girls* (No. 1)
Billboard Hot 100: "Hot Stuff" (No. 1); "Bad Girls" (No. 1);
"Dim All the Lights" (#2); "Walk Away" (#36)

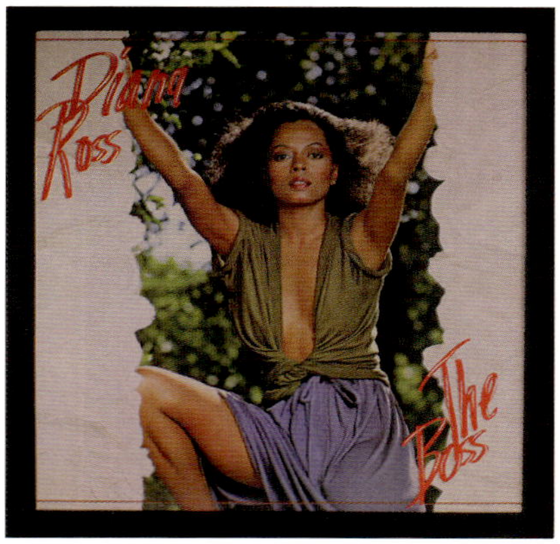

Diana Ross issued *The Boss*, a work that extended her celebrity with club audiences, with the title song and "It's My House" becoming No. 1 dance singles.

Billboard 200: *The Boss* (#14)
Billboard Hot 100: "The Boss" (#19)

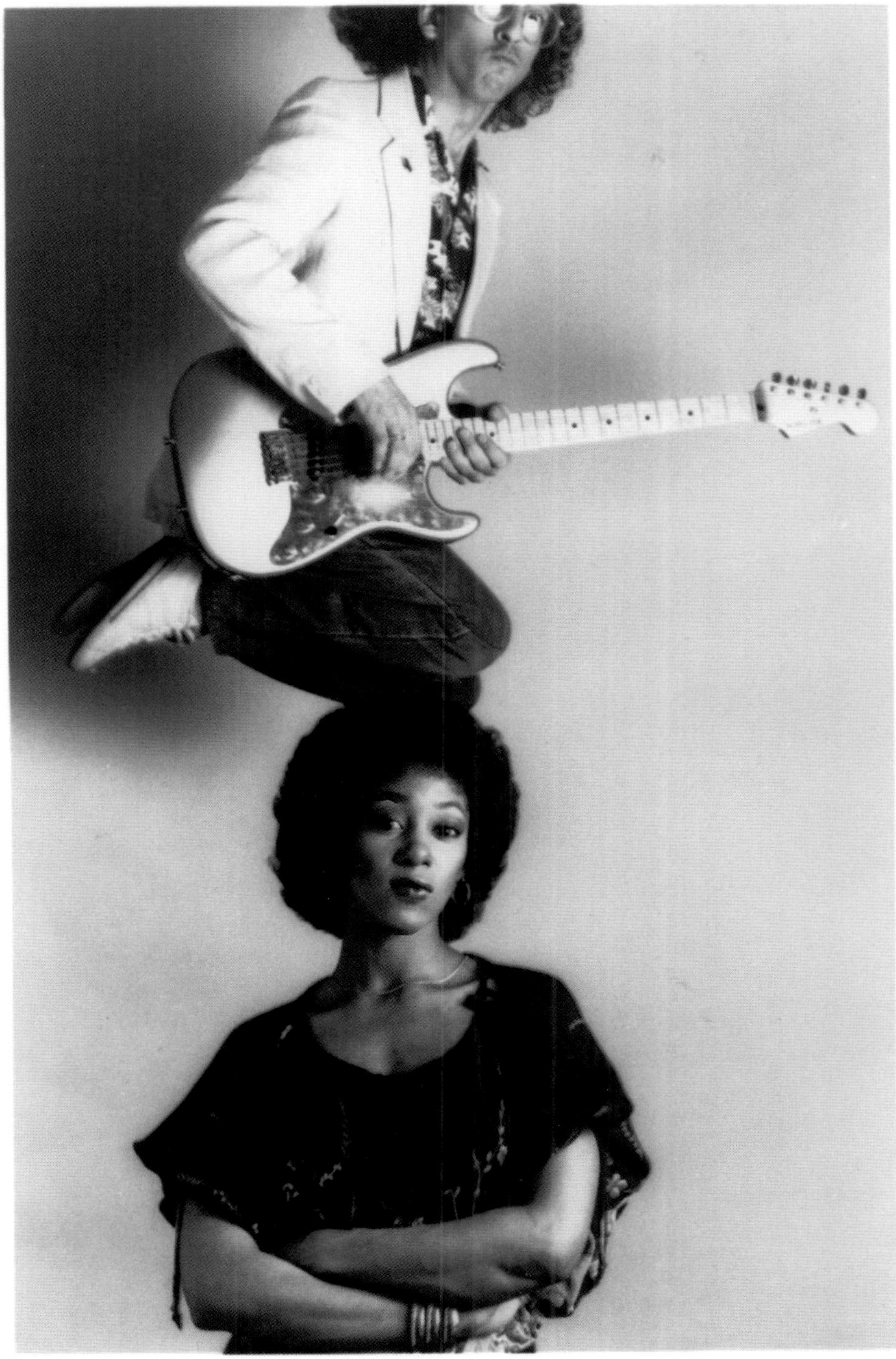

LIPPS, INC.

Casablanca Record and FilmWorks

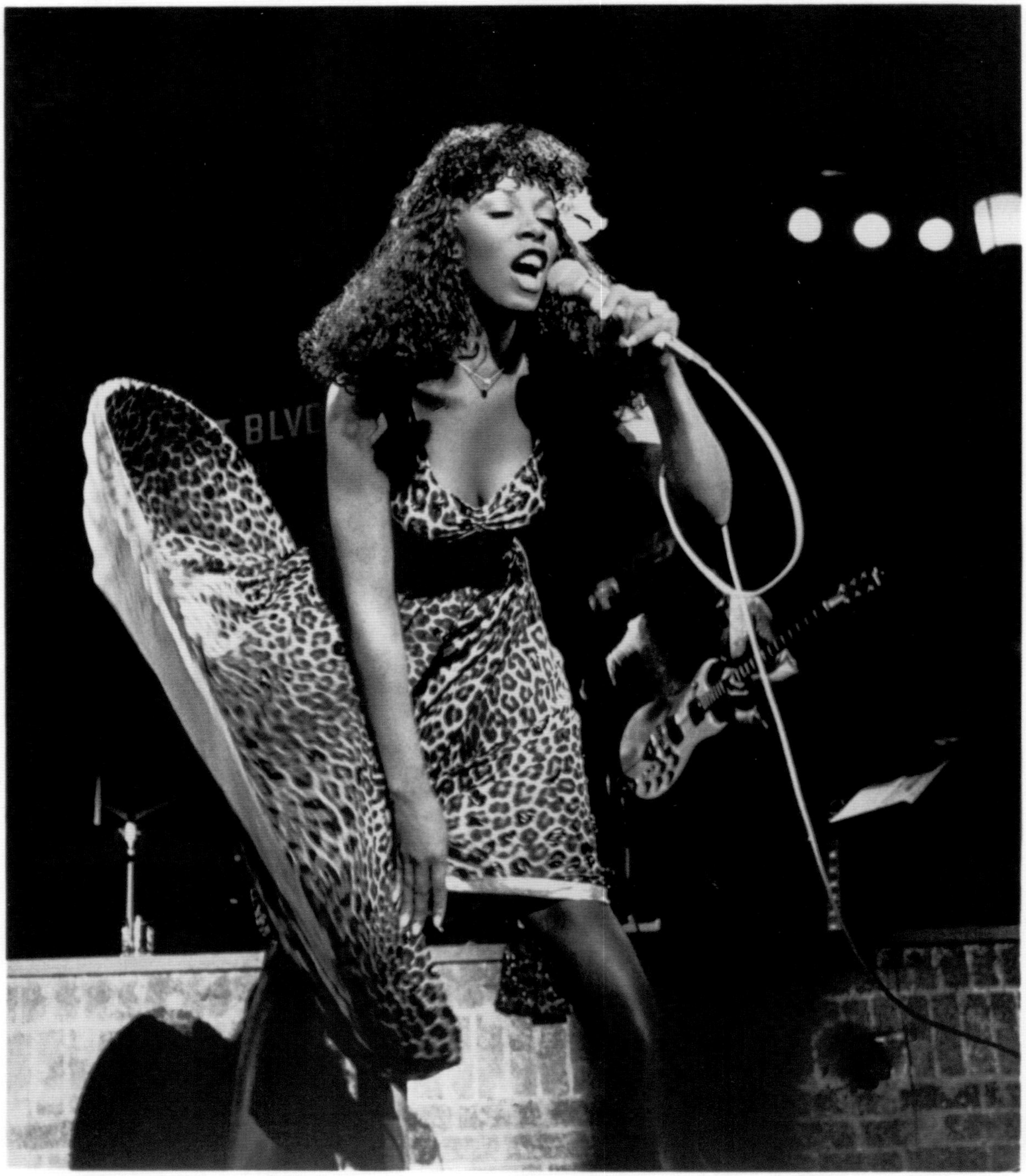

NEAL PRESTON PHOTOGRAPHY

Casablanca Record and FilmWorks

DONNA SUMMER

XXXX

SUSAN MUNAO MANAGEMENT

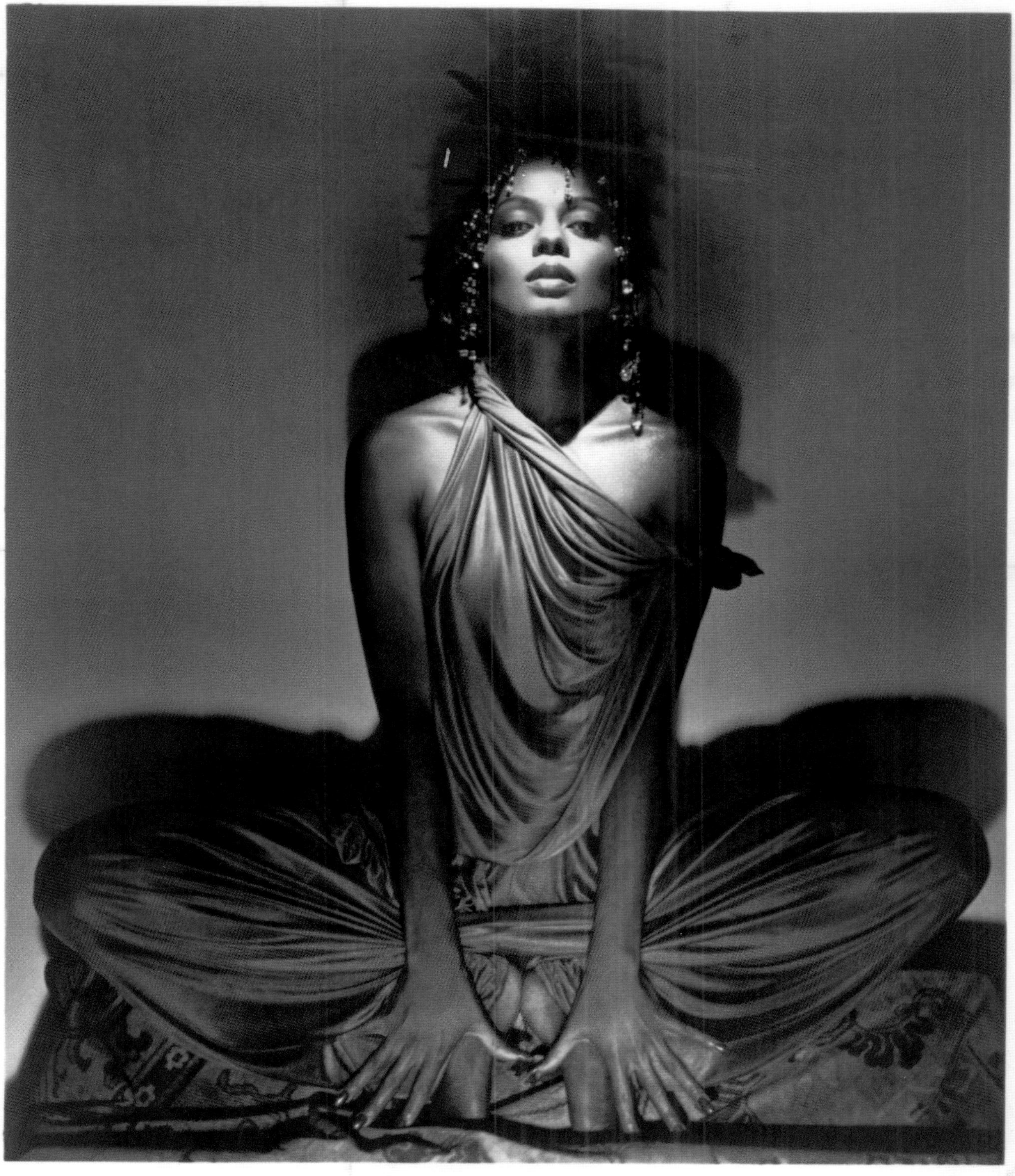

DIANA *ROSS*

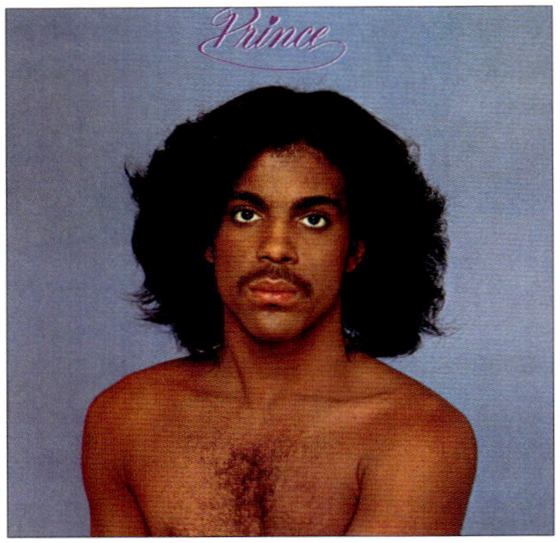

Not yet 20 years old, the precocious **Prince** recorded his second album on his own in five weeks, surfacing with his first major hit, "I Wanna Be Your Lover."

Billboard 200: *Prince* (#22)
Billboard Hot 100: "I Wanna Be Your Lover" (#11)

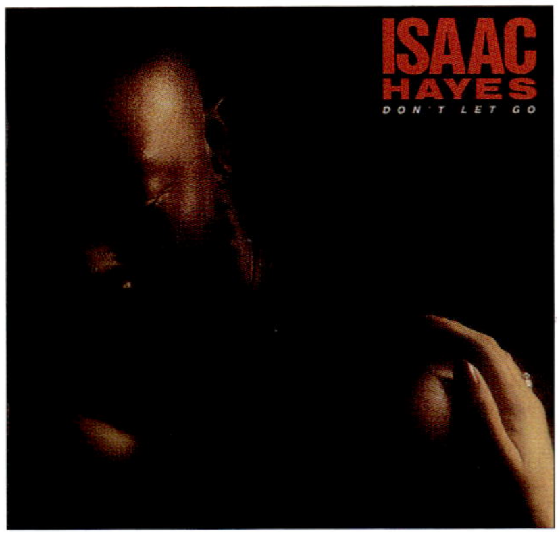

Soul luminary **Isaac Hayes** revisited the Top 40 with *Don't Let Go* and a propulsive disco version of the title track, first a hit for Roy Hamilton in 1958.

Billboard 200: *Don't Let Go* (#39)
Billboard Hot 100: "Don't Let Go" (#18)

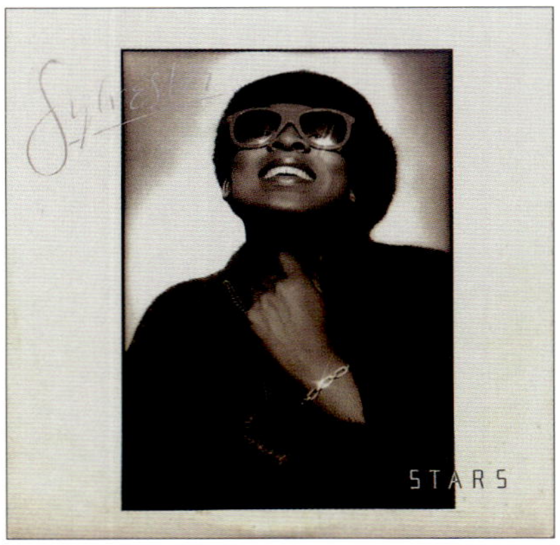

Receiving recognition for his expressive falsetto, the flamboyant **Sylvester** released "I (Who Have Nothing)," a stormy disco treatment of the R&B classic.

Billboard 200: *Stars* (#63)
Billboard Hot 100: "I (Who Have Nothing)" (#40)

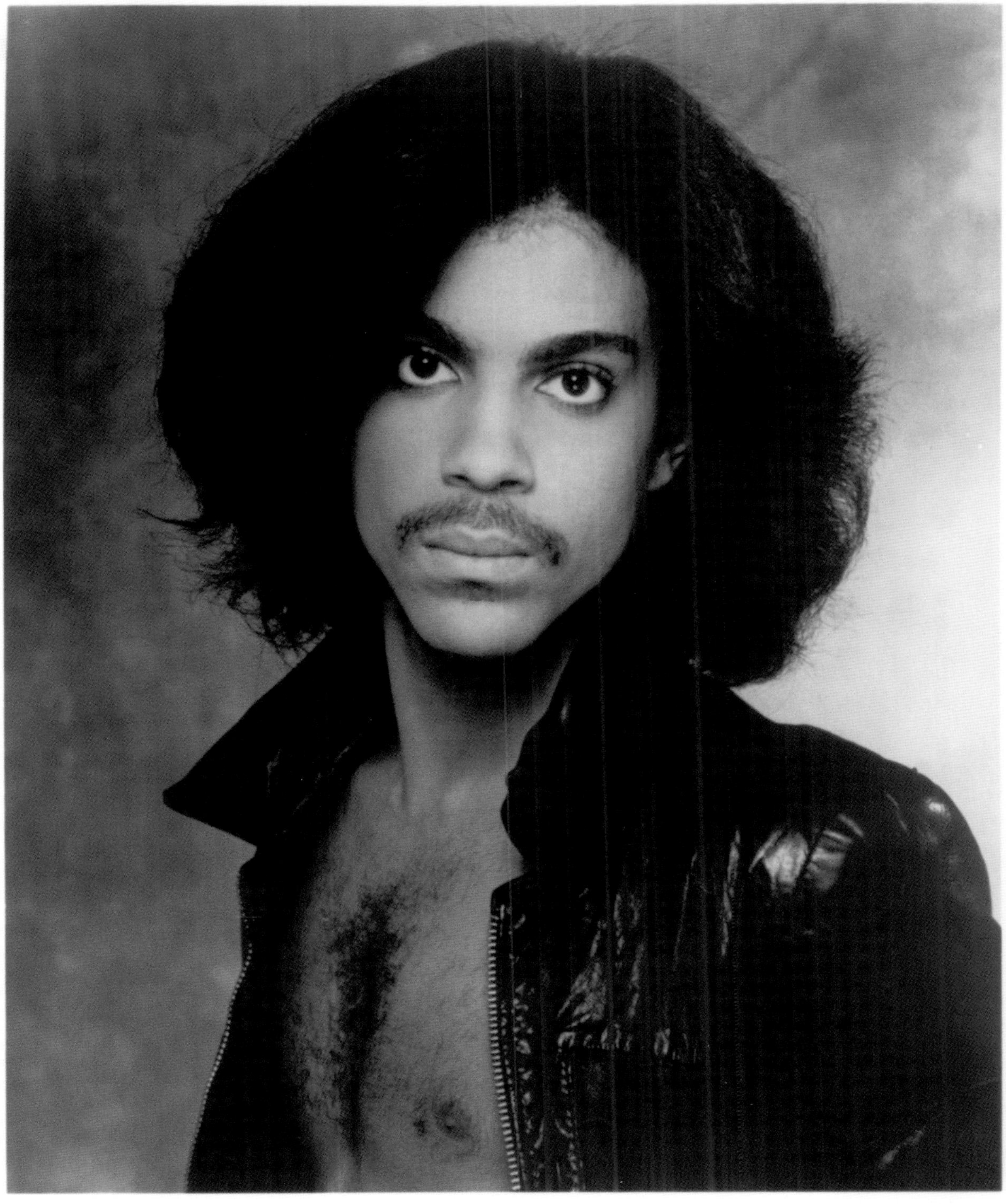

OCTOBER 1979

PRINCE

WARNER BROS.

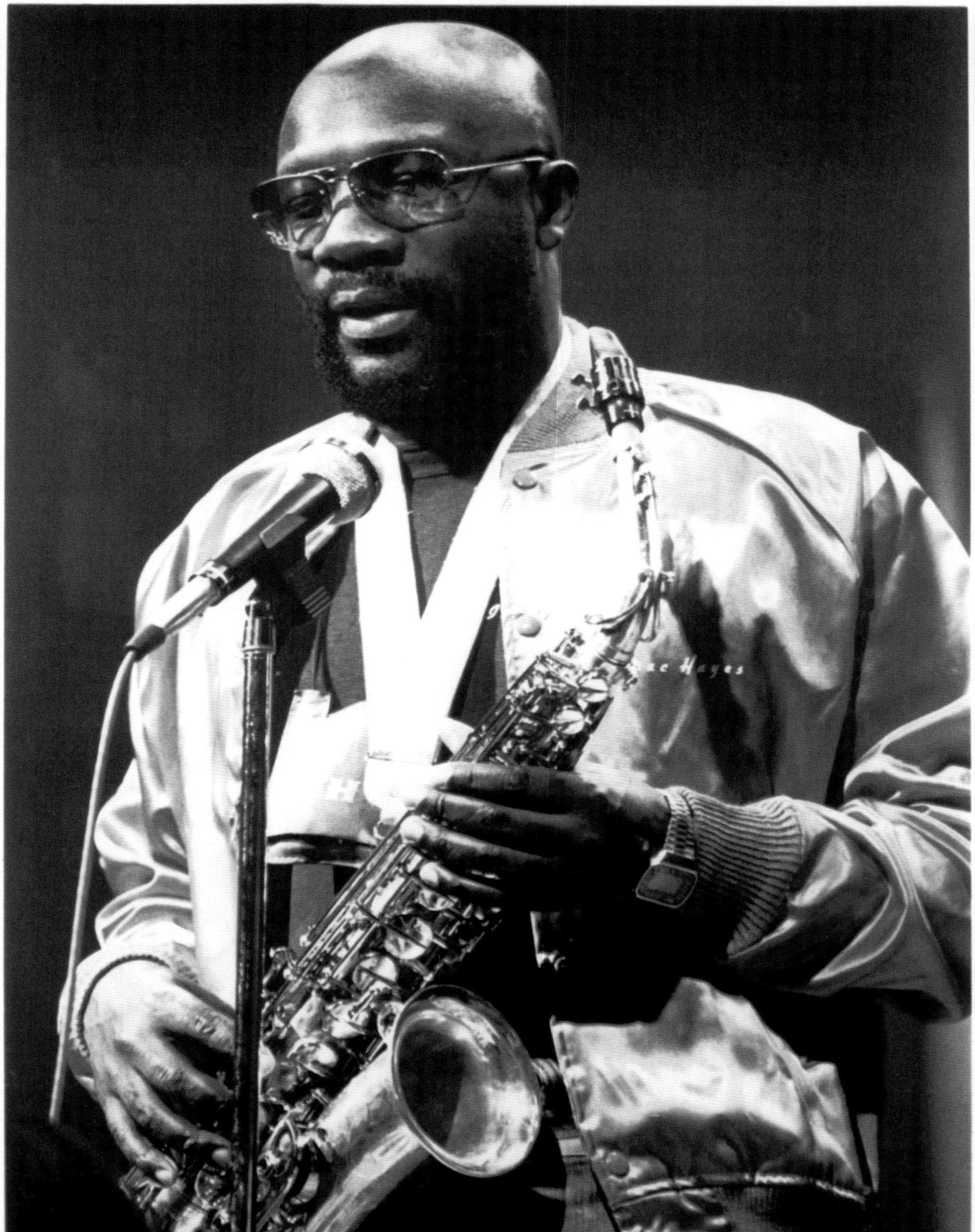

ISAAC HAYES

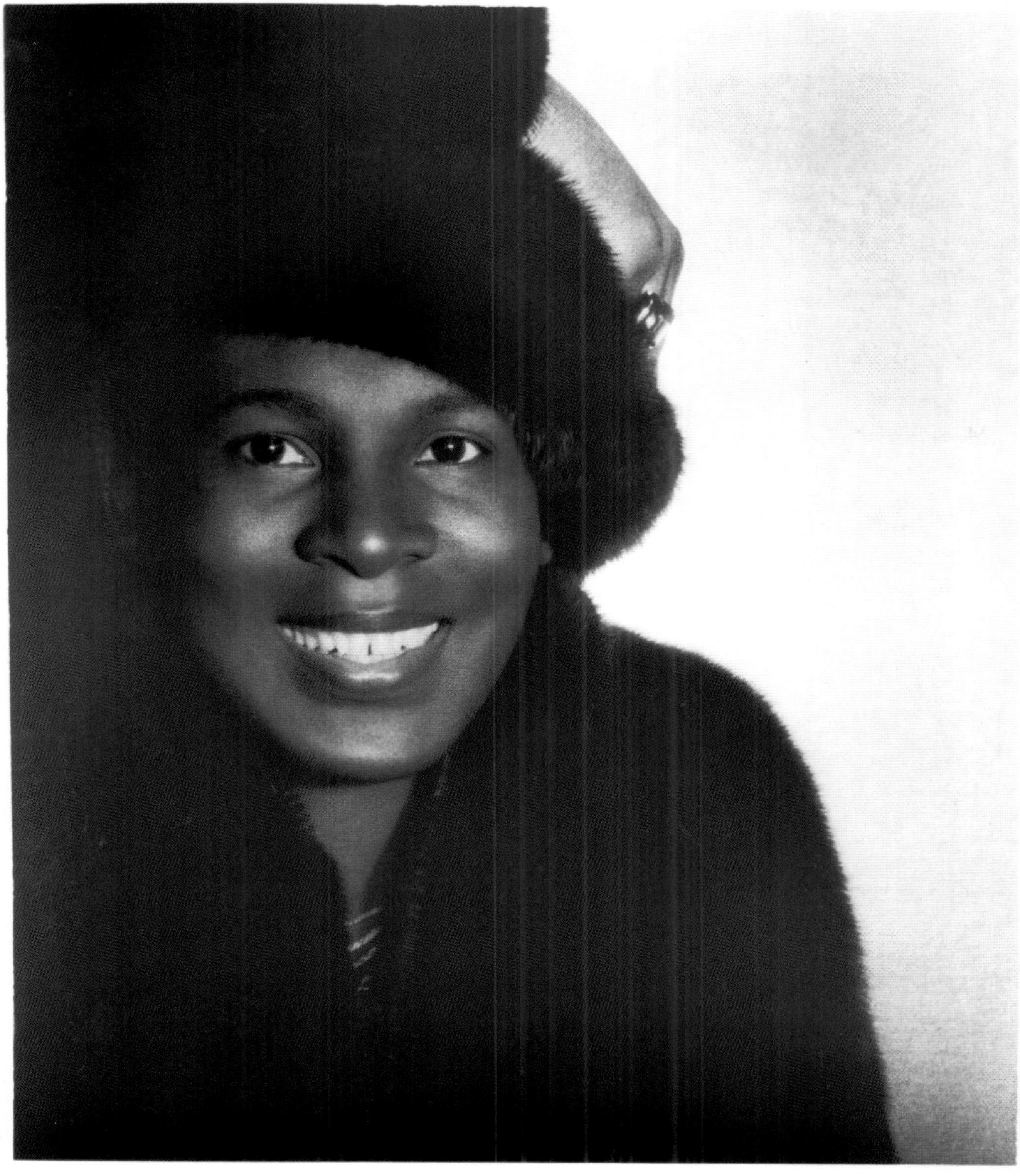

SYLVESTER

MANAGEMENT: NANCY C. PITTS
415/495-7606
BOOKINGS: ICM

Fantasy

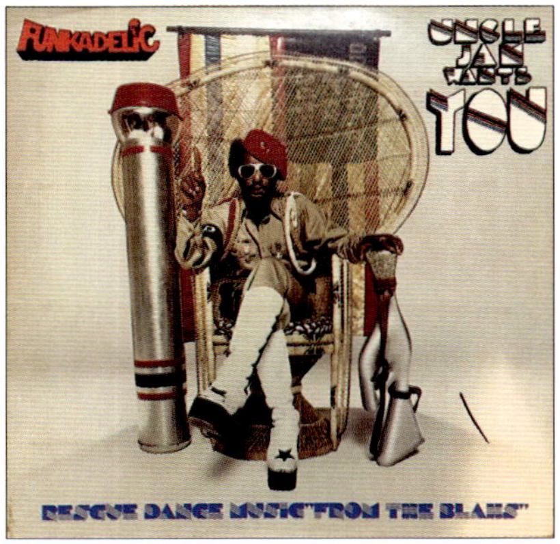

Headed by George Clinton, alias Dr. Funkenstein, **Funkadelic** fired up dance floors with *Uncle Jam Wants You* and the 15-minute "(Not Just) Knee Deep."

Billboard 200: *Uncle Jam Wants You* (#18)
Billboard Hot 100: "(Not Just) Knee Deep" (#77)

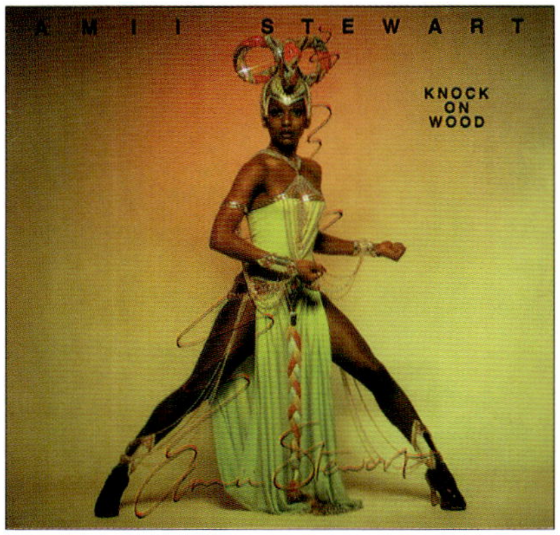

Amii Stewart enjoyed the limelight with her pulsating disco take on Eddie Floyd's "Knock on Wood," reaching No. 1 and earning a Grammy nomination.

Billboard 200: *Knock on Wood* (#19)
Billboard Hot 100: "Knock on Wood" (No. 1);
"Light My Fire/137 Disco Heaven" (#69)

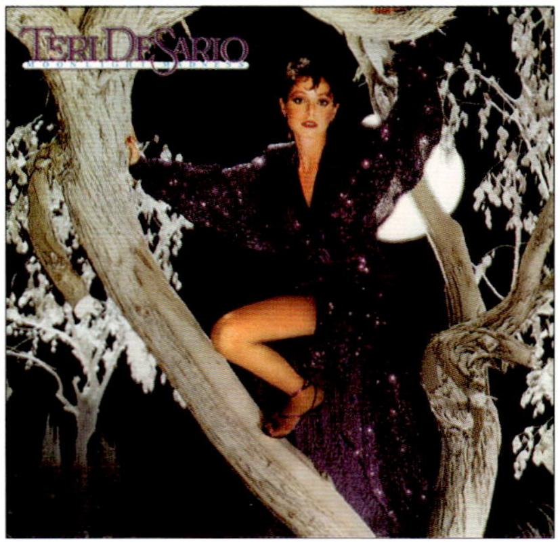

Miami-born singer **Teri DeSario** and childhood pal KC of the Sunshine Band rendered a sparkling cover of "Yes, I'm Ready," Barbara Mason's 1965 hit song.

Billboard 200: *Moonlight Madness* (#80)
Billboard Hot 100: "Yes I'm Ready" (#2);
"Dancin' in the Streets" (#66)

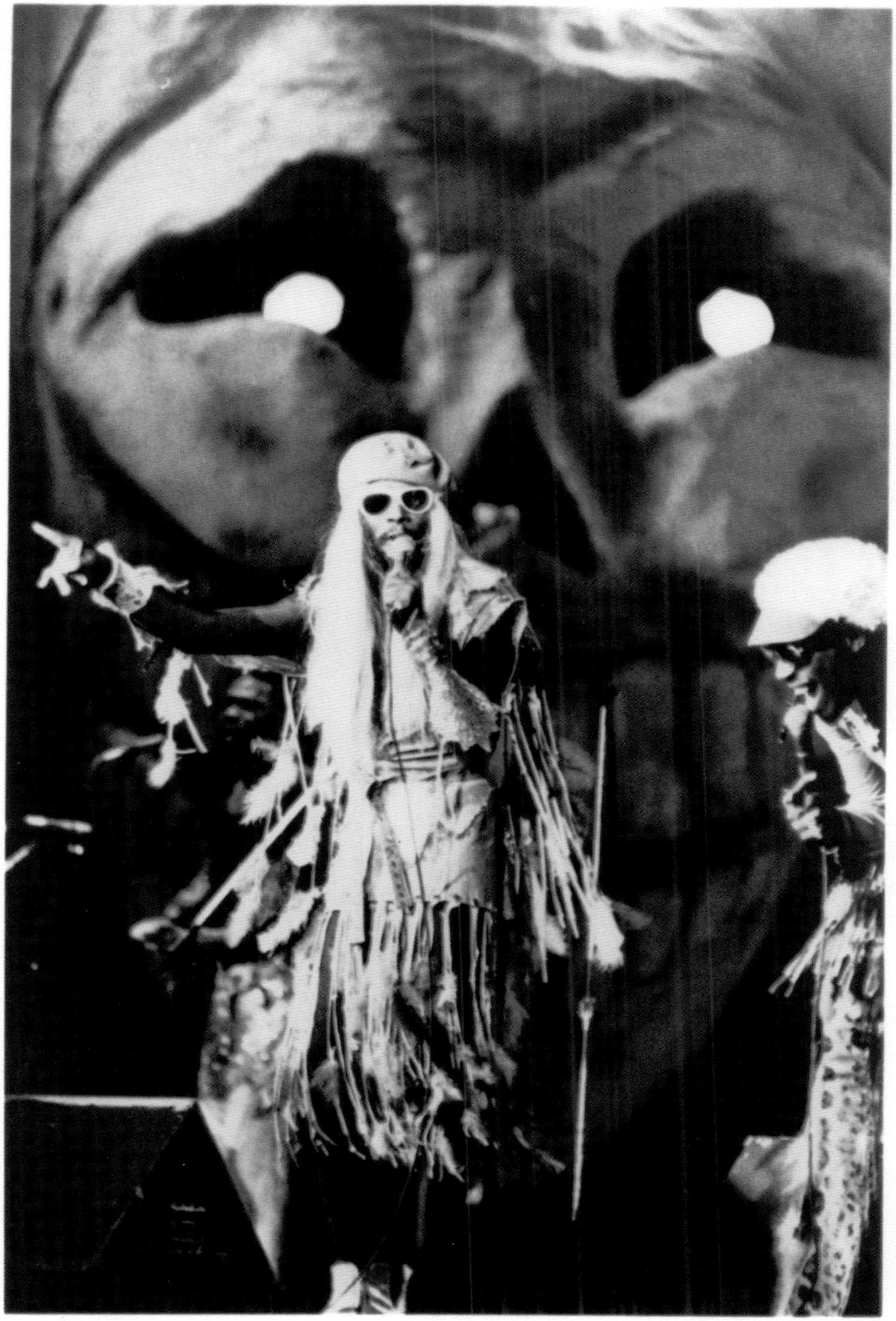

AUGUST 1979

FUNKADELIC

GEORGE CLINTON
(REFEREE)

WARNER BROS.

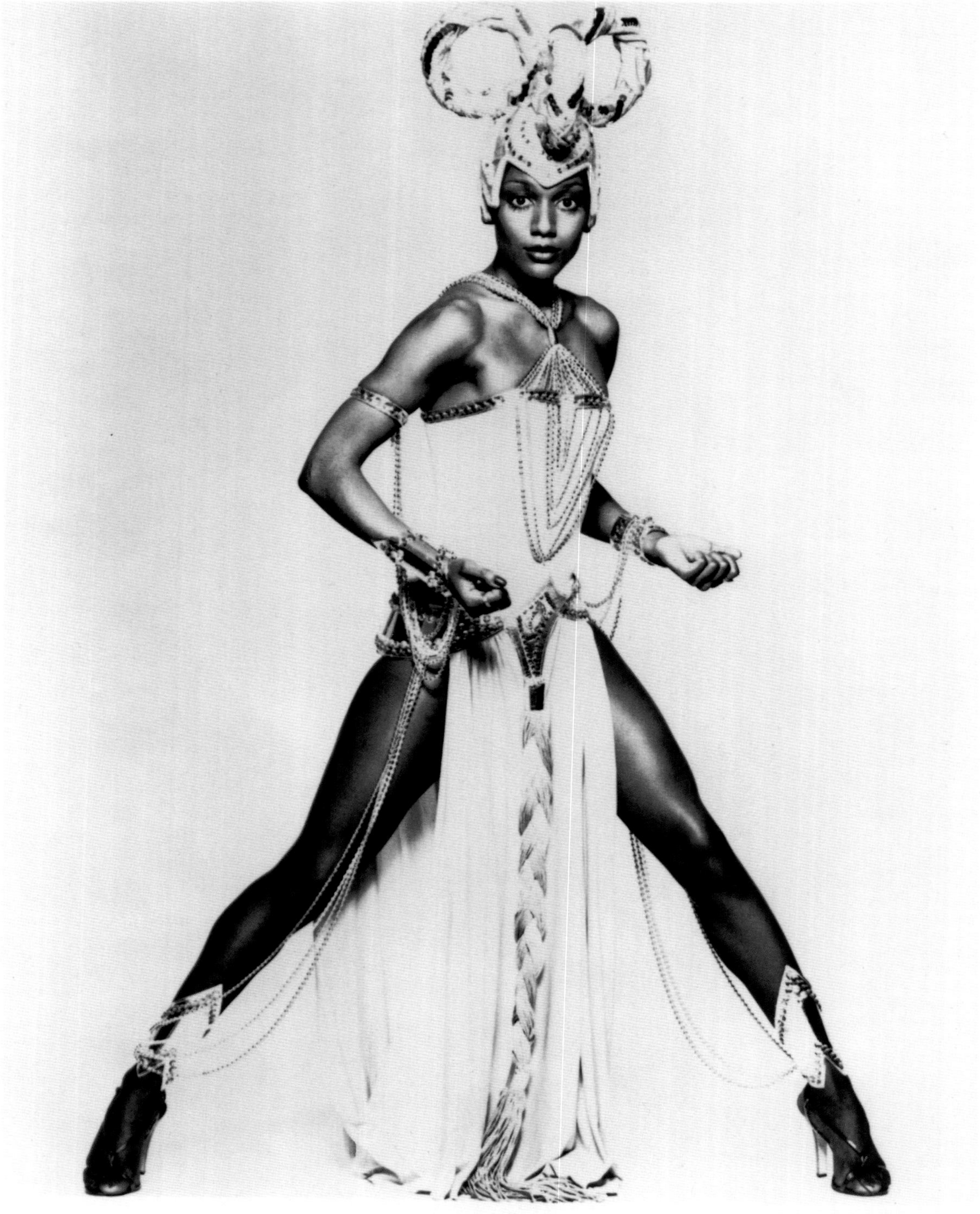

AMII STEWART

HANSA RECORDS

ARIOLA RECORDS America

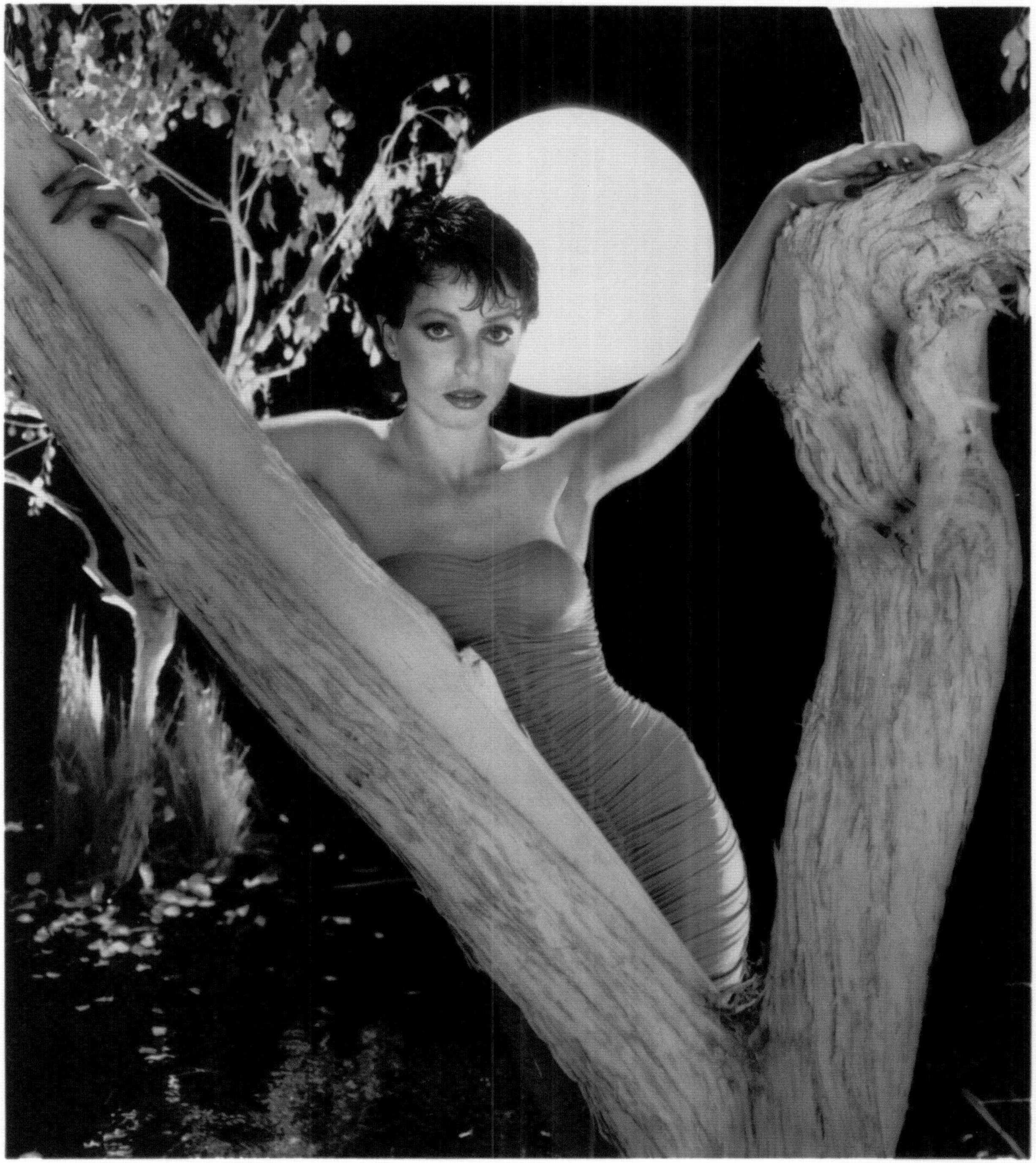

HARRY LANGDON PHOTOGRAPHY

TERI DESARIO

Casablanca Record and FilmWorks

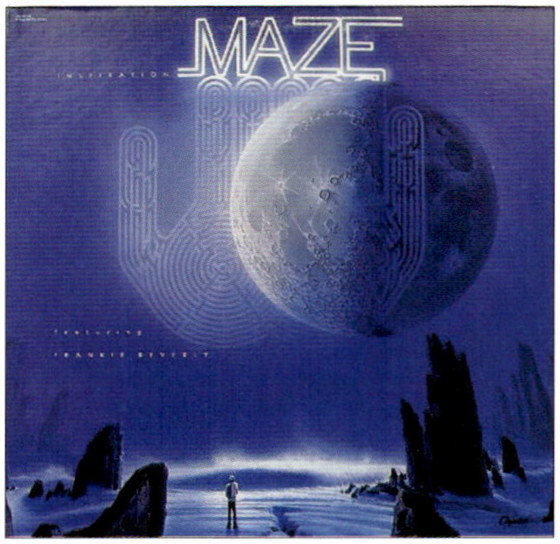

Maze featuring Frankie Beverly, a seven-member group consolidating Philly soul and San Francisco funk, demonstrated its R&B expertise on *Inspiration*.

Billboard 200: *Inspiration* (#33)
Billboard Hot 100: "Feel That You're Feelin'" (#67)

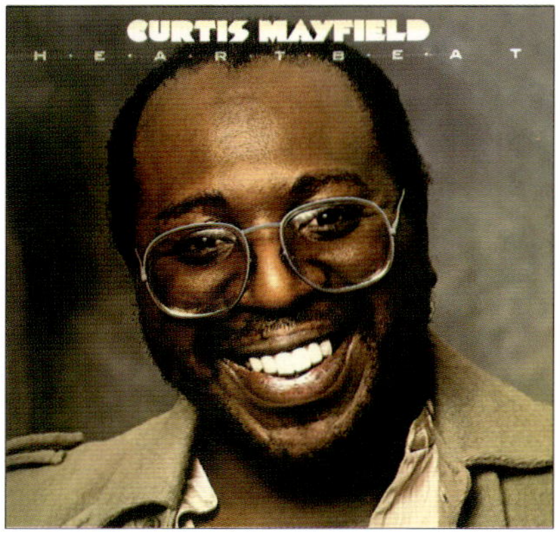

A pivotal pioneer of soul as the leader of the Impressions and as an individual artist, **Curtis Mayfield** sang with Linda Clifford on "Between You Baby and Me."

Billboard 200: *Heartbeat* (#42)

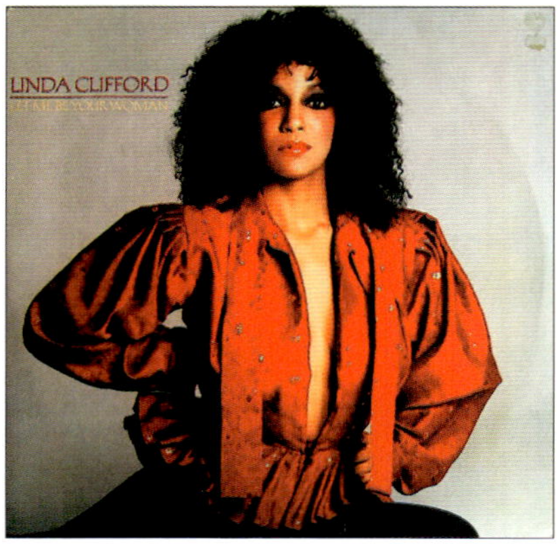

From *Let Me Be Your Woman*, vocalist **Linda Clifford** pulled off an unexpected cover of "Bridge over Troubled Water" in a 10-minute disco arrangement.

Billboard 200: *Let Me Be Your Woman* (#26)
Billboard Hot 100: "Bridge over Troubled Water" (#41)

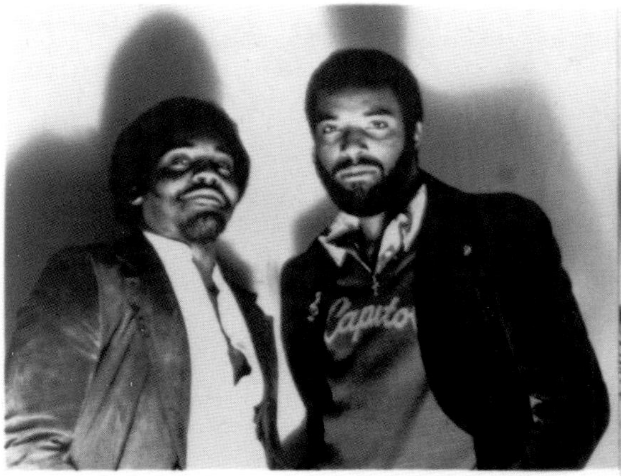

Sam Porter Wuane Thomas

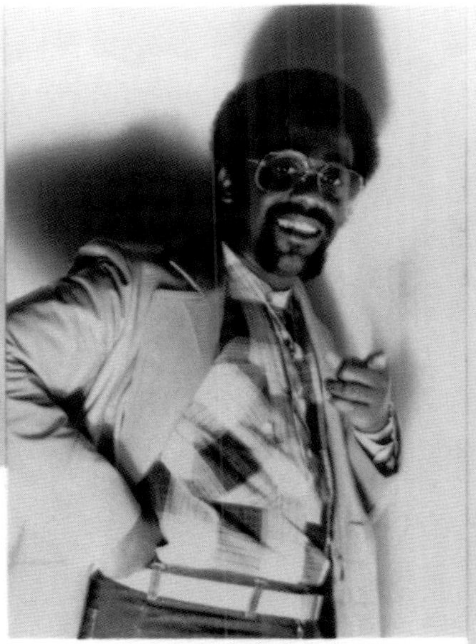

McKinley Williams

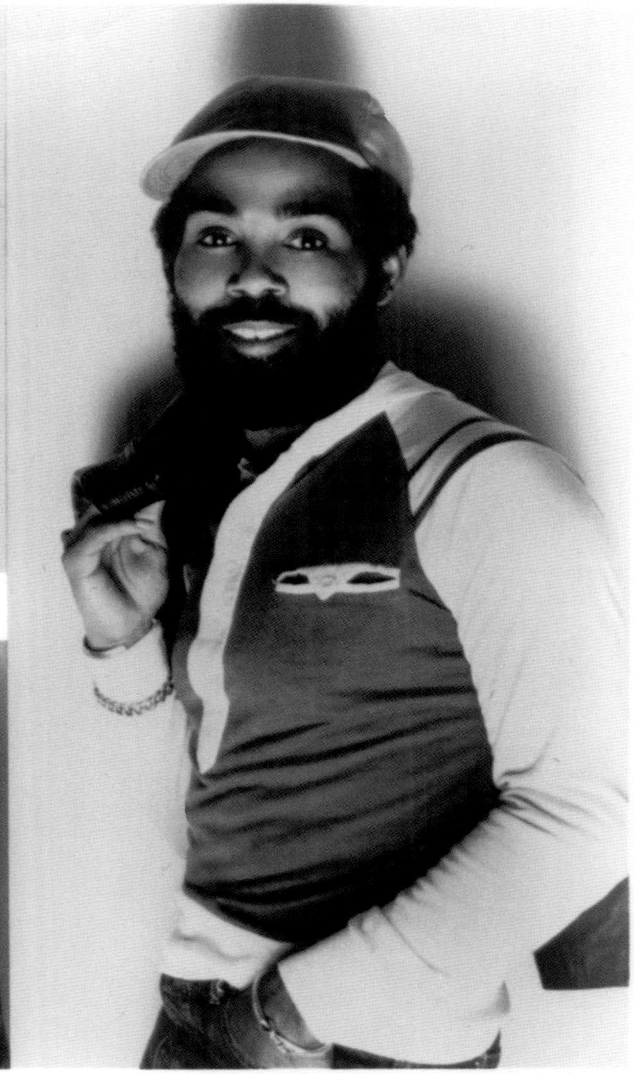

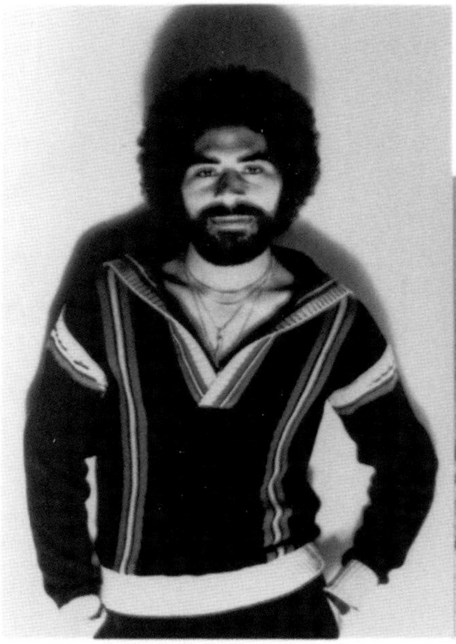

Robin Duhe

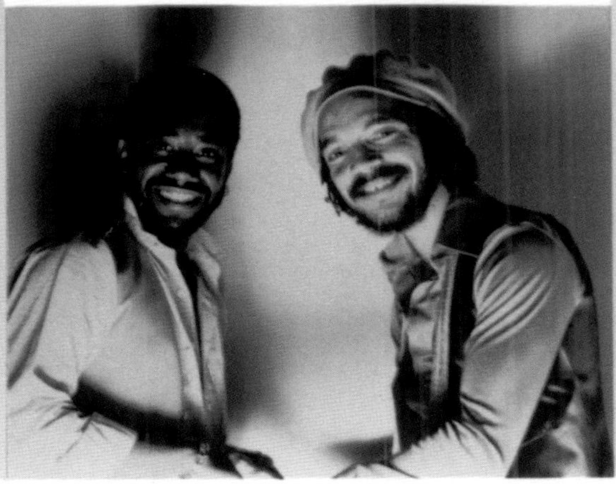

Roame Lowry Ahaguna Sun

Frankie Beverly

MAZE featuring **Frankie Beverly**

Photo: Barbara DuMetz

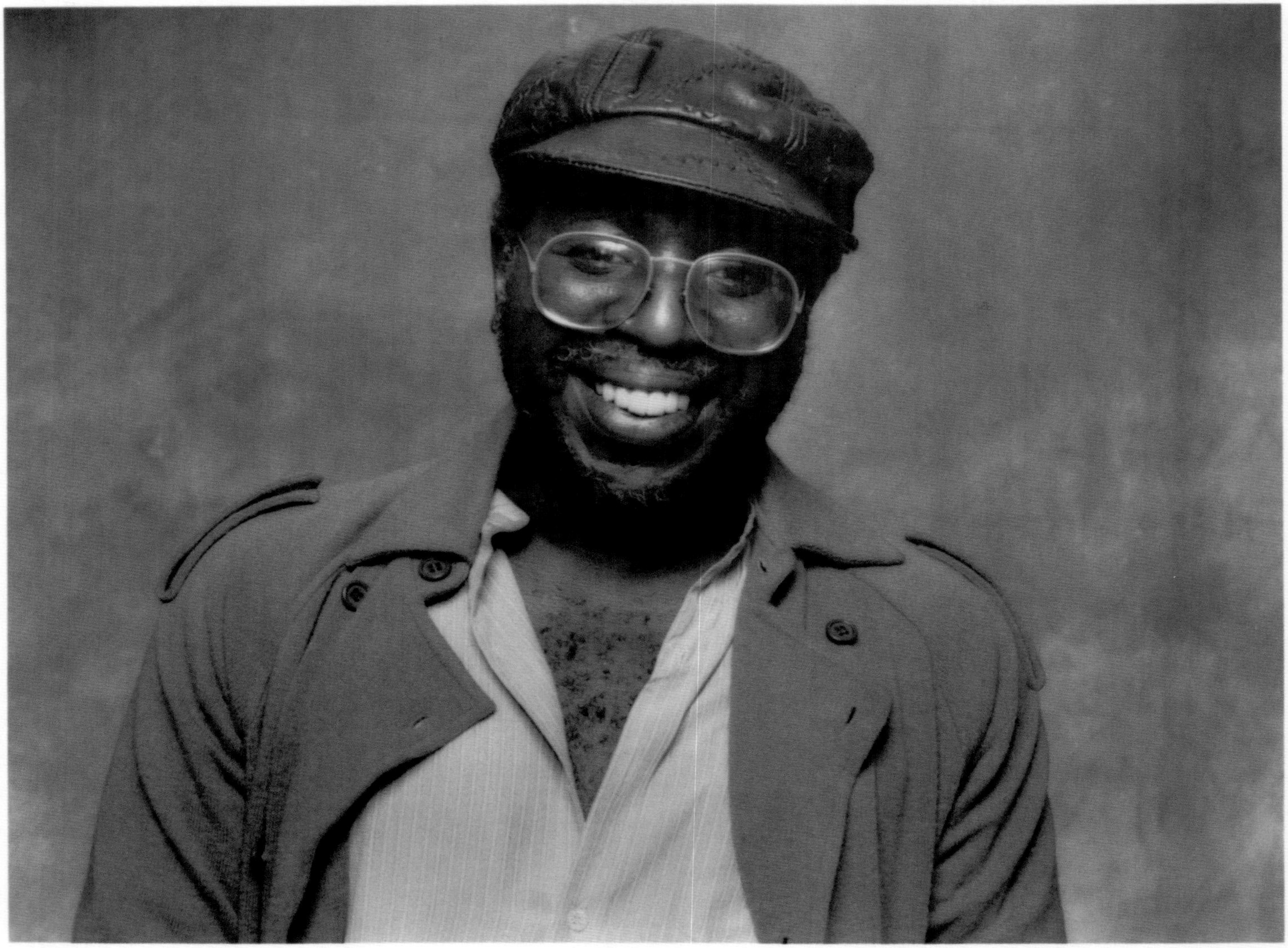

CURTIS MAYFIELD

Curtom Records RSO Records, Inc.

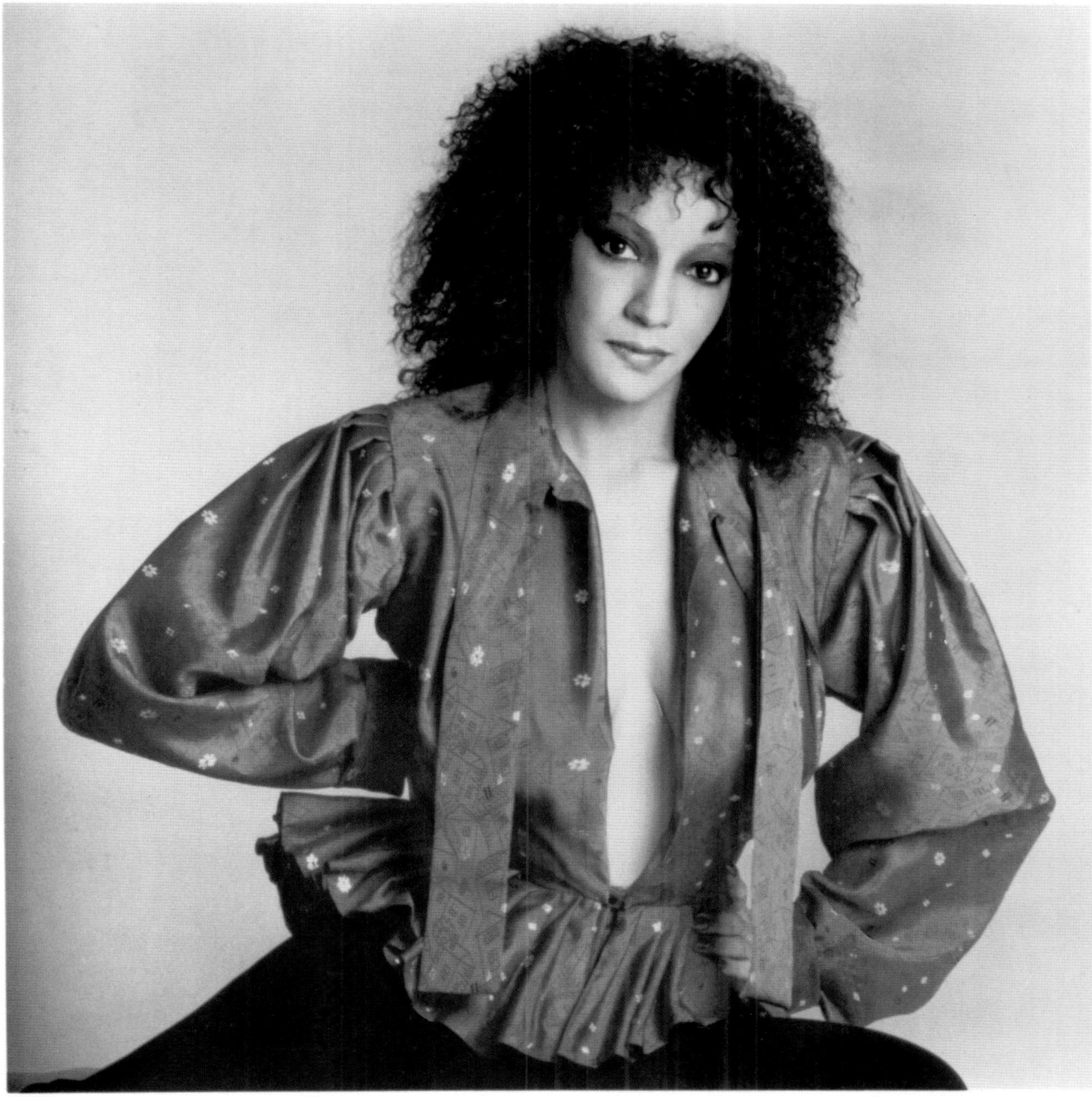

LINDA CLIFFORD

Curtom Records · RSO Records, Inc.

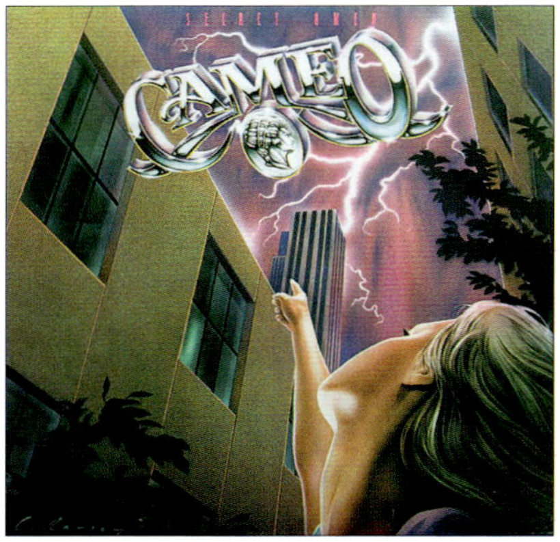

On *Secret Omen*, **Cameo**'s first gold album, the group set its sights on the dance floor, and the funky "I Just Want to Be" materialized as a major R&B smash.

Billboard 200: *Secret Omen* (#46)

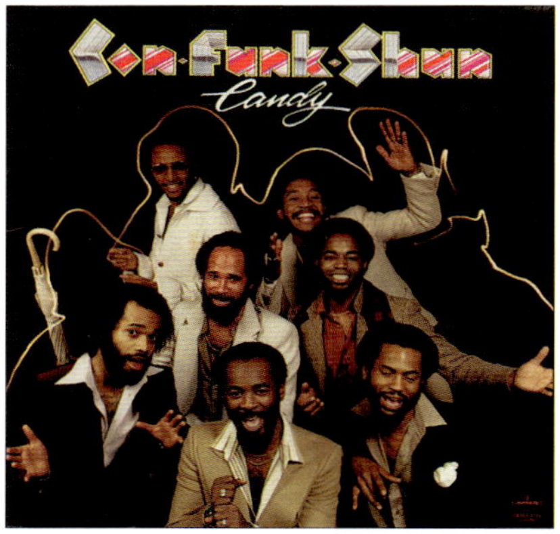

The Northern California band **Con Funk Shun** continued to enjoy a string of hit songs in the R&B world, most notably the blistering dance jam "Chase Me."

Billboard 200: *Candy* (#46)

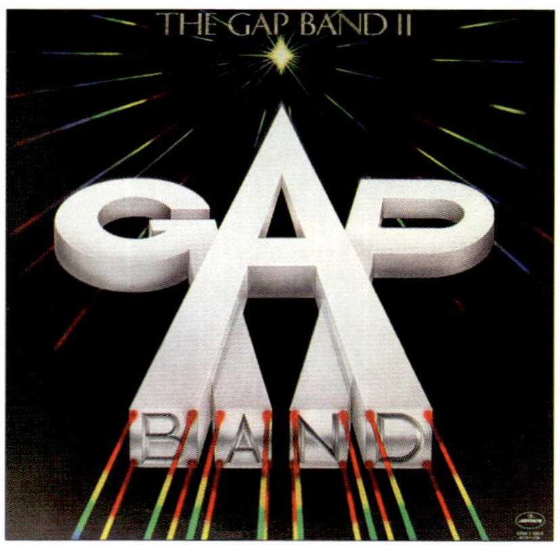

The Gap Band set up its funk sound using synthesizers and dissolute nursery rhymes on the track "I Don't Believe You Want to Get Up and Dance (Oops!)."

Billboard 200: *The Gap Band II* (#42)

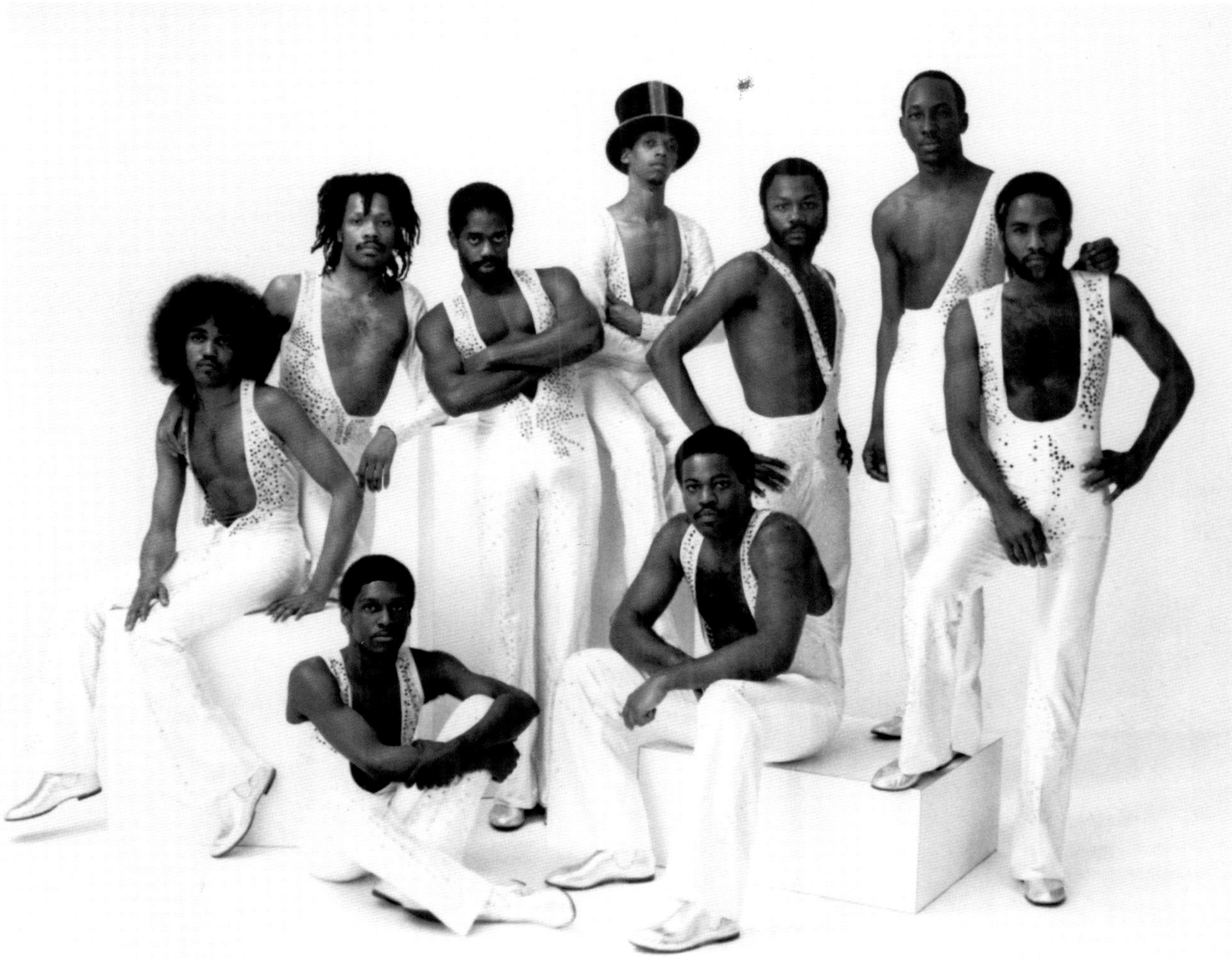

Cecil Holmes' Chocolate City

Distributed by CASABLANCA RECORD and FILMWORKS, INC.

CAMEO

Personal Management:
SANFORD ROSS
(212) 688-4343
STEVE ELLIS
AGENCY, LIMITED
(212) 757-5800

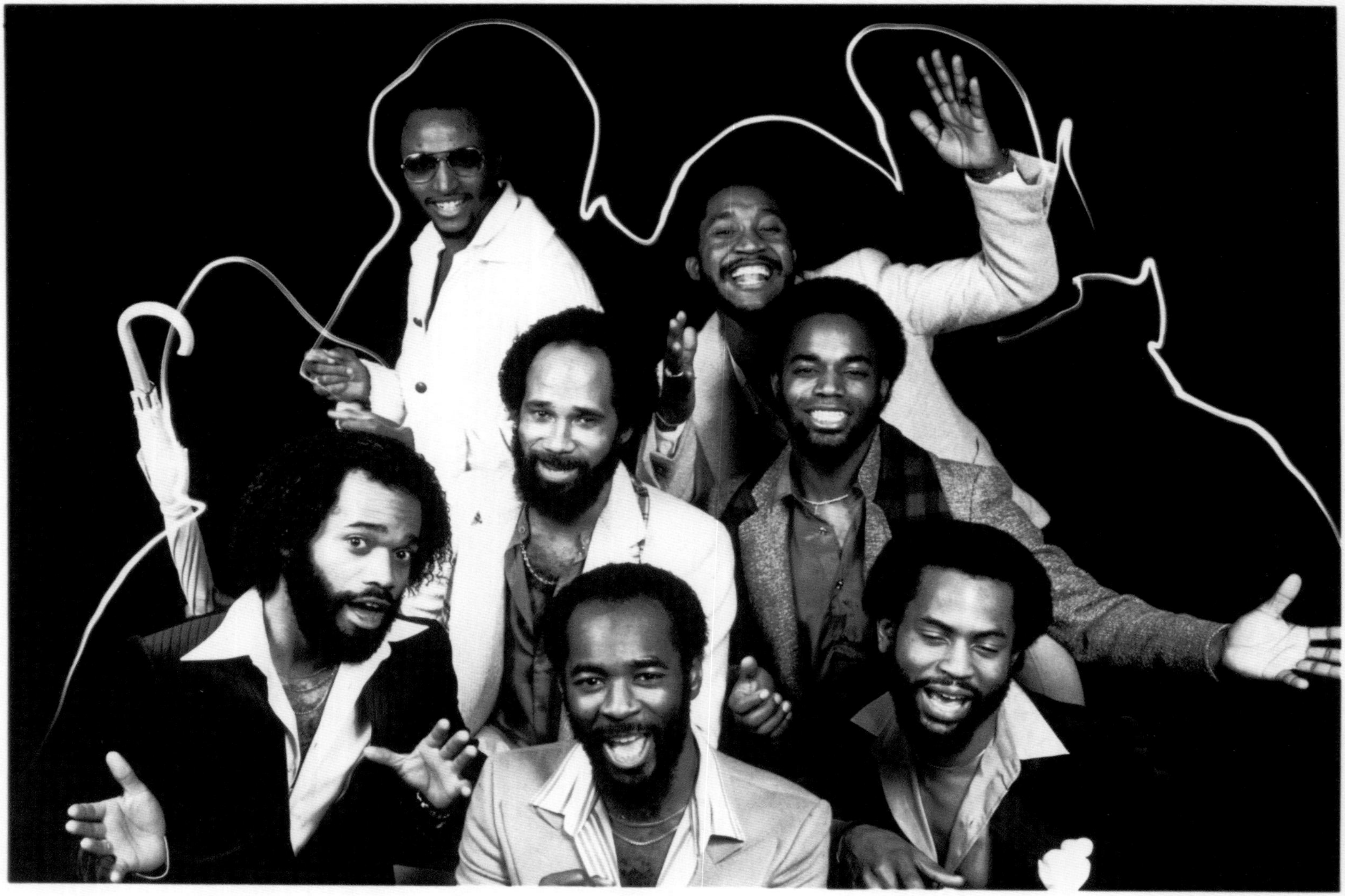

CON FUNK SHUN

Recording Exclusively For

Mercury

A product of Phonogram, Inc.

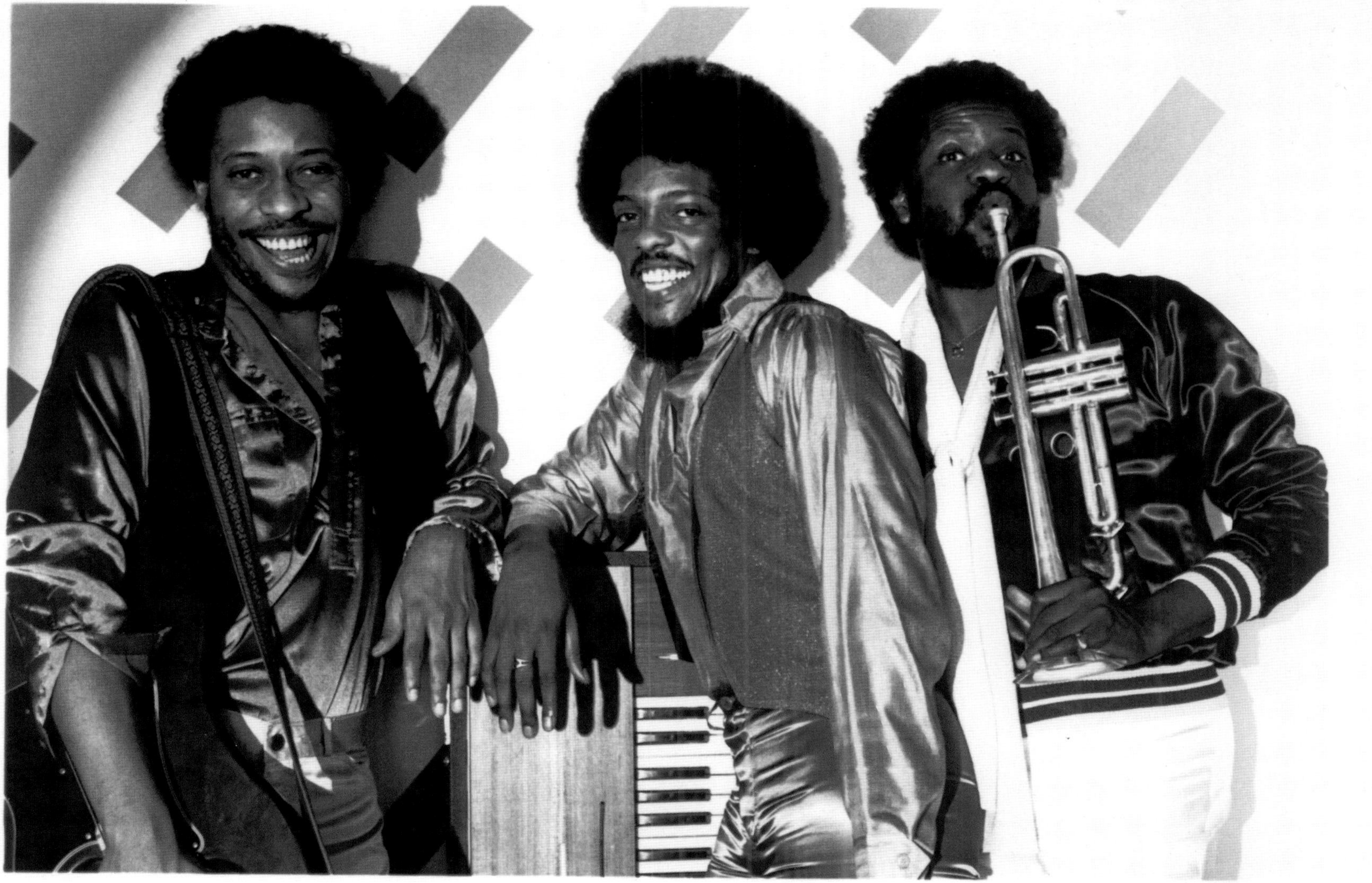

THE GAP BAND

Recording Exclusively For

Mercury

A product of Phonogram, Inc.

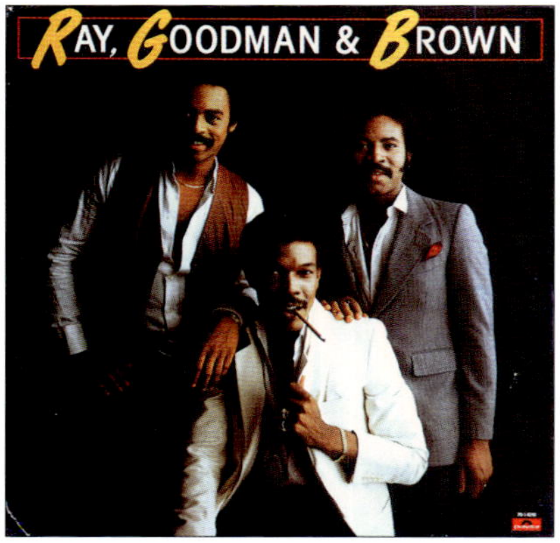

Due to legal reasons, the Moments changed their name to **Ray, Goodman & Brown** and reached No. 1 on the R&B charts with the poignant "Special Lady."

Billboard 200: *Ray, Goodman & Brown* (#17)
Billboard Hot 100: "Special Lady" (#5); "Inside of You" (#76)

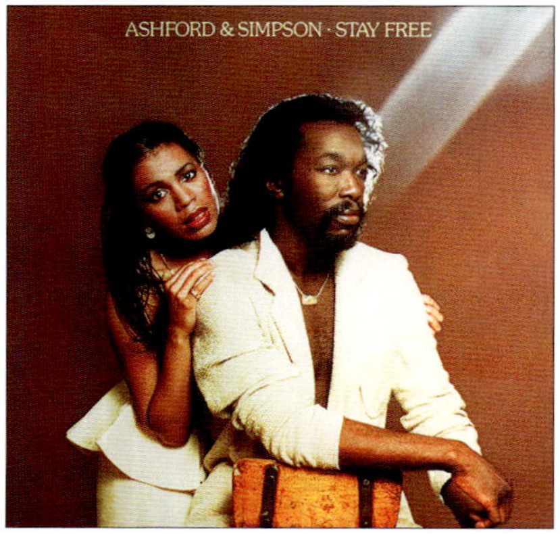

As performers, the writing and production couple of **Ashford & Simpson** racked up an R&B smash with "Found a Cure," from the gold album *Stay Free*.

Billboard 200: *Stay Free* (#23)
Billboard Hot 100: "Found a Cure" (#36)

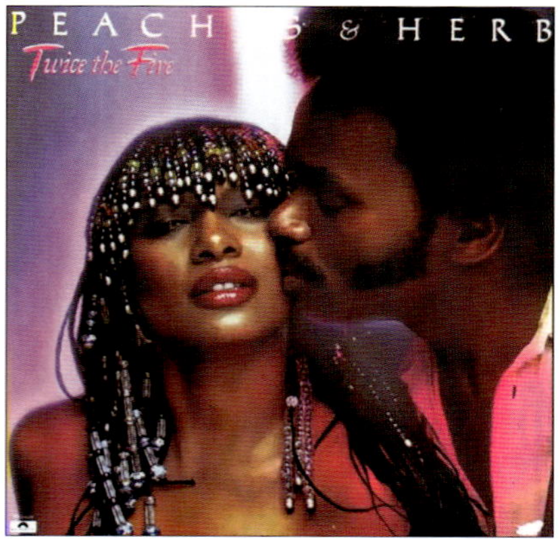

Looking to duplicate the big response to "Reunited," soul vocal duo **Peaches & Herb** managed another chart run with a wedding classic, "I Pledge My Love."

Billboard 200: *Twice the Fire* (#31)
Billboard Hot 100: "Roller-Skatin' Mate" (#66);
"I Pledge My Love" (#19)

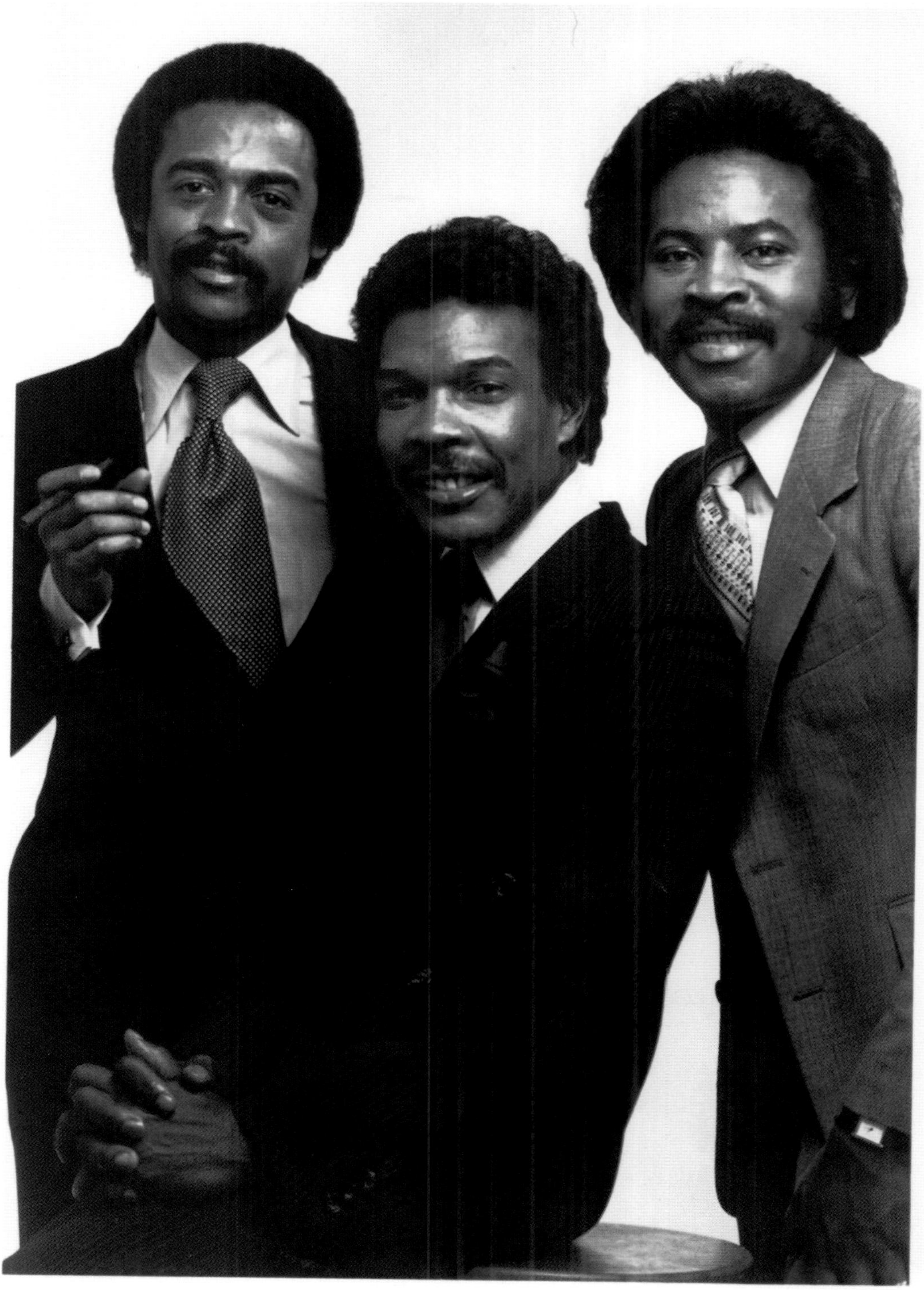

RAY, GOODMAN & BROWN

polydor

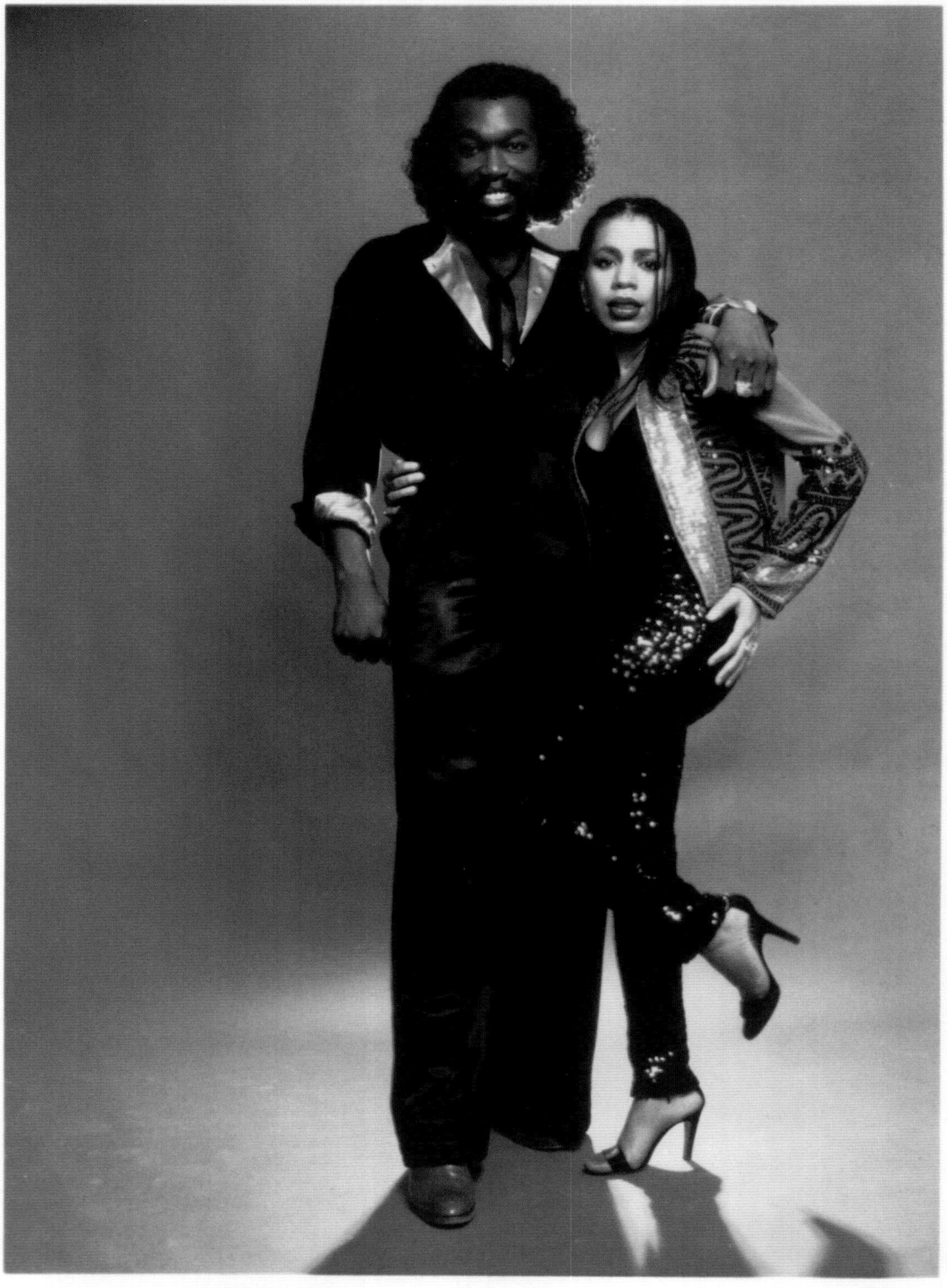

AUGUST 1979

ASHFORD & SIMPSON

WARNER BROS.

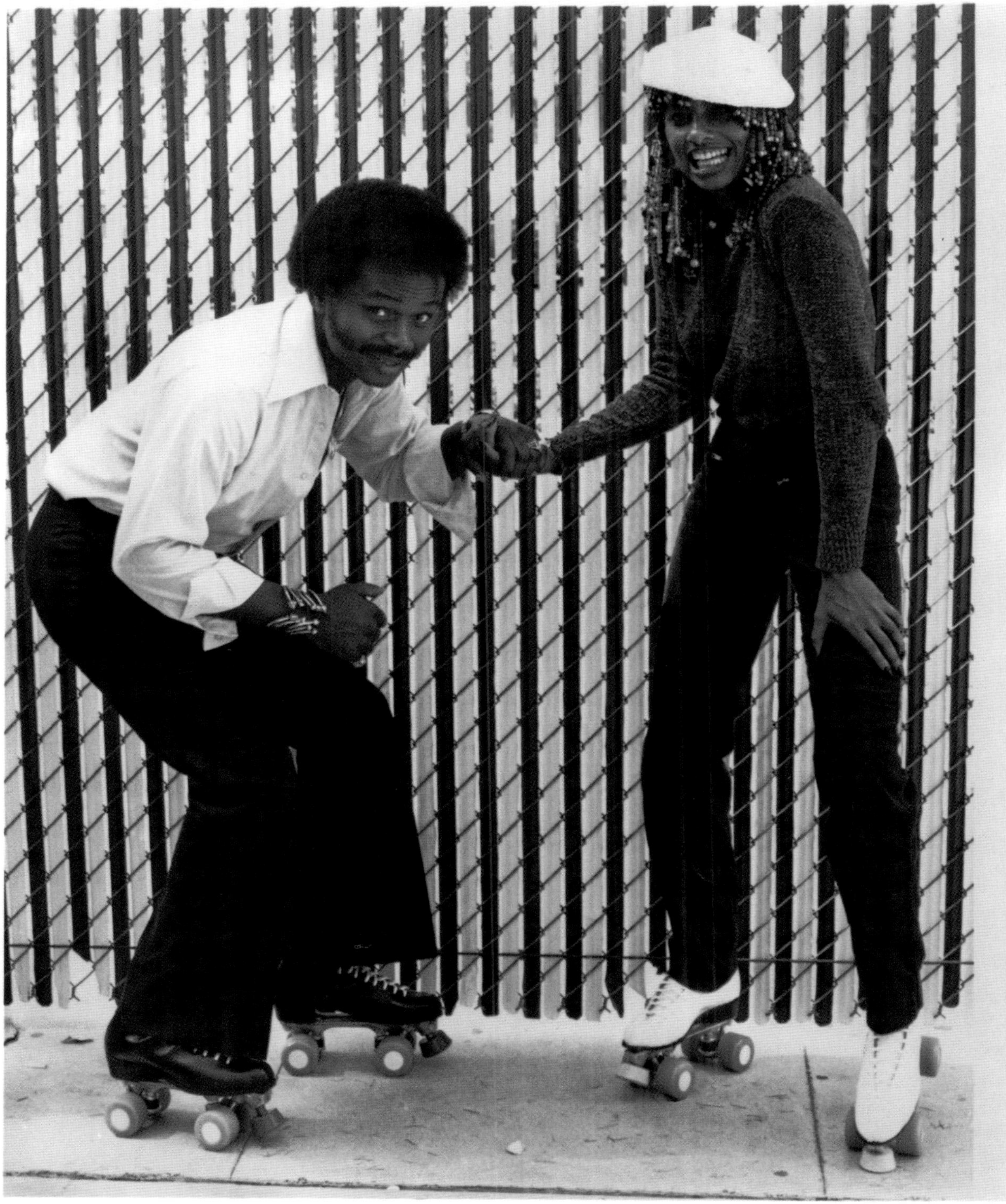

PEACHES & HERB

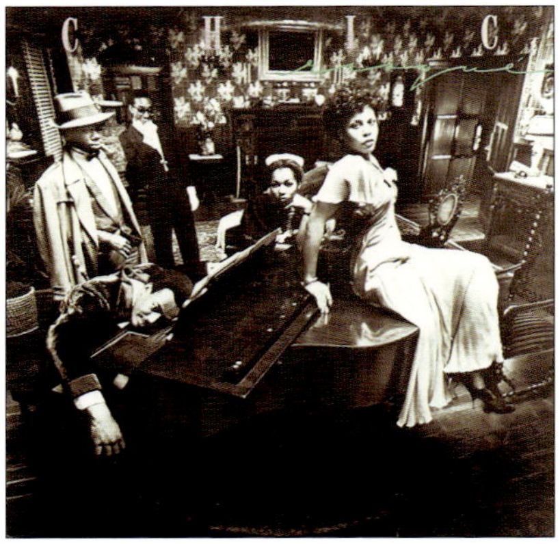

Led by guitarist Nile Rodgers and bassist Bernard Edwards, **Chic** recorded *Risqué* and the definitive disco track "Good Times," a chart-topping pop hit.

Billboard 200: *Risqué* (#5)
Billboard Hot 100: "Good Times" (No. 1); "My Forbidden Lover" (#43)

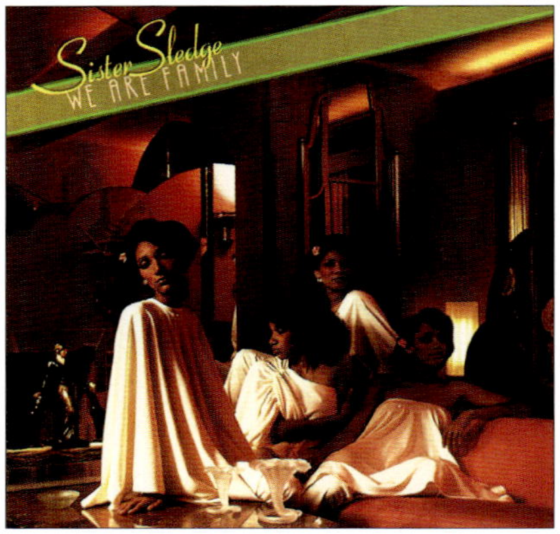

Philadelphia siblings **Sister Sledge** exploded at the height of the disco era with the beguiling "He's the Greatest Dancer" and anthemic "We Are Family."

Billboard 200: *We Are Family* (#3)
Billboard Hot 100: "He's the Greatest Dancer" (#9);
"We Are Family" (#2)

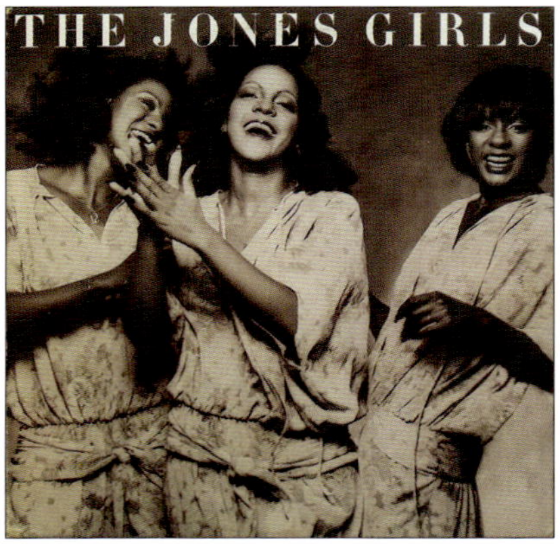

The Jones Girls, a trio of sisters, were in heavy demand as backup singers for other R&B acts before hitting with "You Gonna Make Me Love Somebody Else."

Billboard 200: *The Jones Girls* (#50)
Billboard Hot 100: "You Gonna Make Me Love Somebody Else" (#38)

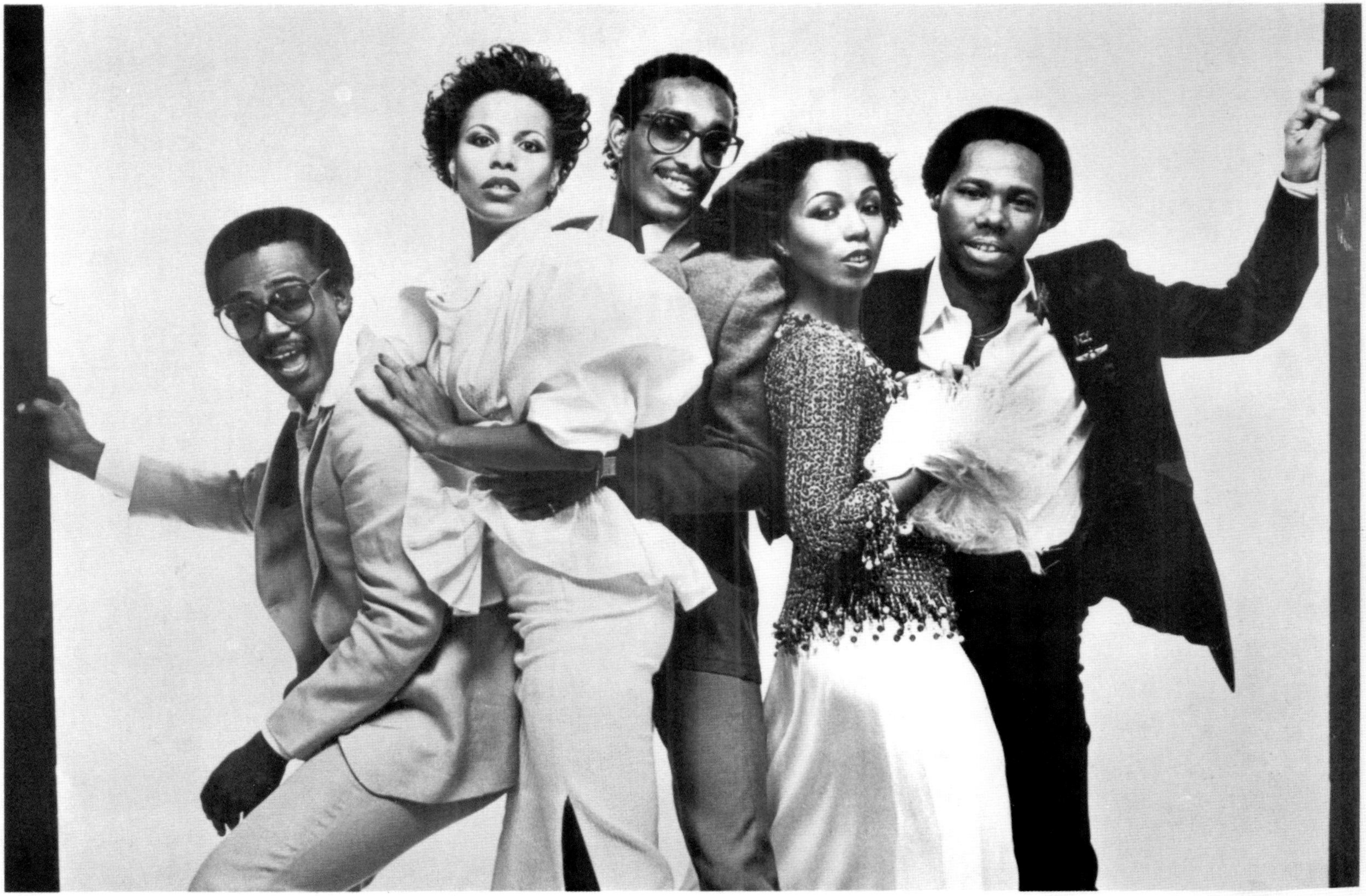

CHIC

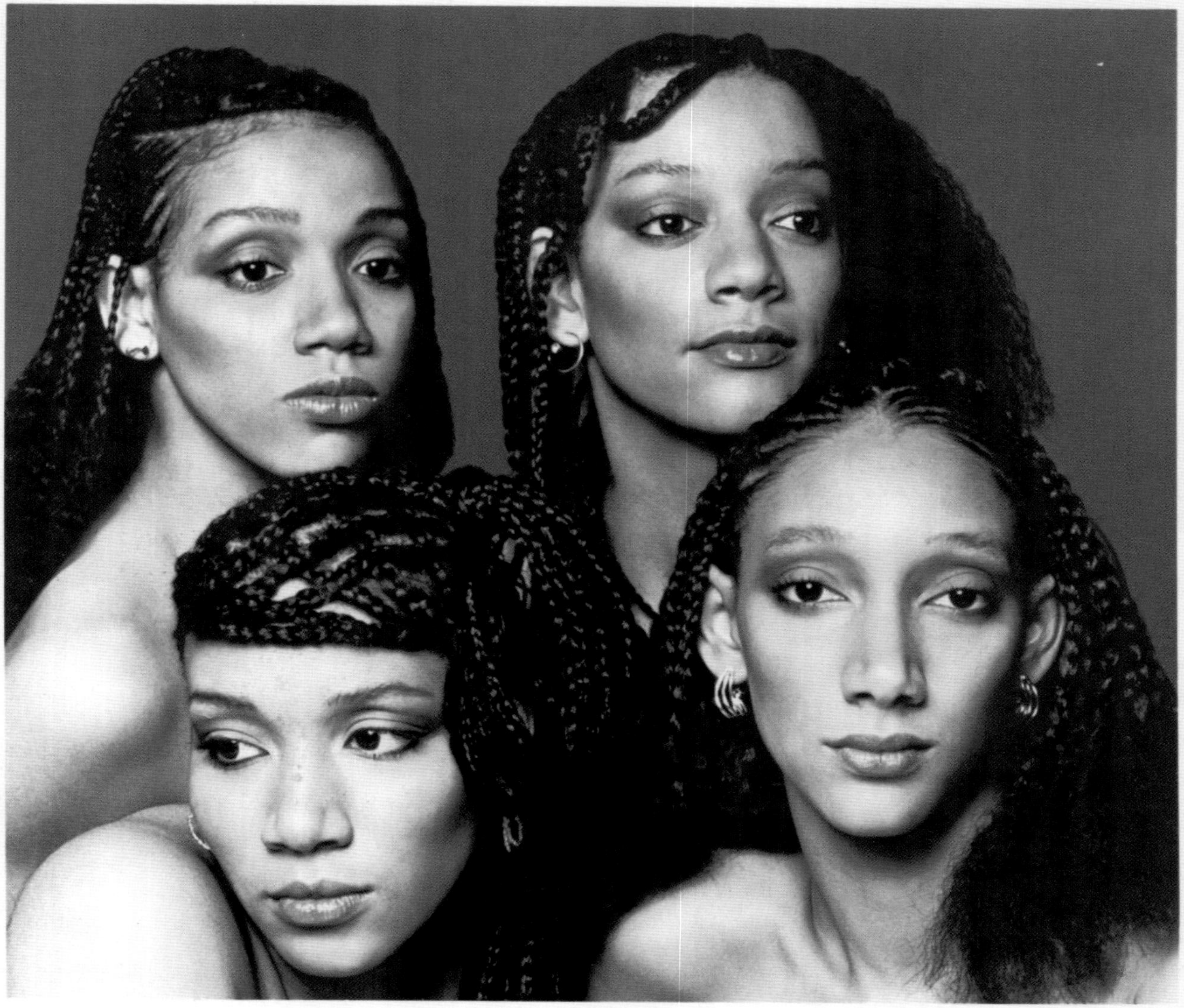

SISTER SLEDGE

COTILLION

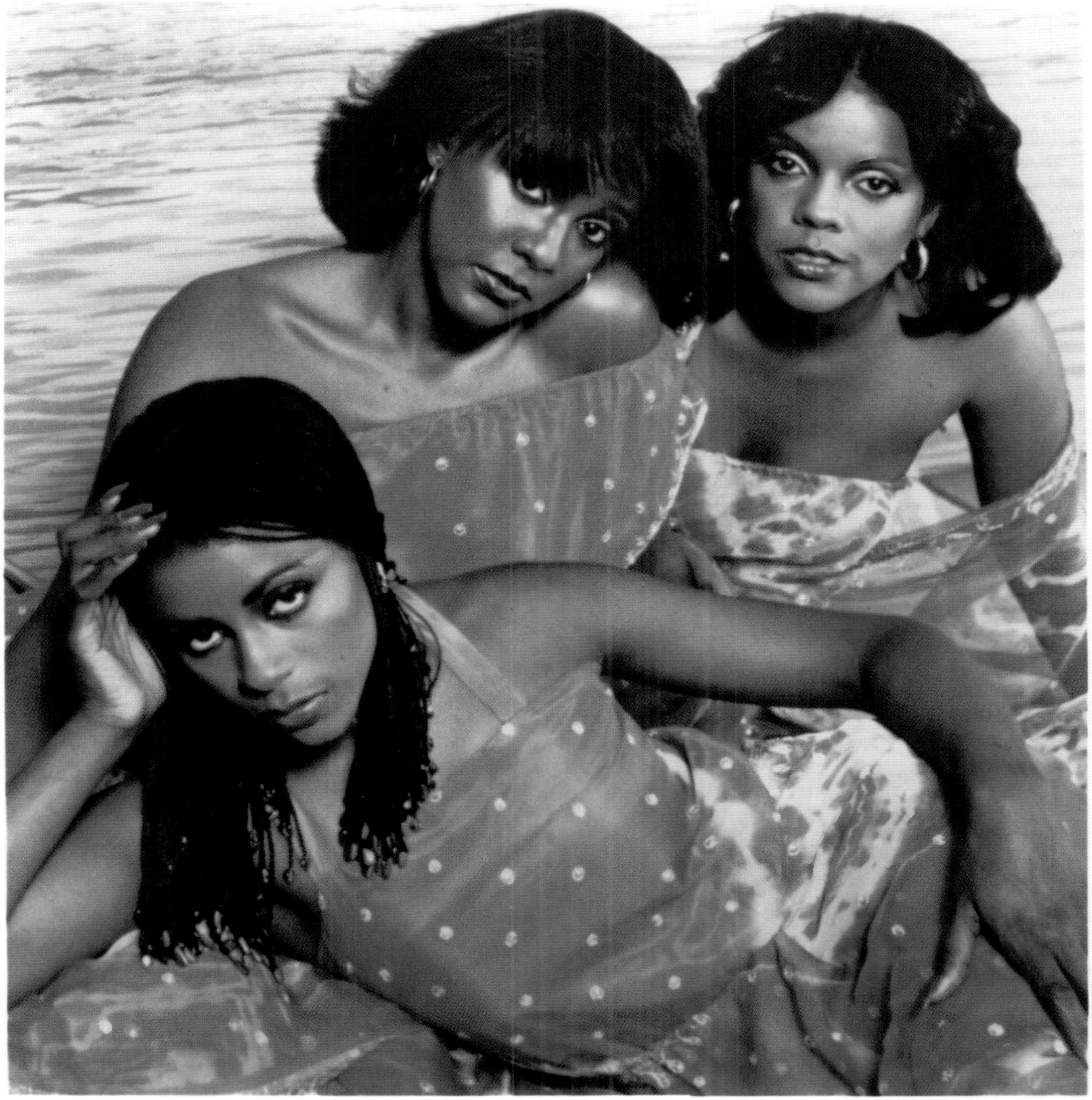

Brenda Shirley Valorie

The Jones Girls

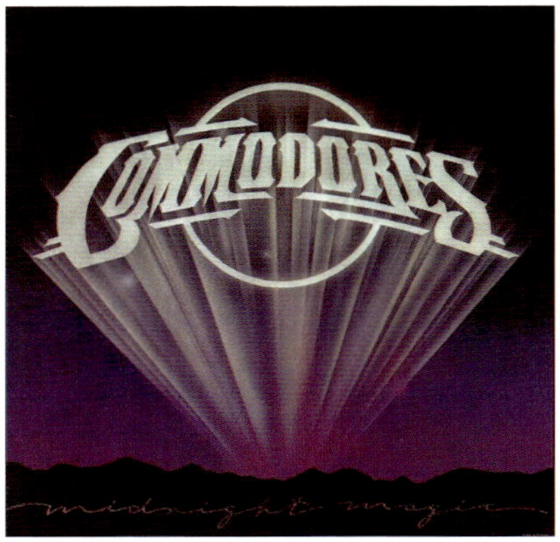

Featuring founding member and co-lead vocalist Lionel Richie, **Commodores** scored a Top 5 single, "Sail On," and reached No. 1 with the ballad "Still."

Billboard 200: *Midnight Magic* (#3)
Billboard Hot 100: "Sail On" (#4); "Still" (No. 1); "Wonderland" (#25)

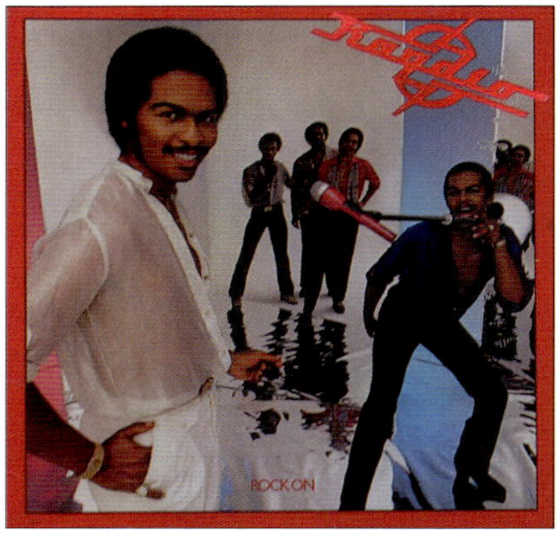

Raydio, led by the multi talented Ray Parker, Jr., released "You Can't Change That," which found its way into the Top Ten on both the R&B and pop charts.

Billboard 200: *Rock On* (#45)
Billboard Hot 100: "You Can't Change That" (#9)

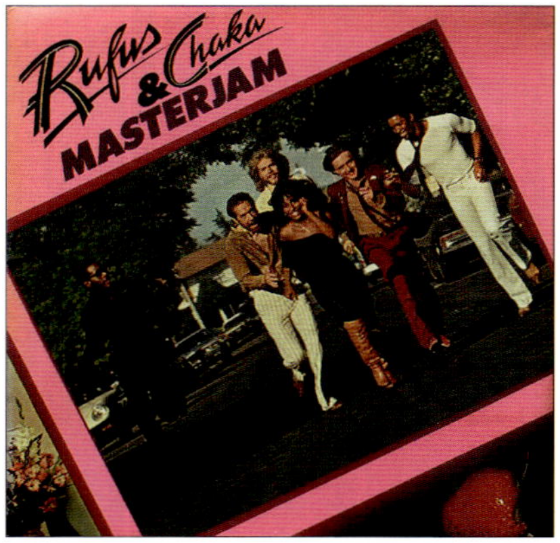

Rufus & Chaka–singer Chaka Khan and her band–reconvened to record *Masterjam* and the hit "Do You Love What You Feel," produced by Quincy Jones.

Billboard 200: *Masterjam* (#14)
Billboard Hot 100: "Do You Love What You Feel" (#30)

COMMODORES

MOTOWN

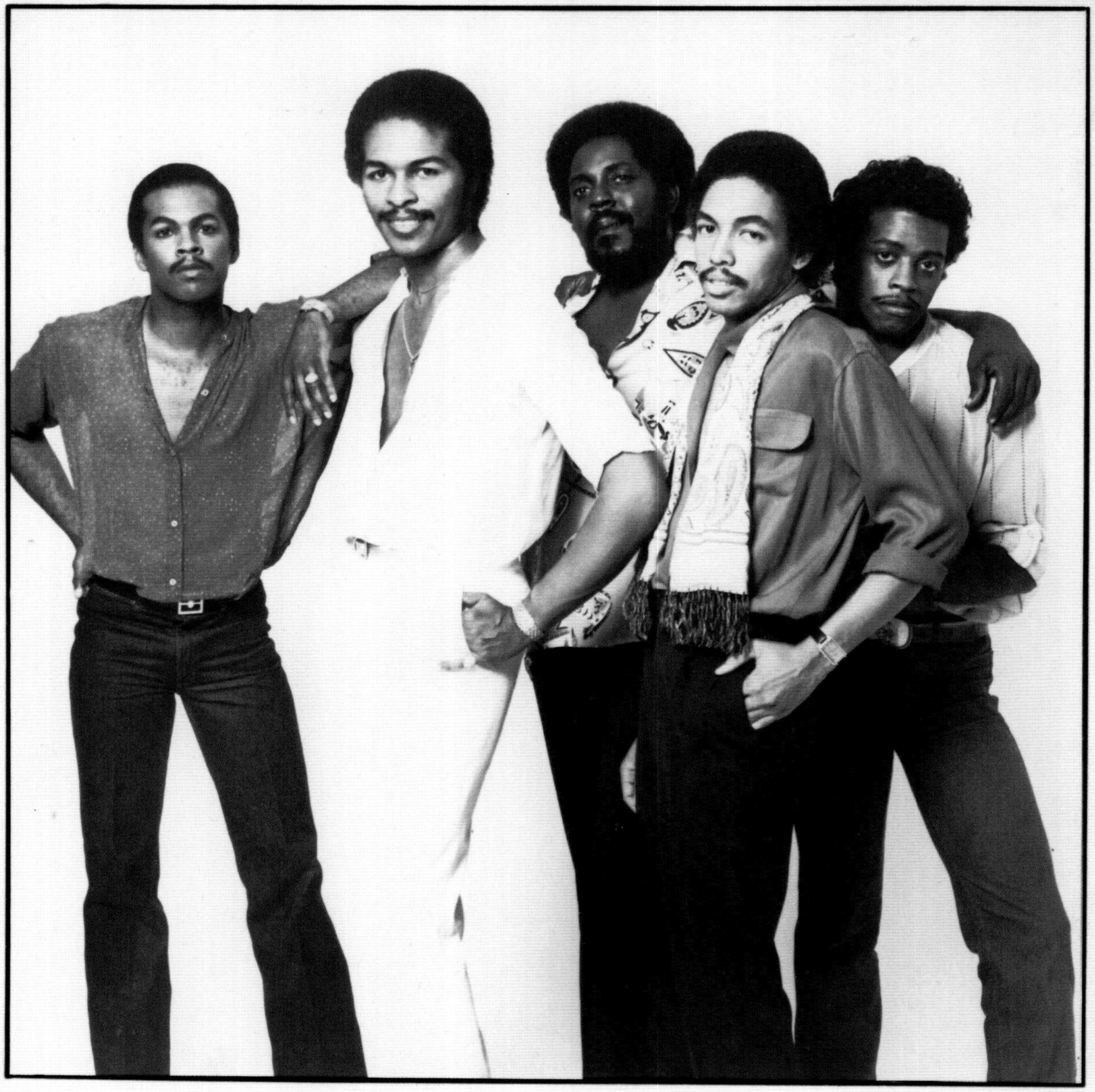

RAYDIO

Exclusive Representation
Cavallo-Ruffalo Management
Beverly Hills, California

ARISTA
RECORDS AND TAPES

Booking Agent:
BRIGHTON ARTISTS
9884 SANTA MONICA BOULEVARD BEVERLY HILLS, CALIFORNIA 90212

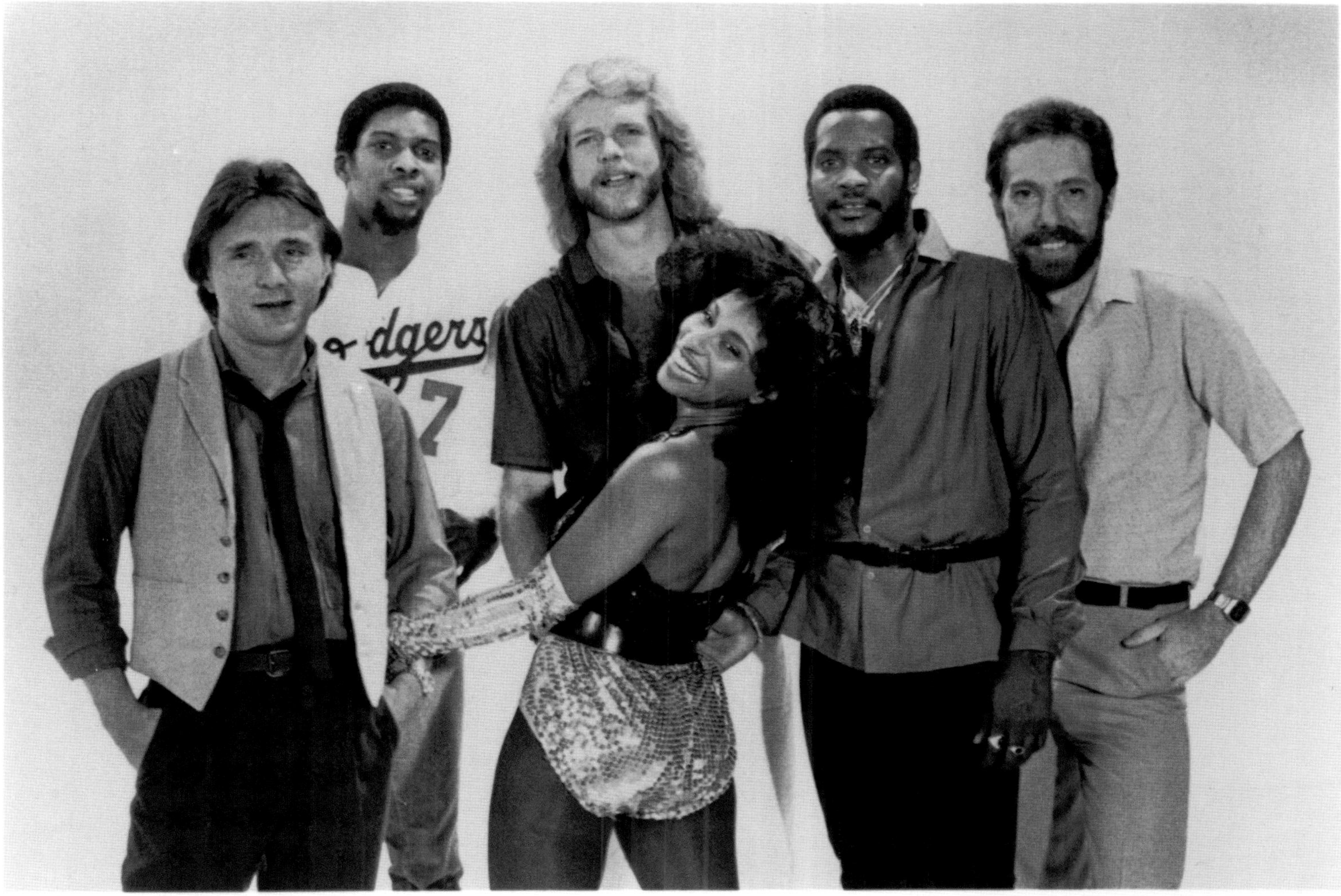

David "Hawk" Wolinski   Bobby Watson   John Robinson   (foreground) Chaka Khan   Tony Maiden   Kevin Murphy

9/79 Photography by Bobby Holland

Rufus & Chaka

RUFUS MANAGEMENT:
The Fitzgerald Hartley Company
(213) 934-8002

CHAKA KHAN MANAGEMENT:
Jack Nelson
(213) 650-0133

PUBLIC RELATIONS:
Ed Eckstine, Melanie Ross
(213) 934-4711

Exclusively On
MCA RECORDS

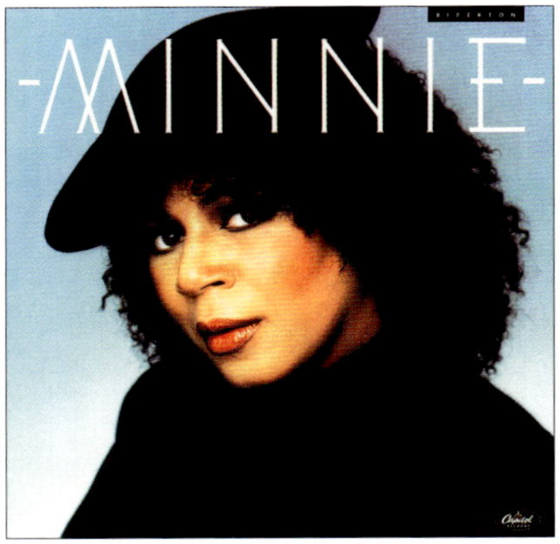

Known for her 1975 hit "Lovin' You" and five-octave vocal range, **Minnie Riperton** released her fifth album, *Minnie*, and died of cancer two months later.

Billboard 200: *Minnie* (#29)

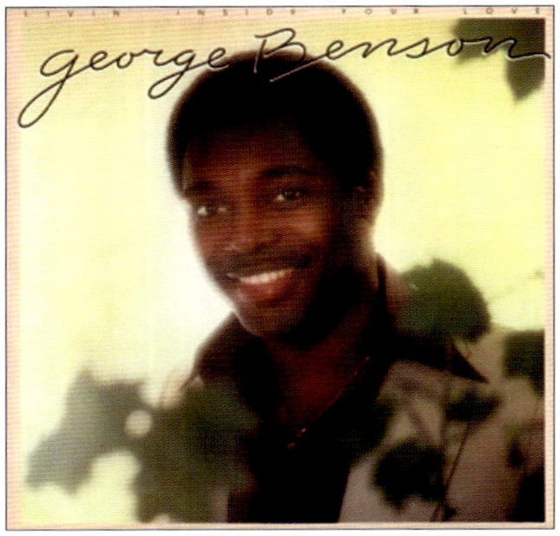

Vocalist and jazz guitarist **George Benson**'s *Livin' Inside Your Love* album prompted a hit single, his up-tempo interpretation of L.T.D.'s "Love Ballad."

Billboard 200: *Livin' Inside Your Love* (#7)
Billboard Hot 100: "Love Ballad" (#18)

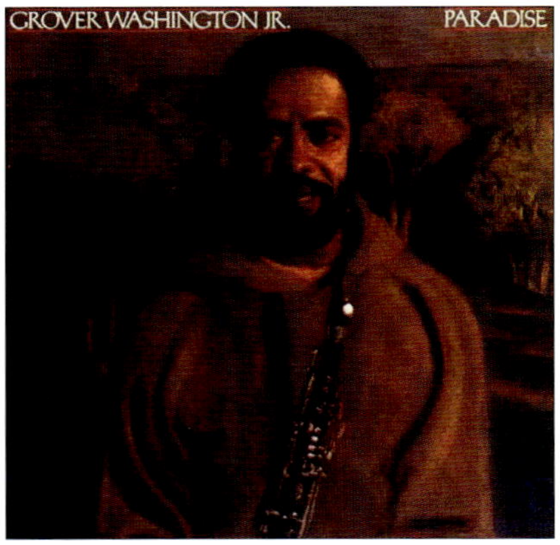

Saxophonist **Grover Washington Jr.**, one of America's most soulful instrumentalists, produced *Paradise* and the funk-jazz track "Tell Me About It Now."

Billboard 200: *Paradise* (#24)

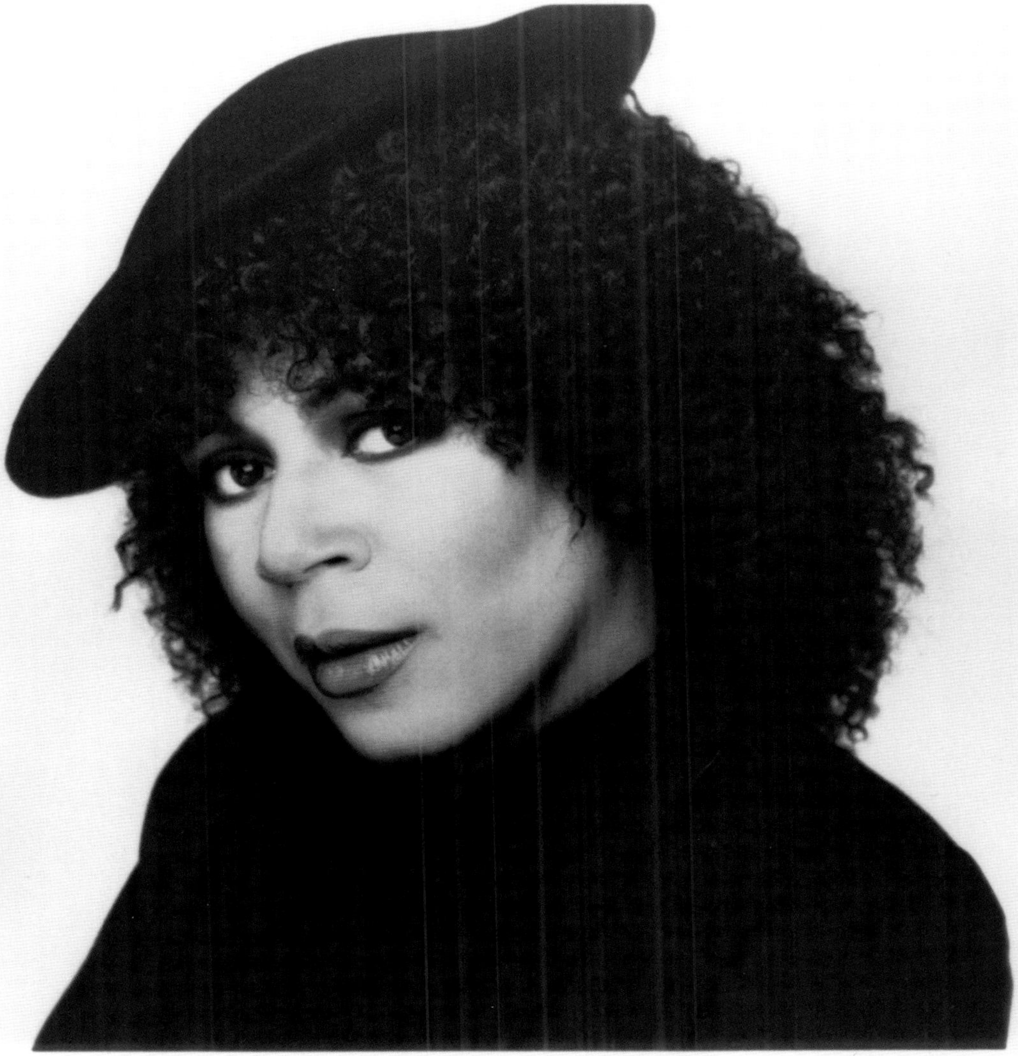

MINNIE RIPERTON

Ken Fritz
Dennis Turner
Connie Pappas

Capitol Records

Photo: Charles Bush

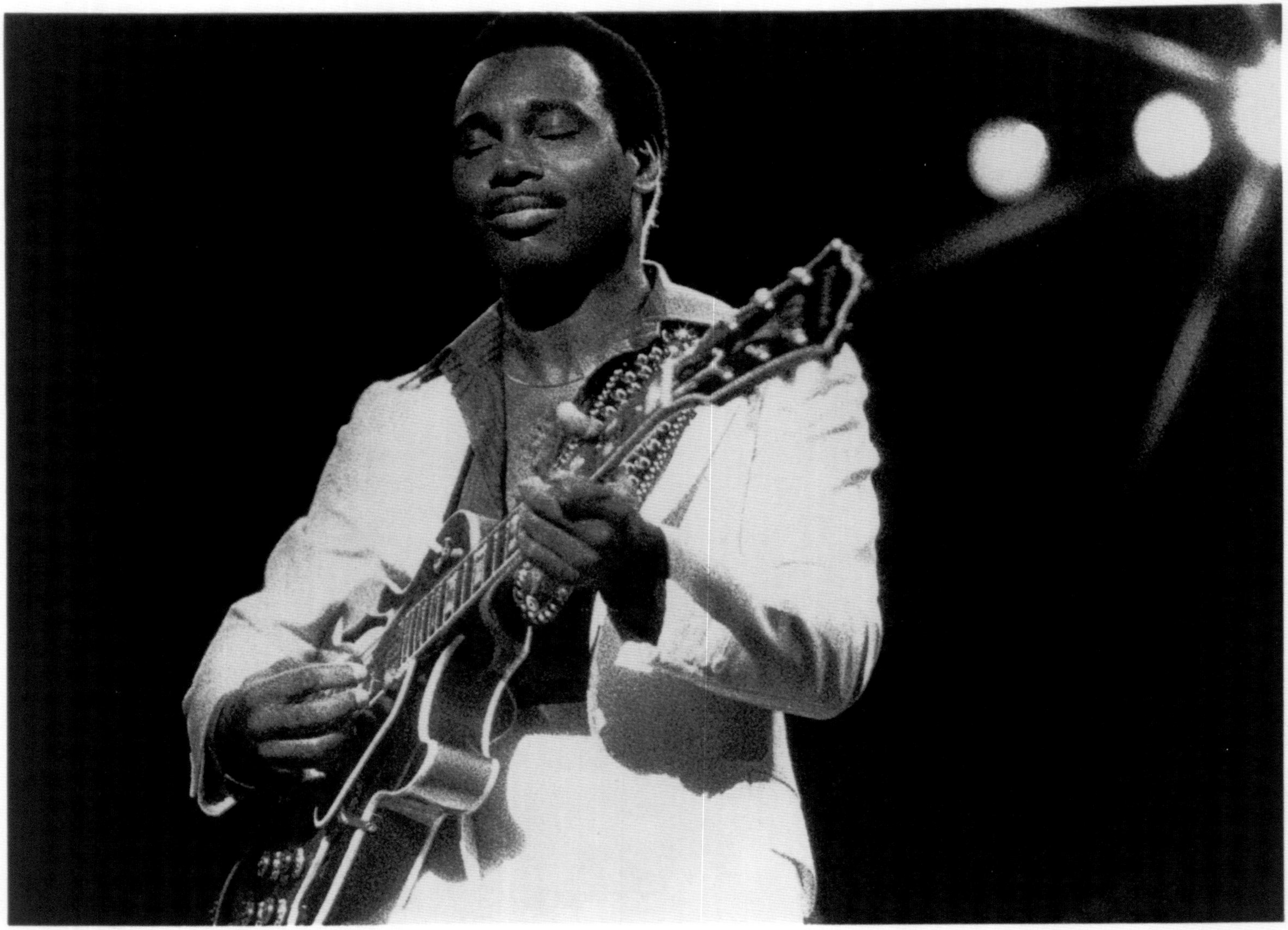

GEORGE BENSON

WARNER/REPRISE

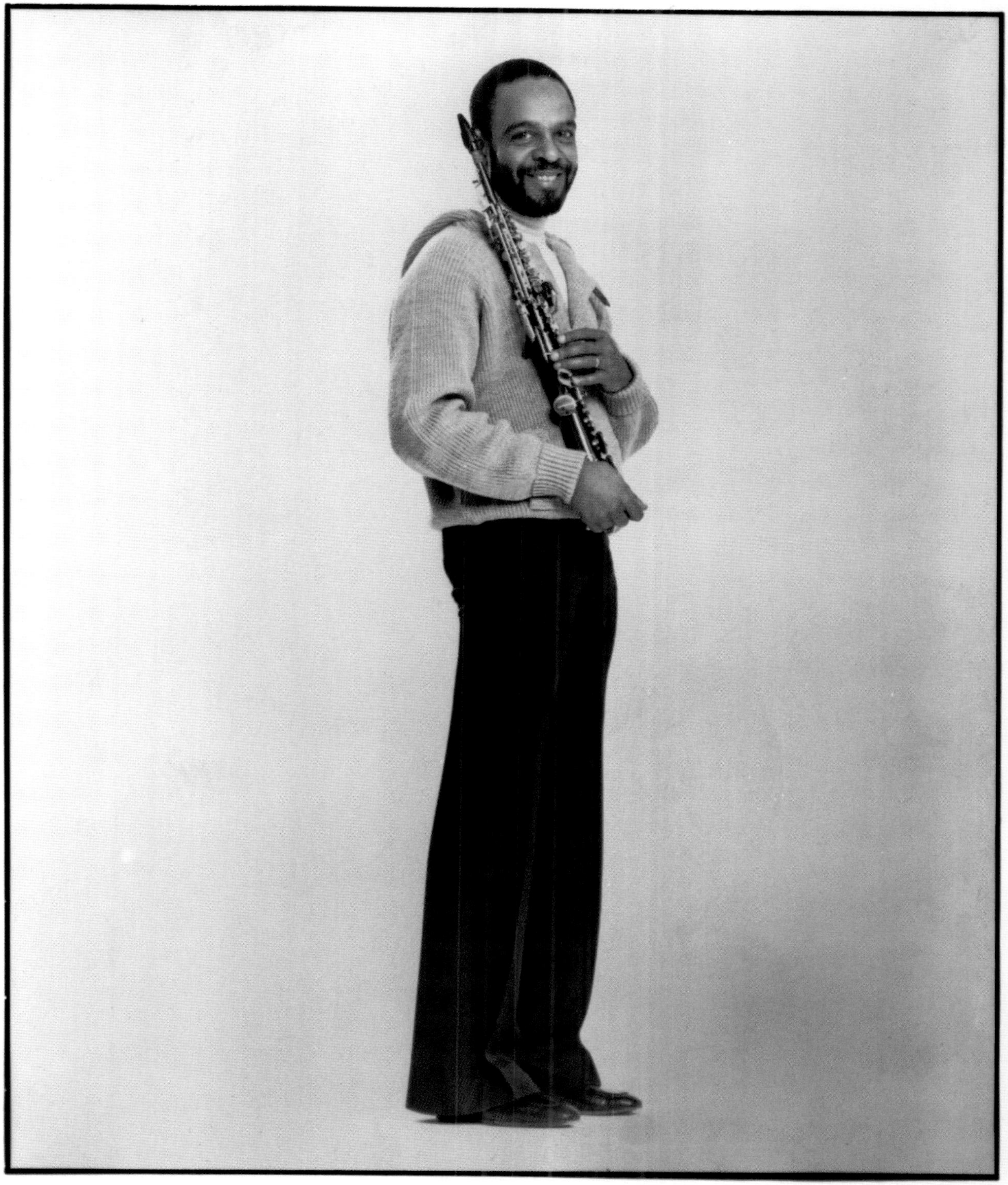

Photo Credit: PAUL S. WILSON

GROVER WASHINGTON, JR.

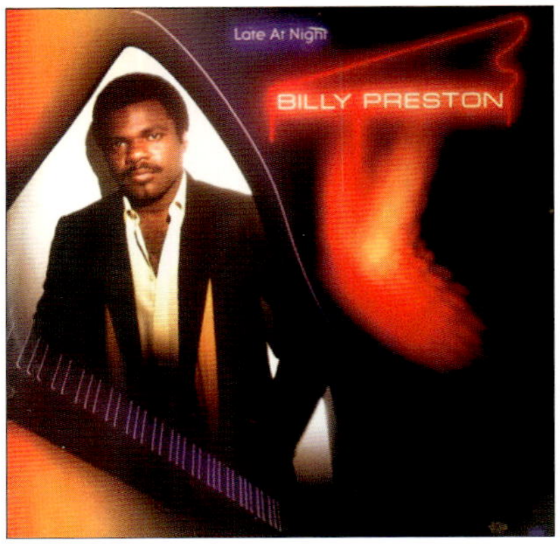

Keyboardist **Billy Preston** paired with Syreeta on the hit "With You I'm Born Again," a sleek ballad originally featured in the sports comedy film *Fast Break*.

Billboard 200: *Late at Night* (#49)
Billboard Hot 100: "With You I'm Born Again" (#4)

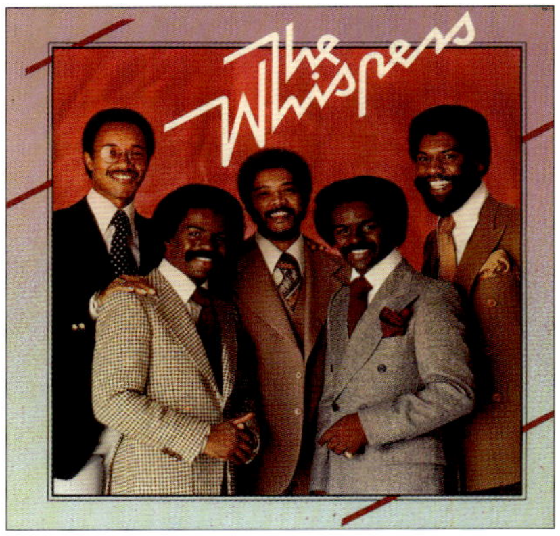

The Whispers enjoyed their first smash album after 16 years together, thanks to the pervasiveness of the No. 1 R&B single "And the Beat Goes On."

Billboard 200: *The Whispers* (#6)
Billboard Hot 100: "And the Beat Goes On" (#19); "Lady" (#28)

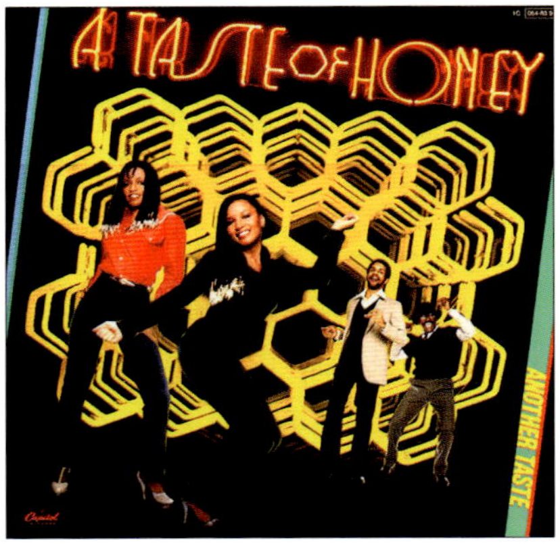

The soul-disco groove of **A Taste of Honey**'s "Do It Good" looked to recapture the universal appeal of the group's chart-topping "Boogie Oogie Oogie."

Billboard 200: *Another Taste* (#59)
Billboard Hot 100: "Do It Good" (#79)

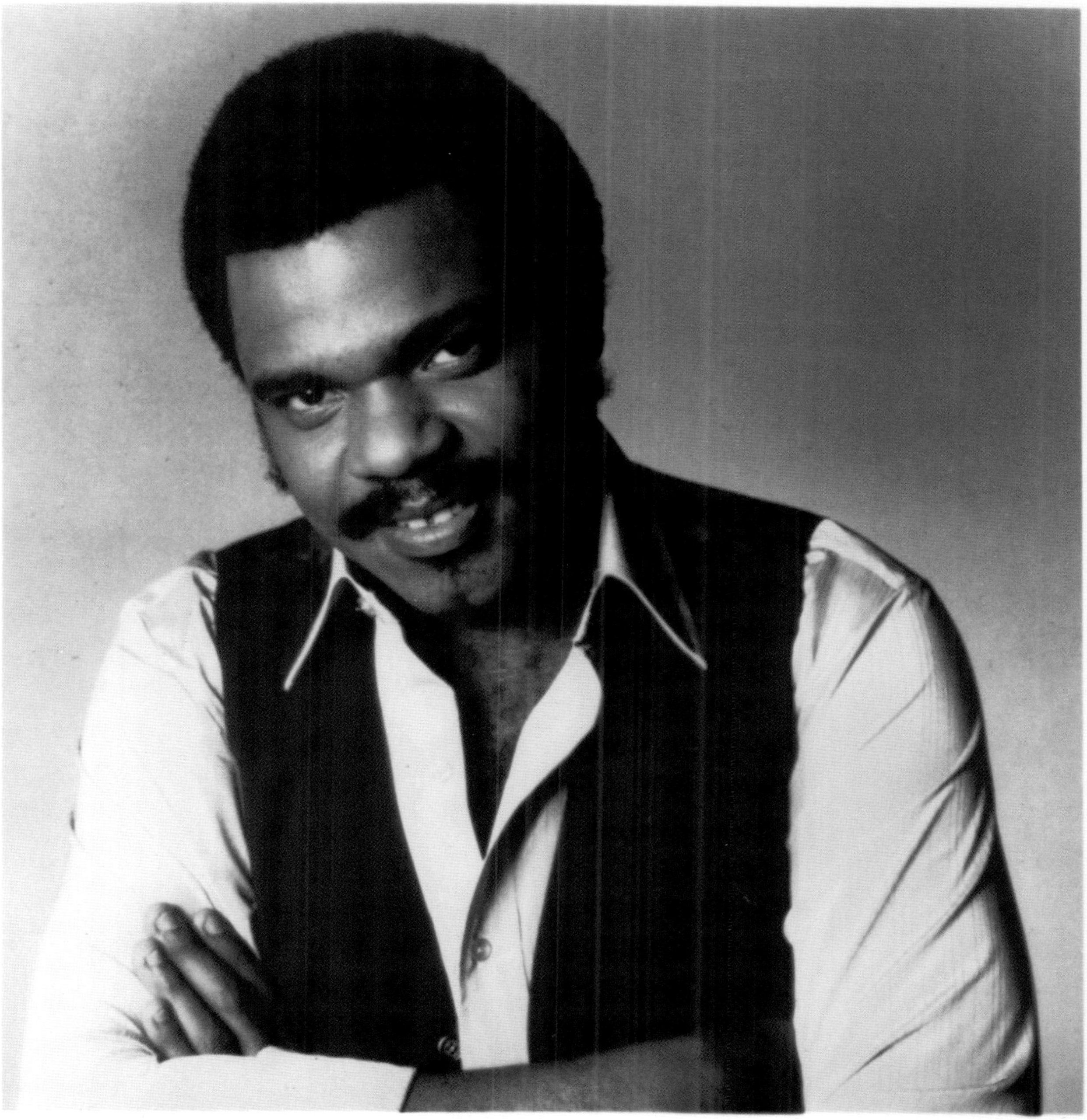

BILLY PRESTON

EXCLUSIVE REPRESENTATION

Rodgers Agency
P.O. Box 76640
Atlanta, Georgia 30358-1640
(404) 992-1050

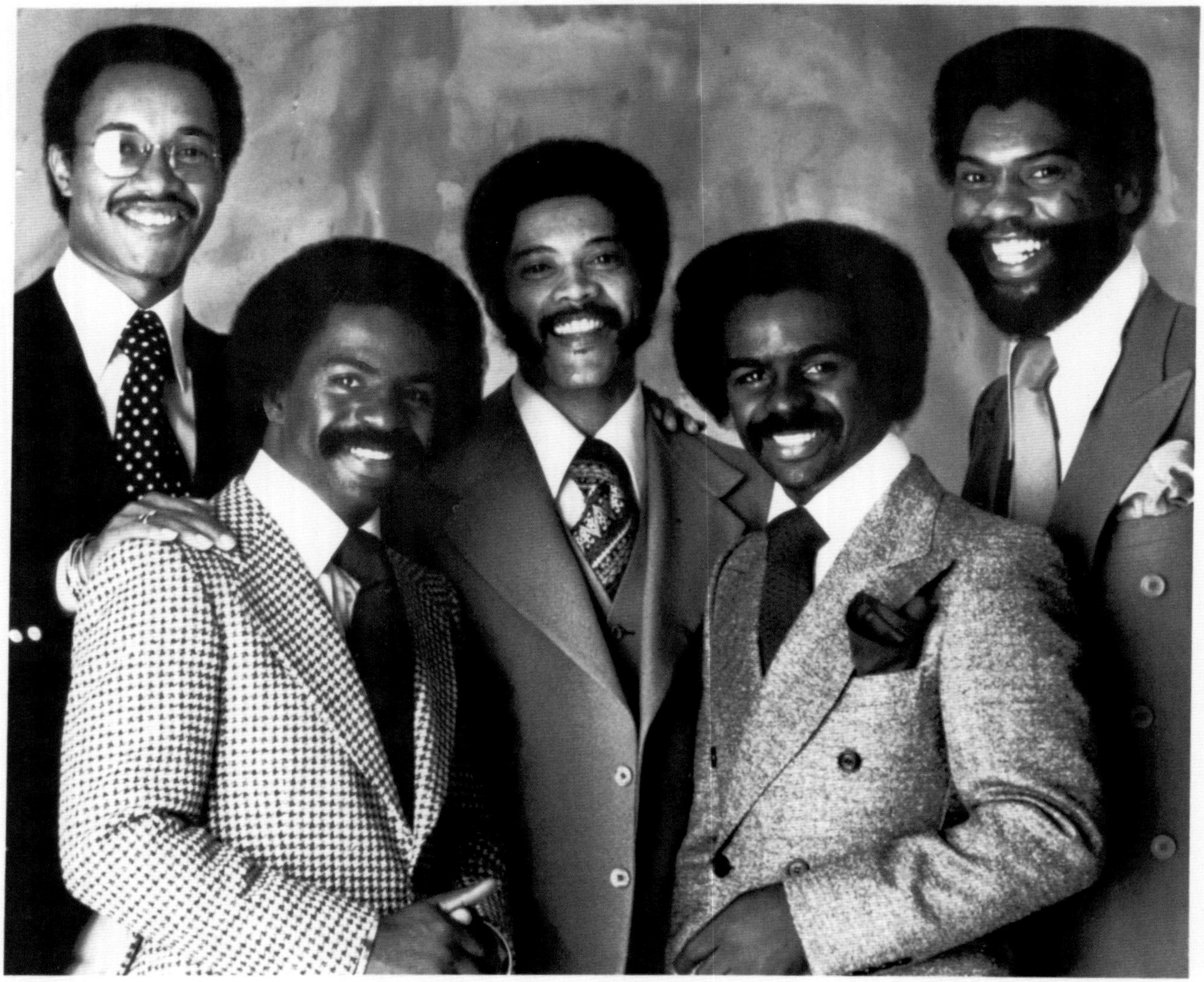

THE WHISPERS

GRIFFCO MANAGEMENT
6255 Sunset Blvd., #923
Los Angeles, Ca. 90028
213 467 6527

SOLAR
SOUND OF LOS ANGELES RECORDS
Manufactured and Distributed by RCA Records

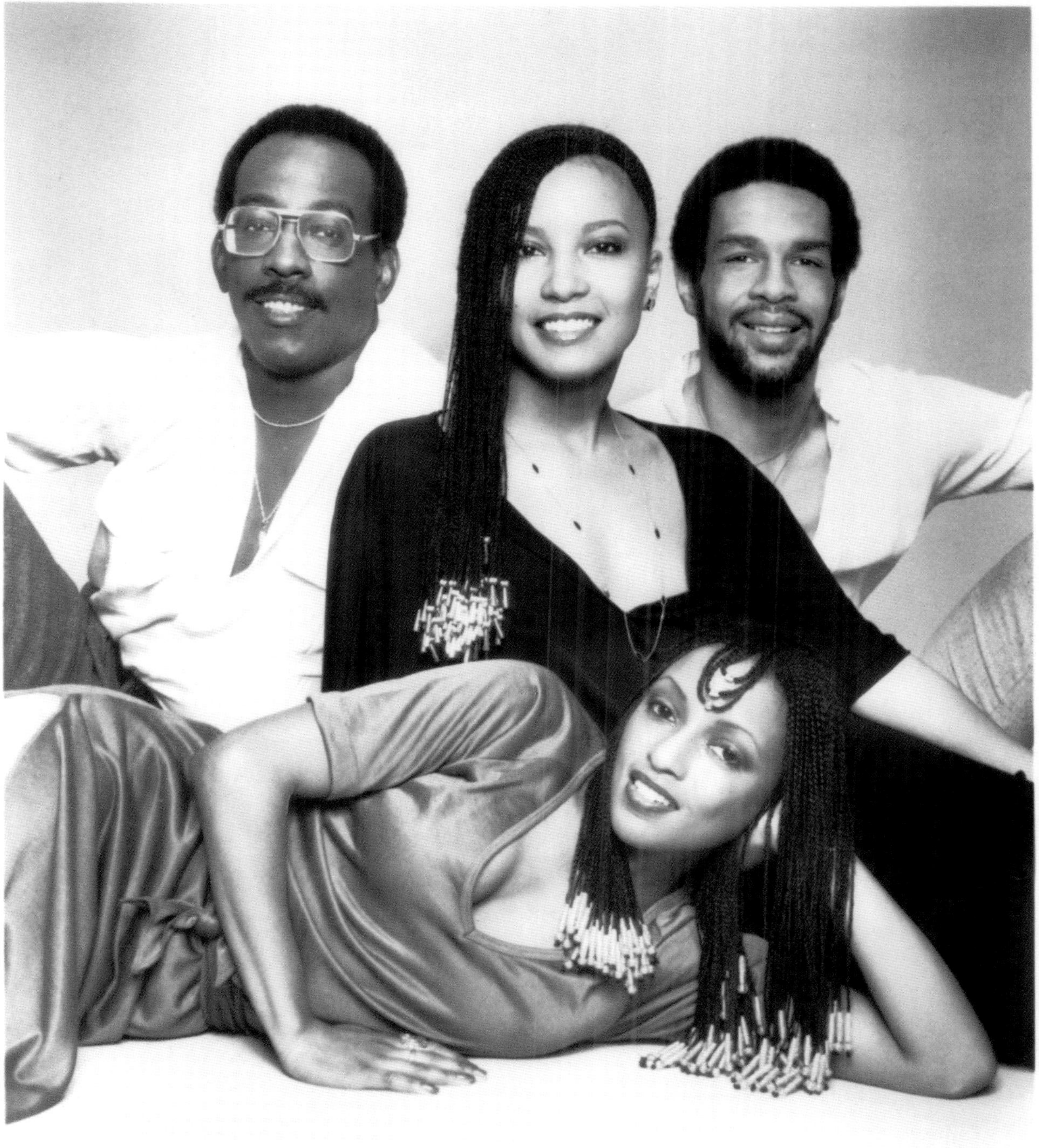

Harry Langdon Photography

Donald Johnson   Janice Johnson   Perry Kibble

Hazel Payne

the management company

A TASTE OF HONEY

Capitol RECORDS

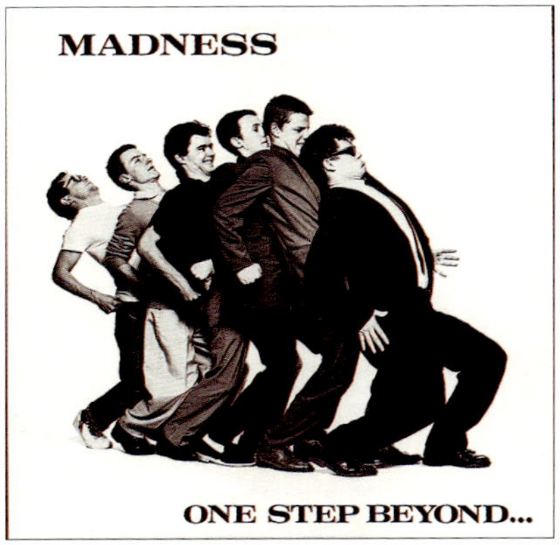

UK ska band **Madness**' debut album drew upon its "nutty" sound for "My Girl" and "One Step Beyond," a fevered tribute to Jamaican singer Prince Buster.

Billboard 200: *One Step Beyond...* (#128)

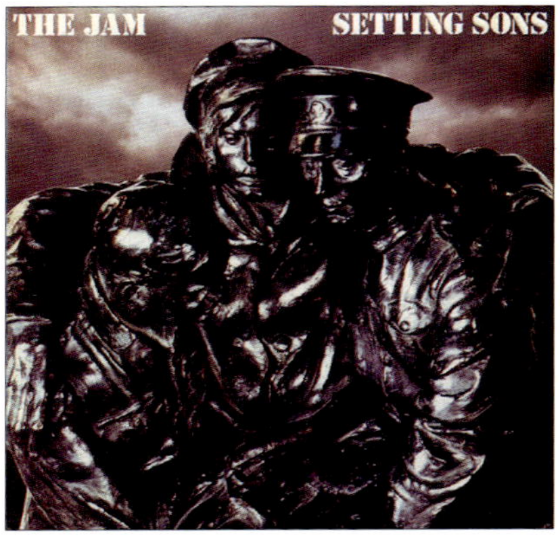

The Jam's *Setting Sons* album surfaced as the British band's chart debut in the US, with the cogent single "The Eton Rifles" marking its first Top 10 UK hit.

Billboard 200: *Setting Sons* (#137)

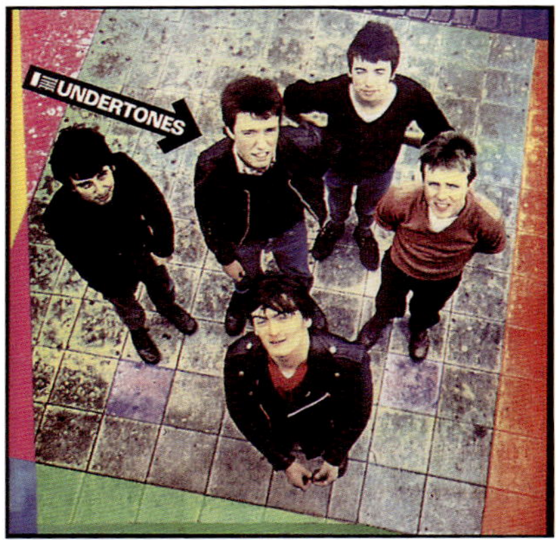

The Undertones' first release was fueled by the punk-pop charm of "Jimmy Jimmy," which quickly catapulted the Northern Irish quintet into the UK Top 20.

Billboard 200: *The Undertones* (#154)

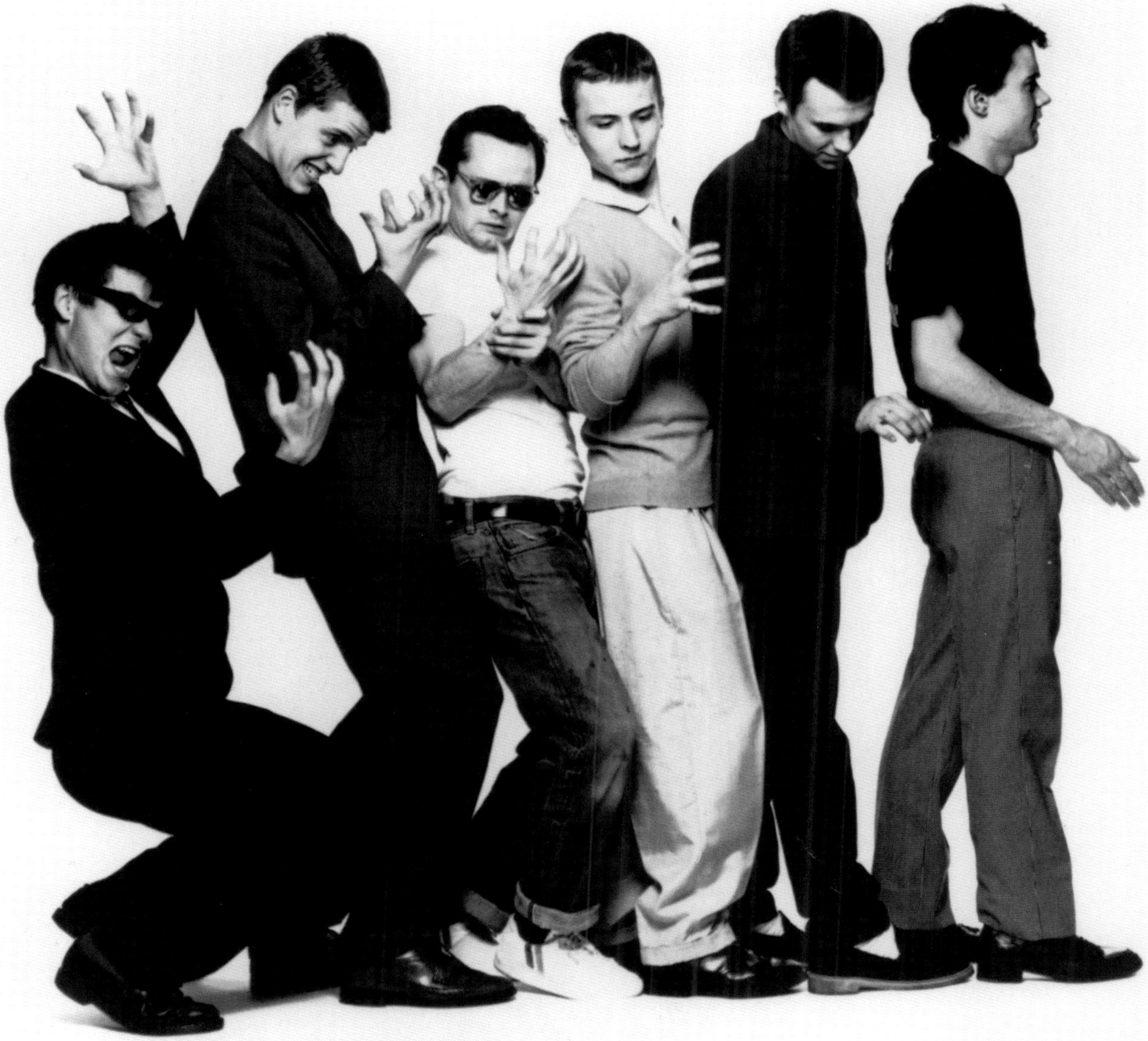

DECEMBER 1979

MADNESS

SIRE®

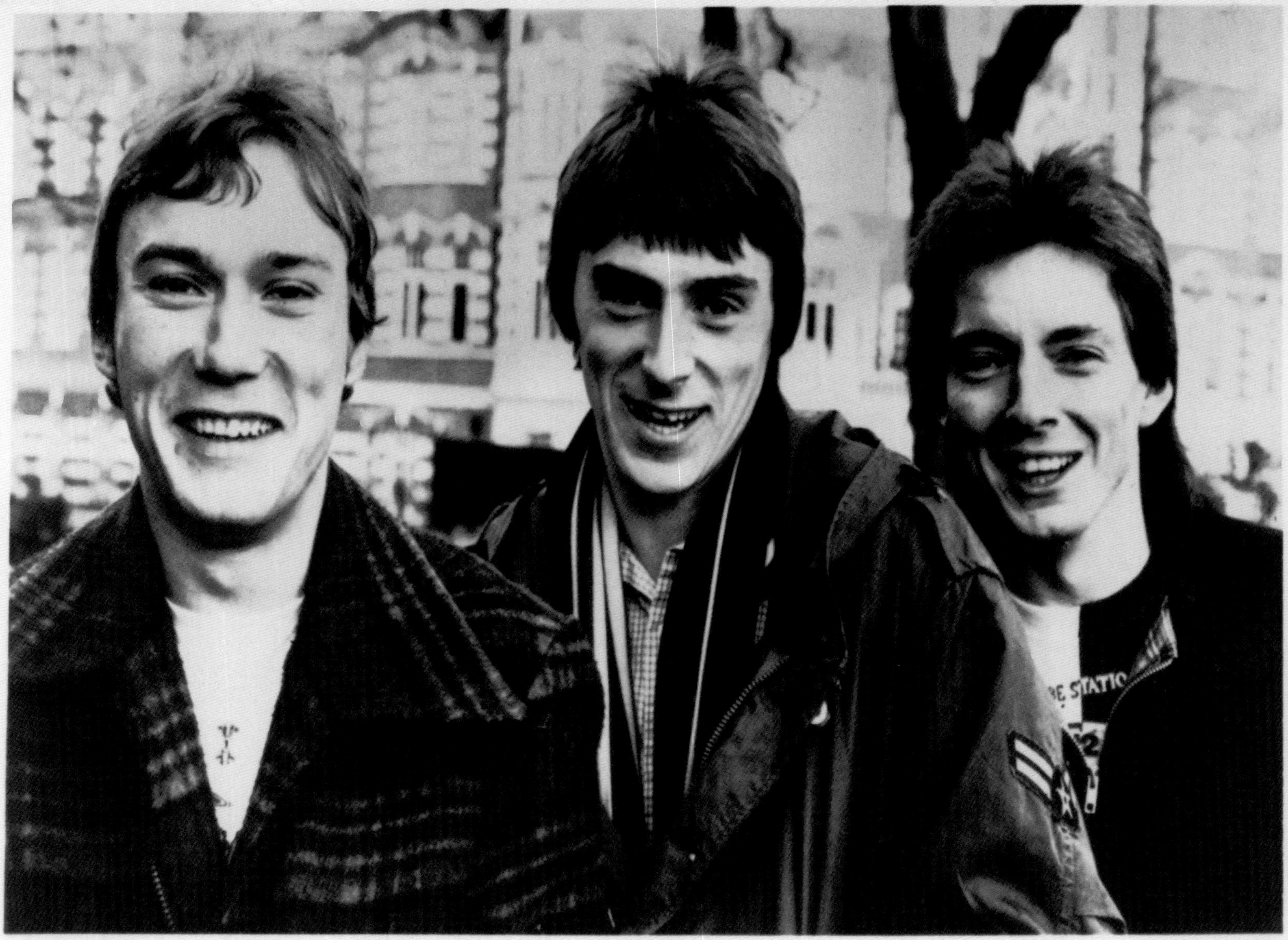

THE JAM

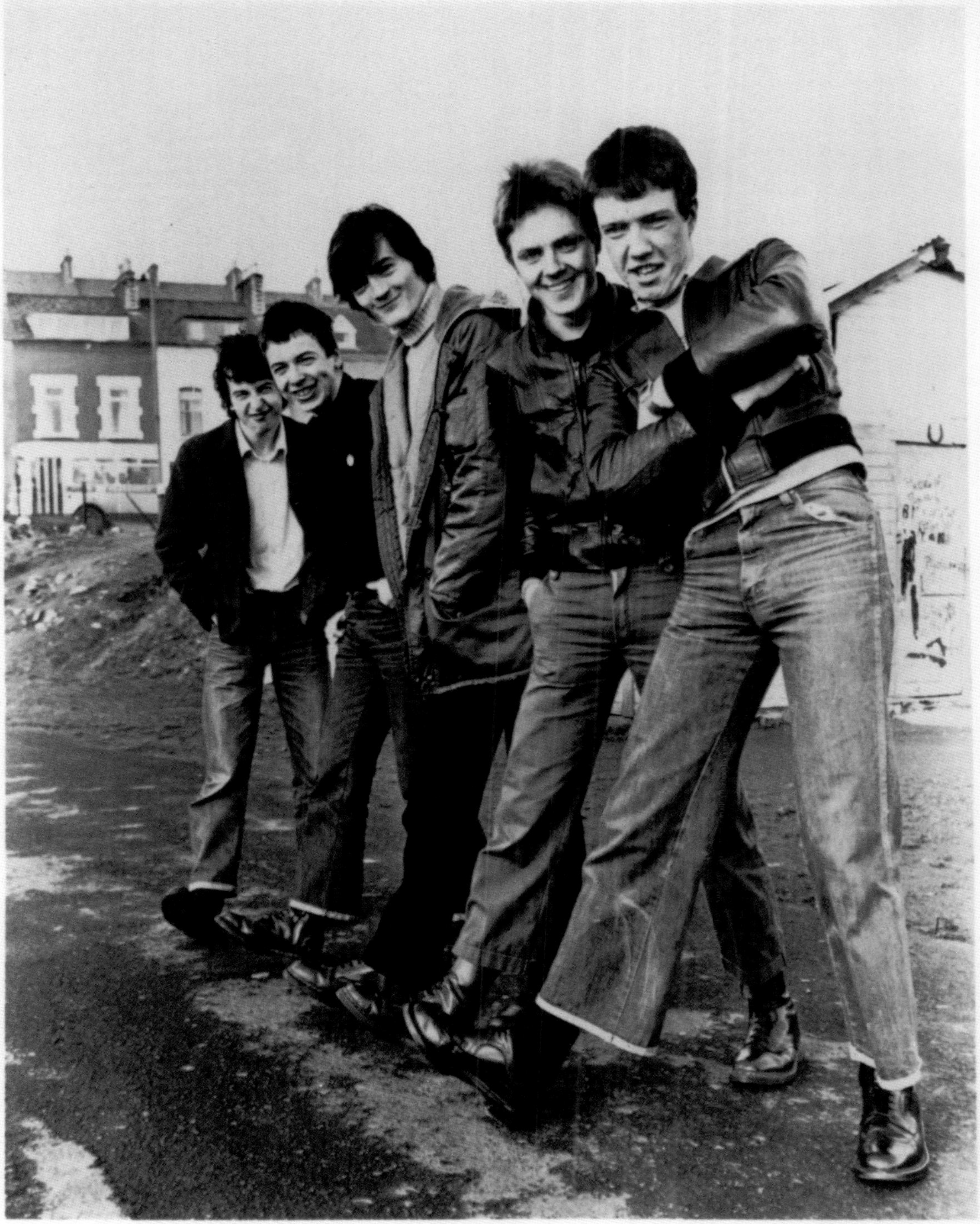

DECEMBER 1979

THE UNDERTONES

SIRE®

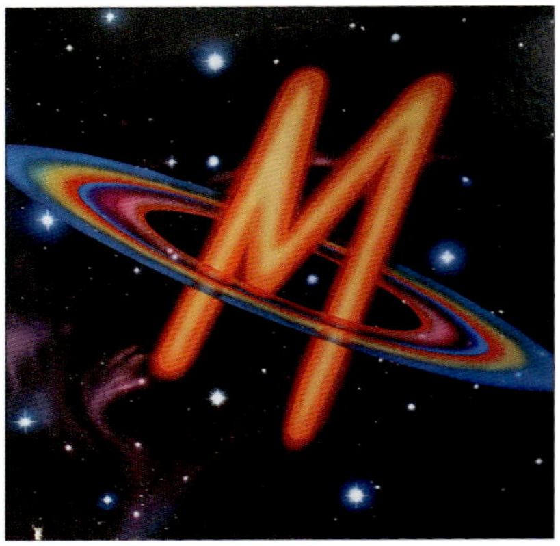

British musician Robin Scott stormed the international charts under the pseudonym **M**, a synth-pop project that reached No. 1 in the US with "Pop Muzik."

Billboard 200: *New York · London · Paris · Munich* (#79)
Billboard Hot 100: "Pop Muzik" (No. 1)

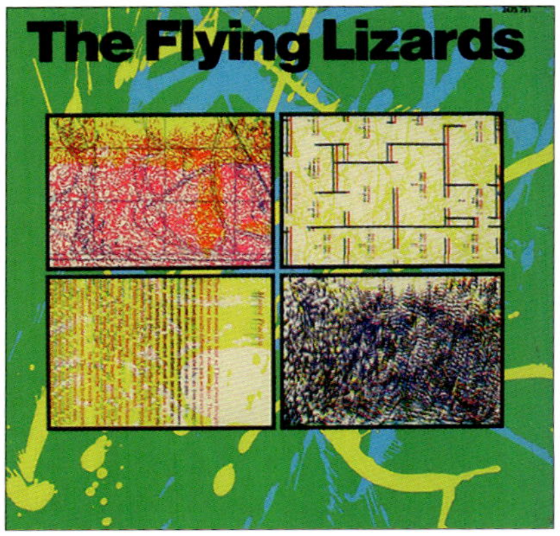

The Flying Lizards, a band of English minimalists, met with unforeseen chart success for a brittle, willfully unusual rendering of Barrett Strong's "Money."

Billboard 200: *The Flying Lizards* (#99)
Billboard Hot 100: "Money" (#50)

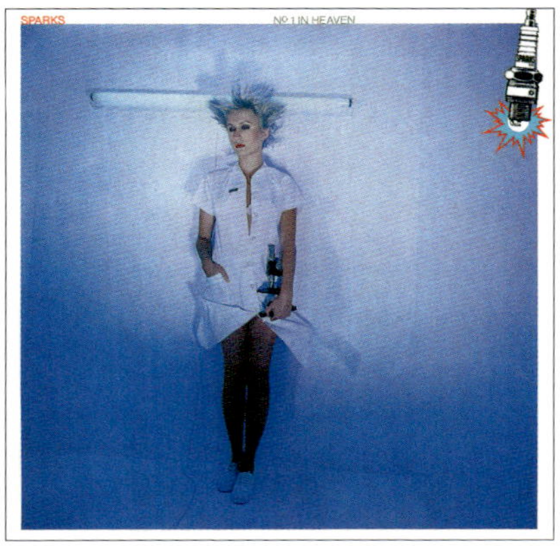

Axing a rock-band format, **Sparks** scored electronic disco hits with "Beat the Clock," "The Number One Song in Heaven" and "Tryouts for the Human Race."

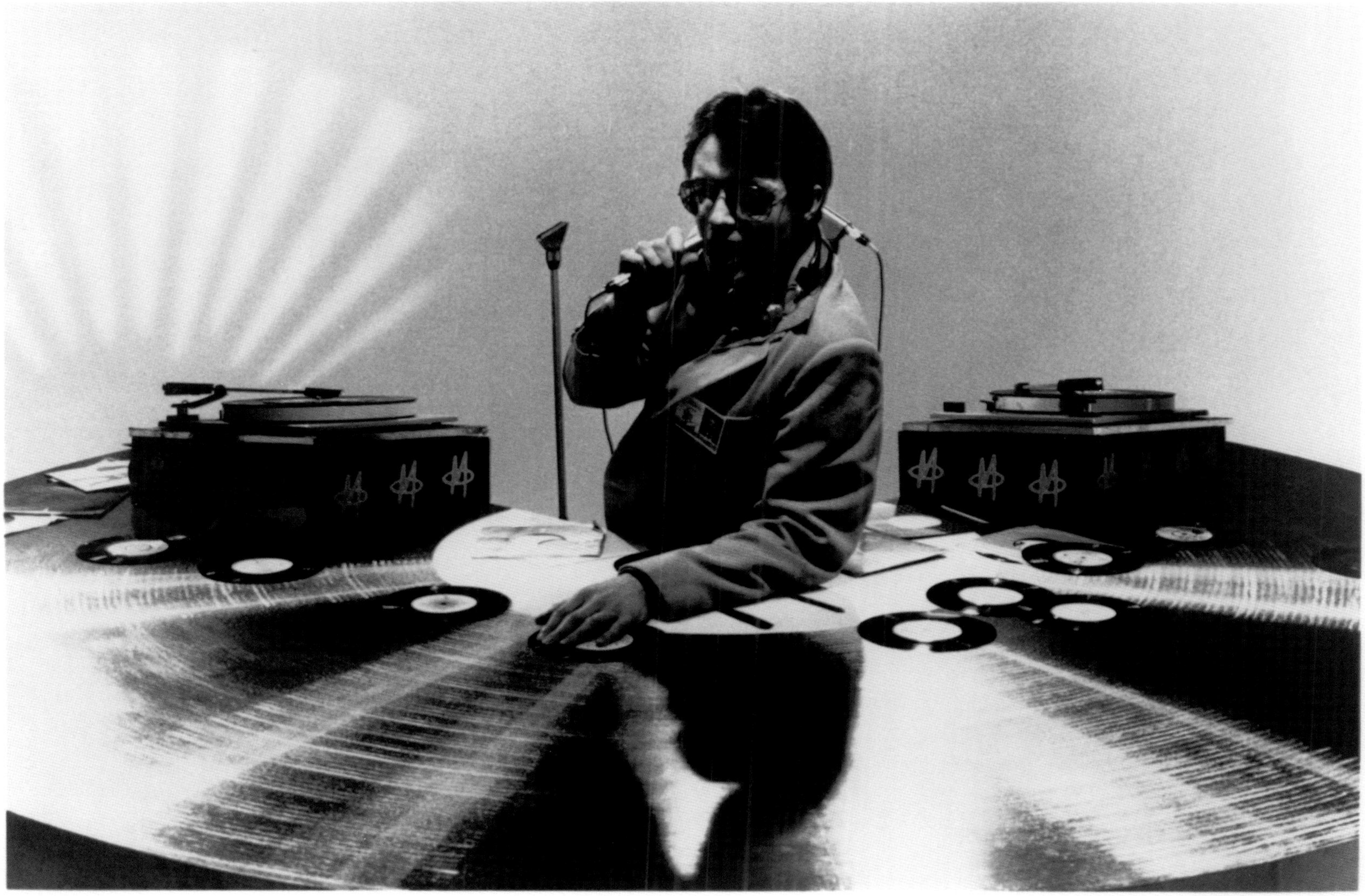

SIRE RECORDS

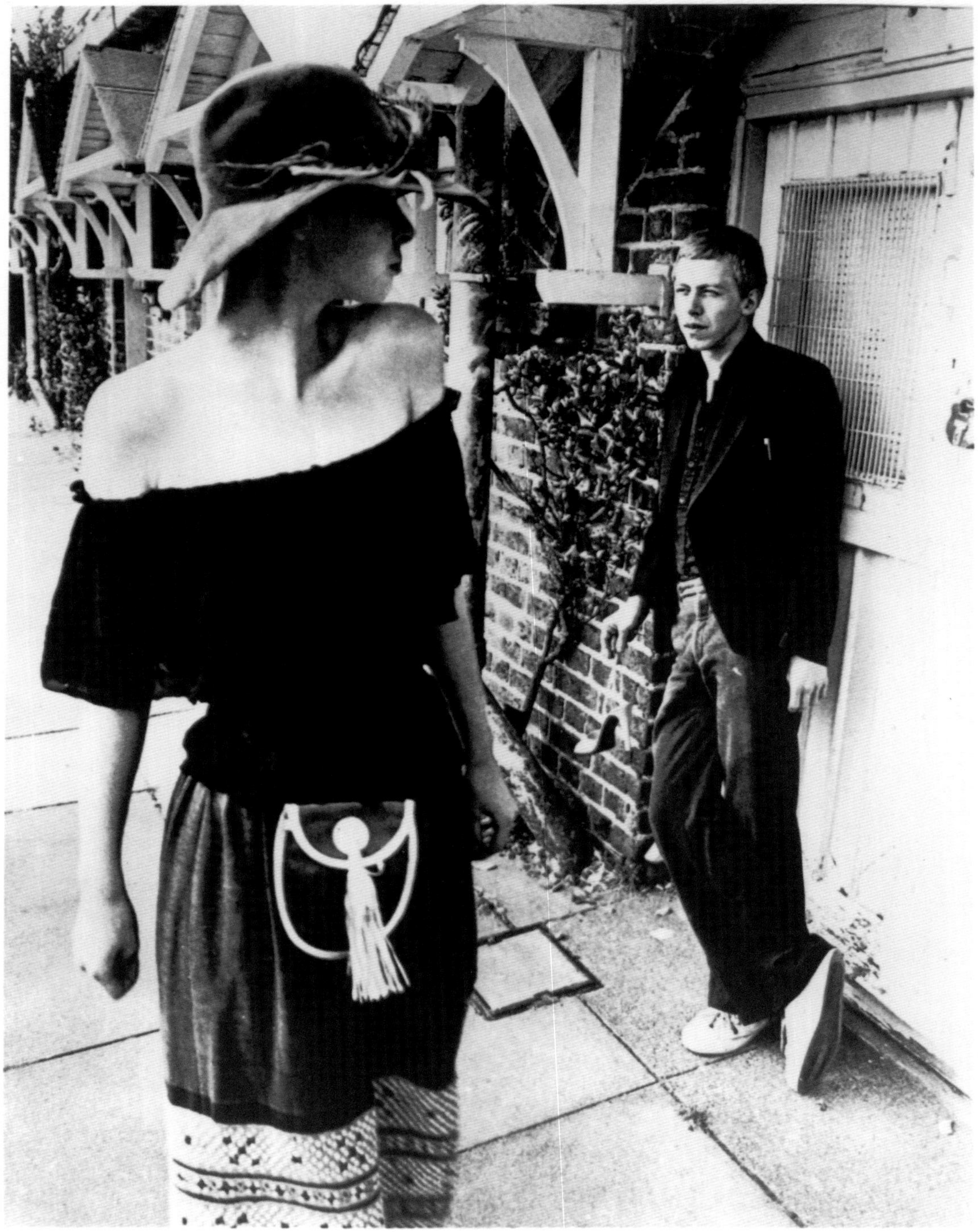

Photo Credit Richard Raynor Canham Oct 1978

The Flying Lizards

Virgin RECORDS

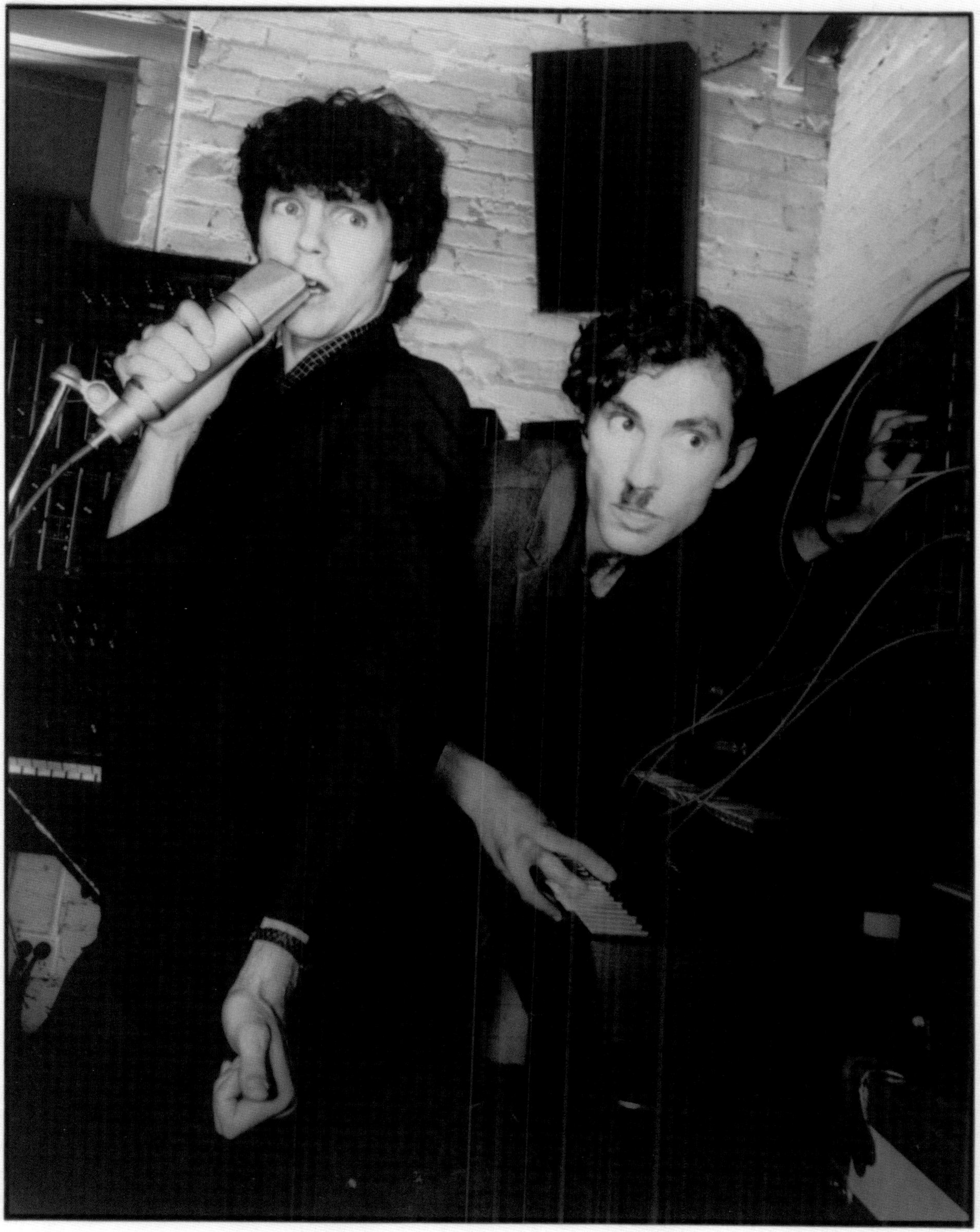

Photo Credit: MOSHE BRAKHA

Russell Mael Ron Mael

SPARKS

elektra

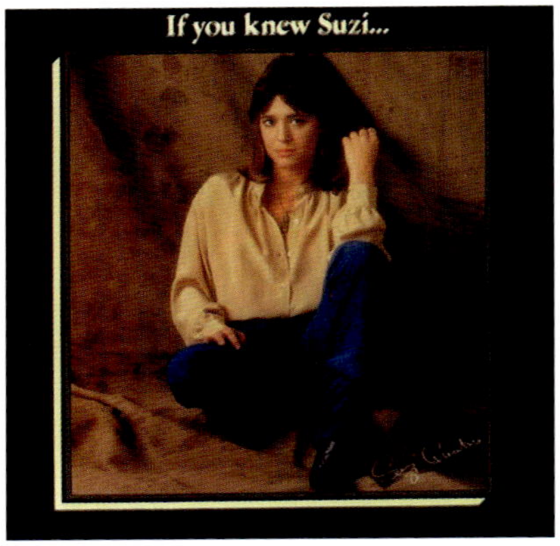

"Stumblin' In," a duet with Chris Norman of Smokie, established **Suzi Quatro** with US audiences who knew her as Leather Tuscadero on TV's *Happy Days*.

Billboard 200: *If You Knew Suzi...* (#37)
Billboard Hot 100: "Stumblin' In" (#4)

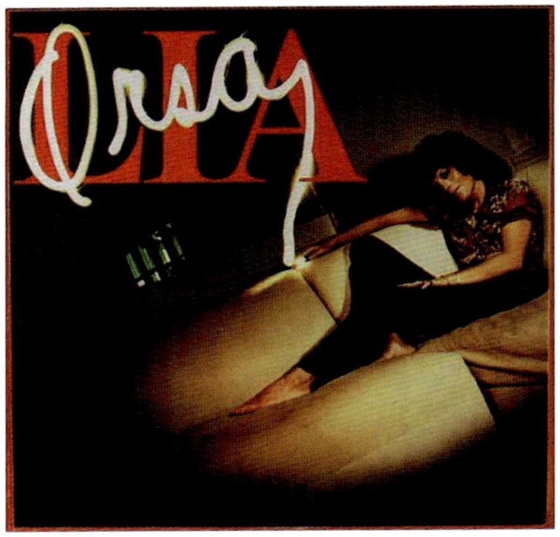

Written and produced by Hal David and Archie Jordan, "I Never Said I Love You" by **Orsa Lia** spent a week at No. 1 on the adult contemporary charts.

Billboard Hot 100: "I Never Said I Love You" (#84)

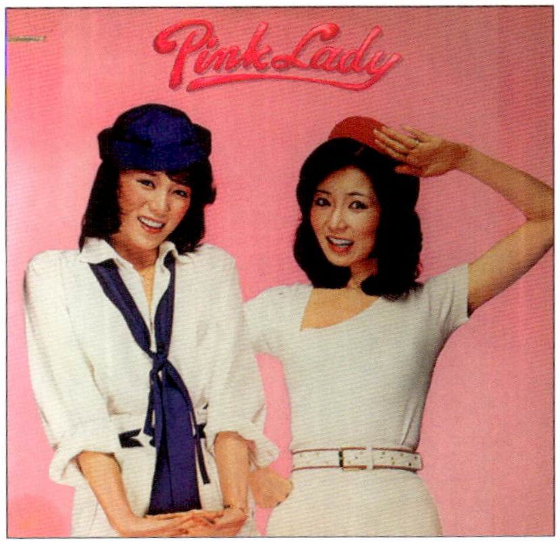

A young Japanese singing duo, **Pink Lady** concentrated on the American market and reached the Top 40 with the temperate disco single "Kiss in the Dark."

Billboard Hot 100: "Kiss in the Dark" (#37)

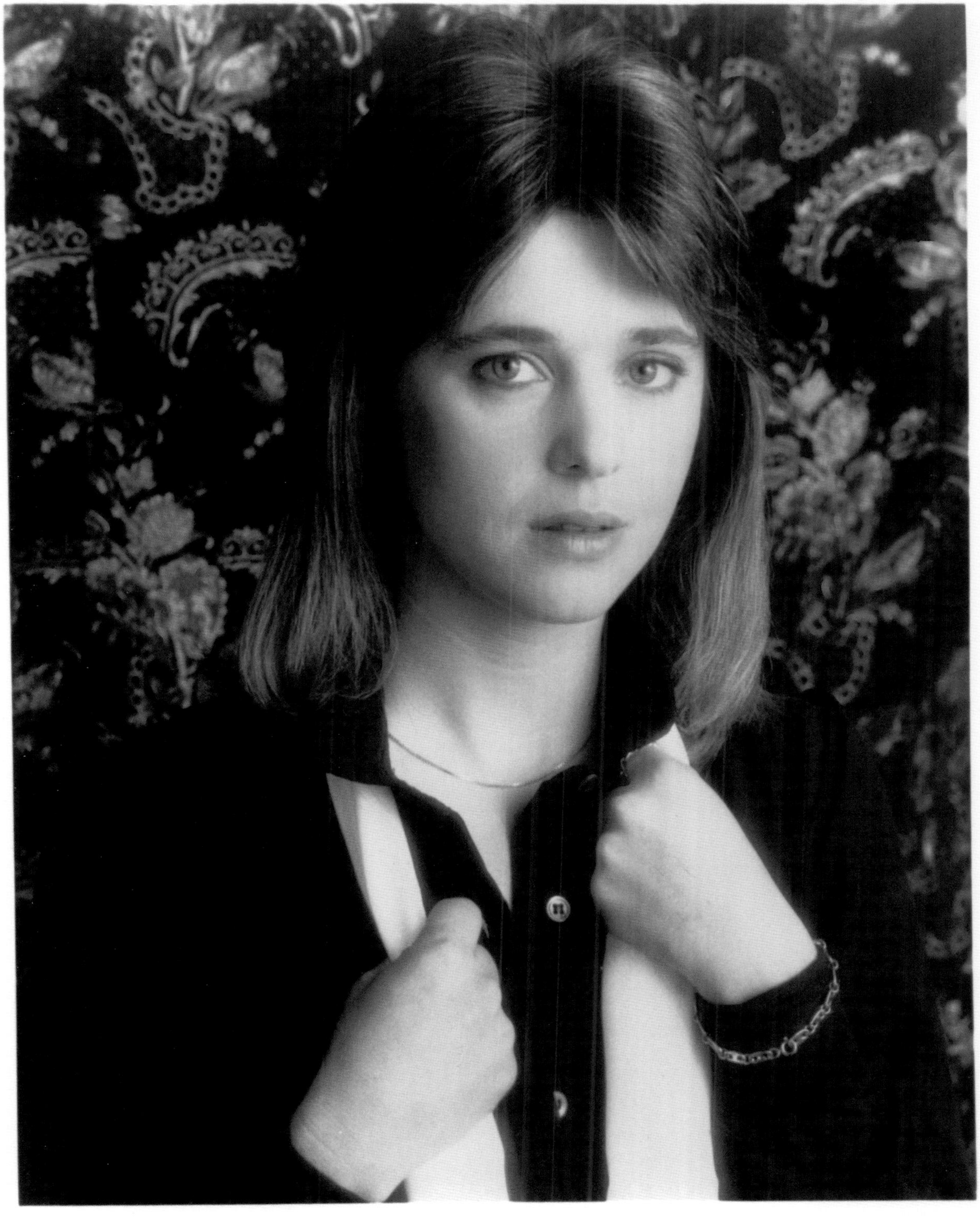

SUZI QUATRO

Records, Inc.

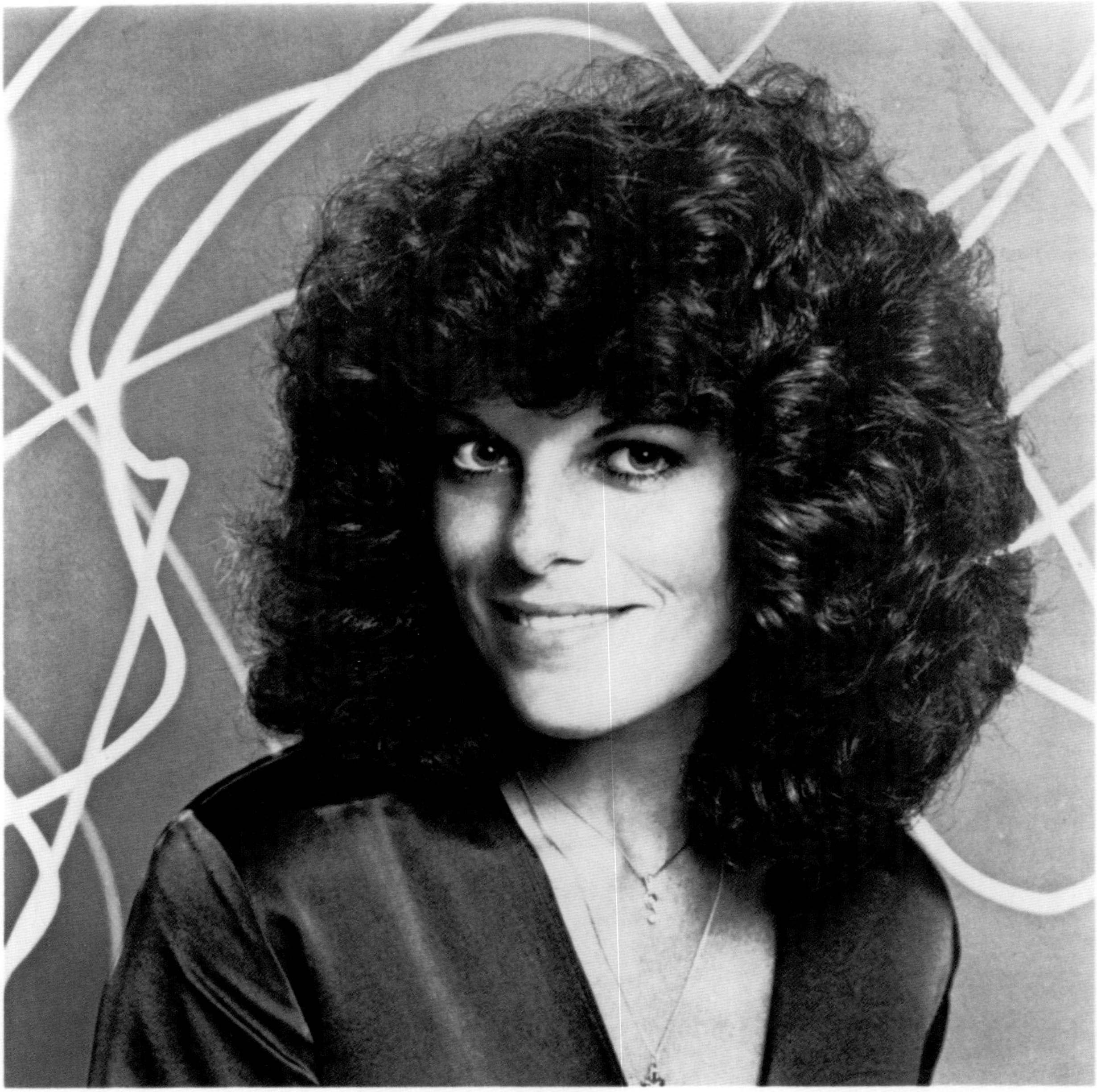

LIA

MANAGEMENT:
James David & William Orr Nelson
6430 Sunset Blvd., Suite 912
Hollywood, CA 90028
(213) 469-8234

INFINITY RECORDS

10 East 53rd Street
New York, New York 10022
(212) 888-9700

100 Universal City Plaza
Universal City, California 91608
(213) 763-8283

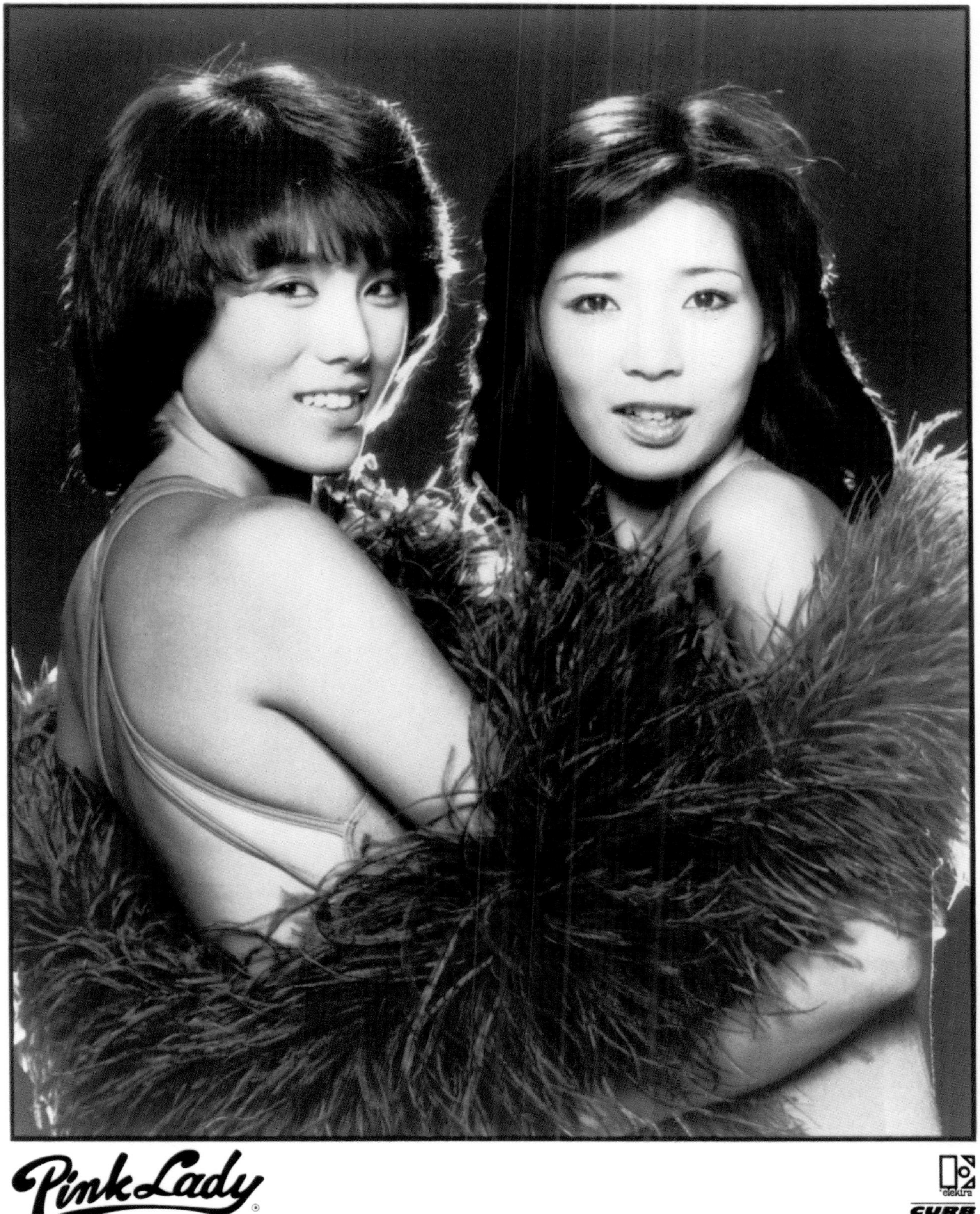

Photo Credit: HARRY LANGDON

Pink Lady®

elektra

CURB RECORDS

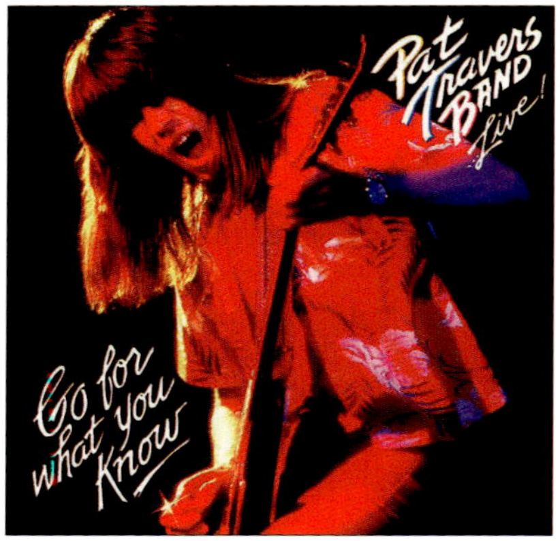

Pat Travers Band's live album included the Canadian rocker's well-liked version of "Boom Boom (Out Go the Lights)," a radio smash and party anthem.

Billboard 200: *Live! Go for What You Know* (#29)
Billboard Hot 100: "Boom Boom (Out Go the Lights)" (#56)

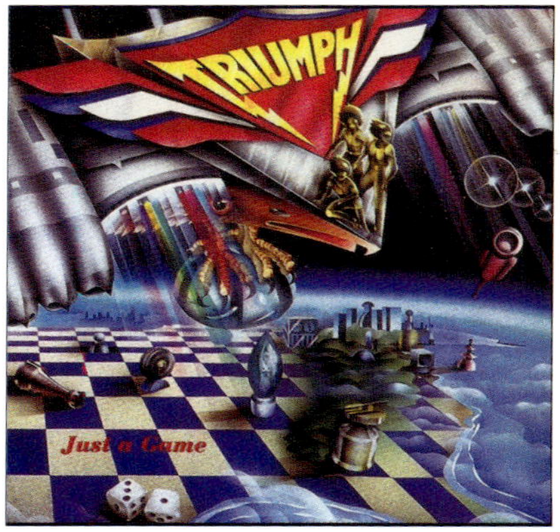

Formed in Canada, the power trio **Triumph** carried the hard-rock banner and gained heavy FM radio play with its second worldwide release, *Just a Game.*

Billboard 200: *Just a Game* (#48)
Billboard Hot 100: "Hold On" (#38); "Lay It on the Line" (#86)

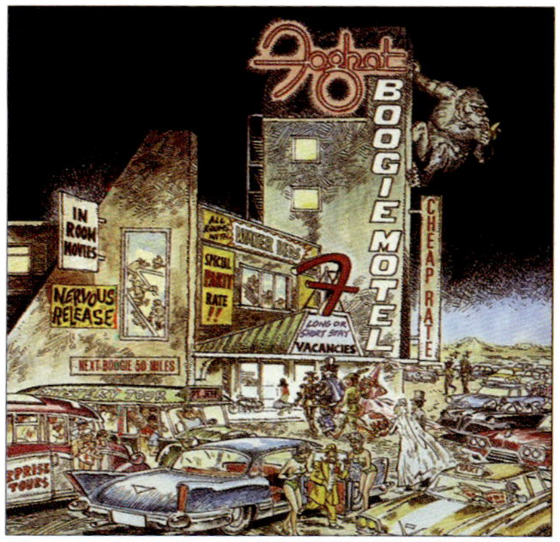

Downplaying **Foghat**'s trademark blues-rock pedigree, *Boogie Motel* gave rise to a hit single, the ballad "Third Time Lucky (First Time I Was a Fool)."

Billboard 200: *Boogie Motel* (#35)
Billboard Hot 100: "Third Time Lucky (First Time I Was a Fool)" (#23)

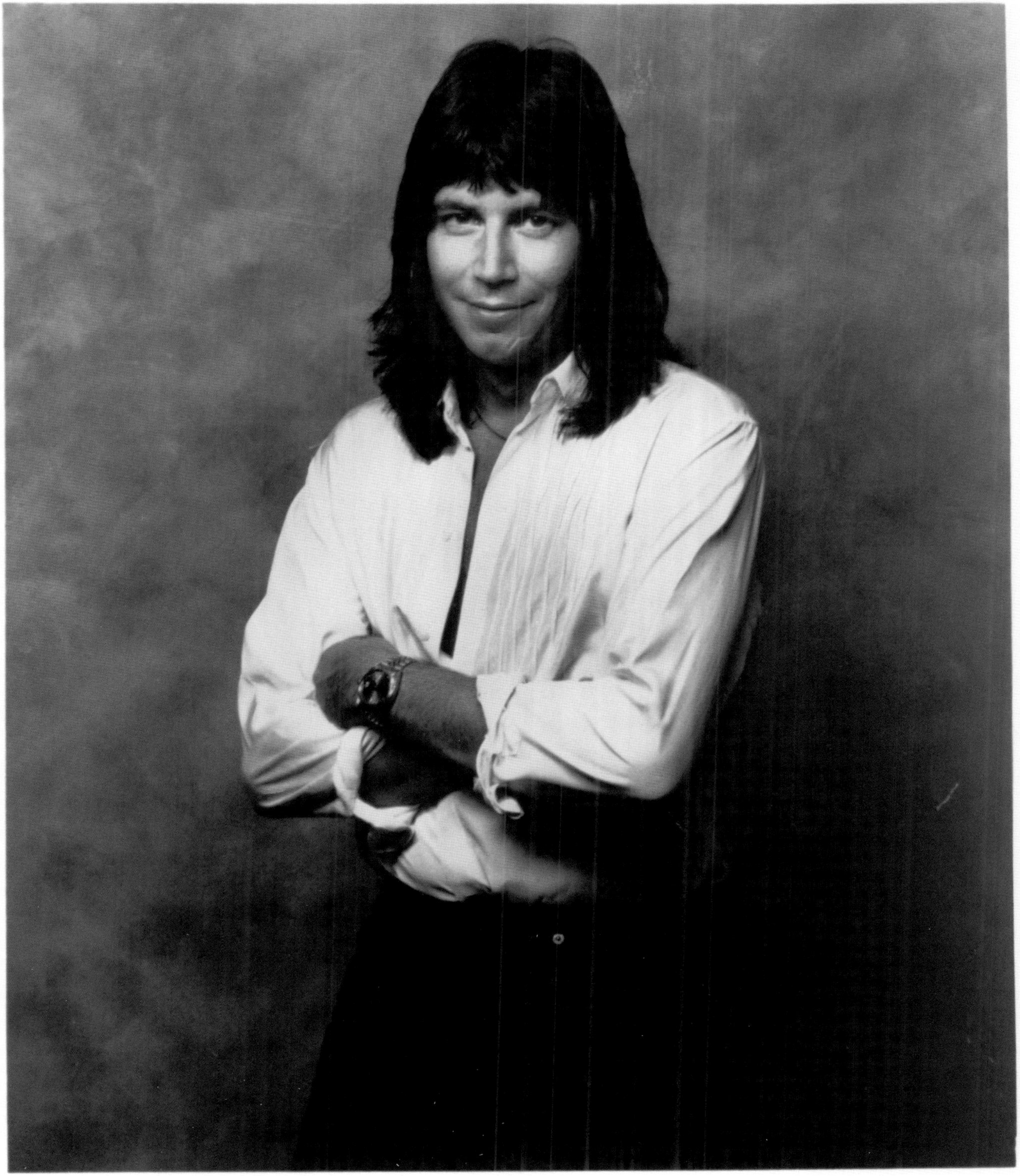

PAT TRAVERS

polydor

PolyGram Records

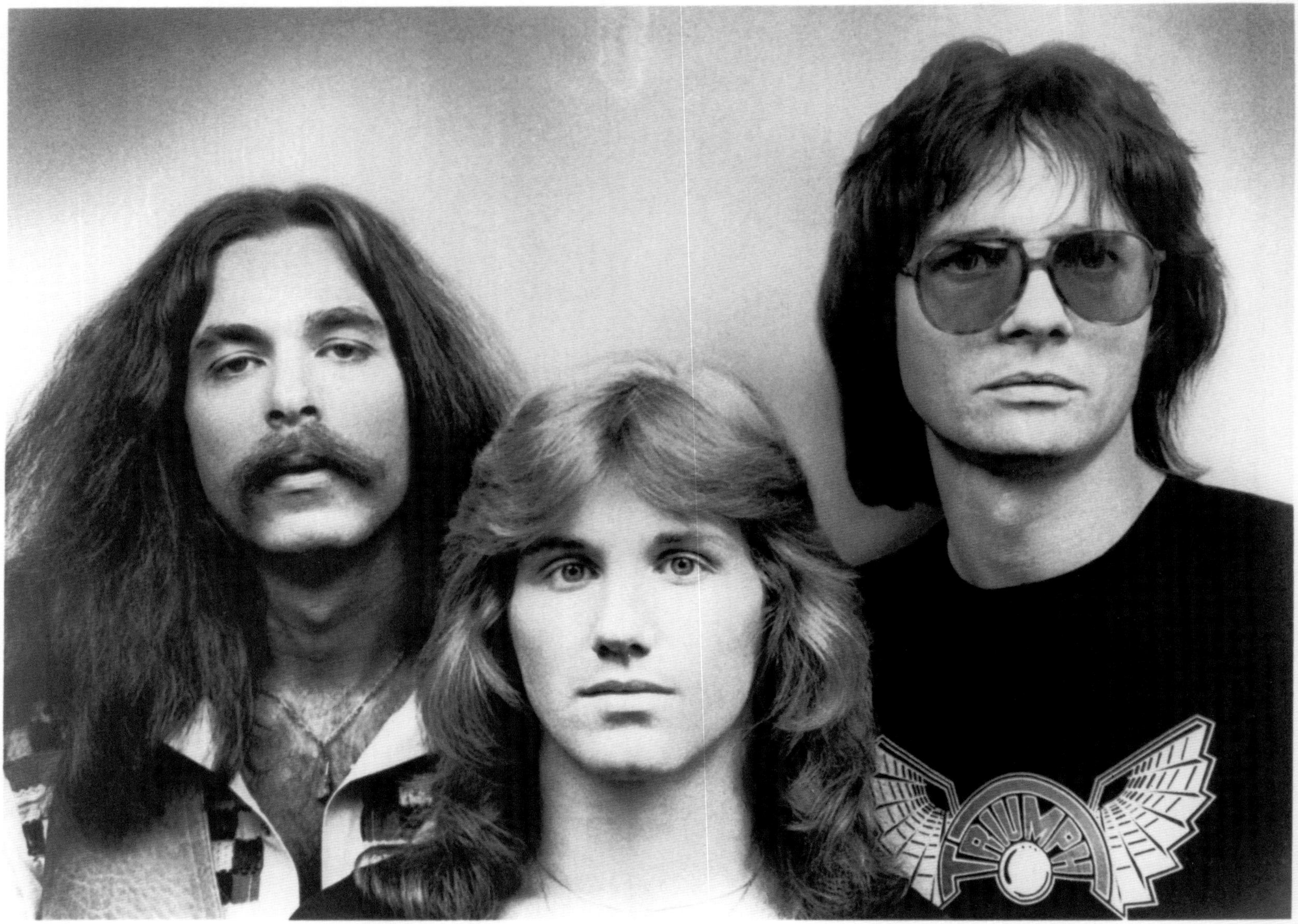

TRIUMPH

RCA
Records

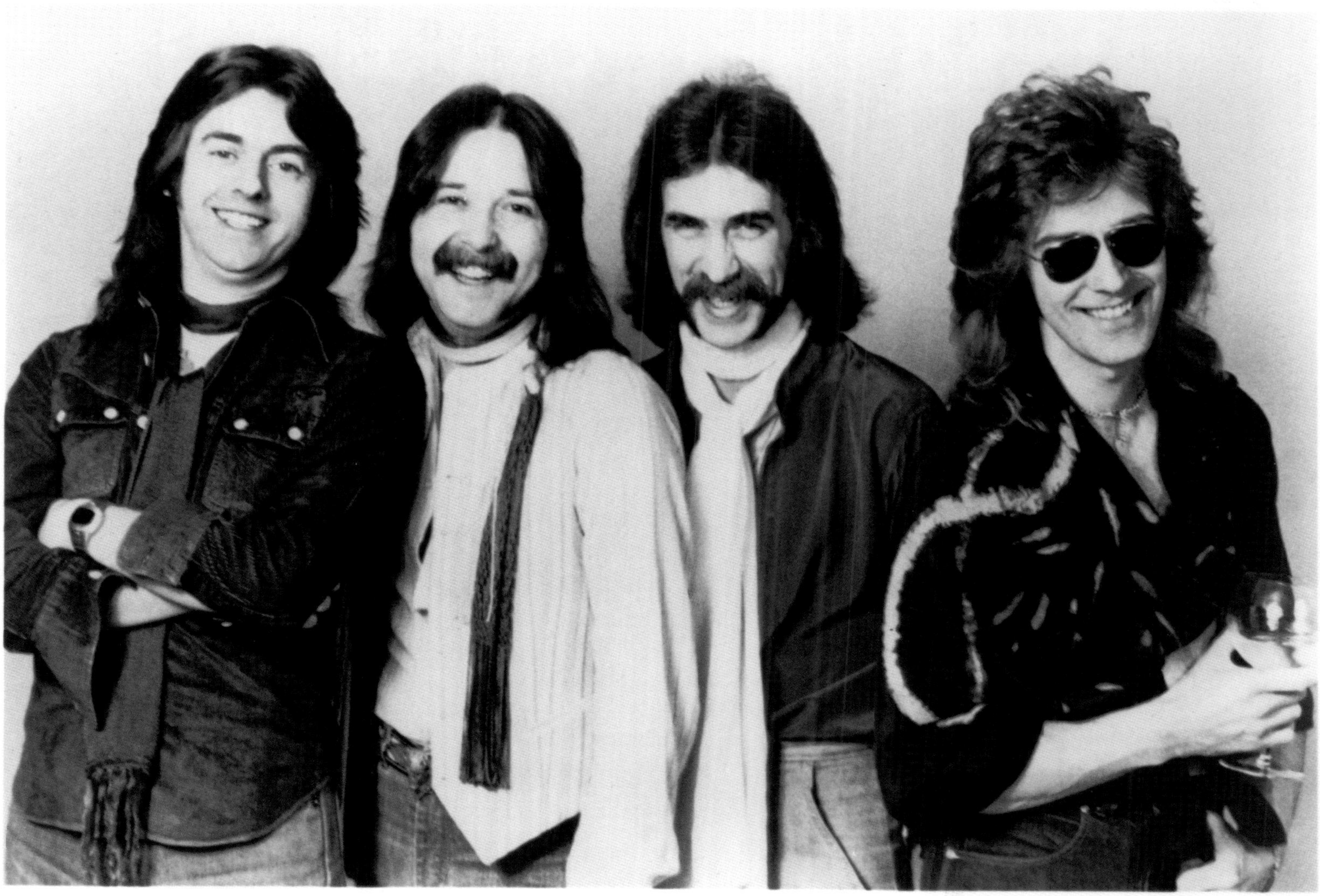

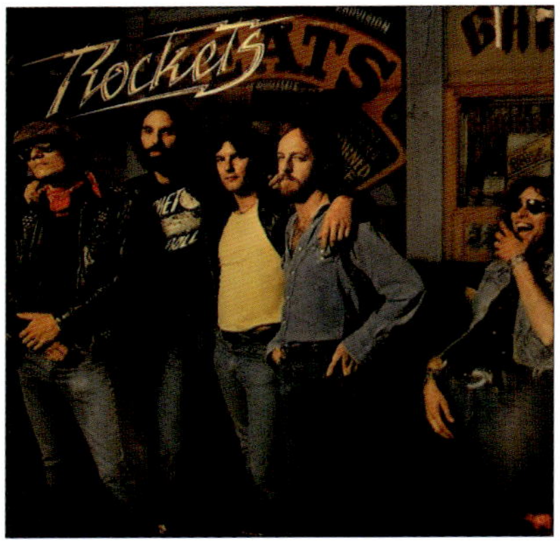

The Rockets, formed by former Mitch Ryder & the Detroit Wheels members, buoyed the Motor City sound with a fiery cover of Fleetwood Mac's "Oh Well."

Billboard 200: *Rockets* (#56)
Billboard Hot 100: "Can't Sleep" (#52); "Oh Well" (#30)

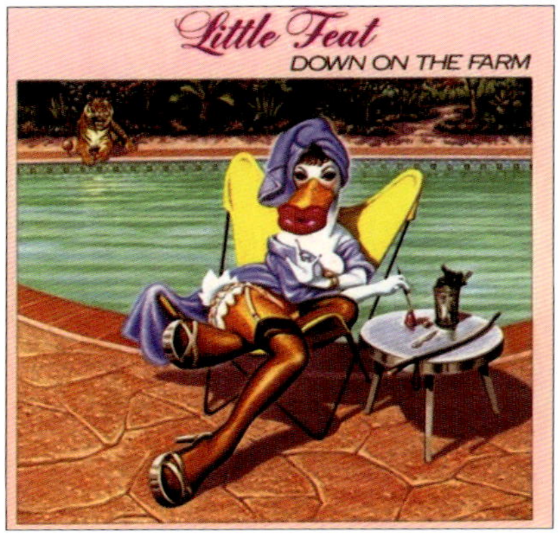

Little Feat disclosed its breakup during the making of *Down on the Farm*, the band's seventh studio project and the last to feature founder Lowell George.

Billboard 200: *Down on the Farm* (#29)

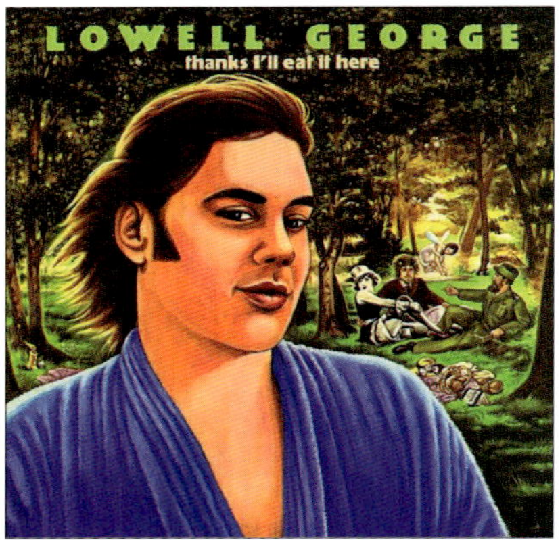

Having left Little Feat after some work on Down on the Farm, leader **Lowell George** released the solo album *Thanks I'll Eat It Here* right before he died.

Billboard 200: *Thanks I'll Eat It Here* (#71)

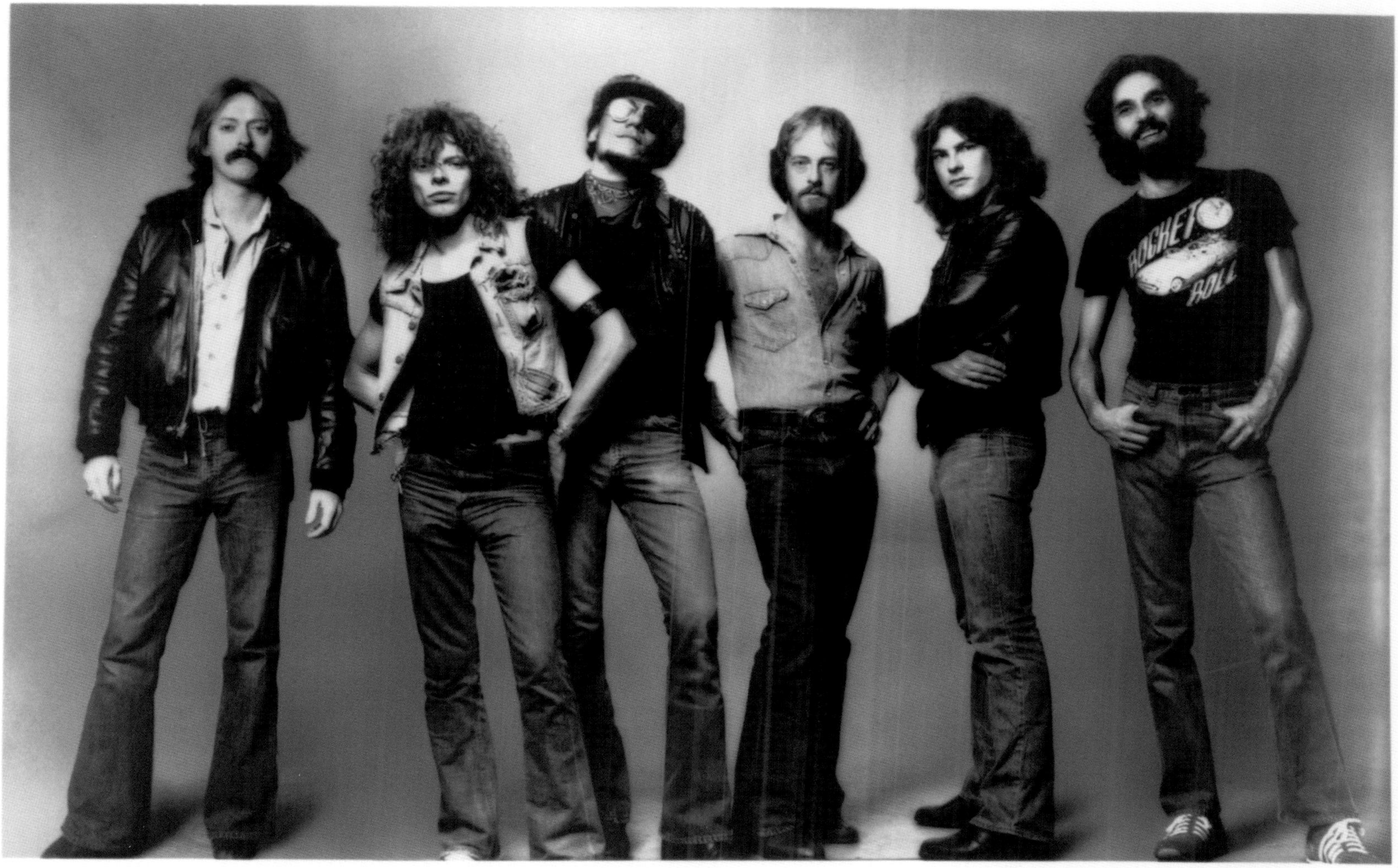

DAN KEYLON DAVE GILBERT JOHN BADANJEK DENNIS ROBBINS DONNY BACKUS JIM McCARTY

Rockets

RSO Records, Inc.

LOWELL GEORGE

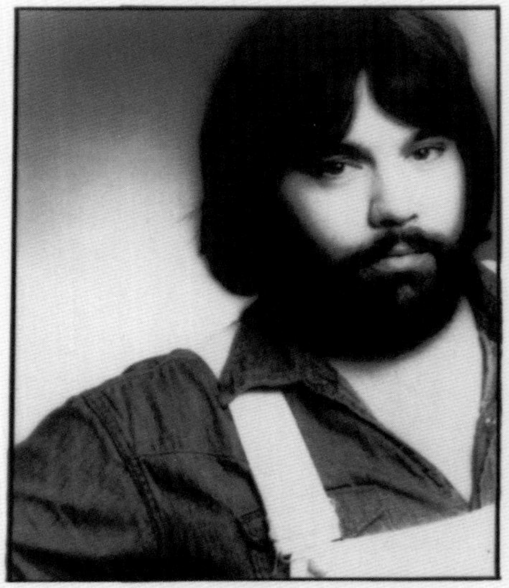

RICHARD HAYWARD

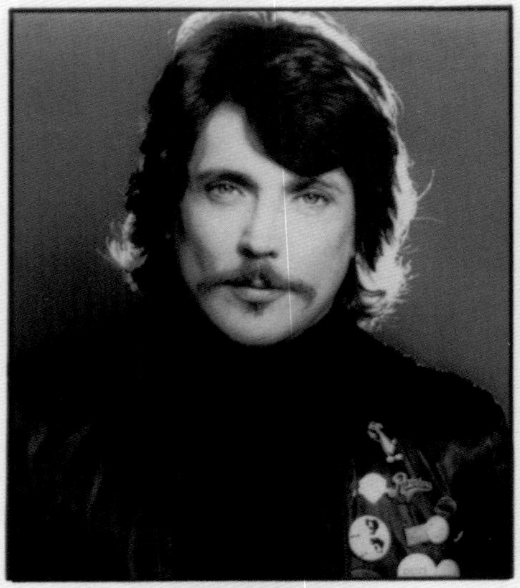

BILL PAYNE

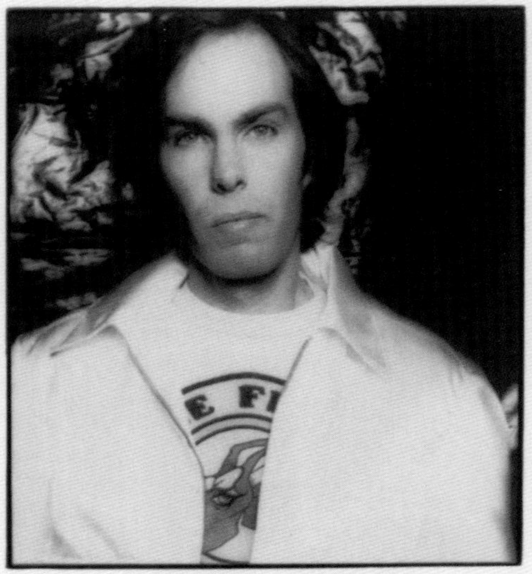

SAM CLAYTON

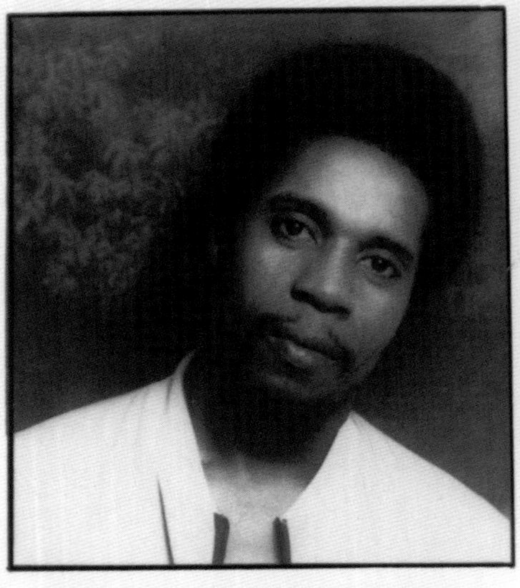

PAUL BARRÈRE

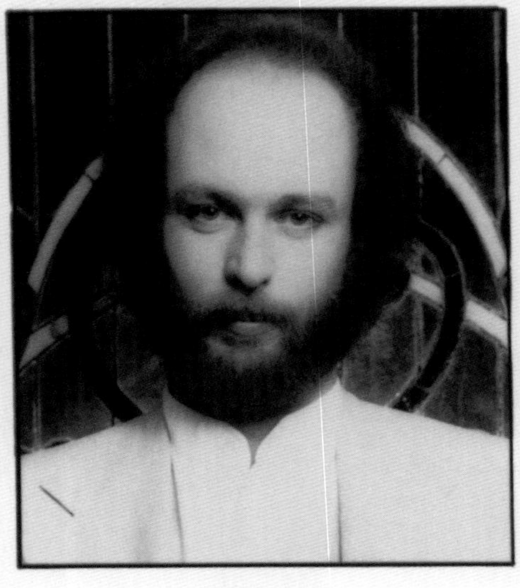

KENNY GRADNEY

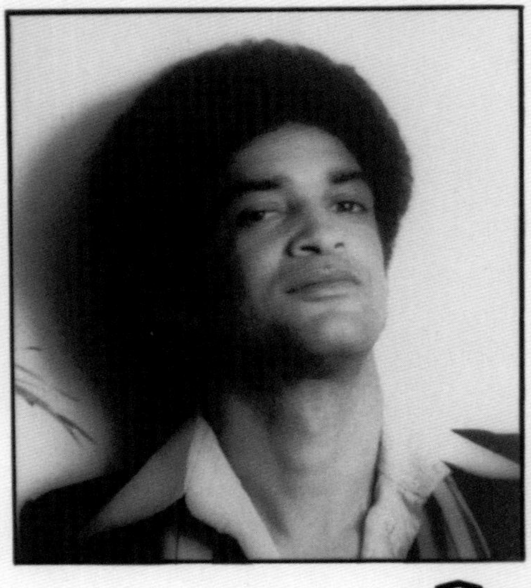

NOVEMBER 1979

LITTLE FEAT

WARNER BROS.

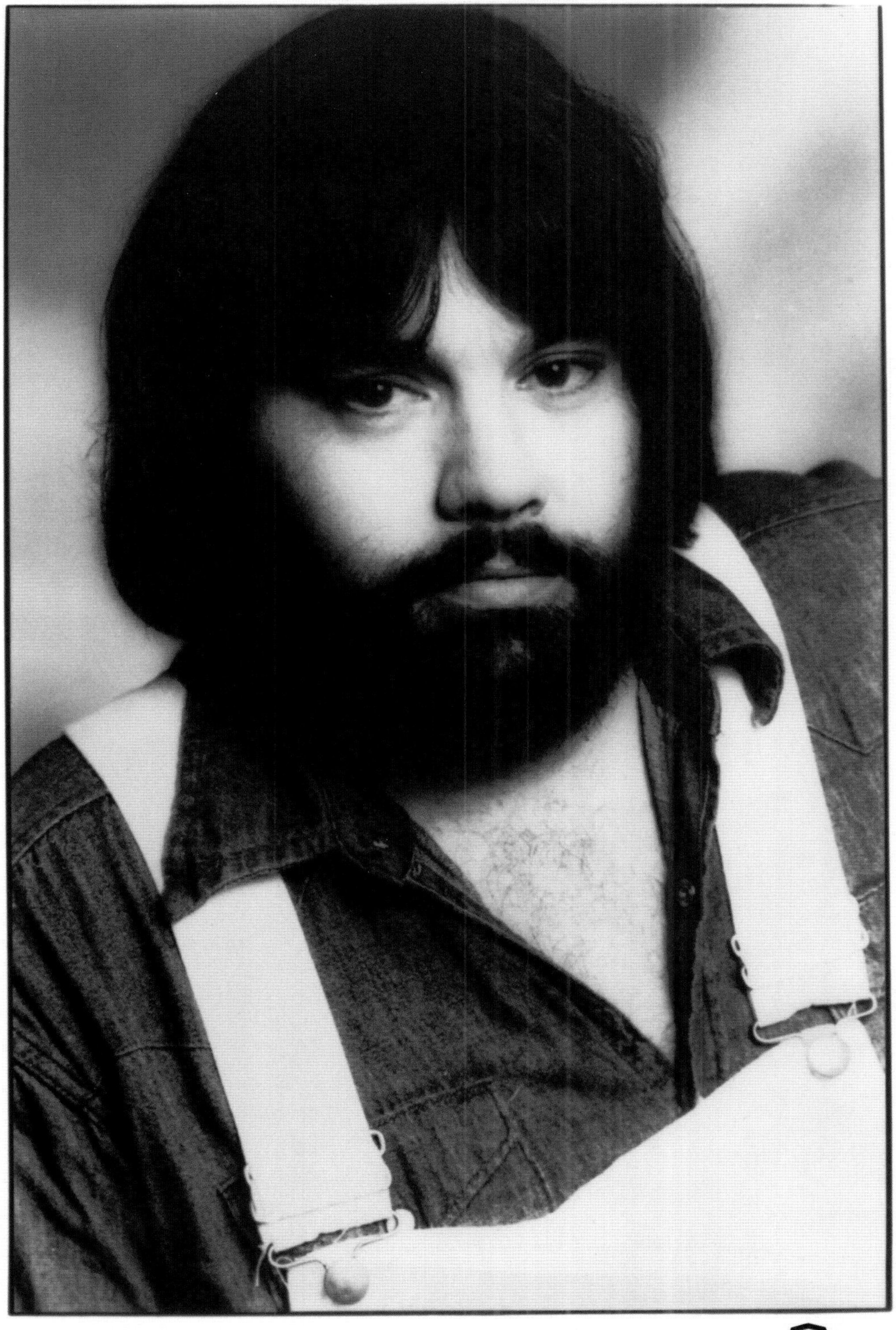

LOWELL GEORGE

WARNER / REPRISE

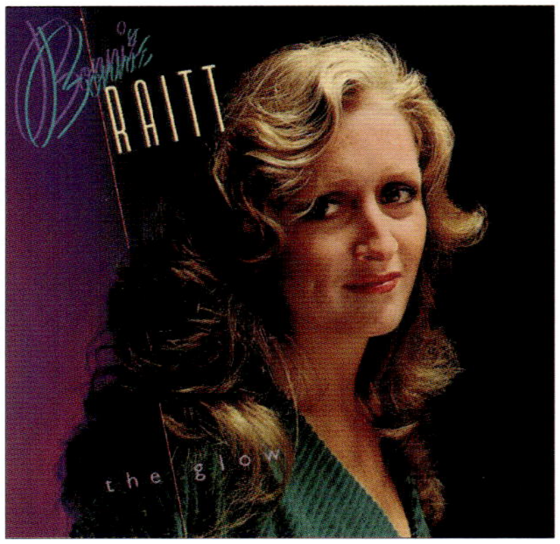

After 1977's revamped version of "Runaway" gave **Bonnie Raitt** her first significant commercial airplay, the singer and guitarist followed up with *The Glow.*

Billboard 200: *The Glow* (#30)
Billboard Hot 100: "You're Gonna Get What's Coming" (#73)

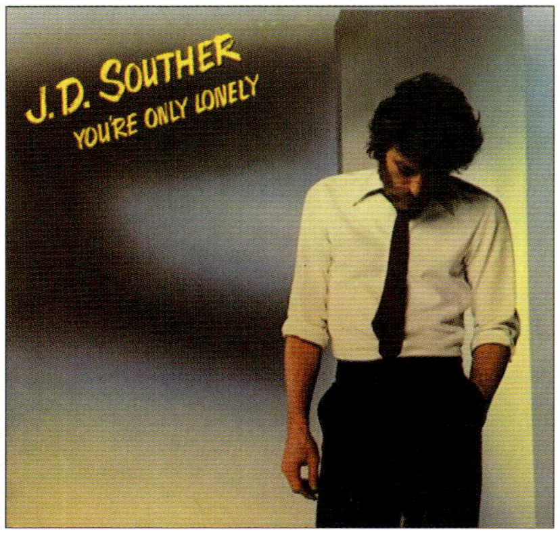

A musician and go-to songwriter for the Eagles and Linda Ronstadt, **J.D. Souther** scored his own No. 1 adult contemporary hit with "You're Only Lonely."

Billboard 200: *You're Only Lonely* (#41)
Billboard Hot 100: "You're Only Lonely" (#7);
"White Rhythm and Blues" (#46)

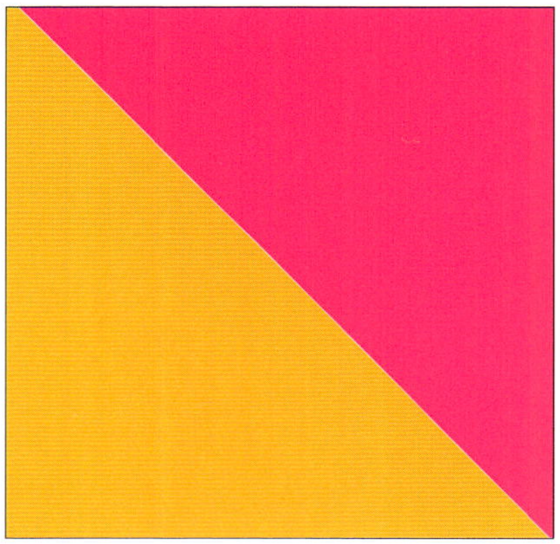

For his album *Flag*, **James Taylor** remade "Up on the Roof," the Drifters' 1963 hit written by Gerry Goffin and Carole King, as a bittersweet reflection.

Billboard 200: *Flag* (#10)
Billboard Hot 100: "Up on the Roof" (#28)

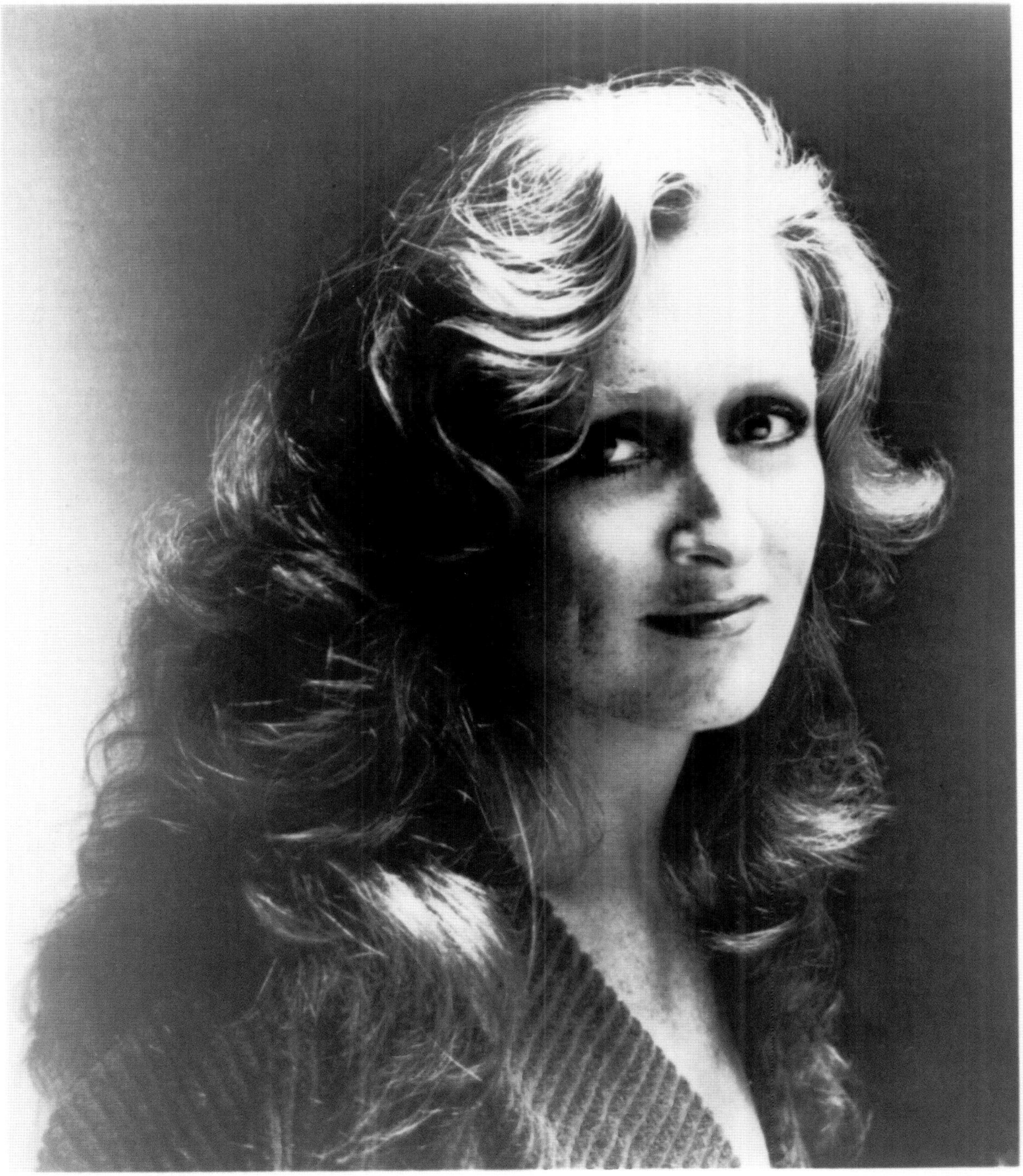

SEPTEMBER 1979

BONNIE RAITT

WARNER BROS.

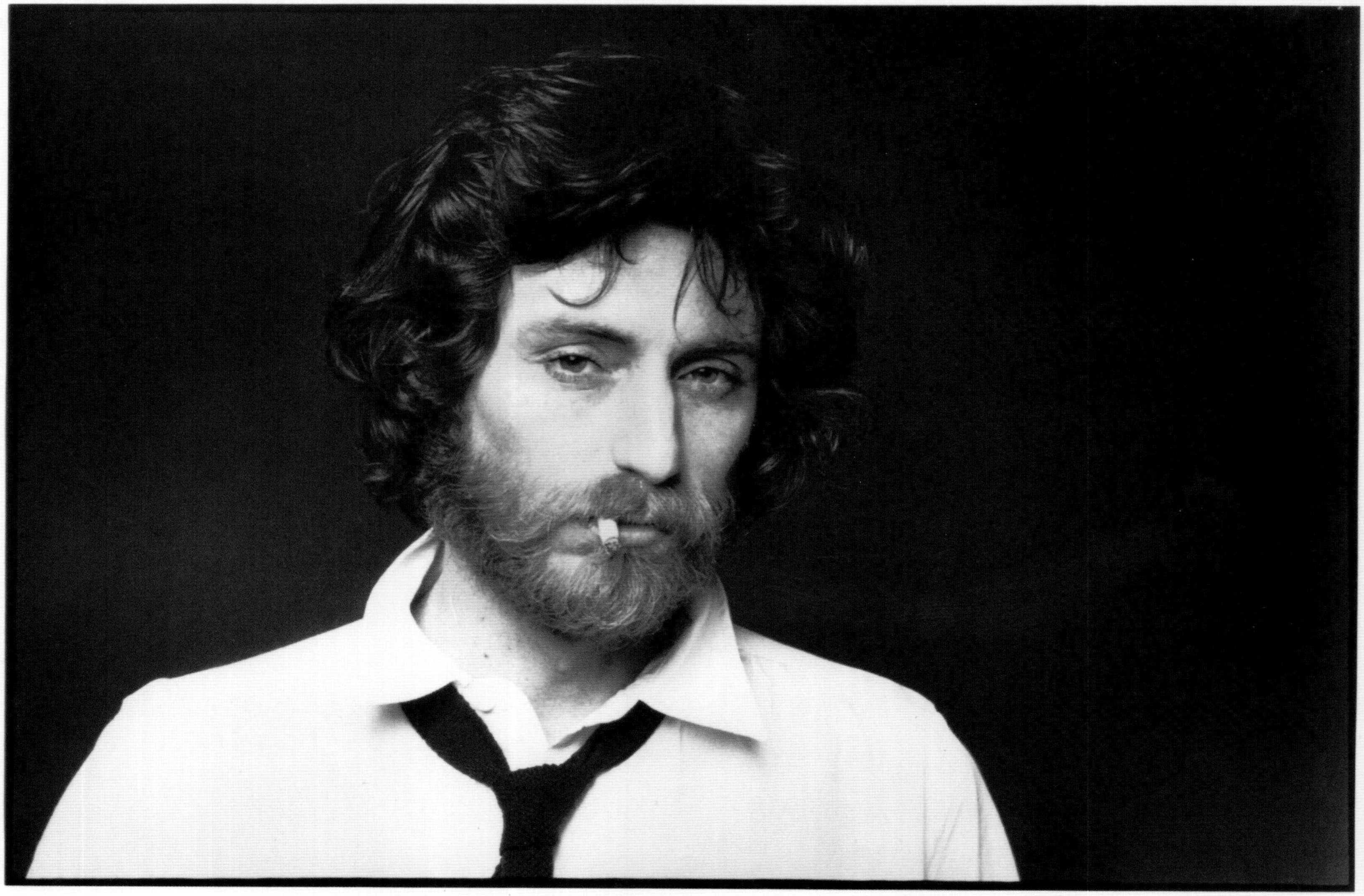

J.D. SOUTHER

Columbia

7908

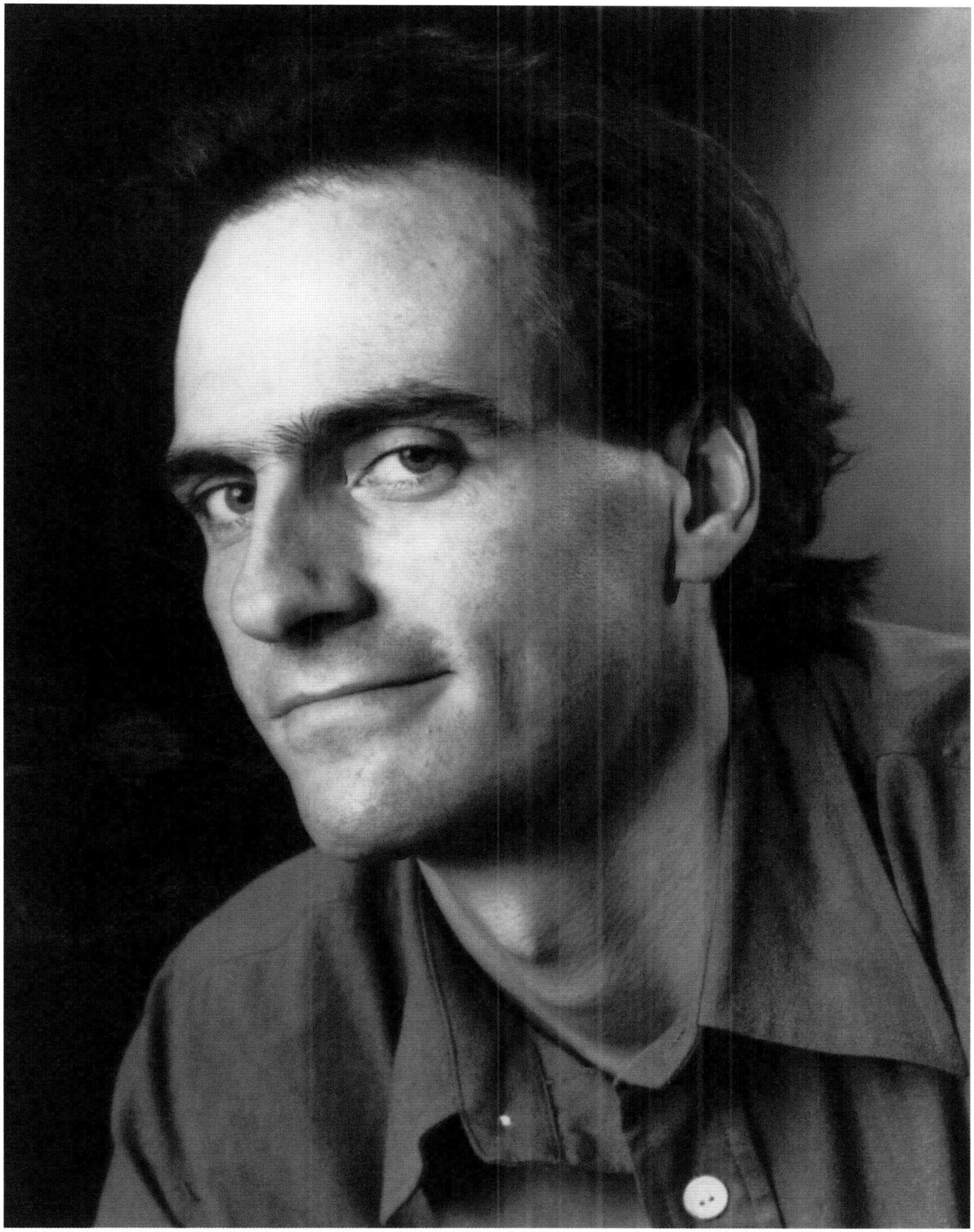

JAMES TAYLOR

Columbia

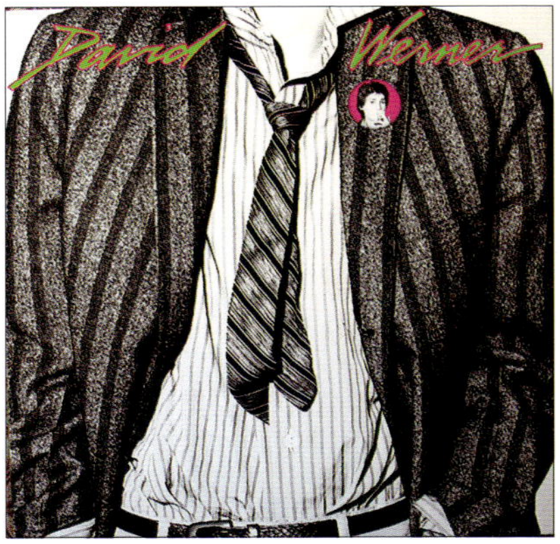

Stirring comparisons to David Bowie, **David Werner** reached the album charts with a self-titled release boosted by the sharp rock single "What's Right."

Billboard 200: *David Werner* (#65)

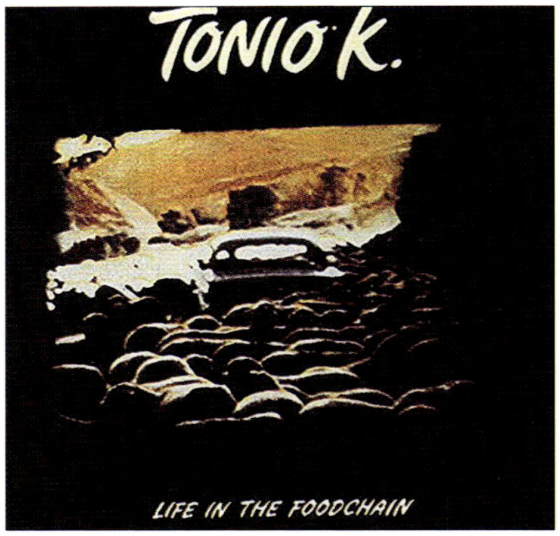

Hailed for the withering wittiness of *Life in the Foodchain*, his debut album, **Tonio K.** anticipated a new dance craze with "The Funky Western Civilization."

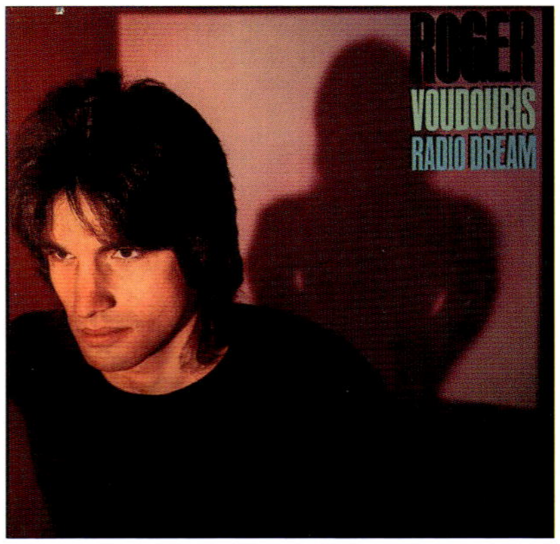

Roger Voudouris partnered with co-writer and producer Michael Omartian to make the pop hit "Get Used to It," featured on his *Radio Dream* album.

Billboard 200: *Radio Dream* (#171)
Billboard Hot 100: "Get Used to It" (#21)

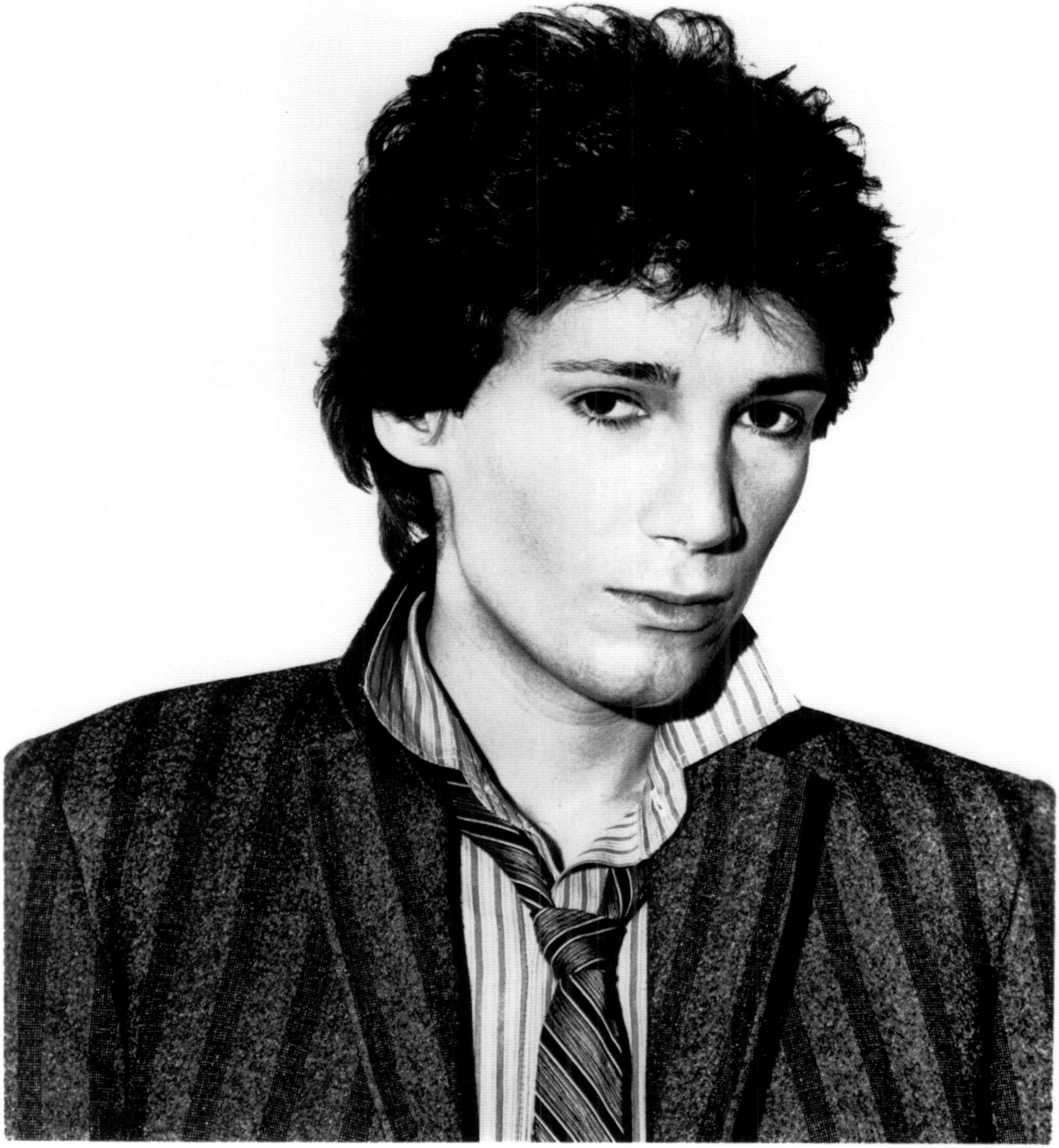

DAVID WERNER

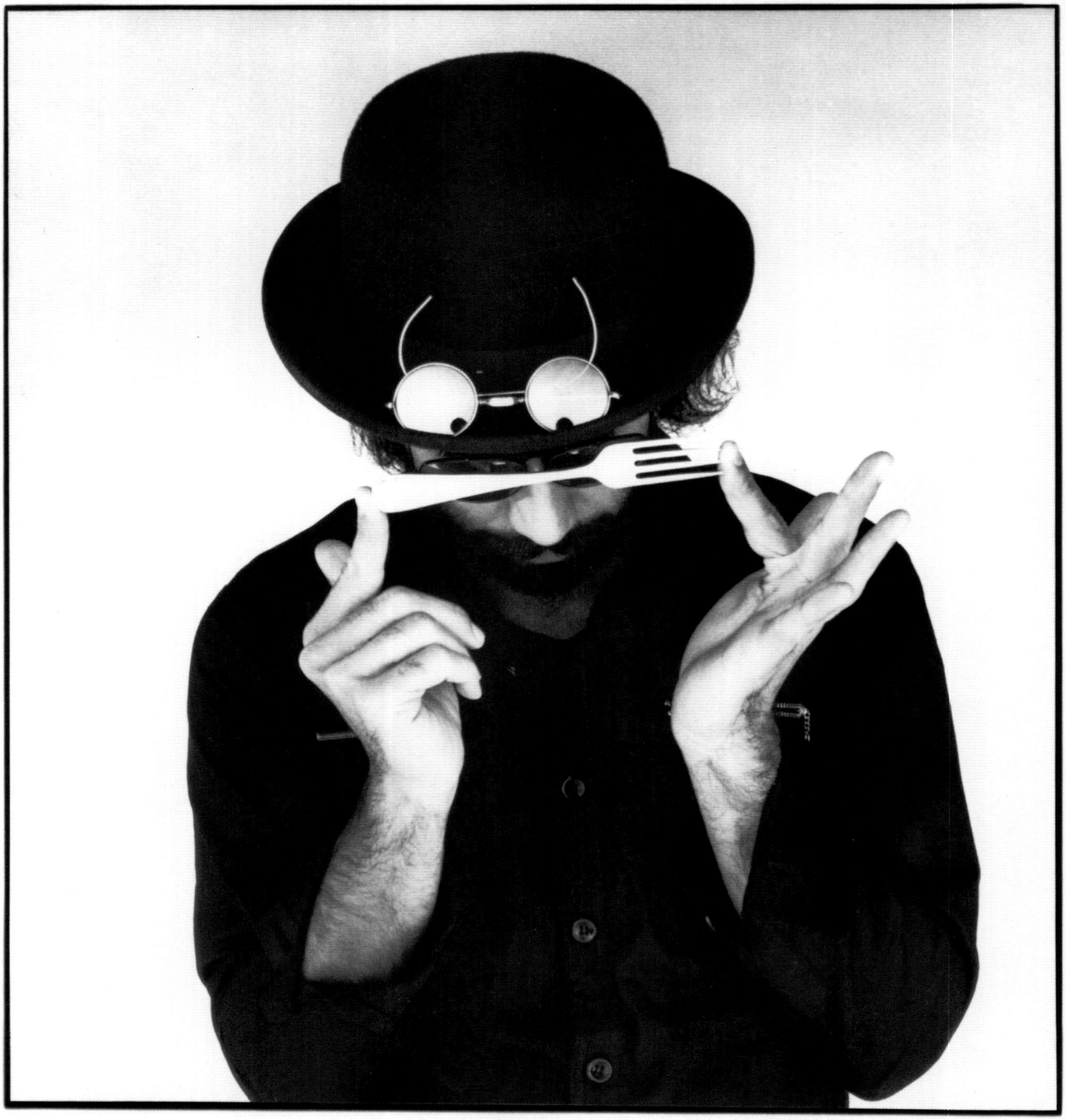

TONIO K

Management:
The Worthless Group

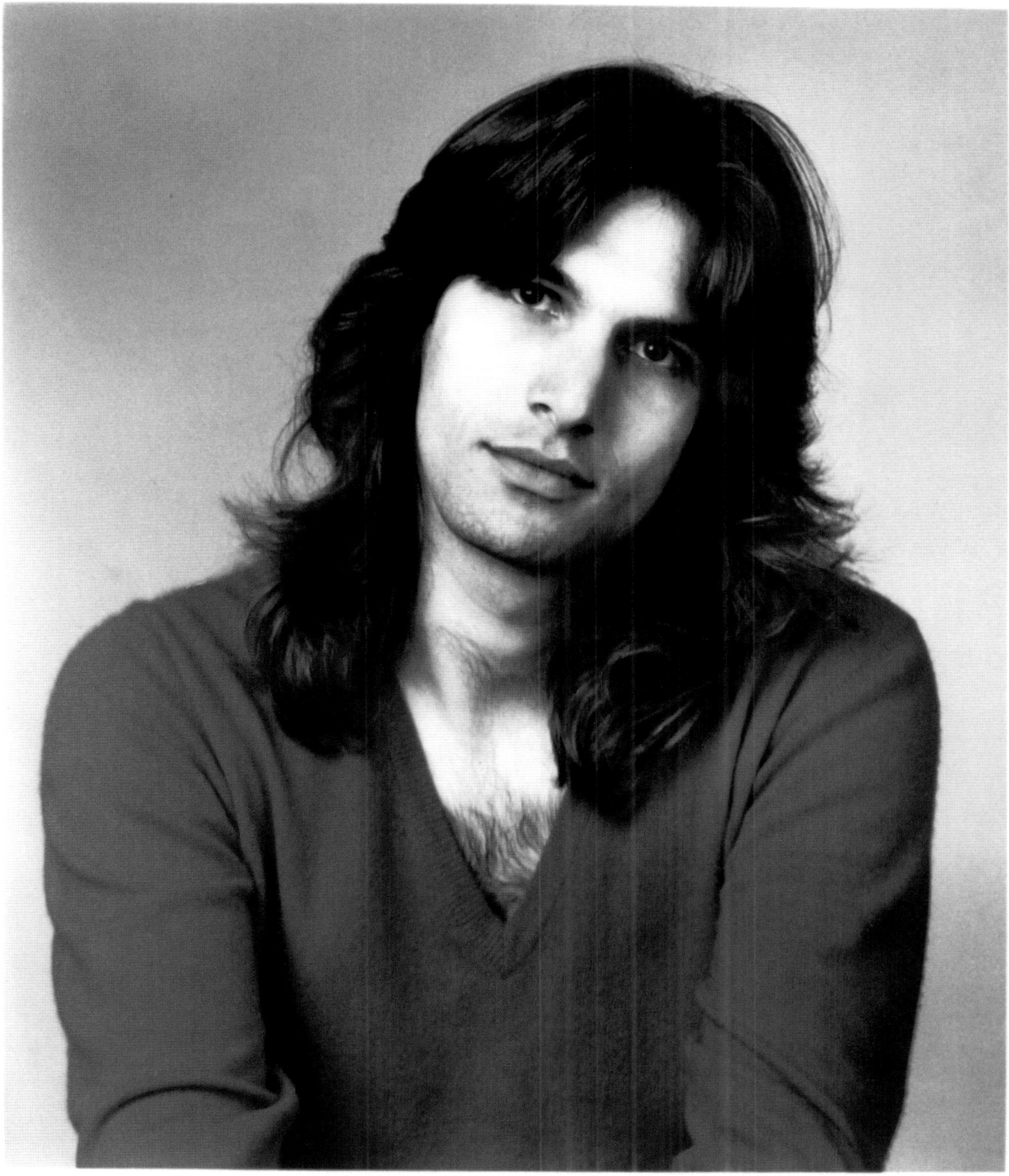

DECEMBER 1979

ROGER VOUDOURIS

WARNER BROS.

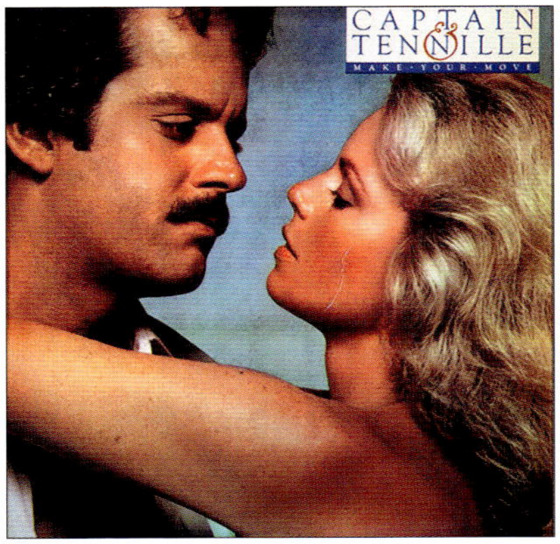

The husband-and-wife duo **Captain & Tennille** demonstrated their pop craftsmanship on "Do That to Me One More Time," achieving a second No. 1 hit.

Billboard 200: *Make Your Move* (#23)
Billboard Hot 100: "Do That to Me One More Time" (No. 1); "Love on a Shoestring" (#55); "Happy Together (A Fantasy)" (#53)

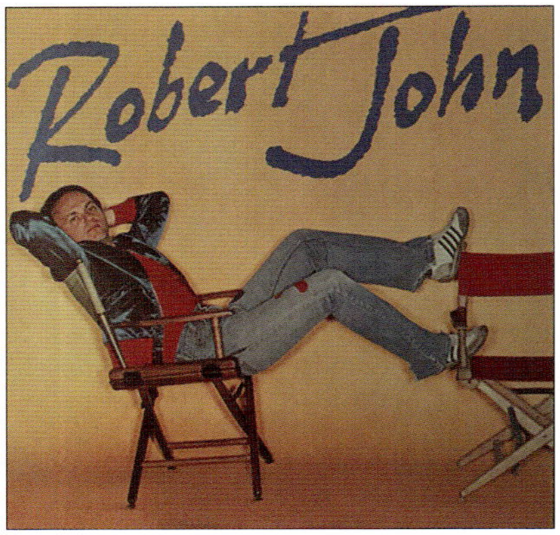

The consolatory ballad "Sad Eyes," recorded by **Robert John**, was one of the year's few songs not influenced by disco to reach the top of the pop charts.

Billboard 200: *Robert John* (#68)
Billboard Hot 100: "Sad Eyes" (No. 1); "Lonely Eyes" (#41)

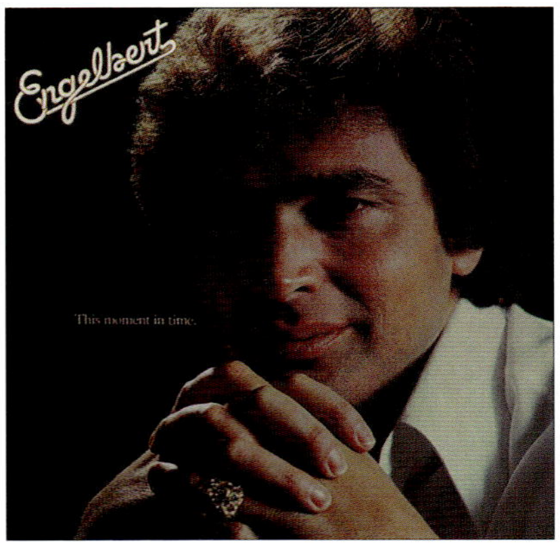

Singer **Engelbert Humperdinck**, whose ballad "Release Me" made him a star in 1967, again topped adult contemporary playlists with "This Moment in Time."

Billboard 200: *This Moment in Time* (#164)
Billboard Hot 100: "This Moment in Time" (#58)

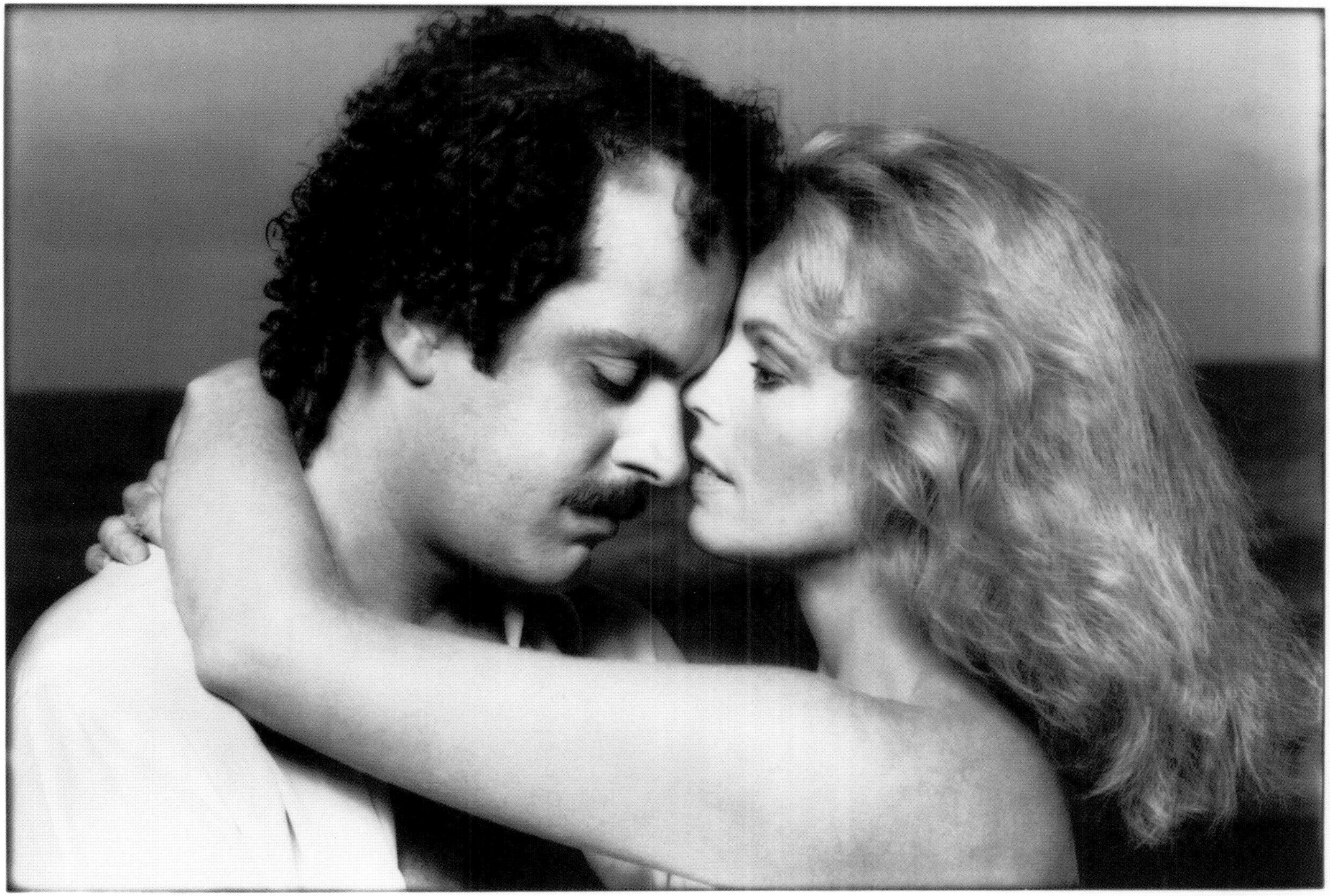

Casablanca Record and FilmWorks

Captain & Tennille

XXXX

Moonlight & Magnolias Inc.

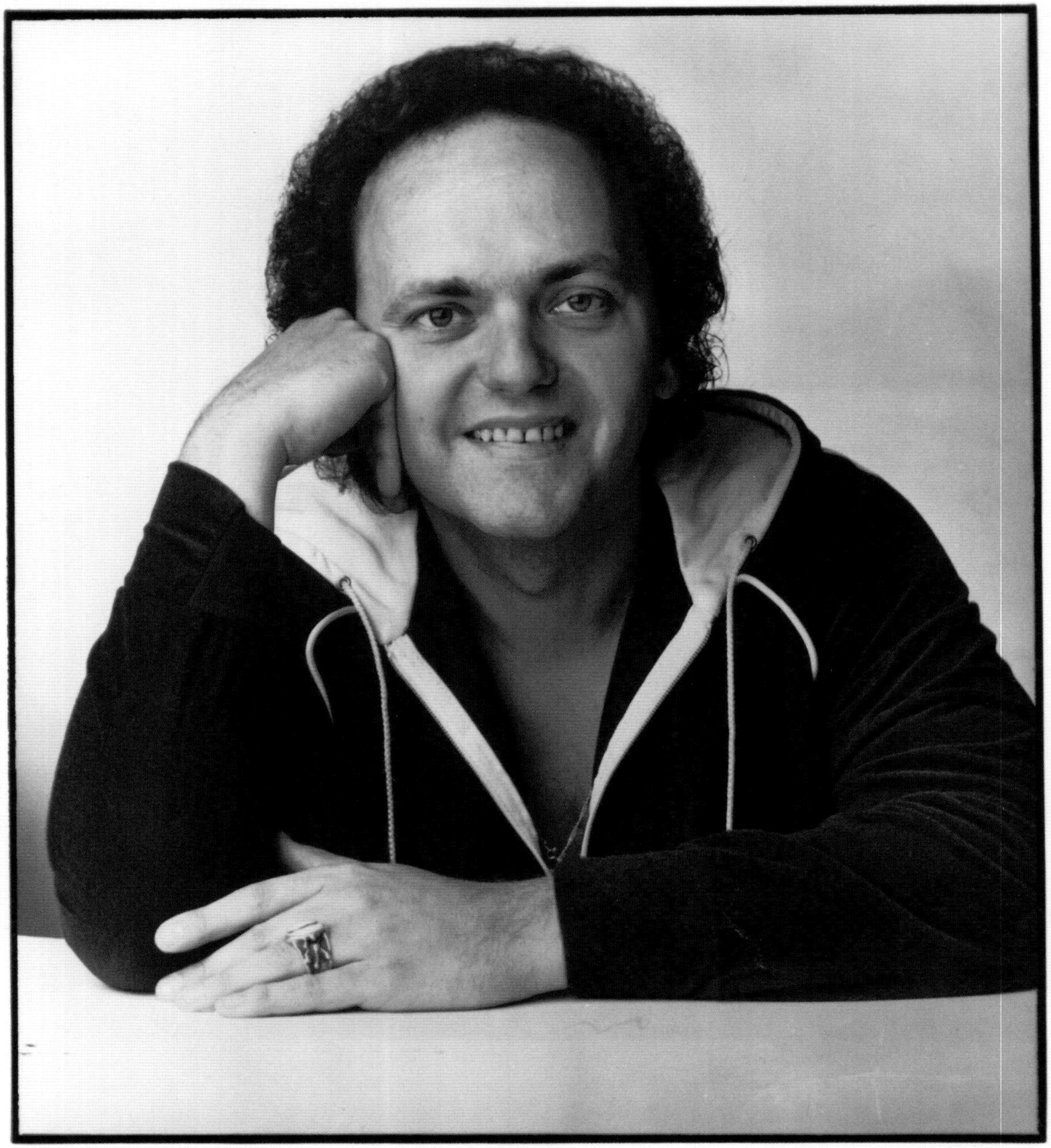

ROBERT JOHN

EMI AMERICA

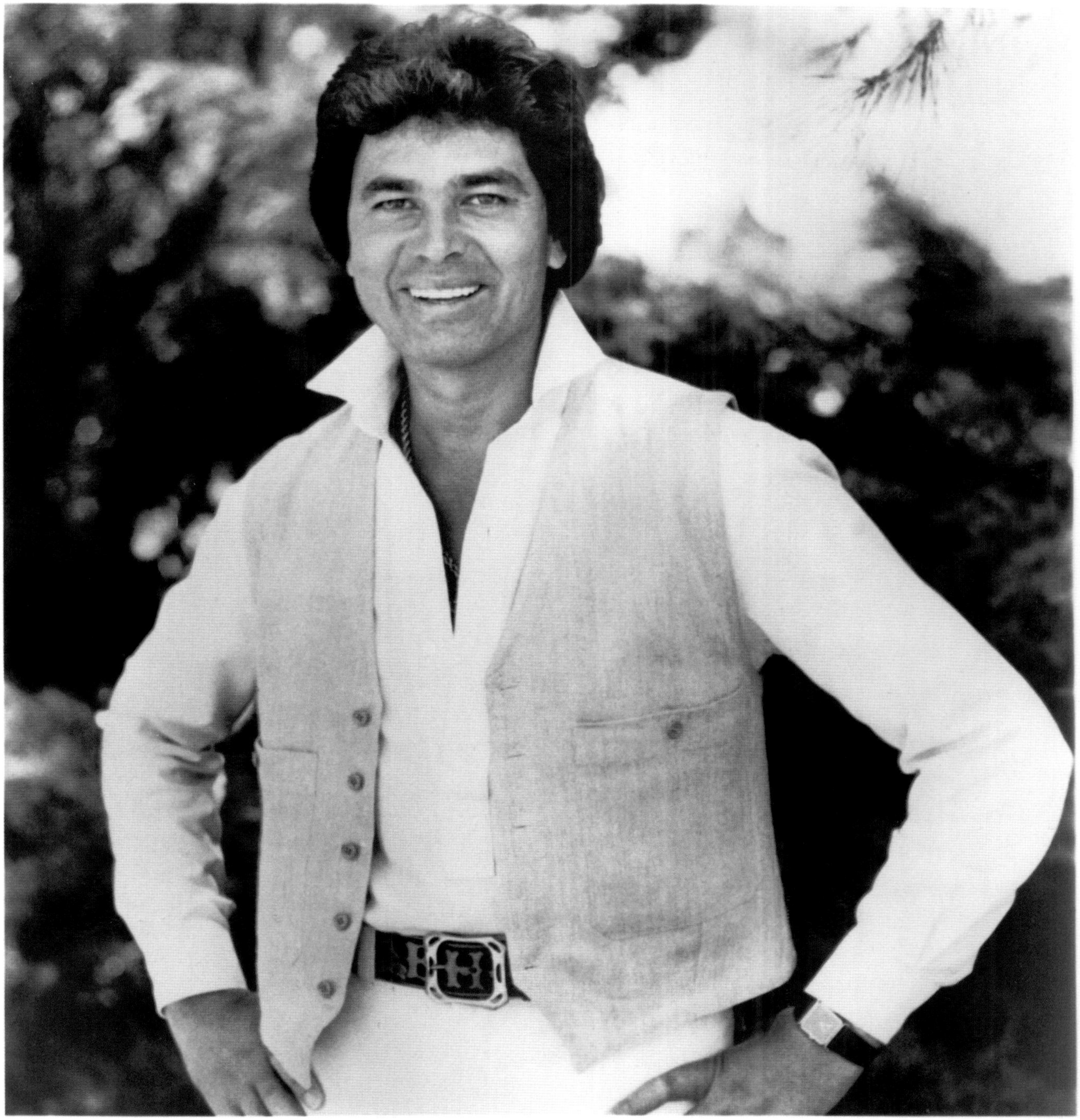

ENGELBERT

Personal Management:
HAROLD DAVISON
9601 Wilshire Blvd , #320
Beverly Hills, Ca , 90210

Representation:
International
Creative
Management

Public Relations:
Press Services Int
1100 Glendon Avenue #1749
Los Angeles Ca 90024

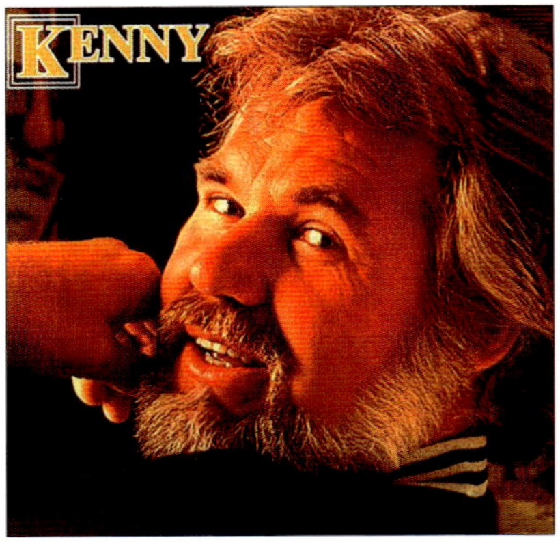

Kenny reinforced **Kenny Rogers**' pop culture success with the No. 1 country smash "You Decorated My Life" and the worldwide hit "Coward of the County."

Billboard 200: *Kenny* (#5)
Billboard Hot 100: "You Decorated My Life" (#7);
"Coward of the County" (#3)

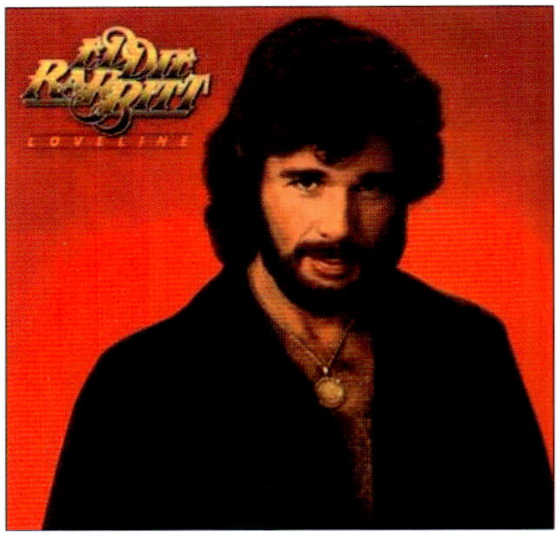

From the album *Loveline*, the R&B-imbued "Suspicions" cemented **Eddie Rabbitt**'s crossover cred, No. 1 on the country music charts and a Top 20 pop hit.

Billboard 200: *Loveline* (#91)
Billboard Hot 100: "Suspicions" (#13); "Gone Too Far" (#82)

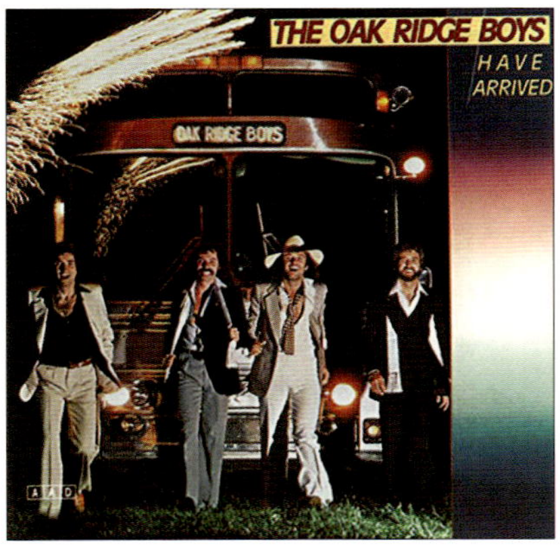

The Oak Ridge Boys' "Leaving Louisiana in the Broad Daylight" provided the group with its second No. 1 country single, co-written by Rodney Crowell.

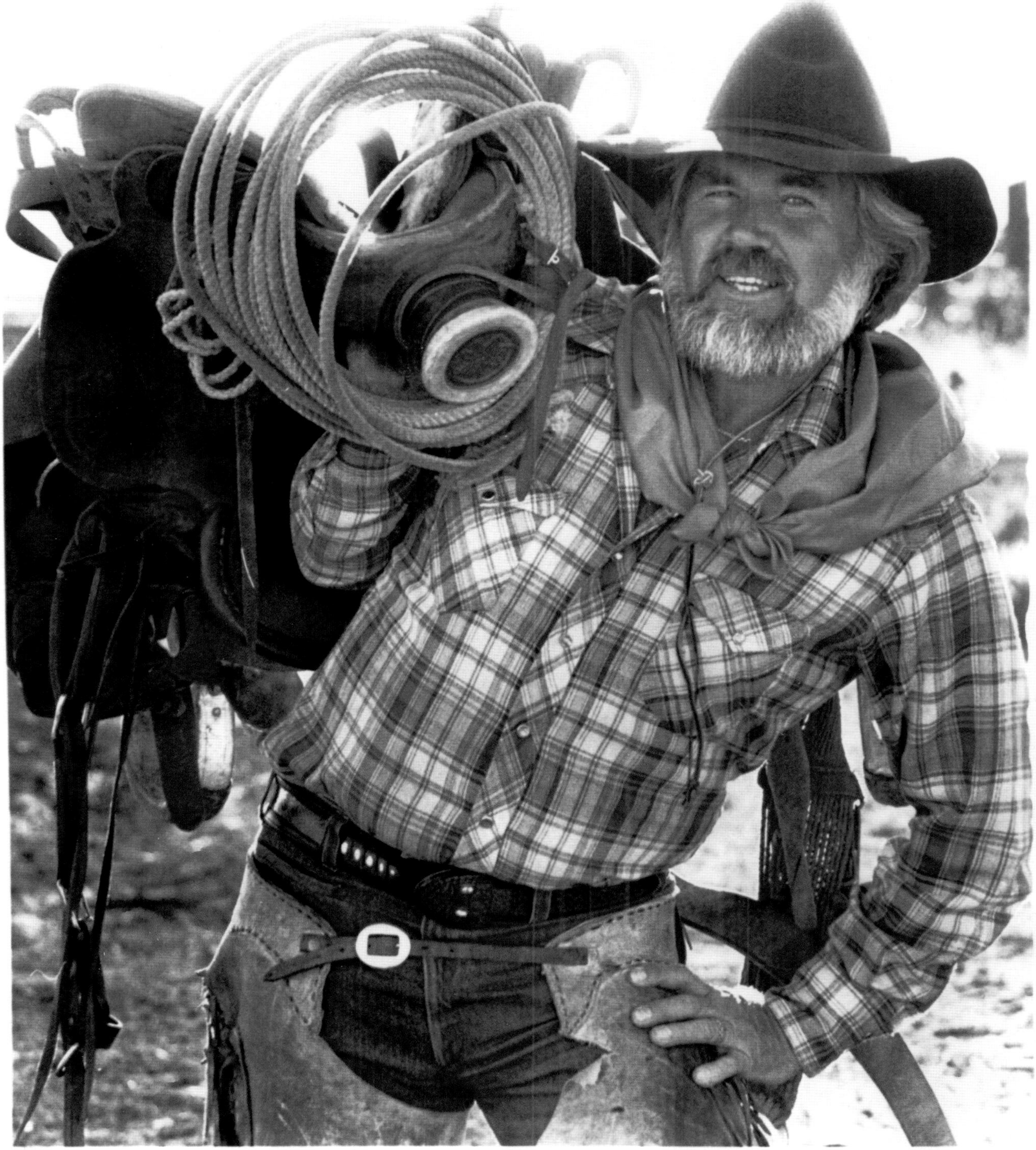

KENNY ROGERS

UNITED ARTISTS RECORDS

Management:
KRAGEN & COMPANY
1112 N Sherbourne Drive
Los Angeles, California 90069
(213) 659-7914

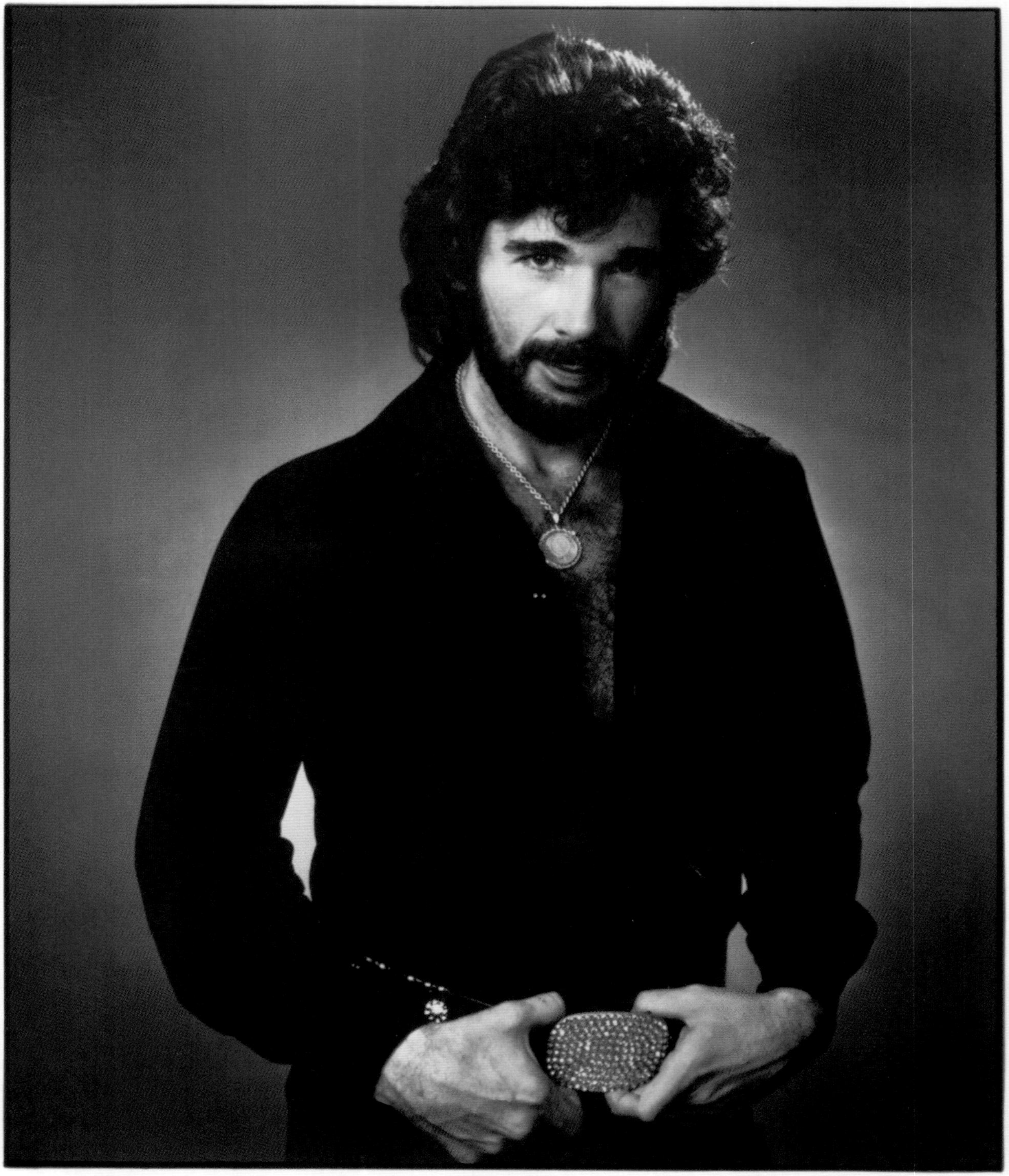
Photo Credit: LYNN GOLDSMITH

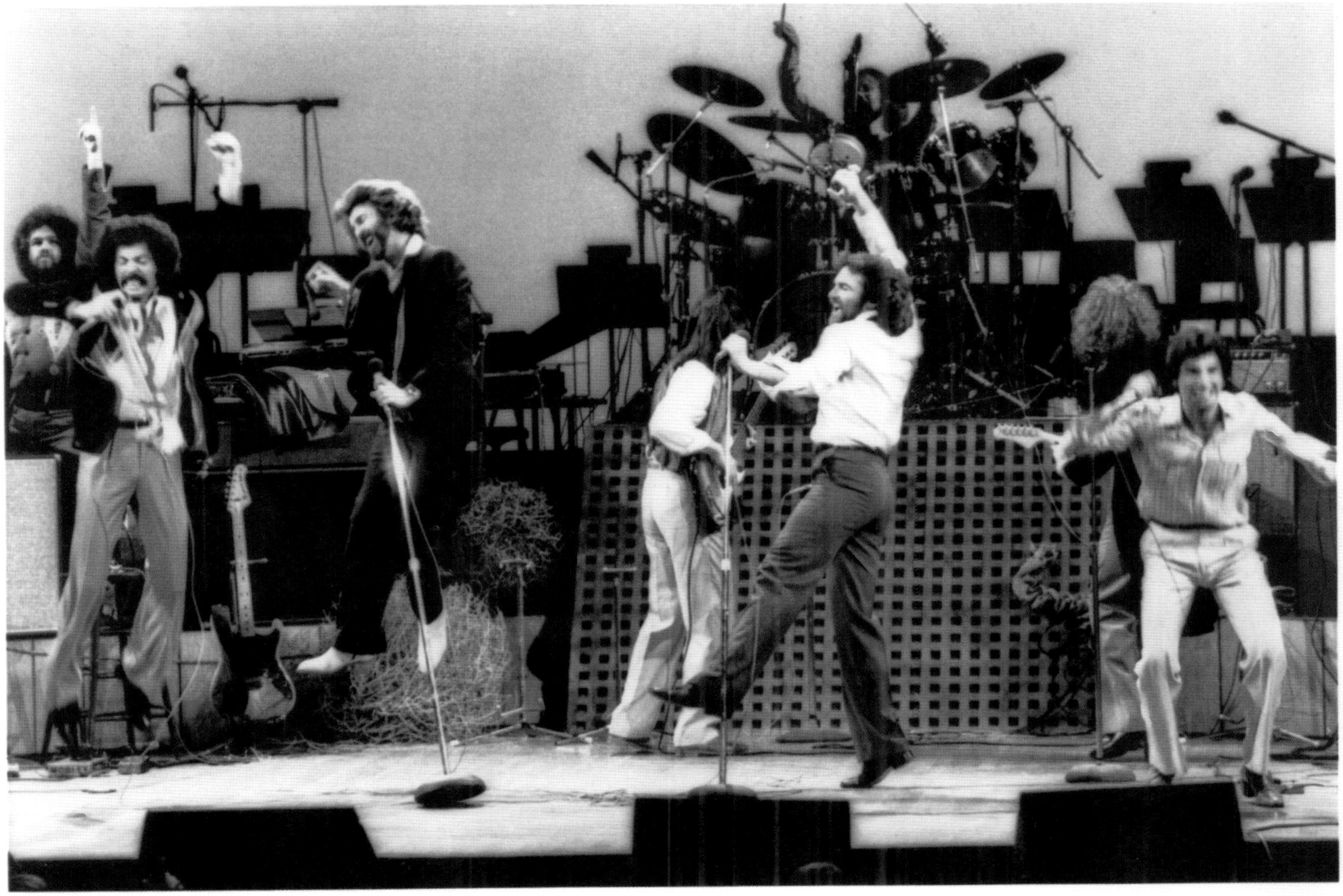

MCA RECORDS

The Oak Ridge Boys

THE JIM HALSEY CO. INC
PENTHOUSE CORPORATE PLACE
5800 EAST SKELLY DRIVE
TULSA, OKLAHOMA 74135
(918) 663-3883

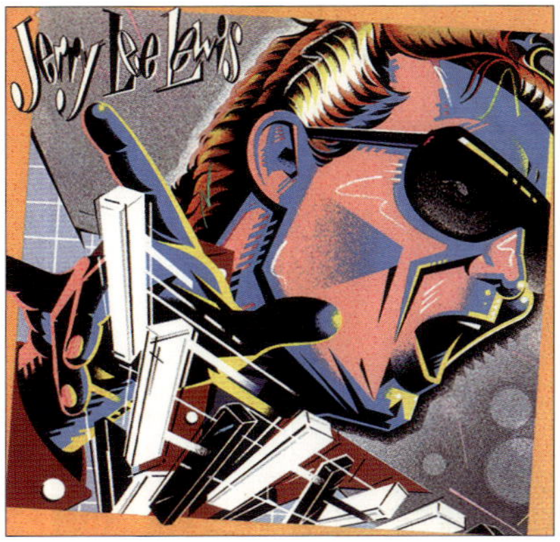

Rock 'n' roll pioneer **Jerry Lee Lewis** switched record labels and delivered two lauded singles, "Rockin' My Life Away" and "Who Will the Next Fool Be?"

Billboard 200: *Jerry Lee Lewis* (#186)

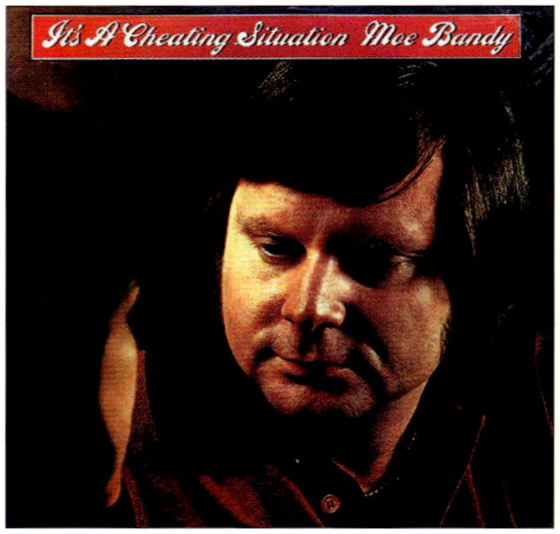

"It's a Cheating Situation," recorded by honky-tonk king **Moe Bandy** with Janie Fricke, won the Song of the Year award from the Academy of Country Music.

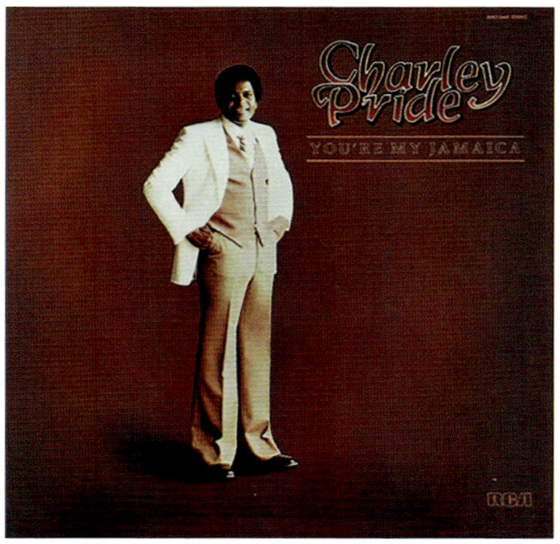

Veteran performer **Charley Pride** continued to earn hits on the country charts with "You're My Jamaica," his 22nd No. 1 single, and the #2 "Missin' You."

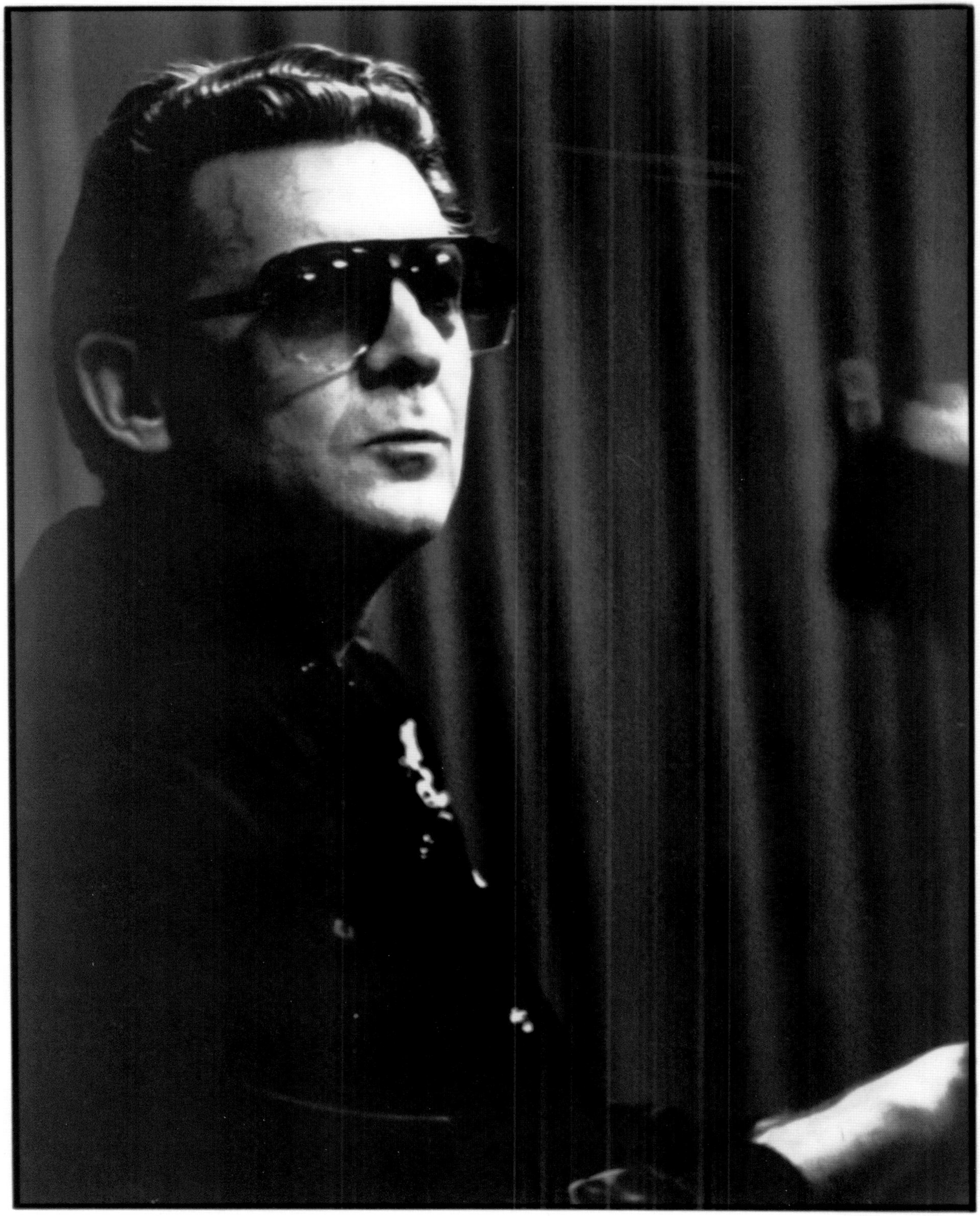

Photo Credit: ETHAN RUSSELL

JERRY LEE LEWIS

elektra

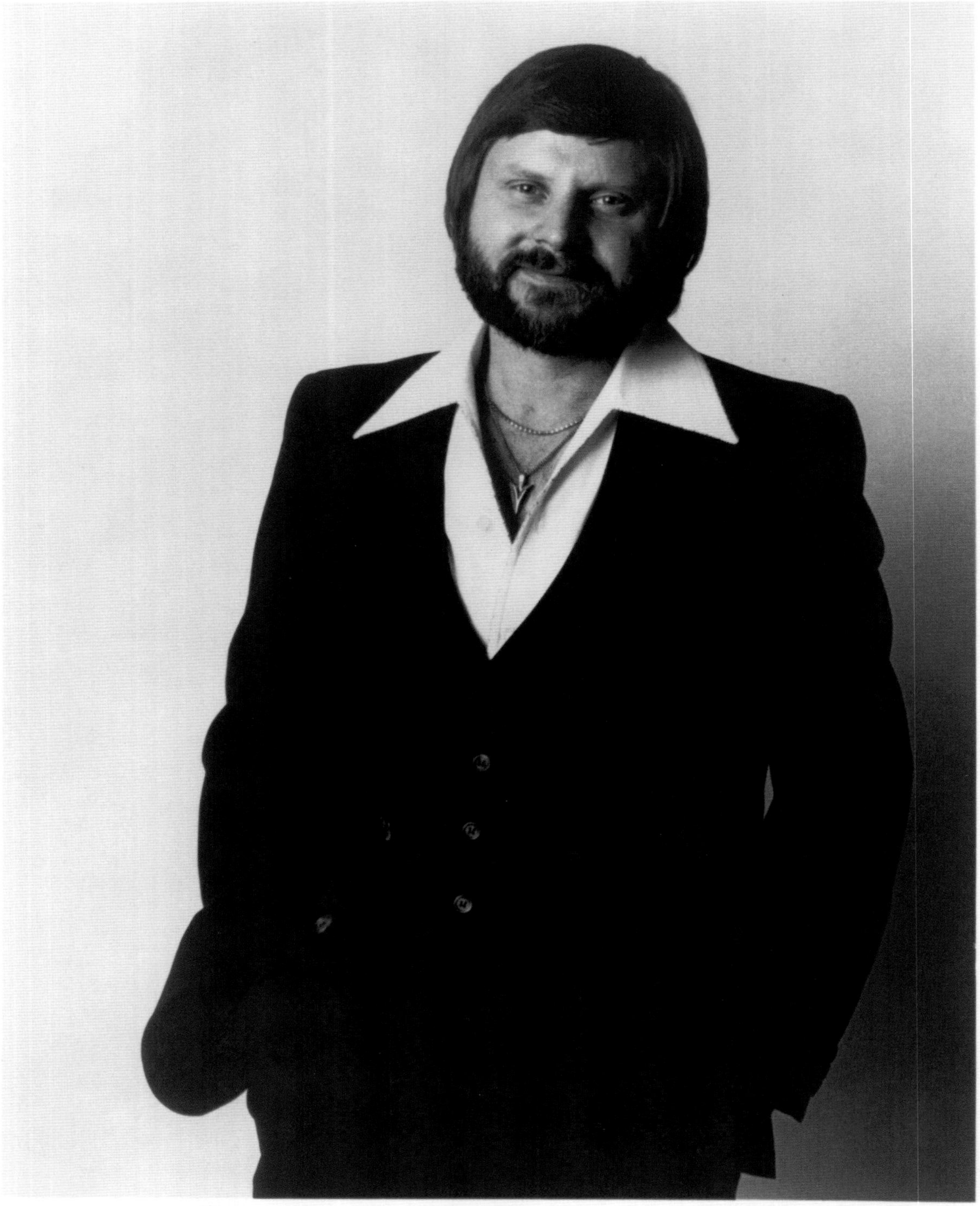

MOE BANDY

Columbia

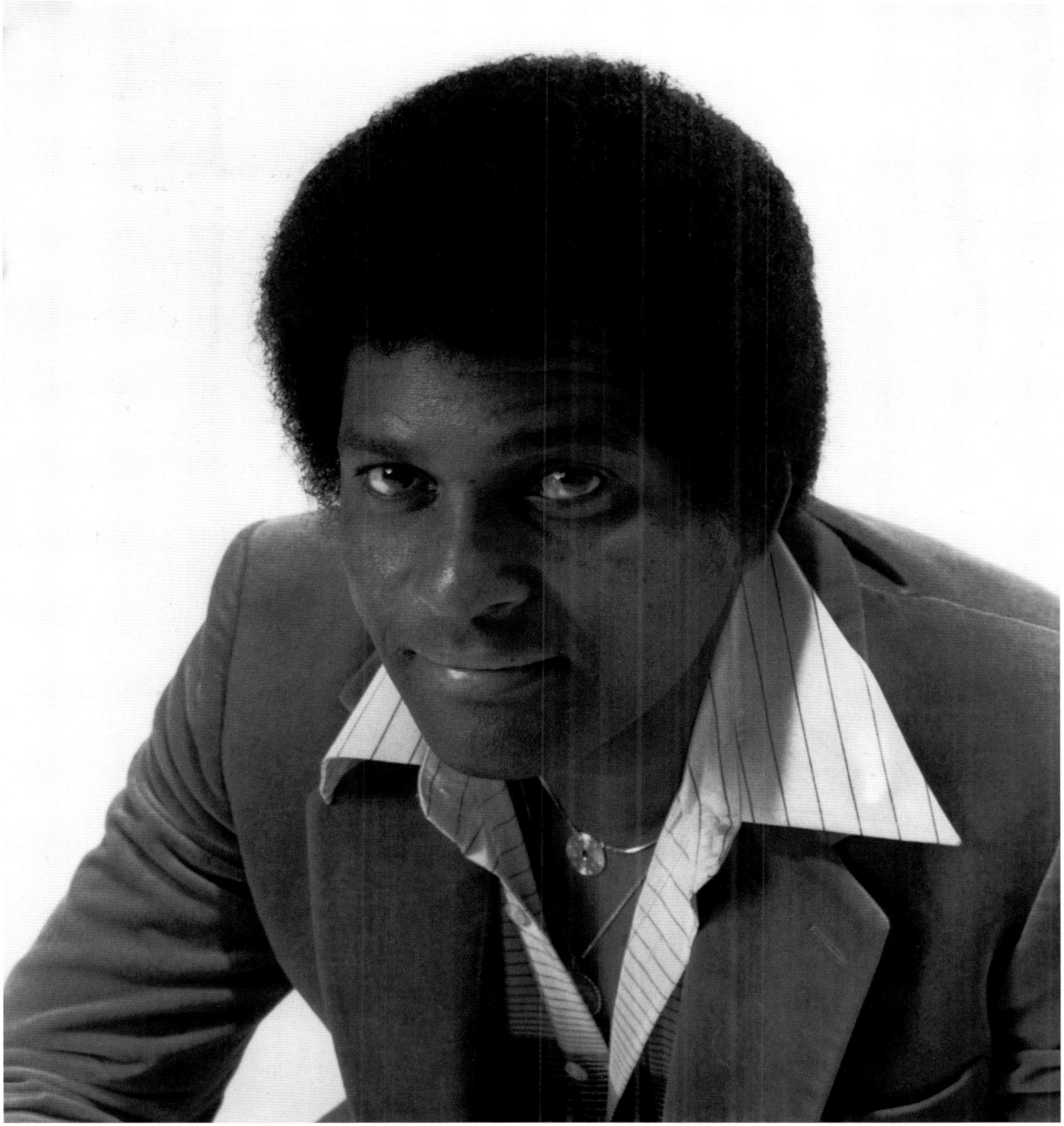

Exclusively on RCA

CHARLEY PRIDE

Chardon INC

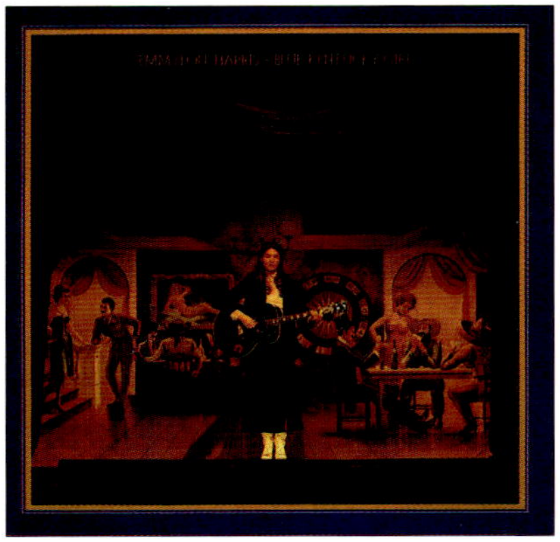

Blue Kentucky Girl marked **Emmylou Harris**' return to a pure country sound, and the recording of "Beneath Still Waters" earned her a No. 1 country hit.

Billboard 200: *Blue Kentucky Girl* (#43)

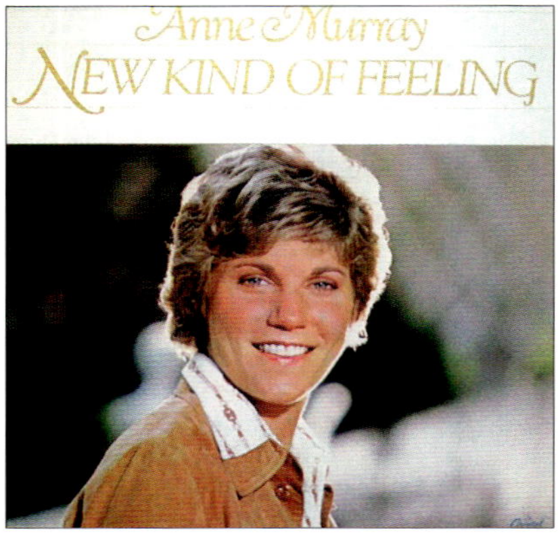

"Shadows in the Moonlight" and "I Just Fall in Love Again," from **Anne Murray**'s *New Kind of Feeling*, topped country and adult contemporary charts.

Billboard 200: *New Kind of Feeling* (#23)
Billboard Hot 100: "I Just Fall in Love Again" (#12);
"Shadows in the Moonlight" (#25)

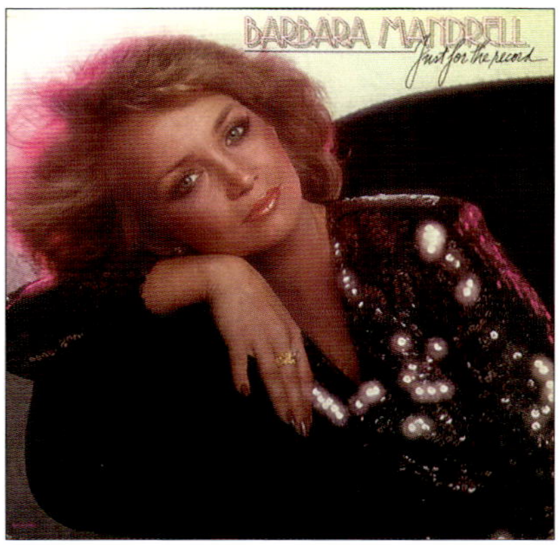

Led to a pop-style sound by producer Tom Collins, singer **Barbara Mandrell** added to her string of No. 1 singles on the country charts with "Years."

Billboard 200: *Just for the Record* (#166)
Billboard Hot 100: "Fooled by a Feeling" (#89)

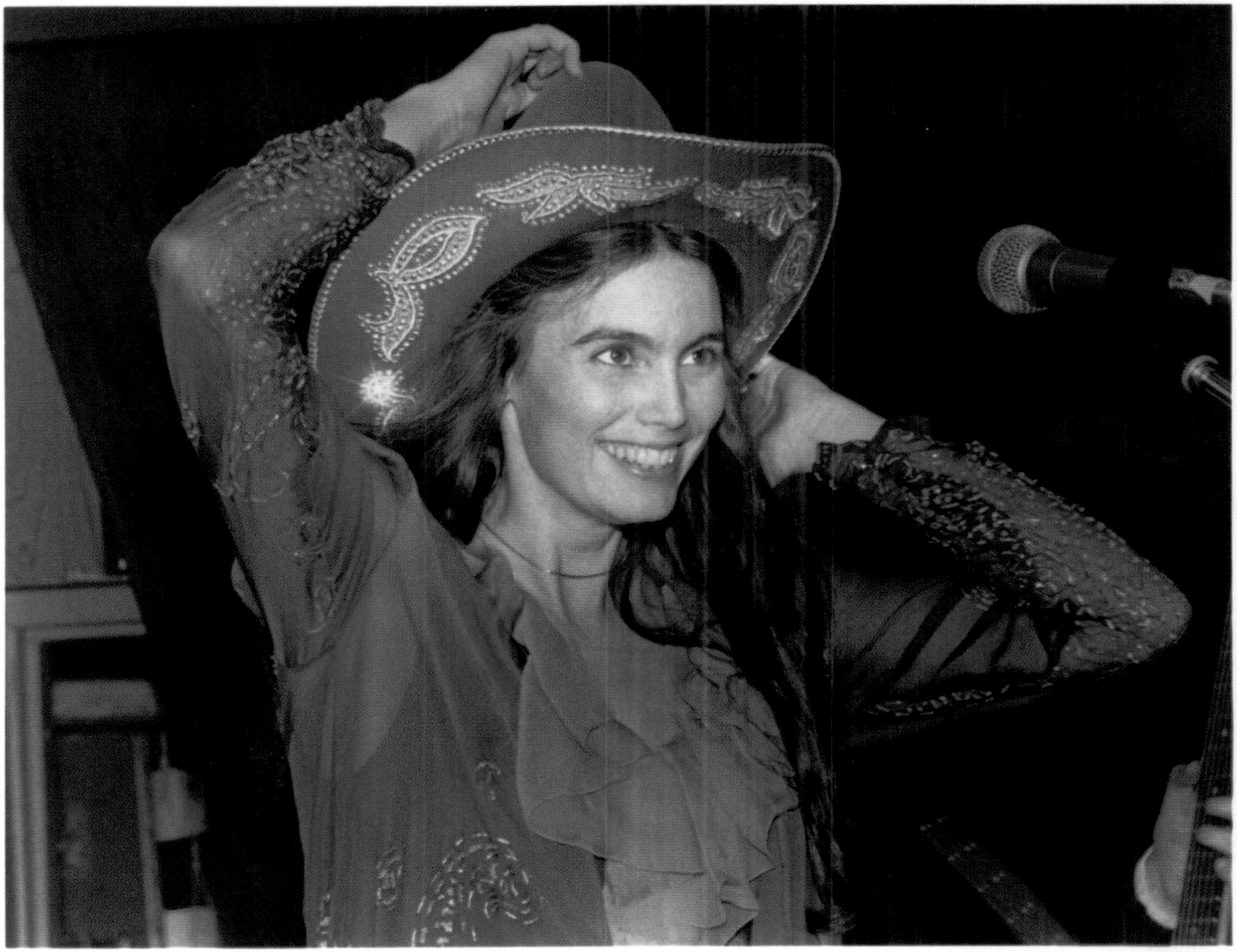

PHOTO CREDIT: BY DON

EMMYLOU HARRIS

WARNER / REPRISE

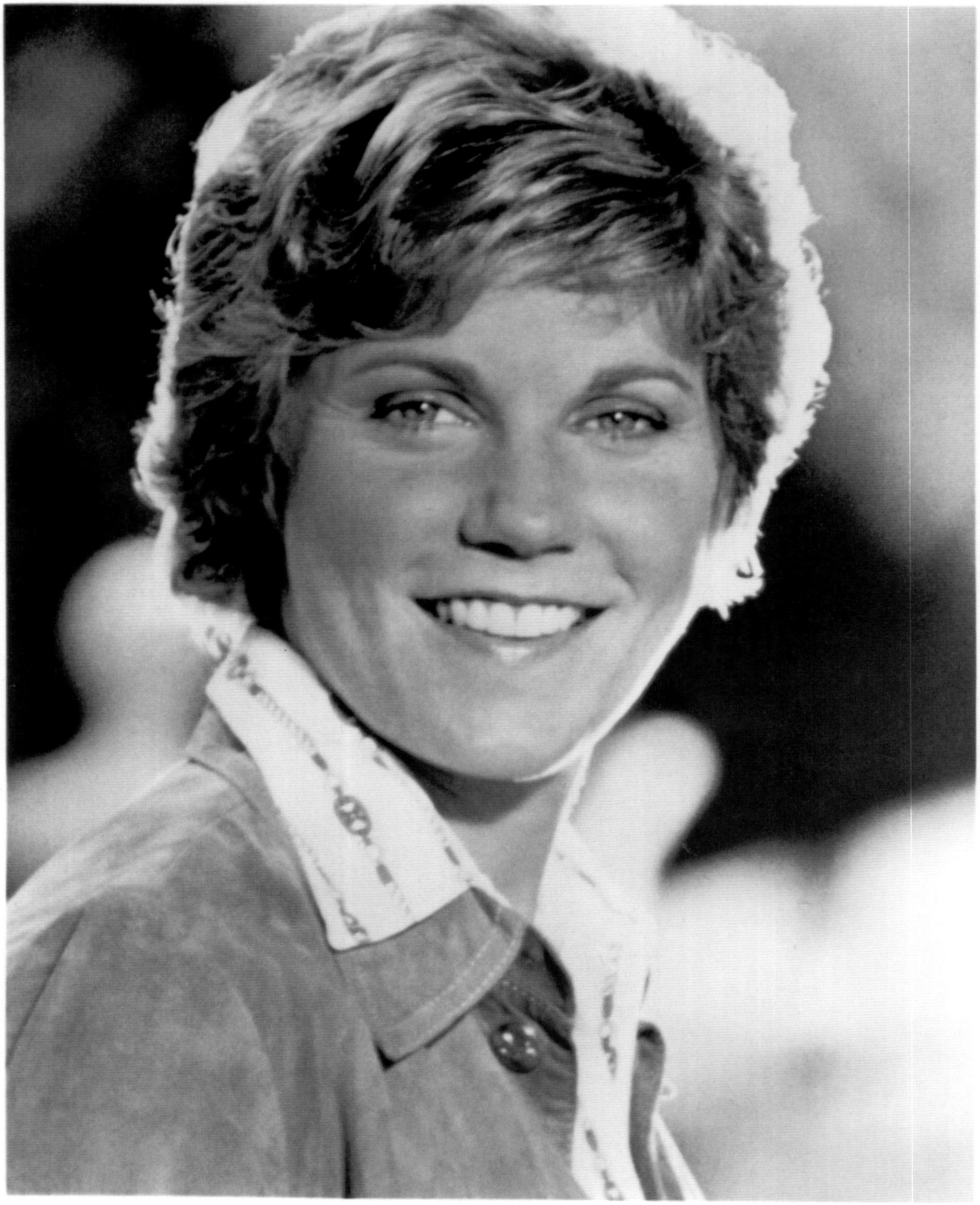

ANNE MURRAY

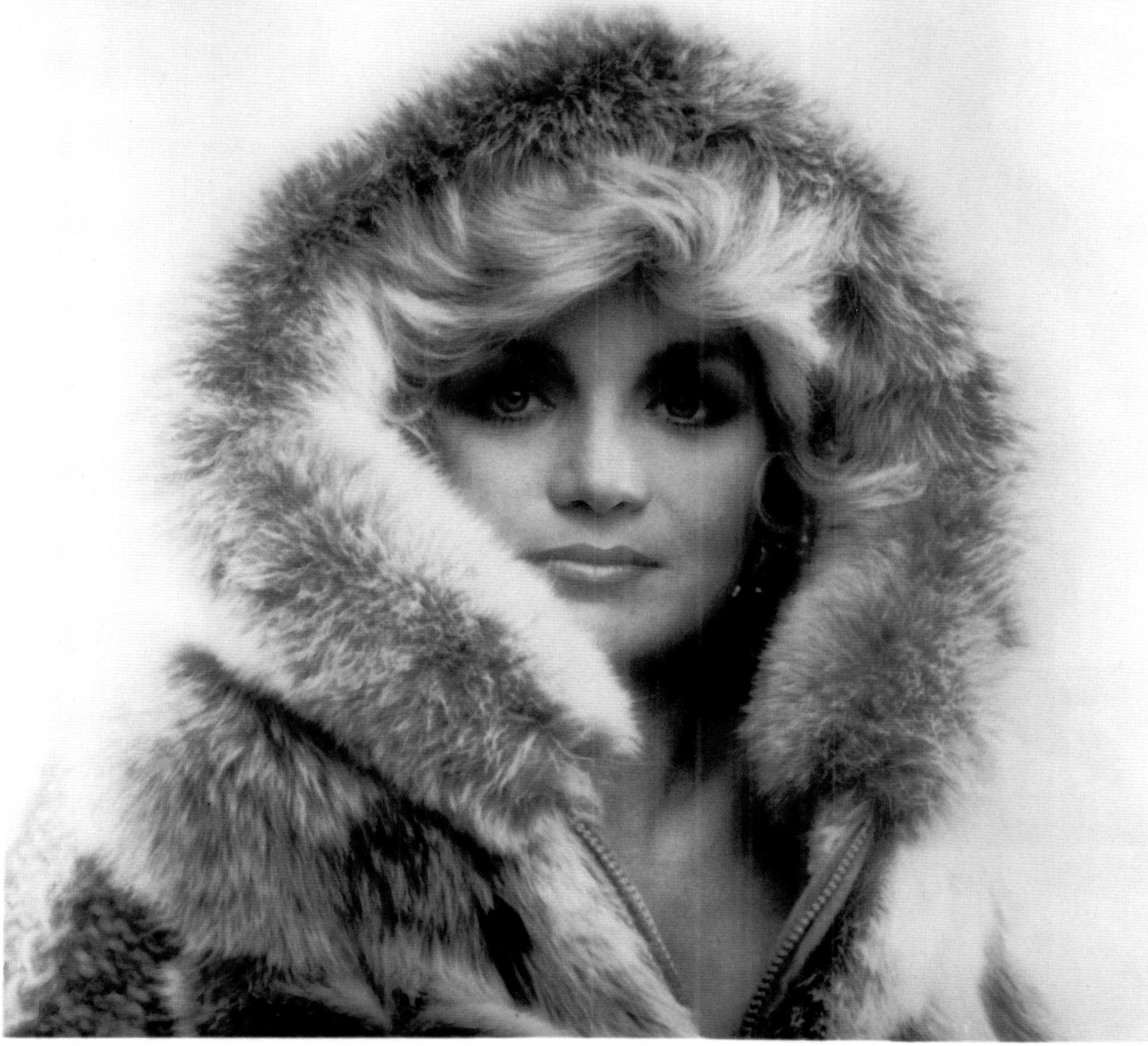

abc Records™

BARBARA MANDRELL

Irby Mandrell
Personal Manager
P O Box 23110
Nashville, Tn 37202
615/244-7530

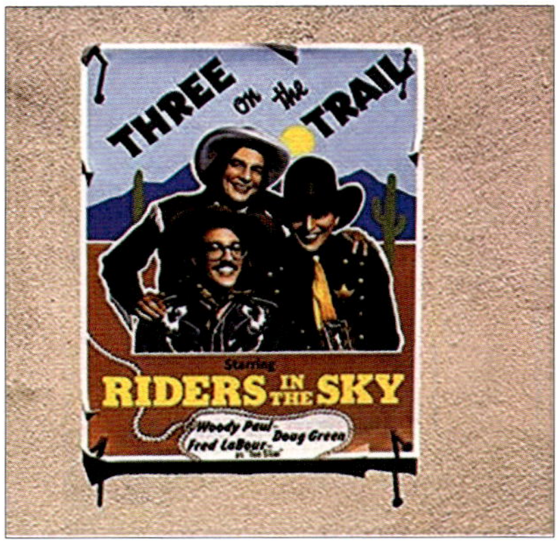

Three on the Trail, **Riders in the Sky**'s recording debut, manifested a sentimental, tongue-in-cheek tribute to Western cowboy songs and harmony singing.

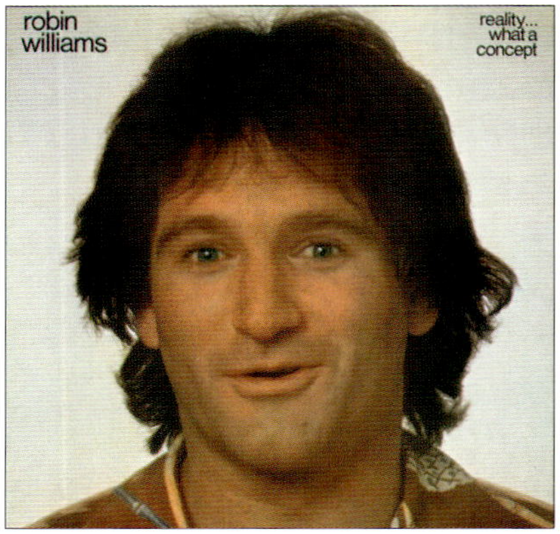

Comedy luminary **Robin Williams** mobilized his maniacal, improvisational style on a Grammy-winning debut album, recorded live at his nightclub shows.

Billboard 200: *Reality...What a Concept* (#10)

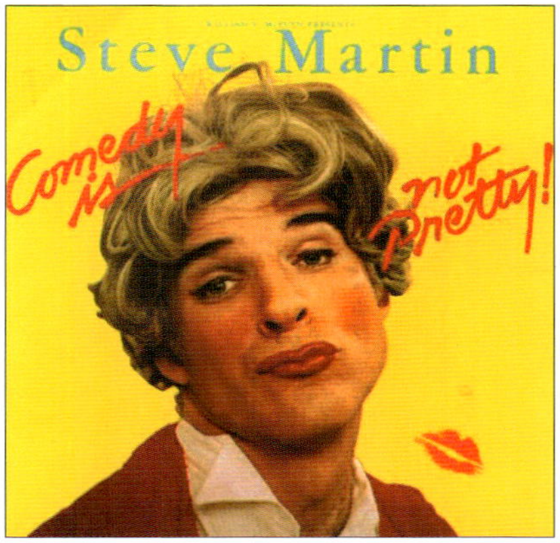

In the midst of writing the screenplay for the motion picture *The Jerk*, **Steve Martin** recorded his stand-up routine for the album *Comedy Is Not Pretty!*

Billboard 200: *Comedy Is Not Pretty!* (#25)
Billboard Hot 100: "Cruel Shoes" (#91)

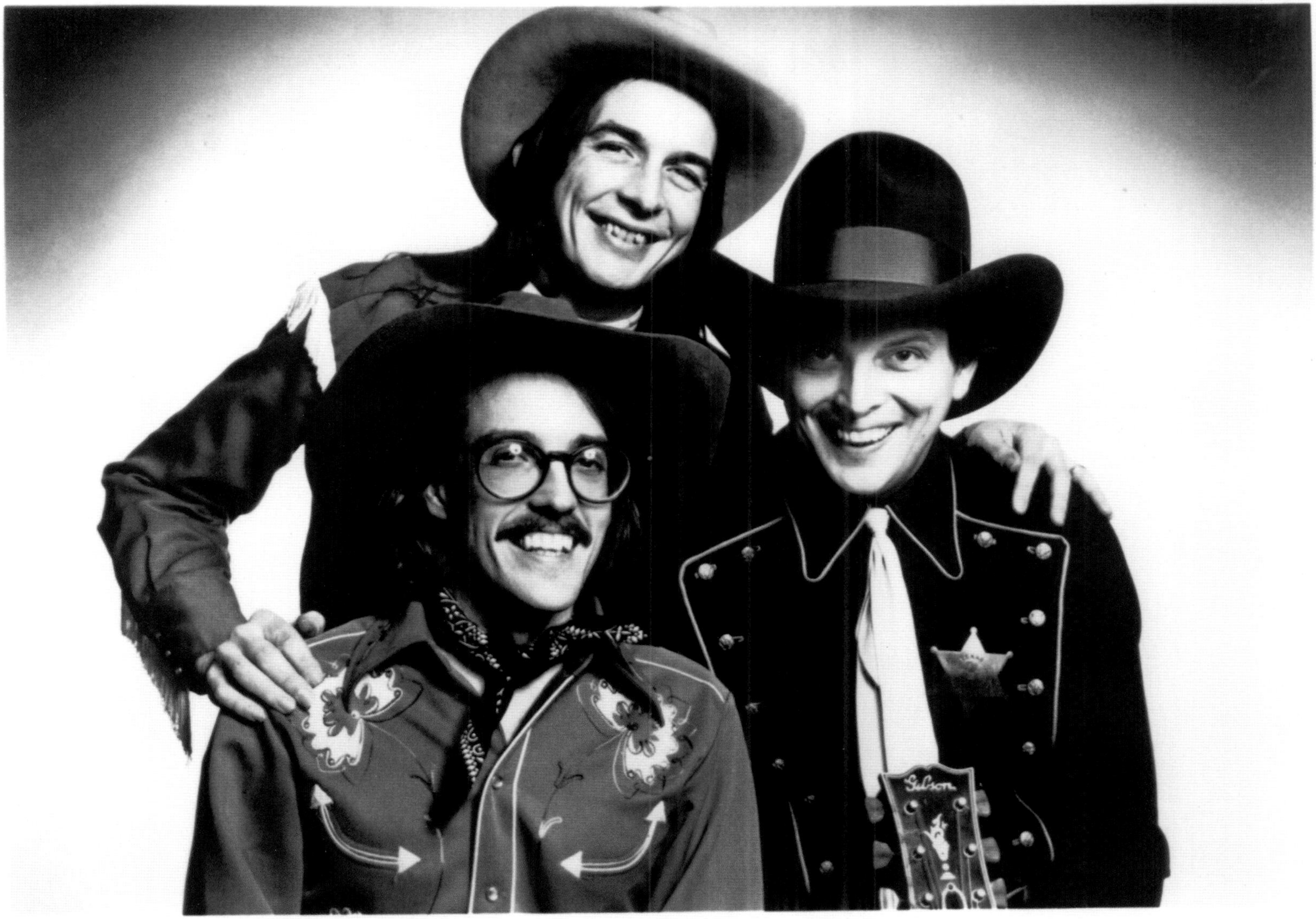

Rounder Records
186 Willow Avenue
Somerville, MA 02144
(617) 354-0700

RIDERS IN THE SKY

RBI MANAGEMENT
DAVID MARSDEN
(212) 768-0473

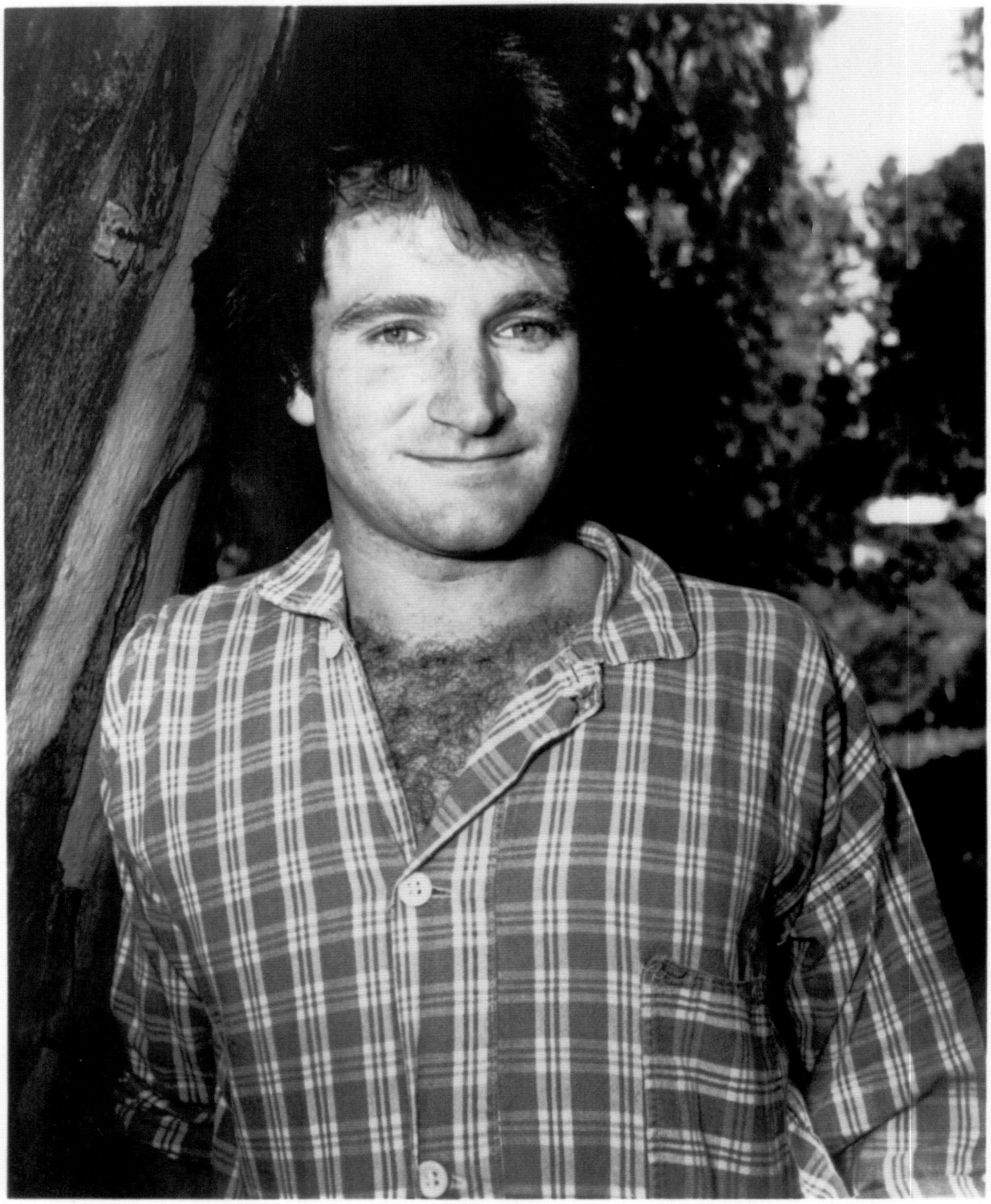

ROBIN WILLIAMS

Personal Management:
Rollins, Joffe, Morra and Brezner

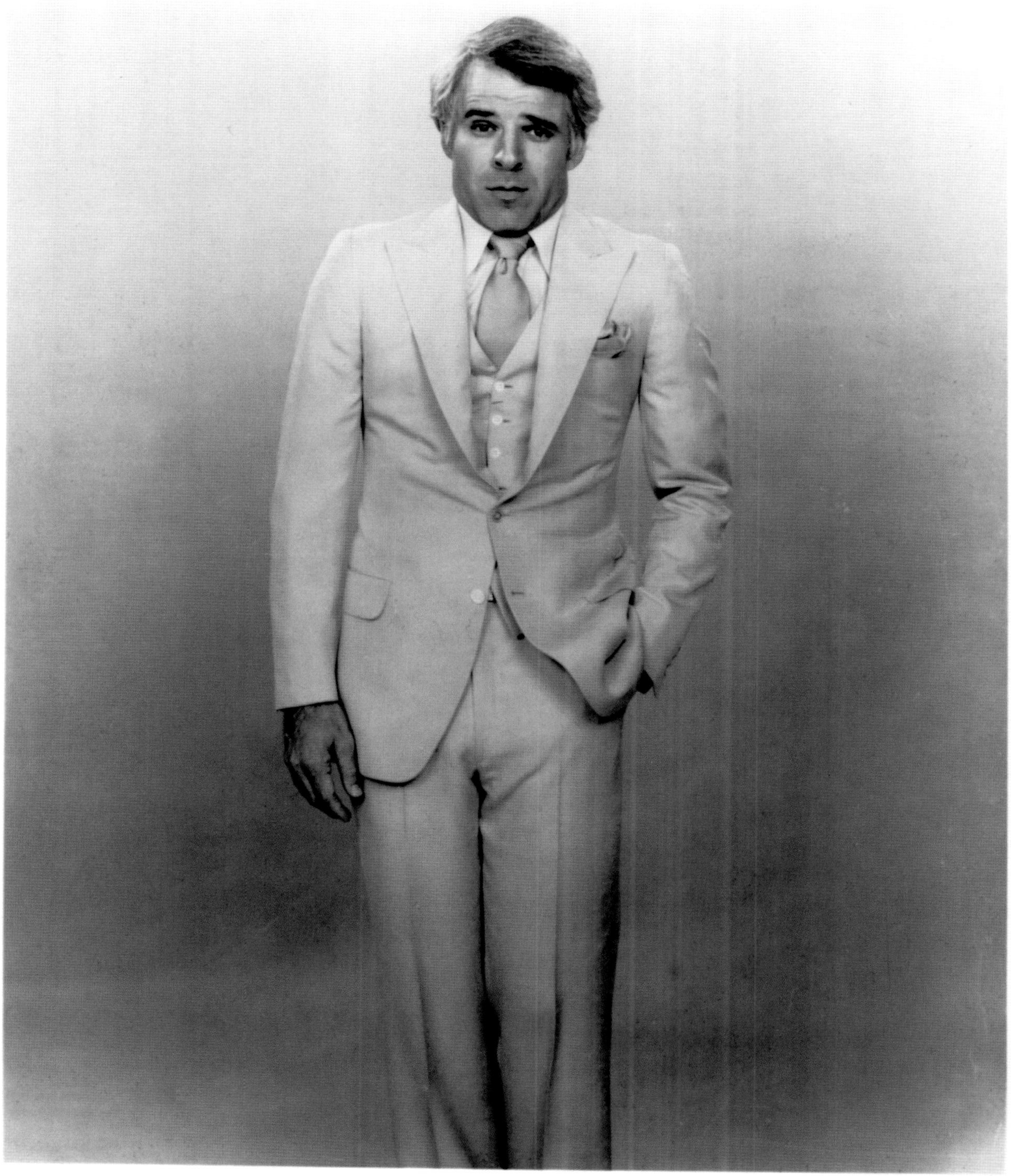

SEPTEMBER 1979

STEVE MARTIN

WARNER BROS.

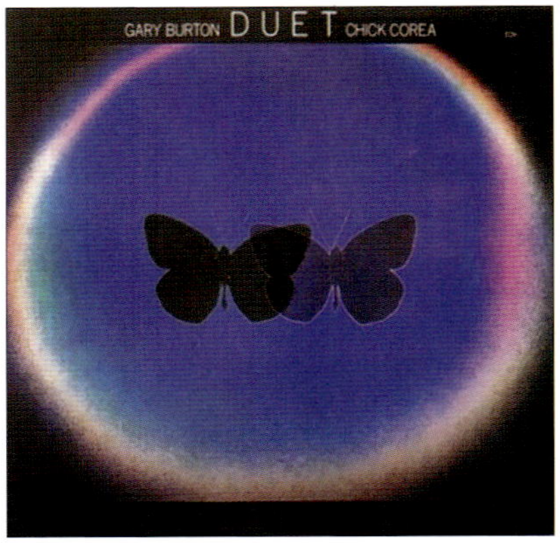

A **Gary Burton/Chick Corea** exchange on vibraharp and piano recorded live for the ECM label, *Duet* won a Grammy for Best Jazz Instrumental Album.

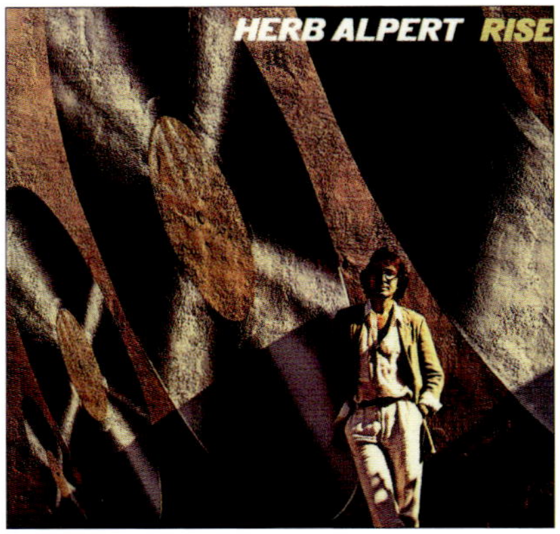

Trumpeter **Herb Alpert**'s "Rise" was his first No. 1 since the Tijuana Brass years, as well as his biggest R&B, adult contemporary and disco instrumental hit.

Billboard 200: *Rise* (#6)
Billboard Hot 100: "Rise" (No. 1); "Rotation" (#30)

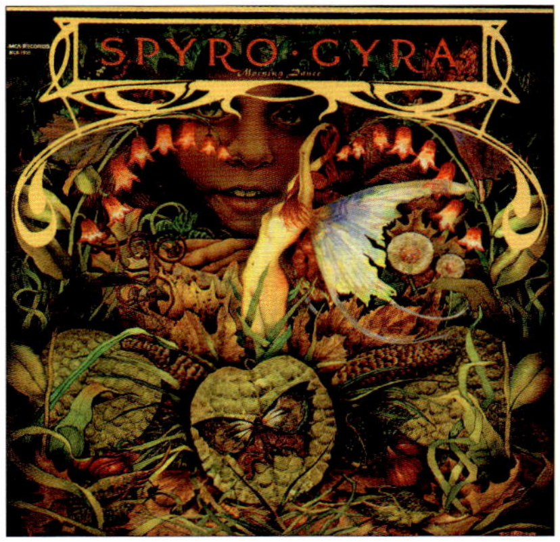

Spyro Gyra, a jazz-fusion band led by Jay Beckenstein, reached No. 1 on the adult contemporary charts with "Morning Dance," a gliding pop instrumental.

Billboard 200: *Morning Dance* (#27)
Billboard Hot 100: "Morning Dance" (#24)

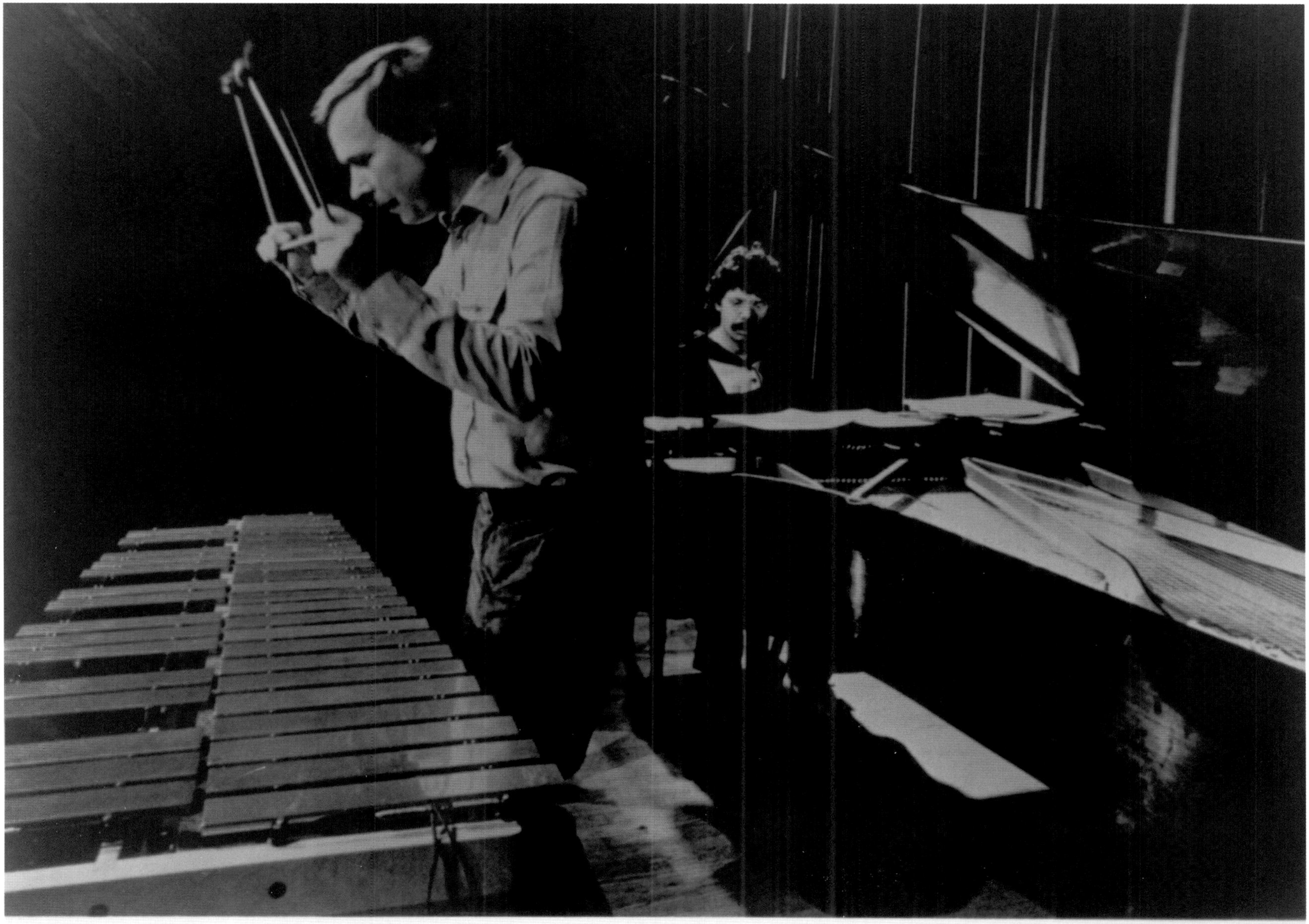

GARY BURTON/CHICK COREA

ECM RECORDS

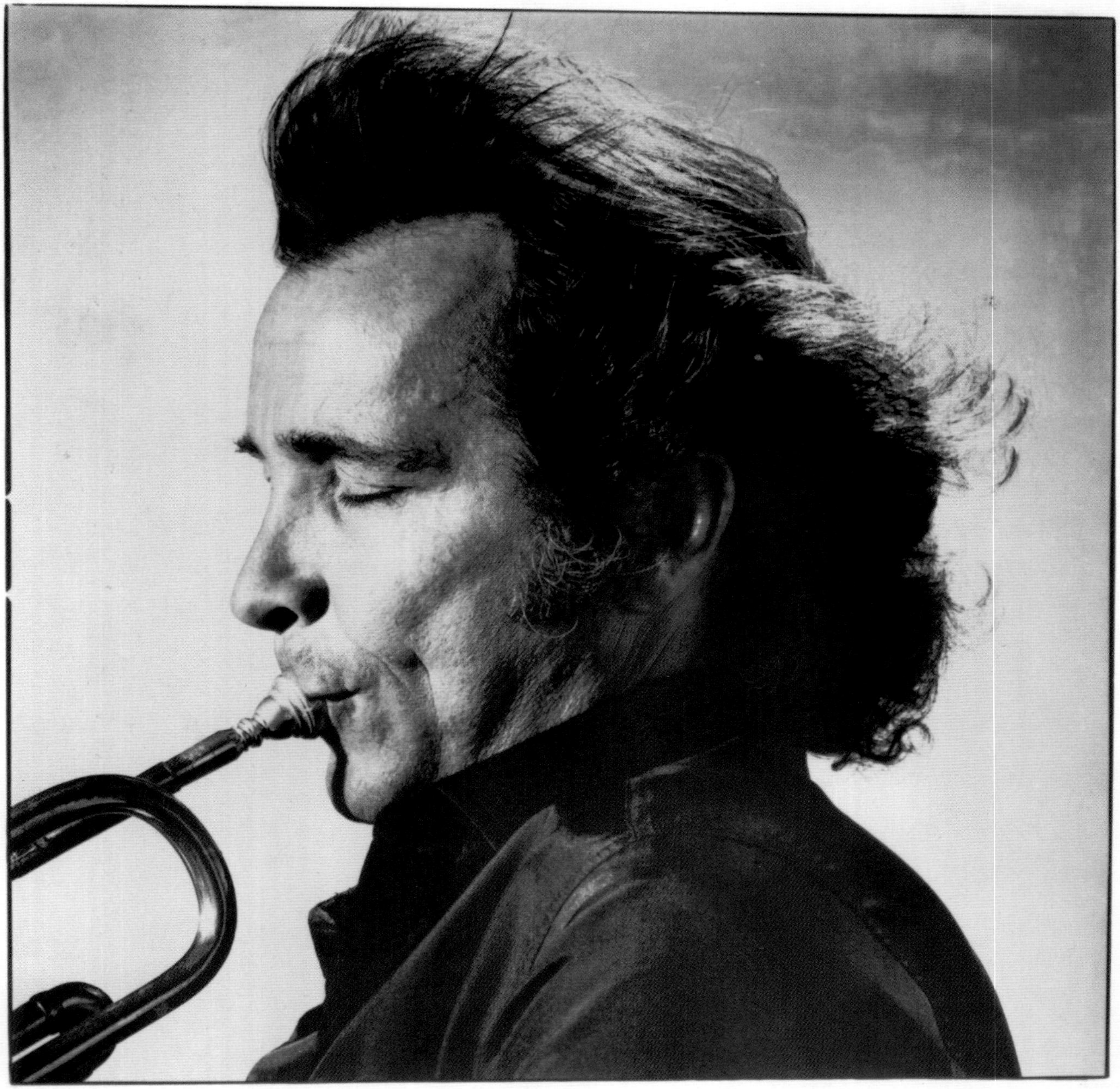

Herb Alpert

A&M RECORDS

Printed in U.S.A.

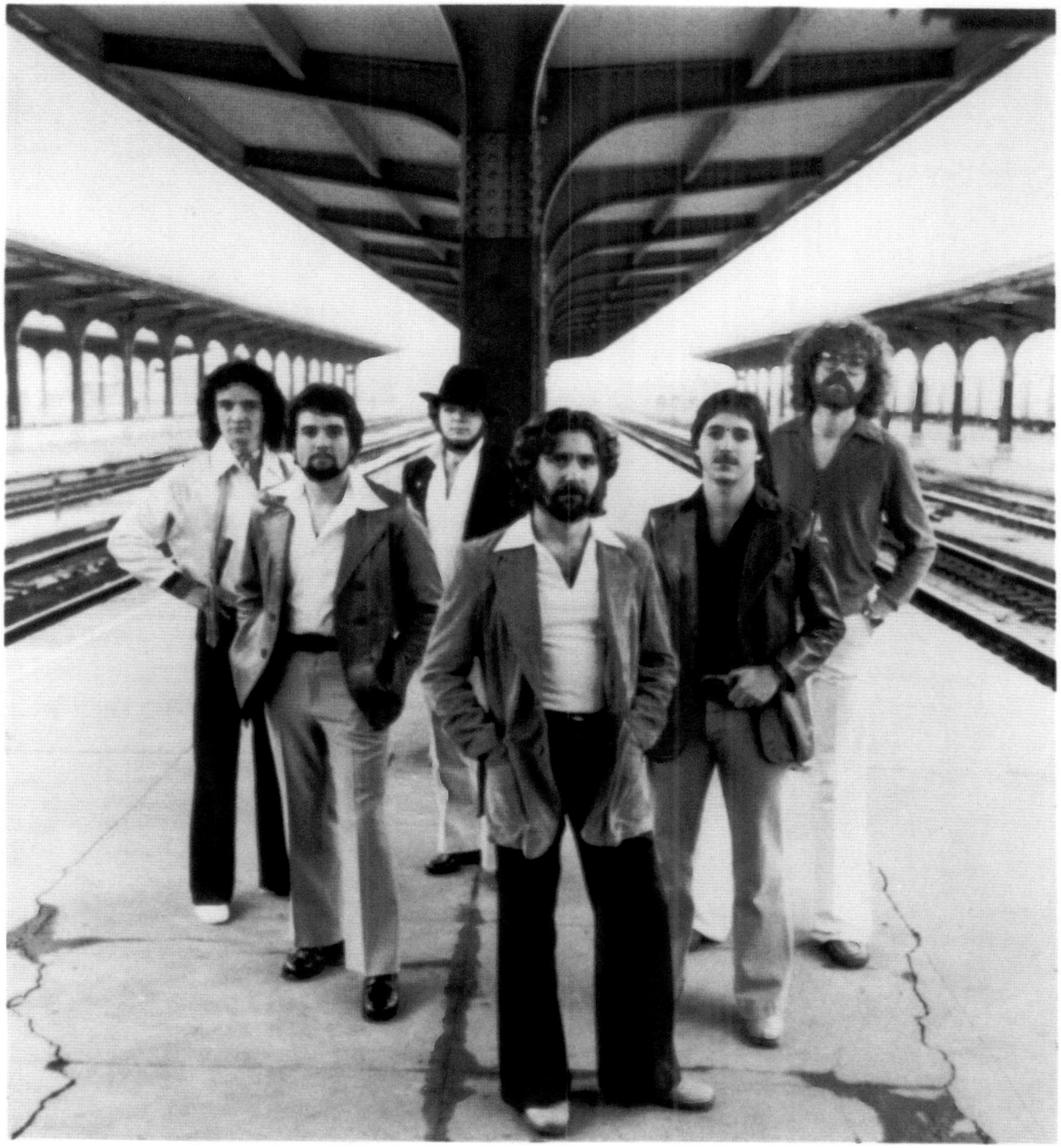

SPYRO · GYRA

INFINITY RECORDS

10 East 53rd Street
New York, New York 10022
(212) 888-9700

100 Universal City Plaza
Universal City, California 91608
(213) 763-8283

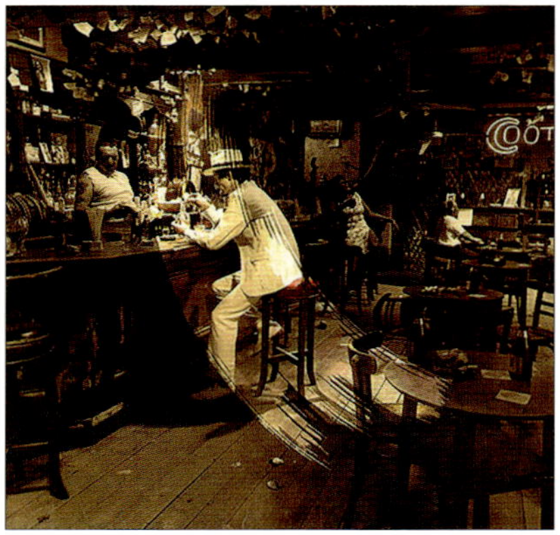

In Through the Out Door, **Led Zeppelin**'s final studio release before the passing of drummer John Bonham, debuted atop the charts in the US and the UK.

Billboard 200: *In Through the Out Door* (No. 1)
Billboard Hot 100: "Fool in the Rain" (#21)

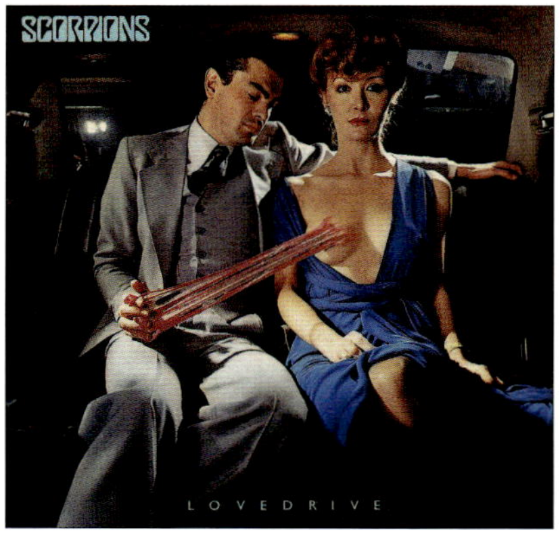

Scorpions banged out *Lovedrive*, featuring the edgy "Loving You Sunday Morning," the near-acoustic "Holiday"—and a provocative album cover.

Billboard 200: *Lovedrive* (#55)

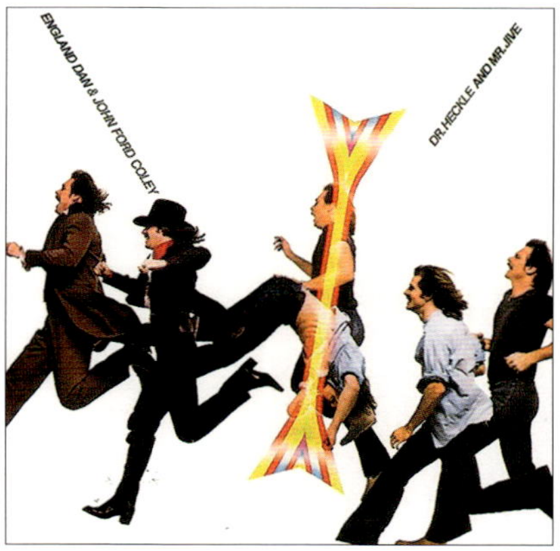

Soft-rock duo **England Dan & John Ford Coley**'s recording of "Love Is the Answer," written by Todd Rundgren, hit No. 1 on the adult contemporary chart.

Billboard 200: *Dr. Heckle and Mr. Jive* (#106)
Billboard Hot 100: "Love Is the Answer" (#10);
"What Can I Do with This Broken Heart" (#50)

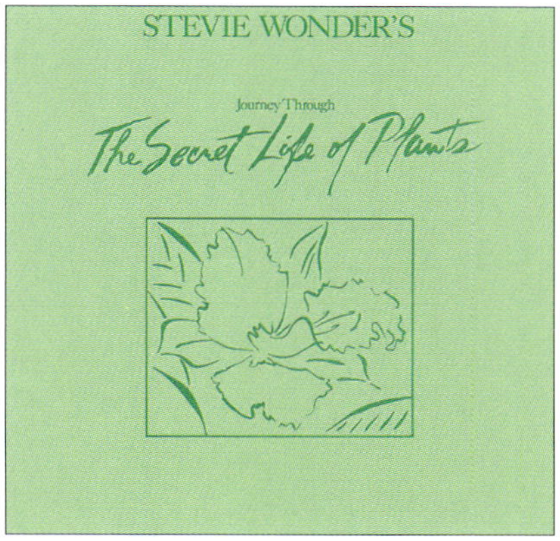

A double album, **Stevie Wonder**'s first digital recording was a mostly instrumental soundtrack to an environmental documentary, *The Secret Life of Plants.*

Billboard 200: *Stevie Wonder's Journey Through* The Secret Life of Plants (#4)
Billboard Hot 100: "Send One Your Love" (#4); "Outside My Window" (#52)

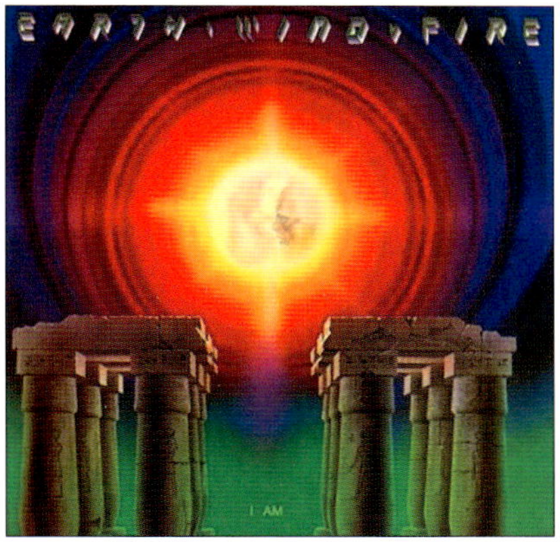

Earth, Wind & Fire's *I Am* featured "Boogie Wonderland," a glistening nod to disco featuring the Emotions, and the ballad "After the Love Has Gone."

Billboard 200: *I Am* (#3)
Billboard Hot 100: "Boogie Wonderland" (#6); "After the Love Has Gone" (#2); "In the Stone" (#58); "Star" (#64)

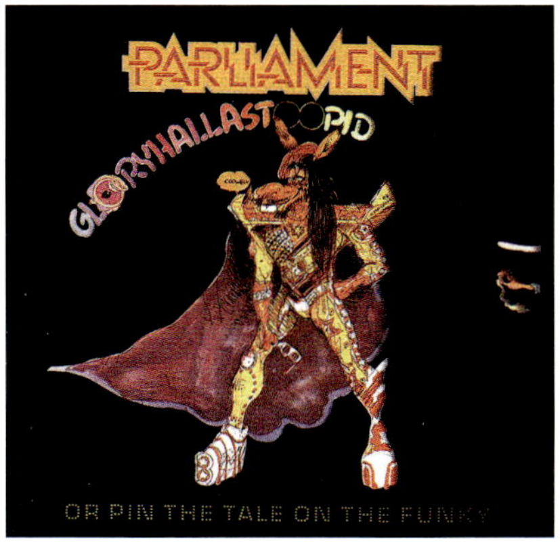

Parliament's concept album *Gloryhallastoopid* further outlined a P-funk mythology begun in the orbit of George Clinton's alter ego "Dr. Funkenstein."

Billboard 200: *Gloryhallastoopid* (#44)

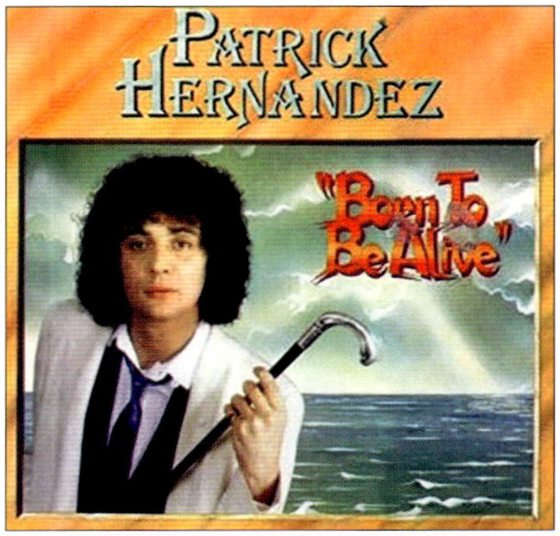

French-based singer **Patrick Hernandez** captured the fancy of listeners globally with the peppy "Born to Be Alive," which topped the disco chart in the US.

Billboard 200: *Born to Be Alive* (#61)
Billboard Hot 100: "Born to Be Alive" (#16)

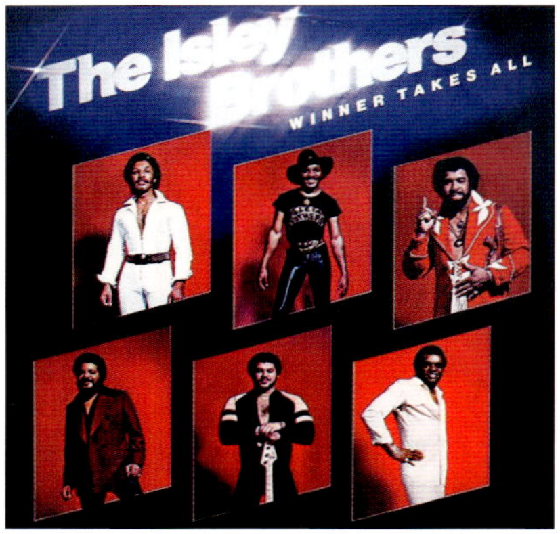

The Isley Brothers' popularity endured as they assimilated disco and slow jams into *Winner Takes All*, featuring the No. 1 R&B hit "I Wanna Be with You."

Billboard 200: *Winner Takes All* (#14)
Billboard Hot 100: "It's a Disco Night (Rock Don't Stop)" (#90)

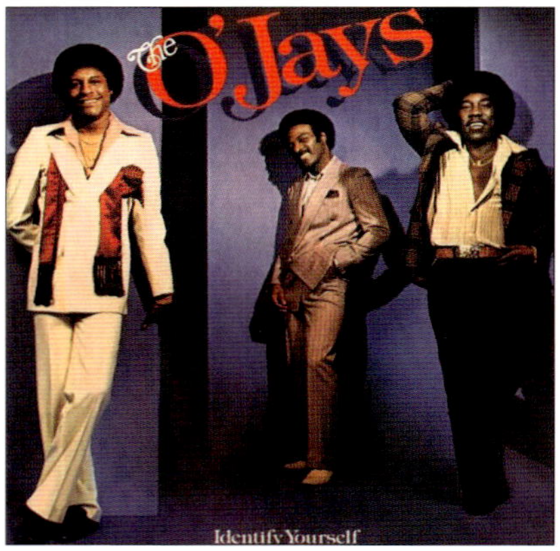

The O'Jays' *Identify Yourself* begat the Top 10 R&B hits "Sing a Happy Song" and "Forever Mine," produced by the Philly soul team of Gamble & Huff.

Billboard 200: *Identify Yourself* (#16)
Billboard Hot 100: "Forever Mine" (#28)

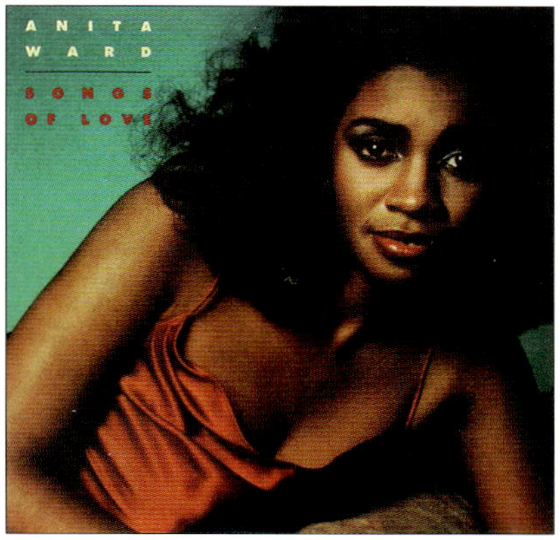

Anita Ward's slinky "Ring My Bell" topped the pop, R&B and disco charts in the US and made No. 1 in the UK, Canada, Spain, Norway and New Zealand.

Billboard 200: *Songs of Love* (#8)
Billboard Hot 100: "Ring My Bell" (No. 1)

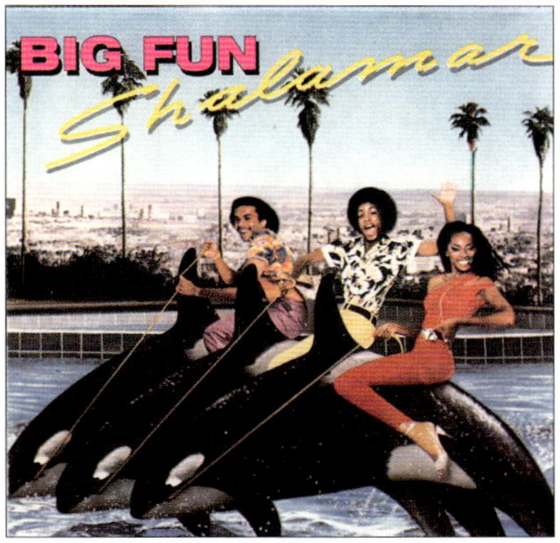

Molded from the cast of TV's *Soul Train*, **Shalamar**—Howard Hewett, Jody Watley and Jeffrey Daniel—got a poppy dance hit, "The Second Time Around."

Billboard 200: *Big Fun* (#23)
Billboard Hot 100: "The Second Time Around" (#8)

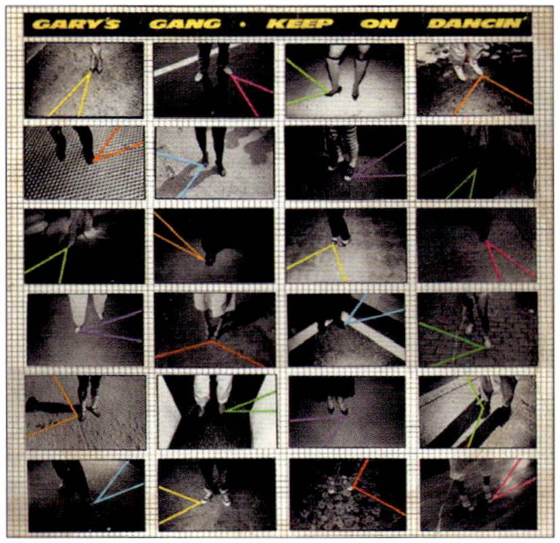

"Keep on Dancin'," the first single by **Gary's Gang**, a disco group from a peaceful residential section of New York, ascended to No. 1 on the dance chart.

Billboard 200: *Keep on Dancin'* (#42)
Billboard Hot 100: "Keep on Dancin'" (#41)

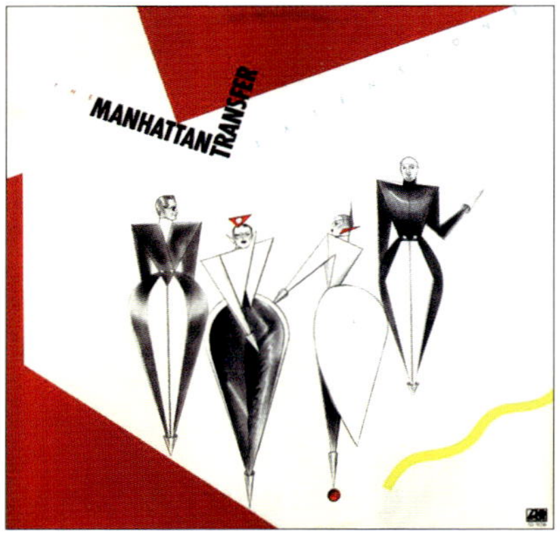

Manhattan Transfer snagged Grammy Awards for Best Jazz Fusion Performance and member Janis Siegel's arrangement of Weather Report's "Birdland."

Billboard 200: *Extensions* (#55)
Billboard Hot 100: "Twilight Zone/Twilight Tone" (#30); "Trickle, Trickle" (#55)

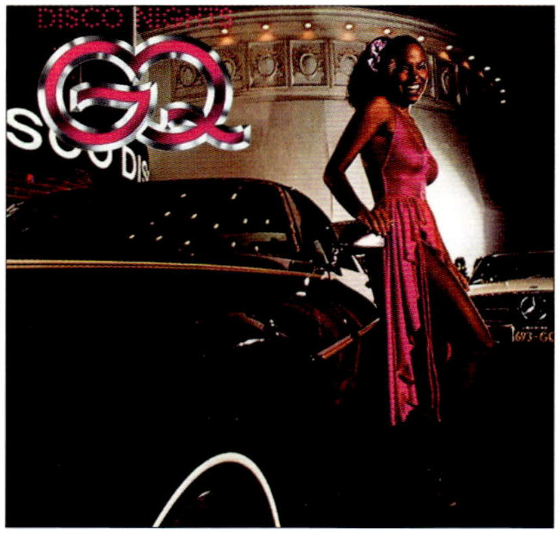

GQ's "Disco Nights (Rock-Freak)" reached No. 1 on the R&B chart, and the Bronx band's cover of the Billy Stewart classic "I Do Love You" came close.

Billboard 200: *Disco Nights* (#13)
Billboard Hot 100: "Disco Nights (Rock-Freak)" (#12); "I Do Love You" (#20)

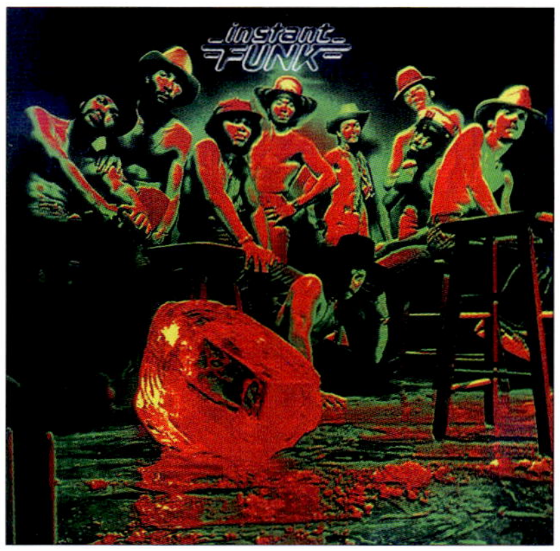

With a remix of "I Got My Mind Made Up (You Can Get It Girl)," which hit No. 1 on the R&B and disco charts, **Instant Funk** caused a stir in dance clubs.

Billboard 200: *Instant Funk* (#12)
Billboard Hot 100: "I Got My Mind Made Up (You Can Get It Girl)" (#20)

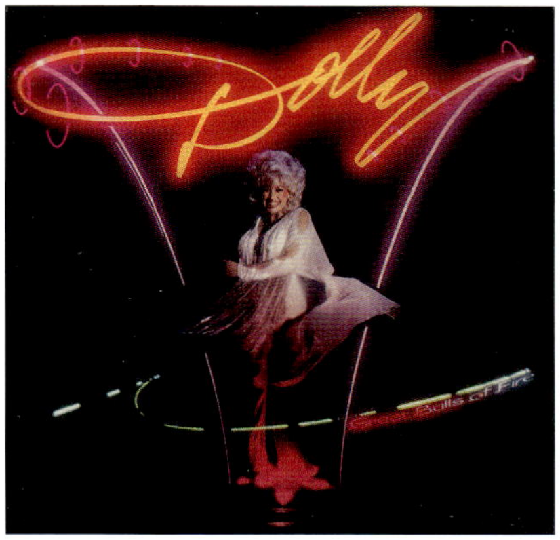

Dolly Parton's *Great Balls of Fire* album yielded the ballad "You're the Only One," her fifth consecutive single to top the country charts in two years.

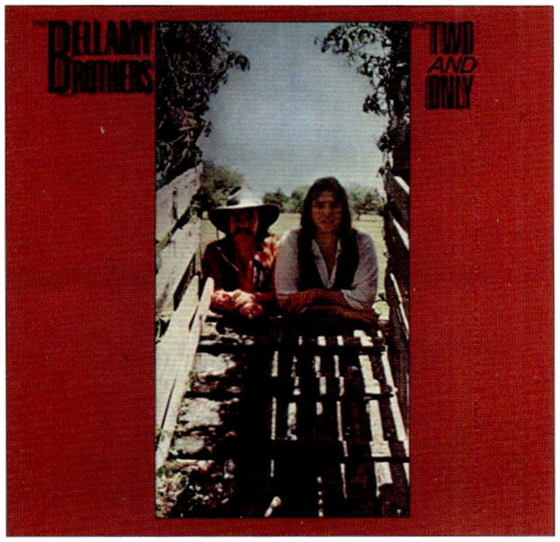

The Bellamy Brothers notched their first No. 1 on the country chart with the playful "If I Said You Have a Beautiful Body Would You Hold It Against Me."

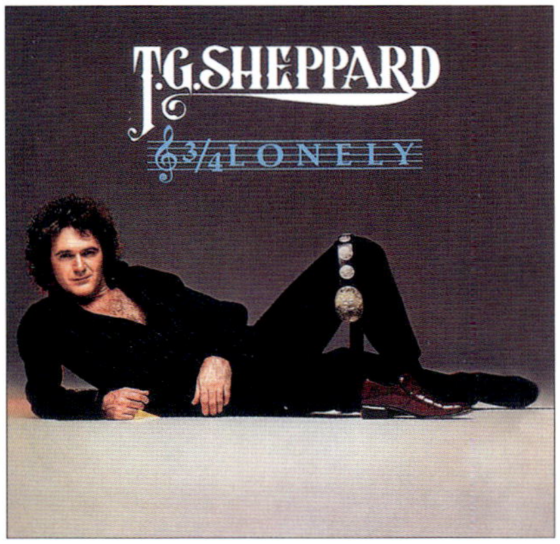

With "Last Cheater's Waltz" and "I'll Be Coming Back for More" from *3/4 Lonely*, **T.G. Sheppard** again found himself at the top of the country charts.

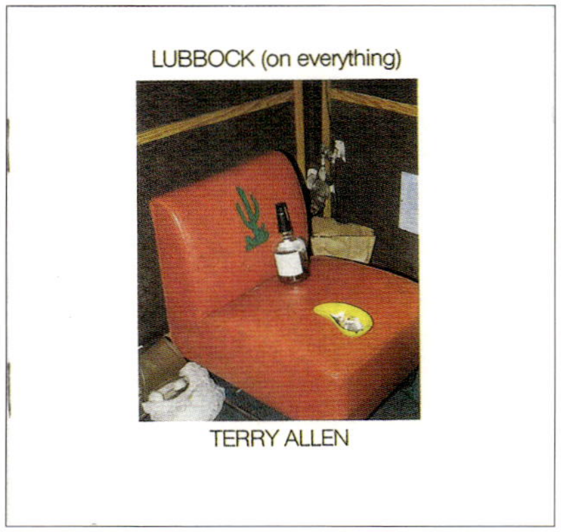

Singer-songwriter **Terry Allen**'s *Lubbock (On Everything)*, a 20-song double album, was an enterprising contemplation of his coming of age in West Texas.

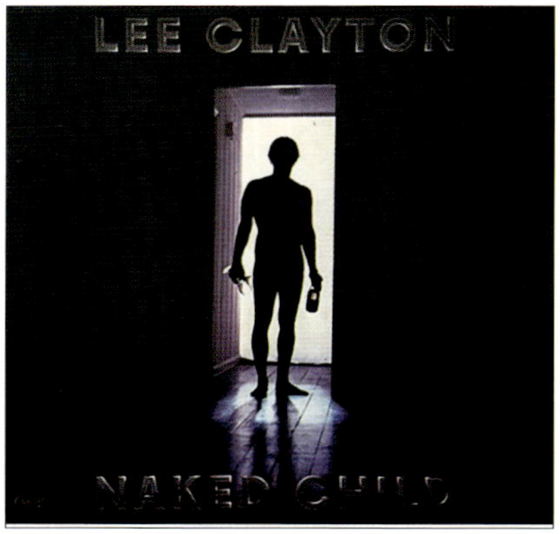

Known for writing the country anthem "Ladies Love Outlaws," **Lee Clayton** released the acclaimed *Naked Child* and the striking declaration "I Ride Alone."

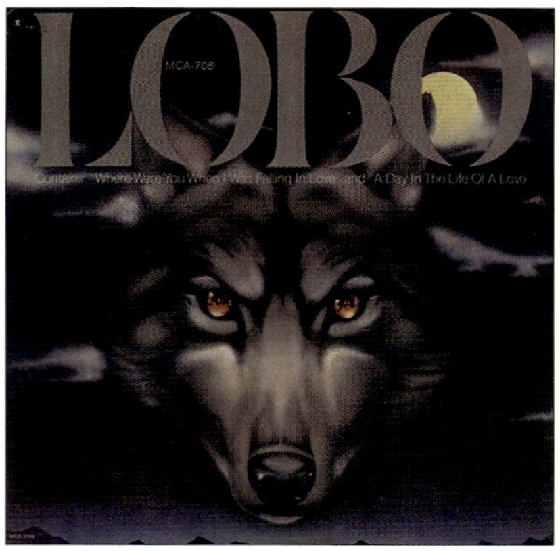

With "Where Were You When I Was Falling in Love," **Lobo**, aka singer-songwriter Kent LaVoie, gained his fourth No. 1 on the adult contemporary charts.

Billboard Hot 100: "Where Were You When I Was Falling in Love" (#23); "Holdin' On for Dear Love" (#75)

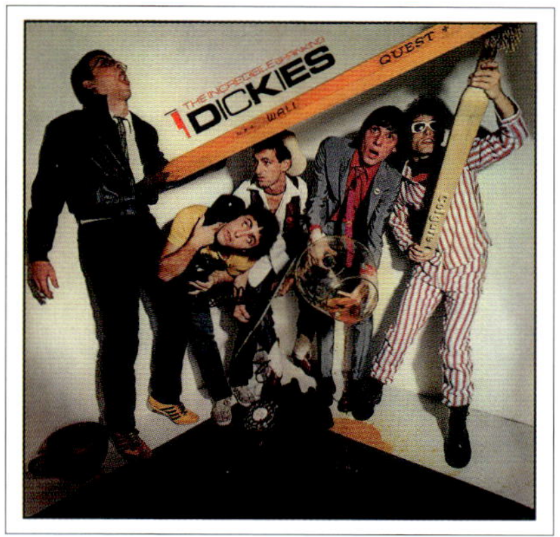

The Dickies, jokers from L.A.'s punk scene, issued the love song "You Drive Me Ape (You Big Gorilla)" and a dizzying cover of Black Sabbath's "Paranoid."

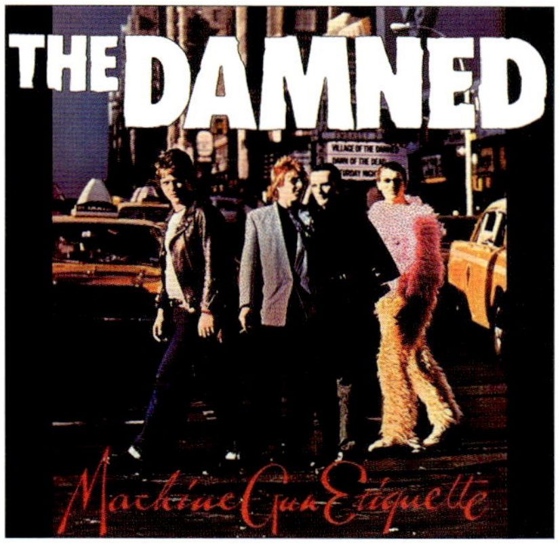

The Damned, the first British punks to score a hit single and album and a US tour, had briefly split before rallying to release *Machine Gun Etiquette*.

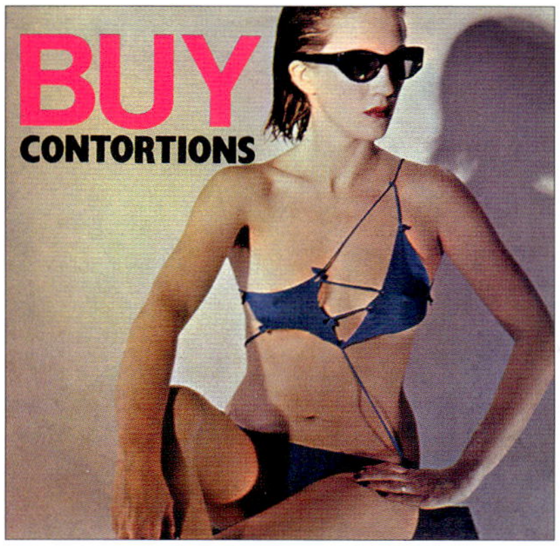

The scathingly turbulent **Contortions**, a key act of New York City's no wave scene, fused James Chance's strident free jazz sax and noisy, unsettling funk.

{ IN MEMORY OF ROBERT HARLAN }

ACKNOWLEDGMENTS

Many people were essential to the creation of this book. My first thanks go to my amazing publishing team—Jon Rizzi for bringing his special brand of editorial wit and intelligence, and Kate Glassner Brainerd for her design artistry and unflagging pursuit of excellence. Special appreciation goes to John Cerullo and Kevin Votel, whose facilitation was indispensable.

Mike Dickson, Chip Garofalo, Jennifer Soulé, Mark Zaremba, Peter Marcus, Matt Rue, Jay Elowsky and Mark Lewis contributed expertise and resources. I am especially indebted to my dear friend Michael Jensen, as well as Sue Satriano, Janice Azrak, Bryn Bridenthal, Byron Hontas, Kathy Acquaviva, Shelly Selover, Sue Sawyer, Glen Brunman, Rick Ambrose, Bob Merlis, Bill Bentley, Heidi Ellen Robinson, Rick Gershon, Judi Kerr and Susan Blond, who all graciously furnished information and assistance.

I specifically treasure the beneficence of Dave Rothstein, Greg Phifer, John Tope, Kevin Knee, Dick Merkle, Jeff Cook, Michael Brannen, Zak Phillips, Rich Garcia, Jason Minkler, Burt Baumgartner, Mitch Kampf, Don Zucker, Sharona White, John Ryland, Geina Horton, Michael Linehan and Jeffrey Naumann—all of whom supported my efforts.

I also salute David Gans, Leland Rucker, Steve Knopper, David Menconi, Gil Asakawa, Mark Bliesener, Butch Hause, Justin Mitchell and Harvey Kubernik, whose writings formed a vital index for the music-obsessed.

Finally, I would like to acknowledge with gratitude my beloved wife, Bridget, for her constant devotion and kindness. I cherish her—the love of my life.

EDITOR | **JON RIZZI**
ART DIRECTOR | **KATE GLASSNER BRAINERD**

ISBN 979-8-9885329-0-3 PRINTED IN CHINA | Asia Pacific Offset

BIBLIOGRAPHY

BOOKS

Bronson, Fred. *The Billboard Book of Number One Hits.* New York: Billboard, 1988.

Davies, Dave. *Kink.* New York: Hyperion, 1996.

Gans, David. *Conversations with the Dead.* New York: Citadel Press, 1991.

Jackson, Joe. *A Cure for Gravity: A Musical Pilgrimage.* New York: PublicAffairs/Perseus, 1999.

Williams Jr., Hank with Bane, Michael. *Living Proof.* New York: G.P. Putnam's Sons, 1979.

MAGAZINES

Feather, Leonard. "Joni Mitchell Makes Mingus Sing." *Downbeat* (September 6, 1979).

Flippo, Chet. "Jimmy Buffett: Misadventures in Paradise." *Rolling Stone* (October 4, 1979).

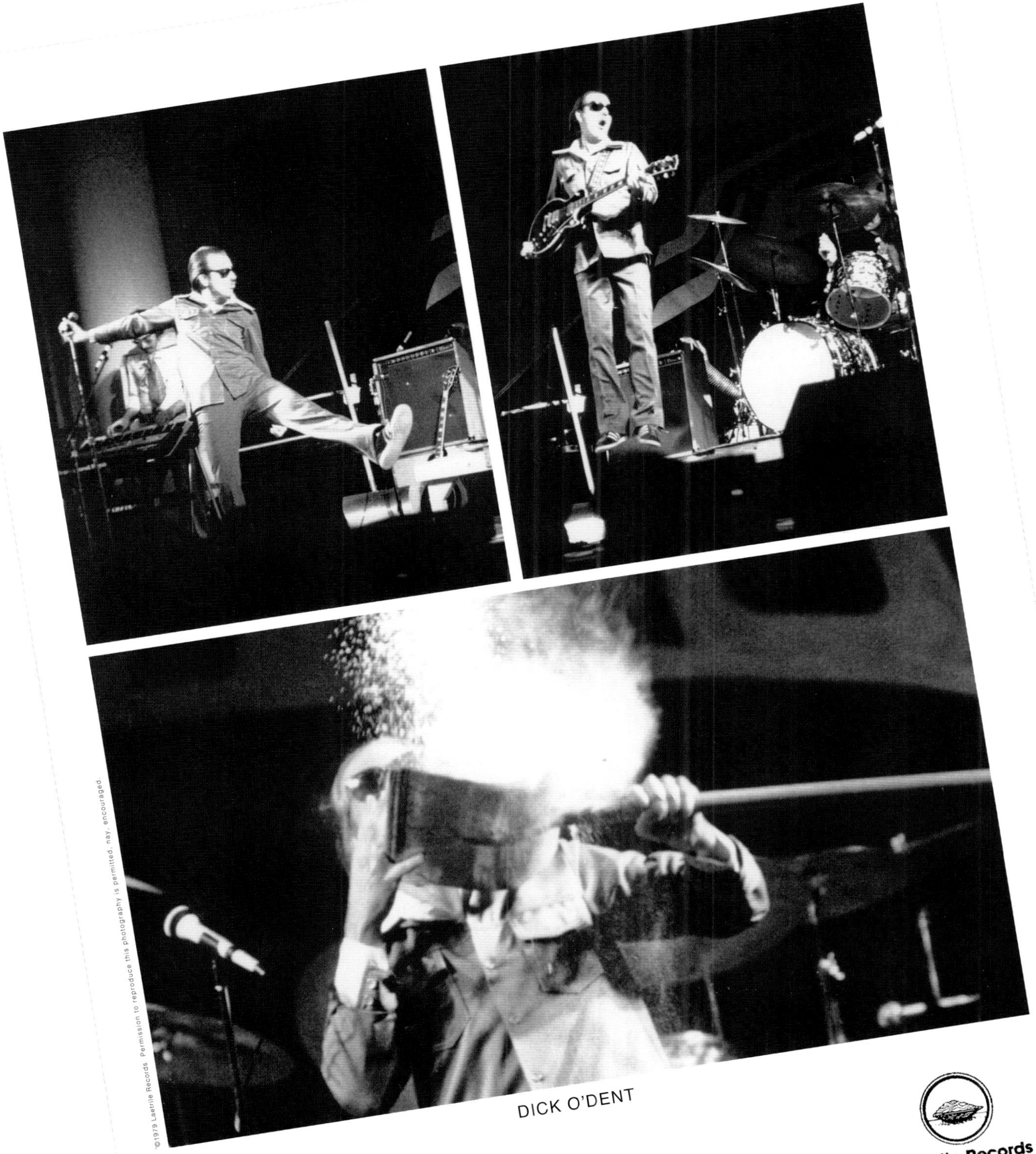

DICK O'DENT

NEW WORLD MUTANTS

Laetrile Records
"it's the pits"

Next in the *ON RECORD* book series

Vol. 8 1986

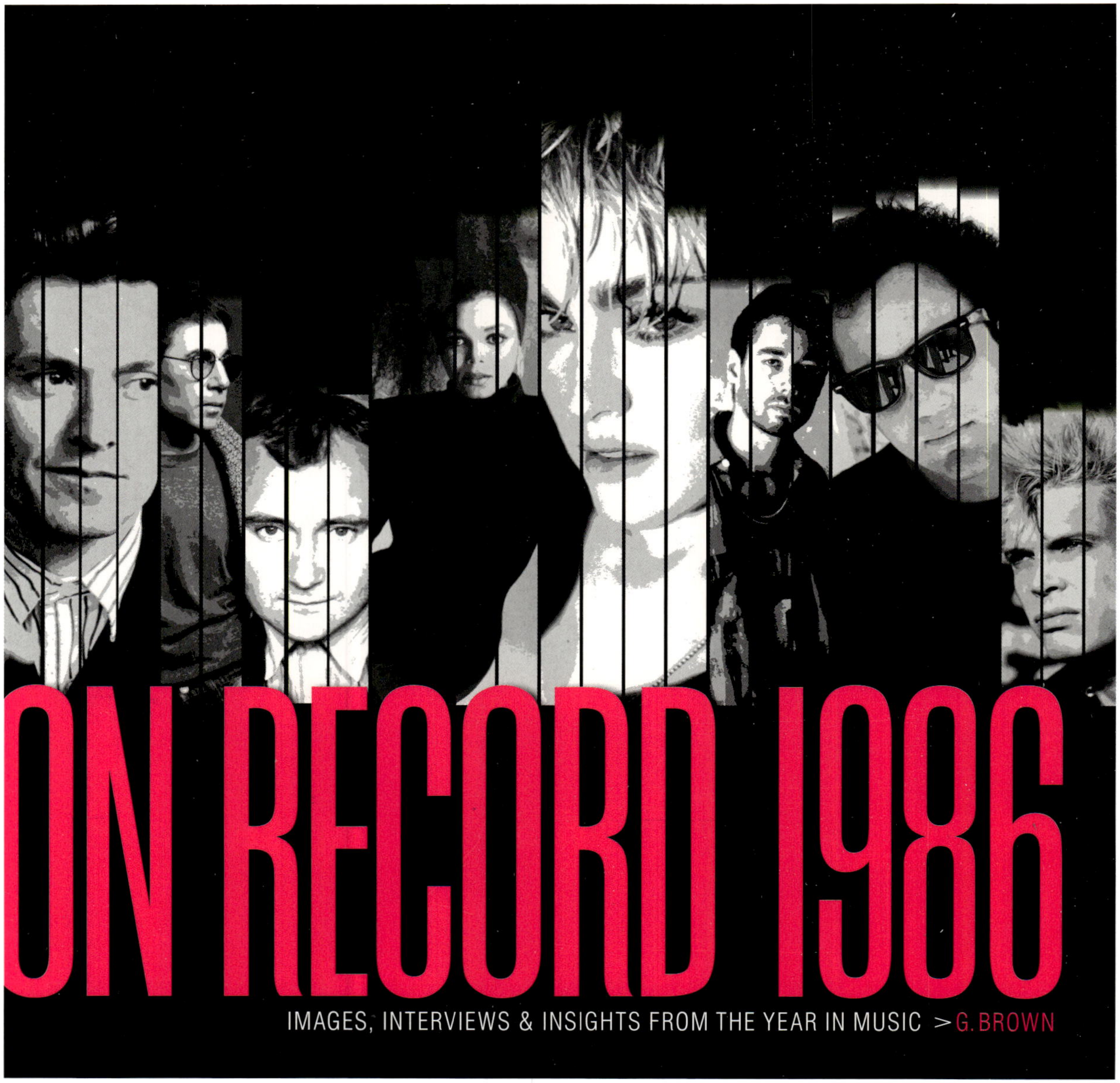